Psychology
The Frontiers of Behavior

Ronald E. Smith

Irwin G. Sarason

Barbara R. Sarason

University of Washington

Harper & Row, Publishers

NEW YORK   HAGERSTOWN   SAN FRANCISCO   LONDON

Kay, Brent, Mark, and Scott Smith
Suzanne, Jane, and Donald Sarason

Special Projects Editor: Marlene Ellin
Project Editors: Renée Beach and H. Detgen
Designer: Rita Naughton
Production Supervisor: Kewal K. Sharma
Photo Researcher: Myra Schachne
Compositor: York Graphic Services, Inc.
Printer: The Murray Printing Company
Binder: Halliday Lithograph Corporation
Art Studio: J & R Technical Services, Inc.
Section-opening illustrations by Howard S. Leiderman

PSYCHOLOGY: The Frontiers of Behavior

Library of Congress Cataloging in Publication Data

Smith, Ronald Edward, Date—
   Psychology: the frontiers of behavior.

   Bibliography: p.
   Includes indexes.
   1. Psychology.   I. Sarason, Irwin G., joint author.
[DNLM: 1. Psychology. HF121 S658p]
BF121.S58   150   77-13860
ISBN 0-06-045732-5

Contents

iii

CONTENTS

Section Two: BIOLOGICAL AND PERCEPTUAL BASES OF BEHAVIOR

Chapter 3 Physiological Systems and Behavior   *69*

CONTENTS

Section Three: LEARNING, COGNITION, AND BEHAVIORAL CONTROL

Chapter 6 Learning: Principles and Applications   *167*

vii

Chapter 10 Motivation, Emotion, and Stress   307

Chapter 11 Human Sexuality   340

xi

CONTENTS

xii

Section Five: PERSONALITY AND PSYCHOLOGICAL ASSESSMENT

Chapter 13 Personality: Understanding the Individual   405

xiii

Chapter 14   **Psychological Assessment: Intelligence and Personality**   432

Section Six: PERSONAL AND SOCIAL PROBLEMS

Chapter 15 Behavior Disorders   467

Chapter 16 Therapeutic Behavior Change   495

Chapter 17   **Psychology and the Problems of Society**   *519*

Credits for photographs appearing on table of contents pages

Chapter 1: (Enkelis, Jeroboam)/   Chapter 2: (Brown, Monkmeyer)/   Chapter 3: (UPI)/   Chapter 4: (*Drawing Hands*, M. C. Escher, Escher Foundation, Haags Gemeentemuseum, The Hague)/   Chapter 5: (Forsyth, Monkmeyer)/   Chapter 6: (Tringali/Palmer, DPI)/   Chapter 7: (Courtesy of Dr. Roger Mellgren/   Chapter 8: (Rawle, Stock, Boston)/   Chapter 9: (Courtesy of Dr. E. R. Sorenson, Smithsonian Institution)/   Chapter 10: (Ritscher, Stock, Boston)/   Chapter 11: (Ritscher, Stock, Boston)/   Chapter 12: (Charles Gatewood)/   Chapter 13: (Siteman, Stock, Boston)/   Chapter 14: (The Psychological Corporation/   Chapter 15: (Culver)/   Chapter 16: (Powers, Jeroboam)/   Chapter 17: (Harrison, DPI)/ Chapter 18: (Charles Gatewood)

Preface

In this book we have tried to sketch the field of psychology and the work of those who are active within it. Of course, the final product is an inevitable outgrowth of our collective personal view of the field.

We regard psychology as the scientific study of behavior and thought. We believe that this study is in an early stage of development and that it would be premature to have strong convictions about a single path to its perfection. This belief has a definite implication for the first course in psychology: Students should be made aware of the diverse paths being taken to explore psychology without being sidetracked from the search for a perspective on the field as a whole. We have tried to pursue this implication throughout the book. In Chapter 2, for example, we present not *the* theory of psychology, but four major theoretical perspectives that guide most of the activities of contemporary psychologists. We do this not to be pedantic or to confuse, but rather to suggest to the reader that although these approaches are often presented as competitive, in reality they complement one another.

Throughout the book we try to show how these four perspectives (biological, behavioristic, cognitive, and psychoanalytic) influence important basic areas of psychological study, including the biological side of life, the ways in which we learn and think, personality and individual differences, social and emotional development, and the ways in which we attempt to solve personal and social problems. As we review these domains, it will become evident to students that different psychologists engage in different activities, depending on their theoretical perspectives and their personal philosophies. We feel that the latter, too often neglected in introductions to psychology, are as important as the former in painting a realistic portrait of the field.

Some psychologists, while they do not deny that psychology should make a contribution to furthering human welfare, believe that the most useful contribution they can make is to the study and ultimate solution of basic scientific questions, regardless of whether or not their solutions will have practical applications. Others feel a need to direct their efforts toward the solution of immediate personal or social problems. Contemporary pyschology accommodates individuals at both extremes, as well as others who combine elements of these two orientations. We believe this diversity is a vital force, and in this volume we try to describe its contribution to the complexity, variety, and growth of the field.

Because most of the readers of this book will have had little or no systematic exposure to psychology, we have tried to use examples and problems that will be familiar to most readers and to avoid overburdening them with seemingly esoteric theories, issues, and methods. We have tried to capitalize on the great interest most students have in understanding themselves and the human relationships that affect their daily lives, but at the same time present a solid treatment of the basic information in the major areas of psychology. If we have succeeded, then perhaps we may also succeed in inspiring a new generation of individuals who will take up the challenge of psychological frontiers.

The book has been designed to assure adequate topic coverage in a one-quarter or one-semester course and to allow instructors flexibility in the design of their course. Some instructors, because of specific course objectives or time limitations, may wish to omit certain chapters. For example, in a course emphasizing an experimental-biological perspective, chapters having a personal-social emphasis (5, 8, 11, 13, 17, and 18) might be treated as elective chapters. Instructors will find many valuable suggestions for the use of the book and for its integration with lecture materials, demonstrations, and films in the *Instructor's Manual* prepared by Judith Siegel of the University of Washington. Judith Siegel has also prepared an extensive *Test Bank*, and Edward Scholwinski and Henry Oles of Southwest Texas State University have prepared a comprehensive *Syllabus* for instructors. A *Study Guide*, prepared by Henry Oles and Jack McMahan, also of Southwest Texas State University, will assist students in deriving maximum benefit from the book.

The introductory psychology course can and should be a vital experience for both student and instructor. We hope that this book and its supporting materials will help to promote the sense of excitement that can be experienced at the frontiers of knowledge.

Many people have contributed in important ways to the production of this book. Several of our University of Washington colleagues provided us with topical suggestions, chapter outlines, and initial drafts of chapters in their areas of expertise. We are grateful to Helen Bee, Ilene R. Gochman, Joy F. Hammersla, John P. Keating, Elizabeth F. Loftus, Judith Siegel, and Stephen C. Woods for their valuable contributions in the critical early stages of our work.

The book has materially benefited from the comments and suggestions of many reviewers. We would like to acknowledge the thoughtful reactions of the following: Robert Bolles, University of Washington; William Dwyer, Memphis State University; Bernadine Fong, Foothill College; Judith Galatin, Eastern Michigan University; John Grotzinger, Black Hawk College; Michael Hughmanick, West Valley Community College; Joline Jones, Worcester State College; Robert Knox, University of British Columbia; Robert Leslie, State University of New York at Oneonta; Joel Lubar, University of Tennessee; Henry Oles, Southwest Texas State; Janet Rafferty, Southern Illinois University; Halbert Robinson, University of Washington; Len Schmaltz, Illinois State University; Carolyn Sherif, Pennsylvania State University; Michael Siegel, State University of New York at Oneonta; John Spivey, University of Kentucky; John Stevenson, University of Rhode Island; Delos Wickens, Ohio State University; and Addison Woodward, Governors State University.

Special thanks are extended to Henry Oles and Jack McMahan of Southwest Texas State University for their meticulous work in producing the *Study Guide* which accompanies this book, and to Judith Siegel for her carefully constructed *Test Bank* and *Instructor's Manual*. To Michael Brown, Marlene Ellin, and the other Harper & Row staff members who worked on this book we express our appreciation for the role they played in helping to create this book. We also thank Isabelle Reynolds, Linda Sollars, and Margaret Thomas, who transformed innumerable handwritten scraps of paper into typed manuscript.

The Sarasons worked on this book while on sabbatical at the Netherlands Institute for Advanced Study, Wassenaar, the Netherlands, an ideal environment for research and writing. We are especially indebted to the institute's director, Professor H.A.J.F. Misset for creating such a congenial working situation, to Marina Voerman for her enthusiasm and skill in transcribing the illegible scrawl of two left-handed authors, and especially to Dinny Young, N.I.A.S. librarian, who uncomplainingly scoured the libraries of the Netherlands for quantities of reference material.

Writing a book entails sacrifices on the part of the author and loved ones alike. Ronald Smith could not have asked for a more loving, understanding and supportive spouse than Kay Smith, who assumed the lion's share of caring for three small children during more than two years of book preparation. This book is in part a product of many evenings and weekends that Brent, Mark, and Scott Smith spent without their father's company. The Sarasons are indebted to their son Don, who so patiently and supportively listened to more mealtime chatter about this book than any teenager should normally be expected to withstand. Our families, like we ourselves, have long looked forward to the day when these acknowledgments could be written.

Ronald E. Smith
Irwin G. Sarason
Barbara R. Sarason

One

Psychologists: Their Methods and Perspectives

Chapter 1

Psychology and the Frontiers of Behavior

(Wolinsky, Stock, Boston)

We have had religious revolutions, we have had political, economic, and nationalistic revolutions. All of them, as our descendants will discover, were but ripples in an ocean of conservatism—trivial by comparison with the psychological revolution toward which we are so rapidly moving.

ALDOUS HUXLEY

When Huxley wrote these words he foresaw a time in which scientific knowledge about behavior and experience would provide us with powerful tools to improve the human condition. He foresaw a powerful psychotechnology that could be used to attack the problems that have beset human beings since the dawn of their existence. He predicted the development of techniques that would extend our mental lives into unexplored realms of experience.

Some people believe that the psychological revolution Huxley predicted is already here. During the past 20 years we have made tremendous strides in unraveling the mysteries of human behavior, in understanding how and why we behave as we do. We have been pushing back the frontiers of behavior, and exploration is continuing in numerous settings around the world. In this book we hope to communicate the sense of excitement that exists on these frontiers of our attempt to know, to understand, and to change ourselves.

The study of psychology encompasses virtually every aspect of our lives. It explores our behaviors and feelings, our motives and thoughts. In a rapidly changing and complex world, psychology has assumed an increasingly important role in solving human problems. Psychologists are concerned with an enormous variety of questions: How are memories registered in the brain? How do we learn? How do our personalities develop and change? What kinds of child-rearing techniques produce happy and creative children? How can we effectively rehabilitate criminals? How can people be persuaded to reduce their consumption of gasoline and electricity? These are examples of the kinds of questions that psychologists ask and attempt to answer through their research.

THE SCOPE OF PSYCHOLOGY

The founding date of psychology as an experimental science is generally agreed to be 1879, when Wilhelm Wundt established a laboratory at the University of Leipzig, Germany, to study consciousness and sensation. The new science soon traveled to the United States, and in 1892 the American Psychological Association was founded by 31 charter members. Today the organization claims some 42,000 members, most of whom hold doctorates. Thousands of other psychologists live and work in virtually every country in the world.

Psychology is usually defined as the scientific study of behavior. This definition is deceptively simple, for psychologists have disagreed over the years about what should be included under the term *behavior*. Should it be restricted to externally observable or *overt* behaviors that can be seen and measured by others, or should it also include internal, or *covert*, events, such as images, thoughts, and feelings? Most psychologists today agree that both overt and covert behaviors are appropriate objects of study, and they use the term *behavior* in its broadest possible sense to include anything that an organism can do.

Because the realm of behavior is so broad, no psychologist can hope to cover the entire field, and there is now a large degree of specialization based on interests and work activities. Table 1.1 lists the divisions of the American Psychological Association. Many psychologists belong to more than one division, for there is a considerable degree of overlap among them. Through specialization psychologists can apply principles and theories from the general body of psychological knowledge to their particular areas of interest. However, there is also a common effort among psychologists to integrate the methods and findings of specialized fields *back* into the body of general knowledge. This effort helps psychologists to reap the full benefits of being able to concentrate on one particular area of interest and still avoid fragmentation within the profession.

What psychologists do

Within each area of specialization in psychology there are a variety of different activities, including research, teaching, and application of psychological principles to help solve human problems. Many psychologists involve themselves in more than one of these activities, so that their professional lives are varied and stimulating. In the following sections we describe several of the major areas within psychology

Table 1.1 Divisions of the American Psychological Association

Division of General Psycology
Division on the Teaching of Psychology
Division of Experimental Psychology
Division on Evaluation and Measurement
Division of Physiological and Comparative Psychology
Division on Developmental Psychology
Division of Personality and Social Psychology
The Society for the Psychological Study of Social Issues
Division on Psychology and the Arts
Division of Clinical Psychology
Division of Consulting Psychology
Division of Industrial and Organizational Psychology
Division of Educational Psychology
Division of School Psychology
Division of Counseling Psychology
Division of Psychologists in Public Service
Division of Military Psychology
Division of Adult Development and Aging
Society of Engineering Psychologists
Division of Rehabilitation Psychology
Division of Consumer Psychology
Division of Philosophical Psychology
Division for the Experimental Analysis of Behavior
Division of the History of Psychology
Division of Community Psychology
Division of Psychopharmacology
Division of Psychotherapy
Division of Psychological Hypnosis
Division of State Psychological Affairs
Division of Humanistic Psychology
Division on Mental Retardation
Division of Population Psychology
Division of the Psychology of Women
Psychologists Interested in Religious Issues

and introduce some psychologists who work in them.

Experimental psychology

Experimental psychologists study basic processes, such as learning, memory, and perception, in both animals and humans. Experimental psychology is a very scientifically oriented area that uses rigorous research methods, usually within controlled laboratory settings.

An experimental psychologist at an eastern research institute whose area of specialization is memory describes his work:

I'm concerned with the basic processes that are involved in memory. These are *encoding*, or registra-tion of the information, *storage* of the information, and *retrieval.* The failure to remember something may be the fault of any one of these processes. We're doing research now on the differences between the principles governing short-term and long-term memory. Short-term memory lasts only about a few seconds, and its capacity seems restricted to between five and nine bits of information, or in other words, about one telephone number. Forgetting occurs rapidly in short-term memory. But once material gets into long-term memory, a great many items can be remembered. What we want to know is how information gets transferred from short-term to long-term memory. Knowledge of this might enable us to help people improve their memories.

I have two other memory projects going right now. One concerns so-called sleep learning and whether it can actually occur. In order to answer the question, of course, we must be able to define and measure sleep in some way. We measure the depth of our subjects' sleep by using electroencephalograph (EEG) recordings. First we attach electrodes to their scalps to monitor the subjects' brain waves. At various times during the sleep cycle, tape-recorded material is presented to the subjects, and we test their recall of the material when they awaken. We find that material learned before a person is truly asleep is remembered quite well, probably because there is little opportunity for later memories to interfere with it. But if the material is presented when people are in deep sleep, and if they remain asleep, then there is no memory for the material upon awakening.

I'm also starting a research project with a psychologist interested in brain functioning on a very controversial topic which might be called *chemical transfer of memory.* Investigators have trained animals to perform a task, made chemical extracts from their brains, and then injected these extracts into other animals who had never been trained for the task. The injected animals reportedly learned the task more quickly than animals not given the brain extracts. However, other investigators have tried this experiment and were unable to obtain the same results, which is why this is a controversial topic. I want to know why some laboratories were successful while others were not. Unless you can reliably reproduce an effect, there are uncontrolled factors that haven't yet been accounted for. I have some ideas about what some of these uncontrolled factors might be, and I hope that my research will provide a definitive test of whether or not it is possible to chemically transfer memory from one brain to another. The implications of such a possibility are vast, but we can't let ourselves get carried away until we are sure if the basic phenomenon actually exists.

5

We will encounter other experimental psychologists and their areas of interest throughout the book, but especially in Chapters 4 through 7.

Physiological psychology

Physiological psychology is closely allied with the biological and medical sciences. Specialists in this area are interested in the neural, genetic, and hormonal bases of behavior. They are also concerned with the effects of drugs on the body and on behavior.

A physiological psychologist who teaches and conducts research at a large midwestern university describes her major area of interest: "I started out as a premed student with the goal of becoming a neurologist," she recalls. "But after a few psychology courses, I became equally interested in behavior. Going to graduate school in physiological psychology enabled me to combine my interests in neurology and behavior. Like most psychologists, I spent about five years in graduate school studying for my doctorate."

Although she received her Ph.D. only three years ago, this psychologist is already becoming well known for her research on electrical stimulation of the brain (ESB).

Modern technology has made it possible to implant tiny electrodes in the brain which can be used to record electrical brain activity or to stimulate areas of the brain through remote control outside of the laboratory. This allows us to control behavior in its natural settings. I'm primarily interested in the control of aggressive behavior through brain stimulation. By stimulating certain areas in the brains of animals, we can instantly produce or inhibit aggressive behavior. A loving mother monkey will throw her baby across the cage when stimulated and return to him only when the stimulation ceases. Bruno, the boss monkey in our colony, can be made to behave very aggressively or very passively, depending on which points in his brain are stimulated. In fact, one of the other monkeys in the colony quickly learned to operate our remote control radio unit when we gave it to her. Whenever Old Bruno threatened her, she merely flicked the switch and turned off his aggression by stimulating an inhibitory center of his brain. Probably the most impressive demonstration of this phenomenon was performed by José Delgado, a pioneer in our field, who waved a cape at a ferocious bull and stopped him in mid-charge by stimulating him through an electrode implanted in an inhibitory center. The bull screeched to a halt only a few feet from Delgado and calmly wandered away. If I ever do a demonstration like that, I'll want to make sure the electrode is implanted in exactly the right place!

I'm intrigued by the possibility of controlling not only animal, but also human aggression through ESB. Perhaps one day violence-prone individuals will be able to inhibit their aggression by flicking a switch. We've already given humans control over some of their brain functions. For example, one man suffered from narcolepsy, a disorder which caused him to drop suddenly from wakefulness into sleep. Electrodes were im-

Physiological psychologists at Stanford Research Institute experiment with communicating with computers through brain waves. (Enkelis, Jeroboam)

Brain researcher José Delgado, armed only with a radio transmitter, waves a cape at a charging bull. The bull is then stopped in midcharge by an electrical signal delivered through an electrode embedded in a specific brain region. (Courtesy of J. M. R. Delgado)

planted in the areas of his brain controlling sleep and wakefulness, and he was outfitted with a portable ESB unit which he could operate by himself. Whenever he felt himself "going under," he simply stimulated himself into wakefulness. In other instances, epileptic patients have been able to prevent their seizures by self-administered ESB. We're on the threshold of a technology of behavioral control which has enormous possibilities, and I'm excited to be working in the area.

Physiological psychologists around the world are unlocking the secrets of the physiological and neurological systems that underlie behavior. We consider their work in greater detail throughout the book, but particularly in Chapter 3.

Developmental psychology

The developmental psychologist is concerned with the study of growth and development, from birth (and even before) through old age. Virtually every area of human functioning, be it intelligence, personality, motor skills, physical change, or language, is of interest to the developmental psychologist.

A developmental psychologist at a Canadian university recalls his path into his chosen field:

> I guess I'm a developmental psychologist because I'm fascinated with change, particularly change in myself. When I was first studying psychology I couldn't help but wonder about how I got to be the way I am. In fact, that question was why I took my first psych course. Was it my heredity? Or my upbringing, the way of life in my home? At first, my interests were directed toward childhood and adolescence. Not being long out of my own adolescence, the process of becoming an adult especially intrigued me. As a psychologist, I try to isolate factors that play roles in the movement from one psychological stage to another. While a number of these factors have been identified—for example, whether the parents really want their child to grow up, the child's rate of physical maturation, and peer relationships—we need to know much more about how these factors combine in individual cases. That's one of the mammoth jobs ahead—determining how factors in development combine and produce unique outcomes in people.
>
> Much of my time is taken up with a research project concerned with the effects of aging on intelligence. We have been testing a large sample of people periodically for over 20 years. This is called a *longitudinal* study, since the same people are tested repeatedly. We're finding that intellectual abilities do not neces-

sarily decline with age, as was suggested by earlier *cross-sectional* studies in which people of different ages were tested at the same time. It looks as if those earlier results may have been due to the differing educational and cultural experiences that the people of different ages had been exposed to.

> I'm also doing work on the other end of the age spectrum. My colleagues and I have received a government grant to design, carry out, and test the effects of a preschool program designed to foster intellectual and social growth in children from disadvantaged backgrounds. Early programs, such as the Head Start program in the United States in the 1960's, were not as successful as we might have hoped, perhaps because the programs were pretty much separated from the child's home environment. What we're trying to do is directly involve the parents in the program, to teach them how they can work with their children to create a more stimulating home environment that our preschool program can build upon.

The findings of developmental psychologists are discussed in Chapter 9.

Educational psychology

Educational psychologists are concerned with all aspects of the educational process, including learning, classroom instruction, vocational counseling, and the testing of abilities and aptitudes.

One educational psychologist employed by a large school district serves as a consultant to the schools in his district and counsels students and parents. He is also responsible for the scholastic aptitude testing program within the district:

> Educational psychology is an incredibly broad field that is concerned with almost everything from adjustment to kindergarten up through adult education. Like most educational psychologists, I don't pretend to know about all, or even most, aspects of school learning. But the area of greatest interest to me is the motivation kids have to ask questions and learn. According to some approaches to education, children's performance in school is motivated primarily by what might be called extrinsic rewards, such as praise from parents, teachers, and other kids, and material rewards like presents and special treats that follow good report cards.
>
> I don't deny the vital importance of extrinsic rewards in motivating all sorts of behavior. But I can't help but be intrigued by intrinsic motives, such as curiosity about things that go on in the world and the

8

This developmental psychologist is studying the problem-solving behaviors of young children. (Shelton, Monkmeyer)

desire to acquire knowledge. No doubt extrinsic rewards influence the individual's inner motivations. But how? We need to know more about what children think about, how they perceive their schools and teachers, what they expect of themselves, and what they think is expected of them by parents and teachers. If we can understand these things, perhaps we can know more, not only about why Johnny and Ruth can learn the multiplication table for number seven, but also about the ways in which their intellectual lives relate to their personalities, their concepts of themselves, and their views of the world around them. By gaining a better understanding of children who are

highly curious and seek knowledge, we may uncover clues to help those youngsters whose academic motivations are weak and poorly developed.

Social psychology

Social psychologists study the ways in which the behavior of individuals and groups is affected by their social context. They focus on topics such as attitude formation and change, affiliation, interpersonal attraction, conformity, and group processes. One social psychologist describes her work in the area of social perception:

Behavior begins with perception, since we behave in accordance with the way we interpret the situation we're in. I'm interested in the factors that influence social perception and the ways in which perception affects social behavior. My associates and I are studying the ways in which our personality influences how we "see" our social world. In particular, we're interested in *attribution*, the process by which we interpret the causes of our own and others' behavior. In one set of experiments, we're studying factors which affect the decisions of jurors. We've constructed a mock courtroom in our laboratory and are conducting mini-trials in which different factors are manipulated to see how they affect judicial decisions. For example, in one experiment, we're studying the effects of sex of defendant and victim on jury decisions in a murder trial. There are four different victim-defendant combinations: a man accused of killing a woman, a woman accused of killing a man, and two conditions in which victim and defendant are of the same sex. We can also vary such things as strength of evidence, possibility of a capital punishment sentence, sexual composition of the jury, etc. We can even place some of our own people on the jury and see what methods of persuasion are most effective in getting the other jurors to change their initial opinions about guilt or innocence. We have a whole series of experiments going, and a number of lawyers are acting as consultants on the project. We're hoping that by specifying the factors which affect the juror's perception of the trial situation, we may be able to make some valuable recommendations for the judicial process. For example, it's been found that evidence ruled inadmissible by the judge can influence judicial decisions almost as much as the same evidence when it is not ruled inadmissible. We're trying to formulate instructions that can be given by the judge to the jury which will reduce this effect.

Social psychologists use scientific methods to study a variety of societal problems. They study social behavior both under controlled laboratory conditions and in its natural setting. We shall examine a number of the areas that interest them in Chapter 12.

Industrial psychology

Industrial psychologists apply psychological principles to work situations. They are involved not only in personnel work and the development of training programs, but also in attempts to create work settings that foster high productivity and job satisfaction.

One industrial psychologist who works for a large consulting firm helps a number of different businesses with a variety of problems. One of his projects is a leadership training program being developed by a large state agency:

We're trying to find out which types of "leader" behaviors are most effective in various types of work environments. It turns out that a given person can be an excellent leader in one type of situation and a rather poor one in other situations. In any situation, it is necessary to consider both the personality and skills of the leader and the conditions with which he or she will be working. By placing the right leader in the right type of work setting, we should be able to increase morale and productivity.

Industrial psychologists are also concerned with the tools people use to help them work more efficiently. For example, have you ever wondered why the letters on the standard typewriter keyboard are located where they are? Not for convenience or efficiency, that's for sure! Actually, the most frequently used letters were placed as far apart as possible to *slow down* typing speed because the keys on the machines of the 1800's used to jam up if the typist went too fast. About 40 years ago, a keyboard called the Dvorak Simplified Keyboard was developed. [See Figure 1.1.] On this keyboard, the most frequently used keys are in the home row, and the right hand does more of the work (56 percent) than the left. Our tests show that typists can greatly increase their speeds (up to five times) with no increase in errors. But in spite of these results, you'd be amazed at how hard it is to get people to change.

Industrial psychologists are involved in many businesses and in industrial and military projects. This field is an increasingly important area of psychology in an age in which people and machines are interacting in new and increasingly complex ways.

Clinical psychology

The clinical psychologist's primary area of interest is the diagnosis and treatment of psychological disturbances. You are perhaps most familiar with this kind of psychologist. In addition to their applied activities, clinical psychologists conduct research on personality, psychological tests, and deviant behavior. Some engage in only one or a few of these activities; others are involved in a number of them. They work in a variety of different settings: universities, hospitals, medical schools, community mental health facilities, and private practices. The clinical psychologist is not

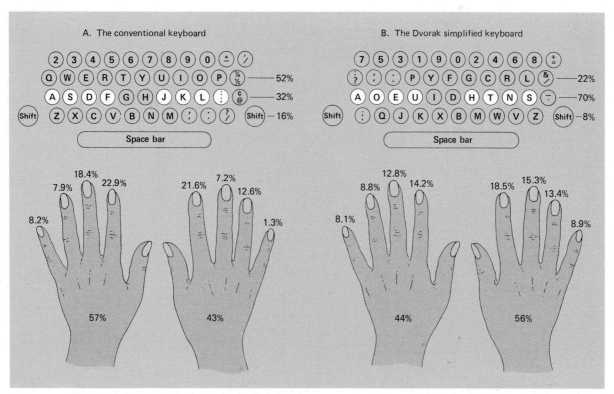

Figure 1.1 The conventional typewriter keyboard and the Dvorak Simplified Keyboard. Advocates of the Dvorak Keyboard claim that their typing speeds increased dramatically and that they were able to type for a longer time. (C. Lekberg, "The tyranny of qwerty." *Saturday Review*, September 30, 1972, p. 38.)

a psychiatrist. Psychiatrists are M.D.'s who specialize in psychiatry; because they are medical doctors, they can prescribe drugs to their patients. Psychologists rely on nonmedical techniques. During recent years a number of new theories and techniques have been developed to aid them in treating a wide range of psychological problems. Clinical psychologists are trained to conduct research and psychological testing as well as psychotherapy.

A clinical psychologist at a large medical school in the Southwest describes some of his experiences:

The other day during a class I teach at the University, a student asked me if maybe clinical psychologists study disturbed people because they're a little crazy themselves. I answered that I don't doubt that there are some clinical psychologists who are unhappy and who have personal problems. After all, psychologists are

people, too, who happen to be primarily interested in asking and answering questions about maladaptive thought and behavior. It might well be that psychologists will make a lot of progress toward understanding normal behavior through the study of persons who have disorganized or disordered personalities, as well as through the study of typical or "average" people, whoever they might be.

There are basically two breeds of clinical psychologists—the practitioners and the researchers. The practitioner works with individuals and groups in order to identify and define behavioral problems and to help people overcome them. The researcher asks questions and carries out projects aimed at answering the questions and figuring out new ways to diagnose problems more accurately and treat them more efficiently. Actually, there is a hybrid type too, the clinical psychologist who both practices professionally and does research. I'm one of those hybrids because I do research on the

BOX 1.1

What psychologists do and where they work

The following figures concerning the distribution of psychologists within subfields and their employment settings are based on a sample of 35,361 respondents to a survey conducted by the American Psychological Association.

Subfield	Percent
Clinical-counseling	49.0
Educational	15.1
Experimental	9.9
Industrial	7.7
Personality-social	7.2
Developmental	4.2
Quantitative	2.6
Physiological	2.0
Other	2.3
Total	100

Employment Setting	Percent
Colleges and universities	46.3
Hospitals and clinics	18.4
School districts	10.3
Business-industry	3.2
Consulting and private practice	8.0
Criminal justice system	1.1
Research establishment	1.0
Government agencies	5.1
Other	6.6
Total	100

Adapted from Boneau and Cuca (1974), p. 823–824.

thought processes of schizophrenic people, people who think and behave in odd ways and who often are not in contact with reality. But how could I ever hope to do research on these people without talking and interacting with them? Seeing them clinically permits me to get to know them and—I hope—to help them.

One thing that keeps my job interesting is the variety of things I do. Here at the medical school, in addition to my research, I do psychological testing, see patients in individual and group psychotherapy, and train medical students and psychiatry residents. We also have a good internship program for clinical psychology graduate students who are studying for their Ph.D.'s.

For the past year and half, I've been helping set up a community mental health clinic in a part of the city where mostly poor minority people live. Finding trained people to staff the center has been a real problem though. We have a terrible need for more minority psychologists to go back into the community, and graduate training programs in psychology are trying to attract qualified minority applicants.

In addition to the preceding specialty areas, there are several other specialties that relate to one or more of them. The *counseling psychologist* receives training similar in many respects to that of educational and clinical psychologists. Aptitude and vocational testing and counseling is a special area of expertise for these professionals. There are probably one or more counseling psychologists at your school's counseling or guidance center.

Personality psychologists engage in research on personality, its development, functioning, and change. They ordinarily do not do clinical work. Their research interests and activities are often similar to those of the social psychologist, but they generally have a greater interest in individual differences among people.

Quantitative psychologists are the mathematical specialists of psychology. They not only develop statistical techniques and computer systems, but also formulate *mathematical models* of behavior to represent relationships between behaviors and their causes in precise mathematical terms.

The distribution of a large sample of psychologists within areas of specialization and the settings in which they work is presented in Box 1.1.

Having briefly surveyed the different fields of psychology, we now turn to the scientific principles and methods that guide the psychologist's study of behavior. First, we outline some of the basic assumptions and scientific concepts that apply to psychology. Then we discuss the major approaches psychologists use in their attempts to understand behavior and its causes.

THE SCIENCE OF PSYCHOLOGY

Although psychology as a formal discipline is only about a century old, people's attempts to understand themselves are as old as the human race itself. People have tried to understand themselves in a number of ways: through informally observing and describing, by looking within themselves, through using philosophical reasoning, and by seeking divine inspiration. The discipline of psychology involves yet another approach, one based on scientific methods.

In a sense, each of us is a kind of psychologist, for in our daily lives we try, like scientific psychologists, to *observe, understand, predict,* and *control* behavior. For example, when you wake up in the morning, probably the first thing you do is make an *observation* about the way you feel and the way you are behaving: Are you feeling good and smiling, or are you grouchy and scowling? Next, you probably try to *understand* why you feel the way you do: Perhaps you are happy because you just finished writing a paper the day before, or grumpy because you have to take an exam for which you are not prepared. Then you probably look ahead at the day and *predict* what will happen: You may foresee a leisurely breakfast and a pleasant afternoon, or indigestion and an afternoon of tension and anxiety about your exam. Finally, you will try to *control* what you do and the way in which you do it: If you want peace and quiet, perhaps you will plan to go to a restaurant where no one knows you; if you want to pass your exam, you will probably plan to spend the morning studying. Moreover, by behaving in particular ways you will try to influence how others behave toward you: If you want them to be pleasant toward you, you will treat them in a friendly fashion. But although the goals of scientific psychology resemble those of everyday life, there are differences in the methods used to attain those goals, particularly the goal of understanding.

Understanding behavior

The basic goal of any inquiry, scientific or otherwise, is *understanding*, or the ability to provide an acceptable answer to the questions "Why?" and "How?" Applied to behavior, understanding means the ability to specify the *causes* of behavior, the conditions responsible for its occurrence. The two basic approaches to understanding the causes of behavior show the distinction between methods a lay person might use and those a scientific psychologist uses.

The historical approach

Many attempts to understand behavior involve an examination of the causes of behaviors that have already occurred. Why did race riots occur in American cities during the 1960s? What motivated Hitler to ignore his military advisors and send his troops to suffer devastating military defeats? Why was John Kennedy assassinated? Why have you chosen your present life goals?

We may view an event in the context of the circumstances at the time the event occurred, and then attempt to identify its causes on a rational or intuitive basis. This is the approach used by professional historians. But a given event in history may be the focus of a large number of different historical accounts and explanations. Hundreds of different theories have been proposed—for example, to explain the causes of the Civil War, both by people who were alive at the time and by modern historians. It is possible to explain this past event in countless ways, and there is no sure way to determine which, if any, of the alternative explanations is correct. After-the-fact explanations of our own and others' behaviors may leave us with a comfortable feeling that we know why something happened, but this kind of "understanding" may not be solid enough.

This does not mean that the historical approach to understanding the causes of behavior is never useful. In many instances we have no alternative; it is often impossible to reconstruct circumstances that occurred in the past. The historical approach can give us valuable leads and insights into certain problems, and it is often the foundation on which further scientific inquiry is built. Although most after-the-fact explanations cannot themselves be tested directly, they can give rise to explanations that can be tested.

13

Understanding through prediction and control
Scientists favor another approach to understanding, one that permits them to test their theories about causes and to obtain more definite answers. For most scientists, understanding consists of the ability to make accurate predictions. If we can understand the causes of a given behavior, it should be possible to specify and predict the conditions under which that behavior will occur. Furthermore, if we understand the causes of a behavior well enough and if we can manipulate those causes, then it should be possible to control the behavior.

The predictive statements of scientists are called *hypotheses*. A hypothesis states the predicted relationship between two events. It is typically stated in the form "if *A* occurs, then *B* will occur." Frequently, there is more than one plausible explanation for a given behavior, so that there will be a number of rival hypotheses. The scientist must be able to specify alternative hypotheses and find ways to pit them against one another in order to test their relative validity. This may be done either by checking the predictions made by the various hypotheses against already known facts or by testing them in new research. It is hoped that through a series of "definitive" tests, the scientist can eliminate all the hypotheses except the one that seems most plausible. But this hypothesis will still only be "true" in a provisional way. Even if it is supported by all the existing data, it can never be regarded as an absolute truth. It is always possible that some new observation will uncover problems with it. But the disproving of established and accepted hypotheses by new observations frequently opens up new frontiers for investigation. The displacement of old beliefs and "truths" is the lifeblood of science.

The assumption of determinism
Normally we think of science as an *empirical* study, one that is based on the perceptions we receive through our senses. Scientific hypotheses can be tested by setting up experiments and observing and measuring the results. But at a more basic level, scientists base all their hypotheses on an *assumption* that, by definition, cannot be proved or disproved. This assumption is that nature operates according to a set of laws and that these laws can be discovered. This is called the *assumption of determinism*.

With respect to psychological phenomena the assumption of determinism means that behavior is not random; it has causes that can potentially be identified and that, if known, would make prediction possible with 100 percent accuracy. Obviously, the determinants of behavior are enormously complex, and this absolute level of predictive certainty can probably never be attained.

Determinism and free will
Does the assumption of determinism imply that none of our behavior is the result of "free will" or "free choice"? The answer is yes. And it is precisely this point that sometimes turns people off to scientific analyses of behavior. The subjective belief in personal freedom is something most people cherish, and an analysis of human behavior based on the assumption of determinism sometimes inspires images of people as robots responding blindly to elements in their present and past environments. Critics of psychologist B. F. Skinner, who holds a totally deterministic view of behavior, frequently assert that his conception robs people of their humanity.

The free will versus determinism issue has raged as a philosophical debate for ages, and it is unlikely that it will ever be resolved. Certainly it can never be resolved scientifically, because science deals in empirical knowledge and there is no way that either determinism or free will can be proved empirically (through the senses). A determinist might point to specific conditions that universally "determine" some behavior, and the believer in free will would simply reply that under those conditions, people always *choose* to behave in the same way. However, although science cannot prove whether or not free will really exists, all scientists must follow a *methodology*, or a set of ground rules for scientific exploration. At the *methodological* level, determinism is an assumption that must be accepted as a working principle. If psychologists are to study human behavior scientifically, they must assume that there is lawfulness and regularity in behavior. If there were not—if behavior were random—then there would be no point in trying to discover causes, or in trying to create conditions to promote human welfare.

Constructs and operational definitions
Throughout this book such words as *aggression*,

*"I can't put it into layman's language for you. I don't
know any layman's language."*

Figure 1.2 Psychologists must be able to define constructs so that they can communicate their ideas
to others. (Drawing by Dana Fradon; © 1975 The New Yorker Magazine, Inc.)

stress, learning, and *motivation* are used. All of
these are concepts or *constructs* that refer to classes
of behaviors or to situations. Because they are words
that represent nonmaterial ideas and not things, they
may have different meanings for different people.
The term *hostility,* for example, represents a concept
that refers to a particular class of behaviors. The
notion of which behaviors belong to that class may
differ from person to person. If someone describes an
acquaintance as "hostile," you may find yourself still
wondering what that person is like. (See Figure 1.2.)

"What do you mean by that?" is a question that
psychologists must answer very precisely if they are
to study psychological constructs scientifically. In
order to begin to answer it they formulate *operational definitions* for their constructs. An operational definition specifies some observable event to
which the concept refers. That observable event may

be something that is *done* to the subject (so that
hunger may be operationally defined in terms of
"the number of hours that subjects are deprived of
food"). It may also be something that the subject
does (*hunger* may be operationally defined in terms
of subjects' ratings of how hungry they are). A construct, then, may be operationally defined both in
terms of conditions imposed on the subject (in
"stimulus" terms) or in terms of subject responses
(in "response" terms). Figure 1.3 shows some of the
operational definitions for the concept of stress that
have been employed in psychological research.
Chapter 10 describes psychological research on stress
in some detail.

Operational definitions of a given construct are, of
course, somewhat arbitrary, and different investigators may not agree on a given definition, just as one
person may not agree with another about whether a

15

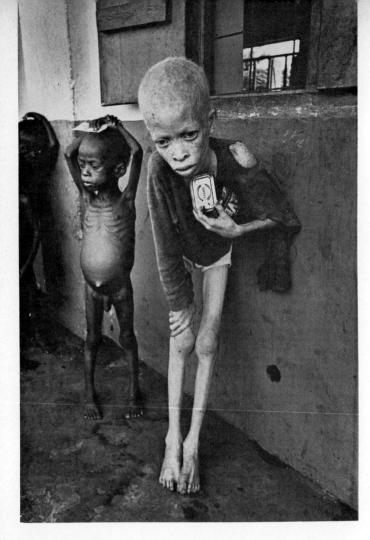

Both of these situations could provide an operational definition for hunger outside of a controlled laboratory situation. One shows people who have actually been deprived of food for a great length of time, the other shows people who are eating because they have decided they are hungry. (McCullin, Magnum: Sheffield, Woodfin Camp)

given behavior is hostile. Likewise, measures based on different operational definitions of the same construct may not always agree with one another. For example, subjects' ratings of their levels of stress may not agree with their measured physiological responses. It is critically important that investigators specify exactly the operational definitions that they use.

Despite these potential sources of controversy psychological constructs must be operationally defined; if they are not they cannot be studied scientifically. If a concept cannot be tied to observable phenomena in a way that people will agree is rational, then it is not the business of science. That is why psychologists cannot study such concepts as *soul* and *free will*. Although it is impossible to study free will itself, it is possible to study scientifically the *belief* in free will. It is possible to operationally define and measure beliefs (for example, by asking people the extent to which they believe they have free will) and to study the causes and effects of those beliefs.

How scientific activity proceeds

Scientific study is a dynamic, often exciting, and sometimes frustrating activity. It involves a continuous interplay between observation and attempts to explain and understand what was observed. Typically, the development of scientific understanding follows a path that has a number of steps: (1) informal observation and formulation of a question; (2) tentative initial attempts to respond to the question; (3) development of hypotheses to answer the question; (4) testing to validate the hypotheses; and (5) theory building.

Scientific activity always proceeds from some kind of observation. Many times researchers stumble onto important discoveries quite by accident. For example, the Curies discovered radioactivity because some photographic plates became spoiled after they were left in the same room with pitchblende ore. Following a hunch that the presence of the pitchblende might be related to the spoiling of the plates, the Curies conducted a series of crude experiments that ultimately led to the discovery of radium.

Once observations have led to the formulation of a problem, scientists try to figure out why or how the phenomenon occurs. They use reason, logic, and

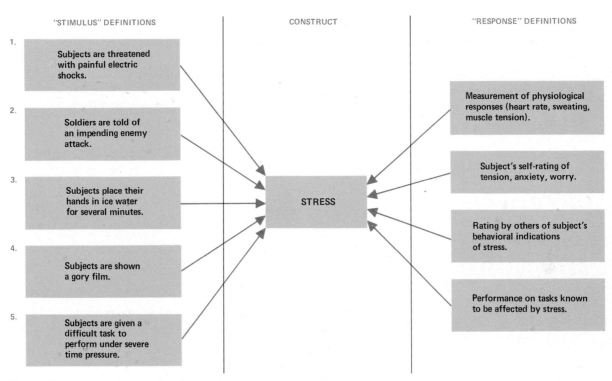

Figure 1.3 Some operational definitions of the construct *stress.* The construct may be defined either in terms of stimulus conditions to which the subject is exposed or in terms of subject responses.

sometimes simple guesswork to arrive at an initial and tentative explanation. Up to this point scientists behave exactly as lay people would, and arrive at preliminary explanations and understandings. But at this point lay people would usually stop, because they would have answered the "How?" or "Why?" question to their satisfaction. But scientists go on to *test* their understanding empirically. They formulate an "if . . . then . . ." hypothesis that can be tested and proceed to collect the observations necessary either to support or to refute it. If their hypothesis is supported by their observations—that is, if the relationships between events that they predict do indeed occur—they then return to their original "Why?" question and attempt to formulate increasingly broad explanatory principles that go beyond their observations. This is the way that theories are developed.

Good theories have a number of functions. First, they are able to incorporate within a single broad framework many existing facts, observations, and relationships. Second, additional hypotheses may be derived from the theory, may be tested, and may lead to new observations. In this way theories provide a foundation on which to build knowledge. In some cases the new observations do not support the theory, so that it needs to be modified or discarded. But it will still have served a valuable function by leading to the discovery of new knowledge and to the development of an even better and more inclusive theory.

In order for a theory to be useful it must be testable and capable of being refuted. It should be able to specify the types of relationships that are *not* possible as well as those that are. If it seems able to account for everything and anything, even seemingly contradictory facts, it is not a good scientific theory.

In comparison with those of other sciences, psychological theories are still rather primitive. Most so-called comprehensive psychological theories are

17

really not theories in the formal sense, but mixtures of observations, generalizations, speculations, and hypotheses that enjoy only limited support. Because of the bewildering complexity of human behavior, a comprehensive theory would be premature at this point; we need far more data on behavior and its causes.

HOW PSYCHOLOGISTS STUDY BEHAVIOR

In their efforts to observe, understand, predict, and control behavior, researchers employ a number of strategies. The strategies they choose are determined by their own goals and preferences, as well as by the objectives of the study. Some behavioral phenomena can be studied only in their natural setting; others can be investigated under more controlled laboratory conditions.

Although all the methods we describe enable researchers to observe behavior, some of them are better controlled and therefore produce more conclusive results than others.

Uncontrolled observation in natural settings

Some disciplines, such as astronomy and anatomy, are basically descriptive sciences. Scientists in these fields concentrate on obtaining precise descriptions of certain phenomena through careful and objective observation. Sometimes even basic observation can present problems. Up until this century, much of the research in anatomy, for example, had to be conducted illegally. Medical students stole corpses from graves in order to dissect and examine them, because it was necessary to have the subject matter of the science in front of them.

Most of us are familiar with the descriptive work of such people as Jane Goodall, the anthropologist who conducted painstaking observations of the behaviors of apes in their native habitat. Such observations of behavior in naturalistic settings can be of great value, particularly in the early stages of research. By describing behaviors and the specific circumstances under which they occur, scientists can obtain leads to explore later under more controlled conditions.

Sanity in insane places

David Rosenhan (1973) of Stanford University described an experiment using naturalistic observation in a paper entitled "On Being Sane in Insane Places." He was concerned with what happens to people who are diagnosed as mentally ill if they begin to act completely sane after they are hospitalized. Are they recognized immediately as sane and released, or does the label of *mentally ill* affect the ways in which their behavior is perceived by the staff?

Eight normal individuals, including Rosenhan, were admitted to mental hospitals when they complained that they were hearing voices. All except one received a diagnosis of schizophrenia, a serious behavior disorder characterized by disorganized thought processes and inappropriate emotional responses. Once admitted to the hospitals, the "patients" acted as normal as possible. They falsified their names and occupations (several were psychiatrists and psychologists) but gave their true life histories.

Were these patients immediately detected as imposters? Not at all. Despite their public show of sanity, no staff member in any of the hospitals ever expressed any suspicion of them. (It is interesting to note, however, that these patients were frequently detected by other patients on their wards.) Although the false patients were highly motivated to obtain a release from the hospital, their hospitalization periods ranged from 7 to 52 days, with an average stay of 19 days.

The hospital staffs were apparently conditioned to see their patients as mentally ill, and they found evidence for mental illness in even the most innocuous behaviors. For example, at one hospital, the most exciting events of the day were mealtimes. One psychiatrist pointed to a group of patients waiting outside the lunchroom and remarked to a group of staff members that this behavior reflected the unconscious "oral-incorporative needs" that are symptomatic of schizophrenia. A later examination of hospital records also disclosed that when the false patients gave their true life histories, the clinicians writing the diagnostic reports often distorted the facts to fit their preconceived idea that the patients were schizophrenic. (Chapter 15 describes current knowledge about schizophrenia). When any of the patients became justifiably angry at staff members, their anger was almost always attributed to their mental illness rather than to the behaviors of the staff.

More than anything else, Rosenhan's investigation reveals the pervasive effect of being labeled mentally ill. Once individuals receive that label, chances are that others will respond to them as non-people. For example, the false patients were instructed to ask ward psychiatrists, nurses, and attendants reasonable questions, such as, "Do you know when my case will be reviewed by staff again?" Of the 185 questions of this type addressed to psychiatrists, only 6 percent were answered with a verbal response. Of a total of 1283 questions asked of nurses and attendants, 88 percent were completely ignored, and fewer than 3 percent received verbal responses.

Once it was attached, the label of *schizophrenic* persisted long after the behaviors that led to the original diagnosis had ceased. Every false patient except one (who was still diagnosed as schizophrenic) was discharged with the diagnosis *schizophrenia, in remission* which meant that the disorder was still present but not in an active form. Perhaps the most damaging effect of such labels as *crazy* and *mentally ill* is that the patients themselves may come to accept them and behave accordingly.

Rosenhan's research raises a number of important questions: How many undiscovered sane people are there in mental hospitals? How many might behave adaptively outside the hospital but behave in a pathological manner in response to the hospital situation?

Although observational research conducted in natural settings cannot yield the same kind of understanding that we can obtain in more controlled settings, it does permit observation of "real-life" behavior, and it can provide a valuable basis for more controlled research.

Observation under controlled conditions
When psychologists move their observational activities from the real world into a laboratory setting, they can control the situation in which the behavior occurs and standardize it for all subjects.

Blind obedience to authority
After World War II the Nuremberg war trials were conducted in order to try Nazi war criminals for the atrocities they had committed. In many instances the defense offered by those on trial was that they had "only followed orders." During the Vietnam War American soldiers accused of committing atrocities in Vietnam gave basically the same explanation for their actions.

Most of us reject justifications based on "obedience to authority" as mere rationalizations, secure in our convictions that we, if placed in the same situation, would behave differently. However, the results of a series of ingenious and controversial investigations performed in the 1960s by psychologist Stanley Milgram suggest that perhaps we should not be so sure of ourselves.

Milgram wanted to determine the extent to which people would obey an experimenter's commands to administer painful electric shocks to another person. Pretend for a moment that you are a subject in one of his studies. Here is what would happen. On arriving at a university laboratory in response to a classified ad offering volunteers $4 for one hour's participation in an experiment on memory, you meet another subject, a pleasant, middle-aged man with whom you chat while awaiting the arrival of the experimenter. When the experimenter arrives, dressed in a laboratory coat, he pays you and then informs you and the other person that one of you will be the subject in the experiment and that the other will serve as his assistant. You are chosen by lot to be the assistant, but in reality you are the subject.

The experimenter explains that the study is concerned with the effects of punishment on learning. Accompanied by you, the "subject" is conducted into a room and strapped into a chair, and a large electrode is attached to his wrist. He is told that he is to learn a list of word pairs and that whenever he makes an error he will receive electric shocks of increasing intensity. On hearing this, the "subject" responds, "When I was at the West Haven V.A. Hospital a few years ago, they detected a slight heart condition. Nothing serious, but are these shocks dangerous?" The experimenter replies in an unconcerned manner that although the shocks may be painful, they will cause no permanent tissue damage.

You and the experimenter then proceed to an adjoining room connected by an intercom so that the "subject's" responses can be heard. You are seated in front of an apparatus with 30 toggle switches ranging from 15 volts to 450 volts. (See Figure 1.4.) Your task is to administer the learning task to the "subject." Whenever he gives an incorrect answer, you must give him an electric shock, starting at the lowest level (15 volts) and increasing the level by 15 volts each time. You are given a sample shock of 45 volts and find it moderately painful.

What you are unaware of at this point is that you are in a carefully contrived situation. The learner is actually an actor who receives no shock at all, and the responses you hear over the intercom are tape-recorded so that they will be exactly the same for each "assistant." The experimenter's actions are also carefully programmed.

As the experiment proceeds, the learner makes error after error. You increase the shock level steadily until he is clearly experiencing pain. The tape-recorded responses are programmed to correspond to the shock intensities as follows:

75 volts Ugh!
90 volts Ugh!
105 volts Ugh! (louder)
120 volts Ugh! Hey, this really hurts.
135 volts Ugh!!
150 volts Ugh!!! Experimenter! That's all. Get me out of here. I told you I had heart trouble. My heart's starting to bother me now. Get me out of here. I told you I had heart trouble. My heart's starting to bother me. I refuse to go on. Let me out.

165 volts Ugh! Let me out. (shouting)
180 volts Ugh! I can't stand the pain. Let me out of here! (shouting)
195 volts Ugh! Let me out of here. Let me out of here. My heart's bothering me. Let me out of here! You have no right to keep me here! Let me out! Let me out of here! My heart's bothering me. Let me out! Let me out!
210 volts Ugh!! Experimenter! Get me out of here. I've had enough. I won't be in the experiment any more.
225 volts Ugh!
240 volts Ugh!
255 volts Ugh! Get me out of here.
270 volts (Agonized scream). Let me out of here. Let me out of here. Let me out of here. Let me out. Do you hear? Let me out of here.
285 volts (Agonized scream).
300 volts (Agonized scream). I absolutely refuse to answer any more. Get me out of here. You can't hold me here. Get me out. Get me out of here.
315 volts (Intensely agonized scream). I told you I refuse to answer. I'm no longer part of this experiment.
330 volts (Intense and prolonged agonized scream). Let me out of here. Let me out of here. My heart's bothering me. Let me out, I tell you. (Hysterically) Let me out of here. Let me out of here. You have no right to hold me here. Let me out! Let me out!

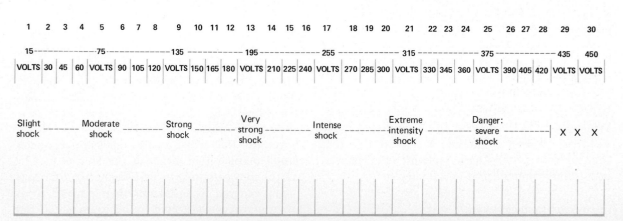

Figure 1.4 The control panel of the shocking apparatus used in the Milgram research. (Milgram, 1974, p. 28.)

Let me out of here! Let me out! Let me out!

345 volts (*At 345 volts and thereafter, there was only silence.*)

(Milgram, 1974, pp. 56–57)

But supposing you express unwillingness at some point to continue shocking the learner? In that event the experimenter, sitting at a nearby desk, would respond in one of the following ways:

"Please continue" or "Please go on."
"The experiment requires that you continue."
"It is absolutely essential that you continue."
"You have no other choice. You must go on."

Having now experienced the Milgram situation at least in your imagination, how long do you think you would continue to administer shocks? Most of our students maintain that they would not go beyond 105 volts before refusing to continue the experiment. A panel of psychiatrists predicted before the experiment began that perhaps only 1 percent of the subjects would proceed to the 450-volt level.

In fact, however, the "shock" produced by the results of this study was much more startling than the simulated shocks in the experiment. Forty men ranging in age from 20 to 50 and representing a cross section of the population, participated in the investigation. The maximum shock levels they administered are shown in Table 1.2. Nearly two-thirds of them administered the 450-volt maximum shock, and the average maximum shock they administered was 368 volts.

Virtually all the people who administered high levels of shock exhibited extreme discomfort, anxiety, and distress. Most verbally refused to continue on one or more occasions. But continue they did when ordered to do so by the experimenter, who assured them that what happened in the experiment was his responsibility.

By contriving a situation with many real-life elements, Milgram succeeded in demonstrating that a high percentage of "normal" people will obey an authority figure even when the destructive effects of their obedience are obvious. The conclusions that he draws from his work are chilling indeed:

A commonly offered explanation is that those who shocked the victim at the most severe level were monsters, the sadistic fringe of society. But if one considers

Table 1.2 Maximum shock levels administered by subjects in the Milgram experiment

Shock level	Verbal designation and voltage level	Number of subjects giving each maximum shock level
	Slight Shock	
1	15	
2	30	
3	45	
4	60	
	Moderate Shock	
5	75	
6	90	1
7	105	
8	120	
	Strong Shock	
9	135	
10	150	6
11	165	
12	180	1
	Very Strong Shock	
13	195	
14	210	
15	225	
16	240	
	Intense Shock	
17	255	
18	270	2
19	285	
20	300	1
	Extreme-Intensity Shock	
21	315	1
22	330	1
23	345	
24	360	
	Danger: Severe Shock	
25	375	1
26	390	
27	405	
28	420	
	XXX	
29	435	
30	450	26
	Average maximum shock level	368 volts
	Percentage of obedient subjects	65.0%

From Milgram, 1974, p. 60.

that almost two-thirds of the participants fall into the category of "obedient" subjects, and that they represented ordinary people drawn from working, managerial, and professional classes, the argument becomes very shaky. Indeed, it is highly reminiscent of the issue that arose in connection with Hannah Arendt's 1963 book, *Eichmann in Jerusalem*. Arendt contended that the prosecution's effort to depict Eichmann as a sadistic monster was fundamentally wrong, that he came closer to being an uninspired bureaucrat who simply sat at his desk and did his job. For asserting these views, Arendt became the object of considerable scorn, even calumny. Somehow, it was felt that the monstrous deeds carried out by Eichmann required a brutal, twisted, and sadistic personality, evil incarnate. After witnessing hundreds of ordinary people submit to the authority in our own experiments, I must conclude that Arendt's conception of the *banality of evil* comes closer to the truth than one might dare imagine. The ordinary person who shocked the victim did so out of a sense of obligation—a conception of his duties as a subject—and not from any peculiarly aggressive tendencies.

This is, perhaps, the most fundamental lesson of our study: ordinary people, simply doing their jobs, and without any particular hostility on their part, can become agents in a terrible destructive process. Moreover, even when the destructive effects of their work become patently clear, and they are asked to carry out actions incompatible with fundamental standards of morality, relatively few people have the resources needed to resist authority. A variety of inhibitions against disobeying authority come into play and successfully keep the person in his place. (Milgram, 1974, pp. 5–6)

Milgram's method of investigation also generated shock waves among psychologists. Many questioned whether it was ethical to expose subjects without warning to experiments that were likely to generate considerable stress and that might conceivably have lasting negative effects on them. But supporters of Milgram's work argue that adequate precautions were taken to protect participants. There was an extensive debriefing at the conclusion of the experiment, and participants were informed that they had not actually shocked anyone. They had a friendly meeting with the unharmed "subject." The purpose of the experiment was explained to them, and they were assured that their behavior in the situation was perfectly normal. Further, supporters argue, the great societal importance of the problem being investigated justified the methods the experimenters used. Finally, they cite follow-up questionnaire data col-

lected by Milgram from his subjects after they received a complete report of the purposes and results. Eighty-four percent of the subjects stated that they were glad to have been in the experiment (and several spontaneously noted that their participation had made them more tolerant of others or otherwise changed them in desirable ways). Fifteen percent expressed neutral feelings, and only 1.3 percent stated that they were sorry to have participated.

The controversy over the ethics of Milgram's research has raged for over a decade. In combination with other controversial issues, it has prompted a deep and abiding concern for protecting the welfare of subjects in psychological research. Because of such concerns, it is most unlikely that Milgram's research could be conducted today. (We return to the question of research ethics at the conclusion of this chapter.)

Correlational research: Finding relationships between events

In many instances psychologists wish to study the relationship between naturally occurring events that they cannot directly control. For example, they may be interested in the relationship between scores on an intelligence test and college grade point average, or in how unemployment figures are related to crime rates. Research designed to study relationships between measurable events not necessarily influenced by the experimenter is called *correlational* research.

Motivation and economic growth

A research project conducted by David C. McClelland (1961) of Harvard University provides an example of the correlational approach. McClelland and his associates have developed a means of measuring human motives by analyzing the content of stories written by subjects in response to certain standard pictures. One of these motives is need for achievement (*n* Ach). The researchers analyze stories for themes and imagery that relate to achievement. They have developed a detailed scoring system that can be applied to virtually any written material, even if it was written centuries ago.

In a series of correlational studies McClelland and his associates related the amount of achievement imagery in children's stories to national economic growth. They reasoned that the level of achievement concern in children's books reflects the motivational level of the adults in the country at that time, as well as the values that are being transmitted to the children. If high achievement motivation is responsible for economic and industrial growth, there should be a *positive* relationship between achievement imagery and economic-industrial indexes. That is, the higher the level of achievement imagery, the higher should be the economic-industrial indexes.

The result of one such study (de Charms and Moeller, 1962) is shown in Figure 1.5. Achievement imagery in second- and fourth-grade school readers was related to the number of patents issued per million population in the United States between 1810 and 1950. There is a striking degree of correspondence between the two measures.

McClelland (1961) reasoned that if school books transmit cultural values and influence the development of motivation in children, it should be possible

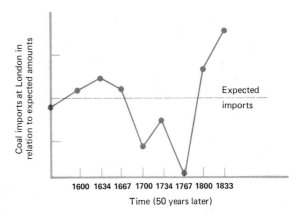

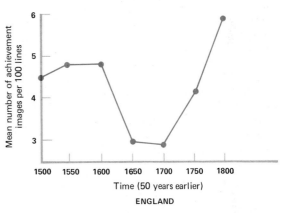

Figure 1.6 Relationship between achievement imagery in children's books and an index of industrial activity (amount of coal imported) obtained 50 years later. (Adapted from McClelland, 1961.)

to predict economic growth by examining school books. Texts from more than 20 different countries were analyzed for achievement motivation and these scores were related to economic and industrial indexes measured within the next 50 years (when the children had reached adulthood). There was a high correlation between the motivational scores and the indexes. As an example, Figure 1.6 presents data relating achievement motivation to changes in the amount of coal later imported by England between the years 1500 and 1800.

Do the relationships between achievement motivation factors in textbooks and economic indexes prove that the need to achieve *causes* economic growth? Not necessarily. Perhaps economic growth attributable to other factors causes changes in achievement motivation. Perhaps other factors cause

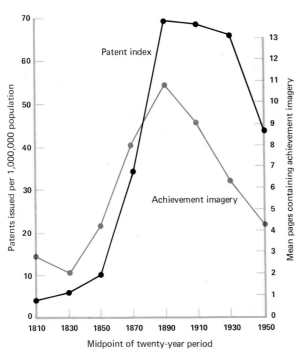

Figure 1.5 Relationship between achievement imagery in children's stories and number of patents per million population issued in the United States between 1800 and 1950. (Adapted from de Charms and Moeller, 1962.)

23

BOX 1.2

Correlation and causality

The following relationships have been reported by researchers. Can you account for the causal factors in each case?

1. On clear days there are more auto accidents than on inclement days.
2. Cigarette smokers have lower college grades than do nonsmokers.
3. A high correlation was found between the hourly salaries of Presbyterian ministers in Massachusetts and the price of rum in Havana.
4. Suicides and weddings both occur at their highest rates during June.
5. Athletic participation is related to good social and emotional adjustment in children.
6. There was a high correlation between the number of storks seen nesting in French villages and the number of births occurring in those locales.

changes in both economic growth and need for achievement, and there is no causal relationship between them. It is very important to remember that *correlation does not mean that there is a causal relationship between two events*. There are numerous possible reasons why two variables might be correlated. (A variable is any characteristic that can vary. It may refer to a behavior that can be measured or to a condition or event that can vary naturally or be manipulated.) Box 1.2 presents some scientifically validated correlations that you might try to explain.

The controlled experiment

The scientist's most powerful tool for establishing cause-and-effect relationships is the controlled experiment. The experimental method differs from the observational and correlational approaches because the experimenter directly manipulates one or more

variables in order to observe the ways in which behavior is affected. The logic behind the approach is that if two groups of "equivalent" subjects are treated identically in all respects except one and if the behavior of the two groups differs, then that difference is likely to have been caused by the factor that was varied. The essence of the experimental method is control.

Independent and dependent variables

In an experiment the variable that is manipulated by the experimenter is called the *independent variable*, and the behavior that is studied is called the *dependent variable*. In other words, the independent variable is the *cause*, or the *stimulus*, the dependent variable is the *effect*, or the *response*. The measurable results concerning the dependent variable are presumably *dependent* on the effects of the independent variable. In an experiment that studies the effects of marijuana on driving performance, marijuana would be the independent variable and the measure of driving performance would be the dependent variable. You will notice that when data are presented in graphs, the dependent variable is plotted on the vertical axis and the independent variable on the horizontal axis.

Experimental and control groups

The experimental method is a powerful scientific tool because it is specifically designed to rule out alternative explanations of the results. Using this method, experimenters strive to hold everything in their experiments constant except the independent variable(s) that they are manipulating. If they are successful in doing this, they can be fairly confident that they have actually established a cause-effect relationship. Although this method may sound simple in principle, it is exceedingly difficult to execute because of the many factors, some perhaps unknown to the experimenter, that can influence behavior within even a highly controlled setting.

Returning again to our experiment regarding the effects of marijuana on driving performance, we might conduct a study in which we allowed a group of subjects to smoke a given quantity of marijuana before we administered a standardized driving test. How would we go about evaluating the performance of these subjects so that we could obtain an answer to our experimental question? Obviously, we would need a comparison group similar in every way to the marijuana group except for the fact that they did not smoke marijuana before the driving test. We might attempt to make the two groups of subjects as equivalent as possible, either by matching them on factors believed to affect driving behavior or by assigning subjects to the two groups on some random basis in the hope that any differences within the groups would cancel themselves out. We would then have an *experimental group*, which received the marijuana, and a *control group*, which did not. By comparing the behaviors of the two groups on the dependent variable measure of driving performance we can assess the effects of the independent variable—marijuana smoking versus no marijuana smoking.

Having discussed the logic and some of the key concepts in the controlled experimental approach, let us now consider some of the basic experimental designs used in psychological research.

Manipulating one independent variable:
The two-group design

The simplest experimental design is the one we have just described. It consists of an experimental and a control group. The experimental group receives the experimental treatment; the control group does not. Everything else in the experiment is held constant.

As an example of this design, we describe a series of experiments on "learned helplessness" performed by Martin Seligman and his associates at the University of Pennsylvania (Seligman, 1975).

First, a group of dogs was given electric shocks while they were strapped in a harness. Another group of dogs, the control group, did not receive this treatment. The next day the experimental group dogs were placed in a shuttlebox, a chamber with two compartments separated by a barrier and a floor that could be electrified. They had to learn to respond to a warning signal by jumping over a barrier to the other side of the shuttlebox within ten seconds. If they did not, they received 50 seconds of painful electric shock.

The animals in the control group, who had not previously been confined and shocked, learned the avoidance behavior very quickly. But about two-thirds of the experimental dogs seemed unable to learn the avoidance behavior. They seemed passively

resigned to suffering the shock, and even if they successfully avoided the shock on one trial, they were unlikely to do so on the next. For some dogs it required up to 200 experiences of being forcibly pushed over the barrier in order for their "learned helplessness" to wear off. In the initial experiment the learned passivity wore off in about 48 hours, but in later studies the researcher found that repeated exposure to the inescapable electric shock could produce a state of learned helplessness that lasted as long as a week.

The obvious conclusion to draw from this study is that exposure to the unavoidable electric shock taught the dogs that they had no control over what happened to them, and this lesson carried over to the shuttlebox avoidance situation. But we must also ask, "Was the only difference between the experimental and control conditions the unavoidable electric shock?" The answer is no; the dogs in the experimental group were hung in harnesses, whereas the control animals were not. This is an example of *confounding*, or mixing, two variables (unavoidable shock and confinement in the harness). When variables are confounded, it is impossible to know for sure which variable produced the effect. One might argue that the confinement of the harness, not the unavoidable electric shock, produced the learned helplessness.

In order to test these alternative explanations the researchers conducted a second experiment in which both experimental and control group dogs were hung in harnesses. The experimental group received the unavoidable electric shock, and the controls were provided with a panel they could push with their noses in order to avoid the shock. Basically the same results were obtained as in the first experiment, showing that it was the unavoidable shock and not merely confinement in the harness that produced the effect.

Seligman's research is a fine example of how rigorous laboratory research performed with animals can have strong implications for human behavior. Learned helplessness has now been experimentally demonstrated with college students (Hiroto, 1974), and its relevance to such psychological problems as poverty and depression is being actively explored (Seligman, 1975). In Chapter 15 we discuss Seligman's learned helplessness theory of depression.

Multivariate and repeated-measures designs

Two other experimental designs, somewhat more complex than the two-group design, are frequently used in psychological research and thus deserve brief mention; they are called *multivariate* and *repeated-measures* designs.

Sometimes psychologists are interested in simultaneously assessing the effects of two or more independent variables on a dependent variable behavior. (This is one way to avoid the problem of confounding, discussed earlier.) For example, a social psychologist may wish to study the effects of overcrowding on both men and women. A *multivariate* experiment could be designed in which the independent variables of degree of crowding and sex of subject were studied simultaneously in relation to certain social behaviors, such as aggressiveness, competitiveness, and interpersonal attraction. In its simplest form the design of the experiment might resemble that shown in Figure 1.7. This design is a very valuable one because it allows us to isolate the separate effects of each of the independent variables as well as to assess whether the independent variables combine or *interact* with one another in some fashion to affect the dependent variable. In fact, an experiment like the one previously described has actually been performed (Freedman *et al.*, 1972), and it was found that as conditions became more overcrowded, males liked others less and became more aggressive and competitive, whereas females became less aggressive and competitive and liked the other people more. This illustrates an *interaction* between degree of crowding and sex of subject, because the response to being overcrowded differed for men and women. Chapter 18 describes other research on overcrowding.

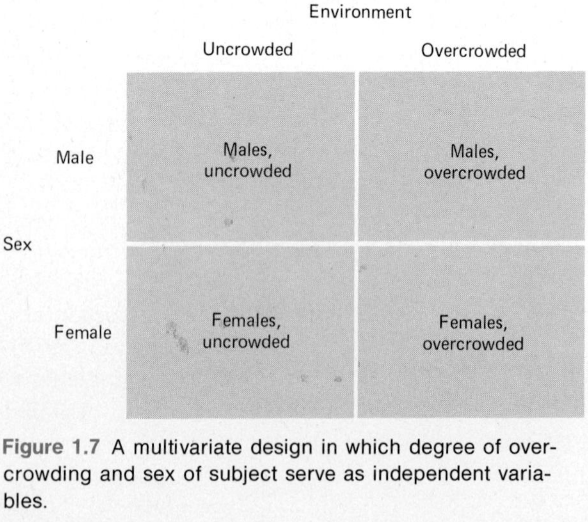

Psychologists are frequently interested in studying changes in behavior over time or as a result of certain experiences. The *repeated-measures* design is used for this purpose. It involves measuring the same behaviors on two or more occasions.

A repeated-measures design to study behavior change was used in an experimental program designed to increase the social interaction of withdrawn elementary school children. The children chosen for the study were observed in their classrooms and the number of social interactions they had with others during specific time periods was recorded. Then they were divided into an experimental and a control group. The experimental group was shown a 20-minute film in which children engaged in a variety of desirable and rewarding social interactions, whereas the control group was shown a 20-minute film about trained dolphins at Marineland.

Following their exposure to the films, the children were again observed in their classrooms and their social interactions were again recorded. The results of this experiment are presented in Figure 1.8. The children exposed to the social interaction film showed a dramatic increase in social interactions, whereas the control subjects showed no improvement. Moreover, by the end of the school year, several months later, teacher ratings indicated that only one of the children exposed to this brief experimental film was still described as withdrawn (O'Connor, 1969).

The various research approaches that we have described enable psychologists to observe behavior in a variety of ways. They also have at their disposal a large number of statistical techniques to evaluate their observations and assess the meaning of them.

Statistical analysis: Drawing conclusions about data

Statistical analysis is the tool that researchers use to draw conclusions and make inferences about their

Figure 1.7 A multivariate design in which degree of overcrowding and sex of subject serve as independent variables.

Overcrowded situations such as this one may bring out aggressive tendencies in males and lower aggression in females. (Menzel, Stock, Boston)

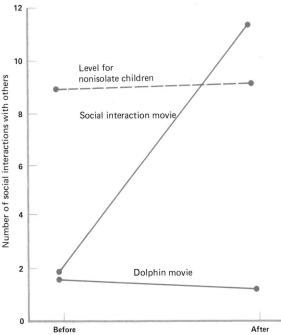

Figure 1.8 Results of a repeated-measures design used in an experimental program intended to reduce severe social withdrawal in children. Social interactions were measured before and after the children watched either a film in which models interacted socially or one showing dolphins performing. (Adapted from O'Connor, 1969.)

data. We do not discuss the statistical techniques themselves, but restrict ourselves to a discussion of the reasons why psychologists use statistical analyses and the meaning of the outcomes of statistical tests. Some of the basic statistical measures psychologists use to summarize data are described in Box 1.3.

Suppose your professor were to conduct an experiment using subjects from your class. The results would be based on this restricted *sample* of college students. However, it is unlikely that your professor would want to confine his or her conclusions to this small group of subjects; more likely he or she would want to generalize to "college students in general" or perhaps even "people in general." These larger groups are called *populations*.

Suppose a pattern of interesting results emerged from the study. Would this be a "real" finding applicable to the entire population, or would it be a chance occurrence resulting from an atypical sample? What is the likelihood that the same results would occur if the experiment were repeated again and again with other samples drawn from the population? These are the types of questions that could be answered through statistical analyses.

All statistical tests yield what is known as a *level of significance*. The level of significance is obtained

27

BOX 1.3
Descriptive statistics

Descriptive statistics provide a shorthand method for summarizing data. Supposing, for example, that your instructor made up two forms of your first exam in the course, one of which contained many humorous items and one of which contained no humor. If half of the class were given each form, it would be of interest to examine and compare the two sets, or *distributions,* of scores.

Our first question would probably be how well the students performed on the two forms of the test. Rather than simply examining all the scores in each distribution, we would prefer to have a single score for each group that characterized their level of performance—that is, a *measure of central tendency.* The most commonly used measures of central tendency are the *mean,* the *median,* and the *mode.* The mean is the arithmetic average, computed by summing all the scores and dividing by the total number of scores. The median is the point that cuts the distribution in half, so that 50 percent of the scores lie above and below it. It is not affected by extreme scores as much as the mean is. The mode is simply the score that the largest number of students obtained. The mean is the most frequently used measure of central tendency, and you will find that most of the data presented in this text are means.

Although measures of central tendency provide useful information about our distributions of scores, they do not tell us how much variability there is among scores. Do the scores cluster closely about the average, or do they vary widely, so that there are some very high and some very low scores? Obviously, the less variation there is among scores, the more the measure of central tendency is characteristic of the group's performance. *Measures of variability* help answer this question. The simplest measure of variability is the *range,* which is the difference between the highest and the lowest score. A measure of variation preferred by psychologists because it takes into account all the scores in the distribution, rather than only the highest and lowest ones, is the *standard deviation.* In computing the standard deviation the difference (deviation) between each score and the mean is squared and the deviations are summed and divided by the total number of scores minus 1 (e.g., by 19 if there are 20 scores). The square root of this "average deviation" value is the standard deviation.

Measures of central tendency and variability not only provide useful information about distributions of scores, but also are used in many tests of statistical significance. When scores are plotted according to the frequency with which they occur, the distribution sometimes resembles a symmetrical, or bell-shaped, curve known as a *normal distribution.* Half of the cases fall on each side of the mean. In a normal curve the median (which divides the distribution in

by comparing the results of a particular statistical test with a set of special statistical tables. The level of significance indicates the likelihood that the results obtained from the sample occurred by chance alone and do not reflect a finding that is characteristic of the population from which the sample was drawn. Significance levels are expressed as percentage figures. When psychologists write that their results are significant at the 5 percent (0.05) level of significance, they mean that the chances are only 5 in 100 that the same results would not occur if the entire population were tested in the experiment. In other

words, the chances are 95 in 100 that the obtained correlation or the differences between the various groups in the experiment hold for the entire population. The 0.05 level of significance is the conventional cutoff point used by psychologists. If the level of significance is above 0.05 (e.g., 0.06, 0.10, etc.), the results are not considered statistically significant.

Ethical standards in psychological research
Earlier, when we discussed Milgram's research on obedience to authority, we indicated some of the

half) and the mode (most frequently occurring score) are exactly the same as the mean. Many human characteristics, including height, weight, and intelligence, have distributions that approximate a normal curve. The normal curve has important statistical properties and is the basis for many of our techniques of statistical analysis. For example, if a normal curve is divided into bands, each equal to one standard deviation (S.D.), a fixed percentage of the cases falls in each band. The accompanying figure shows the percentage of the cases that falls in each band. Thirty-four percent of the cases fall within the band marked off by the mean and one standard deviation above the mean. Sixty-eight percent of the cases fall within one S.D. above and below the mean. Over 99 percent of the cases fall between three S.D.'s above and three S.D.'s below the mean.

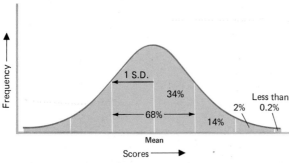

Percentage of cases falling in each portion of a normal distribution.

serious ethical concerns it evoked. Psychologists are now placing increasing emphasis on the protection and welfare of both human and animal subjects used in psychological research. They restrict their experimentation with certain groups of people who are not in a position to give their consent, such as children, the mentally retarded, and mental patients. Both federal and professional organizations are developing strict guidelines.

The ethical and moral issues involved in psychological research are not simple ones and are very similar to those with which medical researchers must deal. In some instances the only way to find out important facts about behavior or to develop new techniques for improving the human condition is to deceive subjects or to expose them to potentially stressful circumstances. In such cases investigators must carefully balance the potential benefits against the risks involved. To assist researchers in this task and to ensure that the welfare of subjects is not jeopardized, virtually every institution at which research is conducted has established panels that review every proposed project. If a given proposal is considered questionable on ethical grounds or if the rights, welfare, and personal privacy of subjects are not sufficiently protected, the proposal must be modified appropriately or the research cannot be conducted.

According to the American Psychological Association's current research guidelines, subjects cannot be placed in jeopardy either physically or psychologically without their informed consent. Subjects must be informed that they are free to withdraw from an experiment at any time without fear of penalty. They must be told about the procedures to be followed and duly warned about any risks that might be involved. If deception must be used, then subjects must be completely debriefed after the experiment, and the entire procedure must be explained to them. Special measures must be taken to protect confidentiality and to preserve the anonymity of the data. When children, seriously disturbed mental patients, or others who are not able to give consent are involved, such consent must be obtained from parents or guardians. Strict guidelines are also being developed for research in prisons. No prisoner can be forced to participate in research or penalized for refusal to do so, and in the case of rehabilitative programs, prisoners must be permitted to share in decisions concerning program goals. Researchers must strictly adhere to the code of research ethics or risk serious legal and professional consequences.

This book is about us. Our behavior is the subject matter of psychology, and this makes psychology a particularly meaningful subject of study for many people. Your decision to study psychology probably reflects, at least in part, a desire to achieve greater understanding of yourself and others. We hope that this book will help you achieve this goal.

In this chapter you met a number of psychologists

29

who are devoting their careers to expanding the frontiers of psychological knowledge. In the pages to follow, you will meet many more. It is said that "the excitement is in the chase," and we hope to communicate the excitement that exists on the frontiers of psychology. We are on the threshold of new breakthroughs and discoveries that promise not only greater understanding of ourselves and our behavior, but also an increased ability to achieve our full potential as humans.

SUMMARY

1. Psychology is the scientific study of behavior, including both overt (externally observable) and covert (internal) behaviors. Psychologists specialize in a variety of different areas—such as experimental psychology, social psychology, and clinical psychology—and their activities include research, teaching, and application of psychological principles.

2. The basic goals of scientific psychology are to observe, understand, predict, and control behavior. Understanding involves specifying the causes of behavior. There are two basic approaches to understanding the causes of behavior. The historical approach, which involves explaining why something occurred in the past, is limited by the fact that there are countless possible explanations and no way to ascertain which one is correct. Scientists prefer to test their understanding through prediction and control.

3. The issue of determinism versus free will is a philosophical question that cannot be settled scientifically, because it cannot be subjected to an empirical test. At a philosophical level a scientist may believe in either determinism or free will. However, at a methodological level psychologists must accept as a working principle that there is

lawfulness and regularity in human behavior if they are to study it scientifically.

4. In order for a construct to be scientifically useful it must be possible to provide an acceptable operational definition of it either in terms of conditions imposed on the subject (in "stimulus" terms) or in terms of observable behaviors of the subject (in "response" terms).

5. Scientific understanding usually proceeds through a number of steps: (a) informal observation and formulation of a question; (b) initial attempts to answer the question; (c) formulation of scientific hypotheses; (d) hypothesis testing; and (e) theory building.

6. A number of research strategies are used by psychologists. The most basic is uncontrolled observation in natural settings. Rosenhan's report of patient and staff behaviors in mental hospitals is offered as an example of naturalistic observation.

7. Observation under controlled conditions allows psychologists to control and standardize the situation to which subjects respond. Milgram's studies of blind obedience to authority utilized this approach.

8. Correlational research is designed to study relationships between naturally occurring events, which cannot be directly controlled. McClelland's research on the relationship between achievement imagery in children's stories and national economic growth is an example of the correlational approach. A limitation of the correlational approach is that causal relationships cannot be determined on the basis of correlation.

9. The controlled experiment is the scientist's most powerful tool for establishing cause-effect relationships. This approach involves the direct manipulation of one or more in-

dependent variables and an assessment of their effects on dependent variable behaviors. Comparisons of experimental and control groups, which differ only in terms of the variable(s) being manipulated, permits a determination of causal relationships between independent and dependent variables.

10. Statistical tests are used to generalize research results from samples to the population from which the sample was drawn. Such tests yield a level of significance, which indicates the probability that the results obtained from the sample occurred by chance alone and do not reflect a similar phenomenon in the population.

11. Psychologists are placing an increasing emphasis on the protection and welfare of human and animal subjects used in research.

Suggested readings

A career in psychology. Washington, D.C.: American Psychological Association; 1200 Seventeenth Street N.W.; Washington, D.C. 20036. This pamphlet describes vocational opportunities within the field of psychology and describes the preparation and training of psychologists.

Doherty, M. E., & Shemberg, K. M. *Asking Questions About Behavior: An Introduction to What Psychologists Do.* Glenview, Ill.: Scott, Foresman and Company, 1970. A readable and interesting introduction to psychological methodology organized around the question "How does stress affect personality?"

Evans, R. I. *The making of psychology: discussions with creative contributors.* New York: Alfred A. Knopf, Inc., 1976. This book consists of transcripts of discussions with 28 outstanding psychologists representing the major areas of psychology. The interviews introduce the readers to the contributors' main ideas and points of view.

Johnson, H. H. & Solso, R. L. *An Introduction to Experimental Design in Psychology: A Case Approach.* New York: Harper & Row, 1971. This book illustrates experimental procedures with examples from the scientific literature in psychology.

McCall, R. B. *Fundamental statistics for psychology* (2nd ed.). New York: Harcourt Brace Jovanovich, 1975. An introduction to statistical methods in the social sciences.

Chapter 2

Perspectives on Human Behavior

(Dietz, Stock, Boston)

On the evening of July 31, 1966, Charles Whitman, a student at the University of Texas, wrote the following:

> I don't really understand myself these days. I am supposed to be an average, reasonable, and intelligent young man. However, lately (I can't recall when it started) I have been the victim of many unusual and irrational thoughts. These thoughts constantly recur, and it requires a tremendous mental effort to concentrate on useful and progressive tasks. In March when my parents made a physical break I noticed a great deal of stress. I consulted a Dr. Cochrum at the University Health Center and asked him to recommend someone that I could consult with about some psychiatric disorders I felt I had. I talked with a doctor once for about two hours and tried to convey to him my fears that I felt overcome by overwhelming violent impulses. After one session I never saw the doctor again, and since then I have been fighting my mental turmoil alone, and seemingly to no avail. After my death I wish that an autopsy would be performed on me to see if there is any visible physical disorder. I have had some tremendous headaches in the past and have consumed two large bottles of Excedrin in the past three months.

Later that night Whitman killed his wife and mother. The next morning he went to the university tower with a high-powered hunting rifle and opened fire on the crowded campus below. Before he was shot to death 90 minutes later, he had shot 38 people, killing 14, and had even managed to hit an airplane.

Because of the shocking nature of the Whitman incident, it attracted widespread attention and there were many attempts to explain the causes of Whit-

A secretary at the University of Texas hides behind the base of a flagpole to avoid the gunfire of Charles Whitman. (UPI)

man's murderous acts. The letter that Whitman wrote provided a number of clues. Whitman referred to intense headaches, and a postmortem examination revealed a highly malignant tumor in a brain region known to be involved in aggressive behavior. Some experts suggested that his acts were caused by his damaged brain. Others viewed the immediate cause of Whitman's acts as a product of the "unusual and irrational thoughts" to which he referred. A study of Whitman's life revealed that he had a long history of rewarding experiences with guns, and some authorities on violent behavior pointed to these previous learning experiences as a possibly important causal factor. Still others cited Whitman's reference to his "overwhelming violent impulses" and suggested that these impulses had been bottled up for many years and had finally exploded into action because of the recent life stresses he described in his letter.

We can't be certain which of these potential causes was most important. Perhaps all of them contributed to varying degrees. The Whitman case dramatically illustrated the many vantage points from which a given act can be viewed and explained.

PERSPECTIVES IN PSYCHOLOGY

Have you ever met a person who seems to view the world much differently from the way you do? Did you find that he or she had different notions about why things happen, or what happened, and attached great importance to things that perhaps you did not even notice? Did it seem as if that person were viewing the same world through a different set of lenses?

Although opposing viewpoints may sometimes be uncomfortable for us in personal situations, they are the lifeblood of social, technological, and scientific progress. If everyone thought and perceived in exactly the same way, originality and creativity would, by definition, be impossible.

In the field of psychology a variety of perspectives for viewing people and their behaviors have emerged over the years, in part because psychology has roots in such varied disciplines as philosophy, medicine, and the biological and physical sciences. When this infant science emerged late in the nineteenth century, the diverse backgrounds and interests of the

33

fathers of psychology—and the enormous complexity of their new object of study—fostered many different approaches to the study of human nature. These differing perspectives caused bitter debates: What should constitute the subject matter of the new discipline? Which methods of study were acceptable? Some people with backgrounds in philosophy believed that psychology should be concerned with the study of subjective experience and the mental life of the individual. Others wished to model the new discipline after the physical sciences. The only acceptable subject matter for psychology, they insisted, was externally observable and measurable, or "overt," behavior. They wished to examine carefully stimulus-response relationships. Still others were fascinated by Darwin's theory of evolution and set out to discover which instincts people shared with other animals and how human traits were genetically determined. Meanwhile, a Viennese physician named Sigmund Freud was shocking nearly everyone with his assertions that people's behavior is largely governed by irrational and unconscious sexual and self-destructive impulses that they strive continually to keep under control. For Freud behavior was merely the surface manifestation of a raging battle within the person.

Perspectives on behavior are of more than merely intellectual interest. They serve as lenses through which the world of behavior is viewed, and they reflect and shape our very conception of human nature. They also determine which aspects of behavior we see as important and worthy of study, which questions we ask, and which methods of study we employ. In a very real sense, perspectives on behavior influence the directions in which psychology develops, what it learns about our behavior, and the kinds of contributions it makes to human betterment.

In this chapter we examine four influential perspectives on human behavior within present-day psychology. These four perspectives reflect in part the disciplines from which psychology developed; they utilize concepts derived from philosophy, the biological and physical sciences, and medicine. Each of the orientations continues to have a major influence on the development of psychology as a science, and each gives us a particular conception of human beings as animals, as reactors, as creatures in conflict, or as problem solvers.

These four perspectives are (1) the biological perspective; (2) the behavioristic perspective; (3) the cognitive perspective; and (4) the psychoanalytic perspective.

The biological perspective: The human animal

You probably do not often stop to consider that as a thinking and acting organism, you go back a long way—long before your own birth. Our species exists today because of our ancestors' ability to adapt, both biologically and behaviorally, to changing and often hostile physical environments. As a result of these adaptations, human beings are the most intricate and complex biological organisms ever to inhabit the earth. If we wish to understand fully our behavior, we must take into account the biological factors that influence it.

Historical development of the biological perspective

Human beings have long sought to understand the role of biological factors in their behavior. Pythagoras, Plato, and Galen all believed that the brain was the seat of the mind and the intellect. Aristotle disagreed, believing that the mind was localized in the heart. The Greek physician Hippocrates sought to account for differences in temperament in terms of proportions of humors—black bile, blood, yellow bile, and phlegm—in the body. Later advances in the biological sciences proved Pythagoras, Plato, and Galen correct, but the ideas of all these men kept attention focused on the relationship between mind and body.

Beginning in the sixteenth century, a number of scientific advances began to occur in the fields of anatomy, physiology, and biology: the study of dissected human cadavers (vigorously opposed by the church); experiments on the circulatory system; the invention of the microscope and the discovery of cells; the development of a biological classification system or taxonomy. A series of scientific breakthroughs about the functioning of the nervous system occurred in the first half of the nineteenth century. At the same time, advances within physics, such as the development of sensitive galvanometers, made it possible to study the electrical activity of nerve transmission. With experimental science coming of age, methods became available to study physi-

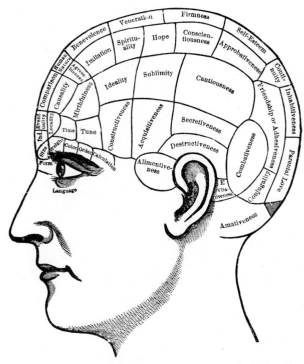

Phrenology charts of the nineteenth century reflected early attempts to locate centers of control in the head for emotions and behavior. (Culver)

ological factors in the behavior of animals and humans.

In 1859 shock waves that are still felt today were generated by the appearance of Charles Darwin's book *The Origin of Species.* Darwin was not the first to suggest the possibility of evolution in animals, but his theory was by far the most plausible, the most far-reaching, and the best documented. It seemed to many a denial of the exalted nature of human beings long fostered by religious dogma.

In retrospect, Darwin's ideas were quite simple. He proposed that new species evolve over time in response to environmental conditions, a process he called *natural selection.* This simply means that any inheritable characteristic that increases the likelihood of survival will be maintained in the species. Those characteristics that do not improve chances for survival will be eliminated from the species over time because those creatures possessing them will not survive to procreate.

As an example of natural selection, let us suppose that a nuclear war were to occur, producing extremely high and long-lasting levels of radioactivity

throughout the world. Presumably, only those humans able to tolerate abnormally high levels of radioactivity could hope to survive; and only the children of the survivors to whom this characteristic was genetically transmitted would survive. Through this process of natural selection, a species of humans having a much higher tolerance for radiation would evolve over generations, so that a characteristic originally present in only a few would become characteristic of human "nature."

Darwin assumed that the principle of natural selection could be applied to all living things, including human beings. Contrary to popular misconceptions, Darwin did not say that we are direct descendants of the apes of today; rather, he believed that both human beings and apes had a common ancestor in the distant past. And indeed, the weight of scientific evidence is on Darwin's side. Recent studies in molecular biology have shown that human beings are physiologically closer to chimpanzees than dogs are to foxes or goats are to sheep; in many ways chimps are related more distantly to gorillas than to us (Johnson, 1972). Our physical evolution from lower animal forms is no longer seriously questioned within science, and most religions today accept the possibility of evolution, with the proviso that at some point in the physical evolution of human beings, God gave them an immortal soul.

Evolution has relevance to more than man's physical development. An organism's biology determines its behavioral capabilities, and its behaviors determine whether or not it will survive. The important point is this: *What evolved in the history of man was successful behavior as well as a changing body.* Anthropologist Sherwood Washburn (1960) speculates that when dwindling vegetation in some parts of the world forced apes from the trees and required that they hunt for meat, a two-legged, or *bipedal,* existence facilitated survival within the changing environment. Bipedalism in turn fostered the development and use of improved weapons, and hunting encouraged the development of social organization. Tool use and bipedal locomotion put new selective pressures on many parts of the body, including the teeth, hands, and pelvis, but the greatest pressure was placed on the brain. Human beings did not simply require larger brains. Rather, selective pressures developed those capabilities in the brain that were

35

The famous Scopes trial on evolution provoked widespread public controversy over Darwin's theory. Clarence Darrow (center) defended Darwin and won his case, but many people still feel the theory conflicts with their religious convictions about the creation of life. (Culver)

most critical to the emerging human way of life: attention, memory, language, and thought. Between Australopithecus of 2 million years ago and Neanderthal man of 75,000 years ago, the brain tripled in size, and the amount of brain tissue devoted to the "higher mental processes" increased dramatically. Human behavior contributed to the development of the human brain, just as the development of the brain contributed to the development of human behavior. (See Figure 2.1.)

Evolutionary theory has had a profound influence on the study of psychology. If human beings are viewed as an elaborate form of animal life, then it should be possible to learn certain things about them by studying lower forms. For example, much has been discovered about the ways in which the human brain functions by electrically stimulating or surgically removing parts of the brains of lower animals. Likewise, because the life spans and reproductive cycles of many animals are shorter than those of humans, it is possible to study several generations of animals over a relatively short period of time. Animals can be studied in ways that humans, for ethical and practical reasons, cannot, so that research with animals is an important tool for obtaining knowledge about human behavior.

The importance of biological factors in human

behavior is underscored by many recent discoveries about brain processes and genetic determinants. Given the technological advances that are occurring, there are many who believe that we are on the threshold of revolutionary discoveries about the biological side of our nature and its effects on our behavior.

The behavioristic perspective: Human beings as reactors

Whenever we try to explain that we did something because somebody "provoked" us to or because "the situation called for it," we are adopting a behavioristic perspective. This perspective views behavior as resulting from an organism's interactions with its environment. Although behaviorists acknowledge biological factors, they believe that human beings are basically reactors to their past and present environments. Behaviorists deny that people freely choose the ways in which they will behave. The factors that control human behavior, they say, reside in the external environment rather than within the individual. People's behavior is jointly determined by (1) how they have been conditioned by their previous life experiences and (2) stimuli within their immediate environments.

THE BRAIN GETS BIGGER

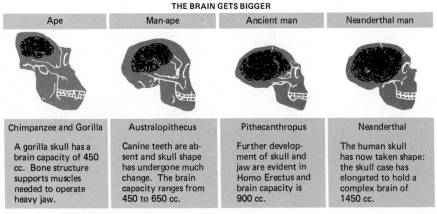

Ape	Man-ape	Ancient man	Neanderthal man
Chimpanzee and Gorilla	Australopithecus	Pithecanthropus	Neanderthal
A gorilla skull has a brain capacity of 450 cc. Bone structure supports muscles needed to operate heavy jaw.	Canine teeth are absent and skull shape has undergone much change. The brain capacity ranges from 450 to 650 cc.	Further development of skull and jaw are evident in Homo Erectus and brain capacity is 900 cc.	The human skull has now taken shape: the skull case has elongated to hold a complex brain of 1450 cc.

Figure 2.1 Evolution of the human brain over several million years. Shaded areas of skulls trace the dramatic development of the brain, particularly those parts concerned with the higher mental processes. (J. S. Wiggins, K. E. Renner, G. Clore, and R. J. Rose, *The Psychology of Personality*, Reading, Mass., Addison-Wesley, 1971, Fig. 3.1, p. 35.)

Historical development of the behavioristic perspective

The behavioristic perspective is rooted in a seventeenth-century school of philosophy known as British empiricism. The empiricists believed that all ideas and knowledge are gained *empirically*, that is, through the senses. According to John Locke, one of the early empiricists, the human mind is a *tabula rasa*, a "blank tablet," on which our experience makes imprints. Human beings know and behave according to the dictates of their environments. Empiricism also maintained that observation was a more valid approach to knowledge than reason, an idea that has been enormously influential in shaping the development of science.

As the developing science of psychology entered the twentieth century, many psychologists were attempting to study human consciousness by presenting specific stimuli to subjects and then asking them to report on their internal experiences in great detail. This method was called *introspection*, or "looking within." Behaviorism emerged as an alternative to this approach. A leader in the new movement was John B. Watson, who argued that the proper subject matter of psychology was observable behavior and not consciousness. A person was likened to a machine that is conditioned by experience to react to certain stimuli. Watson even suggested that thought was nothing more than subvocal talking and that we would eventually prove that it consisted of tiny movements of the larynx. Emotions or feelings were thought to consist of glandular activity or changes within genital tissues. Watson put a lid on the box that is the human being and declared that it was empty. Human beings, he said, were products of conditioning factors in their histories, and their behavior could be controlled completely by manipulating their environments.

This strong emphasis on the role of experience in behavior led behaviorists to devote their efforts to discovering the laws of learning and performance. They believed that the same basic principles of learning applied to both humans and animals, and their subsequent research with both humans and animals led to many discoveries and applications of these principles. Many view these accomplishments as the greatest single contribution of American psychology.

The leading contemporary figure in behaviorism is B. F. Skinner, of Harvard University; he has devoted over 40 years to the study of learning and behavior control and has long been the leading spokesman for the behavioristic perspective. Two of his most widely read works, *Walden Two* (1948) and

37

BOX 2.1
A biological view

When I think of how basic biological factors influence my own behavior, I can't help but think that many other psychologists are barking up the wrong tree when they try to relate what people do solely to the social conditions of their lives. When I'm very hungry I'm a completely different person than after eating a big dinner. Look at the influence of the genes—physical things—on the kind of people we are. For me, biology is the starting point for understanding man.

This really came through to me when my grandmother had a stroke a few months ago. When that blood vessel broke in her brain, she became almost a different person. She can't seem to remember things any more, and her thinking seems much slower. She isn't the same sharp person she used to be. The fact that such a small change in her brain could have such large effects on her really hit me.

BOX 2.2
A behavioristic view

The easiest thing in the world is to find examples of how the environment controls the behavior of organisms. We learn to conform to the requirements of the environment and we learn relationships that pay off, relationships that get us things we need or want. The trick is finding which environmental events most effectively control our behavior.

behaviors are caused by factors within individuals, Skinner says, serves to divert attention from the real causes of behavior, which reside in the outer world. Presumed "inner" factors have acquired the status of an "explanatory" *homunculus*, a "man within the man." The behaviorist strives to replace the inner autonomous man with the external environment in accounting for behavior. Skinner and other behaviorists point to the failure-ridden history of human beings' attempts to solve their problems by changing their "inner selves." If human beings are to be changed, indeed saved, behaviorists maintain, we must manipulate the environment that controls behavior through its pattern of rewards and punishments. Moreover, Skinner believes that large-scale control over human behavior is possible today. The chief barrier to social engineering is, according to Skinner, an outmoded conception of people as free agents.

Strict behaviorists such as Skinner are in the minority. Although they agree that the environment influences behavior in important ways, most psychologists do not consider people to be only reactors to their external world. They believe that important processes occur within people that influence the ways in which they respond to their environments.

The cognitive perspective:
Human beings as problem solvers

"What is it about ourselves that makes us uniquely human?" In our classes this question never fails to stimulate a lively discussion. When we think about human nature, we can hardly help focusing on our marvelous abilities to think, to imagine, to judge, to anticipate, to decide, to reflect on ourselves and our world, to plan, to create—in short, on our cognitive, or "higher," mental processes.

The term *cognitive* comes from the Latin word *cogitare*, "to know." Whereas the behavioristic perspective views human beings as reactors to external stimuli, the cognitive perspective emphasizes the ways in which people mentally process such stimuli, evaluate them, and respond in terms of their plans and anticipations. In this perspective human beings are viewed as active and rational problem solvers who create, interpret, and transform many of the stimuli to which they respond.

Beyond Freedom and Dignity (1971), have aroused storms of protest from those who dispute the concept of the human being as reactor.

Although Skinner does not deny that mental events, images, and feelings occur within each person, he maintains that these are themselves behaviors, not causes. The erroneous belief that human

BOX 2.3

A cognitive view

I think, I plan, and I interpret what's going on in the world about me. As I see it, psychologists need to know a lot more about these mental processes. How we view the world influences our behavior regardless of what the world really is like or how it seems to other people. Psychology might well be defined as the study of information-processing in humans and other animals. How can we talk about things like intelligence and creativity if we don't know anything about how we think and solve problems?

Historical development of the cognitive perspective Psychology has been concerned with cognitive processes from the very beginning. The first formal experimental laboratory was founded in Leipzig, Germany, in 1879 by Wilhelm Wundt, who wanted to reduce consciousness to its basic elements, to create a kind of "mental chemistry." He believed that sensations were basic units of consciousness, and with his associates he set out to study the nature of "pure" sensory experience through the method of introspection. It was this tradition that was attacked so vigorously by Watson and the behaviorists some 30 years later. Nevertheless, Wundt and his successors helped to establish within psychology a cognitive tradition that endures to this day.

Galton's mental tests. Darwin's theory of evolution, which was extremely influential in the development of the biological perspective, also stimulated important work within the area of cognition. Darwin's half-cousin, Sir Francis Galton, became a pioneer in studying the inheritance of mental abilities. In *Hereditary Genius* (1869) he provided evidence that eminent men tend to have eminent offspring. However, he wished to measure mental abilities more directly than by biographical eminence, and this led him to develop a variety of "mental tests" that are the ancestors of the modern ability and intelligence tests described in Chapter 14. Galton's work demonstrated that mental skills could be measured objectively, an accomplishment of no small importance to an infant science trying to achieve scientific respectability.

Gestalt psychology. In the 1920s, when behavioristic stimulus-response psychology was growing more influential in the United States, one of its chief rivals was a German school of thought known as Gestalt psychology. The word *Gestalt* may be translated as *whole* or *organization*. Whereas Wundt and his successors attempted to analyze consciousness into its basic elements and the behaviorists reduced everything to stimulus-response relationships, the Gestalt psychologists used demonstrations to show that our perception is organized so that "the whole is greater

Wilhelm Wundt set up the first formal experimental laboratory for psychology in Leipzig, Germany in 1879. (Granger)

Figure 2.2 Perceptual organization: Nine lines or three groups?

In a demonstration of insight learning, a modern-day Sultan prepares to join two sticks together in order to reach a prized delicacy. (Yerkes Regional Primate Center)

than the sum of its parts." For example, most people perceive Figure 2.2 as three groups of vertical lines rather than as nine vertical lines. The Gestalt psychologists believed that principles of perceptual organization are built into our nervous systems. We consider the Gestalt principles of perceptual organization in greater detail in Chapter 4.

During World War I Wolfgang Köhler, one of the leaders of Gestalt psychology, was stranded at a research station on Tenerife, one of the Canary Islands. There he conducted research with apes and chickens. He learned that such animals perceive *relationships* between stimuli rather than isolated stimuli. His apes and chickens could easily be taught to choose the *brighter* or the *larger* of two stimuli, no matter how they were arranged. (This is called *transposition*, a phenomenon that also enables us to recognize a tune played in different keys.) Köhler concluded that the perception of relationships is the essence of intelligence, and he called the sudden perception of a useful relationship *insight*. Several examples of insight were demonstrated by one of Köhler's apes, named Sultan. Köhler hung a banana from the top of Sultan's cage, beyond his reach. Sultan scratched his head a few times, looked about his cage, noticed a box in one corner, and placed the box beneath the dangling banana so that he could reach the delicacy by standing on the box. On another occasion Sultan joined two sticks together to reach a banana that had been placed out of reach, a feat that has gone down in history as an act of simian genius. Because demonstrations of insight learning were difficult to explain in the conditioned reflex terms of the behaviorists, they stimulated new interest in human cognitive processes.

Piaget and the development of thought. A final figure in our brief historical excursion is a man who has reshaped our conceptions of the development of thought in children. A zoologist by training, Jean Piaget, together with his Swiss colleagues, has spent

nearly 50 years studying how children think, reason, and solve problems. He has done this through naturalistic observation and *empathic inference*, the term for Piaget's practice of carefully observing how children approach problems and then attempting to infer how they must have experienced the situation in order to respond as they did. Piaget theorizes that specific transforming stages of cognitive development *emerge* in the course of development, stages that cannot be explained by the accumulation of past experience at a lower stage. We consider Piaget's work in greater detail in Chapter 9.

The cognitive perspective gives us a far more active role in shaping our own behavior than do the biological and behavioristic perpsectives. In this view people are less what their experience makes them than what they make of their experience. Far from being passive reactors to their environments, people impose their own organization and interpretations on it; and their cognitive constructions are, in turn, affected by their experiences.

Cognitive social learning theory. During the past decade a theoretical approach to behavior has emerged that combines behavioristic and cognitive principles into a more comprehensive framework. *Cognitive social learning theory* looks for causes of behavior not only in the external environment, but also within each individual.

Cognitive social learning theory also emphasizes that people can learn by observing the behaviors of others and storing this information in their memories and that individuals are capable of regulating their own behavior through self-administered response consequences (e.g., self-approval or self-reproach).

The psychoanalytic perspective: Human beings in conflict

The psychoanalytic perspective of human behavior is the one that most people usually associate with psychology and psychiatry. Through countless books and articles such terms as *unconscious, defense mechanism*, and *Freudian slip* have become part of our everyday vocabulary.

Like the cognitive perspective, the psychoanalytic conception of human behavior focuses on inner causes, but with two important differences. First, cognitive theories focus on thinking and problem solving, whereas psychoanalytic theory places greater emphasis on underlying motivations, feelings, and conflicts. Second, the psychoanalytic perspective places great importance on *unconscious* factors in behavior. In this view the mind is a battleground where conflicting psychic forces strive for superiority, and actual behavior often represents a compromise between these forces.

Historical development of the psychoanalytic perspective

Although human beings have sought to probe the shadowy underworld of their hidden motives periodically throughout history, the traditional notion has been that we are creatures ruled by reason and conscious thought. But late in the nineteenth century, as the shock waves produced by Darwin's evolutionary theory were still being felt throughout the intellectual world, Sigmund Freud mounted a second and equally shocking assault on the prevailing conception of human beings as rational creatures.

As a young Viennese medical student in the early 1880s Freud became interested in the treatment of hysteria, a disorder marked by physical symptoms such as blindness, pain, or paralysis without any apparent organic cause. Freud worked with hysterical

Freud contemplating the bust of Freud sculpted by O. Nemon for the famous doctor's 75th birthday. (Wide World)

patients, using hypnosis at first and later a technique he developed called *free association*. In free association the patient was instructed to say whatever came to mind and to let one association lead freely to another, even if the order did not seem logical or rational. To Freud's surprise, his patients (most of whom were women) consistently reported and relived extremely painful and long-"forgotten" childhood sexual experiences and desires, after which their symptoms showed a marked improvement. But many of these childhood sexual experiences proved to be fictitious. This suggested to Freud the existence of a compelling sexual drive which prompted them to create these fantasies.

Freud also found that sexual material often emerged in dreams and "slips of the tongue." These observations, plus an intensive period of self-analysis, led him to propose that much of human behavior is influenced by forces of which we are unaware. He attached particular importance to an inborn sexual instinct, and he believed that our adult personalities are strongly influenced by the way in which we cope with our instincts as we grow up. Freud speculated

41

BOX 2.4

A psychoanalytic view

Motivation is a fundamental fact of life. Our goals, our desires influence what we do. Freud demonstrated that often we aren't even aware of our motivations—they are unconscious. Why do I make embarrassing slips of the tongue? Why do hostile jokes strike me as funny? Why do I tend to forget unpleasant thoughts and events? Sure, we don't know much about the unconscious—but it's there.

that because early sexual desires and needs are forbidden, they are *repressed,* or pushed down into the unconscious portion of the mind. There they remain as sources of energy, continually striving for release. Elaborate defenses are constructed by the personality to keep the forbidden instincts under control and to allow their release in disguised and socially acceptable forms (a process called *sublimation*). Psychiatric symptoms appear when the defenses either fail to control the instincts or force the person to behave in some abnormal way in order to maintain control of them. But behavior, whether it is normal or abnormal, is a reflection of a constant internal struggle between instinct and defense.

The psychoanalytic theorist thinks that human behavior is largely the result of complex psychological forces from within ourselves, and there is considerable emphasis on the influence of past conflicts on current behavior. We should note, however, that Freud's theory has a strong biological emphasis. Freud, who was himself heavily influenced by Darwin, regarded people as animals whose inherently destructive nature is kept under control by the constraints of society.

Whereas the behavioristic and cognitive perspectives tend to focus on *how* a person behaves, the psychoanalytic approach focuses on the *meaning* of the behavior in terms of inner dynamics. Psychologists of this persuasion believe that the thoughts and

behaviors of which we are aware reflect only a fraction of our mental life, and that our major psychological influences are irrational and unconscious, rooted in our instinctual drives and long-forgotten childhood experiences.

Applying the perspectives

In reading about these four different perspectives on human behavior, did some seem more true than others? Did you agree or disagree with some of the conceptions of human nature implied by the perspectives? If you were a psychologist which perspective(s) would you adopt?

The standards by which we judge theories or perspectives within science are not absolute "truth" or "popularity." Most important are their capacity to stimulate new discoveries, and to some extent our ability to verify them. Each of the four perspectives asks us to look at different types of causal factors in behavior. Each helps us to understand different aspects of the ways in which we function, aspects we would miss if we were to view behavior from only one or two of the perspectives.

In the next section we illustrate how the four perspectives can be applied to help us understand human aggression. We have chosen this topic because our destructive behavior is perhaps the greatest threat to our continued survival as a species.

THE PERSPECTIVES IN ACTION: UNDERSTANDING HUMAN AGGRESSION

Should the human race ultimately perish in a nuclear holocaust, the final chapter will have been written on the most destructive creature ever to inhabit the earth. Although physically puny in comparison with other past and present inhabitants of their world, human beings have advanced brains that allow them to create weapons capable of wreaking death and destruction on their fellows without the necessity of personal contact. Between 1820 and 1946 alone, human beings killed over 59 million of their kind in wars and murderous attacks (Richardson, 1960). As we have become more "civilized," we have also become more destructive. About $200 a year is spent to educate each child on earth, whereas about

Does this constitute aggression? These children are playing a game that involves competitive behavior, but they seem to have no deliberate intentions of harming one another. Many psychologists feel that intent to harm is a critical factor in defining aggression. (Brown, Monkmeyer)

$7800 is spent to train and equip each soldier (Smith, 1970). Domestic violence is no less alarming than is international aggression. Crime rates continue to soar, and over 800,000 violent crimes are committed against Americans each year. In any given year the likelihood that an American will be the victim of a serious personal attack is 1 in 550, and the risk of death by willful homicide is about 1 in 20,000. Government statistics show that there are now over 40 million handguns in the United States, and the number is increasing by about 2.5 million annually.

(The social problems posed by crime are discussed in Chapter 17.)

Human aggression may be defined as any behavior intended to harm or injure another. Because we are defining aggression as a particular form of *behavior*, it should not be confused with emotions that may underlie it, such as frustration, anger, or resentment. People can be enraged with each other without necessarily expressing the rage through aggressive behavior. In addition, aggressive behavior may be physical, may be verbal, or in some instances may consist in

43

not doing something that another person might like an individual to do. Finally, the requirement that there be an *intent* to harm another presents a somewhat thorny problem. Intent to harm is a private, hidden motivation that must be inferred from events that precede or follow the behavior. Sometimes it is very difficult to establish whether or not there was intent to harm. However, the requirement of intent is an important part of the conventional definition of aggression.

Important discoveries concerning causal factors in aggression have been made in fields as diverse as biology, criminology, psychology, sociology, political science, and medicine. From a general perspective, aggression is a complex *biosocial* phenomenon having many causes, some biological, some social, some cognitive, and some psychodynamic. These causes interact and combine with one another in complex ways, many of which are not yet understood.

The biological perspective on aggression

Basically, all human behavior is performed by an organism whose brain and nervous system are affected by a host of biochemical, genetic, and experiential factors. The biological perspective looks for the causes of aggression in our evolutionary history, in the biological workings of our brain, and in genetic and physiological factors.

Evolution and aggression:
Hunting, dominance, and territoriality

From an evolutionary standpoint, aggressive behavior has been one of the key factors in human survival.

Figure 2.3 A male baboon mounts another male to assert his dominance. Ritualized gestures of this kind reduce violent conflict. (DeVore, Anthro-Photo)

The careful arrangement of private space in public bathrooms is another example of the way territoriality functions in everyday life. (Bailey, Stock, Boston)

Prehistoric man survived by becoming a hunter, and many scientists have suggested that our aggressiveness and cruelty can be traced to this prehistoric adaptation. Second, among human beings, as among lower animals, dominance hierarchies are the most characteristic form of social organization. That is, there is a definite power structure, in which all animals are in a dominant or submissive position in relationship to each other. Aggressiveness is closely associated with one's place in these hierarchies. Once a dominance hierarchy is established, much fighting is avoided through the use of ritualized threats by one animal and signs of submission by another. (See Figure 2.3.) Dominance hierarchies also determine mating patterns. Because the most dominant males are those most likely to mate, we would expect aggressiveness to become more common within the species. This kind of selective mating is important to us for another reason. In order for brain development to have evolved as rapidly as it did in the human species, there must have been some special breeding system. It is likely that that system was based on a dominance hierarchy.

When space or food resources are scarce, many species limit their growth and survive by marking off living spaces or territories, which they defend against

BOX 2.5
"Territoriality" in the library

You can find some interesting parallels to animal territoriality in your own daily life. Have you ever noticed how you and others "stake out" an area for yourselves at tables in your college library? Do you hang your coat on an adjacent chair and spread books over the table to mark off your "private" space?

Felipe and Sommer (1966) studied the effects of intrusion on personal space in a university library. Females sitting alone at tables served as unsuspecting subjects. A female experimenter would take a seat at the subject's table at varying distances from her, sometimes in the seat right next to hers. In general, the closer the intruder sat, the more quickly the subject got up and left. Subjects showed many signs of discomfort, such as turning away from the intruder and placing books as a barrier between themselves and the intruder.

intruders. *Territoriality* is a behavior common to many (but not all) animal societies. Obviously, aggressiveness is instrumental in competing for resources, in defending territory, in surviving.

Some popular writers, such as Robert Ardrey in *The Territorial Imperative* (1966), point out parallels between human behaviors and certain territorial behaviors in animals. For example, people strive to acquire land and goods, they form attachments to their property, and they show a willingness to defend what they feel is theirs. However, although such parallels are interesting, they certainly do not allow us to conclude that a single territorial instinct is at work. The causes of human aggression are undoubtedly more complex, and it does not enhance our understanding to attribute them to a single instinct

whose existence is dubious, even on an animal level. This is not to deny, however, that aggressiveness had adaptive value during our development as a species. It is ironic that a form of behavior that figured so importantly in our development and survival as a species has now become the problem that most endangers our survival. As biologist Loren Eiseley has written, "The need is now for a gentler, a more tolerant people than those who won for us against the ice, the tiger, and the bear" (1946, p. 140).

Konrad Lorenz's theory: Lack of controls. In species other than man, killing seldom results when members of the same species aggress against one another. Although many members of the animal kingdom have developed deadly weapons, they seldom use them against others of their own species. Rattlesnakes, for example, could quickly kill one another with their deadly fangs. However, when fights occur between rattlesnakes, the combatants engage instead in a kind of Indian wrestling, attempting to force the other's head to the ground. (See Figure 2.4.) Such formidable creatures as lions and wolves frequently battle their own kind to establish dominance hierar-

Figure 2.4 Rattlesnakes could quickly kill each other with their deadly fangs. But most species have evolved mechanisms that inhibit deadly combat between their own members. These rattlesnakes limit their combat to attempts to force each other's head to the ground. (Eibl-Eibesfeldt, "The fighting behavior of animals." Copyright © 1961 by Scientific American. All rights reserved.)

45

BOX 2.6
Ethology and instinctive behavior

Developments in the field of *ethology,* the study of animal behavior in the natural environment, have provided valuable information about instinctive behavior. Ethologists discovered that instinctive behavior does not run itself off blindly and inflexibly, but rather occurs as a result of interactions between external and internal stimulus conditions, changes in any of which cause corresponding changes in the details of instinctive acts. The first concern of ethologists is with behavior patterns typically performed by all animals of a species. In 1973, three ethologists—Konrad Lorenz, Nikolaas Tinbergen, and Karl von Frisch—shared a Nobel Prize for the comparative studies of behavior among animals in their natural environment.

The work of von Frisch was one of the most important pioneering contributions to ethology. He was concerned with bees' communicative behavior and showed that bees use discrete wiggle and dance signals to communicate to other bees not only information concerning the existence of food but also its distance and the direction in which it can be found. Von Frisch showed that each subspecies of bee has its own dance language and that dances performed by members of one subspecies are incomprehensible to members of other subspecies. Von Frisch concluded that the language of the bees was instinctive and not learned.

Ethologists have shown that innate fixed patterns of animal behavior do not just happen, but are triggered by stimuli called *releasing stimuli* or *sign stimuli.* A male robin will attack a bundle of red feathers but not a perfect dummy of a male lacking the characteristic red breast. Such examples show that animals respond with quite specific reactions to specific releasing stimuli. The ethologists have also been interested in early experience, but from a particular perspective. They employ the concept of *imprinting,* by which a specific response of an animal becomes attached to an object that later functions as a releasing stimulus. This occurs within a limited critical period, usually at a young age, and seems to be independent of reinforcers such as food or water. If ducks or doves are reared by other species they will later show a pairing preference toward a partner belonging to the foster species, even when a partner of their species is available. The accompanying figure shows a group of goslings that became attached or imprinted to Konrad Lorenz because he was the first large moving object they encountered after birth.

Some ethologists have tried to generalize their findings with animals to human beings. There have been speculations that aggression and other human social behavior can be understood in terms of instinctive mechanisms and specific releasers.

chies, but such struggles are ritualistic and rarely lead to death or serious injury. Except for certain rodents, no animal kills its own kind as frequently as we do. Why are we different?

Ethologist Konrad Lorenz (also see Box 2.6) believes that aggression is instinctive to human beings as well as to other animals. However, lower animals who lacked internal controls against killing members of their own species probably became extinct long ago. The most successful animals were those who learned to assert superiority without seriously injuring one another, and most species have developed ritualized behaviors through which members can signal submission and thereby escape unharmed. But people often fail to respond to signs of submission from their fellows. Lorenz (1966) believes that because human beings are physically relatively unmenacing creatures, they did not develop internal

46

Genetic factors in aggression

Hereditary traits are carried by complex organic molecules called *genes*, which affect our biological processes throughout life and may thereby affect our behavior. Biological characteristics that influence aggression may thus be transmitted genetically. Animal breeders have for many years bred animals for specific traits through *selective breeding*, which involves mating animals with selected characteristics with other animals having selected characteristics. Strains of pedigreed dogs, fighting cocks, and "brave" bulls have been developed in this way. In Thailand, gambling on contests between fighting fish has for centuries been a national pastime, and the selective breeding of winners has resulted in the development of the Siamese fighting fish, which will instantly attack its own mirror image.

Selective breeding in animals. Controlled laboratory studies have shown that aggressive behavior can be strongly affected by selective breeding procedures. In research that has continued for nearly two decades, K. Lagerspetz and his associates have selectively bred mice for aggressiveness. Their procedure was to pair male animals in a cage for brief periods and to rate aggressive behavior on a seven-point scale that ranged from avoiding the other animal and attempting to escape if attacked to attacking the other and biting hard enough to draw blood. Each mouse was paired with at least seven others. Once males had been selected for high and low aggressiveness, they were mated with sisters of other mice who were high or low in aggressiveness in order to produce highly aggressive or nonaggressive offspring.

By the seventh generation the two strains of animals differed markedly not only in aggressiveness, but also in physical characteristics. A comparison between animals from the thirteenth and fourteenth generations disclosed that the mice from the aggressive line had heavier forebrains and their brains were found to contain greater concentrations of several neurochemicals associated with aggression (Lagerspetz, Tirri, and Lagerspetz, 1968).

Genetic factors in human aggression. There is at least some evidence that genetic factors may contribute to aggressiveness in humans. Male identical twins, who are genetic carbon copies of one another, are more

(McAvoy, Time Life)

inhibitions and controls against killing. Hence there was nothing to curb their acquired deadliness once they began to use their brains to construct weapons.

Many evolutionary theorists besides Lorenz view people as innately aggressive. As we shall see, Freud also thought that human aggression is instinctual. Are human beings truly aggressive "by nature"? We return to this question later in the chapter.

47

BOX 2.7

The case of the XYY "supermale"

Genes, the units of heredity, are carried in egg and sperm cells and are arranged in ladderlike strands called *chromosomes.* In humans there are normally 46 chromosomes, 23 from each parent. When an egg cell is fertilized, these chromosomes line up in pairs. One pair of chromosomes determines the sex of the person. Females have a matching pair of X chromosomes (XX), whereas males have an X chromosome and a Y chromosome (XY). The Y chromosome affects the distribution of hormones that impart male characteristics.

Sometimes accidents or mutations occur, resulting in chromosomal abnormalities that cause a physical or mental disorder in the child. The Down syndrome, or mongolism, is the result of a chromosomal abnormality. Another abnormality involves an extra Y chromosome in males. In recent years scientists have been trying to find out if there is a relationship between the so-called XYY supermale chromosome abnormality and tendencies toward violent antisocial behavior.

Surveys of newborn children reveal that approximately 1 in 500 males possesses an extra Y chromosome. In the 1960s investigators reported that a larger percentage (2.9) of mentally defective men institutionalized for various forms of criminal behavior carried the extra Y chromosome than would be expected in the general population (0.2 percent) (Jacobs, Brunton, and Melville, 1965). Later reports confirmed these findings. Unfortunately, because tallness is associated with the XYY pattern, many of these studies biased their results by selecting only tall prisoners for chromosomal testing; and the subjects, of course, were all institutionalized men. Predictably, this procedure would result in a higher incidence of the XYY pattern than would be the case if all institutionalized males were tested. When the XYY males were compared with normal XY males, it was found that they had been arrested earlier and more often.

On hearing about these results, alarmists began calling for the testing of all children and the "genetic counseling" of parents of XYY children. A moral question was hotly debated: Were XYY men responsible for their crimes? In Paris in 1968 a convicted murderer named Daniel Hugon received a reduced sentence because his attorneys argued that an extra Y chromosome was responsible for his violent tendencies (Johnson, 1972). A rumor circulated that Richard Speck, the convicted murderer of eight Chicago nurses, was an XYY male. (The rumor was

similar in their aggressive and dominant behavior patterns than are male fraternal twins, who differ genetically from one another (Gottesman, 1963). However, this difference in similarity between identical and fraternal twins does not occur in female twin pairs. Presumably this is because genetic predispositions toward aggressiveness are reinforced by male sex role training and discouraged in female sex role training.

Recently there has been considerable interest in the possibility of a link between a specific genetic abnormality involving an extra Y chromosome in males and aggressive behavior. Box 2.7 describes the search for this genetic linkage and illustrates some of the pitfalls that await those who draw sweeping conclusions on the basis of insufficient data. It also points to the difficulties involved in establishing a direct linkage between genes and behavior without considering how genetic characteristics influence life experiences.

The brain and aggression

Many attempts have been made to locate and study areas of the brain involved in aggressive behavior. One research approach is to damage or electrically stimulate certain areas of the brains of animals and

later disproved.) Lost in all the publicity about the XYY's "violent" tendencies was the fact that 88 percent of the crimes that XYY males in the original survey had committed were *nonviolent*. Later reports disclosed that XYY prisoners in fact engaged in less assaultive behavior than did their normal XY male counterparts. More recent studies have failed to find XYY males among institutionalized tall boys with severe behavioral problems. The existence of a genetically caused tendency toward aggression in XYY males now appears highly unlikely.

Psychologists have begun to suggest alternative explanations for the criminal behaviors of some XYY males. Albert Bandura, for example, suggests that an important factor may be the tall physical stature that is associated with the XYY abnormality.

> Apart from the psychological strains and older companionship fostered by conspicuous tallness, large offenders are likely to be treated by arresting officers as older and more dangerous than are smaller ones. Early commitment to a reformatory populated with delinquents is apt to launch one on an antisocial career, regardless of genetic makeup. (Bandura, 1973, p. 25)

Bandura's statement serves to remind us that genetic influences may affect a person's behavioral development indirectly, by increasing the likelihood that the person will have certain kinds of social learning experiences.

to study the subsequent effects on aggressive behavior. These studies have shown that several structures deep within the brain are involved in triggering and inhibiting aggressive behavior. Surgical destruction of these areas of the brain can produce either extremely tame or very aggressive animals. By implanting tiny electrodes (*microelectrodes*) in specific areas, it is possible to stimulate an animal to make vicious attacks and exhibit killing behaviors. Physiologically, however, the matter seems to be quite complicated. The same aggressive behaviors can be produced by stimulating or removing very different areas of the brain, and the stimulation or removal of

a specific area may produce a variety of different behaviors.

Although certain areas of the brain have coordinating functions in aggression, it is clear that these aggression centers are closely regulated by other areas of the brain that process information coming from the environment. The manner in which neural and environmental factors are jointly involved in aggression is illustrated in a famous experiment conducted by Jose Delgado (1967).

Delgado implanted electrodes in members of a monkey colony and observed the social behaviors of the monkeys both under normal circumstances and when an aggression center in selected monkeys was electrically stimulated through radio transmission. The monkeys had been living together for some time and a dominance hierarchy had developed. Delgado

The monkey on the floor cowers fearfully as he is attacked by a monkey whose brain is being electrically stimulated. Delgado has shown that depending on relative position in the dominance hierarchy, stimulation at the same brain location can result in either attack or submission. (Courtesy of J. M. R. Delgado)

49

found that the monkey's position in the dominance hierarchy had a strong influence on the way it behaved when its hypothalamus was stimulated. When a male monkey who occupied a dominant position in the hierarchy was stimulated, he would attack subordinate male members, but not females. But stimulation of the *same* area in a subordinate monkey elicited cowering and submissive behavior. Delgado found that he could influence a given monkey's behavior under stimulation simply by placing him with other monkeys who were either above or below him in the dominance hierarchy. Thus organisms possess brain mechanisms that allow them to behave aggressively, but the triggering of these mechanisms is dependent on other areas of the brain that receive and process information from the environment.

In humans certain kinds of brain damage or disorders can produce violent and unpredictable behavior. The Charles Whitman case received widespread publicity because of its terrible toll in human lives, but unfortunately, it is not unusual for persons to suffer from uncontrollably violent impulses because of physical disorders. During one eight-month period a total of 45 people appeared at Massachusetts General Hospital complaining of such impulses. About a quarter of these self-referred patients had symptoms of neurological disorders, and 11 of them either owned or carried deadly weapons (Lion, Bach-y-Rita and Ervin, 1969).

We have looked briefly at some of the ways in which aggression and its causes are viewed from a biological perspective. Perhaps the most important point for us to keep in mind is that although biological factors are important determinants of aggressive behavior, they interact in important ways with environmental factors.

The behavioristic perspective on aggression

No matter what inner forces you may sense in yourself or in others, if you view a single action or event in terms of its time sequence, you will obtain a somewhat different perspective on it. Does aggressive behavior occur because it is first prompted and later "seconded"? Although the behavioristic perspective acknowledges the role of genetic and physiological factors in human behavior, it focuses primarily on

causes in the external environment. The behavioristic approach to the study of aggression involves an analysis of the following elements:

Present stimulus conditions and previous learning $\longrightarrow$ Aggressive behavior $\longrightarrow$ Consequences of aggression

To the behaviorist, biological factors are "givens" that set physical limits on behavior, cognitions are irrelevant, and psychodynamic factors are regarded as little more than fictional myths. This perspective has isolated important environmental factors that strongly influence aggression.

Response consequences and aggression

The cornerstone of the behavioristic perspective is that our behaviors are largely influenced by the outcomes they provide for us. Behaviors that lead to positive outcomes become more likely to recur in the future, whereas those that do not or that have negative consequences are less likely to be repeated. Following this assumption, persons who are rewarded for aggressive behaviors are more likely to behave aggressively.

Both animal and human research supports this prediction. A number of studies have shown that formerly nonaggressive animals can be trained to become vicious aggressors if conditions are arranged so that they are consistently victorious in fights with weaker animals. Conversely, if conditions are arranged so that an animal is defeated in early battles, it becomes extremely submissive; and the younger an animal is when it first suffers defeat, the more submissively it will react to attacks by other animals.

The extent to which aggression is rewarded affects people in much the same way as it does animals. In one study of four-year-old nursery school children, the investigators recorded a total of 2583 aggressive acts and their consequences. Children whose aggressive behaviors produced positive outcomes for them (such as forcing another child to give up a desired toy) became increasingly more aggressive. Those whose aggressive behaviors were unsuccessful or led to punishing consequences were less likely to be aggressive in the future (Patterson, Littman, and Bricker, 1967). A particularly ominous finding was that about 80 percent of the aggressive behaviors produced rewarding consequences for the aggressor.

Aggressive behaviors may also be learned and strengthened when they succeed in stopping abusive treatment from others. In some instances aggression may be the only successful technique for dealing with an antagonist. A person who does not have social or verbal skills, as is the case with many delinquents, may be especially prone to violent methods.

Aggression can be increased not only by the rewards of victory, but also by the encouragement and approval of other persons. Albert Bandura and Richard Walters (1959) made an intensive study of antisocially aggressive boys who came from apparently well-functioning middle-class homes. Although the parents of such boys were seldom aggressive themselves, it was almost always the case that one or both of the parents demanded, encouraged, and rewarded aggressive behaviors directed toward other children, teachers, and adults outside the family.

Within some social systems aggressive behavior receives a great deal of social support. In San Francisco a juvenile gang used unprovoked attacks on strangers as its main requirement for admission. Each attack, which had to be witnessed by another gang member, earned the aspiring member ten points. One hundred points were required for admission to this choice club (*San Francisco Chronicle*, November 26, 1964). The following statement made by a youth involved in a gang killing clearly demonstrates the relationship he perceives between aggressive behavior and social status: "If I would of got the knife, I would have stabbed him. That would have gave me more of a build up. People would have respected me for what I've done and things like that. They would say, 'There goes a cold killer'" (Yablonsky, 1962, p. 8).

A second set of factors studied extensively within the behavioristic perspective consists of stimulus factors in the environment that trigger aggressive behaviors.

Stimulus control of aggression

As a social behavior aggression always occurs at least partly in response to stimuli in the environment. We have seen that even behaviors directly elicited by electrical stimulation of "aggression centers" within the brain are affected by such factors in the environment as the presence of dominant or submissive others. Certain stimuli, as a result of previous learn-

ing, acquire the ability to trigger aggression when they are present, so that aggressive behavior may then be said to be under *stimulus control*.

Stimuli may acquire aggression-eliciting properties simply by being *present* when there is aggression caused by other factors. For example, Delgado (1963) experimented with monkeys and found that when a neutral stimulus, such as a tone, is present when aggression is elicited by electrical stimulation of the brain, that stimulus can later trigger aggression in the absence of brain stimulation.

Social psychologist Leonard Berkowitz proposes that the likelihood that a person will behave aggressively is jointly determined by two factors. The first of these is an *internal readiness to respond*, based on the strength of a person's aggressive habits and present emotional state (e.g., frustration or anger). The second determinant is the presence or absence of *eliciting* cues in the environment. These elicitors, or *releasers*, of aggression may be objects that the subject dislikes or objects that have previously been paired with aggression. If one of the preceding factors is weak, the other must be strong in order for aggression to occur (see Figure 2.5).

Important to our present discussion is Berkowitz's suggestion that eliciting stimuli may be cues, objects, or persons who have *previously been paired with aggression*. In one experiment designed to assess the effects of aggression-associated stimuli, subjects seated in the presence of guns administered more electric shock to another person who had previously insulted them than did those subjects who were in the presence of nonaggressive objects (Berkowitz and LePage, 1967). According to Berkowitz's theory, the insults produced a heightened readiness to respond aggressively, and the presence of weapons—stimuli normally associated with aggression—enhanced the tendency to respond aggressively. Although other experiments indicate that the presence of weapons does not always increase aggression—and in some instances may actually inhibit it—there is the suggestion that in some instances "the finger pulls the trigger, but the trigger may also be pulling the finger" (Berkowitz, 1968, p. 22).

Frustration and aggression

One stimulus condition that psychologists have found prompts an "internal readiness to respond"

51

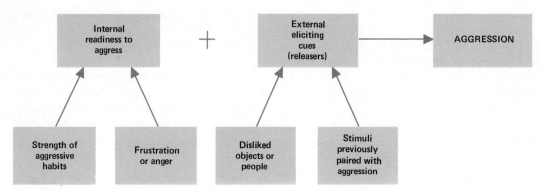

Figure 2.5 Berkowitz's (1969) theory of aggression, indicating the role of both internal and external determinants.

(Berkowitz's first factor for predicting aggressive behavior) is *frustration*, defined as the blocking of goal-directed activity. In 1939 a group of Yale researchers advanced the *frustration-aggression hypothesis* (Dollard, Doob, Miller, Mowrer, and Sears, 1939). This hypothesis consisted of two sweeping generalizations: (1) Every frustration produces an urge to behave aggressively; (2) all aggression is the result of frustration.

Although a good deal of subsequent research has shown that if lower animals and people are frustrated from achieving desired goals, the likelihood of aggression is increased, it is also clear that the original frustration-aggression hypothesis is too simplistic, especially where humans are concerned. First, it is clear that frustration can trigger a variety of reactions besides aggression, including apathy, anxiety, and depression. It is equally clear that not all aggression results from frustration. People behave aggressively for more power and resources, for approval from others, and for countless other reasons.

Although frustration is clearly not the sole determinant of aggression, it is one type of stimulus condition that can trigger aggressive behavior. The connection between frustration and aggression, when it occurs, is likely to involve some of the cognitive factors discussed in the next section.

The cognitive perspective on aggression

Our ability to think, plan, and reason is the focus of the cognitive perspective. In a very real sense we create the environment to which we react through our own thoughts, interpretations, and perceptions.

Every human being is an information-processing system that codes, interprets, and stores information from the external environment and reacts in accordance with conscious plans and anticipations of the future.

Some of the causal factors in aggression that we considered in relation to the behavioristic perspective are also important in the cognitive perspective. But this perspective assumes that their effects are mediated through cognitive processes.

Learning aggression through observation and imitation

Research conducted within the framework of cognitive social learning theory shows that observational learning, or *modeling*, is extremely important in understanding how aggression is learned. Behavior can be *learned* simply by observing others' behavior. Whether or not the observer *performs* the behavior depends on the consequences he or she has observed. If a child sees another child deliver an exotic karate chop to a victim, that child is more likely to *imitate* the aggression if he or she sees the model rewarded for aggression. But regardless of what happens to the model, the child will have *learned* the aggressive behavior, and if you offer him or her a reward for reproducing the karate chop, chances are the child will be able to do it. A number of studies have shown that aggressive and delinquent children tend to have parents who frequently model aggressive behaviors. Mothers who frequently use verbal and physical aggression as a child-rearing technique tend to have children who use similar aggressive tactics in con-

52

trolling the behaviors of their peers. (Hoffman, 1960).

Modeling can be accomplished through description as well as through direct demonstration. News accounts of criminal activities provide detailed information about how antisocial behaviors are performed and the consequences they are likely to produce. News of a sensational crime, such as an airline hijacking, is often followed by a sharp increase in acts of a similar nature. (See Figure 2.6.)

Cognitive factors are critically important in observational learning. The observer must code and store information, retain images of the modeled behaviors, and anticipate consequences.

Perceptual and thought processes in aggression
The ways in which an individual perceives and interprets situations and the behaviors of others strongly influence the way in which he or she behaves. Aggression is just one possible response to the world that people create for themselves.

Perception of intent. Imagine that you are riding in a crowded bus on a hot, humid day and are forced to stand up. Your daydreams are suddenly interrupted by a stabbing pain in your right foot as it is ground under the heel of the person standing next to you. How would you respond to this painful event? Would you assume that the other person's action was accidental or intentional? Your assumption would certainly be affected by such factors as your internal readiness to respond aggressively and your general views of human nature. In addition, the characteristics and subsequent behaviors of the other person would affect your response. (Would the sex of the other person make a difference?) Studies with both children and college students have shown that aggressive responses can be reduced if people are given reasonable explanations for the provocative behavior of others (Mallick and McCandless, 1966; Kaufmann and Feshbach, 1963).

How we justify our aggression. Although aggression can be an effective means for achieving goals, it is not generally regarded as a socially desirable course of action. Many people feel guilty about their aggressive impulses, and most of us cannot conceive of behaving in a cruel and brutal fashion. However, social forces frequently cause people to perform terrible acts that would be totally repugnant to them under normal circumstances. Under these and other circumstances a number of *cognitive mechanisms* that involve self-deception may be used to neutralize guilt reactions.

People often try to minimize their own aggression by comparing it with even more repulsive deeds. During the Vietnam War, for example, proponents of U.S. involvement minimized the horror of slaying countless Vietnamese noncombatants by pointing to even more hideous atrocities perpetrated by the

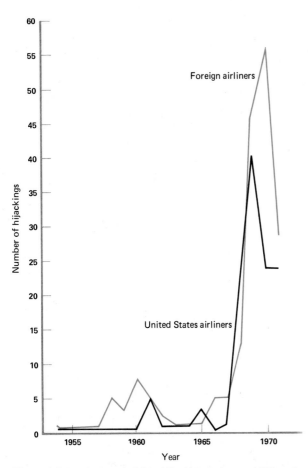

Figure 2.6 Incidence of airline hijacking between 1955 and 1972. The dramatic increase in the late 1960s followed several well-publicized successful hijackings. (Data from Federal Aviation Administration)

53

BOX 2.8

One man's justifi-cation for his acts

By warding off the Jews, I am fighting for the Lord's work. . . . What we have to fight for is the security of the existence and the increase of our race and our people, the nourishment of its children, and the preservation of the purity of the blood, the freedom and independence in the fatherland in order to enable our people to mature for the fulfillment of the mission which the Creator of the universe has allotted also to them. (Adolph Hitler)

(UPI)

nous acts performed in "holy wars" and "moral crusades." (See Box 2.8.)

Guilt over aggression can also be minimized by *displacing* responsibility for the deeds onto another person. Incidents such as those that occurred in Nazi concentration camps and at My Lai show how easy it is for individuals to disclaim responsibility for an act by displacing it onto those in command. ("I was only following orders.") At the Nuremberg war trials following World War II it was decreed that subordinates who obeyed inhumane orders from higher authorities were still responsible for their own acts.

A related method of minimizing guilt is through *diffusion of responsibility*, or group decision making. If a decision is made by a group, no single individual feels responsible for the actions decided on. Sometimes the diffusion of responsibility can enable a group to commit collective violent acts that single individuals within the group would normally not commit.

A final self-justifying cognitive mechanism is *dehumanization*. The aggressor strips his or her victim of all human qualities so that the person can be dealt with as an object rather than as an individual with needs, sensitivities, and feelings like those of the aggressor. Often the process involves attaching demeaning labels, such as *gooks*, *pigs*, or *niggers*, to the victims so that they can be viewed as members of a despised group rather than as individual human beings. (See Box 2.9.)

How we create our enemies. No doubt you have heard about football teams "psyching" themselves up before a game to hate the other team in order to play hard enough to win. Do we do this in real life too?

Through selective perception and by dwelling on real or imagined wrongs, people can create in their minds hated enemies, fully deserving of whatever aggression is directed toward them. Before and during wars both sides usually develop a "diabolical enemy-image" and a "moral self-image" (White, 1968). The participants come to view themselves and their opponents in black and white terms. The enemy side becomes the incarnation of evil and its behaviors are attributed to the most diabolical motives, whereas one's own side is regarded as the defender of all that is right and good.

During the Vietnam War the Communist forces

Communists. Meanwhile, militant antiwar protesters were justifying their domestic acts of violence by comparing their deeds with the carnage in Vietnam.

The belief that "the end justifies the means" also helps to minimize guilt and self-condemnation. Even the most heinous acts can be viewed as justifiable if they are performed in the service of some noble end. The pages of history are filled with accounts of hei-

BOX 2.9
The "final solution" revisited

Like most people, you are probably horrified at the brutality of the Nazis and secure in the conviction that you could never be made to participate in such a horrible enterprise. Or could you? A recent experiment shows that the mechanisms discussed earlier may operate in all of us under certain circumstances.

At the University of Hawaii 570 students like yourself were assembled in groups of 20 to 30 to hear a brief speech by an expert on world population. They were told that they were being asked as intelligent and educated persons to assist in the development of procedures to eliminate the mentally and emotionally unfit through euthanasia, or mercy killing. Because these segments of the population were increasing faster than were the "emotionally fit and intelligent humans," they constituted a definite threat in a world whose resources are dwindling. The students were told that "such killing is considered by most experts as not only being beneficial to the unfit, because it puts them out of the misery of their lives, but more importantly, it will be beneficial to the healthy, fit, and more educated segment of the population."

After hearing the speech the subjects were given a questionnaire. The findings were quite sobering. In response to the convincing speech, 91 percent of the subjects agreed that "it is entirely just to eliminate those judged dangerous to the general welfare." Eighty-five percent indicated that, if required by law, they would be willing to assist in deciding who should be killed, and 8 percent indicated a willingness to assist in the killing (Mansson, 1972).

The "final solution" proposed by this speech was similar to that of the Nazis. Although responding to a questionnaire is not the same as actually carrying out such behaviors, it is nonetheless striking to see how easily cognitive mechanisms such as those discussed earlier can apparently be mobilized to blind people to the true implications of their behavioral choices.

and the United States each constructed a diabolical-enemy image of the other. Psychologist Ralph K. White (1968) analyzed official statements made by both sides for evaluative characterizations of the enemy. Of a total of 337 evaluative references to the U.S. enemy made by the Communists, 337 (100 percent) stated or implied that the Americans were evil. Of the 130 characterizations of the Communists made by President Lyndon Johnson and Secretary of Defense Robert McNamara, 127 were negative.

These extreme images allow both sides in a war to justify aggression in terms of higher principles, to dehumanize the enemy, and to see themselves as persons of good will who are forced into aggressive actions by a villainous enemy. Because victims can be blamed for bringing suffering on themselves, it is not surprising that there is often unspeakable brutality in warfare.

Certain violent acts committed by psychologically disturbed persons are the product of this process taken to its extreme. In 1912 John Schrank attempted to assassinate presidential candidate Theodore Roosevelt. Schrank later reported that he had had a dream years earlier in which he saw assassinated President William McKinley rise from his coffin and accuse Theodore Roosevelt of arranging his death. Schrank decided that his dream was a divine mandate to avenge McKinley's death by killing Roosevelt. After his unsuccessful attempt, Schrank was committed to a mental hospital and remained there until his death 30 years later.

In the cognitive view, human beings are thinking and reasoning problem solvers. But the tragedy of our existence is that our cognition frequently results in our choosing violent solutions to our problems.

55

The psychoanalytic perspective on aggression

You probably often feel that there is a kind of struggle going on inside you. To the psychoanalytic theorist, explaining human aggression entails understanding the continuing conflict between impulse and defense within the personality. Much human aggression is viewed as the result of powerful psychological forces that operate at an unconscious level. Whereas the behaviorist points to environmental factors and the cognitive theorist emphasizes thought processes that are more or less conscious in nature, the psychoanalytic theorist stresses nonrational personality functioning.

Freud's theory of aggression

Freud, who was trained in medicine, viewed human behavior as largely directed toward satisfying drives or instincts. Because those instincts reflect the biological needs of the organism and satisfaction of them enhances and prolongs life, Freud referred to them as *life instincts*, or *Eros*. Failure to satisfy an instinct results in *tension*, and behavior is largely directed toward tension reduction. Freud then proceeded to carry this formulation to its logical extreme. If the organism is constantly striving to reduce tension, what is the ultimate state of quiescence? It is death, of course. This realization led Freud to state that "the goal of all life is death" and to posit the existence of an inborn *death instinct*, called *Thanatos*. Aggression occurs when the death instinct is displaced outward against other persons or objects. Thus, Freud, like Lorenz, viewed aggression as instinctual. But Lorenz regards it as an adaptive instinct whereas Freud viewed it as a destructive urge.

Most modern Freudian theorists treat aggression as an instinct but reject the idea of a death instinct. Other non-Freudian psychodynamic theorists, such as Alfred Adler saw aggressive instincts manifested in such important human motives as the lust for power and the struggle for superiority.

But if aggression demands release and satisfaction like other biological drives, how does one go about satisfying this instinct in a world in which people are made to feel fearful and guilty about their aggressive impulses?

Psychological defenses and aggression

Clearly, people cannot give unlimited reign to their impulses. In order to control them and to create acceptable alternative means for expression, a system of defenses, or *defense mechanisms*, is set up within the personality. If successful, these defenses allow people to satisfy their internal needs, the demands of society, and their own moral standards. We consider the defense mechanisms more extensively in Chapter 13. For now we restrict ourselves to examining several defenses that have received prominent attention in relation to aggression.

Sublimation. In order to understand the Freudian notion of personality, imagine a tea kettle on a hot stove. The impulses arising from the instincts constantly build up, as steam pressure from the boiling water in the kettle does if the spout and lid are sealed. If some means of release is not found, a psychological explosion will occur, similar to the explosion that will occur in the sealed tea kettle. The most adaptive way of dealing with this situation is to find some way to "unseal the kettle," to channel unacceptable impulses into disguised, socially acceptable—even admired or rewarded—behavior. This is what is meant by *sublimation*. Many people find expression for their aggressive impulses in such activities as competitive sports, intellectual debates, games of skill, political activities, and hunting.

But what if people's defenses become so rigid that they cannot express their aggressive impulses? Will their "tea kettles" eventually blow their tops off?

Although aggressive acts are often committed by individuals who have a history of such behavior, some of the most shocking and brutal crimes are committed by those who are described by acquaintances as passive, inhibited, friendly, or unassertive. Edwin Megargee (1966) concluded on the basis of his research that brutally aggressive crimes are often committed by overcontrolled individuals. These people show little reaction to provocations; instead they repress or hide their anger. Over time the pressure to aggress builds up until, at a critical point, their excessive defenses shatter. Often the provocation that "breaks the camel's back" and results in the destructive outburst is a trivial one. Then these people erupt into violence, often of an extreme and brutal form. After their aggressive outburst they revert to their former passive state, appearing again as individuals totally incapable of violence.

Megargee found that male juveniles who had been arrested for extremely brutal crimes (e.g., the murder of their parents, savage killings) seemed to be *overcontrolled* to a far greater extent than did boys who were arrested for moderately assaultive acts. The former group generally had no previous history of antisocial aggression and were rated as far more friendly and cooperative by their counselors. Megargee and his associates have developed a psychological test designed to identify these overcontrolled individuals before they explode into violence (Megargee, Cook, and Mendelsohn, 1967). Perhaps the early identification of overcontrolled violence-prone individuals can enable us to train them to deal more appropriately with provocations as they occur rather than "storing up" their anger and frustration so that they become walking time bombs.

Displacement of aggression. Probably more than once you have felt that it was necessary to tell somebody else, "Don't take it out on me!" Sometimes we direct aggressive responses toward a substitute target. This is called *displaced* aggression. Displacement usually happens either when the true target is not available or when aggression toward the true target is inhibited by anxiety or guilt. A familiar example is of the office worker who is frustrated and angered all day by a boss against whom he cannot safely retaliate. He grins and bears it all day, but when he comes home he kicks the dog, yells at his kids, and beats his wife. In many instances individuals are unaware of the real cause of their displaced aggression.

Some psychologists have also suggested that the displacement of aggression may be an important factor in prejudice. That is, minority groups furnish a convenient substitute target for aggressive impulses that cannot safely be directed toward their true targets.

Some years ago Carl Hovland and Robert Sears (1940) found that between 1882 and 1930 at least 3386 lynchings of blacks occurred in the South. In a correlational study, they related the number of lynchings to economic indicators. As Figure 2.7 shows, during periods in which cotton prices dropped, the number of lynchings rose sharply; when prices were up, lynchings were usually down. Although correlation does not prove causation, it is possible that drops in cotton prices generated frustration and anger, which was then displaced onto blacks.

Evidence was found to support the displacement theory of prejudice in a controlled experimental study by Neal Miller and Richard Bugelski (1948). Young men were asked by a group of prestigious experimenters from Yale University to make evaluative ratings of various minority groups. Then they were frustrated by being given a long series of tests that caused them to miss an eagerly awaited movie. When the subjects were then readministered the minority group attitude scale, they showed an increase in prejudice toward the minority groups. Presumably, their hostility toward the experimenters, which could not safely be expressed, was channeled toward a safer target—the minority groups.

Reaction formation. Have you ever noted that somebody's fervor about a cause or social issue seemed a little too intense, somehow out of character or "unreal"? Perhaps it was the result of *reaction formation*. This defensive mechanism involves the repression of an impulse and the expression of its opposite, often in an exaggerated form. Aggressive impulses that are unacceptable or that cause anxiety for an individual may be repressed into the unconscious and the "energy" expressed in an exaggerated form of the opposite behavior: love. An example of reaction formation is sometimes seen in the smothering, overprotective parent whose oversolicitous behaviors serve to mask underlying feelings of hostility toward the child and protect the parent from becoming aware of them.

SOME ISSUES CONCERNING HUMAN AGGRESSION

Because the four perspectives have differing assumptions about human nature and the causes of our behavior, there are issues on which they strongly disagree. We have chosen three important issues concerning human aggression to illustrate the nature of these disagreements: (1) Are we aggressive by

57

Figure 2.7 Hovland and Sears (1940) found a striking relationship between an economic index based on cotton prices and the number of lynchings of blacks in the South over a 48-year period. (UPI photo)

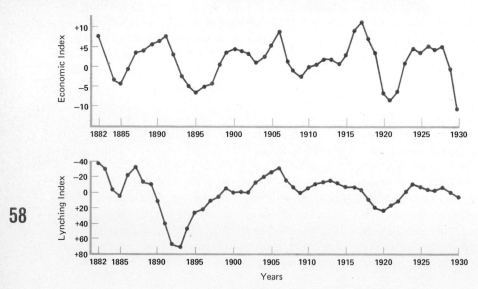

58

nature? (2) Does televised violence breed aggression? and (3) How can human aggression be reduced?

Are we aggressive by nature?

Both Freud and Lorenz think that aggression is inborn. In contrast, the proponents of the behavioristic and cognitive social learning orientations view aggression not as an instinct, but as a learned behavior. These conflicting assumptions, as we see later, have definite implications for finding the ways in which aggression might be reduced.

Whereas Freud's notion of an aggressive instinct was based largely on his clinical observations, Lorenz noted the parallels between certain human aggressive acts and those of lower animals. The idea that human aggression has an instinctual basis has been severely criticized on both logical and scientific grounds. Critics of the instinct theory argue that similarities between human behaviors and those of lower animals in no way prove that the same causes are involved. Innate territorial tendencies may cause a dog to mark off his boundaries with urine, but they are not necessarily the reason people place "No Trespassing" signs in their yards.

There is virtually no evidence to verify that there is an aggressive instinct, nor is it clear how such an instinct could ever be proved to exist. We have seen that even behaviors that result from direct electrical stimulation of the brain are strongly affected by the environment in which animals find themselves. Likewise, we have seen how fighting experiences early in life can strongly affect the aggressive tendencies of animals later in life.

Even more pertinent to our present discussion are scientific findings that "instinctive" aggressive behaviors in lower animals can virtually be eliminated through certain early learning experiences. In a series of classic experiments Zing Yang Kuo reared young animals with their "natural" enemies. Kittens and puppies reared together became friends rather than enemies, as did cats and rats. When predatory birds were raised with smaller birds who normally serve as their prey, they became very friendly with the small birds. On cold nights the large birds "would spread out their wings and let the little birds roost under them" (Kuo, 1967, p. 66). The higher we move up the phylogenetic scale, the more important learning becomes. The position that human aggression is

learned socially rather than instinctual has strong scientific support.

Does televised violence breed aggression?

The television screen is a window through which all of us acquire much information about our world. *Broadcasting Yearbook* (1971) estimates that the average American television set is turned on about six hours per day. Children in the primary grades watch television between 15 and 25 hours per week, older children about 25 hours, and high school students about 12 to 14 hours (Witty, 1966). The amount of aggression and violence seen during these many hours in front of the television set is considerable.

Between the ages of 5 and 15, the average American child witnesses the violent destruction of about 13,400 human beings, as well as innumerable nonlethal aggressive acts (Sabin, 1972). A study published in 1970 showed that during one average week on television over 600 acts of violence were shown, not including those reported on news programs. Eighty percent of all plays contained some violence, as did

Researchers have shown that even the most traditional of "natural" enemies become friends if they are reared together. (Perkins, Stock, Boston)

Is television a "school for violence?" During an average week, over 600 acts of violence are shown on the screen. Psychologists disagree as to the effects of TV viewing upon children. (Roos, Peter Arnold)

important issue in discussing children's reactions to television violence. By watching aggressive models on television, they say, observers can learn not only specific aggressive behaviors, but also the more general lesson that violence succeeds. Analyses of television content have shown repeatedly that violent methods are those used most frequently to attain goals (Liebert, Neale, and Davidson, 1973). Although in the end they are generally punished, villains succeed at first through violent means. And heroes almost inevitably use violent means to subdue the villain and to obtain various rewards. The ultimate lesson is that aggression is an appropriate means of attaining goals for one who is "in the right." But who among us does not generally see himself as being "in the right"?

The notion of catharsis, a "letting out" of the emotions, has been with us for a long time. The early Greeks believed that observing dramatic productions that arouse intense emotions "purges" the audience of its feelings. Freudians (and others) adopted this notion and proposed that observers of violent acts can drain off their own aggressive impulses and reduce the likelihood of behaving aggressively themselves.

Research evidence

Researchers have used a variety of approaches to study the effects of television violence on aggressive behavior. Some have studied the relationship between television viewing preferences and aggressive behavior, whereas others have experimentally manipulated the content of the programs viewed by subjects to study the influence of violence. Results from both approaches show a fairly consistent pattern.

One group of researchers (Lefkowitz, Eron, Walder, and Huesmann, 1972) determined the amount of violence watched by 875 third-grade youngsters and obtained ratings of the youngsters' aggression from other children. A positive relationship between the two variables was found for boys but not for girls. Ten years later, when the same male subjects were 19, their television viewing preferences were again recorded, and ratings of aggression were obtained from their peers. There was a positive relationship between violence watched on television in the third grade and aggressive behavior at the age of

95 percent of the cartoons and 67 percent of the comedy shows (National Commission on the Causes and Prevention of Violence, 1970). It is clear that Americans are being fed a steady diet of televised violence. What are the effects of this diet?

There are those who maintain that constant exposure to brutality blunts one's sensitivity to it and serves as a "school for violence." (See Box 2.10.) Opposing this view are those who contend that observing televised violence provides a useful and healthy outlet for releasing one's own feelings of anger and frustration. This controversy pits the cognitive perspective directly against the psychoanalytic perspective. More specifically, it pits the *modeling* hypothesis of cognitive social learning theory against the *catharsis* hypothesis of the psychoanalytic perspective.

Modeling versus catharsis: A critical issue

Cognitive social learning theorists like Bandura (1973) believe that observational learning is the most

BOX 2.10

Public concern about televised violence

Ernest B. Furgurson: TV—accessory to murder?

Washington—When is censorship tolerable in America?

My own deep belief is never, the Supreme Court on obscenity notwithstanding.

However:

At 8:30 on an autumn evening, the A. B. C. Sunday movie was shown on Channel 5 in Boston and other cities coast to coast. It was "Fuzz," which The Globe said "stars Burt Reynolds as a thoroughly inept police detective in comic pursuit of a master criminal, Yul Brynner. Raquel Welch and Jack Weston co-star in the film, which was made mostly on location in Boston." The time, the subject, the locale and Raquel Welch guaranteed a big audience, particularly among young men, in the Boston area.

One of the scenes in the movie was not as comic as the advance billing made it all sound. It showed young hoodlums—in Boston—setting fire to derelict winos.

And less than 48 hours after the television movie ended, a gang of six young hoodlums stopped a 24-year-old woman carrying a can of gasoline for her disabled car in the Roxbury section of Boston. We all know the story—they dragged her to a vacant lot, beat her, forced her to pour the gasoline over herself and set her afire. She died several hours later, after telling police she recognized three of the men as those who stopped her the day before and warned her to move out of the black neighborhood.

The inevitable and most publicized result was flaring anger between the races, made worse by other incidents that followed in the next few days.

Just as inevitably, authorities drew a straight line between the movie Sunday night and the fiery murder Tuesday night. The mayor, Kevin White, said he had seen the movie, and blamed its sequences for this similar crime in real life. The police commissioner, Robert diGrazia, declared, "It's about time that the public demanded an end to violence such as this in our movies and on television."

The commissioner was right—in what he said and what he did not say. Although he may have had it in mind, he did not say there ought to be a law; he did not clamor for outright censorship. Not quite.

In tracing blame for the crime, the hoodlums themselves obviously must be punished, severely.

But assuming they did indeed see "Fuzz" and were inspired by it, who is to blame beyond them? In order:

1. The writer who did the movie script, the producer who accepted it and the actors who played it.
2. The network that chose the movie for its Sunday-night special or for any other time slot.
3. The local stations that run it.
4. The public that encouraged that it, and hundreds of other films making sport of nauseating violence, be shown on television or for general admission anywhere else.

The commissioner was right, and thousands of people in Boston and elsewhere will say so—and then go right back to watching and thus encouraging murder on film. They will not organize boycotts, pickets or letter-writing campaigns.

(Copyright, 1973, *The Baltimore Sun.*)

---

19. (See Figure 2.8.) On the other hand, *no* relationship was found between aggressive behavior at age 8 and television preferences at age 19. This pattern of results strongly suggests that television violence is a long-term cause of aggressive behavior; it also indicates that preference for televised violence at age 19 is not influenced by earlier aggressive tendencies.

This is of great importance, since it has sometimes been suggested that there is a relationship between observed TV violence and aggression because already aggressive children prefer such shows.

This same conclusion is supported by studies in which television content was experimentally controlled and its effects assessed. In one experiment

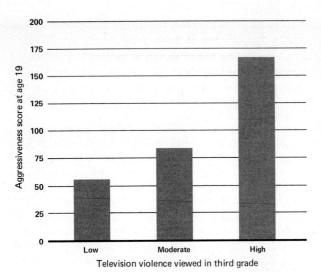

Figure 2.8 The relationship between television violence viewed in the third grade and interpersonal aggressiveness at age 19. No relationship was found in this study between aggressiveness at age 8 and television violence preferences at age 19. This suggests that the viewing of television violence is a long-term cause of aggressiveness, and not vice versa. (Based on data from Lefkowitz, Eron, Walder, and Huesmann, 1972.)

that used a repeated-measure design (Stein and Friedrich, 1972), 97 nursery school children were studied over a nine-week period. For the first three weeks the behaviors of the children were carefully observed and recorded. Then the children were randomly assigned to one of three experimental groups in which the content of programs they saw during nursery school was either aggressive (Batman and Superman cartoons), neutral (e.g., children working on a farm), or pro-social (episodes from the children's program "Mister Rogers' Neighborhood"). After four weeks of viewing these programs three times a week for 20 to 30 minutes, the children's behavior was again assessed over a two-week period. The initial aggression levels of the three groups were quite similar. But after the four-week experimental period, children who had been exposed to the aggressive cartoons behaved significantly more aggressively than did those in either of the other two groups. However, only those children who had been in the upper half of the sample on their initial level of aggression increased in their aggressiveness after see-

ing the violent cartoons. This latter finding is of particular significance, because the already aggressive children are precisely those whose aggressive behavior should be *reduced* most by exposure to televised violence according to the catharsis hypothesis.

More than 50 studies concerning the relationship between television violence and aggressive behavior have been conducted, involving over 10,000 subjects from every type of social background (Liebert, 1974). The evidence from these studies consistently indicates that television violence often makes viewers more aggressive and supports the modeling hypothesis rather than the catharsis hypothesis.

How can aggression be reduced?

We now come to perhaps the most important question of all: What can be done to reduce people's aggressive behavior? The various perspectives provide us with very different answers to this question.

Research and clinical studies within the biological perspective have shown that aggressive behavior can be reduced through brain stimulation and the destruction of diseased brain tissue. Drugs can also be used to control aggressive behavior. These biological means of controlling aggression have been enthusiastically supported by some psychologists. But many scientists have very serious reservations about such control on both ethical and scientific grounds. Currently, the strongest controversy rages over the use of "psychosurgery" techniques designed to alter brain functioning. An example of this approach to reducing aggression is presented in Box 2.11. This is one of a number of successful though controversial psychosurgery cases described by Vernon H. Mark and Frank R. Ervin of Harvard Medical School (1970). But other experts (e.g., 1974; Valenstein, 1973) have expressed serious concerns about the use of psychosurgical procedures. One potential problem is that a given area of the brain may be involved not only in aggression but also in other behaviors that are more adaptive. There is evidence that some of the patients treated by psychosurgeons have suffered crippling behavioral side effects (Chorover, 1974). Because nerve tissue does not regenerate when it is destroyed, the effects of such operations are irreversible.

In addition to the scientific misgivings regarding psychosurgery, there are controversial legal issues concerning its use. Civil libertarians have questioned whether society has the right to subject prisoners and disturbed persons to an irreversible surgical procedure. A number of court suits have been instituted to prevent the use of psychosurgery, and the federal government has grown wary of supporting psychosurgical research.

If we view aggression as an instinctive biological drive, we have little basis for optimism regarding its elimination. If aggression comes from within people, then we cannot hope to eliminate it by changing social conditions; at best we can strive to channel aggressive energy into socially acceptable forms of behavior. In this vein Lorenz (1966) recommends participation in activities such as competitive sports as a substitute means of discharging aggressive drives.

In contrast to instinctual theories, which view aggression as stemming from forces within the person, behavioristic theories view aggression as the result of the conditions under which a person develops and lives. Logically, then, if we modify these conditions, we should be able to reduce aggression. An environment that consistently rewards nonaggressive and pro-social behaviors without rewarding aggressive behaviors fosters low levels of aggressiveness. Likewise, exposure to models who achieve their goals through nonaggressive means teaches observers how to approach problems in a similar nonaggressive fashion. In many instances people are aggressive because they do not know how to deal with problems in more adaptive ways. By observing successful nonaggressive models, these individuals could acquire the skills they lack. We have seen how aggressive television fare can teach aggressive behavior and reduce inhibitions against behaving aggressively. It is important that we realize that the mass media might also be more effectively used to promote pro-social behaviors.

As we saw in our discussion of the cognitive perspective on aggression, cognitive factors contribute to aggression in important ways. Not only do our higher mental processes allow us to remember what we have learned both directly and through the observation of models, but they are also intimately involved in emotional behavior. Many people develop philosophies of life and assumptions about "the way

things are" that predispose them to behave aggressively. Presumably, if these assumptions can be modified, aggressive behavior can be reduced. Evidence of such a change is clear in the following statement made by a psychotherapy patient who was helped to change his viewpoint about other people:

I'm beginning to see now what you mean by not blaming others for their mistakes and wrongdoings. My mother called me up the other day—the first time in a year that she has dared to do so, after I gave her a real piece of my mind the last time I spoke to her—and she started going on as usual, after at first being nice for a few minutes, about how I wasn't getting anywhere in life, how terrible it was that I was still going for psychotherapy, and all that kind of jazz. I began, as usual, to feel my temperature rising and I was all set to tell her off again.

But then I said, as you have been teaching me to do, "What am I telling *myself* to make me get so angry at this poor woman? *She's* not making me mad; *I* am." And I could see right away that I was telling myself that she shouldn't be the nagging, bitchy type of woman that she is and has always been. So I said to myself: "All right: *why* shouldn't she be the way she is and has always been?" And of course, just as you keep pointing out, I couldn't find any good reason why she shouldn't be exactly as she is. For there isn't any such reason. Sure, it would be nice if she were approving, and calm, and everything else. But she isn't. And she's not going to be. And I don't *need* her to be, in order to get along well in the world myself.

Well, as soon as I clearly saw *that*, all my anger against the old gal of course vanished. I tried, just as an experiment, to work it back up again, to get angry at her all over. But I just couldn't make it. Instead, I was very nice to her—much to her surprise, you can imagine!—and even invited her to my home for Christmas dinner—which I haven't done or even thought of doing for years now. (Ellis, 1962, p. 185)

The reduction and control of aggression constitutes one of our greatest challenges. The various perspectives from which psychologists study behavior provide a broadly based understanding of aggression as well as a range of potential approaches to its reduction. The study of aggression and its control is and will continue to be an important frontier of psychology.

63

BOX 2.11

Brain surgery and control of aggression: A psychological frontier.

Recent technological advances have made it possible to treat persons suffering from violent behaviors caused by certain kinds of brain damage. It is now possible to implant tiny electrodes in specific areas of the brain (see accompanying figure). These electrodes can be used to monitor the electrical activity of the brain, to stimulate the brain electrically, or, if necessary, to destroy diseased brain tissue. The use of such procedures in the treatment of aggressive behavior is illustrated in the following case history.

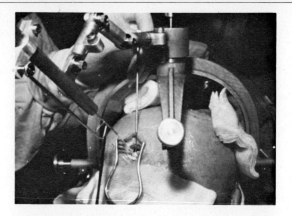

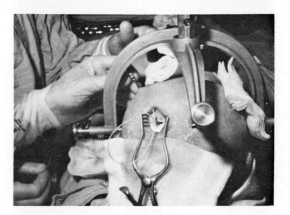

When she was 33 years old, Clara T. slipped on a patch of ice and sustained a head injury which soon led to epileptic seizures. Despite the use of anti-seizure medication, her seizures increased in frequency and intensity during the next 29 years, and she became increasingly more assaultive. She attacked her mother-in-law, her husband, and many other acquaintances. After being hospitalized, she stabbed a nurse with a scissors, and it took six people 45 minutes to subdue this 62 year old woman who weighed only 86 pounds. Neurological examination revealed extensive damage in her temporal lobes. A bank of 40 electrodes was implanted in and around her limbic system and the electrical activity of her brain was monitored for several months. Abnormal brain waves were discovered through certain electrodes, and when electrical stimulation was applied through these electrodes, a seizure began. Using radio frequency current, heat was generated through the electrodes to destroy the cells around them. Following destruction of the cells, Clara's seizures decreased in frequency and intensity. In addition, her rage responses and unprovoked assaults ceased entirely, and she was able to return to a normal life. (Sweet, Ervin, and Mark, 1969)

Surgical techniques are making it possible not only to learn more about how the brain functions,

SUMMARY

Electrodes can now be implanted in human brains with great precision. The target area is first pinpointed with X rays and EEG recordings, after which an electrode is lowered through a small opening in the skull and locked into place. The electrode carrier is removed and the tail of the electrode is then brought out about 6 centimeters from the wound for external connections. The patient suffers no discomfort and the electrode connections are easily concealed with a wig. The electrodes can be removed if this is desired at a later time. (V. H. Mark, F. R. Ervin, *Violence and the Brain,* Harper & Row, 1970. Courtesy of the Neuro-Research Foundation, Inc.)

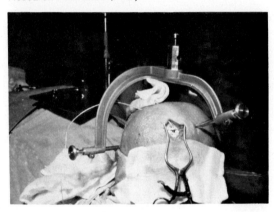

but also to treat people for whom there would have been little hope only a few years ago. Moreover, innovative researchers like José Delgado are developing electronic devices such as the *stimoceiver,* which allows persons to stimulate areas of their own brains when they feel particular symptoms coming on. However, serious scientific and legal issues surround psychosurgical techniques. (See text.)

1. A number of influential perspectives on human behavior have influenced the development of scientific psychology. These perspectives serve as lenses through which the psychological world is viewed, and they help determine which aspects of behavior are studied, the manner in which they are studied, and what is learned about our behavior. The biological, behavioristic, cognitive, and psychoanalytic perspectives were examined in this chapter.

2. The biological perspective views humans as complex animals and focuses on genetic and physiological influences on behavior. Evolutionary theory and advances in the study of biological influences on behavior have contributed importantly to our understanding of the biological side of our nature.

3. Within the behavioristic perspective humans are viewed as reactors to their past and present environments. Behaviorists deny that we freely choose how to behave; instead we are conditioned by our environment to respond in particular ways.

4. The cognitive perspective views humans as active problem solvers whose higher mental processes allow them to think, judge, imagine, and plan. Complex human behavior is seen as the result of these higher mental processes.

5. The psychoanalytic perspective stresses the role of unconscious motives on behavior. The mind is a battleground with conflicting psychic forces and counterforces striving for superiority, and behavior often represents a compromise between these forces.

6. Aggression is defined as any behavior intended to harm or injure another.

65

7. The biological perspective on aggression emphasizes the evolutionary role of hunting, dominance, and territoriality on human aggression. Konrad Lorenz theorizes that, unlike other deadly creatures, humans have not developed internal controls against killing members of their own species. Research has shown that animals can be selectively bred for aggression, but the role of genetic variables in human aggression is less clear. Much research is being done on brain mechanisms in aggression, and there is evidence that aggression can be controlled through brain surgery.

8. The behavioristic approach to the study of aggression involves an analysis of present stimulus conditions and previous learning, particularly the rewarding and punishing consequences of previous aggressive acts. There is much evidence that these factors are crucial determinants of aggression. The role of frustration as an eliciting condition for aggression has received much attention in both theory and research.

9. The role of perceptual and mental processes in aggression is emphasized by the cognitive perspective. It is possible to learn aggressive behaviors through modeling, and the ways in which we perceive and interpret situations strongly influences whether we will behave aggressively. Guilt about aggression can be reduced through cognitive mechanisms such as displacement and diffusion of responsibility, dehumanization, and self-justification.

10. Freud's psychoanalytic perspective views aggression as the result of an innate aggressive instinct. Psychological defenses such as sublimation, displacement, and reaction formation are erected to control the instinctual impulses.

11. There is no evidence that humans have an aggressive instinct, as Lorenz and Freud suggest. There is much evidence that observing violent television and movies increases the likelihood of aggression, which supports the modeling hypothesis. The catharsis hypothesis, which states that such viewing "drains off" aggressive impulses, has received little research support.

12. Each of the perspectives offers suggestions (which sometimes conflict with one another) on ways in which aggression might be reduced.

Suggested readings

Bandura, A. *Aggression: A social learning analysis.* Englewood Cliffs, N.J.: Prentice-Hall, Inc., 1973. A comprehensive review of the research on aggression from the viewpoint of cognitive social learning theory.

Johnson, R. N. *Aggression in man and animals.* Philadelphia: W. B. Saunders Company, 1972. A comprehensive summary of research and theory on aggression that discusses in greater detail many of the concepts covered in the present chapter.

Liebert, R. M. Neale, J. M., & Davidson, E. S. *The early window: Effects of television on children and youth.* Elmsford, N.Y.: Pergamon Press, Inc., 1973. A highly readable review of the research literature concerning the effects of television on children, and particularly on aggressive behavior.

Lorenz, K. *On aggression.* New York: Harcourt Brace Jovanovich, 1966. In this book Lorenz presents his evolutionary view of animal and human aggression.

Mark, V. H., & Ervin, F. R. *Violence and the brain.* New York: Harper & Row, Publishers, 1970. In addition to reviewing case history and research evidence on the brain and aggression, the authors discuss their controversial work in the area of psychosurgery.

Marx, M. H., & Hillix, W. A. *Systems and theories in psychology* (2d ed.). New York: McGraw-Hill Book Company, 1973. A historically oriented discussion of major psychological perspectives and theories.

Megargee, E. I., & Hokanson, J. E. *The dynamics of aggression.* New York: Harper & Row, Publishers, 1970. A collection of important theoretical and research oriented articles on aggression.

Murphy, G., & Kovach, J. *Historical introduction to modern psychology* (3d ed.). New York: Harcourt Brace Jovanovich, 1972. An interesting and readable account of the development of psychology as science and profession.

TWO

Biological and Perceptual Bases of Behavior

Chapter 3

Physiological Systems and Behavior

(Carlson, Stock, Boston)

A damp autumn fog hugged the ground as the soldier slipped silently through the spruce forest. A full moon framed by the tops of shattered trees leered down at the lone figure as it moved cautiously from shadow to shadow.

The soldier had become separated from the other members of his patrol during a brief but fierce skirmish just before nightfall. He wasn't certain if any of the others had survived, and he was now trying to retrace the route back to his own lines. A clammy sweat born of fear had long since drenched his uniform, and his heart pounded in his chest. His eyes probed the light and shadow patchwork of the forest and his ears strained to pick up telltale sounds of human presence. He was now almost oblivious to the dull ache from a flesh wound in his thigh.

Ahead was a small clearing strewn with boulders whose tops projected like ghostly islands above the ground fog. The soldier carefully scanned the area. "I'd be too exposed," he thought. "I'd better keep to the woods and skirt the clearing."

He quickly planned a route around the left side of the clearing and began to pick his way cautiously through the trees. Almost before the faint click and the reflection of light upon metal registered in his awareness, his legs propelled him into a headlong dive for cover behind a shattered tree stump. The enemy submachine gun chattered its evil symphony and a stream of bullets ripped through the night air inches above the soldier's diving form. As his body thudded to the ground, the soldier realized that he was now hidden under the protective mantle of the ground fog, and he began to worm his way through a thick blanket of fallen needles. Behind him he could hear the enemy patrol searching the woods as he continued his journey back to his own lines.

This brief episode occupied only a few minutes of one person's lifetime. Viewed in its broadest sense, it demonstrates an individual coping successfully with an extremely stressful life situation. But if we more carefully examine that episode, we find that a great many psychological processes occurred even within that brief interval of time. All those processes—attending, sensing, thinking, feeling, acting—involve the functioning of complex physiological systems in that invisible world within our skins. It is at this level that the behavior of organisms becomes perhaps the most awe-inspiring because of the amazing complexity and precision that is required on a physiological level for even the most simple of behaviors to

occur. Returning to our soldier, we may marvel at a creature who has a sensory system capable of translating light and sound waves from the outer world into visual and auditory experiences. Somehow he is able to focus attention on certain of these stimuli, whereas others (such as the pain from his wound) barely register. He has a nervous system that relays these messages from his sensors in the form of electrical impulses, interprets them in the light of previously acquired knowledge, and translates them into complex emotional and muscular responses. These *input*, *integration*, and *output* stages are the basis of all complex behaviors. The master control system for his consciousness and behavior is a marvelously sophisticated brain that can remember, think, plan, and even wonder about itself.

In order to understand behavior it is essential to know something about the physiological systems and processes that underlie it. Your sense organs, nervous system, muscles, and glands allow you to be aware of and adjust to your environment. In this chapter we describe the major physiological systems that are involved in the input, integration, and output functions. We first examine the basic building block of the nervous system, the neuron, and how neural transmission occurs. The sensory and nervous systems are then described. Finally, we discuss the endocrine system and the role of hormones in our biological functioning and behavior.

BASIC NEURAL PROCESSES

You began life as a single cell—a fertilized ovum. After about eight days you attached yourself to your mother's uterine wall, divided into two cells, and were on your way to becoming the most biologically complex creature we know.

As cellular multiplication continued, your developing embryo differentiated into three germinal layers of cells—*endoderm*, *mesoderm* and *ectoderm*. The innermost cell layer, the endoderm, was destined to become your digestive system; the mesoderm, your skeletal, respiratory, muscular, and cardiovascular (circulatory) systems; and the outer ectoderm layer, your skin, sensory receptors, and nervous system.

The structures derived from the ectoderm have

been of special interest to psychologists because of the key role they play in behavior. The most elementary of these structures are nerve cells, or *neurons*, which form an ultrasophisticated system for routing and processing information through the body in the form of electrical "impulses."

The neuron

Specialized cells called *neurons* are the basic building blocks of your nervous system. At birth your brain contained 10 to 12 billion of them. You will never again have that many, for unlike other kinds of body cells, neurons are not replaced when they die. It is estimated that you lose about 10,000 of them each day.

Each neuron is a structurally separate and integrated unit within which the vital processes of growth and metabolism occur. As a specialized cell, the neuron has three main parts: a *soma*, *dendrites*, and an *axon*. The *soma*, or cell body, contains a nucleus that regulates the vital life processes that occur within the cell. Small fibers called *dendrites* extend from the soma. The dendrites receive messages from adjacent cells and conduct them to the cell body. Extending from one side of the cell body is a single *axon*, which branches at its end to form a

(UPI)

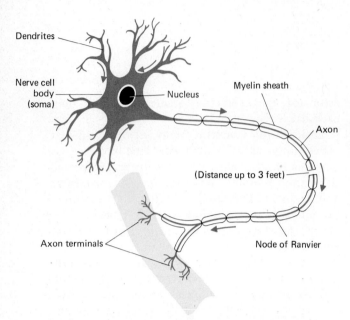

Figure 3.1 A typical neuron. Stimulation received by the dendrites or soma (cell body) may trigger a nerve impulse which travels down the axon to stimulate other neurons, muscles, or glands. Some axons have a fatty myelin sheath interrupted at regular intervals by nodes of Ranvier. The myelin sheath helps to increase the speed of nerve conduction. (Thompson, 1975, p. 93.)

number of *axon terminals*. (See Figure 3.1.) The axon conducts electrical impulses away from the cell body to other neurons, muscles, or glands. Nerve impulses normally move in only one direction— from dendrite or cell body (which can also receive impulses from other neurons) to axon.

All of your neurons have these three structural components, but they vary greatly in size and shape. One neuron might have its cell body in your spinal cord and an axon extending several feet to a fingertip; another might occupy no more than a thousandth of an inch. The *nerves* running through our bodies are actually bundles of axons extending from hundreds or even thousands of neurons. Although a given neuron has only one axon, it may contain 1000 or more dendrites that receive nerve impulses from the axons of many other neurons. Thus the number of potential connections between neurons is very great.

The axons of many neurons are covered by a sheath of fatty tissue called *myelin*. This myelin sheath is thought to serve as a kind of insulation against the leakage of electrical impulses. The sheath is interrupted at regular intervals called *nodes of Ranvier*. As we see in the next section, these nodes play an important part in the conduction of nerve impulses.

Transmission of neural impulses

Simply stated, neurons do two things. First, they generate electricity; second, they secrete chemicals. Neural conduction is thus an *electrochemical* process. We have known about the electrical properties of neurons for over a century, but only in recent years have we begun to learn about the chemical processes involved in the activity of neurons.

How do neurons generate electricity? The answer to this question requires a brief excursion into chemistry. Like other cells, neurons are surrounded by a cell membrane that regulates the passage of substances from surrounding body fluids in and out of the cell. This cell membrane is *semipermeable;* that is, it selectively allows certain particles to pass through relatively unrestricted while refusing passage to other substances. Analysis of the contents inside and the fluid outside of neurons has revealed a large difference in numbers of charged atoms, or ions. Inside the membrane wall there is a concentration of positively charged potassium ions (K^+) and negatively charged protein molecules. Outside of the neurons there are concentrations of positively charged sodium ions (Na^+) and negatively charged chloride ions (Cl^-). In its normal resting state the cell membrane is impermeable to the large, negatively charged protein ions that are thereby trapped inside the cell. It is also impermeable to the positively charged sodium ions that are thus trapped outside the cell. On the other hand, the membrane is almost completely permeable to potassium and chloride ions. The overall effect of the uneven distribution of ions is that the inside of the cell is electrically negative compared to the outside by about 70 millivolts, or $\frac{70}{1000}$ of a volt. Although this is a relatively small electrical potential, in some animals this *transmembrane voltage* forms the basis for specialized organs that generate very high voltages. Some electric fish, such as the eel, can generate 600 to 700 volts because the cell membranes of their muscle tissue are stacked in series, so that the individual voltages add together.

The voltage generated by the unequal distribution of ions inside and outside of the cell membrane is called the *resting potential*. All other cells in the body also have this resting voltage. However, neurons (and muscle cells) have a unique property: Sudden and violent changes can occur in the voltage.

A nerve *impulse* is nothing more than an explosive reversal in the membrane voltage of the neuron during which the membrane voltage momentarily moves from −70 millivolts (inside) to +40 millivolts (See Figure 3.2.)

What causes this sudden reversal? A sophisticated series of experiments that won British scientists A. L. Hodgkin and A. F. Huxley the Nobel Prize provided the answer. Recall that in a resting state positively charged sodium ions are kept outside the cell by its membrane. During an impulse a change takes place in the membrane to make it permeable to sodium—a kind of sodium "gate" opens. Sodium ions flow into the interior of the cell, and because they are positively charged they cause the interior of the cell to become more positive than the outside. This change in polarity, which is called the *action potential*, starts a chain reaction and causes the sodium gate to open at adjacent membrane sites. Once it is started at any point on the membrane, the electrical impulse travels down the full length of the axon as if it were a burning fuse. In the wake of the passing impulse there is a recovery period, lasting a few thousandths of a second, during which the membrane is not excitable and cannot discharge another impulse. This is called a *refractory period*, and it places an upper limit on the rate at which impulses can be

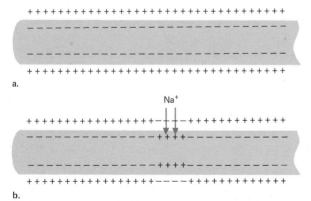

a.

b.

Figure 3.2 Schematic diagram of a nerve impulse. In its resting state (*a*) the inside of the fiber is negative in relation to the body fluids surrounding it. At (*b*) the "sodium gate" has opened in the membrane and positively charged sodium ions rush into the fiber and for a brief instant the polarity is reversed, resulting in the action potential.

triggered in a neuron. In humans the limit has been found to be about 300 impulses per second.

Some of your axons can flash impulses at speeds greater than 200 miles an hour. These high speeds of conduction are possible in nerve fibers that have the insulating myelin sheath previously described. Recall that the myelin sheath is interrupted at regular intervals by the nodes of Ranvier, where the myelin is either extremely thin or absent. In myelinated fibers electrical conduction skips from node to node rather than along the entire axon, and these "great leaps" from one gap to another account for high conduction speed. The myelin sheath occurred late in the evolutionary process, and it is characteristic of the nervous systems of higher animals. In the human brain the formation of the myelin sheath of many nerve fibers is not completed until sometime after birth. This may be one reason why some of our sensory and motor abilities mature so slowly.

Synaptic transmission

The action of the nervous system requires the transmission of nerve impulses from one neuron to another. The complex connections between neurons are not of a physical nature; axon terminals do not actually touch the dendrites or soma of other neurons in the communications chain. Instead there is a small space between them that is known as the *synapse*. Most nerve cells have several thousand synapses on them and can thus be stimulated by axons from many different neurons. In order for a given neuron to fire, certain patterns or intensities of stimulations from adjacent neurons are required. But once an individual neuron fires, its action potential proceeds in an "all-or-none" fashion.

The events that occur at the synapse determine whether or not a neuron will fire. When the dendrites or soma are activated or stimulated by other nerve cells, small shifts occur in the electrical potential of the cell membrane. These shifts are called *graded potentials*, and they are proportional to the amount and kind of incoming activity. If the graded potential is sufficiently large, the neuron discharges with an action potential. If the graded potential does not reach the required level of intensity, the *action potential threshold*, the neuron simply does not fire. In this sense, activating a nerve cell is like firing a gun. Unless a certain amount of energy is applied to

73

the trigger, the gun will not fire; once it does fire, however, the velocity of the bullet bears no relation to how hard the trigger was pulled.

To extend the gun analogy further, guns also have safeties, which prevent their being fired no matter how hard the trigger is pulled. In like manner, the synaptic activity of some neurons serves to inhibit rather than excite the firing of other neurons. This process of *inhibition* prevents a runaway discharge of the nervous system, as occurs in an epileptic seizure. Indeed, certain drugs that block inhibition, such as strychnine, produce this very effect—massive discharges of neurons, such as those that occur in epileptic seizures. Virtually every neuron is constantly being bombarded with excitatory and inhibitory influences from other neurons, and whether the cell fires or does not fire is determined by the interplay of all these influences. An exquisite balance between excitatory and inhibitory processes must be maintained if the nervous system is to function properly.

Chemical transmitters

As we have noted, neurotransmission is an electrochemical process. The chemical aspect of neural activity is intimately involved in synaptic transmission, because in most instances a chemical serves as the transmitter agent. These transmitter chemicals are stored in *synaptic vesicles* in the axon terminals. When a nerve impulse travels down the axon into the axon terminals, it does not "jump" across the synaptic space and directly excite the next neuron. Rather, it stimulates the secretion of the chemical transmitter substance into the synapse. The chemicals move across the synapse and combine with a receptor chemical in the membrane of the dendrite or soma of the receiving cell. The resulting chemical reaction produces the graded potential that, if sufficiently intense, fires the neuron. (See Figure 3.3.)

What kinds of chemical transmitters are there? Although there is much to be learned, we are aware of several kinds. The best understood synaptic transmitter is *acetylcholine* (ACh), which is known to be the transmitter where neurons activate muscle cells and is believed to be a transmitter in certain brain regions as well. Drugs that block the action of ACh can result in fatal muscular paralysis. For example, *curare*, the poison used by South American Indians

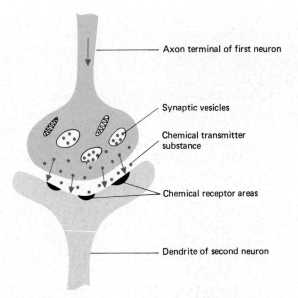

Axon terminal of first neuron

Synaptic vesicles

Chemical transmitter substance

Chemical receptor areas

Dendrite of second neuron

Figure 3.3 Schematic drawing of a synapse between branches of two neurons. An action potential travels to the axon terminals, where it stimulates the secretion of transmitter substances from the synaptic vesicles. The transmitter substances travel across the synapse and combine with a chemical receptor in the membrane of the dendrite of the second neuron. The resulting chemical reaction produces a graded potential in the dendrite.

on their arrows, prevents ACh from activating the receptors in the muscles, apparently by covering the sites normally stimulated by ACh. The muscles no longer respond to nerve commands; the result is a deadly paralysis. A different kind of blocking action is performed at ACh synapses by the deadly food poison known as *botulism*. In this instance the botulinus toxin appears to block the release of ACh from the axon terminal. As with curare, total paralysis is the result.

One other substance known to be a synaptic transmitter is *norepinephrine*. Norepinephrine is found in high concentrations in brain structures that have their prime influence on the motivational and emotional aspects of behavior. It has been noted that many drugs that influence mood and emotions also have an effect on brain levels of norepinephrine and related compounds. Specifically, tranquilizers and depressants cause decreases in the amount of norepinephrine available at synaptic junctions. Antidepressant drugs have the opposite effect on brain concentrations of norepinephrine.

The electromagnetic spectrum

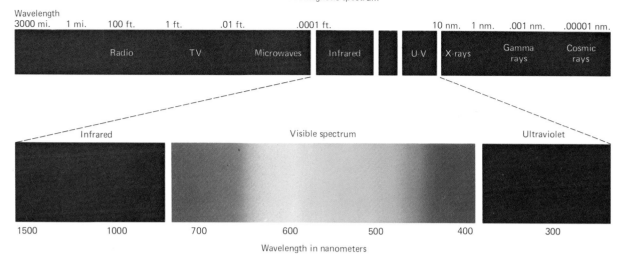

The full spectrum of electromagnetic radiation. Only the narrow band between 400 and 700 nanometers (nm.) is visible to the human eye. One nanometer = 1/1,000,000,000 meter.

Additive color mixture. A beam of light of a single wavelength directed onto a white surface will be perceived as the color that corresponds exactly to that wavelength on the visible spectrum. Two light beams of different wavelengths directed together onto a white surface will be perceived as a color that corresponds to a wavelength different from that of either of the two beams, or an additive color. If beams of wavelengths that fall at certain points within the red, green, and blue color range are directed together onto the surface in the correct proportions, additive color mixtures for the whole visible spectrum can be produced. The Young-Helmholtz theory of color vision assumes that color perception results from the additive mixture of impulses from cones that are sensitive to red, blue, and green (see text).

Subtractive color mixture. Mixing pigments or paints produces new colors by *subtraction*. Colored paints absorb (subtract) colors that correspond to wavelengths different from those of the original color. For example, blue paint mainly absorbs wavelengths that correspond to nonblue hues. Mixing blue paint with yellow paint (which absorbs colors outside the yellow wavelengths) will produce a subtractive mixture that falls within wavelengths between yellow and blue (i.e., green). Theoretically, certain wavelengths of the three primary colors (red, yellow, and blue) can produce the whole range of colors by subtractive mixture.

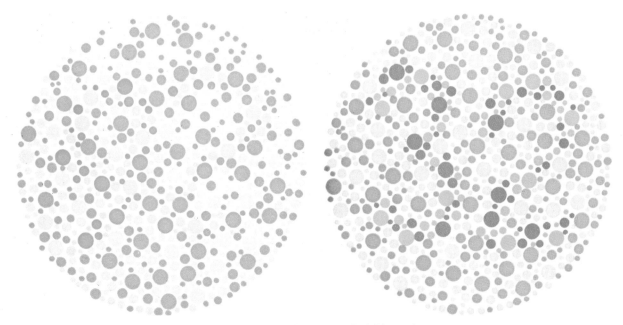

These figures are commonly used to test for color blindness. The one on the left is used to detect yellow-blue blindness, and the one on the right to detect red-green color blindness. Because the dots in the background are just as bright as the dots in the numerals, the only cue for perceiving the numerals is color. (The Dvorine Pseudo-Isochromatic Plates)

A painting as it would appear to a person with normal color vision.

The painting as it would appear to a person with red-green color insensitivity, the most common type of color blindness.

The painting as it would appear to a person with yellow-blue insensitivity.

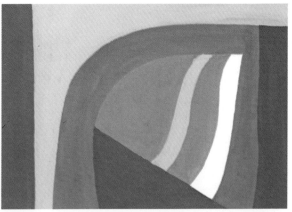

The painting as it would appear to a person with total color blindness.

Day vision and night vision. Color perception is different in daylight than it is at night or at other times when there is only dim light. In daylight the cone receptors are active, so that we perceive a variety of colors. When there is very little light the rod receptors of the retina become active instead. Because rods are color blind, we can perceive only varying shades of gray through them. (Johnson, Woodfin Camp)

Severe perceptual distortions can occur in certain forms of emotional disturbance or under the influence of drugs. This picture was painted by an art student who took LSD, locked himself in a room, and painted what he "saw" outside his window. (See Chapter 5, page 161, for a discussion of drug-produced perceptual distortions.) (From Jones, Shainberg, and Byer, *Health Science*, 4th ed., Harper & Row, 1978.)

This painting illustrates the principle that in perception the whole is often greater than the sum of its parts. Once you have perceived the organized image of a portrait rather than a collection of sea creatures, you will be less likely to perceive the creatures as separate elements. (*Water* by Arcimboldo, Kunsthistorisches Museum, Vienna.)

Many mysteries of synaptic transmission, particularly its chemical aspects, remain to be solved. Solving these mysteries may be the key to understanding the physiological basis of psychological processes such as learning, memory, emotion and motivation, and certain forms of mental illness. To cite one example, learning most certainly involves changes in interactions among neurons, and because the most significant neuronal interactions occur at the synapse, it is possible that learning involves changes in chemical synaptic transmission. Technological advances are permitting increasingly detailed study of this and other questions related to neural communication.

The "language" of neural communication

All of your experiences, thoughts, and behaviors are the result of complex communication patterns among neurons. Your nervous system has two basic ways of coding information for transmission. First, we know that neurons are "spontaneously" active, firing impulses at characteristic intervals known as their *base rate*. One way a neuron can signal that something is happening is by increasing its fixed rate of firing above the base rate or by decreasing the rate of firing. The size of the increase or decrease provides additional information. For example, a neuron whose function is to transmit information regarding pressure might show a larger increase in rate of firing when a heavy weight is placed in your hand than when a light weight is placed there. In addition, a heavy weight might cause more individual neurons to fire, thus increasing the total number of impulses traveling to your brain.

The second way in which information is coded in the nervous system results from the fact that many neurons have very specialized functions and are responsive to only certain kinds of stimulation. For example, we know that certain neurons in the visual system respond only to certain colors, brightnesses, or shapes. In addition, the nervous system is arranged so that particular groups of neurons transmit messages to particular areas of the brain. The "language" of the nervous system thus consists basically of the rate of firing of individual neurons in relation to their base rate of firing, and the particular neurons that are responding. We give examples of both of these means of transmitting information as we explore our sensory systems.

THE SENSORY SYSTEMS

When I turn my gaze skyward I see the flattened dome of sky and the sun's brilliant disk and a hundred other visible things underneath it. What are the steps which bring this about? A pencil of light from the sun enters the eye and is focused there on the retina. It gives rise to a change, which in turn travels to the nerve layer at the top of the brain. The whole chain of these events from the sun to the top of my brain is physical. Each step is an electrical reaction. But now there succeeds a change wholly unlike any which led up to it, and wholly inexplicable by us. A visual scene presents itself to the mind; I see the dome of the sky and the sun in it, and a hundred other visual things beside. In fact, I perceive a picture of the world around me. When this visual scene appears, I ought, I suppose, to feel startled; but I am too accustomed to feel even surprised. (Sherrington, 1950, p. 3)

Like Sir Charles Sherrington, the eminent neurophysiologist who made these observations, you probably take for granted much of the time the window to the world that is furnished by your sensory system. How is it that you can identify and experience one stimulus as a musical symphony, another as a green light, and still another as a fine wine? Your senses provide you with the only means of contact with the environments inside and outside of your body. This contact is possible because certain neurons have developed into specialized sensors that respond to particular types of physical energy. All sense organs share in common the ability to transfer different kinds of energy (sound, light, temperature, heat, etc.) into a common form of neural energy, the nerve impulse. Information about the environment thus becomes translated into the code language of neural impulses, a process called *transduction*.

Sensory organs may be categorized in a number of ways. One way is in terms of the particular kind of energy to which they are responsive (light, sound, etc.). A second way is in terms of the source of the stimulation to which they are sensitive. Environmental events occurring outside of your body are sensed by means of specialized receptors called *exteroceptors*, such as the eye and the ear. Stimulation arising from inside your body is sensed by *interoceptors*, such as pressure-sensitive receptors within the stomach. Movements of the body itself stimulate *proprioceptors*, sensory organs located within the muscles, joints, and inner ear.

Psychologists often use the term *sensation* to refer to the physical process of detecting environmental stimuli and transmitting them through the nervous system, and *perception* to refer to the interpretation of sensations into subjective experience. Realizing that this distinction is an artificial one and that the two processes are virtually inseparable, we nevertheless focus our attention on the physiological aspects of sensation in this chapter and focus on aspects of perception in Chapters 4 and 5.

The visual sense

Vision is our most important means of identifying and locating objects in the external environment. Because of its obvious importance to humans, the visual sense has been studied more than the other sensory systems. Our treatment covers only the highlights of this fascinating sensory system.

The normal stimulus for the visual sense is that portion of electromagnetic energy that we call light. The visible light spectrum is a very tiny fraction of the total spectrum of electromagnetic energies. These energies may be described in terms of *wavelengths* measured in nanometers (nm). A nanometer is one billionth millionth of a meter. The human visual system is sensitive to wavelengths extending from about 380 nanometers to about 780 nanometers. (See color plate.) Your eye will respond to forms of stimulation other than light waves, but they will nevertheless be sensed as light. For example, if you close your eye and rub on the eyelid sufficiently hard, flashes of light will appear. This is because the action potentials caused by the rubbing are interpreted by your brain as light. The experience of light is a quality produced by any stimulus that can excite the visual system.

The human eye

Your eye is a complex and marvelously specialized sensory receptor. Its main parts are shown in Figure 3.4. Light rays enter the eye through the transparent *cornea*. The amount of light allowed to enter is regulated by the *pupil*, which can dilate or contract, depending on the brightness of the stimulus and other factors, such as your emotional state. (Emotional arousal causes the pupil to dilate.) The *lens* is an elastic structure that changes shape in accordance with the distance of the object being viewed; distant objects require a thinner and nearby objects a thicker lens for proper focusing. This adjustment of the lens shape is called *accommodation*, and it is carried out through the action of the *ciliary muscles*. Just as the lens of a camera focuses an image on a photosensitive material (the film), so does the lens of the eye focus the image on the *retina*, which contains the visual receptors. The mechanics of focusing are similar in the camera and the human eye in that a reversed image is cast on a light-sensitive surface (film or retina).

Embedded in the retina of each eye are over 120 million photoreceptor cells, known as *rods* and *cones* because of their shapes. The rods outnumber the

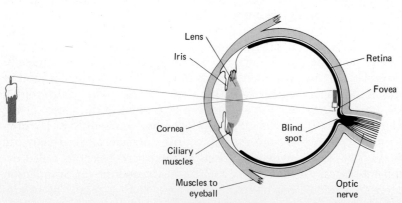

Figure 3.4 The human eye. This cross section shows the major parts of the eye. The iris regulates the size of the pupil, whereas the ciliary muscles regulate the shape of the lens. The image entering the eye is reversed by the lens and cast on the retina, which contains the photoreceptor cells.

X ●

Figure 3.5 The blind spot. This visual test will demonstrate the existence of a blind spot in each eye. Close your left eye and, from a distance of about 12 inches, focus steadily on the X with your right eye as you slowly move the book toward your face. At some point the image of the dot will cross your blind spot and disappear, then reappear after the image crosses the blind spot. The blind spot in your left eye can be located by closing your right eye and fixating on the dot as you move the book toward your face.

cones more than ten to one and are found throughout the retina except in a small central region called the *fovea*, which contains only cones. Strangely enough, the rods and cones form the *rear* layer of the retina, and there are two other layers between the retina and the lens. The first of these layers is the *bipolar cells*, which make direct synaptic connections with the rods and cones. The frontmost layer is composed of the *ganglion cells*, which synapse with the bipolar cells and whose fibers form the optic nerve. The optic nerve exits through the retina not

far from the fovea, and because there are no receptors at this point, there exists a "blind spot," whose existence can easily be demonstrated. (See Figure 3.5.)

After the optic nerves leave the eyes they cross at a point called the *optic chiasma*. As shown in Figure 3.6, the axons of the optic nerve are arranged in such a way that some of them cross over at the optic chiasma and travel to the opposite side or hemisphere of the brain, whereas others do not. You can see that fibers from the right sides of both eyes go to the right hemisphere of the brain and fibers from the left sides of both eyes go to the left hemisphere. This means that if damage were to occur to the visual area of your right hemisphere, you would have blind areas in the right side of both eyes. Because images are reversed when they pass through your lens, this means that you would be unable to see anything in your left visual field. As we shall see later in this chapter, properties of the optic chiasma have made it possible to study some of the unique functions of the two sides of the brain.

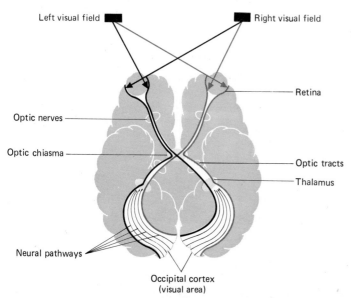

Figure 3.6 The visual pathways. Images are reversed by the lens so that the left visual field is projected on the right side of the retinas of both eyes and the right side of the visual field falls on the left side of both retinas. The optic nerves meet at the optic chiasma, where the nerve fibers from the inner (nasal) half of the retina cross over and to the opposite side of the brain; fibers from the outer half of the retina do not cross over but travel to the same side of the brain. Thus the right half of the visual field is transmitted to the left hemisphere of the brain, and the left visual field is projected to the right hemisphere.

Rods and cones

The two types of visual receptor cells, the rods and the cones, play different roles in visual function. The more numerous rods are especially sensitive to low intensities of light and to movement, but they are insensitive to color. The cones, which function only at relatively high levels of illumination, are the color receptors of the retina.

The rods and cones are unevenly distributed throughout the retina. As we noted earlier, the fovea contains only cones. Outside of the fovea are both rods and cones, with the cones decreasing in number as we move away from the center of the retina. Figure 3.7 shows the photoreceptor connections. Each rod and cone is connected to one or more *bipolar* cells, which are, in turn, connected to the *ganglion* cells whose axons make up the optic nerve. Typically, many rods are connected to the same bipolar cell. The same is true of the cones in the periphery of the retina, but in the fovea each cone has its own bipolar cell. This "private line," plus the fact that the cones in the fovea are very tightly

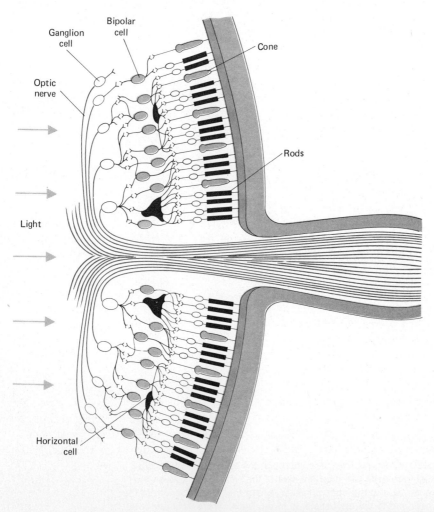

Figure 3.7 Photoreceptor connections in the retina. The rods and cones synapse with bipolar cells, which in turn synapse with ganglion cells whose axons form the optic nerve. The horizontal cells connect rods and cones and help to integrate the activity of the photoreceptors.

packed together, means that our ability to see fine detail (*visual acuity*) is greatest when the image projects directly onto the fovea. Thus both color and fine detail are best seen when objects are looked at directly, because this places the image on the fovea. On the other hand, because cones do not function under dim illumination, we can more easily detect a faint stimulus, such as a dim star, if we do not look directly at it but let its image fall outside of the fovea, where rods are packed most densely.

Although we have described the properties of rods and cones, we have not yet accounted for how they translate light waves into nerve impulses. Although not all the details of the process are fully understood, we do know that in each rod and cone there are several million molecules of a chemical known as *photopigment.* The photopigment contained in the rods is *rhodopsin;* that in the cones is called *iodopsin.* When light is absorbed by one of these molecules, the absorption produces a chemical reaction in the receptor cell that, if strong enough, triggers a nerve impulse. The impulse travels from the photoreceptors to the bipolar cells in the next layer of the retina and then to the ganglion cells. If nerve impulses are triggered at each of the three levels, the message is instantaneously on its way to the visual area of the brain.

Brightness vision

Brightness is probably the most elementary attribute of visual sensation. Many lower organisms have sense organs that are responsive only to differences in illumination. In your eye, brightness vision is a more complex process, because you have more than one type of photoreceptor. As we noted earlier, rods are far more sensitive to low illumination than are cones. Psychologists have studied the relative sensitivity of these two kinds of photoreceptors by establishing their *absolute thresholds*—the minimum amount of light energy needed to produce a visual sensation. By this process *visibility curves* for the two kinds of receptors have been calculated. The curves shown in Figure 3.8 illustrate several important points about rod and cone sensitivity. First, it is clear that the rods have a greater sensitivity than cones throughout most of the color spectrum, except at the red end, where they are about equally sensitive. The curve also shows that cones are most highly

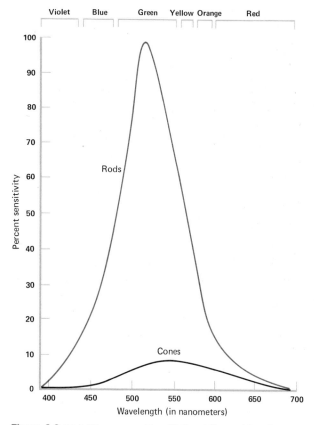

Figure 3.8 Visibility curves. Sensitivity of the rods and cones to various colors. Note the greater general sensitivity of the cones and the different parts of the spectrum to which the rods and cones are maximally sensitive.

sensitive in the greenish-yellow range of the spectrum, whereas the rods are most sensitive in the bluish-green area.

Dark adaptation. Perhaps you have had the experience of entering a dark movie theater from bright sunlight, groping around in the darkness, and finally seating yourself in someone else's lap. As a result of such experiences, many people learn to stand in the rear of the theater until their eyes become accustomed to the dimly lit interior. This improvement in sensitivity is called *dark adaptation.*

Studies of the course of dark adaptation provide further evidence for differences in sensitivity between rods and cones. Figure 3.9 shows a typical dark adaptation curve. Such curves are calculated by having subjects look at a bright light until their retinas have become light adapted. The subjects are then placed in darkness and their ability to detect light flashes of different brightnesses and wavelengths (colors) is measured. Note that the curve has two parts. By changing the color of the light and the area of the retina tested, it can be shown that the first part of the curve is due to dark adaptation of the cones and the second part is due to adaptation of the rods. The cones gradually become sensitive to fainter lights as time passes, but after about five minutes in the dark their sensitivity has reached its maximum as measured by the absolute threshold. The rods,

however, continue to adapt to the dark and do not reach their maximum sensitivity for about a half hour. Research has also shown that the dark-adapted eye is much more sensitive to light with wavelengths in the bluish-green region than to the longer wavelengths of the red region.

The principles of dark adaptation had an important wartime application for fighter pilots who had to be ready for night duty at all times. If they were to function most efficiently and safely, they needed to be able to take off at night on a moment's notice and see their targets under conditions of very low illumination. An experimental psychologist familiar with the facts of dark adaptation provided a solution. Knowing that the rods are very important in night vision and that they are relatively insensitive to red wavelengths, he suggested that fighter pilots either be equipped with goggles with red lenses or work in rooms illuminated by red lights. Because red light stimulates only the cones, the rods remained in a state of dark adaptation, ready for service in the dark.

The mechanism by which dark adaptation occurs involves changes in the photopigment molecules of each photoreceptor. When light is absorbed by a receptor molecule, the molecule bleaches in color so that it cannot absorb any more light for a period of time. During the time that the photopigment is being regenerated, visual sensitivity is lost. If the eye has been in conditions of high illumination, a substantial amount of the photopigments will be bleached at any one time. During dark adaptation the photoreceptor molecules are regenerated and sensitivity increases dramatically. It is estimated that after complete adaptation the rods are able to detect light intensities only one ten-thousandth as great as those that could be detected before dark adaptation began.

Color vision

Within the narrow band of electromagnetic energy that we call the *visible spectrum*, bands of wavelengths are associated with particular colors (see color plates). The color—or more technically, the *hue*—that we see is the result of the wavelength of the electromagnetic radiation. The translation of wavelength signals into sensations of color occurs in the retina.

At one time there was thought to be a different

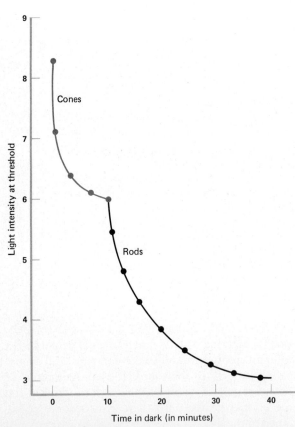

Figure 3.9 Dark adaptation curves. The course of dark adaptation over time is shown. The curve has two parts, one for rods and one for cones. The cones dark adapt completely in about five minutes, whereas the rods continue to increase their sensitivity.

kind of photoreceptor for each hue to which we are sensitive. This is clearly not the case, for we know that human beings are sensitive to over 200,000 different or distinct hues, and it is clear that there are not that many different kinds of color receptors. Around 1800 it was discovered that any color in the visible spectrum can be produced by some combination of the colors blue, green, and red. This fact gave rise to an important theory of color vision developed in 1867 by Thomas Young, an English physicist, and Hermann von Helmholtz, a German physiologist. The *Young-Helmholtz* theory assumes that there are three types of color receptors in the retina—one sensitive to blue, one to green, and one to red. Pre-

sumably, each of these receptors sends messages to the brain, which "mixes" them to re-create the original color.

Although the *Young-Helmholtz* theory is consistent with laws of color mixture (see color plates), there are some other facts with which it is not consistent. For example, the theory held that the hue yellow is produced by activity in red and green receptors. We know, however, that certain color-blind people with red-green color blindness have no difficulty in seeing yellow. A second influential color theory, formulated by Ewald Hering in 1870, attempted to solve this problem. Hering's theory also assumed that there are three types of cones, one for

The cockpits of commercial planes are often illuminated by red lights at night so that pilots can keep the rods of their eyes in a state of dark adaptation. (Bojilova, DPI)

BOX 3.1

Color blindness

About 7 percent of the male population and 1 percent of the female population are unable to discriminate all the wavelengths from one another. The normal eye is capable of discriminating three systems of color: red-green, yellow-blue, and black-white; the person with normal vision is called a *trichromat.* Color blindness results from a deficiency in the red-green system, the yellow-blue system, or both. A person who is color blind in only one of the systems is called a *dichromat.* A *monochromat* has only the black-white system and is totally color-blind. The vast majority of color-blind people have a deficiency in the red-green system. The color plate shows how people with varying types of color blindness would see the same scene.

Many color-blind people are adept at discriminating colors by characteristics other than hue. Indeed, because of such abilities, some individuals are unaware that they are color-blind. For example, red-green color-blind people can easily discriminate between red and green traffic lights once they learn their relative positions. They can also detect differences in the brightnesses of different hues. In addition, the light waves reflected from most objects in our environment usually contain mixed wavelengths, so that a red-green color-blind person may be able to use the small amounts of blue or yellow wavelengths mixed with the predominant bands of green and red to discriminate the latter two colors.

A number of different tests of color blindness have been developed. Typically, these tests involve a circle of color dots within which is "buried" a number or design composed of dots the same size but of colors that the color-blind person cannot see. The color plate presents one such set of figures. A color-blind person cannot read the hidden figures.

red-green, another for blue-yellow, and a third for black-white. Each receptor was assumed to function in two ways, depending on the type of chemical reaction that occurs in response to stimulation. For example, a red-green cone would respond with one chemical reaction to a red stimulus and with another chemical reaction to a green stimulus. Because the receptor cannot react both ways simultaneously, Hering's theory has become known as the *opponent-process theory.* Since Hering's time the theory has been modified somewhat and its proponents now assume that the opponent processes take place not in the cones themselves but in neural coding mechanisms closer to the brain.

Recent evidence suggests that both theories may be partially correct. The development of tiny microelectrodes has made it possible to record the electrical activity of single cones as well as that of single neurons within the visual relay system. This procedure has led to the identification of three kinds of light-sensitive pigments in three different types of cones. These cones are sensitive to either blue, green, or yellow-red, a finding consistent with the Young-Helmholtz theory. However, microelectrode studies have also shown that some bipolar cells in the retina as well as some neurons in visual relay stations in the brain respond to short wavelengths with a burst of impulses above their base rate of spontaneous firing but turn off completely when stimulated by long wavelengths. This finding suggests an opponent-process operating not in the cones themselves, as the original Hering theory suggested, but further along in the pathway from the eye to the brain. It thus appears that the retina contains receptors sensitive to three different hues. However, interactions at the bipolar cells and beyond recode the messages from the receptors so that the neurons in the higher visual centers of the brain respond in an opponent-process manner. As is generally the case in science, the more we learn about a process such as color vision, the more we come to appreciate the complexities of our functioning as biological organisms.

Audition

The energy that is the stimulus for our sense of hearing is fundamentally different from light; it is a form of mechanical energy. What we call sound is actually pressure waves in air, water, or some other conducting medium. When a drum is struck, for example, the resulting vibrations cause successive waves of compression and expansion among the air molecules surrounding it. These sound waves have two characteristics, *frequency* and *amplitude*. Frequency is measured in number of vibrations per second and the unit of measurement is *cycles per second*. The frequency of the sound waves determines the *pitch* that we perceive; the higher the frequency in cycles per second, the higher the perceived pitch. Humans can hear frequencies that range from about 20 to 20,000 cycles per second. Amplitude refers to the *intensity* of the sound waves; that is, the amount of compression and expansion of the molecules in the conducting medium. The amplitude of the sound wave determines the *loudness* of the sound. Differences in intensity of a sound are expressed as *decibels*, a unit developed by

scientists at the Bell Telephone Laboratories to denote the physical pressures that occur at the eardrum. Figure 3.10 shows the loudness of various common sounds scaled in decibels.

The human ear

Your ear is an intricately designed system for translating pressure waves into neural impulses (Figure 3.11). Sound waves travel into an auditory canal leading to your *eardrum*, a movable membrane that vibrates in response to the sound waves. Beyond the eardrum is the *middle ear*, a cavity housing three small bones called the *hammer, anvil,* and *stirrup*. The hammer is attached firmly to the eardrum, and the stirrup to another membrane called the *oval window*. When the eardrum is activated by sound waves, the vibrations are passed along by the bony transmitters of the middle ear to the oval window, which forms the boundary between the middle ear and the inner ear. The inner ear consists of two major organs: the *vestibular apparatus*, which will concern us later when we discuss balance, and the *cochlea*, a coiled tube filled with fluid. The cochlea

Rock groups can play at extremely high decibel levels. Repeated exposure to their sounds at close range may cause permanent hearing damage. (Menzel, Stock, Boston)

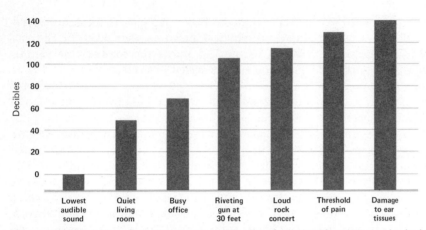

Figure 3.10 Decibel scaling of common sounds. The decibel scale relates a physical quantity—sound intensity—to the human perception of that quantity—sound loudness. It is a logarithmic scale; that is, each increment of 1 decibel represents a tenfold increase in loudness. The graph indicates the decibel ranges of some common sounds. (McNally, 1974, p. 386.)

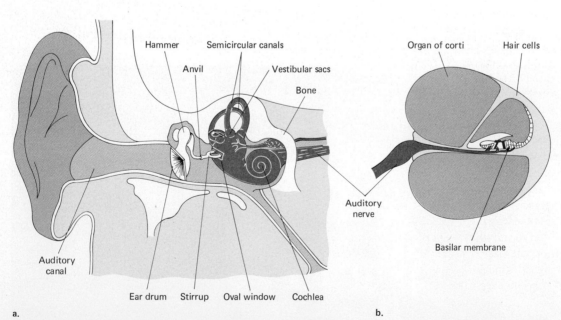

a.   b.

Figure 3.11 The auditory receptors. A cross section of the ear (*a*) shows the structures that transmit sound waves to the cochlea. There they stimulate hair cells in the organ of Corti (*b*). The resulting nerve impulses reach the brain via the auditory nerve. The semicircular canals and vestibular sacs of the inner ear contain sense organs for equilibrium.

contains two membranes, the *basilar membrane* and the *tectorial membrane*. Embedded in the basilar membrane is the *organ of Corti*, which contains thousands of tiny hair cells whose ends are in contact with the tectorial membrane. These hair cells are the actual sound receptors.

When sound waves strike the eardrum, pressure created at the oval window by the bony transmitters of the middle ear sets into motion the fluid inside the cochlea. These movements shift the basilar and tectorial membranes in relation to one another so that the hair cells are bent, setting up an electrical potential that results in nerve impulses being sent to the brain through the auditory nerve.

Coding of auditory information

The sound characteristics that your auditory system must encode are loudness and pitch. Loudness appears to be coded in terms of the total number of auditory nerve fibers that fire and by the activation of certain fibers that fire only when considerable bending of the hair cells occurs in response to an intense sound.

The coding of pitch is more complicated. It appears to involve two different processes, one for frequencies below about 4000 cycles per second and another for higher frequencies. Low-frequency sounds cause the hair cells in the cochlea to vibrate at the same frequency as the physical stimulus and thereby cause a firing of neural impulses at the same frequency within the auditory nerve. Frequencies above 4000 cycles per second are apparently coded in terms of the *region* of the basilar membrane that is maximally displaced by the sound wave. The effect of different sound frequencies on the basilar membrane is similar in some respects to what happens when you shake a rope at different rates. It thus appears that, as in the case of color vision, two processes are involved in pitch perception. Both the frequency of nerve impulses and the place of maximal excitation on the basilar membrane are involved in transmitting information about the frequency of a tone into the language of neural impulses.

The chemical senses

Taste and smell are called the chemical senses because their receptors are sensitive to chemical substances with which they come in contact. Although these senses, particularly smell, have great significance for many species, they are of less consequence in the patterning and organization of human behavior than are the "higher" senses of vision and audition. Our chemical senses are far less developed than are those of some lower animals who depend heavily on them for survival.

Those who fancy themselves gourmets are frequently surprised to find that their sense of taste is responsive to only four qualities: sweet, sour, salt, and bitter. Every other taste experience is composed of a combination of these qualities and those of other senses, such as smell, temperature, and touch.

The stimulus for taste is a variety of chemical substances that come into contact with sensory receptors in the mouth. These receptors, known as *taste buds*, are concentrated along the edges and back surface of the tongue. (See Figure 3.12.) Each taste bud consists of several receptor cells arranged like the segments of an orange. Hairlike structures project

Everyone knows fish smell, but is smell important to fish? A psychologist experiments with a catfish's sense of smell by implanting electronic sensors into its brain, feeding it foul-smelling chemicals, and analyzing the responses with a computer. (Wide World)

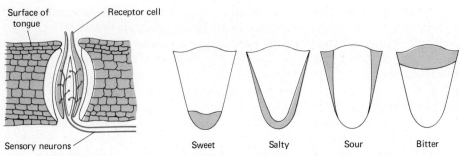

Surface of tongue   Receptor cell

Sensory neurons   Sweet   Salty   Sour   Bitter

Figure 3.12 Taste receptors. The receptors for taste are specialized cells located in taste buds in the tongue. The taste buds are grouped in different areas of the tongue according to the taste sensation to which they respond.

from the top of each cell into the taste pore, an opening to the outside surface of the tongue. When a substance is taken into the mouth it interacts with saliva to form a chemical solution that flows into the taste pore and stimulates the receptor cells. The exact process by which this occurs is not well understood, but we do know that an electrical potential results that excites nearby sensory neurons to send impulses to the area of the brain concerned with taste.

The stimulus for smell is also chemical molecules, and this is one reason we sometimes have difficulty determining whether we are tasting or smelling something. Both chemical senses are undoubtedly involved in our enjoyment of a good meal (or our displeasure with a bad one).

The receptors for smell are long cells that project through the lining of the nasal cavity and into the mucous membrane. The manner in which we discriminate odors is not well understood. It appears that it is the particular combination of neural firings among the neurons in the olfactory system that is responsible for our ability to discriminate.

The skin and body senses

We conclude our discussion of the sensory system with a brief description of the senses of touch, kinesthesis, and equilibrium. We refer to the latter two as body senses because they inform us of the position and movement of the body.

The sense of touch is important to us in a great many ways. Sensitivity to extreme temperatures and pain not only enables us to avoid external danger, but also alerts us to disorders within our bodies that require treatment. In addition, tactual sensations are a source of many pleasures.

We are sensitive to at least four sensations: touch, pain, warmth, and cold. These sensations are conveyed by receptors in the skin and in our internal organs. Mixtures of these four basic sensations are the basis for all other skin sensations that we commonly describe, such as itch and pressure.

Considering the importance of our skin senses, we know surprisingly little about how they operate. We know that there are a number of receptor structures in the skin, but it has not been possible to find consistent relationships between the various structures and types of sensations. We are relatively certain that the primary receptors for pain are free nerve endings that terminate in the skin and that nerve fibers situated at the base of hair follicles are receptors for touch and light pressure. We also know that there are "warm" and "cold" spots on the skin and that their simultaneous activation results in our sensation of hotness. However, it is not yet understood how these points act together to produce the resulting sensation.

The skin receptors send their messages to particular points in the brain that correspond to the area of the body in which the receptor is located. The brain "locates" the point of stimulation in this manner. Persons who have had arms or legs amputated sometimes experience a "phantom limb phenomenon" in which they experience vivid sensations coming from the missing limb. The experience can be quite maddening. Imagine having an intense itch that you

Even the most discriminating of wine-tasters can respond to only four qualities: sweet, sour, salt and bitter. (Mercado, Jeroboam)

can never scratch! Apparently, many of these sensations are due to the irritation of some of the nerves that previously originated in the missing limb. The brain interprets the resulting impulses as real sensations in the limb.

We would be totally incapable of coordinated movements of our bodies if we did not receive constant feedback about the position and movements of our muscles and joints. The sense of *kinesthesis* functions by means of nerve endings in the muscles, tendons, and joints. The information it gives us regarding what our body is doing is the basis for making corrective movements.

Like other critical but underestimated functions, kinesthesis is most appreciated when it fails. When a foot "goes to sleep" we experience reduced sensitivity in our lower legs. A more striking kind of kines-

thetic failure occurs to the victim of *tabes dorsalis*, which results from an advanced case of syphilis. The disease involves a loss of sensation from one's muscles. The patient receives no kinesthetic feedback and is unable to perform even very simple motor skills, such as reaching, except by visually observing the position of his or her body parts.

Cooperating with kinesthesis is the vestibular sense—the sense of body orientation. Those of us who have experienced sea sickness, vertigo, or dizziness from spinning have encountered one unwelcome effect produced by the vestibular sense.

The sense organs for equilibrium are located in the *vestibular apparatus* of the inner ear (Figure 3.11). One part of this system consists of three *semicircular canals*, each in a different plane, which are filled with fluid and lined with hair cells that func-

87

While most people seek to protect their skin against the cold, there are groups across the country whose members refresh themselves by swimming and playing in the snow in subfreezing weather. (UPI)

tion as receptors. When the body moves left-right, backward-frontward, or up-down, the fluid in the appropriate canal shifts, stimulating the hair cells and firing associated neural fibers. The second part of the system is the *vestibular sacs*, located at the base of the semicircular canals. These structures, which are also lined with hair cells, respond to the position of the resting body and tell us whether we are upright or tilted at various angles.

We are constantly kept aware of changes in our external and internal environments through our senses. At any one time we are aware of only a tiny portion of the millions of messages that are being sent out by our sensory receptors. Our sense organs do not select what we will be aware of, but merely transmit as much information as they can through

our nervous system. There the information is processed and integrated. We turn next to this most complex of all our physiological systems.

THE NERVOUS SYSTEM

The biological causes of consciousness and behavior are rooted in the nervous system. This incredibly complex system is the ultimate biological base for all that we are and do. Its study is one of the most exciting frontiers of psychology. Each year many important discoveries are made about how the nervous system functions and how it can be influenced and altered. Such discoveries promise to provide us with new insights into who and what we are, and how we can gain greater control over our behavior. (See Box 3.2.)

The nervous system consists of three kinds of neurons which carry out the input, integration, and output functions of the system. *Afferent* (sensory) neurons carry messages from the periphery of the body and the internal organs to the spinal cord and brain. *Efferent* (motor) neurons transmit impulses from the brain and spinal cord to the muscles and organs of the body. *Interneurons* perform a connective or associative function within the nervous system.

Special groupings of neurons form the structures of the nervous system. Large groups of neuron cell bodies that cluster together in one place are called a *nucleus* if the cluster lies within the brain or spinal cord and a *ganglion* if the cluster lies outside the brain and spinal cord. Collections of axons that form bundles and travel together from place to place are called *tracts* within the brain and spinal cord and *nerves* outside the brain and spinal cord.

Divisions of the nervous system

Although the parts of the nervous system are highly interrelated, they may be broken down for purposes of anatomical discussion into a number of divisions and subdivisions. (See Figure 3.13.) The two major divisions are the *central nervous system*, which includes all the neurons in the brain and spinal cord, and the *peripheral nervous system*, which comprises all the neurons connecting the central nervous system with the muscles, glands, and sensory receptors. The peripheral nervous system may be further subdivided into a *somatic system*, which provides input from the sensory system and output to the skeletal muscles responsible for voluntary movement, and the *autonomic* nervous system, which directs the activity of the glands and internal organs of the body. The autonomic system plays a critical role in emotional behavior; we discuss it in greater detail later.

The central nervous system

The central nervous system, consisting of the brain and spinal cord, is the integrating center for all behavior and bodily functions. It is a hierarchical system, with increasingly complex structures being built on one another in the course of evolution. Some relatively primitive processes, such as reflexes,

can be performed at the level of the spinal cord. In most instances, however, the input-integration-output functions involve several levels of the brain. The higher mental processes that distinguish us from lower animals seem to take place within the highest and most recently evolved portion of the brain, the cerebral cortex.

The spinal cord

Most nerves enter and leave the central nervous system by way of the spinal cord, where they are protected by the spinal vertebrae. When the spinal cord is viewed in cross section (Figure 3.14), its central portion resembles an H. The H-shaped portion is *gray matter*, which consists largely of gray-colored neuron cell bodies and their interconnections. Surrounding the gray matter is the *white matter*, composed almost entirely of white-colored myelinated axons that serve to connect various levels of the spinal cord with each other and with the higher centers of the brain. Emerging from the side of the spinal cord all along its length are the *dorsal* and *ventral roots*. The dorsal root consists of sensory nerves whose cell bodies form the dorsal root ganglion. The ventral root (which faces the front of your body) contains only motor nerves. Once they have left the dorsal and ventral roots, most nerve bundles contain both sensory and motor nerves and are therefore called *mixed nerves*.

Some very simple stimulus-response sequences, known as *spinal reflexes*, can be carried out at the level of the spinal cord. For example, when you touch something hot and quickly withdraw your hand, your response is the result of impulses triggered by sensory receptors in your skin that enter the spinal cord through the dorsal root and synapse with interneurons in the gray matter, which in turn excite motor neurons in the ventral root. At the same time the sensory neurons have synapsed with other neurons, which carry the messages to your brain. However, because the latter messages take slightly longer to reach the brain, you may find that you react by withdrawing from the hot stimulus before you are even aware that it is burning your hand.

The brain

Your brain consists of about 3 pounds of protein, fat, and water, plus a few other minor components. Yet

BOX 3.2

Methods for studying the brain

A variety of approaches are used by brain investigators to study the functions of particular areas of the brain. The following methods are the ones most frequently used in such research.

Lesioning and surgical ablation

We can often learn a great deal about a particular structure in the brain by destroying it and studying the behavioral effects of such destruction. In lesioning, tissue is usually destroyed electrically, whereas in surgical ablation a part of the brain is surgically removed. Many experiments of this kind are performed on animals. Humans can be studied in this way when an accident or disease produces a lesion or when the removal of abnormal brain tissue is essential to their well-being.

The stimulation method

A specific region of the brain may be stimulated either by electric current or by chemicals that excite neurons. Sometimes permanently implanted elec-

trodes are used to stimulate repeatedly the brain area of interest. In chemical stimulation studies a tiny tube, or *cannula*, is inserted into the animal's brain so that a small amount of some chemical can be delivered through the tube to the area of interest.

Electrical recording techniques

It is possible to measure the electrical activity of the brain either by inserting electrodes into particular areas or by recording the activity of many neurons from the scalp, as occurs in the electroencephalograph (EEG). (See the accompanying figure.)

Technological advances have now made it possible to record the activity of single neurons by using tiny microelectrodes about one-thousandth of a millimeter in size. This technique permits an investigator to study the activity of single neurons while the organism is being exposed to different stimuli or as the result of such processes as learning.

Histological procedures

The structural features of neurons and fiber connections can be studied through microscopic examination of brain tissue. Histological examination allows the connections between cells to be traced. An exciting recent development lies in the use of the electron microscope to study the very fine details of nerve cells and how they are modified by such processes as perception and learning.

these 3 pounds of chemicals contain all that you know of yourself and the world. Your brain is the biological seat of your consciousness, intellect, personality, and all else that makes you a unique human being. It might represent the wisdom of a Socrates, the creativity of an Einstein or an Edison, or the tendencies of a Hitler. It is the most complex structure in the known universe.

Your brain is basically composed of two kinds of cells: neurons and fatty cells called *glia*. For a long time it was thought that glia served only to support

the neurons and hold them in place, as do connective tissue cells in many organs of the body. Recent discoveries suggest, however, that although glia do not themselves transmit nerve impulses, they may play a very important role in the activity of neurons by directly modifying their electrical and chemical activity. Your brain contains perhaps 10 to 12 billion neurons and about 120 billion glia. According to one brain researcher, the number of possible interconnections among the neurons in your brain is greater than the number of atomic particles that constitute

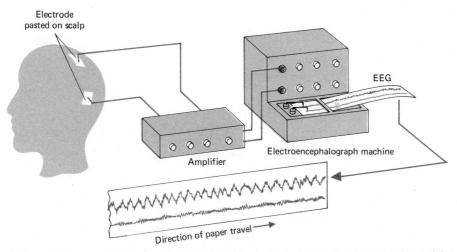

How an electroencephalogram is obtained. In this method of recording human brain activity, electrical signals are picked up by electrodes on the scalp, amplified, and written out on a moving paper by a electroencephalograph. This records the changing voltage generated by the brain over time. (From Timothy J. Teyler, *A Primer of Psychobiology: Brain and Behavior*, W. H. Freeman and Company. Copyright © 1975.)

the entire universe (Thompson, 1975).

Fortunately, the brain is not a random structure, or we could never hope to understand how it functions. Instead the brain has certain structural characteristics that are at least loosely related to particular kinds of functions. We touch briefly on those parts of the brain that seem to be most important in psychological functioning.

The human brain (shown in Figure 3.15) consists of three major divisions: the *hindbrain*, which is the lowest and most primitive level of the brain; the *midbrain*, which lies above the hindbrain; and the *forebrain*, which contains the most highly developed part of the human brain, the cerebrum.

The hindbrain

As your spinal cord enters the skull, it enlarges to form several structures that comprise the *brain stem*. The lowest of these enlargements is the *medulla*, a narrow structure about an inch and a half long that plays an important role in vital bodily functions such as heart rate and respiration. It also contains

91

TWO: BIOLOGICAL AND PERCEPTUAL BASES OF BEHAVIOR

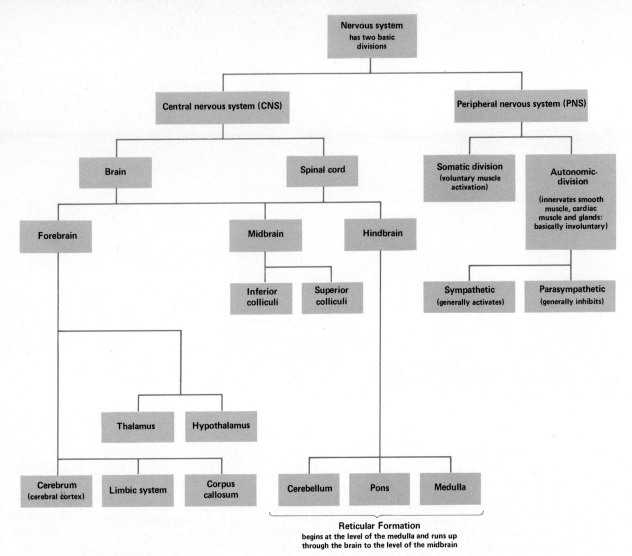

Figure 3.13 Structural organization of the nervous system. (R. Isaacson et al., *A Primer of Physiological Psychology,* New York, Harper & Row, 1971, p. 63.)

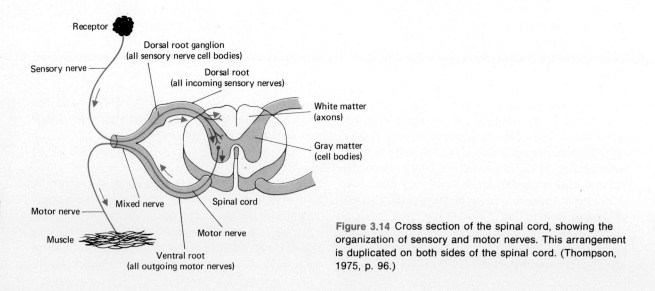

92

Figure 3.14 Cross section of the spinal cord, showing the organization of sensory and motor nerves. This arrangement is duplicated on both sides of the spinal cord. (Thompson, 1975, p. 96.)

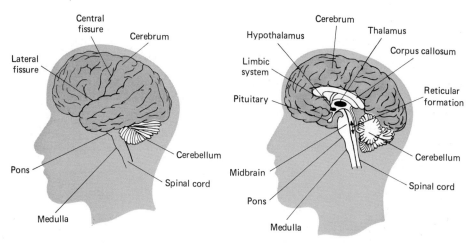

Figure 3.15 The human brain. The lateral surface of the brain (left) and a midline section (right). The parts of the brain discussed in the text are labeled. (Adapted from Thompson, 1975, p. 90.)

all the sensory and motor nerve tracts coming up from the spinal cord and descending from the brain. At the level of the medulla these tracts cross over so that the left side of the brain receives sensory input from and exerts motor control over the right side of the body, and the right side of the brain receives sensory input from and controls the left side of the body. Damage to the medulla has very serious, and often fatal, consequences because of the important role its nuclei play in vital bodily processes.

The *pons* lies in the brain stem just above the medulla. Like the medulla, it contains many ascending and descending fibers that connect higher and lower levels of the central nervous system. It also contains several important nuclei that carry sensory information to the brain from the sense organs of the head as well as motor neurons that control the muscles and glands of the face and neck. Finally, some nuclei involved in respiration are located in the pons.

The *cerebellum* is attached to the rear of the brain stem directly above the pons. It is covered by a *convoluted* cortex having a large number of lobules separated by fissures. This covering consists primarily of cell bodies. Beneath the cortex is primarily white matter (myelinated axons), and buried at the center of the cerebellum are collections of neuron cell bodies, or nuclei, which are concerned primarily

with motor coordination. Your cerebellum is very similar to that of lower animals, including snakes and fish, and it is believed that in the course of evolution this was probably the first structure to be specialized for sensorimotor coordination. Specific motor movements are initiated in the cerebrum, but their coordination depends on the cerebellulm. Damage to the cerebellum results in severe motor disturbances, with jerky, uncoordinated movements, and an inability to perform automatically even such simple movements as walking.

Buried within the brain stem is the *reticular formation*, a complex mixture of fibers, cell bodies, and nuclei extending from the spinal cord up into the forebrain. It receives its name from its structural resemblance to a reticulum, or net. Although the reticular formation seems to be involved in the control of certain aspects of motor behavior, it has attracted a great deal of attention because of its central role in consciousness, attention, and sleep. Anatomical studies tell us that most of the sensory input tracts send secondary branches into the reticular formation while their main projections are routed to higher centers of the brain. The reticular formation acts as a general arousal center, exciting the rest of the brain. Without reticular excitation sensory messages do not register in consciousness, even though they reach the appropriate higher areas of the

93

brain. Some general anesthetics have their effect by deactivating neurons of the reticular formation so that the person is unaware of the sensory impulses that would ordinarily be experienced as pain.

Electrical stimulation studies have shown that the application of particular kinds of currents to the reticular formation can produce sleep in a wakeful animal and wakefulness in a sleeping animal. Severe damage to the reticular formation can produce a permanent coma.

The reticular formation also appears to play an important role in attention. On a physiological level, attention is an active process in which only certain sensory inputs "get through" to our consciousness; others are toned down or completely blocked out. It appears that the reticular formation plays an important role in this process.

The midbrain

The midbrain lies just above the hindbrain and contains a number of important sensory and motor nuclei, as well as many sensory and motor fiber tracts connecting higher and lower portions of the nervous system. The sensory portion of the midbrain contains the *superior colliculi*, a pair of important relay centers in the visual system, and the *inferior colliculi*, which serve a similar function in the auditory system. The midbrain also contains motor nuclei that control eye movement. Extending well into the core of the midbrain is the upper portion of the reticular formation.

The forebrain

The most conspicuous biological difference between your brain and the brain of lower animals is the size and complexity of your forebrain, particularly your cerebral cortex. The forebrain consists of two large cerebral hemispheres that envelop the brain stem as well as a number of very important structures buried in the central regions of the hemispheres. We consider these structures first.

The thalamus. The *thalamus* is comprised of a large group of nuclei located above the midbrain. In appearance it resembles two small footballs, one within each cerebral hemisphere. The thalamus is an important sensory relay system and has sometimes been likened to a giant switchboard that routes sensory

inputs to the appropriate areas of the brain. We know that the visual, auditory, and body senses all have major relay stations in the thalamus. A nearby group of nuclei, known as the *intrinsic nuclei*, have interconnections with the reticular formation and with other structures of the forebrain. Like the reticular formation, they appear to play an important role in the regulation of the spontaneous electrical activity of the cortex and appear to be involved in the control of such processes as sleep and attention.

The hypothalamus. The hypothalamus consists of a group of small nuclei that lie at the base of the brain, above the roof of the mouth. These tiny groups of neuron cell bodies play an enormously important role in many aspects of motivational and emotional behavior. They are known to be critically involved in sexual behavior, temperature regulation, sleeping, eating, aggression, and emotional behavior. The hypothalamus has intimate connections with the *pituitary gland*, the master gland of the endocrine system (discussed later in the chapter). Through its connection with the pituitary gland, the hypothalamus exerts direct control over many hormonal secretions that regulate sexual development and behavior, metabolism, and reactions to stress. Recently it has been discovered that the hypothalamus manufactures some of the hormones previously thought to be manufactured by the pituitary gland. The role of the hypothalamus in motivation and emotional behavior is discussed in Chapter 10.

The limbic system

The *limbic system* consists of a number of structures lying deep within the cerebral hemispheres around the central core of the brain. The limbic system has many neural interconnections with the hypothalamus and seems to be involved in organizing the activities needed to satisfy the basic motivational and emotional needs that are regulated by the hypothalamus. Instinctive activities of lower animals, such as fleeing from danger, mating, attacking, and feeding, appear to be governed by this system. Were you to sustain injury to certain parts of your limbic system, you would be unable to carry out intended sequences of actions. A small distraction would make you forget what you had set out to do. The functional relationship between the hypothalamus and limbic system seems to be that the hypothalamus regulates the needs and the limbic system organizes the behaviors required for need satisfaction.

The limbic system is also intimately involved in emotional behavior, particularly aggression. Lesions in certain areas of the limbic system produce extreme rage reactions to the slightest provocation, whereas damage to other areas results in an inability to respond aggressively even when attacked. Texas mass murderer Charles Whitman (discussed in Chapter 2) was found to have a large tumor in the limbic system, and it has been suggested that this played a major role in his murderous outburst.

The cerebral hemispheres

The cerebral hemispheres constitute the largest part of the brain. These twin hemispheres envelop the brain stem and are the seat of the most complex features of human behavior, such as language and abstract thought. The cerebral hemispheres consist of an outer gray *cortex* composed primarily of neuron cell bodies and unmyelinated fibers and an internal white core composed primarily of myelinated fibers that connect areas of the hemispheres with each other and with other parts of the brain.

The cerebral cortex represents the most recent evolutionary development of the nervous system. Fish and amphibians have no cerebral cortex, and in the progression from more primitive to more advanced mammals, the amount of cortex relative to the total amount of brain tissue increases quite dramatically.

Most sensory systems send information to specific regions of the cortex. Motor systems that control the activity of muscles and glands are situated in other regions of the cortex. The basic organization of the sensory and motor areas of the cortex is quite similar from rat to man. However, the relative amount of *association cortex*, interneurons that are neither sensory nor motor but are believed to be involved in higher and more complex behavioral functions, increases dramatically from lower animals to humans.

Organization of the cerebral cortex

The brain contains a tremendous amount of cortical tissue compressed into a relatively small space inside the skull. This is possible because the cortex is wrinkled and convoluted so that much of it is contained in *fissures* or foldings of the cortical surface. It has been estimated that more than three-quarters of the total amount of cerebral cortex lies within the folds or fissures. Two of these fissures serve as major landmarks in the cerebral hemispheres. The *central fissure* divides the cerebrum into anterior (front) and posterior (rear) halves, and the *lateral fissure* runs in a front-to-rear fashion along the side of the brain. (See Figure 3.16.) Each hemisphere is divided into four *lobes:* the *frontal, parietal, occipital,* and *tem-*

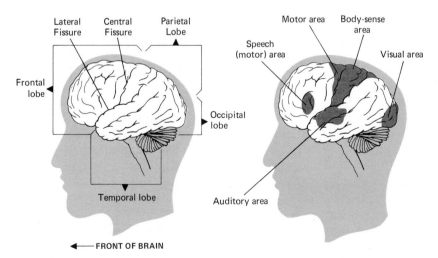

Figure 3.16 Localization of function in the human cerebral cortex. The nonshaded areas are association cortex.

95

BOX 3.3
Reward and punishment centers in the brain: A psychological frontier

The year was 1953 and in the laboratory of psychologist James Olds an experiment was under way to study the effects of electrical stimulation of the rat's midbrain reticular formation. Quite by accident one of the most significant discoveries in the history of brain research was about to occur. One of the implanted electrodes missed its target and was placed in the limbic system rather than in the reticular formation. The investigators noticed that whenever the rat was stimulated, it quickly repeated the behavior that it had performed prior to the stimulation. In a variety of learning situations animals with similarly implanted electrodes quickly learned and performed behaviors in order to obtain what was clearly an electrical reward. Indeed, the reward value of the brain stimulation was so potent that, when given a choice, starving rats often chose electrical stimula-

tion over food, even to the point of dying of starvation (Routtenberg and Lindy, 1965).

Olds and his associates next "mapped" the reward centers of the brain by implanting electrodes in various regions and testing their effects. They found some areas that were rewarding, others that were punishing, and many that were neutral. The "hot spots" for reward were found to be primarily in the hypothalamus and limbic system.

At Tulane University Robert Heath (1972) and his associates have studied the effects of electrical stimulation in epileptic patients who have had electrodes embedded in their brains to search for abnormal brain tissue. In areas roughly corresponding to the reward centers found in animals, patients have reported experiencing intensely pleasurable sensations resembling those of sexual orgasm. One female patient reportedly proposed marriage to the male experimenter while being stimulated.

The study of reward and punishment centers in the brain may ultimately unlock the secrets of how and why we experience pleasure. The potential use of electrical brain stimulation in controlling behavior constitutes an area of great ethical as well as practical concern. For some, electrical stimulation looms as an ominous threat to human freedom, inspiring images of human puppets controlled by the electronic strings of an all-powerful authority. It has already been demonstrated that voltage is more powerful than will. For example, individuals cannot voluntarily inhibit motor movements evoked by stim-

poral. The frontal lobe is separated from the parietal lobe by the central fissure, the temporal lobe lies beneath the lateral fissure, and the occipital lobe is at the rear of the brain.

Each of the four cerebral lobes is involved in particular sensory and motor functions, and these are illustrated in Figure 3.16. Speech and skeletal motor functions are localized in the frontal lobe. The central fissure divides the motor area from the body sense area, which is located in the parietal lobe immediately behind the central fissure. Messages from

the auditory system are sent to a region in the top portion of the temporal lobe, and the visual area of the brain is located in the occipital lobe. The noncolored areas in Figure 3.16 that seem to be neither sensory nor motor in function are called association areas.

The motor area. The motor area, which controls all bodily movements, lies just in front of the central fissure. Each hemisphere governs movement on the opposite side of the body; that is, movements on the

96

ulation of the motor cortex. In the words of Jose Delgado, a pioneer in electrical stimulation of the brain, "The individual is defenseless against direct manipulation of the brain, because he is deprived of his most intimate mechanisms of biological reactivity."

What of the future? As more is learned about the brain and as the technology of brain stimulation increases in sophistication, today's speculations promise to become tomorrow's realities.

In terms of what will come to pass, it matters little what the final limits are on this technology. Whether higher thought processes will someday be controllable by scientific means not known as yet, or whether men can be robotized in frightening or beneficial ways, the course of this industry is clear for years to come. Sooner or later, someone will decide to put a small computer in the human brain to try to raise intelligence. Epileptic seizures will be overcome, some kinds of mental retardation will be conquered, and some psychoses will be subjugated too. But this technology, mindless and without morality, like all things not human, or even living, will not direct itself. People will use it, just as people made it, and some of them will see that it has possibilities for more than merely medical control, helpful perhaps only to the controllers, not to those controlled. There is an intrinsic ambiguity about behavior control; whether its implications are more ominous or more promising to individuals and to society depends on how it will be understood, prescribed, exploited, and contained as it emerges in the future. (London, 1969, p. 191)

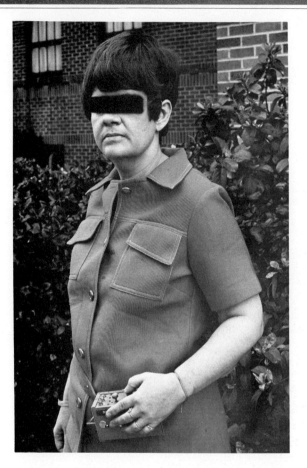

By means of implanted electrodes and a portable stimulator, this person is able to directly stimulate reward centers in her brain. (Robert G. Heath)

right side of the body originate in the motor area of the left hemisphere, whereas movements on the left side originate in the right hemisphere. Specific body areas are represented in different parts of the motor cortex, and the amount of cortex devoted to each area depends on the complexity of the movements that are involved. Figure 3.17 shows the relative organization of function within the motor cortex.

Electrical stimulation of the motor cortex results in muscle movements in the extremities represented by the part of the cortex that is stimulated. On the

other hand, injury to the motor cortex results in a paralysis, which is at least temporary, of the same extremities. Usually there is some recovery in function as other areas of the brain concerned with movement take over the functions of the motor cortex.

The sensory cortex. Input from each of the sensory systems terminates in particular areas of the cortex known as cortical *projection areas*. With the exception of taste and smell, at least one projection area in

97

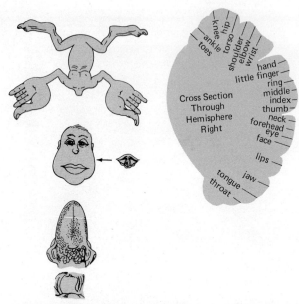

Figure 3.17 Representation of amount and position of motor cortex devoted to various parts of the body. The amount of cortex is directly proportional to the range and fineness of possible movements. (After J. F. Fulton, *Physiology of the Nervous System*, New York, Oxford, 1938.)

the cortex has been identified for each of the senses.

The projection area for the body sense lies in the parietal lobe immediately behind the central fissure. Each side of the body projects to the opposite hemisphere. Heat, touch, cold, and the sense of body movement are represented in this area. As in the case of the motor area, this sensory area is organized in an upside-down fashion, with the amount of cortex devoted to each body area being directly proportional to the use and sensitivity of that region. The representation of sensory functions is schematically presented in Figure 3.18. As far as sensory cortex is concerned, we humans are mainly fingers, lips, and tongue.

The auditory area lies on the surface of the temporal lobe at the side of each hemisphere. Both ears send impulses to the auditory areas of both hemispheres, so that the loss of one temporal lobe has very little effect on hearing. The sensory projection area for vision lies at the rear of the occipital lobe. Here messages from the visual receptors are analyzed, integrated, and translated into sight. As in the auditory

system, both eyes send input to both hemispheres, although only one side of the visual field is represented in each hemisphere.

The sensory cortex is organized so that particular points on the receptor surface for a given sensory system are ultimately connected to specific points on the surface of the cortex. This is known as *topographic organization*. Thus stimulation of a particular point on the skin or the retina activates a particular point in the cortex. Conversely, electrical stimulation of a particular point in the sensory cortex gives rise to a particular sensory experience as if it were occurring through the sensory receptors. Research is now under way that may provide "artificial vision" for blind people by building on this phenomenon. (See Box 3.4.)

In addition to this point-to-point connection be-

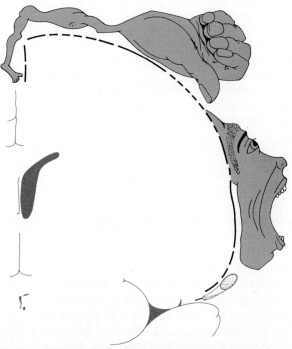

Figure 3.18 Representation of amount and position of sensory cortex devoted to various parts of the body shown by a cross section through the hemisphere. (Reprinted with permission of Macmillan Publishing Co., Inc. from W. Penfield and T. Rasmussen, *The Central Cortex of Man*. Copyright 1950 by Macmillan Publishing Co., Inc.)

BOX 3.4

Artificial vision for the blind

The development of microelectrodes has made it possible to study the activity of single neurons in the cerebral cortex. Studies of single-cell activity in the visual cortex have shown that certain cells respond only to certain types of stimuli. For example, a particular cortical cell may fire only when a horizontal slit of light is viewed by the eye, not when a vertical slit of light is presented; another cell may fire only when a vertical slit is presented; and so on. It appears that the visual cortex is "prewired" to perceive organization and form.

When the visual cortex of patients who are undergoing brain surgery is electrically stimulated, they report "seeing" flashes of light. These electrically produced visual sensations are called *phosphenes*.

Recent research at the University of Utah Medical School has aroused hope that in the future it will be possible to provide artificial vision to blind people (Dobelle, Mladejovsky, and Girvin, 1974). Two patients, one blind for 7 years, the other for 28 years, had thin strips of Teflon containing 64 electrodes placed against their visual cortexes following an operation. By stimulating pairs of electrodes and receiving reports from the patients of their visual experiences, it was possible to "map" the phosphene make-up of each patient's visual cortex. Once the visual "map" was established, the experimenters were successful in presenting forms and letters that could be "seen" by the blind subjects by simultaneously stimulating certain electrode arrays.

The promising results obtained in this research suggest that by developing an artificial visual receptor that could respond to visual stimuli by stimulating electrodes implanted in individual cells of the visual cortex, a kind of artificial vision would be possible for blind people.

---

tween sensory receptor areas and the cortex, we know that within each sensory area there are cells that respond to particular aspects of the sensory stimulus. Certain cells in the visual cortex, for example, fire only if the individual looks at a particular kind of stimulus, such as a vertical line. Other cells respond only if the individual looks at a line of some other orientation. In the auditory cortex certain neurons fire only in response to high tones, whereas others respond only to tones having some other specific frequencies. Recent research has shown that certain of these single-cell responses are present at birth, suggesting that we are "prewired" to perceive many aspects of our sensory environment. The manner and the extent to which such responses are developed or modified through experience constitutes an area of considerable current interest.

Association cortex. The *association areas* of the cortex cover the largest area of the cerebral hemisphere. They are known to be critically involved in percep-

tion, language, and thought. Damage to specific parts of the association cortex causes a disruption or loss of higher functions, such as speech, understanding, thinking, and problem solving. Physiological psychologists are doing extensive research to find out what kinds of electrical and chemical events occur in the association areas during the exercise of our higher mental functions.

Hemispheric localization of brain function

Your cerebrum consists of two symmetrical cerebral hemispheres separated by a deep division that runs from the front of the brain to the rear. The two hemispheres are connected by a large band of fibers called the *corpus callosum*. This communication link between the two hemispheres allows them to function as a single unit. However, both clinical observations and research evidence indicate that there are dramatic differences between the psychological functions of the two cerebral hemispheres. We have seen evidence of hemispheric localiza-

99

tion of function in several of the systems already discussed. In the motor system there is a complete crossing of fibers from the motor cortex to the opposite side of the body, so that the left hemisphere controls movements of the right side of the body and the right hemisphere controls the left side of the body. In the visual system we have seen that some of the fibers of the optic nerve cross at the optic chiasma so that the right halves of the visual fields of both eyes project to the left hemisphere and the left halves of the visual fields project to the right hemisphere of the cerebral cortex. (See Figure 3.6.) The visual areas of the two hemispheres are normally connected by the corpus callosum, so that a unified visual world is experienced rather than two half-worlds.

Evidence that certain complex psychological functions are localized within one or the other of the hemispheres comes from medical studies of patients who have suffered various types of brain damage. Damage to a portion of the frontal lobe of the left hemisphere in a right-handed person abolishes the ability to speak or understand language. Damage to a corresponding part of the right hemisphere has no effect on language. However, damage to the right hemisphere of a right-handed person results in great difficulty in performing certain spatial tasks. The person may have difficulty understanding complex pictures, and may even forget a well-traveled route. The speech centers for left-handed people are sometimes located in the right hemisphere, but the majority of left-handed people seem, like right-handers, to have left hemisphere speech centers. Clinical studies of patients who have had portions of the left or right cerebral cortex removed surgically as treatment for severe epilepsy also indicate that verbal abilities and speech are localized in the left hemisphere, as are mathematical and symbolic abilities. Complex perceptual and musical abilities seem to depend more on the right hemisphere. Figure 3.19 summarizes the functions attributed to the two sides of the cerebral cortex by various scientists.

100 Studies of split-brain patients. A series of remarkable studies on hemispheric localization of function have been performed by Roger Sperry (1970) and his associates at the California Institute of Technology. Certain patients suffer from a form of epilepsy charac-

terized by a seizure that begins on one side of the brain and then spreads to the other hemisphere. Neurosurgeons found that some of these patients could be greatly helped by severing the nerve fibers of the corpus callosum to prevent the spread of the seizure to the other hemisphere. The operations were successful in preventing spread of seizures and seemed to have no negative side effects on other psychological functions. Sperry's studies of these patients involved procedures to test separately the functions of the two hemispheres. He took advantage of the fact that the right side of each visual field is projected across the optic chiasma to the left hemisphere, and vice versa.

In Sperry's experiments split-brain subjects looked at a fixation point, and visual stimuli (words, pictures, etc.) were flashed briefly to the right or left side of the visual field by a slide projector. The subject could respond verbally or with movements of either hand behind a screen. It was found that when words were flashed to the left hemisphere, patients could immediately say them and write them with their right hands. However, if words were flashed to the right hemisphere, the patients could neither say nor write them. This did not mean, however, that the right hemisphere was incapable of recognizing objects. If a picture of an object was flashed to the right hemisphere and the left hand (which is linked with the right hemisphere) was allowed to feel many different objects behind the screen, including the object whose picture was flashed, it would immediately select the correct object and hold it up. But as long as the object was held in the left hand, the patient was unable to name it. However, if the object was transferred to the right hand, the patient immediately named it. In a very real sense the left hemisphere had no knowledge of what the right hemisphere was experiencing until that point.

The evidence obtained from split-brain patients indicates that separation of the hemispheres creates two independent minds within a single brain. Some psychologists have suggested that what we called the conscious self resides in the left hemisphere, because it is based on our ability to verbalize the past and present, and that the right hemisphere is the unconscious mind, except when it communicates with the left hemisphere across the corpus callosum. When the connections between the two hemispheres are

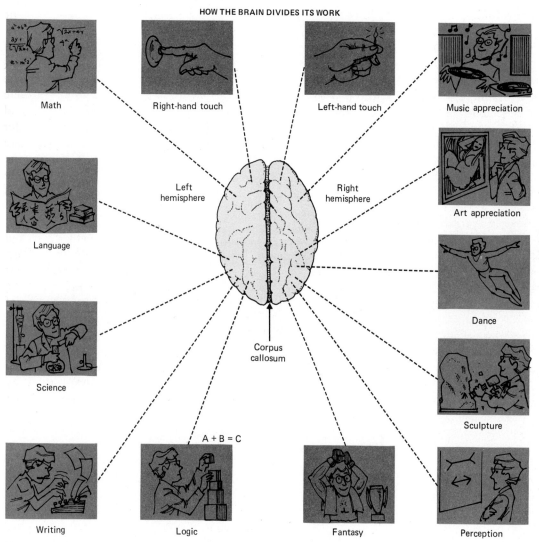

HOW THE BRAIN DIVIDES ITS WORK

Math

Right-hand touch

Left-hand touch

Music appreciation

Language

Left hemisphere

Right hemisphere

Art appreciation

Dance

Science

Corpus callosum

Sculpture

Writing

A + B = C

Logic

Fantasy

Perception

Figure 3.19 Hemispheric localization of brain function. (Drawing by Ray Doty)

cut, the experiences of the right hemisphere are not part of conscious awareness. A person may then experience emotions or other experiences without being able consciously to explain them. One split-brain subject appeared to experience an "unconscious" emotional experience:

> In one of our experiments we would present a series of ordinary objects and then suddenly flash a picture of a nude woman. This evoked an amused reaction regardless of whether the picture was presented to the

left hemisphere or to the right. When the picture was flashed to the left hemisphere of a female patient, she laughed and verbally identified the picture as a nude. When it was later presented to the right hemisphere, she said in reply to a question that she saw nothing, but almost immediately a sly smile spread over her face and she began to chuckle. Asked what she was laughing at, she said, "I don't know . . . nothing. . . . Oh— that funny machine." Although the right hemisphere could not describe what it had seen, the sight nevertheless elicited an emotional response like the one evoked from the left hemisphere. (Gazzaniga, 1967, p. 29)

In 1975, one of Sperry's research associates developed a complicated apparatus called a "Z lens" which allows researchers to project visual stimuli onto the retina of the eye in such a way that the visual input is seen by only the right or the left hemisphere. This important technical advance allows researchers to communicate with the separate hemispheres of normal people whose corpus callosums have not been cut, and use of the Z lens will advance the study of hemispheric brain functions.

The autonomic nervous system

Earlier we noted that the peripheral nervous system, which connects the organs and muscles of the body with the brain and spinal cord, consists of two divisions. The somatic system includes the major sensory systems and the motor nerves that activate skeletal muscles. The other major division is the autonomic nervous system. This system controls the glands and the smooth (involuntary) muscles that form the heart, blood vessels, and the lining of the stomach and intestines. The autonomic system is involved in such bodily functions as respiration, circulation, and digestion, and it is especially important in emotional behavior.

The autonomic nervous system consists of two subdivisions, the *sympathetic* division and the *parasympathetic* division. (See Figure 3.20.) Often these two divisions affect the same organ or gland in opposing ways.

Sympathetic division

The sympathetic neurons have their cell bodies in the spinal cord and run out through the ventral root to a chain of *sympathetic ganglia* that run parallel to the spinal cord. In the sympathetic ganglia these fibers synapse with nerves that course out to activate the internal organs of the body.

The sympathetic division has an arousal function and tends to act as a unit. When you encounter a stressful situation, your autonomic nervous system simultaneously accelerates your heart rate, dilates your pupils, slows down your digestive system, increases respiration, and, in general, mobilizes your body to confront the stressor. It also activates the *adrenal glands*, which then secrete stress hormones,

such as *adrenalin*, into the bloodstream to maintain or increase the level of arousal.

Parasympathetic division

The motor fibers of the parasympathetic division originate at points above and below those of the sympathetic system. (See Figure 3.20.) Although the sympathetic system tends to act as a unit, the parasympathetic system is much more specific in its actions, affecting one or a few organs at a time. The action of your parasympathetic nervous system slows down bodily processes and maintains a state of quiescence. Thus whereas your sympathetic system speeds your heart rate, your parasympathetic system slows it down. The two divisions of the autonomic nervous system work together to maintain a state of equilibrium in the internal organs. Some acts require a sequence of sympathetic and parasympathetic activity. An example is the sex act in the male, which involves erection (a parasympathetic function) followed by ejaculation (a sympathetic function).

THE ENDOCRINE SYSTEM

The *endocrine system* consists of numerous glands distributed throughout the body. Like the nervous system, the function of the endocrine system is to convey information from one area of the body to another. Rather than utilizing electric nerve impulses, however, the endocrine system conveys information in the form of chemical messengers called *hormones*, which are secreted into the bloodstream.

The nervous system is characterized by rapid transmission of information. The endocrine system is slower than this, because it depends on the rate of blood flow. Another important difference between the nervous and endocrine systems lies in the generality of the messages that are transmitted. A particular neuron in the nervous system usually synapses directly with a relatively small number of other neurons. Hormones, on the other hand, travel throughout the body via the bloodstream and reach millions of individual cells. When important information must be transmitted by the brain, it has the choice of sending it to a relatively small number of neurons via nerve impulses or to a large number of cells by means of hormones.

A list of the endocrine glands with their hor-

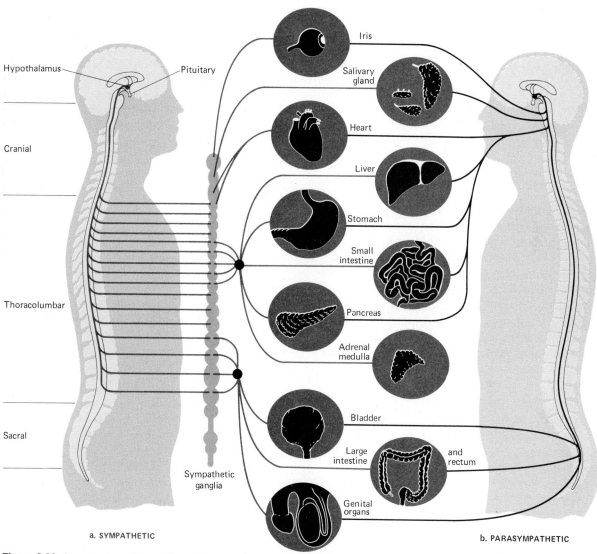

Figure 3.20 Organization of the autonomic nervous system. The sympathetic division functions to arouse the body and speed up its vital processes, whereas the parasympathetic division slows down bodily processes. The two divisions work together to maintain an equilibrium within the body. (Thompson, 1975, p. 97.)

mones and functions is presented in Table 3.1, and the approximate locations of these glands within the human body are shown in Figure 3.21. We restrict our attention to the *pituitary gland* and the *adrenal gland,* which are of special importance in psychological functioning.

The pituitary gland is often characterized as the master gland, because, as you can see in Table 3.1,

several of its hormones stimulate other endocrine glands. The pituitary gland is suspended from the hypothalamus and is heavily influenced by it. The pituitary consists of two subdivisions or lobes. The anterior lobe is composed of glial cells. It receives no neural input from the brain, but rather it receives a special blood supply from the hypothalamus. Blood that has bathed the hypothalamus is collected into a

103

BOX 3.5

Brain damage and behavior: the case of Phineas Gage

The behavioral effects of brain injuries have provided a great deal of information about human brain functions. One of the most celebrated historical cases occurred in 1848 during the building of a railroad in Vermont. An accidental dynamite blast propelled a spike over 3 feet long and weighing over 13 pounds through the face and head of Phineas Gage, a 25-year-old foreman. The spike entered through the left cheek, passed through the brain, and emerged through the top of the skull. Dr. J. M. Harlow, who treated the case, describes the incident as follows:

> The patient was thrown upon his back by the explosion, and gave a few convulsive motions of the extremities, but spoke in a few minutes. His men (with whom he was a great favorite) took him in their arms and carried him to the road, only a few rods distant, and put him into an ox cart, in which he rode, supported in a sitting posture, fully three quarters of a mile to his hotel. He got out of the cart himself, with a little assistance from his men, and an hour afterwards (with what I could aid him by taking hold of his left arm) walked up a long flight of stairs, and got upon the bed in the room where he was dressed. He seemed perfectly conscious, but was becoming exhausted from the hemorrhage, which by this time, was quite profuse, the blood pouring from the lacerated sinus in the top of his head, and also finding its way into the stomach, which ejected it as often as every fifteen or twenty minutes. He bore his sufferings with firmness, and directed my attention to the hole in his cheek, saying, "the iron entered there and passed through my head." (J. M. Harlow, pp. 330–332)

Sometime later Dr. Harlow made the following report.

> His physical health is good, and I am inclined to say that he has recovered. Has no pain in head, but says it has a queer feeling which he is not able to describe. Applied for his situation as foreman, but is undecided whether to work or travel. His contractors, who regarded him as the most efficient and capable foreman in their employ previous to his injury considered the change in his mind so marked that they could not give him his place again. The equilibrium or balance, so to speak, between his intellectual faculties and animal propensities, seems to have been destroyed. He is fitful, irreverent, indulging at times in the grossest profanity (which was not previously his custom), manifesting but little deference for his fellows, impatient of restraint or advice when it conflicts with his desires, at times pertinaciously obstinate, yet capricious and vacillating, devising many plans of future operations, which are no sooner arranged than they are abandoned in turn for others . . . his mind is radically changed, so decidedly that his friends and acquaintances said he was "no longer Gage." (J. M. Harlow, pp. 339–340)

The profound changes in Gage's personality following his brain injury helped to guide later brain researchers in their studies of brain function. We now know that the injury destroyed parts of the brain that later research has shown to be involved in the organization of emotional behavior.

---

special vein called the *portal vein,* which then passes directly into the anterior pituitary and bathes the cells there. The hypothalamus, which is now known to be a part of the endocrine system as well as the nervous system, secretes certain hormones called *releasing factors* into this portal system, and these hormones can either increase or decrease the rate of secretion of the individual anterior pituitary hormones.

The posterior pituitary consists of neurons rather than glial cells. The rate of secretion of posterior pituitary hormones is also controlled by the hypothalamus, but by direct neural input rather than by the portal system. Perhaps the term *master gland of*

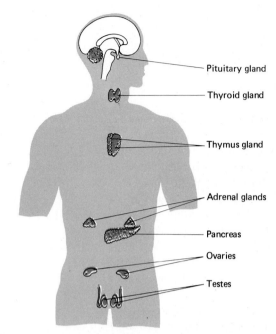

the body should be applied to the hypothalamus rather than the pituitary, because of the control that the hypothalamus exerts not only over the pituitary, but ultimately over many other parts of the endocrine system as well.

The *adrenal glands* also have two distinct anatomical divisions. The *adrenal cortex*, the outer portion of each gland, secretes about 50 different hormones that regulate many metabolic processes within the body, including metabolism of carbohydrates, functioning of the reproductive organs, and balancing of sodium and potassium body fluids that surround the neurons and other cells of the body.

Lying beneath the adrenal cortex is the *adrenal medulla*. It secretes two very important hormones,

Figure 3.21 The human endocrine system.

Table 3.1 Hormones secreted by the endocrine system

Gland	Hormone	Effect
Pituitary	Adrenocorticotropic hormone (ACTH)	Stimulates adrenal cortex
	Thyrotropic hormone (TTH)	Stimulates thyroid
	Luteinizing hormone (LH)	Stimulates testes and ovaries
	Follicle-stimulating hormone (FSH)	Stimulates follicle of ovary in ovulation
	Growth hormone (somatotropin)	Promotes growth in bone and muscle
	Prolactin	Stimulates breasts to produce milk
	Vasopressin	Controls excretion of water in kidneys
	Oxytocin	Stimulates contractions of the uterus at birth
Ovary	Estrogen	Promotes female sexual characteristics
	Progesterone	Stimulates thickening of uterus lining
Testis	Testosterone	Promotes male sexual characteristics
Thyroid	Thyroxine	Controls basal metabolism
Adrenal	About 50 cortical hormones, e.g., cortisone, aldosterone	Controls many basic chemical mechanisms
	Adrenaline	Increases sugar in blood, raises heartbeat, dilates arteries
Pancreas	Insulin	Lowers level of sugar in blood

Courtesy Carolina Biological Supply Company.

105

epinephrine (also known as adrenalin) and *norepinephrine* (noradrenalin). As we noted earlier, these two chemicals are believed to be neural transmitter substances within the nervous system. They also produce many of the same effects as are produced by the sympathetic nervous system. In an emergency the adrenal medulla is activated by the sympathetic branch of the autonomic nervous system and epinephrine or norepinephrine are secreted into the bloodstream. Because hormones can remain in the bloodstream for some time, the action of the adrenal medulla and its hormones is especially important in circumstances of prolonged stress.

Having explored, however briefly, some of the major physiological systems that underlie behavior, we should now have a greater appreciation of the many complex biological processes that are involved in our everyday behavior. As we learn more about how these biological systems function and how they influence behavior, the potential is increased for more and better application of this knowledge to human betterment. When we consider that everything that we experience and do ultimately involves our biological substrate, the importance of this psychological frontier becomes ever more evident. No area of study in which psychologists are involved offers greater potential for momentous discoveries and applications.

SUMMARY

1. Neurons are the basic building blocks of the nervous system. Each neuron has *dendrites*, which receive nerve impulses; a cell body, or *soma*, which controls the vital processes of the neurons; and an *axon*, which conducts impulses to adjacent neurons, muscles, or glands.

2. Neural transmission is an *electrochemical* process. The nerve impulse is a brief reversal in the electrical potential of the cell membrane as sodium ions from the surrounding body fluid flow through the membrane. Passage of the impulse across the *synapse*, the microscopic space between neurons, is mediated by chemical transmitter substances released from the axon terminals.

3. Information is coded within the nervous system by the rate of firing of individual neurons in relation to their base rate and by the particular neurons that are active.

4. The visual receptors are light-sensitive receptor cells located in the retina. The *rods* are responsible for brightness vision; the less numerous *cones* are color receptors. Light energy striking the retina is converted into electrical nerve impulses by chemical reactions in the *photopigments* of the rods and cones. Color perception appears to be a two-stage process involving three color responses from cones that are encoded through an opponent-process mechanism further along in the visual system.

5. The receptors for hearing are tiny hair cells in the *cochlea* of the inner ear. Loudness is coded in terms of the number and types of auditory nerve fibers that fire, whereas pitch involves two different processes involving the frequency of neural impulses for low sound frequencies and the region of maximal displacement of the basilar membrane for frequencies above 4000 cycles per second.

6. The receptors for taste and smell respond to chemical stimuli with which they come into contact. The skin and body senses include touch, kinesthesis, and equilibrium. Receptors in the skin are sensitive to touch, pain, warmth, and cold. These receptors send their messages to particular areas of the sensory cortex that correspond to the area of the body in which the receptor is located. *Kinesthesis* functions by means of nerve endings in the muscles, tendons, and joints: The sense organs for equilibrium are

located in the *vestibular apparatus* of the inner ear.

7. The nervous system consists of *afferent* (sensory) neurons, *efferent* (motor) neurons, and *interneurons* (association neurons). Its two major divisions are the *central nervous system*, consisting of the brain and spinal cord, and the *peripheral nervous system.* The latter is divided into the *somatic system*, which has sensory and motor functions, and the *autonomic nervous system*, which directs the activity of the glands and internal organs of the body.

8. The human brain consists of the hindbrain, midbrain, and forebrain. Major structures within the hindbrain include the *medulla*, which plays an important role in vital bodily processes; the *pons*, which contains important nuclei and sensory and motor tracts; and the *cerebellum*, which is concerned primarily with motor coordination.

9. The reticular formation extends from the hindbrain area up into the forebrain. It plays a vital role in consciousness, attention, and sleep. Activity of the reticular formation excites higher areas of the brain and readies them to respond to stimulation. It appears that the reticular formation helps determine which sensory inputs "get through" to our consciousness.

10. The midbrain contains a number of important sensory and motor nuclei, as well as many sensory and motor tracts connecting higher and lower parts of the nervous system.

11. The forebrain is highly developed in humans. It consists of two cerebral hemispheres and a number of important subcortical structures. The *thalamus* is an important sensory relay station. The *hypothalamus* plays a major role in many aspects of motivational and emotional behavior.

The *limbic system* seems to be involved in organizing the behaviors involved in motivation and emotion.

12. The cerebral hemispheres have a convoluted surface, the *cerebral cortex*, which controls the higher mental processes. It is divided into *frontal*, *parietal*, *occipital*, and *temporal* lobes. Some areas of the cortex are sensory in nature, some control motor behavior, and others consist of interneurons. The cerebral hemispheres are connected by the *corpus callosum.* Studies of *split-brain* subjects, who have had the corpus callosum severed, have demonstrated major differences in functions of the right and left hemispheres. The left hemisphere is skilled in language and mathematics, whereas the right hemisphere has well-developed spatial abilities but no ability to communicate through speech.

13. The autonomic nervous system is made up of two parts—a *sympathetic* and a *parasympathetic* division. The sympathetic division has an arousal function and tends to act as a unit. The parasympathetic division slows down bodily processes and functions in a more specific manner. The two divisions work together to maintain a state of equilibrium.

14. The endocrine glands secrete *hormones* into the bloodstream. These chemical messengers affect many bodily processes. The *pituitary* and *adrenal* glands are two of the most important endocrine structures.

Suggested readings

Christman, R. J. *Sensory experience.* Scranton, Pa.: International Textbook Company, 1971. A description of the sensory system, with special emphasis on the visual and auditory systems.

Hart, L. A. *How the brain works.* New York: Basic Books,

Inc., Publishers, 1975. An interesting and readable book dealing with neural mechanisms of human learning, emotion, and thinking.

Thompson, R. F. *Introduction to physiological psychol-* ogy. New York: Harper & Row, Publishers, 1975. A comprehensive overview of theory and research in physiological psychology. Deals in depth with all of the physiological systems discussed in this chapter.

Chapter 4

Perception

(Culver)

On a brisk autumn afternoon some years ago Princeton and Dartmouth met in the annual renewal of their football rivalry. From the opening kickoff it was clear that it was going to be a very rough game. Tempers flared frequently, and the officials had their hands full trying to keep the game under control. In the second quarter Princeton's star player was led from the field with a concussion and a broken nose. Later in the game a Dartmouth player was carried off with a broken leg. Several other players on both sides suffered serious injuries.

After the game the air was filled with accusations. Princeton coaches, officials, and fans accused Dartmouth of deliberately trying to maim the Princeton player, Dick Kazmaier. Dartmouth supporters denied the charges, but in turn accused Princeton of flagrantly dirty football. Charges and countercharges were exchanged for several weeks after the game, and the resulting publicity attracted national attention.

Fortunately, a few of the people at the two institutions were still talking to one another without clenching their teeth. Psychologists Albert Hastorf of Dartmouth and Hadley Cantril of Princeton were struck by the manner in which Dartmouth and Princeton supporters disagreed violently over what had actually occurred during the game. It was almost as if the fans had been in two different stadiums that day.

Their curiosity aroused, Hastorf and Cantril (1954) conducted a study of the perceptions of Dartmouth and Princeton students. First, they administered a questionnaire designed to tap the reactions of students at the two schools. Next, they showed a film of the game to students from the two institutions. As the students watched the film they were given a questionnaire to check off any infractions of the rules that they saw on the film.

The responses to these questionnaires for both the Princeton and Dartmouth samples are presented in Table 4.1. Dartmouth students saw both teams make about the same number of infractions. Princeton supporters, however, saw the Dartmouth team make twice as many infractions as the Princeton team, and they detected twice as many rule violations by Dartmouth as did Dartmouth fans. Even on the "replay" it was clear that students from the two schools were still seeing "different" games.

Disagreements over what "really happened" are not confined to the world of sports. The same sensory information transmitted to the brains of two different people may be experienced in radically different ways. Our experiences are not simply a one-to-one reflection of what is "out there." Rather, perception is an active process of coding, organizing, and giving meaning to the raw sensory data that we receive from our external and internal environments. Our brain not only converts nerve impulses from our sensory organs into images, colors, sounds, tones, feelings, and the infinite variety of other experiences that we can have, but it also attaches meaning to them.

Although we know quite a bit about the biological processing of sensory input, we still do not know enough about the ways in which the real world and our perceptions of it are linked. A variety of factors influence our perceptions, only one of which is the physical characteristics of the stimulus. Some of these factors are biologically innate, built into our nervous system. Others are the result of our experience; as you can see by looking at the responses to the questionnaire on the football game, our attitudes, motives, values, and psychological defenses influence what we perceive.

Experience is the core of human existence and the starting point for all behavior. Perception, therefore, is intimately related to virtually every topic that we discuss in this book. In this chapter we discuss perception of our physical and social worlds. The next chapter deals with altered states of perceptual experience that occur under conditions of sleep, hypnosis, meditation, and drug usage. In Chapter 15 we discuss the disordered perceptions that accompany certain varieties of psychological disturbance.

PERCEPTUAL SENSITIVITY AND ATTENTION

Psychologists have always been concerned with the process of perception. Wilhelm Wundt's first laboratory of experimental psychology was founded to study sensation and perceptual experience. Although our methods and instrumentation have become increasingly sophisticated over the years, psychologists interested in perception are still asking some of the same questions that intrigued Wundt and his co-

Table 4.1 Questionnaire responses of Princeton and Dartmouth students who saw a film of the controversial game between the two schools

A. Data from first questionnaire

Question	Dartmouth Students N = 163	Princeton Students N = 161
1. From what you saw in the game or the movies, or from what you have read, which team do you feel started the rough play?		
Dartmouth started it	36	86
Princeton started it	2	0
Both started it	53	11
Neither	6	1
No answer	3	2
2. What is your understanding of the charges being made?†		
Dartmouth tried to get Kazmaier	71	47
Dartmouth intentionally dirty	52	44
Dartmouth unnecessarily rough	8	35
3. Do you feel there is any truth to these charges?		
Yes	10	55
No	57	4
Partly	29	35
Don't know	4	6
4. Why do you think the charges were made?		
Injury to Princeton star	70	23
To prevent repetition	2	46
No answer	28	31

†Replies do not add to 100 percent because more than one charge could be given.

B. Data from second questionnaire checked while seeing film

Group	N	Mean Number of Interactions Checked Against	
		Dartmouth Team Mean	Princeton Team Mean
Dartmouth students	48	4.3*	4.4
Princeton students	49	9.8*	4.2

*Significantly different at the .01 level.

From A. H. Hastorf and H. Cantril, "They saw a game: a case study," *Journal of Abnormal and Social Psychology*, 1954, *49*, 129–134. Tables 1 and 2, p. 132. Copyright 1954 by the American Psychological Association. Reprinted by permission.

111

workers. One such question concerns the limits of perceptual sensitivity under varying conditions. Just how sensitive are we?

Psychophysics

The scientific study of the relationship between the physical properties of stimuli and the perceptual experiences they give rise to is known as *psychophysics*. Because every stimulus is a source of energy, the psychophysicist is concerned with the measurement of stimuli in physical terms.

Stimulus detection: The absolute threshold

How much energy must a stimulus exert before we can detect its presence? This minimum amount of energy is called the *absolute threshold*. When the stimulus energy level is below the absolute threshold, there is no sensation; when it is above the threshold, a stimulus can be sensed and experienced. In research the absolute threshold is defined statistically as the intensity at which the stimulus can be detected 50 percent of the time.

Absolute thresholds vary in accordance with a variety of factors, including the conditions under which the stimulus occurs and the characteristics of the perceiver. However, it is possible to arrive at approximate values for absolute thresholds for the five senses. Some examples are presented in Table 4.2.

For many years psychologists conducted studies of the absolute threshold on the assumption that there was a consistent absolute threshold for stimuli. However, more careful observations revealed that there could be wide variations in sensitivity among individuals and even in the same individual at different times, depending on experimental conditions. Subjects may say they heard a weak tone presented to them on one occasion but may not report it on another. Subjects may also report hearing the tone on trials when it is *not* presented. Such findings have challenged the concept of an absolute threshold and have led to a new approach known as *signal detection theory*.

Signal detection theory. Suppose we wish to determine the likelihood that a subject can detect a weak auditory stimulus. Subjects are run individually and are told that following a warning light, a tone may or may not be presented. Their task is to tell us if they heard the tone or not.

Under these conditions there are four possible outcomes, which are shown in Figure 4.1. On trials in which the tone is presented, the subject may say yes (a *hit*) or no (a *miss*). On trials where no tone is presented, which are called *catch trials*, the subject may also say yes (a *false alarm*) or no (a *correct reject*). We would find that subjects vary in the proportion of hits and false alarms they give and that even the same subject may vary at different times. *Signal detection theory* deals with the factors that produce such variations.

Psychologists and engineers studying signal detection discovered that there is no fixed probability that a subject will detect a signal of a particular intensity

Table 4.2 Some approximate values for absolute thresholds

Sense Modality	Absolute Threshold
Vision	A candle flame seen at 30 miles on a clear dark night
Hearing	Tick of a watch under quiet conditions at 20 feet
Taste	Teaspoon of sugar in 2 gallons of water
Smell	One drop of perfume diffused into the entire volume of a large apartment
Touch	Wing of a fly or bee falling on your cheek from a distance of 1 centimeter

Based on Galanter, 1962.

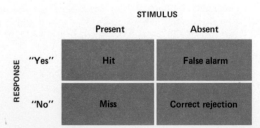

Figure 4.1 This matrix shows the four possible outcomes of perceptual judgments as a result of whether the signal is or is not actually presented.

and that the concept of a "fixed" absolute threshold is largely meaningless. They found that at marginal levels of stimulation the subject's decision criterion is far more influential than the actual physical intensity of the stimulus. If subjects are very cautious they give more "no" responses, which results in fewer hits, but also fewer false alarms. Bold subjects show the opposite tendency. Experiments have shown that the decision criterion can be strongly affected by varying the number of catch trials (a large number of catch trials results in a conservative criterion) as well as by manipulating rewards and costs for giving correct and incorrect responses. Modern signal detection theory has given us a more realistic view of perceptual sensitivity and an increased understanding of how people make judgments about sensations.

Discrimination: Weber's law

Have you ever gone to a store to find a sweater to match a pair of pants or a skirt? Did you find that you had to drag the clothing out into different parts of the store and examine it in different lights to see whether it really matched? We often must make these sorts of subtle discriminations between stimuli. The smallest difference that people can perceive between two stimuli is called the *differential threshold* or the *just noticeable difference* (jnd). In the search for a sweater you might have chosen one that was "really" a different color from that of your pants or skirt, but the difference was below the differential threshold, so that you could not see that the sweater was a different color.

One of the most important facts that has been learned about the differential threshold is that there is a constant *ratio* between the intensity of a stimulus and the amount that a second stimulus must differ from it before the perceiver can detect the difference. This relationship is known as Weber's law, and it is expressed in the formula $\Delta I/I = K$, in which I is the initial intensity of the stimulus, ΔI is the amount that the second stimulus must differ from it in order to be distinguished, and K is the constant for the particular sense through which we perceive the stimuli. For example, the K value for weights that we lift is approximately 0.02, or $\frac{1}{50}$. This means that if the first weight we lift is 100 grams a second weight must weigh at least 102 grams in order for us to discriminate between them. If the first

weight is 200 grams, then the second must be at least 4 grams heavier, and if the first weight is 400 grams, the second one must be at least 408 grams. Weber's law holds up well within the middle ranges of stimulation, but breaks down at extremely high or low intensities of stimulation.

Weber constants have been calculated for many different kinds of stimuli. Sound receptors are most sensitive to differences in stimulation; the Weber's constant for differences in pitch is approximately $\frac{1}{333}$. Taste is the least sensitive of our senses, with a Weber's constant of $\frac{1}{5}$ for detecting differences in saline concentrations. The constant (K) for brightness discriminations is about $\frac{1}{60}$.

Attention

At any given moment our senses are being bombarded by countless stimuli. Yet we register only a small proportion of these at the center of our awareness; the rest we perceive either dimly in the background or not at all. But at any time we can shift our attention to one of those "unregistered" stimuli (for example, how does your big toe feel right now?). Attention, then, involves two processes: (1) selectively focusing on certain stimuli and (2) filtering out other incoming information.

Attentional shifts

Imagine that you are at a party and engaged in an interesting conversation with a group of people. Other groups are conversing nearby, but you are almost unaware of them until you hear your name mentioned by someone in a group across the room. You quickly shift your attention to the group across the room while trying at the same time to listen to what a person in your own group is saying to you.

This "cocktail party phenomenon" has been studied experimentally through a technique called *shadowing*. Subjects listen to two messages simultaneously and are asked to repeat (shadow) one of them word for word. Most subjects can do this quite successfully, but at the cost of remembering what the other message is about. Subjects can also shift their attention rapidly back and forth between the two messages, trying to attend to bits of each. They then draw on their general knowledge of the English language and the topics to fill in gaps in the sentences they hear. The results of these shadowing experi-

113

ments have demonstrated quite conclusively that we cannot attend *completely* to more than one thing at a time, but we can shift our attention rapidly enough to get the sense of two different messages.

Attention is strongly affected by both stimulus properties and personal factors. The properties of stimuli that attract our attention are intensity, novelty, movement, contrast, and repetition. Think about the ways in which advertisers use these properties in their commercials and packaging.

While the numerous stimuli in our environment are competing for attention, internal factors are also acting as filters to determine what we will notice. One of these factors is the motives that are most prominent at a given time. When we are hungry, for example, we are especially sensitive to food-related cues (see Box 4.1). Our interests function in the same way. A botanist walking through a park is especially attentive to plants; a landscape architect attends primarily to the layout of the park; a male college student may be most interested in the young women in the park. Our previous learning experiences also determine which stimuli we notice. A person who has narrowly escaped from a fire may be very sensitive to the smell of smoke. A person who has been painfully jilted in an important romance is likely to be very sensitive to words or body language that threaten rejection.

Studies have shown that we cannot attend completely to more than one thing at a time. This limitation presents difficulties at events such as cocktail parties where large numbers of stimuli vie for attention at the same time. (Peress, Magnum)

BOX 4.1
Perceptions of a dieter

Ever since I went on this diet, I've become more sensitive to food as a stimulus. Although I've cut down drastically on certain foods I used to eat in enormous quantities, I enjoy the tidbits that I have much more. I can make one small piece of a Hershey bar last a long time. As I eat, I notice and appreciate its flavor more than I ever have before. Because I eat half of what I used to, beginning about an hour after each meal my attention is increasingly directed to planning and thinking about what I'll eat the next meal. I should mention that it's not as bad as it might sound. I have a positive attitude toward food. I'm not suffering. It's just that food means something different to me now than it used to.

Perceptual defense

In some cases the previously described filtering process serves a defensive function and protects us from threatening stimuli. This phenomenon is known as *perceptual defense.*

The first studies of perceptual defense were conducted over a quarter of a century ago by Elliot McGinnies (1949). McGinnies presented words to male subjects with a tachistoscope, an instrument that can project visual stimuli for very brief time intervals (as brief as 0.01 second). The words were presented for increasingly longer time periods until the subject identified the word correctly. The exposure time required for the subject to recognize the word was called the *recognition threshold* for that word. Some of the words, such as *whore, bitch,* and *Kotex,* were judged to be unpleasant or anxiety arousing; others were neutral words. During stimulus presentation McGinnies recorded through attached electrodes the subjects' *galvanic skin response* (GSR), a measure of the drop in electrical resistance of the skin caused by the activity of the sweat glands when a person becomes emotionally aroused.

The findings were quite dramatic. First, McGinnies found that the taboo words had higher recognition thresholds (i.e., they required longer exposure times for recognition) than did the neutral words. In addition, even when the taboo words were exposed so briefly that the subject did not recognize them, there was a noticeable change in the GSR. McGinnies concluded that subjects were subconsciously perceiving the taboo words and responding to them emotionally, but that some defensive process was blocking their conscious awareness of the words.

McGinnies's dramatic results attracted much attention, but they also posed a curious paradox: How can people avoid perceiving a threatening stimulus before they have actually perceived what it is? Is there a homunculus, a little "person-within-the-person" that decides what will be perceived? Because of this paradox psychologists began to seek other explanations for McGinnies's results. The controversy that resulted illustrates some of the problems involved in studying the private experiences of others.

Because perception is a private event, not accessible to others and incapable of being measured di-

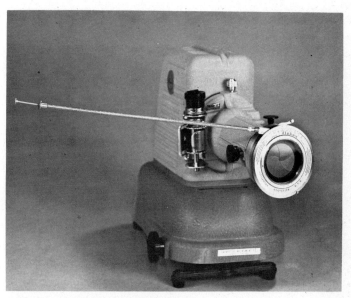

A standard tachistoscope. (Lafayette)

rectly, we must study it through some behavior that we can measure—in this case, recognition thresholds identified through verbal reports. How do we know what McGinnies's subjects were *really* perceiving or not perceiving? Could it be that they correctly perceived the taboo words, at least vaguely, earlier than they reported but were simply hesitant to say them out loud until they were absolutely certain what they were? After all, mistakenly "seeing" a vulgar word could be quite embarrassing. Is "perceptual defense" really a more conscious process than McGinnies suspected?

To get around this possible hesitancy to report taboo words, Richard Lazarus and R. A. McCleary (1951) used nonsense syllables (e.g., BJX, ZEJ) instead of words that already had cultural meaning. Before recognition thresholds were measured, some of the nonsense syllables were paired with electric shocks to make them emotionally arousing. When the nonsense syllables were later presented to the subjects tachistoscopically, Lazarus and McCleary found that the average GSR response to nonsense syllables that the subjects did *not* identify correctly was significantly larger when the syllable had previously been paired with shock than when the stimulus had not been associated with shock. These results reinforced the theory that individuals are capable of making perceptual discriminations at two levels, one at the level of conscious awareness and the other at a subconscious or emotional level, and that emotional discriminations are more sensitive. The paradox was not yet solved.

In 1960 Charles Eriksen proposed an explanation of perceptual defense results that did not require a preperceiving person-within-the-person. He pointed out that in order to receive credit for a correct perception through a verbal report, the subject must say the entire stimulus correctly. However, if a nonsense syllable has been paired with shock to make it emotionally arousing, the emotional response picked up on the GSR may occur when the subject perceives only one or two letters of the nonsense syllable. In addition, subjects who are unsure can give a cautious verbal report ("I couldn't tell what it was"), but they have less direct influence over their physiological (GSR) response. These factors may make it appear as if the emotional system were perceptually more sensitive than the verbal ("conscious") one. Eriksen's

explanation accounts for our ability to respond "emotionally" to partial information in a less mysterious way than the "person-within-the-person" theory of perceptual filtering.

Repression and sensitization

One of the most intriguing findings of studies on perceptual defenses concerned individual differences in the way people reacted to the threatening stimuli. Some individuals not only failed to demonstrate perceptual defense, but actually showed *greater* perceptual sensitivity to anxiety-arousing stimuli than to neutral ones. These individuals are called *sensitizers*, because they seem to be on the lookout for threatening events and are sensitive to their occurrence. Sensitizers deal with anxiety-arousing situations by approaching and seeking to master them. Another group of individuals, called *repressors*, deals with similar situations by avoiding them and trying to minimize the possibility of experiencing negative emotions. Repressors are most likely to exhibit strong perceptual defense reactions.

To understand the contrast between sensitizers and repressors, let us consider the following hypothetical conversation between two students as they walk to an important test for which neither is prepared.

> *Student A:* Oh my God, I don't know anything. This is awful. What am I going to do? I'll blow the test, flunk out of school, and my parents will reject me. No one will want to have anything to do with me. I'll be a failure for life. If only I had studied!

> *Student B:* I don't want to talk about it. No sweat. There's nothing to worry about. I'm glad I didn't study. Probably no one else did either. The test will be a snap. I'm not worried.

Which is the sensitizer and which the repressor? Do you know anyone who is like either of these people? Do you recognize your own attitudes in either of these speeches?

Some researchers have hypothesized that individuals who characteristically use sensitizing defenses in a particular conflict area will perceive stimuli in that area more quickly than will individuals who use repressive defenses. To test this hypothesis clinical psychologists evaluated psychological test results to determine how selected subjects characteristically dealt with sexual and aggressive conflicts, and divided the subjects into sensitizers and repressors. Next they tested the subjects' recognition thresholds for words with sexual and aggressive connotations, as well as for neutral control words. The hypothesis was supported: Although sensitizers showed little difference in perceptual sensitivity to the critical and control words, the repressors required longer exposure times for the critical (sexual or aggressive) words than for the control words (Carpenter, Weiner, and Carpenter, 1956).

Subliminal perception

A phenomenon closely related to perceptual defense is *subliminal perception*. In Latin, *limen* means "threshold" and *sub* means "under," so that this expression literally means "below-the-threshold perception." Certain stimuli are so weak or brief that they cannot be perceived consciously. The effect of such stimuli has been a matter of great controversy in psychology; some researchers have suggested that subliminal cues may affect our behavior without reaching our awareness, whereas others have insisted that this is impossible.

In the late 1950s James Vicary, a public relations executive, arranged to have messages flashed on a theater screen during a movie. These "secret" messages were flashed so quickly that they were imperceptible. They urged the movie audience to "Drink Coca-Cola" and "Eat popcorn." Vicary claimed that these subliminal messages increased popcorn sales by 50 percent and soft drink sales by 18 percent. Naturally his claims aroused a public furor. Consumers and scientists worried about the possible abuse of subliminal messages for "mind control" and "brainwashing." Advertising agencies and manufacturers gleefully foresaw an opportunity to influence the buying habits of millions of Americans.

In the midst of the excitement psychologists conducted numerous experiments to assess the effects of subliminal stimuli on behavior. They found that subliminal stimuli can provide us with partial information even if we cannot perceive them completely. As you will recall, this is the same theory that Erikson suggested to explain perceptual defense. When subjects see stimuli tachistoscopically for very brief intervals and are allowed a second guess if they do not identify the stimulus correctly, their guesses are

more often correct than they would be by pure chance. At least partial information, it seems, is conveyed during these intervals. But researchers have repeatedly found that if exposure time is so brief that it does not allow the subject to obtain even partial information, the number of correct second guesses does not exceed that which would occur by chance.

The most important issue, of course, is whether or not subliminal stimuli can affect behavior. Numerous studies conducted in laboratories, on television and radio, and in movie theaters seem to indicate that behavior is not significantly influenced by subliminal stimuli. Psychologist Norman Dixon conducted an extensive review of the evidence concerning subliminal stimulation. He concluded, "There is little evidence to suggest, and strong arguments against, the possibility of seriously manipulating drives, or drive-oriented behavior, by subliminal stimulation" (1971, p. 178). Despite the scientific evidence, however, public furor is still aroused over the possible use of this technique, as a recent United Nations report demonstrates. (See Box 4.2.)

Extrasensory perception

Researchers have taken an interest not only in the perception of actual physical stimuli that are below the perceptual threshold, but also in the perception of nonphysical stimuli, or extrasensory perception. The question of whether or not extrasensory perception (ESP) does exist has long been the subject of spirited controversy in psychology.

Four basic types of ESP have been studied: clairvoyance, telepathy, precognition, and psychokinesis. *Clairvoyance* refers to nonsensory perception of external objects or events, whereas *telepathy* is the ability to read another person's thoughts. *Precognition* is the perception of future events. *Psychokinesis*, or PK—the ability to control matter through the mind—is not actually a form of perception but is generally studied along with the other three phenomena.

The typical ESP experiment uses a 25-card deck. Each card contains one of five symbols, either a circle, a star, wavy lines, a square, or a cross. In a clairvoyance experiment subjects are required to guess the symbol on a card that the experimenter selected. A telepathy experiment uses a sender who

BOX 4.2

A continuing fear of subliminal stimulation. Brainwashing via satellite TV feared

United Nations (UPI). Satellites orbiting the Earth can beam messages directly to television sets in viewers' homes to brainwash people without them even knowing it, according to a United Nations report.

By sending out so-called subliminal messages that are recorded only in viewers' subconscious, the tech-nique can be used to mass-hypnotize and influence poli-tics of other countries, the report said.

It described subliminal messages as inserts in film which are flashed by light or sound so quickly and faintly that they are received below the level of con-sciousness.

The report, prepared for Secretary General Kurt Waldheim, cited some experts' opinions that the use of such 1984-style techniques amounts to brainwashing.

An American satellite is already in orbit transmitting educational and health programs directly into homes in India and Latin America, a development which has sparked an international debate on how to control tech-nological invasion of sovereignty and privacy.

The use of subliminal messages is banned in some Western European nations but not in the United States. The only prohibition against such use here is under the TV code of the National Association of Broadcasters.

Although broadcasting via satellite produces great benefits, the U.N. report said, the development of direct television to home sets rather than through government-controlled ground stations raises fearful prospects. (*Seattle Times*, November 4, 1974)

---

concentrates on a given symbol so that the subject can attempt to read his or her thoughts. In a precog-nition test the subject is asked to write down the order in which he or she thinks the symbols will appear in the deck. Then the deck is shuffled and the actual order of the symbols is compared with the order in the subject's list. In a test for psychokinesis the subject tries to concentrate on making dice rolled in a cage by the experimenter yield a particular number combination. (Rumor has it that successful subjects immediately depart for Las Vegas.)

In experiments utilizing the deck of cards, five out of 25 correct guesses would be expected by chance alone. The most successful clairvoyance and telepa-thy studies have yielded about 7 out of 25 correct guesses consistently over a number of trials.

Although a few psychologists feel that there is strong experimental evidence to support the exist-ence of ESP, most seem to doubt the scientific credi-bility of the findings. Many of the early studies had serious shortcomings that cast doubt on the validity of the results. For example, some of the symbols in the card decks used in these experiments were im-printed so heavily that they were recognizable through the backs of the cards. Some experiments had no control for recording errors made by the experimenter. Finally, results from trials during which the subject seemed to be "tired" were often discarded during data analyses.

Interestingly, as ESP studies have become more controlled, the results have become less favorable. This is unusual in scientific research; tighter proce-dures usually eliminate sources of error and make for more convincing results. In addition, the tech-nique of using thousands of trials to increase the chances of obtaining statistically significant results has been criticized by some researchers. Even with greater controls, ESP research seems to be vulnerable to human tampering. Schmeidler and McConnell (1958) have shown that experimenters' attitudes toward ESP influence their findings. Many "demon-strations" of the powers of ESP cannot be replicated

118

BOX 4.3

Uri Geller and the "delayed control group"

For several years, Uri Geller, the Israeli "psychic," has mystified and amazed audiences with his "mind over metal" psychokinesis demonstrations. Among his most notable feats are mentally "bending" metal objects such as spoons, starting broken watches, and reproducing drawings hidden in double envelopes. Many scientists have sought to study Geller under controlled laboratory conditions, but he has been quite selective in his cooperation.

Australian psychologists David Marks and Richard Kammann recently reported a series of demonstrations that suggest some of Geller's "psychic" feats may not be psychic at all (Asher, 1976).

Marks and Kammann utilized what they termed the "delayed control group." They reasoned that if a nonpsychic control group of subjects can reproduce results similar to Geller's, the most scientifically plausible explanation is that special psychic powers are not responsible for his success. In their first study, conducted after a Geller demonstration on a television talk show, the psychologists retrieved from a studio wastebasket the drawings, sealed in double envelopes, that Geller had supposedly reproduced clairvoyantly. Forty-eight college students examined the envelopes under identical lighting conditions and attempted to draw the figures by looking at the faint lines barely visible through the layers of paper. They found that the best students equalled or surpassed Geller's reproductions.

Next, the psychologists applied their approach to Geller's psychokinetic feat of fixing broken watches by simply holding them. They found from jewelers that many watches stop because they are gummed up with oil and dust and that simply holding such a watch in a warm hand and then shaking it can loosen the deposit enough to start the watch, at least temporarily. A sample of local jewelers systemat-

ically applied this technique over a one-week period to 106 broken watches. They were able to restart 60 of them—a 57 percent success rate. The psychologists noted that Geller himself averages about 49 percent "psychic repairs."

As for Geller's spoon- and key-bending demonstrations, Marks and Kammann attribute them to sleight of hand. They believe the objects are prebent and weakened by metal fatigue, then bent forcibly when the audience's attention is distracted. The psychologists state, "We have between us bent about 30 keys and ten spoons, all undetected, in front of audiences ranging from 15 to over 200 people" (Asher, 1976, p. 6).

Do these replications prove that Geller does not have the psychic powers he claims? Not necessarily, for a given phenomenon may have more than one cause. They do illustrate, however, the importance of including control groups in studies of ESP phenomena to rule out alternative explanations.

Uri Geller displays a "psychically" bent key. (Wide World)

119

when they are tested by different investigators. In addition, when human experimenters are removed and experimental procedures are completely automated, there is often no longer any evidence of ESP (Hansel, 1966).

It is not certain whether or not this interesting phenomenon will ever be integrated into the mainstream of psychology. But before there can be widespread acceptance of ESP, we will need to gather more convincing scientific evidence than we have at present.

VISUAL PERCEPTION

Organization of perception

The world around us is composed of different shapes, patterns, colors, and sizes. Rather than perceiving each stimulus as a separate element, we seem to perceive certain cues as parts of larger wholes. For example, what you are reading right at this moment is actually a series of black lines, some straight and some curved, with varied spacing between them, on a white page. But you are perceiving these lines as letters comprising words, which in turn comprise sentences and paragraphs. And somehow you are able to make sense out of this complex arrangement of individual stimuli.

The Gestalt psychologists were vitally interested in the principles of perceptual organization that allow us to perceive separate stimuli as parts of larger wholes. They suggested that we group stimuli perceptually in accordance with four laws: similarity, proximity, closure, and continuity. We define these laws in terms of visual perceptions, but they are applicable to perceptions through our other senses as well. The law of similarity states that when parts of a stimulus configuration are perceived as similar, they will also be perceived as belonging together. The law of proximity is quite similar; it states that elements that are near each other are perceived as part of the same configuraton. The law of closure states that we tend to close the open edges of a figure or fill in gaps when a stimulus is incomplete, so that what we see is more complete than what is actually there. The law of continuity states that we tend to see shapes, lines, and angles following in the same direction established by previous elements. These four laws help explain why we perceive discrete stimuli as parts of a larger whole or pattern. These organizational laws are illustrated in Figure 4.2.

We also tend to organize visual stimuli into a foreground figure and a background. The figure is usually in front of or on top of what we perceive as background. It has a distinct shape and is more striking in our perceptions and memory than is the background. The background flows around the shape of the figure; it has no edges of its own. We interpret the contours that we perceive as part of the figure rather than as part of the background. We see contours whenever there is a distinct change in the color or brightness of the background. Consider Figure 4.3, which can be perceived as either two profiles or as a vase. Whichever way we interpret the representation, the contour is always part of the figure, not the background. This same principle of perception operates in relation to auditory stimuli. Most music is heard as a melody against a background of other chords.

As many of the Gestalt laws of perception demonstrate, what we perceive is not determined entirely by the properties of the object itself. All perception is really a selective grouping and interpretation of cues we receive from the environment. R. L. Gregory

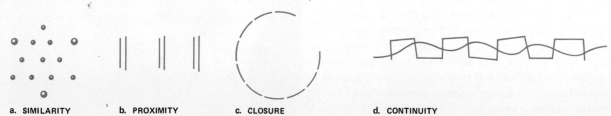

a. SIMILARITY　　b. PROXIMITY　　c. CLOSURE　　d. CONTINUITY

Figure 4.2 These figures illustrate the Gestalt organizational laws of similarity, proximity, closure, and continuity. (See text for a description of these principles.)

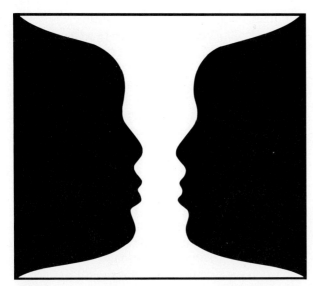

Figure 4.3 Two profiles or a vase? Look closely at this drawing. Do you see two black profiles against a white background or a white vase on a black background? At any given moment, you can see only one of these alternatives. The shape of the contours depends on which one you are seeing. In both cases the figure stands out in front of the background.

(1966) theorized that each perception is essentially a *hypothesis* about what an object is like, based on the cues we receive from our senses. We try to arrive at the best interpretation of the stimuli we perceive, but both what we perceive and the ways in which we interpret our perceptions are variable. The Necker Cube (Figure 4.4), illustrates this variability in our perceptions and interpretations of them. Stare at the figure for a while. Which is the front and which is the back? Do your perceptions change? As you switch from one way of perceiving to another, you are considering two separate hypotheses. In this case you settle on one interpretation until the reversal occurs and you experience a different perception.

Perceptual constancy

As we move about in the world, the optical patterns for everyday objects change as they are sent to our retinas. Yet we have no difficulty recognizing familiar objects from a variety of angles, distances, and under different kinds of light. In other words, partic-

ular sensory stimuli for objects may change, but our recognition and perception of the objects does not change. This phenomenon is referred to as *perceptual constancy*. Perceptual constancy simplifies our interactions with the objects around us. We do not have to figure out what the same object is every time we encounter it under different conditions. For example, you would recognize this book as a book whether you saw it lying on the grass in the sun, sitting on a high shelf in the library, or spread open on your desk.

In the visual realm there are three basic perceptual constancies: size, shape, and brightness. Size is a constant because there is a regular relationship between the size of an image on our retina and the distance between the object and our eye. For example, when the distance between an object and our eyes is doubled, the size of the image on the retina is halved. Usually distance cues are necessary for correct size perception. We can judge the size of an object correctly at varying distances from us if we know how far away it is. When there are no distance cues, we may perceive objects inaccurately and be subject to illusions. But if an object is familiar to us, we often do not need distance cues to perceive it correctly. We already know the object's size, and we can use this information to judge the object's distance from us. Size constancy develops at an early age; even six-week-old infants have it in a rough, undeveloped form.

Shape is another important constant in our visual

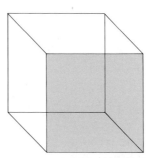

Figure 4.4 Necker cube. An illusion by the Swiss naturalist L. A. Necker in 1832. Note that the tinted surface can appear as either the front or the rear surface of a transparent cube. Gaze steadily at the figure or blink your eyes repeatedly to experience the reversal.

perceptions. For example, we often see our friends from different angles but have little difficulty recognizing them. We can walk in back of them on the street, see them face down on the grass, or in profile in a chair and still recognize them as the same people. The sensory stimuli we receive in each of these situations are different, yet because shape is constant, we can translate all of them into the perception of one person.

Brightness is a constant because the ratio of light intensity between an object and its surroundings is usually constant. That is, the same light usually illuminates both an object and its surroundings. If there is a spotlight on an object, however, the brightness will not be constant. Under normal lighting conditions brightness is constant no matter how bright the light actually is. We perceive snow as brighter than most of the things it falls on whether we see it on a sunny day, or an overcast day, or at night because in each instance the lighting is the same for both the snow and the surrounding trees,

buildings, and people. Another reason the snow would seem brighter in all these cases is that we have "memory colors," which are memories of the way colors are supposed to look, and we use these memories in our perceptions. If we cannot see enough of an object to know what it is, we cannot draw on our memory color for it. When this happens we might perceive very familiar objects in the wrong colors, depending on lighting conditions.

Illusions. An *illusion* is a false perception of a stimulus that is actually present. (In contrast, a hallucination is a false perception for which the stimulus is *not* physically present.) Illusions illustrate the fact that we do not always decide on the correct "hypotheses" to explain our sensations. (See Figure 4.5.)

The classic example of an optical illusion occurs when the moon looks larger on the horizon than it does when it is overhead. Yet research has shown that the size of the image on the retina is exactly the same in both instances. But the distance cues are

Figure 4.5 Things are not always as they seem. "But I was sure it was a soccer ball," said the motorist of an object that came bouncing toward her as she drove up a hill. Police were seeking the bowling enthusiast who had "misplaced" this ball. (*The Seattle Times*)

misleading. When the moon is on the horizon, we see terrain when we look at it, but when we look at the moon when it is overhead, we do not see anything between us and the moon. We correct for distance when we judge the size of the moon on the horizon, but we do not do this when we see it overhead. (When the moon on the horizon is viewed through a hole in a piece of cardboard, which eliminates landscape cues, the illusion is eliminated.) Usually we judge distances in accordance with the cues we have first, then apply this information in order to make judgements about size. When there are no distance cues, we may be subject to optical illusions and perceptual distortions.

Two other optical illusions are shown in Figure 4.6. In the Müller-Lyer illusion the top horizontal line appears to be longer than the bottom one. But both lines are actually the same length. (Check them

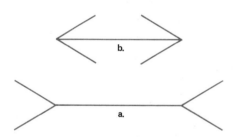

a. MULLER–LYER ILLUSION: WHICH LINE IS LONGER?

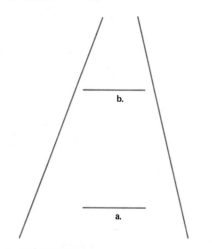

b. PONZO ILLUSION

Figure 4.6 (*a*) Muller-Lyer illusion. Which line is longer? (*b*) Ponzo illusion.

with a ruler and see.) It is the angle of the lines at each end that causes the illusion. In the Ponzo illusion the upper line again appears to be longer than the lower one. But, again, the two lines are the same length. The distortion is caused by the converging lines in the background that provide incorrect depth perception cues. Because the background lines appear as if they are about to converge in the distance at the top, we think that the top bar must be further away and compensate for the perceived distance by increasing our estimate of the bar's size.

In 1896 A. Thiery suggested that we are subject to optical illusions when we attempt to perceive a two-dimensional object in terms of three dimensions and apply distance cues incorrectly. The Ponzo illusion demonstrates the effect that Thiery hypothesized, because we learn to think of the converging lines as a distance cue and allow them to mislead us. Further support for Thiery's learning hypothesis was found in a study that showed that adults are more susceptible to the Ponzo illusion than are children (Parrish, Lundy, and Leibowitz, 1968). Other studies have shown that knowledge of depth perception also increases with age, so that it is logical to assume that adults might misread the converging lines as depth cues and children might not.

Depth and distance perception
One of the most complicated aspects of our perception is the ability to perceive the third dimension of depth. Our retinas receive information in two-dimensional form, but we translate these cues into three-dimensional perceptions. We now know that we do this by using both monocular cues (which require only one eye) and binocular cues (which require both eyes).

Monocular cues
Each of our eyes is capable of perceiving *perspective*. Perspective is really a combination of several kinds of cues that help us to judge distances. One of these cues is that parallel lines appear to converge at the horizon as in the Ponzo illustration. This phenomenon is called *linear perspective. Decreasing size* is another cue. The further away an object is from an observer, the smaller it seems. An object's *height in the horizontal plane* is also a perspective cue. For example, a ship five miles offshore appears in a

123

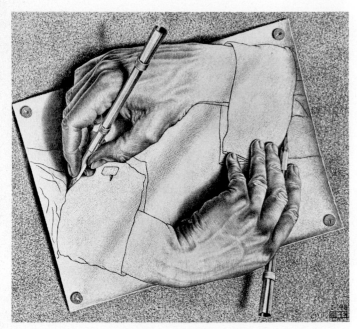

Figure 4.7 By skillful use of light and shadow, this artist has created a three-dimensional effect. (M. C. Escher, *Drawing Hands,* Escher Foundation Haags Gemeentemuseum, The Hague.)

This is called *retinal disparity,* because images of external objects are projected onto our two retinas. We can perceive depth by using both eyes and combining the two different images on our retinas.

Try an experiment to demonstrate your own retinal disparity. Hold a pencil up vertically at arm's length in front of you. Close one eye and line the

Figure 4.8 This painting by Van Gogh illustrates seven monocular cues that we use in depth perception. First, the parallel lines of the corridor seem to converge in the distance (linear perspective). Next, the arches in the back of the corridor are smaller than those in front (decreasing size). The end of the corridor is in a higher horizontal plane than the foreground (height in the horizontal plane), and the more distant parts of the corridor are painted in less detail than the closer ones (texture and clarity). Light and shadow are also skillfully used by the painter. Finally, the arches and hallway in the front of the painting cut off parts of the corridor behind them (interposition). (Vincent Van Gogh, *Hospital Corridor at Saint Remy,* 1889. Gouache and water-color, $24\frac{1}{8} \times 18\frac{5}{8}''$. Collection, The Museum of Modern Art, New York. Abby Aldrich Rockefeller Bequest.)

higher plane and closer to the horizon than one two miles from shore. *Texture* is another perspective cue, because the texture or grain of an object appears finer as distance increases. Finally, *clarity* is an important cue for judging distance; we can see hills that are close by more clearly than ones which are far away. These five perspective cues provide us with information that we can use to make judgements about distance, and therefore depth.

Patterns of light and shadow often constitute a depth cue. (See Figure 4.7.) *Interposition* is another example of a monocular depth cue. It tells us that when one object cuts off part of another, the first object is closer to us. Figure 4.8 illustrates seven monocular depth cues.

Binocular cues

124 Binocular perception enables us to take advantage of the fact that we see different images in each eye. Because our eyes are separated from one another, they each have a slightly different view of any object.

pencil up with a vertical edge in the room, such as a door jam or window frame. Then open the other eye and close the one that was just open. Did the pencil "move"? Next, open both eyes and line the pencil up again with a vertical edge. Then close each eye separately. If the pencil moves when you close your right eye, that means that the images in your right eye dominate your visual perception. This is the case for most people. If the pencil moves when you close your left eye, then your left eye is dominant.

A stereoscope is an apparatus that demonstrates how we combine the two different images from our eyes into a unified three-dimensional picture. Separate photographs are taken from each eye's perspective and mounted on a frame behind two viewpieces. When we look with both eyes through the appropriate viewing hole in the stereoscope, each eye sees a different two-dimensional photograph. But our brain merges the two different views of the same object and we see them as one three-dimensional picture.

Another binocular cue to depth comes from the muscles that turn our eyes. At distances beyond about 70 feet our eyes are essentially parallel to one another as they focus on objects. As the distance to the object decreases, our eyes gradually turn toward one another. This is called *convergence*. The muscles that turn our eyes send impulses to the brain that indicate the angle of focus of our eyes, so that we can then judge the distance of the object on which our eyes are focusing.

Perceptual development

Philosopher and psychologist William James once described the perceptual world of the newborn infant as "one great blooming, buzzing confusion." Obviously, we do not know how true this is, because newborn babies are notoriously poor at describing their experiences. However, this problem has not kept psychologists from grappling with the critical question of how our perceptual abilities develop. Are they inborn or do they develop with learning and experience? Or do innate and learned abilities interact in complex ways? As a result of some ingenious research techniques, the pieces of the perceptual puzzle are gradually fitting into place. However, there is much that we still do not completely understand about perceptual development, and it promises to remain an important frontier for years to come.

Beginnings of perceptual experience

The physical structures of most sense organs are well developed even before birth. But when do they begin to function and what kinds of perceptual experience do they give rise to?

We know that the human fetus can react to tactile (touch) stimuli within eight weeks after conception. Tactile sensitivity begins in the facial region and gradually develops downward until, by the fourth prenatal month, the entire body except for the top and the back of the head is sensitive to touch and pressure. The fetus is also sensitive to temperature, but it has a limited sensitivity to pain. The same is true for newborn infants. Some researchers think that this early insensitivity to pain is a biological defense against the stress of the birth process.

Our senses of taste and smell are well developed at birth. Hearing is less well developed, partly because of the amniotic fluid in the ears, but in the last month before birth, the fetus can already discriminate between tones (Dwarnicka, Jasiencka, Smolarz, and Wawryk, 1964). By the third to seventh day after birth infants respond to ordinary noises in their environment, and by the end of the second month they are able to discriminate between various sounds.

It was once assumed that newborn infants cannot see clearly because their retinas are not fully developed. Research has shown, however, that they do have some visual abilities at birth or shortly thereafter. One of these is the ability to perceive forms. Robert Fantz (1963) filmed eye movements to determine how long infants look at objects or patterns in their visual field. He found that infants less than five days old preferred black-and-white patterns to plain-colored surfaces. Moreover, infants tested on the patterns shown in Figure 4.9 preferred to look at the normal human face rather than at the scrambled face or other pattern. These findings seem to indicate that at least some of our form perception and preference is innate.

Researchers do not agree how early in life infants can perceive color. However, we do know that by 2 months of age, babies can discriminate between red and white lights when the brightness of the lights is constant (Peeples and Teller, 1975).

Eleanor Gibson and Robert Walk (1960) performed an intriguing series of studies on depth per-

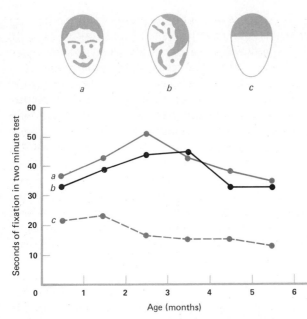

Figure 4.9 The research of Robert Fantz (1961) showed that infants spent more time looking at a "real" face (a) than at a scrambled face (b) or a control figure (c). The results presented here show the average time scores for infants at various ages when presented with the three face-shaped objects paired in all the possible combinations. (Robert L. Fantz, "The origin of form perception." Copyright © 1961 by Scientific American, Inc. All rights reserved.)

ception in infants using a "visual cliff." The apparatus, shown in Figure 4.10, consisted of a slightly raised platform laid across the center of a table top covered with heavy plate glass. On one side of the platform, a checkerboard pattern was placed immediately below the glass. On the other, a sheet of the patterned material was placed several feet below the glass, so that it looked as if there were a drop-off or cliff.

Gibson and Walk tested 36 crawling infants who were 6 months old. The infants were placed individually on the center platform, and their mothers called to them first from the "deep" side and then from the "solid" side. The researchers reasoned that if the babies could not perceive depth, they would be equally likely to crawl to either side of the visual cliff. However, of the 27 children who moved off the center platform, only three crawled onto the glass

above the cliff. Many of the babies cried when their mothers called to them from the deep side, but they still refused to crawl there; some actually crawled *away*, to more secure territory. A number of babies patted the glass above the deep side to assure themselves that it was solid but still refused to crawl onto it. The evidence clearly showed that the infants could perceive depth.

Because the infants were 6 months old when they were tested, there was a possibility that they had learned this depth perception. But Gibson and Walk's conclusion that the ability is innate was supported by visual cliff experiments with young animals. Nearly all the animals tested avoided the cliff as soon as they could stand and walk. Chicks, goats, and lambs less than a day old avoided it. When animals were placed on the glass above the deep side, they froze in fear.

Experiential factors in perception

Although it appears that certain perceptual abilities are innate, it is also clear that certain experiential

Figure 4.10 A kitten in one of the visual cliff experiments hesitates on the glass above the "deep" end. Most animals, even after feeling the solid glass surface, refused to crawl above the cliff. (Vandivert, courtesy, *Scientific American*)

and learning factors are critical to perceptual development. Not only perceptual abilities, but also the underlying sensory and neural apparatus can be affected by experiential factors. In many instances there is evidence of a "critical period," during which certain kinds of experiences are required in order for normal development to occur.

Visual deprivation studies. A number of early experiments in perception studied the effects of visual deprivation on animals. Animals were reared in total darkness and then tested for perceptual abilities. The animals had serious perceptual deficiencies when they were first exposed to light. At first, researchers attributed these deficiencies to the animals' lack of previous perceptual learning, but later they found that the animals had defective retinas that limited their visual input. Apparently, a certain amount of light stimulation is required in order for the visual system to develop normally; otherwise, nerve cells in the system begin to atrophy. For this reason, later studies of visual deprivation used transluscent goggles, which allowed animals to receive light stimulation but not to perceive shapes or patterns.

When animals are raised with these goggles, their retinas do not degenerate, but they still have severe perceptual deficiencies. Monkeys, chimpanzees, and kittens deprived of patterned stimulation early in life perform almost as well as ordinary animals in distinguishing differences in brightness, size, and color. However, they cannot perform more complex tasks, such as distinguishing objects and discriminating between various geometric shapes (Riesen, 1965).

As we saw in the previous chapter, researchers can now monitor electrical activity in single cells of the visual cortex of the brain by inserting tiny microelectrodes (as small as 4/10,000 of an inch) into those cells. British physiologists Colin Blakemore and Grahame Cooper (1970) used this method to study the effects of restricted visual stimulation on the development of the visual cortex. A group of kittens was raised in the dark except for a five-hour period each day during which they were placed in round chambers that had either vertical or horizontal stripes on the walls. A special collar prevented them from seeing their own bodies. When the kittens were 5 months of age, Blakemore and Cooper tested the electrical responses of individual cells in the visual cortex. In normal kittens different individual cells respond to bars of light placed at different angles in the visual field. In other words, some cells fire when the bar is in the 2 o'clock position, others when it is in a 4 o'clock position, and so on. Blakemore and Cooper found that the experimental kittens did not respond in the same manner. Those who had been raised in the horizontally striped chamber did not have any cells that responded to vertical stimuli. The opposite was true for cats raised in the vertically striped chamber. The kittens also had visual impairments. For example, those raised with vertical stripes acted as if they could not see a pencil held in a horizontal position and waved in front of them.

Figure 4.11 shows the positions of the bars of light that elicited cortical responses in the kittens raised in the two environments. It is easy to see the "holes" in their visual fields. Later studies have shown that there is a "critical period" for this effect, which in kittens comprises the first four months of life. Restricted stimulation after this period of time does not affect the responsiveness of cells in the visual cortex.

When the blind see. Supposing people who had been blind from birth suddenly had their vision restored during adulthood. What would they see? Could they perceive visually the things they had learned to identify by touch?

People who are born with congenital cataracts perceive the world in a manner very similar to that of experimental animals who are fitted with translucent lenses. From birth on, the clouded lenses of their eyes permit them to perceive light, but not patterns or shapes.

A German physician, von Senden (1960), compiled data on patients with congenital cataracts who were tested immediately after the cataracts were surgically removed. These people were immediately able to perceive figure-ground relationships, to scan objects visually, and to follow moving targets with their eyes, indicating that such abilities are innate. However, they could not identify by sight objects with which they were familiar through touch, nor were they able to distinguish between simple geometric figures without counting the corners or tracing them with their fingers. After several weeks of training, the patients were able to identify simple objects by sight, but their perceptual constancy was

127

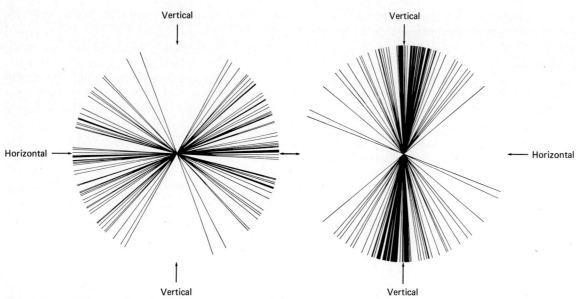

Figure 4.11 Positions of bars of light that elicited responses from single cells within the visual cortex of kittens who had been raised in horizontally (left) or vertically (right) striped environments. Restricted visual exposure resulted in perceptual "holes" in the kittens' visual system. (Blakemore and Cooper, 1970.)

very poor. A shape that they recognized in one color was often not recognizable in another color, even though they could discriminate between colors. Years after their vision was restored, some of the patients could identify only a few of the faces of persons they knew well. Many also had great difficulty judging distances. Apparently, no amount of subsequent experience could make up for their lack of visual experience during childhood.

PAIN PERCEPTION

Pain is one of the unpleasant realities of life, and one that most of us do our best to avoid. In spite of its negative aspects, however, pain also has certain important survival functions. First, it serves as a warning signal when something is amiss and our body is being threatened or damaged. Second, pain is part of a defensive system that triggers reactions to help us cope with the threat. Pain is thus an important part of the natural "biofeedback" system that helps us adjust to our environment. Because of its crucial

survival function, as well as its role in physical illnesses and certain psychological problems, many psychologists are conducting research to discover the physiological and psychological causes of our perception of pain as well as ways in which we can control our subjective experience of pain.

Theories of pain

The sensory receptors for pain appear to be free nerve endings that respond to intense mechanical, thermal, or chemical stimulation and carry messages through special thin fibers in the sensory nerves. According to one theory of pain—the *specificity theory* (Perl, 1971)—the location, intensity, and quality of pain are determined by the activity of the specific fibers stimulated and the neural reactions in the areas of the central nervous system to which they send their nerve impulses.

Another theory of how we sense pain is the *gate-control theory* of Ronald Melzack (1973). This theory states that aversive stimuli that we receive through free nerve endings activate both small-diameter and large-diameter sensory fibers. The thin fibers

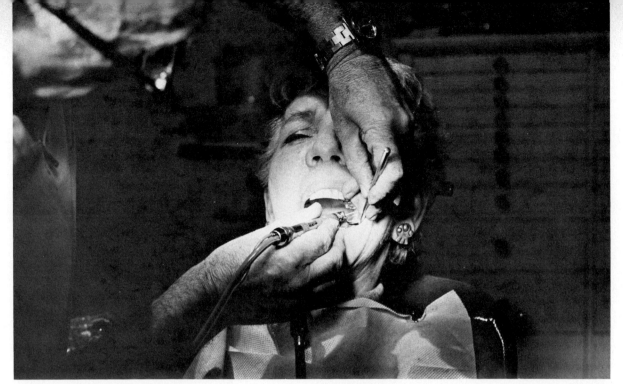

Pain may seem purposeless at times such as this, but it is actually one of the body's most important defenses. (Beckwith)

carry pain impulses; the thick fibers carry information about touch. A neural mechanism in the spinal cord acts like a gate that can increase or decrease the flow of nerve impulses from pain receptors all over the body to the central nervous system. The degree to which the gate increases or decreases the flow of sensory impulses is determined by the relative amounts of activity in the thin and thick fibers. Impulses from thin fibers open the gate, whereas thick-fiber impulses close it. When the ratio of thin-fiber activity to thick-fiber activity exceeds a critical level, the gate opens and the areas in the brain responsible for experiencing pain are activated. Gate-control theory hypothesizes that the gate can be opened or closed by nerve impulses coming down from the brain. If this is true then it helps to explain how psychological factors can modify our subjective experience of pain. Next time you are writhing in the dentist's chair, try concentrating hard on something other than the pain. You may not notice it as much because, according to the theory, the brain mechanisms involved in concentration are able to close the gate, at least partially.

Gate-control theory has been used to explain a variety of phenonomena involving pain. We examine the gate-control explanation of acupuncture later in this chapter.

Psychological factors in pain perception

Like all perceptions, pain is a subjective phenomenon whose quality and intensity are influenced not only by the physical stimulus, but also by psychological factors, such as personal and cultural experiences and beliefs, customary methods of coping with difficulties, and meanings that one attaches to painful situations.

Cultural factors

Childbirth is an event dreaded by many American women because its potential for excruciating pain is widely publicized and frequently exaggerated in our culture. Yet in some cultures that have been studied by anthropologists, women show virtually no distress during childbirth and work in the fields almost up until the moment the baby arrives. In some cultures the woman's husband gets into bed and groans as if he were in great pain while the woman calmly gives birth to the child. The husband stays in bed with the baby to recover from his terrible ordeal and the mother returns to her work in the fields almost immediately (Kroeber, 1948).

Cultural values do have a great influence on an individual's interpretation of the meaning of pain. In certain parts of India, for example, people still practice an unusual hook-hanging ritual. A celebrant is chosen to bless the children and crops in a number of neighboring villages. Steel hooks attached by strong ropes to the top of a special cart are shoved under the skin and muscles on each side of his back and he travels on the cart from village to village. At the climax of a ceremony in each village, the celebrant swings free, hanging only by the hooks embedded in his back, to bless the children and crops. (See

This dancer in Surinam can perform on blazing sticks and hot coals without flinching from heat or pain. (UPI)

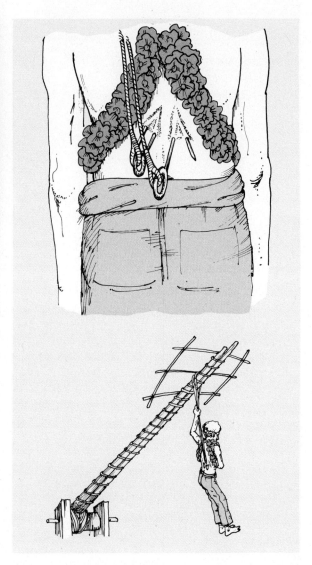

Figure 4.12 The annual hook-swinging ceremony practiced in remote Indian villages. The top drawing shows two steel hooks thrust into the small of the back of the "celebrant," who is decked with garlands. The celebrant is later taken to a special cart which has upright timbers and a crossbeam. The bottom drawing shows the celebrant hanging on to the ropes as the cart moves to each village. After he blesses each child and farm field in a village, he swings free, suspended only by the hooks. The crowds cheer at each swing. During the ceremony, the celebrant is in a state of exaltation and shows no sign of pain. (After Kosambi, 1967, p. 105.)

Figure 4.12.) Incredibly, there is no evidence that the celebrant experiences any pain during the ritual; on the contrary, he appears to be in a state of ecstasy. When the hooks are removed, the wounds heal rapidly and are scarcely visible within two weeks (Kosambi, 1967).

Studies in the United States indicate that various ethnic groups have developed different attitudes toward pain that affect their pain tolerance. In a comparative study of surgical patients in a New York City hospital, it was found that male Anglo-Saxon Americans had an accepting, matter-of-fact attitude toward pain and regarded painful experiences as tests of their masculinity. They usually would moan or cry out only when they were alone. Jewish and Italian males, however, were very vociferous in their complaints and openly sought sympathy and sup-

130

port, but for different reasons. The Jews were usually concerned about the meaning and implications of the pain—what was wrong with them and how long it would last—whereas the Italians focused on the immediate sensations of pain and on their desire for relief from them (Zborowski, 1952).

Placebo effects on pain

Faith and hope are important in other contexts than religious ones. Physicians have long used our cultural belief in the power of medicine to their advantage. Doctors who are convinced that physical complaints are "in their patients' heads" sometimes administer sugar pills, which they described as a "new miracle drug," and frequently their patients report miraculous relief from such "treatment." These sugar pills and other substances that have no medicinal value of their own are called *placebos*.

But what about real pain, with true physiological causes? Can placebos provide relief from this? The answer is clearly yes. In one study of 4588 patients suffering from headaches, relief was reported in 58 percent of the cases in which only placebos were administered. The chronic pain of cancer was relieved in 65 percent of a group of patients who received morphine, a narcotic pain-killer. But 42 percent of a group of similar patients given only a placebo reported equal relief. In another investigation, either placebo or morphine injections were given to 122 surgical patients suffering postoperative pain from their wounds. Sixty-seven percent of those who received morphine reported relief, whereas 42 percent of those given placebos reported equal relief (Beecher, 1959). Thus in many instances the faith that people have in placebos makes them as effective as actual pain-killing drugs.

The power of belief and expectation not only can cause placebos to relieve pain but can also bring about a complete reversal of the usual pharmacological effects of a drug. Ipecac is used to induce vomiting in people who have swallowed poison. In one extraordinary experiment pregnant women suffering from the nausea of morning sickness were given ipecac and told that it was a new drug to relieve nausea. Some of them reported immediate relief from their morning sickness (Haas, Fink, and Hartfelder, 1959).

The mystery of acupuncture: A psychological frontier

Acupuncture is an ancient Chinese medical procedure that involves the insertion of long, fine needles into precise points on the skin to relieve various ailments. Although the technique has existed in China for at least 5000 years, only since 1959 has it been widely used in that country to reduce pain during surgery (Hendin, 1972). Major operations on the abdomen, chest, and head are reportedly carried out with no other anesthetic. On the basis of charts such as that shown in Figure 4.13, needles are placed along the meridians (proposed channels through

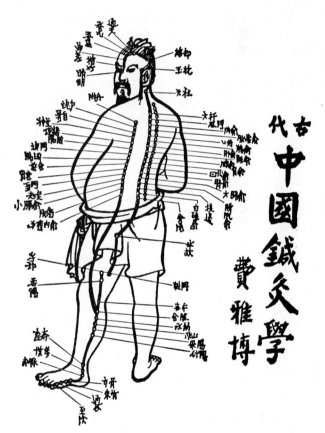

Figure 4.13 Typical acupuncture chart showing sites for the insertion of acupuncture needles along major "meridians" of the body. After two or more acupuncture needles are inserted at selected sites, electrical current is passed through the needles for a period of about 20 minutes. The anesthetic effect produced by the acupuncture procedure is reported to be sufficient for major surgery. (From Ronald Melzack, *The Puzzle of Pain*, © 1973 by Ronald Melzack, Basic Books, Inc.)

131

which life energy flows) at points that are thought to correspond to specific organs. The organ and the site of needle placement may be quite far apart; for example, needles may be placed in the leg to stop a headache. Once they are implanted the needles are usually twirled or electric current is passed through them.

There is great doubt among scientists as to whether or not meridians really exist. Indeed, one prominent researcher concluded, "There is not one scrap of anatomical or physiological evidence for the existence of such a system" (Wall, 1972, p. 129). Moreover, some Chinese surgeons totally disregard meridian points and place their needles almost anywhere to anesthetize their patients (Man and Chen, 1972).

If the Chinese theory of meridians is wrong, then how does acupuncture work? We examine two theories that have been proposed to account for the effectiveness of acupuncture. One of these theories is physiological in nature; the other focuses on certain psychological factors that may be at work.

Melzack's physiological theory. One attempt to understand the physiological effects of acupuncture involves the gate-control theory of pain discussed earlier. You will recall that according to this theory, pain depends in part on the relative balance of activity in thick fibers, which are activated by tactile stimuli, and thin fibers, which are activated by pain stimuli. When the relative activity in the thick fibers increases, a "gate" is closed along the pathways to the brain, preventing further transmission of pain impulses. Ronald Melzack (1973) suggests that the acupuncture needles may stimulate these thick fibers and increase their activity, so that the gate closes to input from pain receptors in various areas of the body. It is also possible that psychological activities in the brain can cause the pain-control gate to close, but at present we do not know precisely how this might occur.

Research on possible physiological mechanisms of acupuncture is continuing. But other psychologists have focused on possible psychological factors which may be involved.

Barber's psychological theory. Theodore X. Barber and his associates conducted a critical evaluation of

the literature on acupuncture and concluded that its effects can be at least partly explained in psychological terms (Barber, Spanos, and Chaves, 1974). They have developed some imposing arguments to support their position.

First, many people assume that Chinese physicians use acupuncture for most surgical patients, but this is not the case. Patients are carefully screened to ensure that they have low anxiety, positive attitudes toward acupuncture, high motivation to undergo the operation, and positive expectations that they will experience little pain. All these factors have been shown to increase pain tolerance in experimental studies.

Patients who are to receive acupuncture typically come to the hospital several days before the operation for an intensive orientation session. They are told what will happen and what effects they can expect. In addition, they are trained to control their breathing and to attend to it during surgery, an exercise that may distract them from the pain cues of the operation. Pain from the acupuncture needles may have a similar distracting effect. Contrary to popular belief, patients receiving acupuncture are also commonly given pain-relieving drugs (Dimond, 1971), so that it is difficult to determine how much the acupuncture needles themselves actually help to reduce pain.

Although there is much to be learned about the physiology of acupuncture, it appears that its pain-reducing effects are at least partially influenced by psychological factors. You may have noted the similarities between the psychological forces that researchers suspect are at work in relation to acupuncture and those that they believe are involved in placebo effects. The fact that our beliefs and expectations can alter our perceptions to such a great extent points once again to the many ways in which we create our own experiential world.

Perception cuts across all areas of psychology, and each of the four perspectives discussed in Chapter 2 is reflected in its study. The biological perspective is concerned with the sensory and neural basis for perception as well as with innate and maturational factors in its development. The behavioristic emphasis is seen in studies of how early experience affects perception and in how we learn to organize and respond to our perceptions. The psychoanalytic perspective gave birth to the perceptual defense studies and has focused attention on the general question of how our perceptual processes serve and are affected by our inner needs. Finally, perception is the cornerstone of the cognitive perspective, because it involves the processing and coding of information and is the basis for thought and planning. The meaning we give to raw sensory input is a cognitive process. In this chapter we have seen some of the multitude of factors that influence those meanings.

SUMMARY

1. Perception is influenced by a host of factors, including biological determinants, learning, motives, values, and psychological defenses.

2. *Psychophysics* is the scientific study of how the physical properties of stimuli are related to perception. The *absolute threshold* is the intensity at which a stimulus can be detected 50 percent of the time. Studies of the *differential threshold* gave rise to *Weber's law*, which states that there is a constant ratio between the intensity of a stimulus and the amount that a second stimulus must differ from it before the perceiver can detect the difference. *Signal detection theory* deals with factors that produce variations in stimulus detection.

3. Attention is an active process in which certain aspects of the environment are attended to while other stimuli are blocked out. We cannot attend completely to more than one thing at a time, but we are capable of rapid attentional shifts. Attentional processes are affected by stimulus factors as well as by such internal factors as motives, interests, and previous learning.

4. *Perceptual defense* refers to a process whereby threatening or anxiety-arousing stimuli are not consciously perceived. At-

tempts to account for such phenomena illustrate some of the problems encountered in studying the private experiences of others. The *repression-sensitization* dimension refers to tendencies to respond to anxiety-arousing stimuli with avoidance or approach responses.

5. There is no evidence that *subliminal perception* can affect behavior without our awareness. The existence of *extrasensory perception* (ESP) has not been demonstrated to the satisfaction of most psychologists.

6. The Gestalt psychologists identified a number of principles of perceptual organization, including figure and ground, similarity, proximity, closure, and continuity. R. L. Gregory has suggested that perception is essentially a hypothesis about what an object is, based on whatever cues are available to us. According to this view, illusions are incorrect hypotheses.

7. Perceptual constancies allow us to recognize familiar stimuli under changing conditions. In the visual realm there are three constancies: size, shape, and brightness.

8. Depth perception is made possible by both *monocular* cues, such as perspective, texture, clarity, and interposition, and *binocular* cues, such as retinal disparity and convergence.

9. Perceptual development involves both physical maturation and learning. Certain perceptual abilities are innate or develop shortly after birth, whereas others require particular kinds of experiences in order to develop. There appear to be "critical periods" for the development of certain perceptual abilities.

10. Perception of pain is heavily influenced by psychological factors, including cultural learning, beliefs, and expectations. Studies

133

of placebo effects have provided evidence for the power of beliefs and expectations. Some psychologists have attempted to account for the effects of acupuncture in terms of psychological factors. A physiological explanation has been offered in terms of the *gate-control* theory of pain.

Suggested readings

Gregory, R. L. *The intelligent eye.* New York: McGraw-Hill Book Company, 1970. Gregory presents his theory that perception is a set of hypotheses about reality, and he uses the theory to explain visual illusion.

Hansel, C. E. M. *E.S.P.: A scientific evaluation.* New York: Charles Scribner's Sons, 1966. Analyzes many ESP experiments and evaluates them in terms of their adequacy of experimental design and interpretation of data.

Lindsay, P., & Norman, D. *Human information processing.* New York: Academic Press, 1972. Presents a clear and readable analysis of perception in terms of information processing. Also applies the information-processing analysis to many other psychological phenomena, such as learning, personality, and cognitive processing.

Melzack, R. *The puzzle of pain.* New York: Basic Books, Inc., Publishers, 1973. Melzack presents the gate control theory of pain and applies it to many pain-perception phenomena, including acupuncture.

Rock, I. *An introduction to perception.* New York: Macmillan, Inc., 1975. An in-depth analysis of visual perception, including movement, depth, size, and form perception. Also deals with illusion and color perception.

Chapter 5

Altered States of Consciousness

(Arthur Tress)

One night author Barry Farrell took LSD at a friend's house. The drug plunged him into a new reality, one of fascinating and sometimes terrifying dimensions.

We got in the car, and I had only driven about three blocks, when suddenly the pavement in front of me opened up. It was as though the pavement was flowing over Niagara Falls. The street lights expanded into fantastic globes of light that filled my entire vision. I didn't dare stop.

It was a nightmare. I came to traffic lights, but I couldn't tell what color they were. There were all sorts of colors around me anyway. I could detect other cars around me, so I stopped when they stopped, and went when they went.

At home I flopped in a chair. I wasn't afraid. My conscious mind was sort of sitting on my shoulder—watching everything I was doing. I found I could make the room expand—oh, maybe a thousand miles—or I could make it contract right in front of me. All over the ceiling there were geometric patterns of light. To say they were beautiful is too shallow a word.

My wife put on a violin concerto. I could make the music come out of the speaker like taffy, or a tube of toothpaste, surrounded by dancing lights of colors beyond description.

A friend showed up. He was talking to me, and I was answering, all in a perfectly normal way. Then, I saw his face change. He became an Arab, a Chinese, a Negro. I found I could take my finger and wipe away his face and then paint it back again.

I made a chocolate sundae and gave it to him for a head. A great truth appeared to me. The reason he had all those faces was this: he was a reflection of all mankind. So was I.

I asked myself, "What is God?" Then I knew that I was God. That really sounds ridiculous as I say it. But I knew that all life is one, and since God is Life, and I am Life, we are the same being.

Then I decided to examine my own fears, because I wasn't really afraid of anything. I went down into my stomach and it was like Dante's inferno—all steaming and bubbling and ghastly. I saw some hideous shapes in the distance. My mind floated to each one, and they were horrible, hideous.

They all got together in a mob and started to come up after me—a flood of bogeymen. But I knew I was stronger than all of them, and I took my hand and wiped them out.

Now, I think there lies the real danger with LSD. Anyone who motioned with his hand and couldn't wipe out those creatures. He has to stay down there with them, forever. (Farrell, 1966, pp. 8–9)

136

What is reality? Is your reality the same as someone else's reality? Is there a single "truth" about anything in the world around us, or is it possible that everything we experience is simply a product of our own creations, that it has no real existence outside of our minds? These are old questions. They are as old, in fact, as our ability to reflect on our experiences.

Until recently most psychologists were content to let philosophers ponder these questions and to focus their own attention on more "scientific" topics. Although subjective experience might well be the core of human existence, scientific psychologists, influenced by behaviorism, have tended to focus on observable behavior rather than internal experiences. Many scientists have not considered the phenomena of hypnosis, dreaming, and mystical experiences as legitimate subjects for study, and those who dared to explore them did so at the risk of their scientific reputations. Because these experiences are hidden, they are very difficult to verify or measure scientifically. Charles Dickens recognized the problem when he observed that "every human creature is constituted to be that profound secret and mystery to every other."

During the past decade, however, there have been fundamental changes in our society and in our values that are being reflected in psychological research. In increasing numbers people are turning to Zen, yoga, meditation, psychoactive drugs, and other methods to alter their state of awareness. People of every description are reporting that a fascinating and mysterious world lies beyond the boundaries of our ordinary perceptions, and many reputable psychologists are being drawn to the study of this exciting new frontier of psychology. Moreover, all perspectives—biological, behavioristic, cognitive, and psychoanalytic—are making contributions to the investigation of altered states.

CHARACTERISTICS OF ALTERED STATES

Our conscious states range from deep sleep to alert wakefulness. Every day we experience a variety of states within that range we regard as "normal" or "ordinary." The most familiar of these is conscious thought. No matter what we are doing, we are constantly thinking. Some of our thoughts relate to our immediate situations, some are memories, some focus on the future, and about 200 of our daily thoughts are "daydreams," fantasies about real or impossible situations (Singer, 1966).

Under certain conditions, however, some individuals experience altered states of consciousness. They may discover new mental functions and perceptual capabilities that have no counterparts in normal experience. Their sense of time and their body image may become distorted, and they may perceive illogical and impossible events as real and absolute.

SLEEPING AND DREAMING

On the average, we spend from 30 to 40 percent of our lives asleep. No wonder we sometimes feel that there are not enough hours in the day! But no one really understands why we sleep so much, or for that matter, why we sleep at all. It has long been thought that sleep provides a chance for our bodies to recuperate. However, we now know that we consume about the same amount of energy during sleep as we do during wakefulness, and that we do not seem to accumulate any body toxins that dissipate during sleep. On the other hand, growth hormones involved in building up body proteins reach their peak concentrations in the blood during sleep. Whatever its function, we know that sleep is very important to us because our mental and physical functioning deteriorate if we go without it for extended periods. (See Box 5.1.)

Our biological clocks

Most of us regulate our periods of sleep and wakefulness in accordance with external events, such as changes in light and darkness, mealtimes, and the unwelcome buzzing of alarm clocks. But these external events overlay a basic 24-hour activity cycle, which we have in common with other mammals. This *circadian rhythm* (from the Latin *circa,* "around," and *dia,* "day") involves cyclical changes in body temperature, blood pressure, blood-plasma volume, hormonal secretions into the bloodstream, and other bodily processes. We normally sleep during the low point of the temperature cycle.

Animal species have differing cycles of sleep and

wakefulness. Many, including human beings, sleep for one long period every 24 hours. This is called a *monophasic* sleep cycle. Other animals have several sleep-wakefulness cycles during their 24-hour circadian rhythm. This is called a *polyphasic* cycle. Rats, rabbits, and other rodents have polyphasic cycles. Human infants have polyphasic cycles that become monophasic as they mature. (See Figure 5.1.)

Our circadian rhythm responds to external influences, so that extreme changes in our sleep habits may result in a kind of "jet lag," the fatigue and disorientation that we may experience if we cross several time zones while traveling. Our bodies may require a week or more to adapt completely to a major change across time zones. In fact, some corporations require their executives to wait several days after they have made a transcontinental flight before they begin important negotiations.

Stages of sleep

Electroencephalogram (EEG) recordings of the electrical activity of the brain show that there are five stages of sleep, as shown in Figure 5.2. In a relaxed waking state, we have a brain wave pattern of 8 to 12

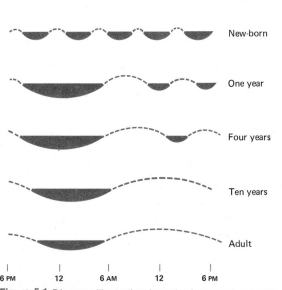

New-born

One year

Four years

Ten years

Adult

6 PM   12   6 AM   12   6 PM

Figure 5.1 Diagram illustrating how the human sleep cycle changes from a polyphasic to a monophasic cycle from birth to adulthood. Solid areas indicate sleep periods. (Kleitman, 1939, p. 515.)

137

BOX 5.1

Two hundred hours without sleep

In 1959 Peter Tripp, a well-known New York disc jockey, vowed to remain awake for 200 hours in a marathon for the Polio Fund. For over eight days he broadcast his regular program and periodic progress reports from a glass-walled booth in Times Square.

Tripp's "Wake-a-thon" attracted the attention not only of many New Yorkers, but also of a group of psychologists and medical specialists. They set up a psychological laboratory in a nearby hotel to study Tripp, gave him a daily battery of psychological tests, and monitored his physiological reactions. He was under the constant scrutiny of doctors, nurses, and psychologists, as well as curiosity seekers, who flocked to Times Square to watch him in what became a carnival atmosphere.

138

(UPI)

By the second sleepless day Tripp began to experience intense fatigue. After about five days he needed a stimulant to stay awake. On the third day he began to have visual illusions and hallucinations. He saw cobwebs in his shoes. He imagined that specks on the table were live insects, and he thought he saw a rabbit in his booth. He began to have trouble remembering things. After being awake for 100 hours, he could no longer perform psychological tests that required attention and mental problem solving. He was unable to recite the alphabet. His mental functions deteriorated rapidly, and after 170 hours simple tests became torture for him and for the psychologists testing him.

By the fifth day Tripp's personality began to grow disorganized, and his hallucinations became more grotesque. He saw a tweed coat as a suit of furry worms. He claimed that a nurse was dripping saliva, and that the tie of one of the scientists was jumping. After about 150 waking hours, Tripp became disoriented, and wondered who and where he was. In order to explain his bizarre experiences, he developed delusions that he was the victim of a sadistic conspiracy designed to test his limits. Although he appeared to be awake, his brain waves sometimes resembled those that occur during deep sleep. Somehow he managed to marshal his resources during his daily 5 P.M. to 8 P.M. show, and neither his listeners nor casual onlookers were ever aware of his private torment.

On the morning of the final day, during an examination performed by a neurologist, Tripp concluded that the doctor was really an undertaker who was about to bury him alive. He jumped from the examination table and raced for the door with several doctors in hot pursuit.

With some persuasion Tripp managed to get through the final day and then sank into deep sleep for 13 hours. When he awoke, his mental anguish and disorientation had disappeared, and he was able to solve mental problems. He was slightly depressed for the next three months; in other respects his functioning returned to normal. However, neither Peter Tripp nor the scientists who witnessed his ordeal will forget the nightmare of his 200 sleepless hours.

Politicians and diplomats must often ignore the effects of "jet lag" in order to fulfil the duties of office. Here, Vice-President Walter Mondale makes a brief statement upon his arrival at the Cologne-Bonn military airport in Germany. (UPI)

cycles per second. This is called an *alpha* rhythm. As we drop into light sleep, the alpha rhythm is replaced by the fast, irregular rhythm of stage 1, which is similar to the rhythm for an active state of wakefulness. As sleep progresses toward stage 4, the brain waves become progressively slower and larger in amplitude. The EEG records the simultaneous electrical activity of billions of brain cells, and the changes in wave patterns from stage 1 to stage 4 reflect an in-

creasing synchronization in the electrical "firing" of those cells.

In 1953 sleep researchers Eugene Aserinsky and Nathaniel Kleitman discovered a fifth sleep stage, which begins about an hour after we fall asleep and occurs approximately every 90 minutes thereafter. The EEG pattern for this stage resembles the pattern for stage 1, but it also involves rapid eye movements (REMs) that occur about 20 times per second. Aserinsky and Kleitman found that individuals who were awakened during REM periods almost always reported that they had been dreaming. This was a major discovery, for it opened the door for research that has yielded great insights into the nature of sleep and dreaming.

REMs and dreaming

Infants spend about 50 percent of their sleeping hours in REM sleep. This proportion drops to about 25 percent by ages 5 to 9 and continues at about this level throughout adult life. Adults have about five REM periods each night. These become progressively longer as the night wears on and may last as long as 60 minutes (Dement, 1974). Subjects awakened during REM sleep report having been dreaming about 80 percent of the time, whereas subjects awakened during non-REM sleep report that they have been

Figure 5.2 Stages of sleep as they appear on the electroencephalograph (EEG). Note how the brain waves become larger and slower as sleep becomes deeper. Note also that the pattern for REM sleep is similar to that for stage 1.

Awake
One
Two
Three
1 Sec
Four
REM sleep

BOX 5.2

Psychoanalytic dream interpretation

People have always searched for meaning in their dreams. But in the twentieth century, Sigmund Freud's theories have had the greatest impact on the way in which we interpret our dreams. Because of his conviction that dreams allow our unconscious thoughts and desires to slip by our defenses in disguised form, Freud regarded dreams as "the royal road to the knowledge of the unconscious activities of the mind."

Analysts distinguish between the *manifest content* of a dream, the story or symbols that the dreamer reports, and the *latent content,* or the true psychological meaning of the dream. The process by which the latent content is transformed for defensive purposes into the manifest content is called *dream work.* In dream interpretation analysts try to search out the symbolic meaning of dreams, often by asking patients to free-associate to various aspects of them.

The following dream, for example, was analyzed as a manifestation of the classic struggle between dangerous impulses and restraining defenses that takes place within every person. The two "people" in the dream are really two sides of the dreamer.

I am walking, holding a leash in my hand, to which is attached a young man, who is very sweet and docile. All of a sudden, he turns into a ferocious beast, threatening to destroy me. I grab hold of him, and we attempt to fight, but it becomes apparent neither of us can win: the best I can do is keep him from destroying me (Whitman and Kaufmann, 1973, p. 94).

In helping their patients interpret dreams, analysts focus on dream symbols. Some common symbols and the meanings assigned to them by psychoanalytic theory are presented. Note that many are sexual symbols, because sexual instincts are of great importance in psychoanalytic theory.

Manifest symbol	Latent meaning
Bath	Birth
Room	Woman
Box	Uterus
Woods and thickets	Pubic hair
Tooth extraction, baldness	Castration
Balloon, airplane	Erection
Elongated objects (e.g., pencils, snakes, telephone poles)	Penis
Playing with children	Masturbation
Fruit	Breast
Climbing stairs; riding a horse	Intercourse; masturbation

dreaming only about 14 percent of the time. Because we spend about 25 percent of our sleeping hours in REM sleep, it is likely that most of us dream far more than we realize. Although some individuals can recall their dreams quite well, others cannot. At present, researchers do not know the reasons for these differences, but they are working to find them.

Typically, bodily responses during REM sleep are not directly related to the content of dreams. A recent study showed, however, a high degree of correspondence between eye movements and subjects' descriptions of what they had been "looking at" in their dreams immediately before being awakened (Thompson, 1976). Interestingly, the time sequencing of recorded and reported eye movements were of the same duration as they would have been had they occurred in a waking state. This suggests that, at least in some instances, the duration of events in dreaming corresponds to their duration in an awake state.

Males of all ages, including infants, commonly have penile erections during REM periods, whether or not the dream is a sexual one. These erections are caused by nerves that are activated during REM sleep, and not by urinary bladder pressure, as many people assume. Although muscle tone decreases during REM periods, the nervous system appears to be quite active, and sleepers often show rapid fluctuations in their breathing and heart rates.

In our dreams there is often vigorous activity, such as running, jumping, or struggling. During this time our bodies remain almost motionless, but recordings of brain activity show that the motor cortex of the brain seems to be "acting out" the dream. The reason we seldom awake to find ourselves on the floor or on the wall is that we have a brain mechanism that blocks nerve impulses to the muscles at the level of the spinal cord. But although our skeletal muscles are essentially paralyzed, we may be quite aroused mentally and emotionally during REM sleep.

Why do we dream? We have sought for centuries to understand the meaning of our dreams. (See Box 5.2.) An even more basic question is why we dream at all. Scientists do not yet have a definitive answer to this question. A number of theories have been advanced. Some have suggested that dreams serve as a means of releasing mental tension, solving problems, resolving conflicts, and compensating for things that are lacking in our waking lives. Experiments have shown that a rise in REM sleep occurs after stressful experiences. Others have suggested that dreaming permits deeper sleep and more complete rest. There is also evidence that REM sleep aids in establishing memories (see Box 5.3). Whatever the reason, we seem to have a definite need to dream. When subjects are prevented from dreaming for several nights by being awakened each time they enter a REM phase, they spend more time in REM sleep on subsequent nights, as if to catch up on their dreaming. They also tend to slip into REM phases much sooner after they go to sleep. This "REM rebound effect" suggests that dreaming may have important adaptive functions, and researchers around the world are seeking to solve the mystery of dreaming.

Can we control our dreams? If dreams are indeed a means of releasing tensions and solving problems, it would be to our advantage to be able to influence the content of our dreams. Researchers have found that it is possible to influence dream content by giving subjects emphatic instructions to dream on a specified topic throughout the night (Barber and Hahn,

1966). Suggestions given to subjects immediately before they go to sleep may also be effective in causing subjects to awaken at the beginning of their dreams or at the end of their dreams (Tart, 1963).

More studies are needed to expand and clarify these findings. It may be possible to discover precise methods (such as by thinking of a particular topic immediately before drifting off to sleep) that will enable us to influence the content of our dreams, the point at which we awaken, and perhaps the amount of time we dream at night.

Hypnagogic and hypnopompic imagery

Have you ever felt as if someone were talking to you just as you were falling asleep, even though no one was in the room? Have you ever imagined that the alarm clock was buzzing as you were just waking up, even though you had not set it? The intermediate state between wakefulness and sleep is called *hypnagogic*, and that between sleep and full wakefulness is called *hypnopompic*. During these times we sometimes experience sudden, vivid images that we produce without conscious control. Often their content is bizarre and frightening.

Not a great deal is known about these odd experiences. One survey study (McKellar, 1957) reported that in a sample of 182 students, 63 percent reported experiencing hypnagogic imagery, whereas 21 percent reported hypnopompic images. Most subjects reported that they had these experiences only occasionally, but a few reported that they had them regularly.

We can experience these images or sensations through any of our senses, but auditory and visual experiences are the most common ones. Many people report hypnagogic sensations of hearing their names called or hearing music, which often wakes them up. The most common type of hypnagogic imagery is the "faces in the dark" that sometimes terrify children (and some adults) as they are falling asleep. The faces are often distorted or brightly colored.

Hypnagogic images are usually of short duration and may occur in rapid succession. Unlike dreams, they usually have no theme, and they are typically unrelated to our ongoing thoughts and concerns. However, we do sometimes have kinesthetic or muscular images that are related to our day's activities.

141

BOX 5.3

Sleep for the memory

According to Boston Psychiatrist Chester Pearlman, evidence from both Europe and America is making 1976 "The Year of REM Sleep." Scientists have long known that REM (for the rapid eye movement during periods of dream sleep, which occur three to five times a night in 20-min. segments) serves crucial needs. One of those needs, Pearlman told the Paris conference, has now been clearly identified: REM dreaming is essential to consolidate memories—no dreaming, no long-term memory.

Some ten years ago, French Psychologists Vincent Bloch and Pierre Leconte showed that laboratory rats forgot how to do certain things if deprived of REM sleep after training. In a similar experiment by Pearlman, a rat that had mastered an intricate system of avoiding electric shocks to get food was deprived of REM sleep and then starved to death when tests were repeated.

Among other things, the evidence indicates that the student who stays up all night cramming for an exam is making a mistake. Says Pearlman: "You introduce a lot of facts that you really can't learn, because staying awake prevents it. The next day you won't be able to remember any of it, and you certainly will not be able to use any of it in the future—it is not part of you." A group of researchers at the University of Ottawa showed the same role of sleep in integrating recently learned material into long-term memory: among students enrolled in an intensive language course, those who were learning had an increase in REM sleep; those who were unable to learn had no such increase. (Reprinted by permission from *Time*, The Weekly Newsmagazine; Copyright Time Inc. 1976.)

For example, people who have been driving cars all day may feel as if they are still moving as they fall asleep in bed.

Hypnopompic images are reported less often than are hypnagogic ones. Frequently, they anticipate the activities of the day, as when a person "hears" an unset alarm clock on a weekend.

Individuals sometimes attribute their hypnagogic and hypnopompic experiences to supernatural causes or to telepathy. Those interested in spiritualism frequently interpret these images as messages from the spirit world. As we noted earlier, hypnopompic images are often linked to anticipations about the coming day, so that those who believe in ESP may interpret them as instances of precognition. Finally, some individuals have viewed these experiences as pathological symptoms and have sought psychiatric help.

These images that visit us in the twilight states between wakefulness and sleep are evidently quite normal, common occurrences. But by studying their causes, we may also obtain a better understanding of abnormal phenomena, such as hallucinations.

HYPNOSIS

For several hundred years hypnosis has been a fascinating topic to many people. The idea of control over other people through hypnotic power has been popularized, and often sensationalized, in books, plays, and movies. We are all familiar with the stereotype of a hypnotized person moving about in a zombielike trance and doing the will of a sinister and evil hypnotist, and with the fantastic "feats" performed by stage hypnotists. Given the widespread publicity that hypnosis has received and the number of years it has been with us, it may surprise you to learn that a controversy still rages among scientists as to what hypnosis is and how it works. Experimental research is providing partial answers to these questions. You may find some of them a bit surprising.

Animal magnetism, mesmerism, and hypnosis

During the eighteenth century a Viennese physician named Anton Mesmer became famous (and apparently wealthy) as a result of a series of magical cures of physical and psychological afflictions. He claimed that these cures were brought about by magnetic forces that radiated from the planets. He treated his patients by exposing them to magnetic objects and fluids in order to restore their "bodily harmony," and called this technique *mesmerism*. Hundreds of patients flocked to his clinic in Paris, and many successful cures were reported. (See Box 5.4.) It apparently never occurred to Mesmer that these "cures" might be the products of suggestion or expectation. However, this possibility did occur to two scientific commissions appointed by the French government, which concluded that Mesmer's "magnetic" cures were a hoax. Moreover, the commissions were concerned that women could be seduced easily while under the influence of these "mysterious" forces. Mesmer's clinic was closed down, and the practice of mesmerism was declared illegal in France.

But James Braid, a Scottish surgeon, was interested by the fact that patients undergoing mesmerism often went into a trance in which they appeared to be oblivious to their surroundings. In 1842 he decided that mesmerism was a state of "nervous sleep" that the subject entered as a result of concentrated attention rather than as a result of magnetic forces. He noted that individuals who entered this "nervous sleep" became highly responsive to verbal suggestions. Braid renamed the phenomenon *hypnosis*, for the Greek god of sleep, Hypnos.

In the mid-1800s hypnosis began to be used for medical purposes. James Esdaile, a Scottish surgeon, performed nearly 300 major operations in India using only hypnosis as an anesthetic. The remarkable results he reported excited many physicians, but the subsequent discovery of new anesthetic drugs limited the further use of hypnosis for that purpose.

In 1885 Sigmund Freud went to Paris to study with Jean Charcot, an eminent neurologist who had begun demonstrations of hypnosis some seven years earlier. Freud used the technique to uncover unconscious material in hysterical patients and to convince these patients that their condition was improving. But because the results of hypnosis were unpredictable and because it seemed to foster dependency in his patients, Freud eventually became disenchanted with hypnosis and gave it up in favor of the technique of free association, in which pa-

Figure 5.3 The sinister side of hypnotism has been popularized in fiction and movies. In the silent film classic *The Cabinet of Dr. Caligari*, the evil hypnotist exercised absolute control over his zombielike subject. (Culver)

tients report every thought that enters their minds.

Much of the scientific knowledge we now have regarding hypnosis has been gained in the last 20 years. Controlled research has been made possible by the development of tests of hypnotic susceptibility. These tests or scales contain standard instructions and suggestions that investigators read to subjects (e.g., "You cannot move your arm.") Each item involves a different suggested behavior, and subjects receive a "pass" or "fail" on each one, depending on whether or not they respond in a certain way. The total hypnotic susceptibility score is based on the number of "passes."

Hypnotic susceptibility scales make it possible to study experimentally the effects of a variety of situational, procedural, and subject factors on hypnotic

143

BOX 5.4

A visit to Mesmer's baquet

The patients who came to Mesmer's clinic were treated in a *baquet,* a trough around which more than 30 persons could be magnetized simultaneously. The bottom of the trough was covered with iron filings, other minerals, and bottles. The patients were tied to the *baquet* with cords, and instructed to join hands. Mesmer, adorned in impressive robes, paced through the crowd from time to time touching the bodies of patients with an iron rod, placing his hands on their abdomens, or magnetizing them with his eyes. The following description of the effects of mesmerism was written by a visitor to the *baquet:*

> Some patients remain calm, and experience nothing; others cough, spit, feel slight pain, a local or general heat, and fall into sweats; others are agitated and tormented by convulsions. These convulsions are remarkable for their number, duration, and force, and have been known to persist for more than three hours. They are characterized by involuntary, jerking movements in all the limbs, and in the whole body, by contraction of the throat, by twitchings in the . . . [abdominal] regions, by dimness and rolling of the eyes, by piercing cries, tears, hiccoughs, and immoderate laughter. They are preceded or followed by a state of languor or dreaminess, by a series of digressions, and even by stupor. Patients are seen to be absorbed in the search for one another, rushing together, smiling, talking affectionately, and endeavouring to modify their cries. They are all so submissive to the magnetizer that even when they appear to be in a stupor, his voice, a glance, or sign will rouse them from it. It is impossible not to admit, from all these results, that some great force acts upon and masters the patients, and that this force appears to reside in the magnetizer. This convulsive state is termed the crisis. It has been observed that many women and few men are subject to such crises; that they are only established after the lapse of two or three hours, and that when one is established, others soon and successively begin . . .

> Young women were so much gratified by the crisis, that they begged to be thrown into it anew; they followed Mesmer through the hall and confessed that it was impossible not to be warmly attached to the magnetizer's person. (Binet and Fere, 1901, pp. 9–11)

susceptibility. The test items can be administered either with or without previous hypnotic induction instructions, so that it is possible to compare the behaviors and experiences of hypnotized and non-hypnotized subjects.

Hypnotic induction

Hypnotists typically begin their sessions by asking their subjects to stare at a stationary or moving object, suggesting in a soothing voice that their eyelids are becoming heavy, that they are relaxing and becoming hypnotized, and that they will find it easy to comply with the suggestions of the hypnotist. In experimental settings this "hypnotic induction" lasts for about 15 minutes.

If the subjects are willing to be hypnotized, they appear relaxed and drowsy and become responsive to test suggestions from the hypnotist. Afterward they report changes in bodily sensations and claim that they have been hypnotized.

Certain procedures seem to increase the subject's responsiveness to the hypnotist's suggestions. Researchers hypothesize that these procedures encourage positive attitudes about being hypnotized, which increase both the subjects' motivation to become hypnotized and their expectations of being able to do so.

Defining the situation as hypnosis

Almost all hypnotists tell their subjects that they are going to be hypnotized. By clearly defining the situation in this way and by suggesting relaxation and

144

A late eighteenth-century Dodd engraving of an "animal magnetizer" putting his patient into a "crisis." (National Library of Medicine)

sleep, hypnotists can lead their subjects to expect that they will respond to suggestions.

The importance of beliefs and expectations for hypnosis was shown in a study conducted by Martin Orne (1959) of the University of Pennsylvania. During a classroom demonstration college students were told that when individuals were hypnotized, they frequently exhibited "catalepsy (stiffening of the muscles) of the nondominant hand." (Actually, catalepsy of the hand rarely, if ever, occurs spontaneously in hypnosis.) An accomplice of the lecturer was then hypnotized and, sure enough, he "spontaneously" exhibited the cataleptic response. When subjects who had seen the demonstration were later hypnotized, 55 percent of them exhibited the catalepsy spontaneously without any suggestion from the

hypnotist. Of a group of control subjects who saw a demonstration without the catalepsy act, not one exhibited the behavior when they were hypnotized later.

Removing fears and encouraging cooperation

Individuals with a negative attitude toward hypnosis or who fear being hypnotized are quite unresponsive to hypnotic suggestions. Many induction procedures include procedures designed to remove fears about loss of control or consciousness.

Subjects are also told that if they cooperate, they will have interesting experiences. Most subjects feel that their responsiveness to the hypnotists's suggestions is desired and expected, and that if they resist they will disappoint the hypnotist and be labeled uncooperative. Thus considerable social pressure to comply with the suggestions exists in most hypnotic induction settings.

Linking suggestions with actual experiences

During induction, experienced hypnotists link their suggestions with actual events. For example, knowing full well that subjects' eyes will begin to water after they stare intently at a stationary target for awhile, a hypnotist may say, "As you become hypnotized, your eyes will become heavier and heavier. Soon they will begin to water." Likewise, hypnotists may phrase their suggestions in certain ways to avoid failures and to ensure that subjects continue to expect that they can be hypnotized. Rather than saying, "Your eyes are so tired that you can't open them. Go ahead, try," a hypnotist will say, "Your eyes are so tired that it would be very difficult for you to open them . . . so difficult that you don't even feel like trying."

Hypnotic induction procedures incorporate many of the strategies that have been shown to foster high motivation, expectations, and compliance with requests and suggestions in nonhypnotic situations. Box 5.5 describes some of the strategies that stage hypnotists use in their theatrical demonstrations.

Some hypnosis investigators, most notably Theodore Barber (1972), have argued that so-called hypnotic phenomena actually result from common psychological factors, such as suggestion and expectancy, rather than from a unique state of con-

145

BOX 5.5

Secrets of the stage hypnotist

Much of the mystique that surrounds hypnosis is created by the sometimes astounding demonstrations performed by stage hypnotists. "Average" individuals selected from the audience often perform startling feats after they have been placed into a hypnotic "trance." Spectators leave these demonstrations with a firm belief in the "powers" of the hypnotist. On closer examination, however, it becomes clear that the hypnotist's powers are not dependent on a hypnotic trance, but on his or her knowledge and use of certain psychological principles.

Stage hypnotists select their subjects very carefully by giving several test suggestions to individuals who volunteer to come up to the stage. Only those who pass all the test suggestions are allowed to remain on stage.

The hypnotist then begins an induction procedure, stating that hypnosis is about to be performed, which increases everyone's (including the subject's) expectations that unusual events and behaviors are about to occur. During the induction the hypnotist carefully notes the subjects' readiness to respond to suggestions. He or she then asks the one who appears to be most highly motivated and extroverted to perform some act that is relatively easy but that the subject would not ordinarily perform on his or her own initiative (e.g., "You are a rooster; the sun is coming up, and you are flapping your wings and crowing"). Subjects find it difficult not to comply; they know the audience and the hypnotist are expecting them to perform, they are in a submissive role in relation to the hypnotist, and they have a perfect excuse to engage in silly behavior: They are "hypnotized." Audience reactions reinforce all these feelings. Soon all the subjects get into the act and begin competing with one another for the best performance.

The audience actually hears only a portion of the interaction between hypnotist and subject. The hypnotist makes numerous whispered requests. For example, he or she may whisper, "Sit down and close your eyes, please." As the subject complies, the hypnotist stands over him or her, makes elaborate hand motions, and loudly declares, "You are entering a deep hypnotic trance," to impress the audience with his or her amazing ability to hypnotize someone quickly.

Most hypnotism shows contain several "amazing feats" performed by "entranced" subjects. One is the so-called human plank routine. A male subject is placed between two chairs, one chair beneath the calves of his legs, the other beneath his shoulders. He is told that his body is absolutely rigid, and an attractive girl is asked to stand on his chest. The audience doesn't know is that an average man sus- attributes the man's ability to support the woman to his "profound somnambulistic trance." What the audience doesn't know is that an average man suspended in this manner can support at least 300 pounds on his chest with little discomfort and no need of a hypnotic "trance."

Let us consider one final item from the stage hypnotist's repertoire of "astounding hypnotic feats." In a demonstration of "anesthesia," the hypnotist tells subjects that their hands are numb and insensitive. The audience gasps as the hypnotist then takes a match or cigarette lighter and places the flame close to or on the subject's outstretched palm and moves the flame back and forth. In reality, as long as the hypnotist moves the flame, the subject cannot be burned. He or she will experience the sensation of heat, but there will be no pain.

Because of the psychological pressures for compliance in hypnotism stage shows, proficient stage hypnotists know that if they exclude uncooperative subjects, then they can carry on an entertaining show, regardless of whether or not their subjects are really "hypnotized" or are actually experiencing the things hypnotists suggest to them.

sciousness, or trance. Armed with the results of well-controlled laboratory studies, Barber and his colleagues have made some telling points in their criticism of "trance" theories. We now examine these.

Hypnotic behaviors and experiences

Most of us are fascinated by hypnosis because we have either seen or heard about the remarkable physical and behavioral changes that it can bring about. The physical and psychological effects of hypnosis can be so striking and profound that they defy explanation in terms of "everyday" psychological principles. Or do they? Let us examine some of the effects more closely.

Perceptual distortions

Hypnosis can produce marked perceptual distortions. Researchers have reported instances of temporary deafness, blindness, and visual hallucinations under hypnosis. For example, hypnotized subjects who are told that they can no longer hear reportedly do not react to unexpected sounds, insults, and so on. However, there is evidence to indicate that at least some "hypnotically deaf" persons can really still hear. To demonstrate this, Barber and Calverley (1964) used a method known as *delayed auditory feedback*. In this technique subjects speak into a microphone and hear their voice through a set of earphones. However, transmission of the voice is delayed for a fraction of a second. When individuals with normal hearing are exposed to delayed auditory feedback, they typically begin to stammer and to mispronounce words. Of course, deaf persons do not react in this manner. Barber and Calverley gave hypnotic induction instructions to subjects and suggested that they could no longer hear. When these subjects were tested on delayed auditory feedback, they showed the same speech distortions as did nonhypnotized control subjects.

Some hypnotized subjects report visual hallucinations so real that they actually believe the object is present. In one recent study 5 percent of a group of hypnotized subjects stated that they saw a suggested object and believed it was actually present. However, 3 percent of nonhypnotized subjects who were given "task-motivational instructions" in which they were asked to try as hard as possible to experience the

suggestions of the hypnotist also reported actually "seeing" objects. Results such as these, coupled with methodological shortcomings in many of the original studies reporting perceptual distortions, have led researchers to question whether such perceptual phenomena are really brought about by a hypnotic "trance."

Physiological effects

Striking physiological effects have been reported in hypnotized persons. These include improved visual acuity in near-sighted individuals, inhibition of allergic responses, curing of warts, and increases in stomach acidity. However, recent well-controlled studies have shown that nonhypnotized control subjects who are given the same suggestions can exhibit all the same effects. For example, Graham and Leibowitz (1972) reported that training in relaxing the muscles around their eyes resulted in equal but small increases in visual acuity in both hypnotic and control subjects. This suggests that in previous demonstrations in which nonhypnotized control groups were not used, relaxation produced by the hypnotic induction instructions may have been responsible for improvements in visual performance.

Another experiment investigated the effects of hypnosis on 13 subjects who were allergic to two poisonous trees. Each subject was blindfolded and told that one arm was being touched by leaves from a harmless tree when in fact it was being touched by leaves from one of the poisonous trees. Four out of five hypnotized subjects and seven out of eight nonhypnotized controls had no allergic reaction. Next, the subject's other arm was rubbed with leaves from a harmless tree and he or she was told that the leaves were poisonous. All subjects, both the hypnotized subjects and the controls, responded to this suggestion with mild to severe allergic reactions (Ikemi and Nakagawa, 1962). These results demonstrate the powerful effects of simply imagining and believing that an experience is occurring.

Several experiments have shown that hypnotized individuals can induce localized changes in their skin temperature. In one study experienced hypnotic subjects were able to raise their skin temperature in one hand and simultaneously lower it in the other. (See Figure 5.4.) Unhypnotized controls were unable to effect the same changes. An important factor in

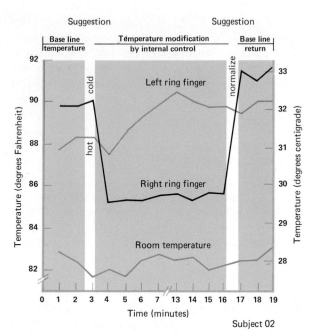

Figure 5.4 Change in skin temperature after hypnotic suggestion. (After Maslach et al., 1972.)

then they can probably tolerate extensive internal cutting with little discomfort. Major operations, such as amputating limbs, removing thyroid glands, removing appendixes, cutting and draining the gallbladder, removing glands in the neck and groin, and removing the female breast have been performed using only a local anesthetic to desensitize the skin. It is interesting to note that in the majority of cases of major surgery reportedly performed under hypnosis, local anesthetics were used to deaden the skin in the area of the incision. In addition, there is evidence that suggestions for anesthesia and surgical pain relief given when patients are *not* hypnotized may at times be as effective as those given under hypnosis (Evans and Paul, 1970).

We should not conclude, however, that hypnosis has no value in increasing pain tolerance. The effects are undoubtedly real. What is at issue is what produces the effects. By reducing anxiety and fear; by

the control shown by the hypnotized subjects may be the practice in concentration and imagination that they received in their previous hypnotic training. Reportedly, they changed their skin temperature by vividly imagining events such as having one hand in ice and the other under a heat lamp (Maslach, Marshall, and Zimbardo, 1972).

Increased pain tolerance

Hypnosis has been used with striking success to control pain during surgery since the nineteenth century.

At face value, clinical reports of surgery under hypnosis are most impressive. Most of us assume that the pain associated with cutting into internal organs is excruciating and would be impossible to tolerate without the use of drugs or some other special technique to inhibit pain. Actually, it appears that, with the exception of the skin, which is very sensitive, most tissues of the body are rather insensitive to *cutting* (although they are sensitive to other sensations, such as stretching or pressure). If patients can tolerate the initial incision through the skin,

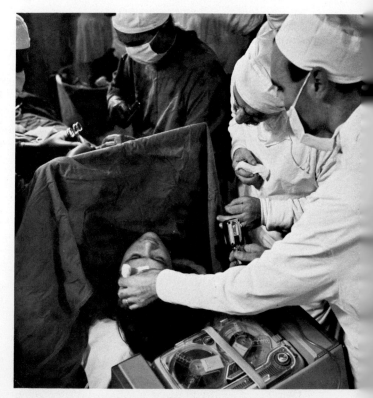

This patient is undergoing an appendectomy under the influence of hypnosis. No anesthestics were used before or during surgery. (UPI)

establishing positive attitudes, motivations, and expectations about stressful situations; by distracting patients from their pain; and by exposing them to believable suggestions that they will not experience pain, hypnosis may be quite effective as a way of increasing tolerance to pain. But perhaps almost the same things could be said about placebos, acupuncture, faith healing, and other methods for pain reduction without drugs. Psychologists are interested in understanding the psychological processes that underlie the positive effects of all these methods.

Performance of antisocial acts

We have all read fictional accounts of people who perform criminal acts "against their will" while under the influence of an evil hypnotist. Is there any factual basis for such accounts?

In an experiment conducted by Orne and Evans (1965), six "good" hypnotic subjects (defined in terms of responses to prior test suggestions) were given a deep hypnotic induction, then ordered to throw acid in the face of the experimenter. (The experimenter was protected by a pane of invisible glass.) Five of the six subjects threw the acid. This seems to suggest that hypnotized individuals can be made to commit acts they otherwise would not perform. Fortunately, however, the investigators included several control groups in the experiment, which shed a somewhat different light on the results. In one control condition, six "poor" hypnotic subjects were told to pretend they were hypnotized and were then ordered to carry out the "antisocial" act. All six immediately threw acid at the experimenter. Another unhypnotized control group of six subjects was simply ordered to throw the acid. Five of the six subjects complied, the same proportion as in the group that was hypnotized.

In another experiment (Calverley and Barber, 1965) half of a group of nursing students was hypnotized, and the whole group was then told to sign slanderous statements about their supervisor that were addressed to the assistant superintendent of the hospital. Nonhypnotized subjects signed the statements as often as the hypnotized subjects. Several of the subjects who had received the hypnotic induction justified their signing of the statements by claiming that because they were hypnotized, they were not responsible for what they had done.

The results of these and other studies suggest that hypnosis does not significantly increase the likelihood that subjects will perform harmful or bizarre acts. Whether subjects are hypnotized or not, if they trust and want to please the person who is giving orders, they will often comply with requests to perform unusual acts. It is also important to remember that when individuals believe they are hypnotized, they are likely to feel less personal responsibility for their behavior and therefore be less inhibited.

Explanations of hypnosis

If all this evidence showing the similarity between hypnotic and nonhypnotic behavior is valid, then what is hypnosis and how does it produce its effects? The best place to begin to answer this question is by stating what hypnosis is *not*. It is not sleep, nor is it any other state of consciousness with specific physiological properties. The EEGs of subjects under hypnosis are not like those for subjects in any of the recognized stages of sleep. Rather, they are the same as those for subjects in a waking state, and they change continuously, depending on the activities the person is engaging in. No physiological measure shows a unique pattern for hypnosis that would enable us to differentiate reliably between hypnotized and nonhypnotized subjects. This failure has important implications. If we wish to say that a trance is the scientific explanation for hypnotic behavior, we must be able to define and measure it in some way other than in terms of the behaviors it is assumed to produce. Otherwise we find ourselves enmeshed in circular reasoning of the following type: "Why does the hypnotic subject behave as he does? Because he is in a trance. How do we know he's in a trance? Because he behaves as he does."

Because there is no physiological evidence that hypnosis is a special state of consciousness and because hypnotized and nonhypnotized control subjects often behave in identical ways, psychologists have sought to understand hypnosis in terms of other psychological processes. Contemporary theorists emphasize the importance of *role playing* and *imagination* in hypnotic behavior.

Role playing

A number of theorists have suggested that hypnosis involves "taking on" the role of a hypnotized person.

149

In our culture most people have a general conception of the ways in which hypnotized individuals are supposed to behave. They are supposed to be responsive to suggestions, to listen carefully to the hypnotist, to have a trancelike appearance, and to lose their self-consciousness. Individuals who are motivated to conform to this role, who are free of fears and inhibitions, and who expect to be able to experience hypnosis are likely to adopt successfully the role of hypnotized subject and to experience the suggested effects.

Martin Orne has performed a number of experiments that support this role adoption theory. We discussed earlier the experiment in which subjects led to believe that the hypnotic role included "catalepsy of the nondominant hand" exhibited this behavior spontaneously when they were hypnotized. In another experiment young adult subjects were hypnotized and told that they were returning to the age of 6. The subjects exhibited childlike behaviors, but they also made many "mistakes." For example, they painted like children, But they spelled complex words perfectly. When asked the time of day, they looked at their wrists, even though they had not worn wrist watches at the age of 6 (O'Connell, Shor, and Orne, 1970). It was clear that their behaviors were imperfect attempts to play the role of themselves when they were 6. However, Orne also concluded that individuals who are hypnotized believe that they are actually *experiencing* what the hypnotist suggests rather than merely playacting.

Imagination

Hypnotic experiences seem to be the result of thought and imagination. If an individual is able to become actively involved in imagining, then it is *as if* the imagined events actually occur. During hypnosis this "as if" process is supported by the hypnotist's suggestions. When a hypnotist suggests to a subject that his or her arm feels heavy, the subject is likely to recall previous experiences in which his or her arm did feel heavy and to reexperience the sensations and feelings. Research has shown that imagining an event often produces the same bodily changes that occur during an actual event. For example, individuals who *imagine* that their legs are moving actually do have small but measurable movements in their legs (Arnold, 1946).

Research is revealing some of the ways in which cognitive events such as images are involved in hypnosis. Subjects who are most responsive to hypnotic suggestions tend to vividly imagine situations that would prompt them to behave in the suggested manner (Spanos, 1971). For example, a subject who is told that his or her arm is getting heavy might imagine weights being tied to the arm to pull it down. Researchers have found that subjects who are especially responsive to hypnotic suggestions have rich imaginative lives and become involved in the themes of their imagery. One responsive hypnotic subject reported the following experience after reading a novel:

> I identify myself with the character in 1984, with Winston Smith, who was tortured at the end, fearing rats. His head was in a cage and he felt he would have to submit. I *felt* the fear that he felt as it came closer, closer. Walking back from the Union after finishing the book, I had a problem relating myself to my present environment, to the stuff around me, for I was so entangled in the story that I had become exhausted. (J. R. Hilgard, 1970, p. 26)

Current theories about hypnosis emphasize the importance of role adoption, fantasy, and imagination. This cognitive-behavioral approach may enable psychologists to relate hypnosis to other areas of psychology in a more systematic fashion. Perhaps research on hypnosis will provide us with valuable insights into how we can use imagination more productively in other areas of our lives.

MEDITATION

Meditation has a long and far-reaching history; it has been performed throughout the world for centuries in connection with religious, military, and recreational activities. In the United States, however, most of the current interest in meditation has occurred during the past few decades. Transcendental meditation, a quasi-religious technique founded by the Maharishi Mahesh Yogi, may have as many as half a million disciples in this country practicing it daily. The increasing popularity of meditation seems to reflect a search for peace and harmony in a world that has become increasingly chaotic and stressful.

All types of meditation involve dwelling on a

The practice of transcendental meditation has caught on among all age groups. It is especially popular in big cities where stress is great. (Forsyth, Monkmeyer)

thought, a sensation, a word, an object, or some mental state. Some techniques are very *active* and require that practitioners make strenuous efforts to focus their attention on a specific thing. Certain Yoga techniques, for example, require that practitioners maintain specific postures and deliberately control their breathing or other bodily functions. Other meditation techniques, such as transcendental meditation (TM), are *passive* approaches. Practitioners remain in a quiet atmosphere and make a relaxed attempt to achieve a state of inner peace. Zen practitioners seek a state of *satori*, or "enlightenment," which involves simultaneous feelings of "nothingness" and "oneness" with all of nature. In the state of *satori* there are no boundaries between the person and the material world.

Practitioners of TM close their eyes and concen-trate their attention on the imagined sound of a *mantra*, a word chosen for them by their TM teacher that they are not supposed to reveal to anyone else. Although followers of the Maharishi Mahesh Yogi claim that the individualized mantra is of vital importance and that it should be nonsensical so that it does not distract the practitioner, there is no direct evidence to support these claims. Teachers may assign mantras, such as *hairdhign* or *aahnah,* but some meditators substitute personally meaningful words, such as *peace, love,* or *let go.*

Most passive techniques are practiced for two 20-minute periods each day, once in the morning and again before dinner. The results, practitioners claim, are astounding. Proponents of passive meditation techniques like TM report positive personality changes, improved interpersonal functioning, in-

151

BOX 5.6

One person's experience with meditation

The following account was written by a 22-year-old female college student who had been practicing TM for 16 months:

In April, 1966, I had to leave college to enter a mental hospital. I was hypertense, overemotional, self-destructive, and was putting on weight extremely fast. I left the hospital not really able to function or to relate to reality at all. For a year or two I lived alone and took a lot of drugs—put on 35 pounds in less than three months. After that I was never able to lose the weight, as it was a result of tension as well as of an emptiness inside. I did not know myself, I did not respect myself,

and felt that anything that happened to me didn't matter—if it was bad, fine—if good, I destroyed it because I felt I was not worth it. I really felt I was very sick for a long time after I left the hospital. In February, 1968—after almost 2 years of doing nothing—I began TM. Within three months I lost over thirty pounds and felt physically and mentally as if I were able to move again. I was able to be with people, to begin to have some self-respect, and to have circumstances work out for me—the support of nature. Last February I returned to school, came out first in all but one class and had to do very little work even so. I feel great about everything—there are still hassles and some uncertainty but I feel confident about my ability to do whatever is necessary and to enjoy a lot of it. Actually I can't really remember what it was like to be so unhappy and incompetent, and I don't think much about it now. I expect that everything will keep improving as it has.

This sounds a bit dramatic, but I feel that the benefits I have received through meditation are more than dramatic—to my family, it is almost incredible. (Kannelakos and Lukas, 1974, p. 129)

---

creased energy and mental efficiency, and reduction in tension and stress. (See Box 5.6.)

A growing number of researchers are investigating these extraordinary TM claims. Although some of them appear to be valid, others have yet to be proved scientifically.

Physiological effects

EEG recordings made during meditation show brain wave patterns typically associated with relaxation and drowsiness (Wallace, 1970). The results of a recent study suggest that meditators may actually be in EEG sleep stages 2, 3, and 4 during up to 40 percent of their meditation time (Pagano, Rose, Stivers, and Warrenburg, 1976). Their metabolism becomes lower and there are 5 to 20 percent decreases in oxygen consumption. These are comparable to metabolic decreases that occur during deep sleep. There are also decreases in rate of respiration, heart rate, and blood lactate—a chemical associated with fatigue and anxiety (Wallace and Benson, 1972).

There is also some preliminary evidence that in-

dicates that meditation may increase the ability to adapt to stress. In one study meditators who were subjected to loud, unpleasant noises showed significantly faster drops in physiological arousal than did subjects in a control group of nonmeditators (Orme-Johnson, 1973).

The physiological responses of TM subjects suggest that meditation causes an increase in parasympathetic nervous activity, a decrease in sympathetic activity, or both. This results in a state of relaxation that is quite the opposite of the body's "fight or flight" response to danger and stress. (See "The Autonomic Nervous System" in Chapter 3.)

The physiological effects of extremely intense forms of meditation are not well known. Studies conducted in Japan with Zen monks have revealed some remarkable effects from Zen meditation, including the ability to remain so "open" to stimuli from the environment that there is no physiological adaptation or habituation to repetitive stimuli (Kasamatsu and Hirai, 1966). For example, subjects exposed to a loud noise typically exhibit physiological arousal responses that decrease over time as the stimulus is repeatedly presented. The Zen monks, however, did not show this normal adaptation response. Although those meditational techniques that have been investigated appear to have no harmful effects on the body, accounts such as the one in Box 5.7 raise the possibility that certain extreme and unusual forms may have unknown and possibly hazardous effects.

Herbert Benson of Harvard University has referred to the restful physiological state produced by meditation as the *relaxation response*. He suggests that a variety of techniques can produce this response, and he and his associates have developed and tested a simple and straightforward technique that appears to produce physiological effects similar to those of TM. (See Box 5.8.)

Effects on behavior and personality

Enthusiastic endorsements of meditation such as the one by the young woman in Box 5.7 suggest that meditation can cause strikingly positive changes in behavior and personality. But personal endorsements alone do not constitute acceptable scientific evidence; in recent years researchers have been attempting to substantiate the claims of meditation proponents with empirical research.

Giving up drugs

Several researchers have reported that meditation is associated with decreased use of illicit drugs. Moreover, they claim that the longer people practice meditation, the greater the change in their drug habits. These findings might have strong implications for combatting drug abuse in our society. Indeed, they have encouraged the U.S. Army to investigate TM as a possible solution for this problem.

TM proponents claim that people give up drugs because the changes in consciousness that occur through meditation are far more pleasant than those that occur with drugs. But there are other possible explanations. In order to begin TM, for example, practitioners must voluntarily abstain from drugs for two weeks. An individual's willingness to do this may indicate that he or she was ready to quit using drugs even before beginning meditation and that he or she was not highly dependent on drugs in the first place. There are also strong group pressures among

meditators to discontinue the use of drugs. Subjects beginning TM usually expect to be able to give them up, and their success in doing so may be as much the product of this positive expectation as of the effects of TM. Because no study has controlled for these factors, there is no scientific proof that TM can cure drug abuse.

Personality changes

Practitioners of TM frequently report increases in happiness, contentment, and ability to function effectively. In one study meditators were given a personality test before they began TM and again two months later; their pre- and posttest scores were then compared with those of a nonmeditating control group. The meditators showed significant positive changes on scales designed to measure self-acceptance, spontaneity, self-esteem, capacity for intimate contact, inner directedness, and other variables that measure "self-actualization." The nonmeditating control subjects showed no significant positive changes on any of the self-actualization scales (Seeman, Nidich, and Banta, 1972). Although this finding is encouraging, more research is needed to assess the stability of personality changes in meditators. Studies that use direct behavioral measures (rather than self-reports) of personal functioning are also needed.

Changes in intelligence and creativity

One of the main goals of TM is to increase "creative intelligence." This requires a global change in one's perception and understanding of the world. Although the concept of creative intelligence is difficult to define and measure operationally, several studies have been conducted on the cognitive functioning of meditators. (We know of no research that has studied changes in meditators' performance on well-established intelligence tests. Until these changes are studied, we cannot gauge the effects of meditation on intelligence.)

There is evidence that the effects of meditation on creativity depend on the requirements of the task. Researcher Gary Schwartz (1973) administered two measures of creativity to 16 teachers of meditation and to 16 controls. Meditators performed better than nonmeditators on several tasks that required spontaneous creativity, such as storytelling. But meditators

153

BOX 5.7

Yoga expert died of too deep meditation?

ANN ARBOR, Mich. (UPI). A pathologist says a yoga instructor who was found dead June 3 may have meditated so deeply his heart slowed down and cut off a sufficient flow of blood to his brain.

Robert Antosczyck, 29, was found dead in a yoga position used for deep meditation two days after he told friends he was going to attempt a state of "astro-projection" and did not want to be bothered.

Dr. Paul Gikas, a University of Michigan pathology professor, said "The Indian scientists I have consulted tell me that this form of meditation can be very dangerous if the person does not know what he is doing."

Other pathologists said they have been unable to detect any physical explanation for the man's death, but that if he did die from meditating, it may be a first in medical history.

Antosczyck's friends described astro-projection as the journey of one's soul through the "astral plane" of the universe.

"His death is a mystery to me," said his mother, Lillian Antosczyck, 53, of Detroit. "It's a mystery to the undertaker, to the doctor, everybody."

(*The Seattle Times,* Sunday, June 29, 1975)

BOX 5.8

A simple technique for producing the relaxation response

John Beary and Herbert Benson (1974) developed a meditative technique with four essential components:

1. *A mental device.* Choose a constant stimulus (e.g., a word, thought, or object) to direct your attention away from the environment.
2. *A passive attitude.* Disregard distracting thoughts and do not concern yourself with how well you are performing.
3. *Muscular relation.* Attempt to relax all your muscles and "go limp."
4. *A quiet environment.* Closing your eyes may be helpful. Make sure you are not disturbed by noises, images, or smells.

Beary and Benson then asked their subjects to proceed according to the following instructions:

1. Sit quietly in a comfortable position.
2. Close your eyes.
3. Deeply relax all your muscles, beginning at your feet and progressing up to your face. Keep them deeply relaxed.
4. As you breathe out, say the word *one* silently to yourself. For example, breathe *in . . . out,* "One:" *in . . . out,* "One." Continue until told to stop. (*Subjects did this for 12 minutes.*) Do not worry about whether you are succeeding in achieving a deep level of relaxation. Maintain a passive attitude and permit relaxation to occur at its own pace. If distracting thoughts do occur, ignore them and continue to repeat *one.*

Subjects learned the technique easily in about one hour of self-instruction and exhibited physiological changes comparable to those in TM. These changes did not occur when subjects simply rested with their eyes closed.

did not perform as well as the controls on tasks that required logical problem solving. Schwartz suggests that meditation may enhance the "germinal," spontaneous stages of creativity, but that too much meditation may interfere with logical and systematic thinking and actually decrease creative productivity. Schwartz's research also suggests that relaxed meditators perform well on creative tasks whose performance benefits from low levels of arousal, but that their performance declines on tasks that require a high level of arousal. More research on meditation is badly needed to determine what effects it has on cognitive functioning of all kinds.

DRUGS AND ALTERED EXPERIENCES

A drug is any chemical agent that affects human beings or other animals. This includes a wide variety of substances, from tobacco and vitamins to heroin and LSD. Our discussion focuses on drugs that produce changes in our consciousness and behavior.

Depressants

Alcohol

Alcohol has been used in virtually every society as a social relaxant for thousands of years. The cultural acceptance that it has attained masks the fact that, because it affects the lives of so many people, it is perhaps the most dangerous of all drugs.

Alcohol is often thought of as a stimulant because it seems to make people lively and uninhibited. In very low concentrations it does stimulate cellular activity in most organisms, from the simplest bacteria to the most complex mammals. And in moderate quantities it increases heart rate; slightly dilates blood vessels in the arms, legs, and skin; lowers blood pressure by a moderate amount; stimulates appetite; increases gastric secretion; and markedly stimulates urine output. Technically, however, alcohol is classified as a depressant, because it decreases the general level of activity of the central nervous system. The reactions are related not so much to the amount of alcohol consumed as to the concentration of alcohol in the blood. Unlike most other foods, alcohol does not have to be digested slowly before it reaches the bloodstream. Instead it passes directly through the walls of the stomach and small intestine and is absorbed immediately into the bloodstream and carried to the brain.

Because individuals vary they react to alcohol at varying levels of concentration. Table 5.1 shows typical relationships between blood-alcohol level and behavior for a 155-pound moderate drinker who rapidly consumes 90-proof whiskey on an empty stomach. These levels may be slightly higher if the drink is gin or vodka or if the drinker weighs much less than 155 pounds. Conversely, the level will be lower if the beverage is beer, wine, or a "mixed" noncarbonated drink; if the drinking is spaced out over a long period of time; and if the drinker weighs more than 155 pounds or eats solid foods while drinking.

We are all painfully aware of the fact that alcohol has a high potential for addiction and that with-

Table 5.1 Effects of alcohol consumption

Quantity of Whiskey	Percent Blood-Alcohol Level*	Resulting Behavior
3 oz. (2 "shots")	0.05	Sedation and tranquility
6 oz.	0.10	Loss of coordination
12 oz.	0.20	Obvious intoxication
15 oz.	0.30	Unconsciousness
30 oz.	0.50+	Possible death

*Blood-alcohol levels have become important for legal reasons. In most parts of the United States and in some European countries, an individual with a blood-alcohol level of 0.10 percent or more (in some places 0.15 percent or more) is considered legally intoxicated or "under the influence." A blood-alcohol level of 0.05 percent or less is the legal measure for sobriety and fitness to operate a motor vehicle.
From *Alcohol and Alcoholism*, 1972.

155

BOX 5.9

Profiles of persons differing in likelihood of having drinking problems

Profile of persons most likely to have no alcohol-related problems

Lowest rates of alcohol-related problems for respondents in a 1973 national survey were found among:

Women
Persons over 50
Widowed and married persons
Persons of Jewish religious affiliation
Residents of rural areas
Residents of the South
Persons with postgraduate educational levels
Persons who are mostly "wine drinkers"

Profile of persons with high problem rates

Highest rates of alcohol-related problems for respondents in a 1973 national survey were found among:

Men
Separated, single, and divorced persons (in that order)
Persons with no religious affiliation
Persons who are beer drinkers as compared with those who are mostly hard liquor or wine drinkers
Persons who were more likely (compared to other persons in the survey) to say:
"Drunkenness is usually *not* a sign of social irresponsibility."

and

"Drunkenness is usually a sign of just having fun."
(Based on *Alcohol and Health*, 1974, p. 26)

drawal symptoms can be severe when an alcoholic attempts to "go on the wagon." In addition, alcohol and nutritional deficits that frequently accompany its excessive use can produce irreversible tissue damage in the brain, the liver, and other organs.

The scope of the alcoholism problem. To many people the notion of an alcoholic individual conjures up visions of the typical Skid Row derelict: homeless, unkempt, unemployed and unemployable, sprawled on the sidewalk in a drunken stupor. Yet the alcoholic men of Skid Row (and many people on Skid Row are not alcoholics) make up a tiny fragment of the entire population of alcoholic and problem drinkers—probably less than 5 percent. At least 95 percent of the problem population consists of employed or employable, family-centered individuals. It has been estimated that more than 70 percent of them reside in respectable neighborhoods, live with their husbands or wives, try to send their children to college, belong to a country club, attend church, pay taxes, and continue to perform more or less effectively as bank presidents, housewives, farmers, salesmen, machinists, stenographers, teachers, clergymen, and physicians.

Although estimates vary, it is thought that approximately 75 percent of alcoholic individuals are men and 25 percent are women. The proportion of women has been steadily rising. For example, in the 1950s there were approximately five or six alcoholic men for every alcoholic woman. Many authorities on alcoholism have suggested that the increase may be more apparent than real, because during recent years there has been a growing willingness on the part of women with drinking problems to seek treatment. They may therefore be more visible than more numerous.

Because the great majority of persons who consume alcoholic beverages do so in a controlled manner, it would be useful to identify persons who are likely to develop drinking problems. Box 5.9 lists characteristics of persons who are prone to alcohol-related problems and those who are not.

Barbiturates

Barbiturates are also classified as depressants or sedatives. Nembutal ("yellow jacket"), seconal ("red-bird"), and phenobarbitol and amobarbital ("the

156

purple hearts'') slow muscle responses and reduce the general level of activity in the nervous system. Mild doses are effective as "sleeping pills." Higher doses, such as those used by addicts, trigger a period of excitation, followed later by slurred speech, loss of coordination, extreme depression, and severe impairment of memory and thinking. Overdoses, particularly when they are taken in conjunction with alcohol, may cause unconsciousness or even death.

Barbiturates ("downers") initially send users into a state of calmness and serenity. But if they are used in large doses, the effect often produces a temporary "high" followed by deep depression, loss of coordination, and severe impairment of memory and thought. Users can build up a *tolerance* for barbiturates (so that they need progressively larger doses to produce the same effect), and addicts may take as many as 50 sleeping pills a day to "get high."

Barbiturates are highly addictive, and sudden withdrawal symptoms in heavy users may be so severe that they cause death. It can require several months of gradual, supervised withdrawal for addicts to lose their physical dependence on these drugs.

Narcotic analgesics

Opium, morphine, and heroin

Opium, morphine, and heroin are part of a group known as *narcotic analgesics*. Morphine and heroin are both derived from opium. Narcotic analgesics act on the central and autonomic nervous systems and are used therapeutically to ease pain. Users often sink into a general state of euphoria, and lose much of their desire for sex or drink.

Heroin causes emotional rather than perceptual changes. Experienced users feel a "thrill" within several minutes of an injection. It resembles, they say, a sexual orgasm, except that the sensation is in their abdominal region rather than in their genital region. For a time users feel as if they are "on top of the world," with no worries, no concerns. They feel peaceful and nonaggressive. Their psychological

A heroin user "shoots up" with a solution made from heroin and water. The chemicals used to "cut" heroin (quinine and milk sugar) and the hypodermic needles used for injection are often impure or unsanitary and may cause serious illness. (Gatewood, Stock, Boston)

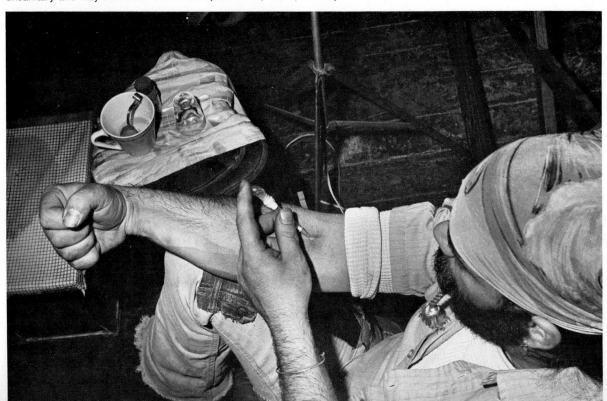

157

functions are not impaired, as they are with alcohol and barbiturates, and heroin users can perform well on certain kinds of skilled tasks.

But tolerance for and physiological and psychological dependence on narcotic analgesics develop quickly. Withdrawal symptoms are traumatic, and many addicts continue to "shoot up" in order to avoid them, even if they do not feel "high" any longer. The following description of withdrawal was made by a young woman who succeeded in "kicking" her heroin habit:

> It's like a terrible case of flu. Your joints move involuntarily. That's where the phrase "kick the habit" comes from. You jerk and twitch and you just can't control it. You throw up. You can't control your bowels either and this goes on for four or five days afterwards. For fifteen days afterwards, you can't sleep and you're gagging all the time and you cough up blood, because if you're on drugs, you can't eat and that's all there is to cough up.

Although heroin use does not seem to cause chronic tissue damage, there are many deaths from overdoses. Undoubtedly, some of these deaths are caused by impurities in "street" heroin and by taking combinations of drugs. Heroin use seems to be declining at present, but in the late 1960s it was a leading cause of death among Americans from 18 to 25 years of age. Because addicts always "mainline" the drug (inject it directly into a vein), dirty needles sometimes cause them to develop local infections or even hepatitis, which can be fatal.

Narcotic addiction. No one knows how many narcotics addicts there really are in the United States. During the mid-1970s close to 100,000 active narcotic cases were reported by governmental agencies. Estimates of the actual number of narcotic users range upward to 500,000 persons. Most addicts come from a handful of states; New York alone accounts for more than 50 percent of the cases.

Adolescence and early adulthood are periods during which use of narcotics shows a peak. The national cost of drug addiction (including the cost of the drugs themselves, crimes committed by addicts, apprehension of the addicts committing those crimes, and attempts at rehabilitation) runs to many hundreds of millions of dollars. These costs and fear of criminal activities by narcotics users have resulted in strong indignation among large segments of the

population and demands that those who employ drugs be punished.

For the most part, hard-core addicts suffer from various types of emotional instability, which may or may not have been apparent prior to initial drug abuse experience. Occasional cases may have a background (often undiagnosed) of psychiatric disorders. Some psychiatrists have suggested that addicts have an inherent inability to develop meaningful interpersonal relationships. Others have maintained that addicts are persons who are unwilling to face the responsibility of maturity. It is significant that many addicts have their first drug experience in their teens. Adolescent addicts may have suffered childhood deprivation or overprotectiveness. Or they simply may not be able to cope with the physical and emotional changes accompanying this period.

The transition from childhood to adulthood is seldom smooth, and many individuals are not emotionally equipped to meet the demands they face. The early and middle teens bring a loosening of family ties, a lessening of parental authority, increasing responsibility, and sexual maturation. Beset with anxiety, frustration, fear of failure, inner conflicts, and doubts, the adolescent may find that narcotics provide relief and escape. Drug use may provide the entrée to an "in group" or be a way of affirming independence by defying authority and conventional norms of conduct.

There is relatively little reliable information on how to rehabilitate the narcotic user. Hospitalization, often prolonged, for purposes of withdrawal from narcotics has been used since the nineteenth century. Aside from being the most expensive treatment approach, it seems generally to be ineffective.

Methadone maintenance is the most significant form of drug treatment currently available. It has proved sufficiently attractive to opiate dependent persons that even voluntary programs show a substantial patient retention rate, compared with other methods of treatment. Because maintenance programs seem suitable to a wide range of opiate-dependent persons, they are capable of large-scale application. Because they can be carried out on an outpatient basis, they also cost relatively little.

Methadone is pharmacologically similar to other opiates, including heroin; however, methadone's effects last from 24 to 48 hours, whereas heroin's last from 6 to 12. Its withdrawal effects are delayed in appearance and less intense, though somewhat more prolonged. Methadone does not produce the intense euphoria of heroin when taken orally at constant doses. If the dosage is sufficient, it will block the action of heroin so that the dependent person does not experience its euphoric effect. At lower doses, although it will not block heroin's effects, it will suppress "heroin hunger." Although the biochemical and physiological properties of methadone are not fully understood, it apparently blocks off the ordinary effects of morphinelike drugs by competing at receptor sites located in the central nervous system where the drugs enter or have their effects. The craving for heroin is relieved and the heroin-dependent person can function in society.

Despite its relative effectiveness, methadone maintenance has not enjoyed universal support. Critics claim that it does not really cure the user but merely transfers dependence from one drug to another. There have been reports of death due to methadone poisoning, and the side effects of methadone are being explored. At the present time methadone maintenance seems promising but needs further study.

Stimulants

Amphetamines

Amphetamines—popularly known as *speed, uppers,* and *bennies*—are powerful stimulants of the brain and the autonomic nervous system. They are sold under such trade names as Benzedrine, Dexedrine, and Methedrine to reduce appetite, fatigue, need for sleep, and depression. In small dosages amphetamines are sometimes prescribed as "diet pills," with variable results. Low dosages are also used to overcome fatigue by groups ranging from truck drivers to students cramming for exams.

When they are used in moderation, amphetamines appear to have no harmful effects. However, people who use higher dosages readily develop a tolerance for and often a psychological dependence on amphetamines. There does not appear to be a physical dependence, as there is with depressants and narcotic analgesics. Eventually, many heavy users start mainlining large quantities of the drug. When speed is mainlined, a sudden flash or "rush" of intense pleasure envelops the body within sec-

onds. Addicts may mainline repeatedly and remain awake continuously for as long as a week. During this period they become increasingly tense and anxious and may suffer a large weight loss. When they stop the injections there is an inevitable "crash" and they may sleep deeply for one or two days, only to wake up profoundly depressed and exhausted. The crash brings on severe headaches and intense irritability.

When amphetamines are mainlined, there is an enormous increase in blood pressure, which can lead to heart failure and cerebral hemorrhage (stroke). There is considerable evidence that repeated use causes brain damage. Thought processes and memory can become permanently impaired, and many addicts suffer paranoid delusions of persecution. These individuals can be extremely dangerous to others, whose acts they misperceive as hostile. Finally, because speed taxes the body heavily, addicts have a relatively short life expectancy.

Cocaine

Cocaine is a stimulant derived from the coca plant, which grows mainly in western South America. It was once used widely as a local anesthetic in eye, nose, and throat surgery, but it has been replaced by newer drugs.

Cocaine is a white or colorless crystalline powder that is either inhaled (sniffed) or injected (mainlined). It has a wide range of possible effects: It can induce euphoria, excitation, anxiety, a sense of increased muscular strength, talkativeness, and liveliness. It causes pupils to dilate and heart rate and blood pressure to increase. In larger doses cocaine can produce fever, vomiting, convulsions, hallucinations, and paranoid delusions. Overdoses can depress breathing and heart functions so much that users die.

Cocaine users may develop a strong psychological dependence on the drug, although there is no evidence that they become physically dependent. Regular users may feel depressed and have hallucinations when they stop use.

Hallucinogenic drugs

The *hallucinogenic*, or *psychotomimetic*, drugs are the most powerful of the mind-altering drugs. *Psychotomimetic* literally means "imitation of psychosis." Some of the effects of these drugs are very close

159

BOX 5.10

The discovery of LSD-25

Like many important scientific discoveries, LSD was discovered quite by accident in 1943 by Albert Hofman, a Swiss chemist. One afternoon Hofman was beset by giddiness and an inability to concentrate. Most alarmingly, he noticed that the shapes of his assistants kept changing. He went home to bed, but instead of sleep he experienced fantastic dreams of intense and fluid colors.

Returning to his laboratory the next day, Hofman examined a chemical substance he had been synthesizing and concluded that he must have absorbed through his skin a small amount of the substance, LSD-25. He therefore orally ingested 0.25 milligram, which he presumed to be a minimal dose. He could not know that the substance was a thousand times stronger than mescaline and that he had taken a huge dose. Soon he began to experience a strong sense of uneasiness, felt that he was splitting into two people, and experienced strange visions. He was taken home, where he was beset by fantastic hallucinations and a highly distorted time sense. He was certain that he had gone insane and that he would never be able to report his discovery. However, he recovered by the following day, and with his report of his discovery and experience, the age of "acid" had begun (Hofman, 1968).

---

to symptoms of psychosis, a severe form of psychological disturbance. Among the psychotomimetic drugs are *LSD*, a synthetic drug; *mescaline*, a substance derived from the peyote cactus; *psilocybin*, known as the "magic mushroom"; and *marijuana*.

Most of these drugs are processed clandestinely, often not under the best laboratory conditions. They may be placed in capsules, tablets, powders, or liquids, and there are no standard dosage forms or markings that make visual identification possible. They are usually taken orally. Users may put drops of the liquid in beverages or on sugar cubes, crackers, and even small paper wads or cloth. These drugs are often used in group situations under special conditions designed to enhance their effect. Individuals under the influence of hallucinogens usually sit or recline quietly and appear to be in a dream or trancelike state. However, these drugs do not always have a euphoric effect. Users may be seized with fear for no apparent reason and then desperately attempt to escape from the group.

Experiences with hallucinogens are not determined solely by the drug. They are modified by the user's mood, mental attitude, and environment. Hallucinogens usually distort or intensify sense perception and blur the boundaries between fact and fantasy. Users may speak of seeing sounds and hearing colors. They may lose their sense of direction, distance, and ability to make objective judgments. Their pupils become dilated and their eyes become extremely sensitive to light. Until the drug loses its effectiveness, they may be restless and unable to sleep. The mental effects of these drugs are always unpredictable, even if the drugs are taken repeatedly, and their effects may recur as "flashbacks" days or even months after the drug has been taken. Hallucinogens may cause illusions, exhilaration, withdrawal from reality, violent movement or self-destruction, or sheer panic. This unpredictability constitutes the greatest danger to users. Unlike depressants and narcotics, hallucinogens are apparently not physically addictive, but psychological dependence may develop.

LSD

Lysergic acid diethylamide (LSD-25) is many times more potent than other hallucinogens, such as cactus-derived peyote. It is derived from ergot fungus, a disease that affects rye and wheat grain. LSD has been placed in or on sugar cubes, candy, paper, aspirin, jewelry, liquor, cloth, and even the back of postage stamps. The drug appears to disrupt brain mechanisms involved in filtering information from inside and outside the body. (See color plate.)

A dose of from 50 to 200 micrograms (a quantity no larger than the point of a pin) can take a user on a "trip" for approximately 8 to 16 hours. These "trips" proceed in phases. During the first hour users may experience visual changes, followed by extreme changes in mood. In the next phase they may lose their depth and time perception and perceive the sizes of objects, movements, colors, spatial arrangements, sounds, tactile sensations, and their own "body image" in distorted ways. During this period their general ability to make sensible judgments and to see common dangers is reduced and distorted, which makes them susceptible to personal injuries and potentially destructive to others.

After these "trips" users may suffer acute anxiety or depression for a variable period of time. Some even suffer short- or long-term psychoses. We do not yet know whether the drug causes the psychotic disorder or merely precipitates it.

The regular use of LSD does not seem to lead to physical dependence, but if "trips" are pleasant for users, they may develop a psychological dependence on the drug. Regular users may also develop a tolerance for it and require increasingly larger dosages over time.

Experiments with animals have shown that LSD can cause malfunctions in the activity of the nervous system. Research is being conducted to resolve a current controversy on possible chromosomal damage from LSD. Some researchers are using alcoholics and mentally disturbed individuals as subjects to determine if LSD has any therapeutic effects.

Marijuana

Although we have known and used marijuana for nearly 5000 years, it is one of the least understood of all natural drugs.

In the past, marijuana has been used to treat a variety of clinical disorders. Very early in China's history it was used to relieve pain during surgery. In India it was used as a medicine, and in the United States it was used as an analgesic and a poultice for corns. It is widely used as a social drug.

The active ingredient of marijuana is a chemical substance called *tetrahydrocannabinol*, or *THC*. As with most drugs, the effects that any individual experiences and the intensity of those effects is dependent on the dosage, the individual's sensitivity to the drug, and his or her psychological state.

Marijuana is either smoked in a cigarette (a "reefer" or a "joint") or a pipe or eaten in cookies, bread, sandwiches, or salads. When it is smoked marijuana appears to enter the bloodstream quickly, and symptoms appear very soon. It affects the user's

Harmless fun or long-term damage? Preliminary research suggests that prolonged use of marijuana may result in serious physical harm. If these findings prove to be true, this boy may regret his early start. (Sacks, EPA)

mood and thought patterns, but its effects on the emotions and senses are quite variable, depending on the amount and strength of the marijuana. The social setting and the effect the user anticipates also influence the ways in which he or she will react to the drug. Marijuana smoking is often a communal activity and all the members of the group are aware of the changes that take place in any group member.

The drug starts to take effect about 15 minutes after the user inhales the smoke. Depending on drug potency and dosage, its effects can last up to four hours. Low "social" doses may cause individuals to feel an increased sense of well-being. Initially, they may feel restless and giddy, then sink into a dreamy, carefree state of relaxation. Their sensory perceptions may become distorted and their sense of space and time may be expanded. Sensations can become more intense and a craving for food, especially sweets, occurs. Finally, subtle changes occur in thought formation and expression. An uninformed observer, however, would probably not notice anything unusual about a user's behavior.

If the dose is higher but still moderate, these same reactions become more intense, but an observer still might not notice any marked changes in a user's behavior. Users might experience rapid changes in emotions and sensory imagery, a dulling of ability to be attentive, and alterations in thought formation and expression (fragmented thoughts, a rush of ideas, impaired memory for very recent experiences, disturbed associations, an altered sense of identity, and perhaps feelings of greater insight into themselves and their surroundings). These distortions can produce feelings of panic and anxiety in some individuals who have had little experience with drugs and might make them fear that they are dying or "losing their mind." This panic is transient and usually disappears as soon as the effects of the drug wear off.

Very high doses may cause distortions in body image and sense of personal identity, fantasies, and hallucinations. In addition, extremely potent doses can cause a disorganization of thought and behavior, which disappears as the drug loses its effect.

Individuals under the influence of marijuana may have a hard time making decisions that require clear thinking and may be highly susceptible to the suggestions of other people. Their ability to perform tasks that require quick reflexes and thinking is impaired. For example, a substantial body of experimental evidence derived from driver test course performance and actual traffic conditions indicates that driving under the influence of marijuana (even "social doses") is hazardous.

During the past several years a debate has been raging over possible health hazards associated with marijuana use. As it is typically used in our culture, as a relaxant or a "social" drug, marijuana does not appear to have dangerous physical side effects, nor does it seem to cause physical dependence, as do narcotics. However, various researchers have suggested that prolonged and heavy usage may cause chromosomal damage, loss of cellular immunity to invading diseases, hormonal dysfunctions, lung and bronchial disorders, and perhaps even brain damage. However, none of these effects have been clearly established. Much more research is needed before we can make any definite statements concerning these possible effects of marijuana.

ALTERED STATES: A PSYCHOLOGICAL FRONTIER

During the past decade researchers, religious enthusiasts, and the general public have become involved in exploring the causes, nature, and effects of altered states of consciousness. This concentrated exploration of inner space promises to teach us more about ourselves and the limits of our awareness. The search for altered states of experience is for many a quest for spiritual growth and a redefinition of themselves and their relationship to nature. They seek altered states in the hope that their experiences will reveal alternate views of reality not shaped by previous learning and cultural influence, as a way of getting around the perceptual habits they have acquired. But learning from altered states may not be easy. Some of the experiences appear to be state-specific; that is, they are so different from normal mental functioning that it is difficult to translate what has been experienced into the thinking, feeling, and remembering of normal experience. A person may feel, for example, that he or she has had a great insight, or new mode of understanding, yet not be able to recall what it was.

Scientists' current attempts to study altered states

of experience may someday be viewed as a landmark in the development of psychology as a science. Throughout history we have been influenced by mystical and spiritual experiences, but now, for the first time in our history, we are making a concerted attempt to understand these experiences in scientific terms. Our explorations into these uncharted frontiers may enable us to expand our ability to perceive and understand more of our inner world, for, in the final analysis, our experience is all we have.

SUMMARY

1. In common with other mammals humans have a basic 24-hour *circadian rhythm*, which involves cyclical changes in vital bodily processes such as body temperature, blood pressure, and hormonal secretions.

2. EEG recordings show that there are five stages of sleep. The fifth stage, which occurs periodically during sleep, involves rapid eye movements (REMs), which are associated with reports of dreaming.

3. Various theories of why we dream have been suggested. Whatever the reason, we seem to have a need to do so. Individuals deprived of REM sleep by being awakened show an increased level of REM sleep on subsequent nights. There is evidence that the content of dreams can be influenced by suggestions, as can the time at which subjects awaken in relation to their dreams.

4. Vivid imagery is sometimes experienced during the intervals between wakefulness and sleep (*hypnagogic imagery*) and between sleep and wakefulness (*hypnopompic imagery*).

5. A number of variables have been identified that increase responsiveness to hypnotic suggestions. These include defining the situation as hypnosis, removing fears and encouraging cooperation, linking suggestions with actual experiences, and reinforcing cooperation. These procedures increase cooperation and motivation to be hypnotized, as well as subjects' expectations that they will enter hypnosis.

6. A variety of altered behaviors, physiological changes, and experiences have been attributed to hypnosis. Some investigators, such as Barber, have argued that these phenomena are brought about by common psychological factors, such as suggestion and expectancy, rather than through an altered state ("trance") that is unique to hypnosis. Alternatives to trance theories have emphasized role playing and imagination as processes giving rise to hypnotic phenomena.

7. Of the various meditation techniques, *transcendental meditation* (TM) has been the most intensively researched. Decreases in physiological arousal during meditation have been repeatedly demonstrated, but it has not been shown that these effects are specific to TM. Benson's simple technique for producing the *relaxation response* appears to be a reasonable alternative to TM. Studies have also reported that TM leads to decreased drug use and positive personality changes, but more methodologically sound research is needed to verify these effects and to assess the effects of TM on intelligence and creativity.

8. Drugs can produce a variety of altered states. Alcohol and the barbiturates are depressants that decrease levels of activity in the nervous system. Both are highly addictive, and withdrawal symptoms can be severe.

9. The *narcotic analgesics* include opium, morphine, and heroin. Users experience a temporary feeling of euphoria and well-being. These drugs are highly addictive, and tolerance and dependence (both physiologi-

163

cal and psychological) develop quickly. Many deaths occur from heroin overdoses. Narcotic addiction is a major societal problem. Many addicts appear to have severe adjustment problems. *Methadone treatment* is an effective, though somewhat controversial, treatment for heroin addiction.

10. Such stimulants as the amphetamines and cocaine increase central and autonomic nervous system activity. Repeated use of amphetamines in large doses can result in brain damage and permanent mental impairment.

11. The experimental effects of hallucinogenic drugs such as LSD and mescaline are variable and depend heavily on the psychological situation. Profound perceptual and mental alterations may occur. Marijuana has less extreme effects than other hallucinogens, but its effects are also variable. Its long-term physical effects have not been clearly established.

Suggested readings

Barber, T. X., Spanos, N. P., & Chaves, J. F. *Hypnotism: Imagination and human potentialities.* New York: Pergamon Press, 1974. A skeptical view of altered states theory of hypnosis and a reformulation of hypnotic phenomena in terms of social psychological variables and imagination.

Biofeedback and self-control. Chicago: Aldine Publishing Company. These yearbooks, which have been published since 1971, reprint the most significant research and theoretical developments in altered states areas, such as biofeedback, meditation, and hypnosis.

Castaneda, C. *The Teachings of don Juan: A Yaqui way of knowledge.* Berkeley: University of California Press, 1968. A gripping account of a man's experience with mind-altering drugs.

Dement, W. C. *Some must watch while some must sleep.* San Francisco: W. H. Freeman and Co. Publishers, 1974. An investigator who has done much of the important research on REM sleep presents an account of what is known about sleep and dreaming.

Reed, G. *The psychology of anomalous experience.* Boston: Houghton Mifflin Company, 1974. A highly readable approach to unusual, irregular, and puzzling experiences such as illusions, delusions, hallucinations, and other anomalies of experience. Contains many introspective verbal reports of such experiences.

Sarbin, T. R., & Coe, W. C. *Hypnosis: A social psychological analysis of influence communication.* New York: Holt, Rinehart and Winston, Inc., 1972. Considers the research findings in light of a social psychological theory involving role playing and imagination.

Teyler, T. J. *Altered states of awareness.* San Francisco: W. H. Freeman and Co. Publishers, 1972. A collection of important articles from the *Scientific American* on sleep and dreaming, drugs, meditation, and other altered states topics.

Three

Learning, Cognition, and Behavioral Control

Chapter 6

Learning: Principles and Applications

(Culver)

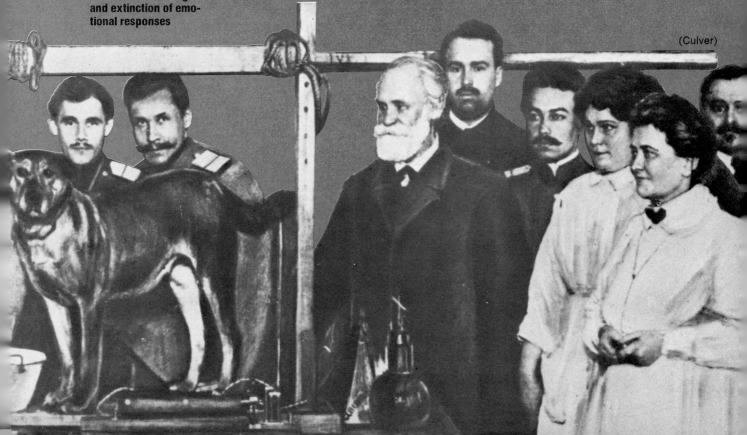

A young woman sits nervously on the edge of a comfortable chair as she begins her first interview with a therapist (therapist = T, client = C):

T: I'm glad you were able to make it here today.

C: You don't know how hard it was. I was so clutched up that I told my husband to forget the whole thing and take me home. Finally, we had to stop the car and walk the rest of the way—over two miles.

T: When you called last week, you mentioned your fear of cars. Can you tell me about the problem?

C: You mean what's happening now, or how it started?

T: Both.

C: Well, about a year ago I was driving on a rainy night when my car went out of control. It crashed into a light pole, rolled over, and began to burn. I . . . couldn't get out . . . (*begins to weep*). . . . I'm sorry, Doctor, but even thinking about it is horrible. I had a broken pelvis and third-degree burns over half my body. I can still remember being trapped in the car and hearing myself being burned alive before I passed out (*pause*). I was in the hospital for months.

T: That's an experience that would upset anybody. When did the fear of cars begin?

C: When my husband came to take me home. As we walked toward the new car he had bought, I began to feel uneasy. I felt nervous all the way home. It started to get worse after that. I found myself avoiding riding in the car, and I couldn't drive it at all. I stopped visiting friends and tried to get them to come to our house. After a while, even the sight of a car started to make me nervous.

T: As nervous as riding in one?

C: No, but still nervous. It's so stupid. I'd even turn off the TV during scenes involving car chases. And I hate to admit it, but even pictures of cars in magazines started to make me queasy. I finally got my husband to cut all the car ads out of our magazines before I looked at them.

T: How has your husband reacted to your problem?

C: He's been understanding, but it's really been getting to him lately. You know, this is the first time I've left the house in about four months. I figure I'd better get over this stupid thing or I might lose him.

T: You say "stupid thing."

C: Of course it's stupid! I know those cars in magazines and on TV can't hurt me in any way. And even if I'm riding in one or driving one I'm unlikely to get into another accident. But I can't help myself. The fear just gets triggered off automatically when I see or hear about cars. I've gotten so uptight, I've even thrown up. And the longer it goes on, the worse it gets.

A middle-aged man has been playing the tables in a Las Vegas casino for nearly 36 hours. His clothes are disheveled and his hair hangs limply over his forehead. Hope and desperation are alternately mirrored in his face as he peers through the smoke-filled air at the whirling roulette wheel.

Nearby, one casino guard nudges another and mutters, "That poor guy's really got the fever. He's been in here since yesterday. A real loser, too—I'll bet he's blown thousands. He's in hock up to his ears. I'll never understand what keeps these guys going. It's a sickness."

In one wing of a large metropolitan research hospital a business executive is comfortably settled in a semi-reclined position. A number of electrodes are attached to his body, and he peers intently at a small box on an adjacent table. The box contains a green, a yellow, and a red light. The executive suffers from atrial fibrillation, a cardiac disorder involving a dangerous disturbance in heart rhythm. He is learning to control his heart rate. He smiles with satisfaction as the yellow light signals that his heart rate is within the desired range. The green light goes on when he should increase his heart rate, and the red light goes on when his heart rate is too fast.

In another wing of the medical center a young research subject sits in a reclining chair in a semi-darkened room. Electrodes attached to his scalp monitor his brain wave activity. He is wearing earphones through which he receives tones that tell him when he is producing the desired wavelengths. This "feedback" will eventually enable him to control his brain waves and to enter an altered state of consciousness without the use of drugs. In this altered state he will experience unusual sensations and images.

These instances of human behavior share one important characteristic: They can be examined and understood in terms of the basic principles of human learning. No topic is more central to modern psychology than learning, because most human behaviors result at least partially from learning processes.

How did the young woman learn her intense fear of cars? How did the exhausted man learn to be a compulsive gambler? How do people such as the business executive and the young man learn to control their heart rates, brain waves, and other "involuntary" bodily processes? We will attempt to answer these questions and will discuss some of the ways in which principles of learning established within the behavioristic perspective have been applied to the

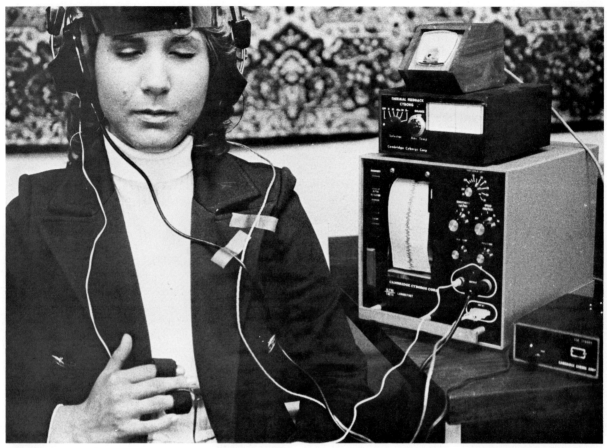

(Tringali, Palmer, DPI)

understanding and solution of personal and social problems. We do not confine our discussion of learning to this chapter, however, because every branch of psychology deals in a fundamental way with issues related to learning.

Learning may be defined as *a change in potential behavior that occurs as a result of experience.* Behavioral changes brought about by physical changes, such as maturation or injury, are not included in this definition; it is restricted to changes that result from interactions with the environment. We define learning as a change in *potential* behavior because we do not always reflect our learning by changing our behavior immediately. For instance, most of us have learned by observing television shows and movies how to rob a bank. Because of other considerations, we have not gone out and robbed one, but we still have the *potential* to do it. When a superior

athlete performs poorly, it is simply because he or she cannot perform all the correct behaviors on an "off day," not because those behaviors have not been learned.

Although the products of learning can be enormously complex, the basic principles underlying almost all learning are fairly simple. There are three major types of learning: (1) classical conditioning; (2) instrumental or operant conditioning; and (3) observational learning. Many learned behaviors involve a combination of these processes.

CLASSICAL CONDITIONING

169

Over 75 years ago Ivan Pavlov, a Russian physiologist, made a landmark discovery in the study of behavior. Originally, Pavlov was studying salivation in dogs as part of his research on digestive processes. He was inducing salivation by presenting food to his dogs. In the course of his experimentation, however, he discovered that if a stimulus that would not ordinarily induce salivation (a neutral stimulus), such as the sound of a bell, were presented to the dogs at the same time they received the meat, eventually the bell alone would make the dogs salivate.

Pavlov's technique is called classical conditioning. The principle underlying the technique is that a neutral stimulus paired with a stimulus that already evokes a response will eventually evoke the same response by itself. The original stimulus (the meat) is called the *unconditioned stimulus* (UCS), and the response it evokes (salivation) is called the *unconditioned response* (UCR). The neutral stimulus (the bell) is called the *conditioned stimulus* (CS), and the response that it eventually evokes (salivation) is called the *conditioned response* (CR). (See Figure 6.1.) The CR is generally not identical in all respects to the UCR. In Pavlov's experiments, for example, the bell usually did not make the dogs salivate as much as did the meat.

Reinforcement, extinction, and spontaneous recovery

Each pairing of the CS with the UCS is called a *reinforcement*, because it strengthens or reinforces the connection between the CS and the CR. The

strongest and fastest conditioning occurs when the CS is presented slightly before the UCS. (The optimal interval is about one-half second.) After conditioning, if the CS is presented repeatedly without the UCS, then the CS-CR bond will become weaker. This process is called *extinction*. Pavlov found that after the dogs had begun to salivate in response to the bell, if he continued to ring the bell without giving them

Figure 6.1 The conditioning process.

Before conditioning:

CS (bell)	→	No salivation response
UCS (meat)	→	UCR (salivation)

During conditioning:

CS (bell) + UCS (meat)	--→ →	UCR (salivation)

After conditioning:

CS (bell)	→	CR (salivation)

(Reprinted by permission of NEA.)

FRANK AND ERNEST   **by Bob Thaves**

YOU'VE GOT TO STOP RINGING THAT BELL EVERY TIME YOU FEED HIM, DR. PAVLOV... YESTERDAY HE ATE THE AVON LADY

THAVES © 1974 by NEA, Inc.

1-28

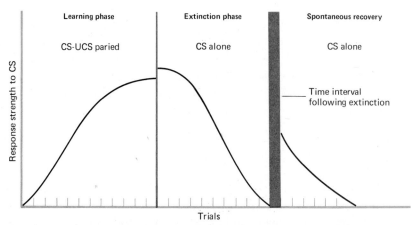

Figure 6.2 Learning, extinction, and spontaneous recovery of a conditioned response. Presentation of the CS after a time interval following extinction elicits a weak CR.

meat they salivated less and eventually stopped salivating at all in response to the bell. Occasional reinforcement is required in order to maintain a classically conditioned response. If a CR has been extinguished, however, and the CS is presented after a period of time, the CR may reappear (usually in weakened form). This phenomenon is called *spontaneous recovery.* (See Figure 6.2.)

Classical conditioning may require only one or a very few CS-UCS pairings. Once a CR has been established, it may last for an extremely long period of time. In one study hospitalized Navy veterans who had seen combat in World War II had strong emotional responses (measured by changes in their skin resistance) when they were exposed to a repetitive "call-to-battle-stations" gong, even though 15 years had passed since this stimulus had been associated with danger. Army veterans, who had not served on ships, were significantly less responsive to this stimulus (Edwards, 1962).

Generalization and discrimination

Once conditioning has occurred, the subject will respond not only to the CS, but also to stimuli that are similar to it. The more similar a stimulus is to the original CS, the more likely the subject is to respond to it with the CR. This phenomenon is called *generalization.* The emotional response of the Navy veterans, for example, could probably also be evoked by sounds that were similar to the sound of the "battle stations" gong. A more famous demonstration of a generalized fear response is described in Box 6.1.

Discrimination is essentially the opposite of generalization. It refers to a subject's ability to detect differences between stimuli. Poor little Albert could not discriminate very well among the white, furry stimuli that were presented to him. It is possible to build in discrimination during classical conditioning by presenting a series of similar stimuli but only pairing one of them with the UCS.

Some applications of classical conditioning principles

Although classical conditioning is a relatively simple form of learning, it is the basis for many complex behaviors. While we may find it difficult to become excited about salivating dogs, Pavlov's principles help us understand how we learn emotional responses that underlie our attitudes and social behaviors. Contemporary Soviet psychology, in fact, is based on Pavlovian principles. Let us briefly consider several practical applications of classical conditioning principles.

Interoceptive conditioning and physical health

In all the examples of classical conditioning previously cited, the CS was an external environmental

171

BOX 6.1

Little Albert and the white rat

One of the most famous examples of the generalization of a conditioned response is provided by a demonstration conducted by John B. Watson and Rosalie Rayner (1920). Albert was an 11-month-old child. One day, as Albert was playing in his crib, Watson and Rayner placed a white rat before him. Albert showed no sign of fear. On several subsequent occasions, however, they showed the rat to Albert and made a loud noise behind him. The noise was sufficient to make Albert cry and act distressed. After the rat had been paired with the noise several times, the sight of the white rat alone made Albert cry and try to escape. Watson and Rayner then presented a number of other test stimuli to Albert. When they placed colored blocks in the crib, Albert showed no signs of fear. But objects such as a white rabbit, a sealskin coat, and a man with a white beard made him cry and struggle to escape, although not as much as the sight of the rat had done. The experimenters not only had classically conditioned a phobia, but had demonstrated how such a conditioned emotional response can generalize to other similar stimuli. (History does not tell us whether this child is the same Albert who later opened a rodent extermination business in Eight Corners, Nebraska.)

172

stimulus. Theoretically, however, any stimulus that an organism can sense, whether internal or external, can serve as a CS if it is paired with a UCS. Russian scientists have reported successful experiments in *interoceptive conditioning,* in which the CS is inside the body rather than outside it. In one experiment a dog was operated on so that gases could be introduced through its trachea into its lungs. Carbon dioxide, which causes rapid breathing, served as a UCS. For a CS, pressure was mechanically applied to the dog's intestine. After only a few CS-UCS pairings the intestinal pressure alone evoked a conditioned rapid-breathing response. In another demonstration of interoceptive conditioning, an abdominal operation was performed on a dog and a jet of air blown on the uterine wall was used as a CS. The UCS was a shock to the dog's leg, which caused it to flex involuntarily. After 10 to 12 CS-UCS pairings the dog flexed its leg in response to the air jet alone.

The range of bodily responses that can be conditioned is enormous. In an experiment performed in the United States a rapid drop in the level of blood sugar and a state of physiological shock were induced by administering insulin to rats as a UCS. A flash of light was paired with the UCS. After a number of such pairings the light flash and the sight of the hypodermic needle alone caused a drop in the rats' blood sugar and threw them into a state of shock (Sawry, Conger, and Turrell, 1956). Findings such as these suggest that classical conditioning processes may be important in the development of some psychosomatic disorders, in which physical symptoms are caused by psychological factors. For example, one study of asthma patients revealed that their asthmatic attacks often occurred in the presence of specific stimuli such as dust, radio speeches by influential politicians, goldfish, the national anthem, and waterfalls. Once the critical stimuli had been identified in a particular case, the investigators were able to induce asthma attacks by presenting the critical stimuli or pictures of them. The investigators describe one such case:

> Patient L had told us that she got an asthmatic attack from looking at a goldfish. After a base line had been obtained, a goldfish in a bowl was brought into the room. . . . Under our eyes she developed a severe asthmatic attack with loud wheezing, followed by a gradual remission after the goldfish had been taken from the room. During the next experiment the goldfish was replaced by a plastic toy fish which was easily recognized as such . . . but a fierce attack resulted. (Dekker and Groen, 1956, p. 62)

Using classical conditioning to study covert processes

When we study nonverbal creatures such as animals and infants, they cannot tell us what they are perceiving or experiencing. One way of learning about their private experiences is through classical conditioning. For example, we can determine if young children can discriminate blue from green by conditioning them to respond to a blue light but not to a green one. This can be accomplished by pairing a blue light with a puff of air to the eyeball (which produces the UCR of blinking) and by not pairing the air puff with a green light. The development of a conditioned blinking response to the blue light but not to the green light would show that the child was able to discriminate between the two colors. Many studies have used methods such as this one to study internal processes.

Sometimes classical conditioning can be used in a diagnostic manner. Cohen, Hilgard and Wendt (1933) report a classic case study in which a man was suffering from blindness in one part of his visual field. His physicians believed that the partial blindness was being caused by emotional factors rather than by actual damage to the man's retina. To rule out retinal damage, the investigators carried out a classical conditioning procedure in which a tiny beam of light (CS) was focused on a "nonblind" area of the retina. The beam of light was paired repeatedly with a loud sound (UCS), which produced a reflex eyelid response (UCR). After conditioning was established, a special instrument was used to focus the beam of light on the "blind" portion of the retina. The conditioned reactions which occurred (even though the patient maintained that he could not see the light) proved that the patient's blindness was not due to retinal damage.

Classical conditioning and attitude formation

Emotional reactions are an important component of attitudes. When we say we have a "positive" or a "negative" attitude toward a person or an object, we are referring in part to an emotional response that the person or object evokes. Some theorists feel that classical conditioning is critically important in establishing attitudes. In classical conditioning terms, the object or person is the CS. If this CS is associated with another stimulus (a UCS) that already elicits a positive or negative emotional response, we may develop a conditioned emotional response toward the object or person. For example, most of us have a song that became a favorite because it was paired with a pleasurable situation or event, or one that arouses negative feelings because it was associated with a negative event.

A number of experiments have shown that it is possible to condition positive or negative attitudes toward neutral stimuli. Staats and Staats (1958) paired national names (e.g., *Swedish*, *Dutch*) and familiar masculine names (*Tom*, *Bill*) with either positive words (e.g., *sacred* and *happy*), negative words (e.g., *failure* and *ugly*), or neutral words (e.g., *table*) in a series of conditioning trials. After the trials, subjects were asked to rate the CS words on a pleasantness-unpleasantness scale. It was found that both the nationalities and the masculine names could be conditioned in either a positive or a negative direction. Moreover, the subjects showed no awareness that they had been subjected to a conditioning procedure. The implications of this finding are sobering. If a certain person or group of people is always referred to with negative words (e.g., *dangerous*, *dirty*, *stupid*, *immoral*), individuals may develop a prejudice toward that person or group even if they have never come into contact with one another.

Classical conditioning procedures have also been used to change behavior. Box 6.2 describes an example of the way in which classical conditioning was applied to an ecological problem.

Now that we have defined the elements of classical conditioning, let us return to the case at the beginning of this chapter—the young woman with the automobile phobia. Suppose you were her therapist. Do you think classical conditioning could help you explain any part of her problem?

Clearly, classical conditioning played a role in establishing her fear response to cars. During her accident conditioned stimuli relating to her car were associated with unconditioned stimuli that evoked pain and terror (UCRs), and she was left with strong conditioned fear responses. It is also clear that considerable stimulus generalization has occurred, so that stimuli other than those involved in the original accident situation can also evoke strong fear responses. Note that the young woman experiences more anxiety when she is riding in a car than when she merely views a car on TV or in magazines. This would be predicted on the basis of generalization, because the latter stimuli are less similar to the original conditioned stimuli.

173

BOX 6.2

From Pavlov's dogs to wild coyotes: Changing food preferences in predators

Wild coyotes, an endangered species, have become a major problem in some areas of the western United States because they prey on lambs and other livestock. This has led to a sharp controversy between ranchers, who want to destroy the coyotes, and environmentalists, who want to preserve them. Fortunately, recent laboratory research on the principles of classical conditioning has produced an alternative that may permit the continued survival of both predator and prey.

Several years ago psychologist John Garcia discovered that rats would quickly learn to avoid eating food contaminated with substances that made them sick. The conditioned aversion occurred after only one experience, even though the sickness (the UCS) did not occur until several hours after they had eaten the food (the CS). (A CS-UCS interval of this length was, before Garcia's studies, virtually unknown in animal research.) Moreover, the conditioning was restricted to the taste of the food that made the animals sick; it did not generalize to similar foods with different tastes, even if they were eaten at the same time as the poisoned foods.

A recent study (Gustavson et al., 1974) showed that this "Garcia effect" could be used to produce a classically conditioned aversion to meat usually eaten by coyotes. Three coyotes were fed lamb flesh that had been treated with lithium chloride, a substance that produces temporary but severe illness. Three other coyotes were fed rabbit flesh treated with the same chemical substance. The predatory and eating behaviors of the animals were then carefully observed. After one or two conditioning trials, the coyotes refused to attack the type of animal whose flesh had made them ill, but they readily attacked and ate the other type.

These results suggest that by treating sheep carcasses with lithium chloride or some other nonlethal toxin, coyotes could be conditioned to avoid the smell and taste of sheep. They would then be forced to return to hunting their regular prey and would no longer threaten the human food supply. We have here an example of how basic laboratory research can later be found to have important practical applications.

Although classical conditioning principles explain the way in which the phobia was established, a number of important questions remain. Why does the fear not decrease? After all, the stimuli that relate to the car are no longer being reinforced by pain. Should we not then expect the response to become extinct? Most puzzling of all, why does the client seem to be getting progressively worse? After all, she realizes that her fear is irrational and seems highly motivated to get rid of it. In order to answer these questions we must consider a second major type of learning, operant conditioning.

OPERANT CONDITIONING

Behaviorists assert that all organisms are basically motivated to maximize pleasure and to minimize pain. We tend to repeat behaviors that produce positive outcomes, and not to repeat those that produce neutral or negative outcomes. This principle, sometimes called the *law of effect*, is the cornerstone of operant conditioning.

Consider your own social behavior. It is likely that you have developed a repertoire of behaviors that, for the most part, allow you to interact harmoniously with others. Can you trace one or two of them back and remember when and why you began using them? Can you remember any social behaviors that you once used but have since discarded? Can you see how the law of effect has operated with respect to your behaviors? That is, do the behaviors that you still perform seem to produce some kind of positive outcome for you? Did you discard the other behaviors because they were no longer producing positive outcomes?

The terms *operant* and *instrumental*, which are interchangeable, refer to the fact that the behaviors in question produce some effect for the organism: The organism *operates* on its environment in some way; the behaviors in which it engages are *instrumental* in achieving some outcome.

Psychologists have learned much about operant conditioning through laboratory studies involving animals. As we shall see, the findings from these studies are helpful for understanding many forms of human behavior.

A typical laboratory demonstration of operant conditioning might proceed as follows: A rat that has been deprived of food for a number of hours is placed in an experimental chamber called a Skinner box (named for its inventor, B. F. Skinner). There is a lever on one wall of the chamber. Beneath the lever is a small cup into which a pellet of food can be dropped by a dispenser, which operates whenever the rat depresses the lever. (See Figure 6.3.) When it is placed into this box, the hungry rat explores its surroundings. In the course of its explorations it inadvertently depresses the lever. A pellet of food clinks into the cup and the rat eats it quickly. Sometime later the rat again presses the bar and receives another pellet. If we record the rat's behavior we discover that it soon begins to press the bar more and more frequently. An operant bar-press response has now been established. Receiving the food pellet is a *reinforcement* because it increases the likelihood that the rat will again press the bar.

Suppose we now place a red light and a green light on the panel above the bar. When the green light is on, pressing the bar dispenses food, but when the red light is illuminated, no food is dispensed. The rat will soon learn to press the bar only when the green

Figure 6.3 A rat explores a Skinner box, which has been used in studies of operant conditioning. When the rat presses the bar on the wall, food is automatically delivered by the apparatus to the left of the Skinner box. (Shelton, Monkmeyer)

Another kind of Skinner box. Skinner designed a dirt-free, noise-free "baby tender" for his daughter Debby. She lived in the box during her entire infancy. (Wide World)

light is on, or respond to the *discriminative stimulus* that signals the availability of reinforcement.

In the laboratory, operant behavior is typically studied by means of a *cumulative recorder*. Each response triggers a pen on a moving piece of paper. (See Figure 6.4.) The more frequently and rapidly responses are made, the more rapidly the pen climbs on the chart. Changes in response frequency can be detected by studying the cumulative response curves. The Skinner box procedure has been used to study operant conditioning in many different species, including human beings. All that needs to be modified for different animals is the response to be made (e.g., in studies with pigeons a disc is pecked) and the type of reinforcer employed (most children do not respond as enthusiastically to rat pellets as they do to pieces of candy).

176 Differences between operant and classical conditioning

As we can see from the preceding example, there are two main differences between operant and classical conditioning:

1. In classical conditioning the behavior (CR) is elicited by a particular stimulus (CS) and is therefore called *elicited behavior*. Operant behavior is *emitted behavior* in the sense that the response occurs in a situation containing many stimuli. In a sense, the organism chooses when to respond.

2. In both classical and operant conditioning the behavior develops as a result of reinforcement. In classical conditioning, *reinforcement* refers to the pairing of the CS with the UCS, an event that occurs *before* the response. In operant conditioning, *reinforcement* refers to any event occurring *after* the behavior that increases the probability that the behavior will occur in the future. The relationship between a behavior and its consequences in operant conditioning is called a *reinforcement contingency*. For example, when a mother says to her child, "If you do your homework, you can stay up late tonight," she is specifying a reinforcement contingency. Obviously, there is no reinforcement contingency in classical conditioning, because the CS-UCS pairing does not depend on anything that the subject does.

Although the procedures for classical and operant conditioning are easily distinguishable, many learning situations involve both processes. For example, when a young child reaches out and touches a hot stove, the painful stimulation it receives is a negative response consequence, so that it becomes operantly conditioned to avoid performing the same behavior. In addition, the painful stimulation is paired with

Figure 6.4 A cumulative response recorder. (Lafayette Instrument)

the neutral stimuli of the stove, so that the child may develop a classically conditioned fear of the stove.

Response consequences and behavior

A given behavior may have many possible consequences. A great deal of research has been directed toward specifying the effects of different types and patterns of response consequences on behavior. We now consider some of the major principles of operant conditioning in greater detail and indicate some of the ways in which these principles have enabled psychologists to understand, and sometimes to change, behavior.

Positive reinforcement

A positive reinforcer is any stimulus or event that increases the frequency of a behavior it follows. The term *reward* is often used as if it were synonymous with positive reinforcement. However, psychologists prefer the latter term because in many instances rewards do not function as positive reinforcers. For example, there was a teacher who began to dispense chocolate candies to her pupils for perfect scores on spelling tests. She noted with pleasure that all of them began to get higher scores—except Johnny. One day she asked, "Johnny, why aren't you studying harder for your spelling tests? You know you can get chocolate candy for perfect scores." Johnny's response made clear why the teacher's "reward" had not affected his spelling performance: "I hate chocolate."

In order to apply positive reinforcement procedures successfully to develop desired behaviors, two basic conditions must be met. First, one must choose a reinforcer that will be strong enough to strengthen the behavior. Once an effective reinforcer has been found it must be made contingent on the desired behavior, so that the subject learns what it must do to earn the reinforcer.

Reinforcers such as candy and other foods sometimes prove ineffective because their potency is affected by the organism's degree of hunger. It is sometimes necessary to increase the reinforcing properties of the positive reinforcer. In one program that was designed to develop social behaviors in profoundly disturbed psychiatric hospital patients, food was chosen as the reinforcer because the patients were unresponsive to conventional social reinforcers such

as verbal praise. But when even food did not work well, the patients were injected with insulin, which increased their hunger. After the injections, the food worked quite effectively to bring about behavioral changes (Peters and Jenkins, 1954).

Secondary reinforcement. *Secondary* or *conditioned* reinforcers acquire their reinforcing properties by being associated with other reinforcers. Attention, verbal praise, trading stamps, and money, for example, serve as reinforcers because we know they can enable us to obtain other things that we already value. *Primary reinforcers*, such as food and water, satisfy biological needs and do not require prior association with other reinforcers in order to have reinforcing properties. Any stimulus associated with the attainment of a primary reinforcer can become a secondary reinforcer. A chimpanzee will learn to value and work for tokens it can place into a vending machine to obtain raisins (see Figure 6.6) in much the same way that we learn to value and work for money we can exchange for valued commodities.

Shaping

Imagine that you are sitting in your introductory psychology class one day when your instructor enters

Figure 6.5 (Columbia *Jester*, date unknown)

"Boy, have I got this guy conditioned! Every time I press the bar down, he drops in a piece of food."

Figure 6.6 A chimp drops a token into the Chimp-O-Mat vending machine to obtain raisins. Through their association with food (a primary reinforcer), the tokens become valued secondary reinforcers for the chimps. (Yerkes Regional Primate Research Center)

carrying a cage. "Today you will meet a remarkable animal," says the instructor, who uncovers the cage. A small white rat peers curiously at the class through the wire mesh. "This is Marcella, the brightest rat in our laboratory. Today she will demonstrate her marvelous abilities for you." The instructor opens the top of the cage and Marcella runs up his arm to his shoulder, then down his arm as he places it over a nearby table that has been set up for her. Marcella runs across the table and jumps into a small electric train. She presses a lever with her right front paw, and the train starts up and moves along the track. Reaching her destination some 5 feet along the track, Marcella stops the train and jumps out. She then climbs a ladder to a platform about 2 feet high, faces the class, and bows solemnly. Next, she runs to the other end of the platform and onto a small diving board. Eighteen inches away from her is a panel with two windows. One window contains a black card, the other a white card. Without hesitation Marcella launches herself into a majestic dive into the white card. The card falls back from the window, allowing her to enter another chamber. (Had Marcella jumped against the black card, she would have bounced off and fallen into a net below.) Inside the chamber, Marcella approaches a lever attached to one of the walls and pulls the lever. A door opens, allowing her access to an elevator. She enters the elevator, pulls a chain suspended from the ceiling, and the elevator brings her down to the first floor, where she again bows to the class and consumes a piece of food. She then repeats the entire sequence, or *chain* of responses, receiving food each time, until she is no longer hungry.

Is Marcella truly a rat genius? Actually, her performance is not extraordinary. If they are trained well, most laboratory rats can perform a sequence of responses much like Marcella's. The method used to train animals to perform novel and complex behaviors is called *shaping*, or the *method of successive approximations*. Marcella's trainer gradually got her to perform each of the behaviors in sequence by manipulating the reinforcement contingencies. The trainer started with a behavior Marcella could already perform and reinforced her to make gradual changes in the direction of the desired behavior. For example, it is highly unlikely that Marcella would ever climb onto the train and drive it spontaneously. But the trainer reinforced her with food whenever she simply faced in the direction of the train. Then the trainer reinforced her only when she approached the train, then only when she stood on her hind legs beside the train, then when she touched the train, then when she climbed onto the train. Once Marcella had been "shaped" to climb onto the train, she had to touch the lever in order to be reinforced, then to press it, and so on. In this way Marcella gradually learned to perform behaviors that increasingly approximated the final desired behaviors.

We learn many complex human behaviors through shaping. For example, shaping is involved in learning a language and in developing educational skills. If we want to train children to be mathematicians, we do not expect them to solve complex calculus problems spontaneously. We start by teaching them basic arithmetic operations and successively

(George Gardner)

building on what they have already learned. On a broader level, the socialization process through which individuals acquire the behaviors, values, and attitudes of their society involves a great deal of shaping. Box 6.3 describes the use of shaping in dealing with a serious behavioral problem.

Positive reinforcement is a powerful means of changing behavior. One issue that has received attention in recent years is how positive reinforcement influences the individual's pattern of motives. For example, if people are rewarded for performing behaviors they would not otherwise perform, they may come to enjoy behaving in that manner. But what happens if people are rewarded for behaviors they already enjoy? Will they come to enjoy them even more, or will something that was once fun now become less pleasurable for its own sake? Box 6.4 describes recent research related to this question.

Operant extinction

In operant conditioning, as in classical conditioning, extinction refers to the gradual disappearance of a learned response that occurs when there is no reinforcement. Extinction effects undoubtedly account for many changes in human behavior. When previously reinforced behaviors no longer "pay off," we are likely to abandon them and replace them with more functional ones.

BOX 6.3
Shaping: The case of Dickie

Dickie was a severely disturbed three-year-old child who was completely unresponsive to other people. His behaviors were generally inappropriate, and he was prone to temper tantrums. When he was first seen by a psychologist, he absolutely refused to wear his corrective eyeglasses. This was a serious problem because he had had the lenses removed from both of his eyes after the doctor had discovered cataracts when he was 9 months old. If Dickie was to see again, he had to wear corrective lenses, but no one had been able to induce him to do it. The psychologist decided to try a shaping procedure.

The psychologist saw Dickie in his room for several 30-minute sessions each day. During these sessions the psychologist placed glass frames around the room and used small pieces of candy and fruit to reinforce Dickie, first for simply approaching the frames, then for picking them up and holding them. Then Dickie was reinforced for bringing the frames toward his face. At this point, however, progress stopped. The food and candy reinforcers appeared to be losing their effectiveness. The psychologist withheld Dickie's breakfast, then used bits of it as reinforcers. By the end of the fifth week, however, Dickie was still not wearing his glasses in the proper position and looking through them; the psychologist tried ice cream as a reinforcer. Dickie began to wear his glasses eagerly. The psychologist provided him with toys and other visual stimuli, in the hope that being able to see them would serve to reinforce his behavior. In the end, Dickie was wearing his glasses an average of 12 hours per day (Wolf, Risley, and Mees, 1964).

It is important not to confuse extinction with *punishment,* which we discuss later. Punishment involves making negative consequences contingent

BOX 6.4

Can extrinsic reinforcement reduce intrinsic motivation?

"I don't enjoy playing football as much as I used to. It's just a way to make a living, and I'll stop playing if they refuse to pay me what I'm asking." This statement, which was made by a well-known professional athlete, reflects a definite shift in his motivations.

People engage in certain behaviors for *intrinsic* reasons (for reinforcement that they can provide for themselves) or for *extrinsic* reasons (for reinforcement that they receive from others). Some people learn for the sheer enjoyment of it; others learn only so that they can make passing grades. Some people fish because they enjoy the activity; others fish for a living.

But what happens when an individual starts to re-ceive extrinsic rewards for behaviors that already provide intrinsic rewards? For example, what happens if Johnny, who loves to read, is given monetary reinforcement for reading? Will the extrinsic reinforcer eventually replace the intrinsic one? If the money is later withdrawn, will the child no longer have an interest in reading?

Recent research with both college students and children indicates that extrinsic reinforcement can indeed undermine intrinsic motivation (Deci, 1975). For example, when children who spent a great deal of time drawing pictures with felt-tipped markers were offered certificates for doing so, the amount of time they spent on the activity remained high. But when they stopped receiving certificates, the time decreased by 50 percent.

Extrinsic reinforcement does not always undermine intrinsic motivation. Sometimes extrinsic rewards can be used to get a behavior started so that the individual can *develop* an intrinsic motivation for it. But it seems important to use extrinsic reinforcement sparingly. The rewards should be just powerful enough to bring forth the desired behavior, and they should be phased out as soon as the person indicates a desire to perform the behavior for its own sake.

on a given behavior, whereas extinction simply involves a failure to reinforce a behavior. Extinction can be a useful way to correct undesirable behaviors, as discussed in Box 6.5. Although both extinction and punishment can cause a decrease in a given behavior, punishment has additional side effects, as we shall see later.

The speed with which extinction occurs is governed by a number of factors. The most important are

1. The individual's level of motivation during extinction. (The higher the level, the slower the rate of extinction.)
2. The amount of effort required to perform the behavior that is undergoing extinction. (The greater the amount of effort, the faster extinction occurs.)
3. The ease with which changes in the conditions of reinforcement can be detected by the individual. (The more quickly the individual can detect changes in contingencies, the faster extinction occurs.)
4. The pattern, strength, and frequency of reinforcement received in the past.

The pattern and frequency with which reinforcements occur are important factors in both rate of learning and extinction. We examine these factors next.

Schedules of reinforcement

In everyday life there are many different types of positive reinforcement contingencies. In some rare instances we receive reinforcement after each response. More frequently, however, only a relatively small proportion of responses receive reinforcement. In other words, reinforcement contingencies operate according to *schedules of reinforcement.* Much research has been directed toward the study of how different reinforcement schedules affect behavior.

A *continuous reinforcement* schedule is in effect if there is reinforcement after every response. *Partial reinforcement,* as the name implies, refers to conditions in which not all responses are followed by reinforcement. Partial reinforcement schedules can be broken down into two major categories: *response-dependent* (or *ratio*) and *time-dependent* (or *interval*) schedules. In response-dependent, or ratio, schedules, reinforcement is contingent on the number of responses the subject makes; in time-dependent, or interval, schedules a certain amount of time must elapse between reinforcements. Both types of schedules may be further subdivided into *fixed* and *variable* schedules. In a fixed schedule the reinforcement always occurs after a fixed number of responses or after a fixed time interval; in variable schedules the required number of responses or the time interval varies around an average. Figure 6.7 shows how all these partial reinforcement categories combine to produce four different reinforcement schedules: fixed ratio (FR), variable ratio (VR), fixed interval (FI), and variable interval (VI).

Fixed ratio. In a fixed-ratio (FR) schedule there is always reinforcement after a fixed number of responses. For example, FR 10 means that reinforcement occurs after every tenth response, regardless of how long it takes the subject to respond ten times.

A special education program designed to help improve the arithmetic skills of underachieving children used an FR reinforcement schedule. The children were given stacks of cards, each of which contained a simple arithmetic problem. When a fixed number of problems were solved correctly, a child could redeem the completed cards for a token that could be used later to purchase other reinforcers. At first, three correct solutions were required for a token (FR 3). The requirements were gradually increased until eventually the children had to solve 20 problems to receive a token (FR 20).

An FR schedule produces a high rate of response with little hesitation between responses. If the ratio is gradually increased, many responses can be ob-

tained with relatively few reinforcements. Pigeons have been known to persistently peck a key in a Skinner box on an FR 20,000 schedule. But if the ratio is increased too rapidly, the response may extinguish between reinforced trials.

FR schedules have a second characteristic effect. As shown in Figure 6.7, the subject pauses after each reinforcement. The larger the ratio of response to reward, the longer the pause.

Variable ratio. In a variable-ratio (VR) schedule, reinforcement is given after a variable or average number of responses. A VR 10 schedule means that, *on the average,* ten responses are required for reinforcement. But any given reinforcement may require less or more than ten responses.

A VR schedule, like an FR schedule, produces a very high rate of response. Because the reinforce-

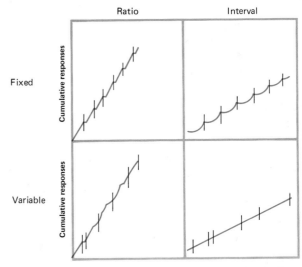

Figure 6.7 Typical cumulative response curves obtained with the four partial schedules of reinforcement. The hash marks on the curves indicate the delivery of a reinforcement. Both of the ratio schedules produce a high rate of responding, as shown in the steep slopes of the curves. Interval schedules have lower response rates. The variable-interval schedule elicits a steady rate of responding, since the time for the next reward is not known. The fixed-interval schedule produces a "scalloped" curve because the animal learns to stop responding (as indicated by the horizontal line) until the time for the next reward approaches.

181

BOX 6.5
The taming of Pascal the Rascal

Mrs. Adams sought help at a child guidance clinic because she was having persistent and severe problems with her 4-year-old son, Pascal. Pascal, she said, seemed to delight in misbehaving. ''He'll go to any lengths just to make my life miserable,'' she complained. His behavior was especially disruptive, she added, when she was concentrating on her housework. Under the circumstances, she found Pascal very difficult to love, and felt guilty about her hostile feelings toward him.

Mrs. Adams was at her wit's end because nothing she had tried with Pascal made him less obnoxious. First she had tried to reason with him. Then she resorted to yelling and screaming at him when he misbehaved. When that produced no effect, Mrs. Adams began using physical punishment. Even that did not work. ''In fact,'' she reported, ''he got worse.''

Mrs. Adams certainly had a problem, but why? How did Pascal get the way he was? Our starting assumption is that brats are made and not born. If this assumption is true, then we must ask two questions about Pascal's behavior: (1) How did it develop? and (2) What was reinforcing it? The second question is the more important one with respect to changing the behavior, for we can decrease undesirable behavior only by altering the current conditions.

We already know that Pascal was most likely to misbehave when his mother was busy. Then his mother attempted to reason with him, scolded him, or punished him physically. If we represent this sequence of events in abstract terms, it seems to be the following: lack of attention → misbehavior → attention.

Like many parents, Mrs. Adams could not understand why such ''punishments'' as scolding and spanking not only failed to reduce her son's negative behaviors, but even seemed to increase them. She did not realize that any sort of attention is such a powerful positive reinforcer for many children that it can overshadow the effects of the punishment. Behavior patterns such as Pascal's usually develop when parents do not reward desirable behaviors with attention; then the only way for a child to get their attention is to misbehave. This again illustrates the difference between the concepts of reward and reinforcement. Parents are not likely to view punishment as a reward for negative behavior, but it certainly can function as a reinforcement.

Like many parents who have similar problems,

ment is variable and predictable, however, there is no postreinforcement pause. Instead there is a relatively steady rate of response, as illustrated in Figure 6.7. Because each response is equally likely to result in reinforcement, this schedule can be physically taxing. Both animals and human beings may continue to respond to the point of exhaustion.

Fixed interval. On a fixed-interval (FI) schedule, reinforcement follows the first response that occurs after a fixed interval of time. On an FI 3 schedule, for example, there is reinforcement for the first response that occurs three minutes after the preceding reinforcement. The reinforcement occurs only if there is a response. The FI schedule produces a characteristic pattern of response, as shown in Figure 6.7. The cumulative recorder shows that after each reinforcement there is a period of time during which the rate of response is very low. As the fixed time interval elapses, the response rate gradually increases until, by the end of the interval, there is a very rapid response rate.

Although ''pure'' FI schedules such as those generated in the laboratory are probably quite rare in everyday life, some situations do approximate them. One such situation, familiar, unfortunately, to all of us, is the schedule of tests in most college courses. Many 12-week courses give three exams, one every

Mrs. Adams believed that there was something wrong with her child. She thought his obnoxious behavior was a symptom of possibly severe emotional problems and was eager for him to begin psychotherapy. The psychologist urged her to consider another explanation: that Pascal was simply responding to the reinforcement contingencies in his life and that the most effective approach would be to modify these contingencies. Mrs. Adams agreed to try to extinguish Pascal's problem behavior while strengthening his positive behaviors.

For a one-week period Mrs. Adams kept a record of Pascal's misbehaviors and of her response to each of them. She was instructed to respond to Pascal as she ordinarily did. These data provided a *baseline* that showed Pascal was engaging in an average of 24 negative behaviors per day and that Mrs. Adams usually responded by giving him some kind of attention.

In the next stage of the program, Mrs. Adams was instructed to ignore Pascal's obnoxious behaviors whenever possible. She was warned that Pascal was likely to increase his negative behaviors for a period of time. When a reinforcement is removed, most people try harder for a while to obtain it before they begin to decrease the behavior. This is the main reason why many people stop extinction procedures before they have a chance to work.

But because Pascal's behavior was so disruptive, it could not simply be ignored. The psychologist suggested a procedure called *time out,* which is short for "time out from positive reinforcement" and involves removing the child from the situation in which he can receive reinforcement. When Pascal's behavior was too disruptive to be ignored, Mrs. Adams was instructed to lock him in another room for a specified period of time. If Pascal threw a tantrum, as he did on the first two occasions, she told him that the time out interval would begin when the tantrum ended. Because it was impossible for Pascal to receive attention during these periods, he soon began to reduce the behaviors that resulted in time out.

Mrs. Adams was also instructed to reinforce Pascal for desirable behaviors by paying attention to him. Because Pascal had strong needs for attention, simply extinguishing his negative behavior without establishing a way to reinforce him for positive behavior would not have been very effective.

Mrs. Adams collected behavioral data on Pascal throughout the program. The frequency of his negative behaviors increased briefly when she started extinction procedures, but declined steadily, along with a corresponding rise in the frequency of positive behaviors. The family atmosphere at the Adams house improved immensely, and Mrs. Adams began to enjoy once again her relationship with Pascal, the ex-Rascal.

four weeks. Suppose that each one offered you the opportunity for reinforcement in the form of a good grade, increased self-esteem, and approval from your instructor. This situation would be very similar to an FI schedule. What kind of pattern would your study behavior follow?

If you are like most students, the cumulative recording of the number of hours you spend studying is likely to resemble the one shown in Figure 6.8. It shows very little study during the first two weeks of the Test 1 interval, somewhat more during the third week, and a great deal of studying during the week of the test. The pattern is repeated for the second and third tests. This "cramming" pattern, which is so common among students, demonstrates the potency of the FI reinforcement schedule.

Variable interval. The variable-interval (VI) schedule, as the name suggests, involves a variable time interval between opportunities for reinforcement. Reinforcement is given for the first response that occurs after the interval. A VI 5 schedule means that, *on the average,* there is a five-minute interval between opportunities for the subject to obtain reinforcement. Because the availability of reinforcements is apparently random, the VI schedule produces a fairly steady response rate that is much different from the scallop pattern generated by an FI schedule. The rate

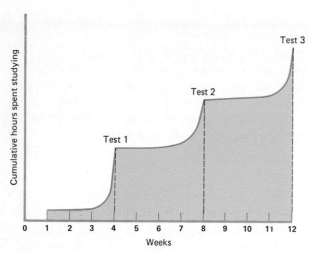

Figure 6.8 The manner in which tests are scheduled in college courses often creates a kind of fixed interval schedule. The cumulative response curve of study behavior for many students shows a gradually increasing amount of study which reaches its maximum rate in "cramming" immediately before the test.

of response for a VI schedule, although fairly steady, is affected by the size of the average interval between reinforcements. The longer the average interval, the lower the rate of response.

Fishing often approximates a VI schedule. You know that the fish are present, but it is difficult to predict when they will start biting. But the fact that the reinforcement is unpredictable may make you very persistent, even if you have not had a bite all day.

Effects of reinforcement schedules on learning and extinction

Reinforcement schedules not only have important effects on response patterns and rates, but also affect rates of learning and extinction. Learning occurs most rapidly under conditions of continuous reinforcement. If there is reinforcement for each response, then there is no opportunity for extinction, and it is easy to perceive the reinforcement contingency rather quickly.

Although learning occurs most rapidly under continuous reinforcement, partial schedules produce behaviors that are harder to extinguish, especially if the behavior is reinforced on a variable rather than

on a fixed schedule. It is very difficult for the subject to discover the fact that reinforcement has ended if it has occurred on a very unpredictable basis in the past. Even if there is no reinforcement, a subject who has been partially reinforced is likely to continue responding for a long time. If, on the other hand, the behavior has previously been reinforced on a continuous schedule, the change is radical and easy to perceive, so that extinction is likely to occur quite rapidly.

The best way to promote fast learning *and* high resistance to extinction is to begin reinforcing the desired behavior on a continuous schedule until the behavior is fairly strong and then shift to a partial (preferably variable) schedule and gradually make it more stringent. With a gradually increasing ratio on a VR schedule, for example, a pigeon may learn to peck a disc 12,000 times per hour in order to obtain a reinforcer given, on the average, once every 110 responses (Ferster and Skinner, 1957).

Let us return at this point to the gambler described at the beginning of the chapter. As the casino guard remarked, he has been responding without reinforcement for a long period of time. Is he indeed sick, as the guard suggests, or can we understand his behavior in terms of the conditions under which he is behaving? On what kind of a reinforcement schedule is he operating, and what are the effects of such a schedule on his behavior?

Gambling is a good example of behavior that is maintained on a variable ratio schedule. Because any spin of the roulette wheel or any pull of the lever on a slot machine is as likely as any other to be reinforced with a jackpot, it is easy to establish a high rate of response for these activities that is highly resistant to extinction. This is especially true if an individual wins a jackpot early on. Suppose, for example, that a slot machine is programmed on a VR 20 schedule. You might drop a coin in, pull the lever, and receive a 10-coin jackpot. After two more attempts, you might hit a 15-coin jackpot. But after 67 more consecutive, unsuccessful attempts, you might walk away muttering angrily about your lot in life. If you were to stay and play the machine indefinitely, you would receive a payoff for every 20 attempts, on the average. The reason these "one-armed bandits" make money for the owner is that the average number of coins in the jackpot is smaller than the 20

What kind of a reinforcement schedule are these people responding to? (Bellak, Jeroboam)

needed, on the average, to trigger the jackpot. Our "sick" gambler, then, may be seen as the unhappy victim of a difficult reinforcement situation rather than as the victim of some mysterious sickness.

Negative reinforcement: Escape and avoidance conditioning

As we suggested earlier, we can understand most kinds of behavior as attempts to maximize positive outcomes and to minimize negative ones. In our discussion of positive reinforcement we have focused on positive outcomes. We now turn to those behaviors that we learn and maintain in order to escape from or avoid negative consequences. These behaviors are maintained through *negative reinforcement*. A negative reinforcement is anything that serves to increase a behavior that results in its *removal*. It is important not to confuse negative reinforcement with punishment. Negative reinforcement *increases* a response that enables the subject to escape or avoid the consequence, whereas punishment simply *decreases* the response on which it is contingent.

Escape conditioning is the direct result of negative reinforcement. The following experiment demonstrates the way in which animals respond to this conditioning. A dog is placed in a shuttlebox, a rectangular chamber with two compartments separated by a low partition. The floor of the shuttlebox has an electric grid through which shock can be delivered to either compartment. The shock produces a strong emotional response, and the dog attempts to escape

from the compartment. Sooner or later during one of its escape attempts, the dog jumps over the barrier into the other compartment, in which the current is not on. When it is turned on, the dog can escape by jumping over the partition in the opposite direction. The shock stimulus is a negative reinforcer for the jumping behavior. As the conditioning proceeds, the dog will require less and less time to escape the shock, until finally it will escape as soon as the shock is administered.

To study *avoidance conditioning* we need only introduce a warning buzzer or some other stimulus that precedes the shock. The dog will learn after the first several trials that the buzzer signals impending shock. After it learns to jump over the partition in response to the shock, it will begin to jump over the partition after it hears the buzzer and before the shock is administered.

The *two-factor theory of avoidance learning* provides the following analysis of shuttlebox avoidance learning: First, because it is paired with shock on the initial trials, the warning stimulus or buzzer evokes a classically conditioned fear (anxiety) response. The fear aroused motivates the operant avoidance behavior, and anxiety reduction following the avoidance serves to reinforce the avoidance behavior. As you can see, this two-factor theory incorporates both classical and operant conditioning factors to account for the development and maintenance of avoidance behavior.

One aspect of this avoidance experiment that has intrigued psychologists is the remarkable strength of

185

the avoidance behavior that may develop in only a few trials. Some animals need experience only a few shocks before they learn to jump into the other compartment of a shuttlebox at the sound of the warning buzzer. After that they may jump thousands of times to the buzzer without ever again experiencing shock. What accounts for the amazing resistance of avoidance behavior to extinction?

The key to this intriguing question, according to the two-factor theory, is the conditioned fear response that motivates the avoidance behavior and whose reduction reinforces it. Fear reduction is a powerful reinforcer, and because each avoidance response is followed by a reduction in fear, as long as the fear remains the avoidance behavior continues. But why does the classically conditioned fear response not extinguish? After all, the buzzer is paired with the shock only a few times at the beginning of the training. This is exactly the same question we asked earlier concerning the young woman's fear of cars. In her case the automobile stimuli were associated with pain on only one occasion, yet the conditioned fear response did not grow weaker.

Recall that in order for a classically conditioned response to be extinguished, the CS (warning buzzer, automobile stimuli) must be presented in the absence of the UCS (shock, pain) long enough for extinction to occur. But if an effective avoidance response is learned, the subject leaves the fear-producing situation before extinction can occur. Thus the dog in the shuttlebox has no opportunity to learn that the buzzer (CS) is no longer followed by a shock because it is long gone by the time the shock would occur, and the young woman never allows herself to be around an automobile long enough for her fear to extinguish. The avoidance behaviors prevent the fear response from becoming extinct, and the avoidance responses are strengthened over time because they reduce fear. This helps to account for the fact that phobic avoidance often becomes stronger over time, as appears to have been the case for our young woman's automobile phobia.

186 Does this theoretical analysis of the woman's automobile phobia have any implications for treating her problem? One approach to treating phobias is based on the two-factor theory and is called *flooding*. It is described in Box 6.6.

Punishment

A punishment can be defined as any consequence that decreases the future occurrence of the behavior on which it is contingent. Punishment can be administered in either of two forms: (1) by applying negative stimuli, such as painful physical contact or verbal reprimands, and (2) by removing positive reinforcers that are customarily available to an individual, such as privileges, social interactions, or possessions. The latter form of punishment is different from extinction because the reinforcer of which the subject is deprived is *not* the one that is reinforcing the undesired behavior. For example, if a child is deprived of watching television for misbehaving in school, it is punishment rather than an attempt at extinction, because watching television is not what reinforces the child's misbehavior.

Because the two types of punishment have somewhat different side effects, we discuss them separately.

Applying negative stimuli

When a negative stimulus is made contingent on a given behavior, an inhibition or suppression of that behavior usually occurs. But a punished behavior may reappear at a later time with full intensity, particularly if circumstances change or if the punisher is not present. This is an important criticism of the use of punishment. In addition, many kinds of punishment have been criticized on humanitarian and ethical-moral grounds. Box 6.7 discusses some of the issues that relate to the use of punishment and shows an example of the conditions under which punishment might be employed by a psychologist to change behavior.

Punishment is frequently effective in controlling undesirable behaviors, but it can have a number of undesirable side effects.

First, the suppressive effects may generalize to related behaviors. For example, a child who is severely punished for inappropriate physical aggression may become generally unassertive, even in situations in which assertive behaviors would be appropriate. Behaviors that are punished because they are culturally prohibited at certain ages may be difficult to resume later on. For instance, a person who is punished for sexual behaviors during childhood may suffer from later sexual inhibitions.

BOX 6.6

Flooding in the treatment of phobias

According to the two-factor theory of avoidance learning, it should be possible to eliminate phobias by forcing extinction. This involves preventing the avoidance responses and exposing individuals to the CS they fear in the absence of the UCS with which it was originally paired. Studies with both animals (Polin, 1959) and human beings (Hogan and Kirchner, 1967) have shown that conditioned fear responses can be extinguished in this way. A clinical treatment based on this principle is called *flooding*, and has been used to treat phobic disorders. Imaginative scenes involving stimuli that the patient fears are presented to the patient in order to elicit the conditioned fear response. For example, the patient with the car phobia might be asked to imagine in vivid detail such scenes as the following:

1. She is drawn as if by some unseen force out of her house. She approaches her car and climbs in.
2. She drives away from her house onto side streets, then onto a freeway, where she involuntarily dodges through rush hour traffic. Her speed gradually increases until she is up to 110 mph.
3. Her car slows down to 90 and exits from the freeway onto a narrow winding mountain road, narrowly missing light pole after light pole. The situation improves very little when she realizes she has no brakes and the steering wheel comes off in her hand. She careens down the mountain road out of control. It is quite dark now and the only light comes from her engine, which has burst into flames. In the dim light a sign flashes past that says: "Dead End."

These scenes would probably elicit intense fear responses from our patient. In each instance the therapist would continue to describe the scene with appropriate embellishments until the patient's anxiety level decreased, indicating that in the absence of a painful UCS, the fear response was extinguishing. These extinction effects should generalize to "real-world" situations involving the stimuli that evoked the fear.

Because of the intense anxiety that patients experience during the treatment, many therapists resort to flooding only if other fear reduction techniques have failed. Flooding seems to be more effective than other treatment techniques in treating strong phobias that are relatively unresponsive to other forms of treatment (Boulougouris, Marks, and Marset, 1971). For milder fears that can be treated on a short-term basis, other techniques may be preferable.

Second, individuals who are punished may simply learn to avoid the punishing person or situation and not learn to change their behavior. In addition, a socializing agent, such as a parent or teacher, consistently associated with punishment is not likely to be an effective administrator of positive social reinforcers, such as approval. In other words, if we do not like someone, we will probably not value his or her approval.

Third, people learn many of their behaviors by observing those of others and their consequences. What will the child learn whose parents successfully control his or her behavior through physical punishment?

But certain steps can be taken to reduce these undesirable side effects. First, let us consider the criticism that punishment results in only a temporary suppression of behavior. The evidence for this assertion comes chiefly from animal studies, such as one in which a rat in a Skinner box is shocked for pressing the bar that results in delivery of food. Under these circumstances the rat temporarily stops

BOX 6.7

Therapeutic use of punishment

There are two important questions that psychologists ask themselves before they decide to use punishment as a treatment technique: (1) Are there alternative, less painful approaches that might be effective? (2) Is the behavior to be eliminated sufficiently injurious to the individual or to society to justify the severity of the punishment?

Treatment programs involving punishment are used only under very specific conditions. One is when the performance of the undesirable behavior is in itself reinforcing, as is the case for some aggressive behaviors. Punishment can also be used to bring under rapid control behaviors that have injurious consequences for the performer or for others. Finally, punishment might also be used when the reinforcers for an injurious behavior cannot be identified or controlled. To illustrate the therapeutic use of punishment, let us consider a case that involves all three of the preceding conditions.

Some of the most startling and self-destructive behavior is exhibited by schizophrenic and mentally retarded children. These children may strike themselves repeatedly, bang their heads on the floor and on sharp objects, bite or tear pieces of flesh from their bodies, and engage in other forms of self-mutilation. Such behaviors are, of course, extremely serious, because they may cause permanent injuries, and self-mutilating children must often be kept under constant physical restraint. It is also difficult to specify what the reinforcement for the behavior is in any given case, because the children continue the behavior in spite of the pain it produces. Although they are perplexing and difficult to understand, self-mutilating children have responded to a variety of operant conditioning procedures, including punishment.

Bradley Bucher and Ivar Lovaas (1968) report several cases in which self-destructive behaviors in disturbed children were eliminated through the use of electric shock. One 7-year-old boy who had been self-injurious for five years performed some 3000 self-pummeling responses during a 90-minute period when his restraints were removed. During treatment he was wired with electrodes and given an electric shock each time he struck himself. Only 12 shocks over four treatment sessions were required to virtually eliminate his self-destructive behavior. In another case a schizophrenic girl who had been banging her head against objects for a period of six years ceased after she received a total of 15 contingent shocks.

---

pressing the bar but may soon begin again (depending on how strong the shock was and how hungry the rat becomes). This is not surprising because the only way that the rat can obtain food is by pressing the bar. Suppose, however, that the rat learned an alternative behavior (such as pressing a foot pedal) that also allowed it to receive food. Under these circumstances we would expect the punishing of the bar-press response to result in relatively permanent suppression of that response. Available evidence (Mowrer, 1940) indicates that when there are alternative ways of obtaining reinforcers, punishment has more potent suppressive effects on the punished behavior. This is an important consideration in attempting to use punishment as a means of social change. For instance, punishment for wrongdoing is not likely to be effective in reducing the antisocial behavior of delinquents who have no alternative means of obtaining things they want. More likely, it would encourage them to develop more sophisticated antisocial behaviors that would reduce their chances of being caught and punished. Fear of punishment might be a more effective deterrent to crime if we provided delinquents with opportunities to acquire needed social, vocational, and educational skills (See Chapter 17.)

Punishment is most effective when it is used in conjunction with other procedures designed to strengthen desirable alternative behaviors. This is especially true if the alternative behavior is one that competes with or blocks the response that is being punished. For example, punishment may be used to suppress temporarily physically aggressive behavior while pro-social cooperative responses are being strengthened through positive reinforcement.

Certain other measures may reduce or minimize some of the negative byproducts of punishment. It is important to help the individual who is receiving punishment to discriminate between appropriate and inappropriate behaviors and to learn when a particular behavior is desirable and when it is undesirable. For instance, to keep the suppressive effects of punishment for physical aggression from generalizing to other forms of self-assertion, a parent should not merely punish the physical aggression, but should also reward desirable forms of assertiveness. Similarly, if individuals are consistently punished for a given behavior in one situation but consistently are not punished for the same behavior in another situation, they will have an easy time learning when and where the behavior is appropriate. For human beings language is one of the greatest aids in learning to make these discriminations. For example, we can say simply, "It's okay for you to play tackle football outside, but not in my china closet."

But although some of the undesirable side effects of punishment can be prevented, it is difficult to keep individuals from avoiding punishing agents and situations and from learning through imitation. In general, then, it is best not to use punishment when other measures, such as extinction, might be effective.

Punishment through removal of reinforcers

The second type of punishment involves the removal of positive reinforcers that are not connected with the behavior being punished. This punishment through deprivation has two distinct advantages over punishment that involves administering negative stimuli. First, it does not create new fears, even though it may cause temporary frustration. It is less likely to cause avoidance of the punisher or of the punishment situation, and it may actually increase the attractiveness of the punisher and/or situation.

Second, there is no aggressive behavior that the punished individual can learn through imitation. For these reasons punishment through deprivation is usually preferable to punishment that involves administering negative stimuli.

Self-reinforcement

Until now we have considered only external consequences of behavior. But although external rewards and punishments are crucial determinants of behavior, they are clearly not the whole story. How can we explain the behavior of a prisoner of war who chooses to die rather than to cooperate with the enemy, or of a person who performs a noble act when there is no chance for recognition, or of an individual who resists temptation when there is no chance that he or she will be discovered and punished? Examples such as these suggest that in some instances the causes of behaviors may be independent of external reinforcement contingencies. In recent years psychologists have begun to focus more attention on internal rewards and punishments, or *self-reinforcement* processes.

Self-reinforcement may involve giving or depriving oneself of external goods or experiences. For example, an individual may make a contract with himself or herself to enjoy a meal at a fine restaurant if he or she completes a homework assignment, or to give up some bodily pleasure for a period of time if he or she does not. But a more interesting set of self-reinforcement processes involves self-approval or self-disapproval for meeting or failing to meet personal standards of behavior. We have all felt proud of ourselves for doing something of which no one else was aware. And we have all disapproved of, berated, or devalued ourselves for failing to live up to our own standards in other situations. What we usually call self-esteem may be viewed in terms of self-reinforcement processes, in that individuals with high self-esteem reinforce themselves positively quite often, whereas those with low self-esteem evaluate themselves quite negatively.

Self-reinforcing responses appear to develop both as a result of direct learning experiences and through observing the behaviors of others. In the former case someone else, such as a parent, sets up standards for acceptable behavior and consistently rewards the individual for meeting or exceeding the standards and does not reward or punishes the individual if he or she falls short of them. Eventually, the individual will selectively reward himself or herself according to similar standards. For example, children whose parents reward them only when they perform at a superior level are likely to regard average achievement as inadequate and to devalue themselves unless they meet or exceed the high standards they have been taught. A second way in which individuals establish standards for reinforcing themselves is by observing others. Many research studies have shown that individuals tend to adopt the standards they see in others, particularly in novel situations in which they are unsure of what constitutes acceptable performance.

Once standards for self-reinforcement have been developed, a given behavior can have two consequences: an external outcome and a self-evaluative response. In some instances these two consequences conflict with one another; an individual may be punished by others for performing an act of which he approves. Under such circumstances the self-reinforcement system might be strong enough to override the external outcome, so that the individual will continue to perform the behavior. In Chapter 8 we explore the role of self-reinforcement in controlling behavior in greater detail.

Sometimes unrealistic standards for self-reinforcement result in maladjustment and unhappiness. Some people experience a great deal of distress because they have excessively high standards for self-reinforcement. Because they had direct learning experiences in which others demanded exceedingly high levels of performance and/or because they compared themselves with "superstar" models, these individuals acquired standards that they can rarely meet; as a result, they suffer depression, feelings of worthlessness, and self-devaluation.

Timing of behavioral consequences

The timing as well as the schedule of the consequences for a given behavior can have important effects on that behavior. Other things being equal, consequences that occur immediately after the behavior have stronger effects than consequences that occur later on. Many behaviors have immediate positive consequences and later negative consequences. Smoking, drinking, drug usage, and criminal acts all have this pattern of consequences. These behaviors are difficult for many people to overcome because the immediate positive reinforcement for the behavior overrides the negative consequences that occur later on.

The psychologist O. H. Mowrer (1950) once sought to resolve what he termed the *neurotic paradox:* If behavior is governed by its consequences, why do some people (called neurotics) repeatedly engage in behaviors that are maladaptive, self-defeating, and frequently punished by the society in which they live? Mowrer explained the paradox in terms of the timing of consequences. The deviant behaviors are maintained, he suggested, because they produce immediate reinforcement, often in the form of anxiety reduction. For example, neurotics may consistently destroy their love relationships because they unconsciously fear being too close to others. The need to deal with this fear can be more potent than the negative consequences that may occur later. This is true even though the negative consequences may be stronger in absolute terms, involving societal rejection, nonattainment of important goals, or even psychiatric hospitalization.

In spite of the greater potency of immediate consequences, however, it is clear that they do not always govern people's behavior. Many people did stop smoking, thus foregoing immediate pleasure, when evidence linking smoking with lung cancer—a long-term effect—was publicized. People often strive for long-term goals in the face of great immediate difficulties. Think of the many day-to-day frustrations that you experience as you work toward your college degree. In general, it appears that human behavior is less influenced by the timing of behavioral consequences than are the behaviors of lower species.

One very important factor that can help free us from the immediacy factor is our ability to imagine future events. Our imagination allows us to cross the time gap and experience future consequences in the present. Many people are able to tolerate unpleasantness in the present by imagining future positive outcomes. Conversely, imagining future aversive consequences may override the effects of immediate short-term positive reinforcement. However, because it is unpleasant to imagine negative consequences, many people avoid doing so. Box 6.8 describes the therapeutic use of imagination to bring a criminal behavior under control.

BOX 6.8
Experiencing the ultimate aversive consequence

The following case study illustrates a behavior change program based on the imagining of future aversive consequences in the treatment of a criminal behavior of long standing.

The patient was a 33-year-old divorcee and mother of seven children who had been shoplifting on an almost daily basis for more than 20 years. This behavior had led to some 15 to 20 arrests and convictions and several jail terms. She reported that she never thought about the consequences of her stealing until she was caught. The client felt that another conviction would result in a long prison sentence.

The first phase of the treatment program involved identifying the ultimate aversive consequences (UAC's) for the client of being arrested. These included being sent to jail, being separated from her children, being visited in jail by her tearful children and told that the court was going to place the children in foster homes, and losing contact with her children. The client was trained to vividly imagine these scenes, which greatly upset her.

Next, the client was trained to associate the imagined UAC's not only with the stealing response, but also with earlier links in the chain of behaviors leading up to stealing. Whenever such a behavior chain is involved, it is best to concentrate on stopping the earliest behaviors in the chain. They are the easiest to eliminate, since they are farthest from the reinforcement which follows the final response in the

Teaching shoplifters to imagine the future punishment they might receive can help them to inhibit their criminal behavior. (Anspach, EPA)

chain. To aid in this training, the client enacted the shoplifting behaviors in the therapist's office while verbalizing and visualizing the UAC's which would occur if she were caught.

According to the client's reports, the program was highly effective in allowing her to bring her shoplifting behavior under control. She reported a complete cessation of stealing for a 5-month period before once again experiencing the urge to shoplift. A number of additional treatment sessions resulted in a 2-month period of abstinence, at which time treatment was terminated.

Both the preceding discussion of self-reinforcement and the present consideration of imagined behavioral consequences illustrate the important roles that cognitive processes play in controlling human behavior. We are not merely passive reactors to external environmental forces; we have the capacity to plan and regulate our own behavior. We must realize that these internal processes are behaviors, and that we may train ourselves to use them more effectively in our own interests.

OBSERVATIONAL LEARNING (MODELING)

As we have mentioned before, our behavior is strongly influenced by our observations of others' behavior and its consequences. In fact, it seems that virtually all the direct learning phenomena that we have discussed can occur through observation of others. This method often saves us time and effort; we are spared the potentially dangerous process of learning through trial and error, and we can instead imitate those behaviors that appear to pay off for others and avoid engaging in those that have negative outcomes.

When we observe models in a particular situation we typically gather information not only about how they are behaving, but also about the consequences of their behavior. We can learn modeled behavior simply by observing it, but whether or not we perform the behavior is strongly influenced by the consequences that the model experiences. If the model is reinforced we are far more likely to imitate the behavior than if the model is punished.

In one study, for example, children watched a film in which a model exhibited a series of novel verbal and physical aggressive responses. The consequences for these behaviors were varied; one group of children saw the model rewarded with praise and candy, a second group saw the model reprimanded for his aggression, and a third group saw no consequences for the model. After the film the children were observed to see how many of the novel aggressive responses they reproduced. Those children who saw the model punished performed fewer imitative responses than did the children who had seen the model rewarded and those who had seen no consequences. The experimenter then offered the children attractive incentives if they could do what they had seen the model do. All the children quickly reproduced the model's aggressive behaviors, so that there was no longer any difference between the children who had seen the model punished and the children from the other two groups. Clearly, the three groups of children had all learned the same amount, but those who had seen the model punished were more reluctant to perform the aggressive behavior (Bandura, 1965).

192

Establishing new behaviors through modeling

Through exposure to *behavioral modeling stimuli,* individuals can be shown how to perform a desired behavior. After language develops they can be told how to do something through *verbal modeling stimuli* (instruction). The following excerpt from a newspaper advice column is an example of verbal modeling stimuli:

Dear Walt: I don't smoke and I'm wondering if I have a right to ask my dates not to smoke in my car. I don't like the smell and it stays in the car for a long, long time after the smokers go.

Joe

Dear Joe: You have the right, but exercise it at point of invitation. "I'm really bothered by cigaret smoke, so I've made my car nicotine-free by banning cigarets. I'd love to take you to the concert (dance, whatever), but I don't know if you can stand the drive without a puff. What do you think?" If she says "yes," remind her of her promise by posting a cancer-control sign on the dashboard. (Hurrah for you!)

Walt

(*The Seattle Times,* November 6, 1972)

Some individuals have behavioral problems because they have not learned the necessary skills to adjust satisfactorily to their life situations. Modeling can be used to help people acquire these skills. (See Box 6.9.)

Observational learning and extinction of emotional responses

Emotional responses as well as overt behaviors can be learned through modeling. For example, children often acquire fears by observing fear responses in their parents or other adults. Laboratory studies have shown that classically conditioned emotional responses can be learned by observing what happens to another person. In a typical observational classical conditioning experiment, the subject observes another person exhibit a pain response to a simulated electric shock. A neutral stimulus, such as a tone, repeatedly accompanies the observed pain response. Later, when the neutral stimulus is presented to the observer without pain cues, the observer usually exhibits an increase in physiological arousal, indicating a conditioned emotional response (Berger, 1962).

Modeling can also reduce emotional responses. A study by Albert Bandura, Joan Grusec, and Frances Menlove (1967) shows how modeling procedures can be used to treat maladaptive emotional responses.

Young children with a strong fear of dogs were the subjects. Before their assignment to treatment groups, they were given a "behavioral avoidance test" that consisted of a series of tasks involving progressively closer interactions with a dog. Their fear level was measured by the number of tasks they could complete. The children were then assigned to one of four experimental groups. One group participated in eight short sessions in which they watched a fearless child engage in increasingly daring interactions with a dog. The atmosphere was festive and light, designed to counteract the children's fear. A second group observed the same activities in a more subdued setting. A third group was exposed to the dog in the festive atmosphere with no model. A fourth group was placed in the festive atmosphere with neither a dog nor a model.

Following the eight sessions, the children were once again given the behavioral avoidance test, this time with a different dog. They were asked to pet the dog, release it from a playpen, remove its leash, feed it dog biscuits, stay alone in the room with it, and, finally, lock themselves in the playpen with the dog. One month later the children were again given the avoidance test as a follow-up to assess the long-term effects of the treatments.

The results of the study are presented in Figure 6.9. Clearly, the two conditions in which models

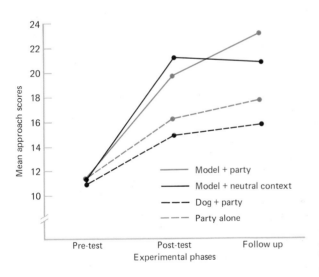

Figure 6.9 Dog-approach scores of children in the various conditions of the Bandura, Grusec, and Menlove (1967) study as measured before and after treatment, and at follow-up. A girl who was fearful of dogs fearlessly interacts with dogs after being exposed to fearless models (Bandura and Menlove, 1968). (Copyright 1967 and 1968 by the American Psychological Association. Reprinted by permission.)

193

BOX 6.9
Modeling and juvenile delinquency

A training program based on modeling was conducted by Irwin G. Sarason and Victor Ganzer (1973) at a juvenile detention facility in Tacoma, Washington. They assumed that many juvenile delinquents engage in antisocial behaviors because they have not mastered certain adaptive behaviors and that if they can learn these behaviors, they might become useful members of society.

The subjects were male first offenders ranging in age from 15 to 18. Some of them were randomly assigned to training that involved modeling, while others in a control group received no treatment. Those in the training program engaged in 14 three-hour sessions on ways of dealing with common problems in their lives, such as how to apply for a job, how to approach teachers or parole counselors for help, how to resist social pressures to engage in antisocial acts, and how to bypass opportunities for immediate gratifications in favor of long-term goals. Each of the sessions dealt with a specific problem and ways of coping with it. The sessions were led by trained psychology graduate students, and four or five subjects attended each one. The series was introduced in this way:

> We think that small groups, working together, can learn a lot about appropriate ways of doing things just by playing different roles and watching others play roles. By role we mean the particular part a person acts or plays in a particular situation—kind of like the parts actors play in a movie scene, only this will be more realistic. These roles will be based on actual situations that many young people have trouble with, like how to control your anger, or resist being pressured into doing destructive things by friends. . . . We want to emphasize better ways of doing these things and coping with similar problems which will be important in the future for most of you. Everyone in the group will both play the roles for themselves and watch others playing the same roles. This is like acting, only it is realistic because it involves situations in which you might really find yourselves. We feel that the situations are realistic because they are based on the real experiences of a lot of fellows.

interacted with a dog were more effective in reducing fear than were the other two. Exposure to the dog alone had relatively little effect unless the model was also present.

CURRENT DEVELOPMENTS IN LEARNING

Because learning is so central to understanding and changing behavior, it is intimately involved in many of the frontiers of behavior. Recent years have seen many advances in the application of learning principles to personal and societal problems. They have also witnessed scientific discoveries that call into question some of the widely accepted principles of learning. In this section we discuss a number of these current developments.

Learning to control "involuntary" behaviors
A great many of our internal behaviors occur in a seemingly automatic and involuntary fashion. For example, the actions of internal organs, such as the heart, the liver, various glands, the digestive system, and so on, occur without conscious awareness. As we noted in Chapter 3, such behaviors are brought about, or mediated, by the autonomic nervous system, which is involved in carrying out basic bodily functions.

During each session the leaders posed a practical problem, demonstrated how it might be handled, and the boys imitated the behavior. One session dealt with how to behave in a job interview. This topic was selected because many delinquents have short academic careers and seek jobs at an early age.

The experimenters administered a series of personality and self-concept measures to the subjects before and after treatment. Ward personnel rated the subjects' behaviors before and after treatment, and the boys were followed up over a three-year period to assess the long-term effects of the treatment.

The results of the study were quite encouraging. The boys who had received treatment showed more positive changes in attitude and behavior than those in the nontreatment control group. The training also seemed to have long-range effects on the delinquent boys. Among the no-treatment control group, 34 percent were arrested again at least once during the next three years, compared with only 19 percent in the training group.

One incident shows how the modeling experience affected some of the boys. About a year after he had participated in this experiment, Jimmy Larsen paid a social visit to Cascadia, the institution in which it had been carried out. He described his recent experience in hunting for work. Jimmy received a number of rebuffs because the labor market was tight and because he had a "record." However, he was able to obtain an appointment with the personnel manager of a large company. On arriving for a 3 o'clock interview, Jimmy was told that the personnel manager would be a half-hour late and was invited to sit in the waiting room. Jimmy's tension increased until the job interview scene he had enacted in the experiment popped into his head. To distract himself he thought about that scene and spent several minutes rehearsing it. The scene dealt with the specific types of behavior that are important for a job applicant (courtesy, neatness, interest, honesty). While he was waiting Jimmy thought about specific things he could say or do that would communicate how interested he was in joining the company. He paid his return visit to Cascadia to tell those who had conducted the experiment that he had gotten the job. He attributed his success to Cascadia's modeling program.

The autonomic nervous system (ANS) has long been viewed as an involuntary system that cannot be directly controlled by the individual. The ANS was known to be capable of being classically conditioned, but operant conditioning of autonomic responses was thought to be impossible. For example, although increases in heart rate could be classically conditioned to a light by pairing the light (CS) with a loud noise (UCS), individuals could not directly increase their heart rates in order to receive rewards, or so it was believed.

Sharply conflicting with this prevailing belief were reports of individuals who apparently had achieved a great deal of control over such behaviors. Such reports described feats performed by Eastern Yogi and Zen practitioners that indicated a degree of control over "involuntary" behaviors unheard of in Western man. For example, Wenger, Bagchi, and Anand (1969) tested four Yogi practitioners who were able to decrease cardiac activity for 10 to 15 seconds to the extent that the heartbeat could not be heard with a stethoscope and pulse disappeared, although electrocardiograph readings showed that the heart continued to beat. Green (1972) described a series of studies with a Yogi named Swami Rama. Laboratory tests showed that the Swami was able to, among other things: (1) speed up and slow down his heart rate at will; (2) stop his heart from pumping blood for 17 seconds; (3) cause two areas of his palm a few inches apart gradually to change temperature in op-

195

posite directions until the areas differed in skin temperature by 10°F. The "hot" side of his palm became rosy red, whereas the "cold" side became ashen gray during this demonstration; (4) produce widely differing brain wave patterns at will.

In the late 1960s Neal E. Miller, an eminent psychologist who has devoted most of his career to discovering the mechanisms of motivation and learning, published a series of striking demonstrations of the use of operant principles in establishing control of "involuntary" responses in animals. Miller and his students developed a procedure for training rats to increase or decrease their heart rates by reinforcing their responses. In order to ensure that the rats' voluntary skeletal muscles were not influencing their heart rates, Miller injected the rat with curare, a drug that paralyzes the skeletal muscles but does not affect the internal organs. He also provided each rat with an artificial respirator so that it would not die as it became paralyzed. The investigators chose to use direct electrical stimulation of a "pleasure center" of the brain as a positive reinforcer.

To condition heart rate the experimenters began to monitor the interval between heartbeats (the interbeat interval, or IBI). Initially, they reinforced spontaneous IBI changes in the desired direction. Some animals were reinforced for heart rate reductions, others for increases. They used a shaping procedure, which required progressively larger IBI changes for reinforcement as the training session continued.

The results were quite encouraging. Miller and his associates were able to produce approximately 20 percent increases or decreases in heart rate in only 90 minutes of training. (See Figure 6.10.) They obtained similar results when they used shock avoidance rather than brain stimulation as the reinforcer. Moreover, rats who were given only one such training session seemed to retain the learned cardiac control when they were retested three months later. The cardiac responses could also be brought under stimulus control. Rats who were reinforced for heart rate changes when a light and tone were present and not reinforced when they were absent rapidly learned to change their heart rates only for the light and tone. Using similar operant techniques, Miller's group was also able to condition control of intestinal contractions, kidney function, and blood volume.

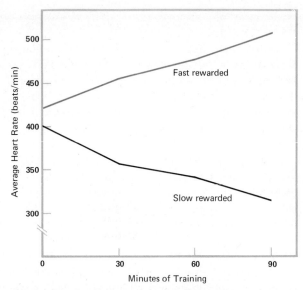

Figure 6.10 Cardiac changes over a 90-minute period in rats rewarded for increases or decreases in heart rate in the first Miller and DiCara (1967) experiments on operant conditioning of cardiac responses.

More recent studies by Miller and other investigators have shown less impressive control of heart rate in curarized rats (about 5 percent changes as opposed to 20 in the original study). Nevertheless, a surge of interest in operant autonomic control has opened up a new frontier of behavior. Miller and other psychologists were quick to see the enormous implications of autonomic control. For instance, the fact that control of visceral and glandular responses can be learned may help us to understand how certain physical disorders with psychological origin (psychosomatic disorders) might develop. An individual who is reinforced for certain physical symptoms with concern, attention, or escape from responsibility may inadvertently (and unconsciously) learn to perform these "involuntary" behaviors under certain circumstances. But the most exciting implication of these studies is that we have the potential to learn through *biofeedback* techniques to control our internal processes for our own benefit. (See Box 6.10.)

Changing behavior within social systems

We have already examined within this chapter numerous ways in which learning principles can be applied to help solve human problems. Most of our examples involved changing the behavior of one individual within a treatment context. In recent years, however, there have been increasingly more ambitious attempts to use the principles of learning for problem solving on a social level.

Many of these broad attempts at behavior modification have occurred within the field of education. Retarded and emotionally disturbed children who could not learn in traditional educational settings have responded very favorably to teaching methods based on behavior modification. One program focused on a special education preschool classroom straight out of a teacher's nightmare. The following is a record of four minutes of behavior in that classroom:

Mike, John, and Dan are seated together playing with pieces of Playdoh. Barry, some distance from the others, is seated and also is playing with Playdoh. The children, except Barry, are talking to each other about what they are making. Time is 9:10 A.M. Miss Sally, the teacher, turns toward the children and says, "It's time for a lesson. Put your Playdoh away." Mike says, "Not me." John says, "Not me." Dan says, "Not me." Miss Sally moves toward Mike. Mike throws his Playdoh in Miss Sally's face. Miss Sally jerks back, then moves forward rapidly and snatches Playdoh from Mike. Puts Playdoh in her pocket. Mike screams for Playdoh, says he wants to play with it. Mike moves toward Miss Sally and attempts to snatch the Playdoh from her pocket. Miss Sally pushes him away. Mike kicks her on the leg, kicks her again and demands the return of his Playdoh. Kicks her again, picks up a small steel chair and throws it at Miss Sally. She jumps out of the way. Mike picks up another chair and throws it more violently. Miss Sally cannot move in time and chair strikes her foot. Miss Sally pushes Mike down on the floor. Mike starts up, pulls over one chair, then another, another; stops a moment. Miss Sally is picking up chairs. Mike looks at her. She moves toward Mike. Mike runs away. John wants his Playdoh. Miss Sally says, "No." He joins Mike in pulling over chairs and attempts to grab Playdoh from Miss Sally's pocket; she pushes him away roughly. John is screaming that he wants to play with his Playdoh; moves toward phonograph, pulls it off the table and lets it crash onto the floor. Mike has his coat on; says he is going home. Miss Sally asks Dan to bolt the door. Dan gets to the door at the same time as Mike. Mike hits Dan in the face. Dan's nose is bleeding. Miss Sally walks over to Dan, turns to the others and says that she is taking Dan to the washroom and that while she is away, *they may play with the Playdoh.* Returns Playdoh from pocket to Mike and John. Time: 9:14 A.M. (Hamblin et al., 1971, p. 102, italics ours)

Initial or baseline observations indicated that, on the average, the children engaged in 55 cooperative and 140 aggressive sequences per day.

The investigators instructed Miss Sally to ignore all the children's aggressive behaviors and to reward their cooperative behaviors with tokens that they could later exchange for various reinforcers. Under these conditions the behavior patterns in the classroom changed radically. Within 12 days the number of aggressive sequences had dropped from 140 to about 15 per day, whereas cooperative behaviors rose from 55 to about 150 a day.

A number of investigators have applied behavioral techniques to solving certain types of environmental problems. One project designed to reduce littering (Kohlenberg and Phillips, 1973) was set up at the municipal zoo in Seattle, Washington. The researchers placed a single trash can near a concession stand as an experimental trash receptacle. During a baseline period that lasted two weeks, trained observers recorded the number of deposits made in the trash receptacle during an eight-hour period each day. (As you can see, science is not always glamorous.) During the third and fourth weeks, a sign was placed near the receptacle that read: "At times persons depositing litter in this container will be rewarded." An experimenter stood nearby and, on a randomly determined variable ratio schedule (VR 20), gave individuals who deposited litter a ticket that they could redeem for a free soft drink at the concession stand. (They were not reinforced if they deposited trash removed from other cans.) During the third two-week period the researchers left the sign, but they did not give any reinforcers. Finally, during the seventh and eighth weeks they reinstated reinforcement on a more generous (VR 10) schedule.

The total number of deposits during the four experimental periods is shown in Figure 6.11. Data collected on the age of depositors showed that those between the ages of 10 and 20 were most responsive.

197

BOX 6.10

Biofeedback: A psychological frontier

Numerous studies conducted during the 1960s indicated that humans as well as animals can learn to control their heart rate, blood pressure, brain waves, and other behavior previously thought to be involuntary. It was further shown that no external reinforcement of the behaviors is necessary. All that is required is that the individual be given information in the form of *feedback* from the particular response system. Just as we could never learn to shoot a basketball accurately if we did not receive feedback from our muscles and visual feedback regarding our accuracy, we cannot learn to control our heart rate or brain waves unless we receive some kind of feedback on physiological changes as they occur. The feedback then serves as the reinforcer for change in the desired direction. By precisely measuring physiological events and converting the electronic signals into visual or auditory feedback, we can be made continuously aware of our own physiological responses. This process is known as *biofeedback,* and it has been used to train people to control voluntarily physiological response systems involved in stress reactions and in physical and psychosomatic problems.

Biofeedback techniques have been used to alleviate a variety of medical and psychological problems. At Baltimore City Hospital, Weiss and Engle (1971) treated eight patients suffering from premature ventricular contractions, a dangerous heart disorder that can produce sudden death. The patients received biofeedback training in speeding up and slowing down their heart rates and in keeping their heart rates within normal limits. The training technique was similar to that described in the example at the beginning of the chapter, with the patient responding to feedback in the form of different colored lights. All eight patients learned to control their heart rate to some degree; five of them were able to decrease the frequency of premature ventricular contractions. The abilities remained in follow-up tests up to 21 months later. One patient who had had three heart attacks in the 11 months before beginning treatment had no cardiac problems during the 21-month period.

Although applications of biofeedback techniques have produced a number of encouraging results, we still have much to learn about their range of application. For example, how do motivational and personality variables, intelligence, and other individual differences affect our ability to control autonomic responses? What are the best ways of providing feedback to subjects? How successfully can autonomic control learned in the laboratory be transferred to real-life situations? Which medical and psychological disorders can be treated using biofeedback techniques, and how effective is such treatment compared with other methods? Just how far can we go in controlling our internal environment and our own states of consciousness? Researchers are cautioning an enthusiastic public that biofeedback may not be the cure-all that many popular writers would have us believe. But we will have to wait for more research to provide us with answers to these and other questions concerning this important frontier.

One young man managed to collect a total of 16 soft drinks during a four-hour period!

These results indicate that programs could be established to reinforce people positively for reducing electrical and gasoline consumption, riding in car pools or using public transportation, observing speed limits, recycling paper and glass, keeping recreational areas clean, and so on. On both a short-term and a long-term basis, such programs would probably be far more effective than our present attempts to coerce people into preserving their environment by threatening them with punishment.

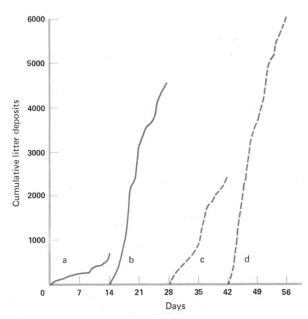

Figure 6.11 The cumulative number of litter deposits made during each of the two-week experimental conditions: (a) baseline I: (b) reinforcement I; (c) baseline II; (d) reinforcement II. The total number of deposits increased from 720 in the first two weeks to over 6000 in the final phase of the experiment. (Kohlenberg and Phillips, 1973.)

Cognitive reinterpretations of learning phenomena

What does learning really involve? Do changes in our behavior come about simply through the formation of stimulus-response bonds? Or do they occur because we have acquired a new set of expectations about relationships between events, expectations about "what leads to what"? Is behavior automatically "stamped in" or "stamped out" by its consequences and by CS-UCS pairings, or do cognitive processes play a central role in both classical and operant conditioning?

Early behaviorists like John B. Watson thought that learning involved only the formation of stimulus-response (S-R) bonds. Later S-R learning theorists like Clark Hull also thought learning was quite automatic in response to reinforcements that reduced biological or learned drives.

Other theorists disagreed with the S-R theories

and emphasized the role of cognition. The Gestalt psychologists argued that learning involved making discoveries about the environment by perceiving relationships among events. They cited experiments on insight learning in both human beings and animals (see Chapter 2, page 40) to support their position.

Perhaps the most influential of the early cognitive learning theorists was Edward Tolman. The basic concept in Tolman's theory is *expectancy*. He argued that organisms learn "cognitive maps" of their environments. Stimuli serve as *signs* that certain events are to follow. In operant conditioning, certain stimuli arouse the expectancy that a particular consequence will follow from a particular response. From this point of view reinforcement does not stamp in behaviors automatically, but provides information about what to expect. Tolman maintained that learning can occur without reinforcement and in a series of important experiments he and his students allowed rats to explore a maze freely. When they later introduced food at a particular place in the maze the rats found their way to it quickly and repeatedly, so that they must have learned the location before the food was there. These demonstrations of *latent learning*, so called because it was not reflected in performance until a reward was introduced, were viewed as evidence that the rats had in fact formed a "cognitive map" of the maze during the first phase of the experiment.

More recently, Robert Bolles (1972) formulated a theory which views learning as the acquisition of two kinds of expectancies. The theory states that in classical conditioning, what is learned is a predictive relationship between two stimuli, the CS and the UCS. The presence of the first stimulus (CS) predicts the occurrence of the second (reinforcing) stimulus (UCS). In the second kind of expectancy, formed in operant conditioning situations, the organism learns a predictive relationship between the way in which it responds (R) and the consequences (S) that follow from that response. In Bolles' opinion, reinforcement in both classical and operant conditioning basically provides information and does not automatically strengthen behaviors. The information acquired in learning situations forms the basis for subsequent behavior.

This theory is similar to Tolman's in many ways.

199

But Bolles (1972) has shown how this cognitive interpretation of learning can account not only for all of the effects explained by the noncognitive S-R model, but also for many phenomena in both human and animal learning which that model cannot easily explain. We will examine some of these phenomena below.

Cognitive factors in human learning

A variety of experimental data indicate that cognitive factors play a central role in many kinds of learning. Like Tolman's demonstrations of latent learning in animals, there are several human learning phenomena that are difficult to account for without introducing cognitive processes.

Semantic generalization. Most researchers, particularly Russian ones, hypothesize that classical conditioning in human beings involves more than the simple establishment of CS-CR bonds. They have gathered proof for this hypothesis through studies that use words as the CS. For example, one experiment paired the word "hare" with a painful electric shock, until it became a CS for a conditioned emotional response (measured by changes in skin conductance, heart rate, and so on). The experimenters then tested for stimulus generalization by visually presenting different words during test trials. The subjects responded more to the word "rabbit" than to the word "hair" despite the fact that the latter word was more structurally similar to the original CS. The response became generalized on the basis of the semantic *meaning* of the words rather than on the basis of their similarity as stimuli, so that the phenomenon was named *semantic generalization*. Apparently, cognitive processes play an active role in even this simple kind of learning.

The role of awareness in learning. Awareness in human beings is operationally defined as the ability to verbalize reinforcement conditions. Noncognitive theorists argue that awareness is not necessary for learning, since reinforcement has an automatic strengthening effect on behavior, while cognitive theorists argue that although awareness may not be absolutely necessary, it greatly speeds up learning processes, and is probably involved in almost all learning. This debate has been difficult to resolve, because if subjects correctly verbalize the reinforcement contingency, it is impossible to pinpoint *when* they discovered it. Despite this methodological problem, however, a number of findings suggests that awareness is of major importance in learning.

One study of classical conditioning showed that when a number of different stimuli were presented repeatedly, only one of which was paired with the UCS of electric shock, subjects who were aware of the specific CS-UCS relationship had conditioned skin conductance responses only to the CS and not to the other stimuli. Subjects who could not verbalize the CS-UCS relationship (or in Bolles' terms, the S-S* relationship) did not respond differently to the various stimuli (Fuhrer and Baer, 1965). Other studies have shown that awareness also affects extinction. If subjects are simply told that the UCS will no longer be paired with the CS, they extinguish the CR almost immediately (Grings and Lockhart, 1963).

In operant conditioning, awareness involves knowing the relationships between responses and their probable consequences. The role of awareness in improving learning in human beings was demonstrated in an experiment by Spielberger and De Nike (1966). The subjects took part in a *verbal conditioning* experiment in which they were rewarded by the experimenter with comments such as "Mmm-hmm" whenever they said a certain kind of word—in this case a human noun. Control subjects did not receive this reinforcement. The change in the number of times subjects mentioned these words over time was measured. In addition, subjects were asked frequent questions to determine whether or not they were aware of the reinforcement contingency.

The results of the experiment are shown in Figure 6.12. Part *a* of the figure shows that the subjects who were aware of the reinforcement contingency showed a large increase in their mention of human nouns, whereas unaware subjects demonstrated virtually no changes. Part *b* shows the impact of awareness. There was a drastic increase in responsiveness as soon as the subjects discovered the reinforcement contingency.

Because of findings such as those we have described, many learning psychologists have concluded that the learning process, even in lower animals, is complicated and that our basic "laws of learning" do

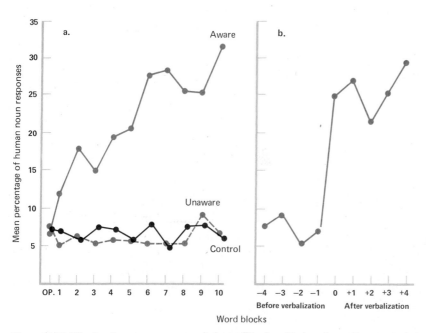

Figure 6.12 Effects of awareness on verbal conditioning. Part *a* shows the percentage of desired responses given by aware subjects, unaware subjects, and a control group. Part *b* shows level of performance before and after the subjects were able to verbalize the reinforcement contingency. (Spielberger and DeNike, 1966. Copyright 1966 by the American Psychological Association. Reprinted by permission.)

not account for all the factors involved. No one disputes the power of the learning *procedures* we described earlier in the chapter, but researchers believe that if we can discover the psychological processes that underlie their effects, then we might be able to make them even more effective. The years to come are certain to witness important developments and applications related to the cognitive perspective on learning.

SUMMARY

1. Learning is a change in potential behavior that occurs as a result of experience. There are three major types of learning: classical conditioning, operant conditioning, and observational learning (modeling).

2. In classical conditioning a conditioned stimulus (CS) paired with an unconditioned

stimulus (UCS) acquires the ability to evoke a conditioned response (CR). Important concepts in classical conditioning include reinforcement, extinction, spontaneous recovery, generalization, and discrimination. Interoceptive conditioning studies have shown that a physical stimulus inside the body can function as a CS. Classical conditioning has been used to study covert processes in nonverbal subjects and there is evidence that attitudes can be acquired through classical conditioning.

3. In operant conditioning, behaviors are strengthened or weakened by their consequences. A reinforcement is anything that strengthens a behavior on which it is made contingent. Secondary or conditioned reinforcers acquire their reinforcing properties by being associated with other reinforcers.

201

Extinction occurs when a behavior is no longer reinforced.

4. Complex behaviors can be operantly conditioned through *shaping*, or the *method of successive approximations*, in which behaviors that increasingly approximate the desired behavior are reinforced.

5. Schedules of reinforcement have important effects on learning, performance, and extinction. *Continuous* reinforcement occurs after each desired response. Partial reinforcement schedules include *fixed interval*, *fixed ratio*, *variable interval*, and *variable ratio*. Learning occurs most quickly under continuous reinforcement, but partial (especially variable) schedules produce higher resistance to extinction.

6. A *negative reinforcement* is anything that strengthens a behavior that results in its removal. It is the basis for escape and avoidance conditioning. The *two-factor* theory of avoidance conditioning incorporates both classical and operant conditioning principles to explain the acquisition of the fear response and the strengthening of avoidance behaviors that reduce fear.

7. Punishment is frequently effective in controlling unwanted behaviors, but it can have a number of undesirable side effects, such as generalization of suppression, avoidance of the situation in which punishment occurs, and observational learning of punitive behaviors. It is most effectively used in conjunction with positive reinforcement of alternative desirable behaviors.

8. *Self-reinforcement* processes are important determinants of many behaviors. The consequences that individuals present to themselves in the form of self-approval and self-disapproval may override external contingencies. Standards for self-reinforcement are

acquired both through direct learning and through observations of others' standards.

9. In general, immediate response consequences have stronger effects on behavior than do delayed consequences. The ability of humans to imagine future consequences helps to overcome the potency of immediate consequences.

10. Many behaviors are learned through modeling. Modeled behaviors can be learned simply by observing them, but performance of the behaviors is governed by the perceived consequences to the model. Modeling stimuli can be either behavioral or verbal in nature. Emotional responses can also be learned or extinguished through observation.

11. Experiments with both animals and humans have shown that subjects can learn to control response systems previously thought to be involuntary. These demonstrations have inspired successful attempts to use biofeedback techniques to treat medical and psychological problems.

12. Operant techniques are increasingly being applied in societal settings to change behavior. Future years promise an increased use of behavioral technology in applied settings.

13. Learning, far from being a mechanical conditioning process, is affected strongly by cognitive processes. Much research is currently under way to identify cognitive variables that are involved in learning phenomena.

Suggested readings

Bandura, A. *Social learning theory*. Englewood Cliffs, N.J.: Prentice-Hall, Inc., 1977. A clear and readable presentation of cognitive social learning theory and its applications.

Bolles, R. C. *Learning theory.* New York: Holt, Rinehart and Winston, Inc., 1975. A description of the major theories of learning and an analysis of learning phenomena from a cognitive viewpoint.

Rachlin, H. *Introduction to modern behaviorism.* (2nd ed.) San Francisco: W. H. Freeman and Co. Publishers, 1976. An analysis of basic learning phenomena from a Skinnerian point of view.

Skinner, B. F. *Beyond freedom and dignity.* New York: Alfred A. Knopf, Inc., 1971. Skinner's classic and controversial book that argues for systematic application of learning principles to societal engineering.

Chapter 7

Cognitive Processes: Memory, Language, Thinking, and Problem Solving

(Charles Gatewood)

One evening the Greek poet Simonides was reciting poetry at a huge banquet given by a nobleman of Thessaly. About halfway through the banquet, Simonides was abruptly drawn away from the hall by a messenger of the gods. Moments later the entire roof of the hall caved in, crushing all the guests. The grief-stricken relatives of the guests were horrified to discover that the bodies were so mutilated that they could not identify a single one. How were the relatives to bury their loved ones properly? At first, the situation seemed impossible, but then Simonides discovered that he could mentally picture the exact place at which each guest had been sitting, so that he could identify the bodies. This tragic experience showed Simonides that this technique could be used to remember all sorts of objects and ideas—they simply had to be assigned to fixed positions in space. From this experience Simonides originated the idea of memory aids, called *mnemonic* techniques, discussed later in this chapter.

How do the cognitive processes, including memory, function? The more psychologists study behavior, the more evident it becomes that a diversity of concepts and methods is needed to understand all that happens within this wide area of behavior. We have seen the applicability of conditioning principles to many of the situations in which humans and animals are placed. Yet these principles by themselves do not provide a sufficiently comprehensive framework for understanding several important complex behavioral categories, such as memory and forgetting, language and its acquisition, thinking and problem solving. The term *higher mental processes* is often used in reference to these dimensions of behavior.

This chapter deals with this topic and places special emphasis on recent developments in theory and research. We explore the world of cognitive processes that is concerned with how we gain and lose knowledge and how we apply it in solving problems.

HUMAN MEMORY

Human memory provides the building blocks for all the other cognitive processes, such as language and thought. What happens when you see the problem 3×7 and 21 pops into your mind? What happens when a baseball in a store window calls to your mind the fun you had on a baseball team when you were 12? What happens as you read this chapter? How is the information stored for another time when you may need it? All these situations and many more involve your memory. Although the idea of memory is easy to comprehend and easily observed in daily life, the details of how memory works are not easy to study or understand.

We shall present memory from an information-processing point of view. This way of looking at the memory process assumes that it functions in a way similar to a computer. Described in this way, the process has three phases—input of information, its processing or coding for storage, and retrieval of a particular piece of information from that storage when it is called for.

Input

Information in the form of simple or very complicated stimuli is received by the person from one or several sense organs. Researchers have looked carefully at the differences in how much information can be received at one time and how long it can be retained. One finding has been that the amount of information taken in and the time it can be retained in its original form varies, depending on the sense organ involved. These differences show up in the study of visual information and auditory information, for example.

How many objects can be seen at a glance?

In fiction the hero of a detective tale can walk into a room filled with clues and take in enough in a single instant to piece together the solution to a complicated mystery. In fact, however, most human beings can take in only a limited amount of information in a single glance.

In the middle of the nineteenth century Sir William Hamilton, a Scottish metaphysician, claimed that if a person threw a handful of marbles on the floor, he or she could correctly state their number without counting only if there were six or fewer marbles. With any greater number the person would make mistakes. It is not clear whether Hamilton actually threw the marbles or simply used his imagination. (See Figure 7.1.) In any event, in 1871 an English economist named William Stanley Jevons

BERNARDA
BRYSON

Figure 7.1 Sir William Hamilton, a nineteenth-century philosopher (not to be confused with Sir William Rowan Hamilton, the mathematician), observed: "If you throw . . . marbles on the floor, you will find it hard to view at once more than six . . . without confusion." G. A. Miller, "Information and memory." Copyright © 1956 by Scientific American, Inc. All rights reserved.)

actually threw not marbles, but beans. He reported that when there were three or four, he could name the number with no mistakes; when there were 5 he was sometimes wrong; when there were 10 he was wrong half the time; and when there were 15 he was almost always wrong.

The Hamilton-Jevons experiments have been repeated hundreds of times with better equipment and better techniques. In many experiments subjects have been shown arrays of letters. These arrays are presented very briefly (perhaps for one-twentieth of a second) with a *tachistoscope*. After seeing a single array, subjects are asked to report as many of the letters as they can remember. If one, two, three, or four letters are presented, subjects answer perfectly. If more than five are presented, subjects do not report any additional letters; they still recall only four or five. This limit of four or five letters is called the *span of apprehension.*

Although subjects presented with a large array of

letters can only report four or five accurately, most of them are aware that they have seen more than that number. The image of some letters fades away as they are reporting others. Immediately after we see a visual stimulus we have a fairly complete memory of it, but this memory is very brief.

To understand this observation better, George Sperling (1960) used a partial report technique. Subjects saw a 4- by 3- inch rectangular array of 12 letters, such as the one in Figure 7.2. The arrays were shown for very short time periods (less than a second) and the subjects were asked to report only the contents of a single row. In order to let subjects know which row to report, Sperling sounded a high-, medium-, or low-frequency tone after the stimulus array. A high-frequency tone meant that subjects should report the contents of the top row; a medium- or low-frequency tone indicated that they should report the middle or bottom row.

Subjects were able to report back almost all the

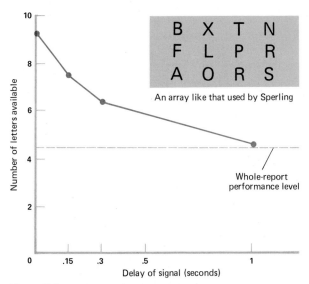

An array like that used by Sperling

Whole-report
performance level

Figure 7.2 Letters recalled in the partial-report situation for various delays of the signal to report. Also shown is performance with a whole-report task for comparable material. (After Sperling, 1960. Copyright 1960 by the American Psychological Association. Reprinted by permission.)

letters in the rows indicated by the tone. Because they did not know at the time the stimulus was being displayed just which row they were to report, they must have stored almost all the letters of the array by the time the stimulus disappeared. These results indicate that immediately after we see something, our memory briefly contains all the information about it. This memory for information entering through the eyes is called *iconic store.*

The subjects in Sperling's experiment reported that immediately after the stimulus was presented, the image of some letters faded away as they were reporting others. Sperling conducted experiments to see how long an image actually lasted by using a variation of his original partial report procedure. He presented a stimulus, waited for some interval of time, and then presented a tone. He hypothesized that if the tone were presented immediately, the image would still be available. If the tone were presented after a long delay, the image would have disappeared.

The results of these experiments are shown in Figure 7.2. To find the estimated number of letters that the subject could name, multiply the number of letters subjects remembered from the row they were

signaled to report by the total number of rows in the array. When the tone occurred immediately (zero delay), subjects recalled almost all the letters. When the tone occurred after a one-second delay, they could recall only about four or five letters, or the same number that they could report for a whole array. We can conclude, then, that the image of the entire array lasted about one second before fading.

How much auditory information can be remembered from one presentation?

Using a modified version of the Sperling technique, researchers investigated the sensory store for auditory information, which corresponds to the iconic store, called the *echoic store.* In one study (Darwin, Turvey, and Crowder, 1972) subjects wore earphones. Three letters (e.g., B, P, J) were read off into their right ear, then three different letters were read into their left ear, and finally three different letters were read off to the "middle" of the subjects' heads through both earphones as shown in Figure 7.3. After the letters had been presented and an interval ranging from zero to four seconds had passed, subjects were signaled by a lighted bar that flashed on the left, middle, or right of a screen to report either the left, middle, or right letters.

The results of this experiment are shown in Figure 7.4. With a zero delay, subjects could recall about five out of nine letters; with a delay of four seconds, the number averaged only 4.25. It may seem odd that only five letters could be recalled when there was no delay, but there is a good explanation for this. In Sperling's visual experiments subjects saw an entire

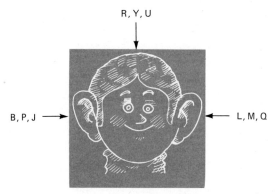

Figure 7.3 A subject in an experiment to determine the duration of an image in the echoic store.

207

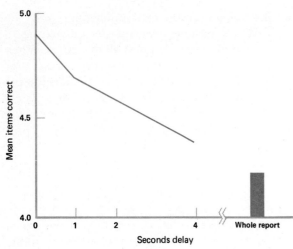

Figure 7.4 Number of items reported in a partial-report task with auditory stimuli, as a function of the delay of the signal to report. Also shown is the performance in the whole-report task for the same material. (Darwin, Turvey and Crowder, 1972.)

visual array all at once. In the auditory experiments, however, letters were presented sequentially in groups of three (e.g., B, P, J to the right ear; then R, Y, U to the middle of the head; then L, M, Q to the left ear). By the time the last group of three letters was presented, the first two groups had had time to be forgotten. The zero delay was not really zero, so that the estimate of the number of letters that can be recalled at this delay is probably low.

The data presented in Figure 7.4 show that when an auditory stimulus is presented, much of the information in that stimulus is absorbed into an auditory image. This image remains after the stimulus is no longer physically present, and fades away gradually. The results of Figure 7.4 indicate that it takes about four seconds for the image to fade completely. The comparable figure for the iconic store was one second.

Processing

Because everyday experiences shows us that we remember information much longer than a few seconds, there must be some process that makes it possible to remember over a longer time period.

Clinical data
Study of the brain has suggested that remembering newly learned information and information learned in the past may involve two different processes. These two kinds of memory are referred to as *short-term* and *long-term* memory. Observations of patients whose brains have been damaged or who have had brain surgery has helped support this view. For example, some correlations between specific anatomical areas and specific memory difficulties have been established. Sometimes a particular brain area is damaged by accident or disease. If patients show memory difficulties these can often be correlated with the location of the damage. Although such correlations do not *prove* a cause-and-effect relationship, if similar results are found consistently some relationship is suggested. For example, a lesion in a particular area of the left parietal lobe is associated with poor short-term auditory memory span (Warrington, 1971).

In some cases a portion of the brain is removed surgically, usually after all known alternate procedures have produced no relief from an incapacitating condition. The effects of the surgical removal on memory functions gives some information about the activity of different parts of the brain. In one such case H. M., a 27-year-old patient of neuropsychologist Brenda Milner, suffered from epileptic seizures so severe that they kept him from working. He was treated with a surgical technique that involved removing a portion of his medial temporal lobes. After the surgery his epileptic seizures stopped, but his memory seemed to suffer. For example, he could repeat a telephone number that he had just heard, but if his attention were diverted for a moment, then he could not remember it. No matter how many times the number was repeated, he could not learn it. In general, H. M. could remember things that happened to him in the past before his surgery, but he could not learn anything new. The following description of his behavior illustrates the severity of his problem.

During three of the nights at the Clinical Research Center, the patient rang for the night nurse, asking her, with many apologies, if she would tell him where he was and how he came to be there. He clearly recognized that he was in a hospital but seemed unable to reconstruct any of the events of the previous day. On another occasion, he remarked, "Every day is alone in itself, whatever enjoyment I've had, and whatever sorrow I've had." He often volunteers stereotyped descriptions of his own state by saying it is "like waking from a dream." His experience seems to be that of a person who is just becoming aware of his surroundings without fully comprehending the situation, because he does not remember what went before. (Milner, Corkin, and Teuber, 1968)

These kinds of clinical data suggested that the process of retaining information for a short and for a long time were different at least in the location in the brain where they took place. A number of questions then had to be answered.

Memory without time to practice

One question is focused on how long learned material is remembered if the subjects cannot rehearse or practice it. To find out, Margaret and Lloyd Peterson (1959) presented subjects with a set of three consonants, such as BFP, followed immediately by a three-digit number. Subjects were asked to count backward from the number; this ensured that they did not rehearse the letters. On a signal from the experimenter subjects stopped counting and tried to recall the three letters. Usually recall dropped very rapidly over a 15-second interval. (See Figure 7.5.) Immediately after the letters were presented recall was nearly perfect. After a 15-second wait recall was very poor, but its probability never reached zero.

The capacity of memory

In addition to the time these short-term memories are retained, the question remains, "How much in-

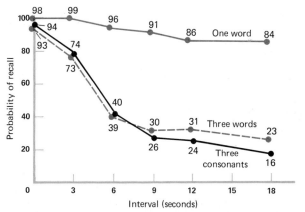

Figure 7.6 Probability of recall as a function of retention interval when the item to be remembered is either one word, three unrelated words, or three consonants. (Adapted from Murdock, 1961.)

formation can be remembered at one time?" Bennet Murdock (1961) conducted an experiment using a variation of the Peterson-Peterson design to test the capacity of short-term memory. The item to be retained was either one word, three words, or three unrelated letters. Subjects were told to count backward for some interval of time and then to try to recall the item. Murdock's results are shown in Figure 7.6. The forgetting function for three words is nearly identical to the function for three letters. When letters form a meaningful word, they are treated as a unit.

Chunks. Look briefly at the top ten letters in Figure 7.7. Now look away and try to repeat them. Now look at the bottom ten letters, look away, and try to repeat them. Most people can recall all ten in the second case but not in the first. These two examples contain exactly the same letters, but we can remember them all only if they form a recognizable word.

N O T G N I H S A W

W A S H I N G T O N

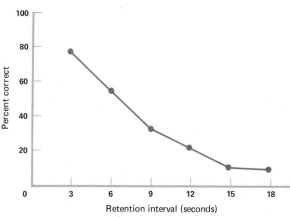

Figure 7.5 Results of the experiment on forgetting in short-term memory, showing that recall decreases as a function of the retension interval. (Peterson and Peterson, 1959. Copyright 1959 by the American Psychological Association.)

Figure 7.7 Look at the top row of letters for just an instant. Try to recall as many as you can. Now look at the bottom row, look away, and try to recall it. In which case did you recall more letters?

BOX 7.1

How memory is measured

What do you mean when you say you remember something—that you can pick out the item from a group of similar items or that when you mentally search for a piece of information it pops into your mind without much difficulty? Researchers must have well-defined measures or their experiments are meaningless. Some of these measures of memory have been used from the beginning of formal experimentation.

Recall

Subjects are asked to reproduce or recall material they had previously learned. They might be asked to recall a list in its original order or in any order (free recall). When Hermann Ebbinghaus, one of the first to study verbal learning scientifically, learned his nonsense syllable lists, he tested his memory by recall, recording the *number of trials* necessary before he could recite the entire list in order when given only the first syllable.

Recognition

When learning is measured by recognition the subjects are asked simply to pick out from a list of old and new items those they had previously learned. As you might expect, subjects will be able to point out more items than they could recall from the same list. Using this approach, some learning can be measured that could not be measured by recall.

Relearning

Another measure of memory, even more sensitive than recall, is relearning. The difference between the number of trials needed to learn material originally and the number needed to relearn the material, called the *savings score,* measures how much of the previous learning was retained. Subjects may believe they do not remember "anything" and be able to recall none of the material. Yet when they relearn it, the number of trials may be considerably fewer than the number needed for the original learning. Reviewing for an examination will take less time and be more effective if the material was studied on earlier occasions. Savings may be found even when the material originally was learned years before.

One unique demonstration of the use of relearning to study memory was presented by H. E. Burtt (1941). Daily for three-month periods Burtt read three 20-line sections of Greek verse to an English

In experiments in which subjects are shown a collection of items and asked to recall them, most people can repeat about seven items, or "chunks." A chunk is not easy to define; it is something that can be recognized as one unit. The letter *W* is a chunk, and so is the word *Washington.* However, NOTGNIHSAW would be considered ten separate chunks. Research suggests that short-term memory can hold about seven chunks. That is why we can retain a phone number until we dial it, but we have trouble with both an address and a phone number.

Remembering information

Experimental data of the kind mentioned earlier have given us some knowledge about how long information is initially remembered and how much information can be remembered at one time. Everyday observations tell us that we remember more information and do so for a longer time than seven chunks retained for 15 seconds. What happens to make this improved performance possible?

The work of several researchers has shown that rehearsal plays a role in retaining information for a period of time. By rehearsing or mentally reviewing the words, they are kept in the memory. To get a better idea of the way in which rehearsal works, an ingenious set of experiments was done. In these experiments subjects had to rehearse out loud while lists were presented to them. They could rehearse any of the words on the list they wanted, as many

boy who was about 1 year old when the experiment began. He continued this until 21 sections had been read to the child. When the boy was 8, 14, and 18 years old, Burtt tested him by the relearning method. The number of repetitions necessary for him to learn one of the familiar passages was compared with the number necessary to learn a comparable passage he had never seen before. At age 8, 30 percent fewer repetitions were necessary for the familiar passage. The savings decreased to 8 percent at age 14, and no savings were found at age 18. The results showed that even though the Greek language was meaningless to the boy, the original presentations had resulted in some learning that could still be measured over a decade later.

An example of recall, recognition, and relearning

The subjects are given a list of words.

TABLE
PAIR
UNDER
SHOES
FOUND

After repeating each word on the list they are tested in one of the following ways.

To test *free recall* the experimenter gives this in-struction: "Say the words from the list in any order you wish."

To test *serial recall* the experimenter gives this in-struction: "Say the words in the order they appeared on the list. The first word is TABLE."

To test *recognition* the experimenter says: "Look at the following list of words. Tell me those that appeared on the list you learned."

ORCHARD
SHOES
BED
CHAIR
UNDER
FOUND
PAIR
SOCKS
SAW

To test *relearning* the experimenter says: "Here is a list of words to memorize."

The number of trials needed to learn the list is then compared with the number originally required to learn it. The results are expressed as a savings score:

Savings score =

$$\frac{\text{original trials} - \text{relearning trials}}{\text{original trials}} \times 100$$

times as they wanted; experimenters used a tape recorder to record their choices.

Experimenters then counted the number of times each word in the list was rehearsed, and the number of times each word was correctly recalled in later tests. Figure 7.8 shows the relationship between probability of recall and number of rehearsals. The more times subjects rehearsed a word, the greater the likelihood that they would recall that word. This is shown by the curve labeled *immediate recall* in Figure 7.8.

Three weeks later, subjects in one of the experiments were asked to come back for a recognition test on the same words. They were presented with another set of words and asked to tell whether or not the words had been on the original list. Recognition was better for words that had been rehearsed many times than it was for words that had been rehearsed less often or not at all. The curve labeled *delayed recognition* in Figure 7.8 shows this result.

In addition to showing a relationship between rehearsal and long-term memory, the "rehearse out loud" experiments also help us understand another important phenomenon: the *primacy effect.* (See Box 7.2.) The primacy effect may occur because subjects rehearse the first few words in a list more than the others. When the first word of a list is presented, it is the only word subjects have to rehearse, so that it gets their undivided attention. The second word must share the subjects' attention with

211

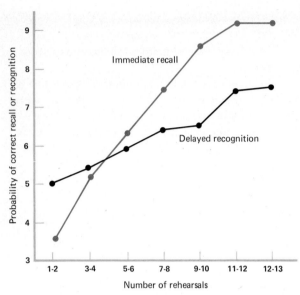

Figure 7.8 The more times a word is rehearsed, the higher the probability it will be recalled and later recognized. (Rundus, Loftus, and Atkinson, 1970.)

the first word, so that it is not rehearsed quite as many times. When the third word appears it is rehearsed along with the first two, so that it is not rehearsed as often as either of them. The data from the "rehearse out loud" experiments show that the first few words do in fact receive many more rehearsals than the others in the list. Apparently, at least part of the explanation for the primacy effect is that the first few items in a list are rehearsed more than others.

But rehearsal does not always lead to long-term retention of information. In fact, there may be two kinds of rehearsal (Craik and Lockhart, 1972). The subjects may intend simply to keep the material available for immediate use—*maintenance rehearsal* (as in looking up a telephone number for one-time use)—or they may be rehearsing it with an intent to remember it permanently—*elaborative rehearsal.*

Organizing to remember. The distinction between maintenance and elaborative rehearsal suggests that subjects may have to do more than simply repeat items over and over for successful long-term retrieval. In fact, when we operate on a higher level, such as when we study a new theorem in mathematics or a new novel in an English course, we are doing

more than simply repeating the material to ourselves. We are trying to *organize* it, which means that we are trying to fit it into some preexisting logical framework or to create some new framework that will bind the material into a cohesive unit.

The process of remembering

S-R, or associationist approach. For many years a major focus of work on memory concerned the probability or likelihood that the subject would recall a correct response or associated linkage under certain conditions. Many experiments used lists of single or paired words or syllables presented by a memory drum. Such topics as the number of lists learned, the similarity of the lists, and the activity taking place between lists to be learned were studied.

The cognitive approach. As the years passed, psychologists became aware of the many questions about memory that could not be investigated using the simple S-R concept. They adapted the basic ideas of *information theory*, which is a mathematical analysis of communication and which has served as a basic idea for the development of computers. These theorists were interested in memory from the cognitive point of view. They wanted to study such problems as how memory is stored and how it is brought out when needed. One way to make such an investigation easier is to construct a theoretical model. Experiments can then be run to test predictions based on the model.

One of the most influential of these models was proposed by Atkinson and Shiffrin (1968). It divides the memory system into three major components: sensory store (SS), short-term memory (STM), and long-term memory (LTM). The model works as follows: Suppose that we were to call the information operator in Washington, D.C., and ask for the telephone number of the White House. When the operator gave us the number, the information would first enter our memory system through our ears. The information would then be placed in the *sensory store,* which holds large amounts of information for a particular sense organ. In this case the sensory store would hold not only the telephone number, but all other information that had entered through the ears as well, such as the operator's words, "The number

BOX 7.2
Serial position curve

When subjects are asked to recall as many words or syllables as they can immediately following learning, the results form a *serial position curve.* The probability that a word will be recalled is plotted as a function of the word's position on the list, as shown in the accompanying illustration. This curve shows that the probability a word will be recalled depends largely on where in the presentation list it occurred. The fact that words from the beginning of the list have a good chance of being recalled is called the *primacy effect.* The fact that words from the end of the list have a good chance of being recalled is called the *recency effect.* Words from the middle of the list cannot be recalled as often.

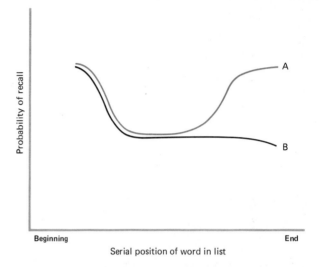

Curve A shows the shape of a serial position curve when subjects recall words immediately after they are presented. When a time period elapses between learning and recall, the curve assumes a shape more like curve B.

Learning the script for a play requires extensive rehearsal because learned material must be stored for long-term use. (Vandermark, Stock, Boston)

213

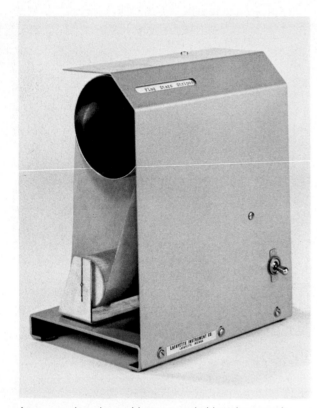

A memory drum is used in many verbal learning experiments. One or several words or syllables appear in the opening for a brief, measured period. Then the drum rotates and new stimuli appear. (Lafayette Instrument)

is . . . ." The sensory store has very short-term storage capacities. The information is lost within a few seconds unless it is quickly transferred to another area.

In the second stage of the process our telephone number would be transferred to the *short-term memory* (STM). The STM has a limited capacity; it can hold about one telephone number, but it would have difficulty holding both a telephone number and an address. It can hold information somewhat longer than can the sensory store, but still only for about 15 seconds. If we were to dial the phone number as soon as we received it from the operator, get a busy signal, wait a few minutes, then decide to redial, we might discover that we needed to ask for the telephone number again. In those few minutes the number would have been lost from the STM. But if we had placed the information instead into a special section

of STM called the *rehearsal buffer*, we could have remembered the number. Information can be stored indefinitely in this buffer by rehearsing it, that is, by repeating the information over and over.

If our telephone number were a matter of lasting importance we might send it on to *long-term memory* (LTM). This area has a huge capacity for holding information. It holds all the words we have learned, along with their meanings. It holds all the important events of our past, and perhaps a great many unimportant ones as well. It holds the alphabet, the multiplication tables, our telephone number, and our friends' names.

The theory illustrated by the model in Figure 7.9 assumes that while information is in short-term memory, it is also being transferred into the long-term memory (LTM) whenever we make an attempt to send it there. If we wanted to remember the telephone number of the White House for a long time, we might begin repeating it over and over to ourselves and look it up several times during the day. While we did this, the information in short-term store would continually be copied into long-term memory. This is what it means to "memorize" material.

This model and others similar to it stimulated a great deal of research. They built on the ideas that (1) short-term memory (for example, for an event that occurred 15 seconds ago) has characteristics different from memory that lasts longer or indefi-

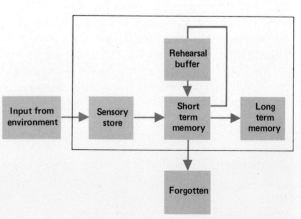

Figure 7.9 A theoretical model of the human memory system. (Adapted from Atkinson and Shiffrin, 1968.)

While switchboard operators must remember the location of many connections in order to work efficiently, they need to remember only briefly the numbers requested. (Herwig, Stock, Boston)

nitely and (2) these differences can be explained best by thinking of two separate storage systems in addition to the sensory register.

Fergus Craik and Robert Lockhart (1972) at the University of Toronto asked whether a different type of model might explain experimental findings better. They suggested a simpler concept in which memory was related to the level at which information is processed rather than where it is stored. Craik and Lockhart emphasized the importance of analyses and integration of the stimuli by the person, that is, the degree to which the person organizes the material and makes it meaningful. According to this view, persons take information and elaborate on it by forming associations with other stored information. If the individual does not expect to recall the words being presented, there is no relationship between recall probability and number of rehearsals. In that case, words are retained only for as long as they are needed. If students expect a test, for example, they often elaborate on the words so that they will be available later. Others have also questioned the need for two storage components in the model.

In addition to such models, other factors stimulated cognitive psychologists to look at memory in new ways. The technology of brain surgery and experimental study of the brain leaped forward and provided some suggestive evidence of internal processes that S-R theory could not handle. The ideas of the Gestalt psychologists concerning perception also proved stimulating because of their emphasis on the need to organize material. Freud's work on repression or motivated forgetting (see Chapter 13) also provided clues to be followed up.

Retrieval

What kind of organization is used to keep "handy" material that we remember? Memory contains a great deal of information. It contains facts about our personal experiences, such as what we did last Christmas or what our first cereal bowl looked like. The term *episodic memory* has been used to refer to our record of personal life experiences. Another term, *semantic memory*, refers to the organized knowledge we have about words and other verbal symbols, their meaning, and the things to which they refer; about relationships among them; and about rules for manipulating them. In Figure 7.10 Sally's episodic memory seems to be functioning more effectively than her semantic memory.

Very little research has been done on the structure and processing of "episodic" experiences. Much more has been done on semantic memory. We know that we can reach into our store of semantic knowledge and produce an appropriate response to a question. We can easily answer such questions as, "Who was the first president of the U.S.A.?" or, "What is an animal beginning with the letter Z?" With the huge number of items in store how are we able to answer

215

PEANUTS®   By Charles M. Schulz

Figure 7.10 Sally, the little girl in the cartoon, shows better episodic than semantic memory. (© 1973 United Feature Syndicate, Inc.)

such questions as these so quickly? Exactly how do we search our memories for specific information?

A model for memory retrieval

If an individual is asked to retrieve an instance of a category, does he or she search through the category sequentially until the desired piece of information is found? Freedman and Loftus (1971) asked subjects to name something in a restricted category (e.g., a fruit that is red) and measured the time they needed to do this. They reasoned that if this involved a sequential search through all the instances in the category, then it should take longer to name an instance of a large category than to name an instance of a small one. For example, if subjects search sequentially, they should be able to find a "season that is cold" faster than they could find a "beverage that is cold," because *seasons* is a smaller category. In fact, however, it took no longer to name an instance of a large category than to name an instance of a small one. It seems that the process of retrieving such information from semantic memory does not involve a sequential search.

Allan Collins and Ross Quillian (1969) suggested that the items in semantic memory are connected by links in a huge network. Figure 7.11 illustrates a portion of this hypothetical memory structure. Notice that the concepts in this structure are organized into subordinate-superordinate relationships. The superordinate of *canary* is *bird;* and the superordinate of *bird* is *animal.* The *cognitive economy assumption* states that a property that characterizes a particular class of things is stored only at the place in the network that corresponds to that class. A property that characterizes all birds, such as the fact that they have wings, is stored only at *bird.* It is not stored

216

again with the different types of birds, even though they all have wings. Collins and Quillian next tried to determine how information is retrieved from the structure. They asked their subjects very simple questions to see how much time it took them to answer.

1. Does a canary eat?
2. Does a canary fly?
3. Is a canary yellow?

The first question took the longest time for a response. Collins and Quillian explain the differences in response time as follows: To answer question 3, subjects first have to enter the level in memory that corresponds to *canary.* There they find the information that canaries are yellow, so that they can answer the question relatively quickly. To answer question 2 (Does a canary fly?), they still enter the memory system at *canary,* but they do not find any information there as to whether or not canaries can fly. Because canaries are birds, however, subjects move up the network to the level where information about birds is stored. There they find that birds fly, and they are able to conclude that canaries fly as well. Question 2, therefore, takes somewhat longer to answer than question 3. Using the same reasoning, we can see why question 1 takes the longest to answer: Subjects must move up through two levels. Some questions take longer to answer than others because they require more traveling from one level of memory to another.

People took about 75 milliseconds longer to answer the question "Does a canary eat?" than to answer "Does a canary fly?" and about 75 milliseconds longer to answer the question about flying than to

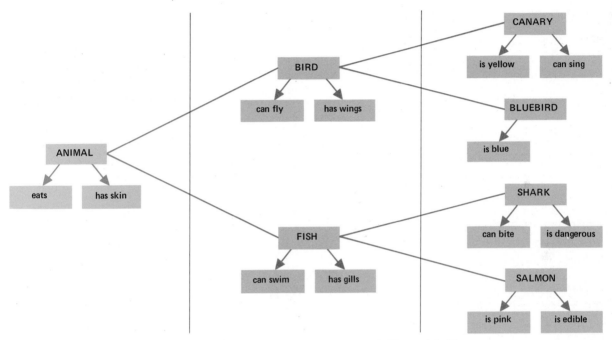

Figure 7.11 A portion of a hierarchically organized memory structure. (After Collins and Quillian, 1969.)

answer "Is a canary yellow?" In other words, the time necessary to travel from one level of the network to another was about 75 milliseconds. This kind of experiment suggests a model to explain one particular kind of memory search. In some ways the memory seems to work like a computer.

Mnemonic devices

There are certain tricks or speech techniques that aid memory. One of the problems encountered in the experimental study of memory is the use by some subjects of these special devices. Experiments are designed to keep the subjects' use of these at a minimum, because they tend to produce much more rapid responses than normal learning. Recently psychologists have been interested in studying these special memory techniques. Remembering information for a long period depends on more than repeating it over and over. Organization of the material so that it can be easily recalled is essential. Students who customarily use special techniques, called *mnemonic devices*, for this organization tend to have higher grade point averages than other students (Carlson et al., 1976).

A *mnemonic* is a technique for organizing information so that it can be memorized easily. (See Box 7.3.) Mnemonic devices are ancient. The anecdote that begins the chapter was told by Cicero in his *De Oratore*. Before the days of teleprompters, such devices as this example of the *method of loci* were used by political orators who had to memorize long speeches.

We all use mnemonic devices to remember. A number of experiments have demonstrated how organizing material in this way can aid in recall. In one study subjects were given a list of ten unrelated words and told to learn them in the exact order in which they were presented. Half of the subjects learned the words by making up and weaving a story around the words. For example, if the list began with the words *school, walk, table, infant . . .*, a subject's story might begin, "One day I arrived at *school* and started to *walk* to my first class, when suddenly I saw a *table* with an *infant* crying on it. . . ." The other half of the subjects were given the words and told simply to memorize them for recall. Both groups could recall the list of ten words almost perfectly when tested immediately after it was presented. This

217

BOX 7.3

Mnemonics: How you can remember better

We have all used mnemonics to aid memory. The rhyme "Thirty days hath September . . ." is a simple way to remember the number of days in each month. The rhyme "*i* before *e* except after *c*" has helped spellers of *receive* and *believe* for generations.

A rhyming system for general use is a *pegword* system such as this: ONE is a BUN, TWO is a SHOE, THREE is a TREE, FOUR is a DOOR, FIVE is a HIVE, SIX is a STICKS, SEVEN is a HEAVEN, EIGHT is a GATE, NINE is a WINE, and TEN is a HEN.

After you have memorized the system it can be used for remembering lists of items more easily. First number the list to be learned in sequence. Then form a compound visual image involving the first item and a bun, the second and a shoe, and so on. The vividness and unusualness of the image are important in memory. For example, to learn a list of raw materials produced by a particular country you might proceed as follows. The list is coffee, tin, rubber, beef, sugar, hides, handcrafts, fertilizer, cocoa beans, and caustic soda.

coffee—picture a *bun* with a man's head inside. The man is coughing
    COUGH-HE
tin—picture a *shoe* with a large letter *T* standing in it
    T-IN
rubber—picture a *tree* using its branches to scratch a girl's back
    RUB-HER
beef—picture a bee carrying a large letter *F* flying through a *door*
    BEE-F

COUGH-HE RUB-HER

T-IN BEE-F

This pegword list is a modern adaptation of the *method of loci* that was illustrated at the beginning of the chapter. It is useful for learning lists of items because the peg words provide a framework that leads from one item to the other. The pegword system calls for a high degree of visual imagery. Sometimes the *narrative technique* of weaving a story using the words to be learned works better (page 219). Sometimes the *beginning letter* of each word can be used as a cue. For example, the sentence "*Jesus Christ made Seattle under protest*" has been useful to many Seattleites because the initial letters correspond to the order of the main east-west streets in the long, narrow business district: Jefferson, James, Cherry, Columbia, Marion, Madison, Spring, Seneca, University, Union, Pike, and Pine.

All these techniques can help you learn information and remember it when you need it. Similar techniques of visual imagery can be used to remember names and faces. Try using some of them to help you remember the material in this chapter.

It is not difficult to remember the names of the seven dwarfs in the Snow White story because each has some visual characteristics that suggest his name. Can you find Dopey, Doc, or Grumpy? The association of facial characteristics and names is often used by public figures who meet and must remember the names of many people. (Culver)

same procedure was then repeated again and again until subjects had been presented with a total of 12 lists of words. After the final list, they were given the first word of the first list and asked to recall all the remaining words in the list. Then they were given the first word of the second list and told to recall the rest of that list. The procedure was repeated until subjects had been tested on all 12 of their lists.

There was an enormous difference in the ability for recall between the two groups. Subjects who had made up stories recalled an average of 93 percent of the words, whereas subjects in the other group recalled an average of only 13 percent of the words. The simple mnemonic of weaving words into a story, or *narrative chaining*, increased recall by a factor of almost 7.

Forgetting

Another way to look at the retrieval process is to concentrate not on what can be pulled out or re-

It is probably easier for this child to learn the metric system than it will be for most of us because previous knowledge of our own system of weights and measures interferes with our ability to learn metric equivalents. (Shelton, Monkmeyer)

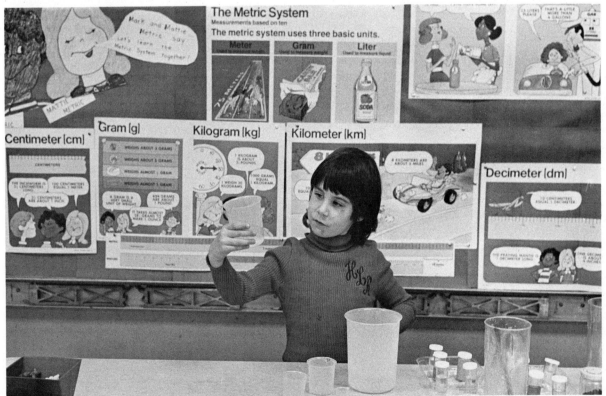

membered, but on what is at least temporarily unavailable or forgotten.

Why is it that a person recalls more information immediately after receiving it than one hour later? How much will you recall of this chapter tomorrow, next week, at the end of the term? The amount you seem to remember decreases as time passes. This is what we mean by forgetting.

It sometimes seems that people who learn quickly also remember well, whereas those who learn slowly seem to forget quickly as well. Although this principle seems true, research shows it is not. When the amount learned is taken into account this difference disappears. In one study (Young and Thompson, 1967) when the number of items recalled immediately after learning was compared with the number recalled 24 hours later, both groups forgot 1.5 items during the 24-hour period. The fast learners did appear to remember more, but they had also remembered more in immediate recall. When this difference was removed the amount of forgetting was the same.

Theories of forgetting. Forgetting, or the inability to remember, has been explained theoretically in different ways. It may be dependent on a *memory trace* or a *memory cue*. The *decay theory* is based on the memory trace idea. *Interference theory* and the idea of *retrieval failure* are based on the memory cue concept.

According to the memory trace theory, the memory trace fades away and no longer exists. This idea has not been connected to any physiological process and therefore cannot be tested at present. It is circular in that we say we forget because the trace decays or vanishes. But how do we know the trace decays? Because we have forgotten. In spite of this circularity the theory has had an appeal and has stimulated much research.

One of the oldest explanations of forgetting is that people forget things because other things interfere with, or block, the items they try to remember. This theory, called *interference theory*, is based on two observations: that earlier learning can interfere with our ability to recall newly learned material, a phenomenon called *proactive interference*, and that new learning can interfere with our ability to recall previously learned material, a phenomenon called

retroactive interference. These two types of interference are illustrated in Figure 7.12.

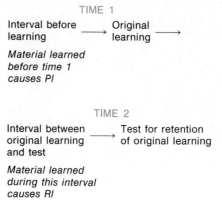

Figure 7.12 Interference theory. At time 1, some material is learned. After some interval of time, there is a test for recall at time 2. Material learned before time 1 produces *proactive interference* (PI), whereas material learned between time 1 and time 2 produces *retroactive interference* (RI).

Conditions under which different amounts of interference occur were of major interest to early associationist or S-R theorists. The theoretical importance of this concept, although still useful, has declined as cognitive theories have become popular. Another theoretical way to view forgetting is as a *failure to retrieve* desired information. Most of us have at some time tried to think of some piece of information but were unable to remember it. Because this happens so often some psychologists have argued that forgetting is much like being unable to find something we have misplaced. It happens because the information we are looking for is temporarily unavailable; if we had the right *retrieval cue*, the information could be found. At other times, when conditions were different and the connect cue was available, that piece of information might again be available. This theory assumes that material once learned is not forgotten. The problem of remembering lies in finding the correct place in the storage system.

Experimental studies of forgetting. Many types of experimental work have been directed toward the puzzle of forgetting. One area of study is the use of *highly similar stimuli*. This method was often used in early verbal learning experiments on the interference phenomenon. Lists of words highly similar in sound or meaning would be learned and the amount of forgetting under these conditions would be compared with that when dissimilar lists were used. Another method was the use of an interfering task, such as reciting numbers backward or doing mental arithmetic problems. The object here was to *prevent rehearsal*, that is, to keep the subject from practicing the list after its original presentation.

Prevention of new learning was another method of study used. The subjects slept after the original learning and were tested on awakening. Their retention was generally better than that of subjects who did not sleep. This could be explained either in terms of lack of competing stimuli or by chemical changes in the brain during sleep. The effects of *drugs* on retention have also been studied. Some drugs seem to improve memory. This may be because these drugs, which excite the brain, may produce faster, more efficient storage of information. Another group of drugs appears to cause temporary amnesia. Memory can also be affected by electric impulses to the brain. *Electric shock* administered to the brain after learning, when strong enough to produce convulsions, affects recent memory but leaves older memories intact.

With the research techniques currently available it is not possible to tell whether any of the events we experience are completely forgotten or whether they all remain in memory to be retrieved when an appropriate cue comes along. It is clear that some things become temporarily inaccessible, either because they are blocked by other memories or because we do not have an appropriate method for getting them out.

Clinical observations. Clinical findings are relevant also in attempting to understand the process of forgetting. As technical progress was made in surgery, a process of electrical stimulation of particular points in the brain was perfected. This has been widely used in animal experiments and can also be used as an aid to the surgeon in locating particular areas before any tissue destruction begins. This technique has yielded some provocative results that raise the question "Is anything ever forgotten?" In the 1950s Wilder Penfield, a Canadian neurosurgeon, exposed portions of the temporal lobe cortex of epileptic patients while using a local anesthetic so that the patients were fully conscious during the operation. He then stimulated different points on the cortex electrically. One patient stimulated in this way recalled in perfect detail a scene from a play he had seen years earlier. Another patient reported that she could see herself in an office in which she had worked a long time ago: "I could see the desks. I was there and someone was calling to me—a man leaning on a desk with a pencil in his hand." Many reexperienced events from early childhood. These were not particularly significant events, and it was unlikely that the patients would have remembered them under normal conditions.

Sigmund Freud found in his psychoanalytic work that during therapy patients remembered incidents from the past that had long been forgotten. Many of these events, it seemed to him, had been forgotten because they were so upsetting to the patient. He called this process of motivated forgetting *repression*. One of his patients remembered during therapy a thought that came to her mind while standing beside her sister's coffin, "Now my brother-in-law is free to marry me." This apparently shocked her so much that she did not remember it again until the therapy session, but instead felt only mild, appropriate affection for her brother-in-law.

The same process occurs in *amnesia*. Soldiers, after undergoing a particularly traumatic battle experience, may have no memory of the entire episode. Sometimes amnesia occurs when people cannot face the reality of their own behavior or the situation in which they find themselves.

An enlisted man in the Air Corps had some previous experience as a private pilot. After a disagreement with his wife, he decided to punish her by committing suicide. Choosing the most dramatic method he could think of, he took off in a large, unattended aircraft and made several passes at the local river, each time pulling up before he plunged in. Very soon, all other aircraft were diverted to other cities, and the local tower was concentrating on trying to persuade him to change his mind. He finally agreed, but then he discovered that although he knew how to take off, he did not know how to land the unfamiliar plane. After some tense interchanges with the control tower, however, he managed to get the plane down. When the welcoming party of military police arrived at the plane, he found himself unable to remember his name or anything

221

BOX 7.4
Teaching children the power of language

Psychologist Roger Brown (1965) invented this ingenious classroom demonstration to impress on young children the advantages of being able to read and write.

> We would let the children hide, wherever they wished within the classroom, a large number of small desirable objects: coins and tricks and stamps and the like. Then we would ask each child to call out the names of the objects he had hidden and also their hiding places. All the children would be instructed to try to memorize all of the information so that they might recover as many valuables as possible on the following day. The teacher, while all this went on, would stand at the blackboard inscribing certain cryptic signs:
>
>> Dime—in dirt around plant
>> Stamp—page 21 of dictionary
>> Metal spider—on top of painting of George
>>   Washington
>
> On the next day one child after another would be given a chance to recover as many treasures as he could directly find while the teacher stayed out of the room. No child would recover more than a fraction of the total. Then everything would be returned to its hiding place and the teacher called into the room. Consulting the blackboard, she would triumphantly collect every last object. The preliterate children would gather that there was some powerful "medicine" in those marks on the board, something enabling the teacher to store far more information than they were able to store. (Brown, 1965, p. 250)

about his identity, his present situation, or the events leading up to it. (Aldrich, 1966, p. 238)

Another clinical example comes from ordinary everyday behavior, the *tip of the tongue* (TOT) phenomenon. Have you ever had the answer to a question on the "tip of your tongue" yet been unable to produce it? Suppose someone asked you the name of the capital of Illinois. You might think of Fairfield, Mayfield, or other similar words. You might think it was a two-syllable word beginning with *S*. If you could not think of the answer it is likely that the question would keep returning to your mind until the correct answer, Springfield, finally occurred to you. This inability to remember, but at the same time to produce clues to the correct answer, is interesting to psychologists who study memory. It implies that the fact is not forgotten but that the retrieval mechanism is temporarily faulty.

LANGUAGE

A tremendous amount of information about language is stored in our memory. In fact, information about the components and rules of language constitutes one of the most important portions of semantic memory. For example, we know that there is an elementary sound corresponding to the letter *F* and one corresponding to the letter *W*, but in English we cannot combine them: FWOG is not an acceptable English combination. Semantic memory contains not only the sounds that make up the language, but also the rules that determine the sequences of sounds we can use.

Within the first two years of our lives we begin to acquire a language system that enables us to communicate an infinite set of messages. This system is enormously valuable. It enables us to transmit information from one individual to another for *social* communication. But language is also intimately involved with our mental processes and has important *problem-solving* functions. (See Box 7.4.)

Language influences many of our "nonlanguage" behaviors. For example, it helps us to discriminate between objects and events. In Arabic there are over 400 words that correspond roughly to the English word *camel*. Arabian camel traders use these 400 words to differentiate among camels by age, sex, and breed; by whether or not they are pregnant; by whether or not they are used to carry heavy goods; and so on. An American who looked at two camels might be able to tell that one was a little bigger than the other, or a different color, but be unable to make the finer distinctions that the Arabian words denote.

222

Simultaneous translators must convert the concepts of one language to those of another in a split second. (United Nations)

Benjamin Whorf, a noted linguist, suggested that a people's language determines the way in which they perceive and think about their world. This is called the hypothesis of *linguistic relativity*, or *linguistic determinism*, or the *Whorfian hypothesis*. Researchers have gathered data that indicate that people who speak different languages do classify objects in different ways.

An alternative theory is that different languages share the same concepts, even if these concepts are more easily expressed in some languages than in others. In fact, new words can be and are invented in all languages when they are needed. For example, when we speak of astronauts and moon shots, we are using words or combinations of words that were not used years ago. But it seems likely that we could have grasped the idea of an astronaut even before we had a word for it. Most linguists believe that language does not *determine* how we can think, but it certainly does determine how efficiently we can code our experiences, and it influences the way we think.

Language influences not only thought and perception, but also memory. The images and symbols that we use to reconstruct a past experience can be influenced by the words that prompt the recall. This was illustrated in a series of experiments in which college undergraduate students were shown films of traffic accidents and later asked questions about them to see how wording affected their judgment. Some were

asked, "About how fast were the cars going when they hit each other?" For others the verb *hit* was replaced with *contacted*, *bumped*, *collided*, or *smashed*. Although these words all refer to two objects coming together, they imply differences in the speed and force of impact. The researchers found that estimates of speed were influenced by the word that was used. Those subjects who were asked how fast the cars were going when they *contacted* each other gave the lowest estimates, whereas those questioned with the word *smashed* gave the highest (Loftus and Palmer, 1974).

The results of this and further studies suggest that the form of a question can actually change a person's memory of an event. The researchers conducted another experiment in which subjects saw a short film about a traffic accident and answered questions. A third of them answered the question "About how fast were the cars going when they *smashed into each other*?" Another third answered the same question with the word *hit* instead of *smashed*. The remaining third, which acted as a control group, was not asked a question about speed. As in the earlier study, subjects who were questioned with the word *smashed* gave higher speed estimates than those who were questioned with the word *hit*.

A week later, the subjects returned to the laboratory and were asked a series of questions about the film without viewing it again. This time they were

223

Original information　　**External information**　　**The ''memory''**

"About how fast were the cars going when they SMASHED into each other?"

Figure 7.13 Memories of complex events contain gaps that are filled in from a person's general information store. The question asked of a witness may supply information that distorts the original memory. The picture on the left shows the original information, the question provides external information, and the picture on the right shows the memory of the information. (Used with permission of the authors and the publishers, from G. R. Loftus and E. F. Loftus, *Human Memory: The Processing of Information*, Hillsdale, N.J., Lawrence Erlbaum Associates, publisher, 1976, p. 161.)

asked whether they had seen any broken glass. (None had been shown in the film.) If *smashed* really influenced subjects to remember the accident as more severe than it had been, the researchers hypothesized, then they might also ''remember'' details that were not shown but that were consistent with an accident occurring at high speed. More than twice as many subjects questioned with the word *smashed* reported seeing the nonexistent glass as those who were questioned with *hit*. Apparently, the influence of a word can actually change a memory. The words used in the question provided additional information to subjects (e.g., that the cars did indeed smash into each other), which was integrated into the information already stored in long-term memory, so that the subjects formed a ''memory'' of an accident that was more severe than the accident they saw. This phenomenon is illustrated in Figure 7.13. These findings have clear implications for the way in which eyewitness questionings are conducted in police interrogations and court trials.

Structure of language

The study of the way in which sounds and symbols are translated into meaning and the psychological processes that are involved in this translation is called *psycholinguistics*. The basic units and structure of language are described below. In Chapter 9 we discuss language development.

Units of language

The smallest units of sound are called *phonemes*. They are the vowel and consonant sounds that are recognized in any given language. The English language has 45 phonemes; some languages have fewer and some have many more. In the English language, phonemes correspond to vowel and consonant sounds as well as to such sounds as *sh* and *th*.

Phonemes can be combined into *morphemes*, the smallest units of meaning in a given language. English morphemes include whole words (*tree, run, learn*); prefixes (*un-, pre-, anti-*); and suffixes (*-ing, -ed, -ous*). The 45 English phonemes can be combined into over 100,000 morphemes, which in turn can be combined to form over 500,000 words. The number of morphemes is limited in all languages by certain rules that restrict the combination of phonemes. In English, for example, a phoneme never begins with more than three consonant sounds (such as *spl*); Russian phonemes, however, can have four consonants (such as *stch*).

The term *syntax* refers to the way morphemes are put together into coherent phrases or sentences. In English the sentence ''He caught the ball'' conforms to the syntactic rules of the language, whereas the sentence ''Ball caught he the'' does not. Syntax provides the ground rules for combining morphemes in order to express particular meanings shared by the people speaking a particular language.

Surface and deep structures

Psycholinguists draw a distinction between the *surface structure* and the *deep structure* of language. The surface structure of a spoken or written sentence, they say, consists of the words and their organization, whereas the deep structure refers to the underlying meaning of the sentence. The meanings that comprise deep structure are stored as concepts and rules in long-term memory. Some psycholinguists believe that the deep structure of language is built into our nervous system.

To understand the difference between surface and deep structure, consider the following sets of sentences:

A. John hit the ball.
   The ball was hit by John.

B. There is the white house cat.
   There is the White House cat.

In set A the surface structures are quite different, but the sentences mean the same thing. That is, they have the same deep structure. The sentences in set B have identical surface structures, but very different deep structures.

Chomsky's transformational grammar theory. Noam Chomsky formulated a theory of Transformational Grammar in 1957 which was based on the distinction between surface and deep structures. According to his theory, deep structure is represented by a *kernel* in surface structure. A kernel sentence is a simple declarative one, such as "John committed the crime." The *meaning* of this sentence is the kernel, whereas the *form* of the sentence is merely a "husk" that is discarded by the memory. The basic structure of the kernel sentence can be *transformed* into seven other surface structures that all represent the same kernel. These seven structures are presented in Table 7.1.

Many of the sentences we use are made up of one or more kernel sentences. Consider the sentence "The man who developed transformational theory is Noam Chomsky." It contains transformed versions of two kernel sentences: "The man developed transformational theory" and "The man is Noam Chomsky." We use certain transformational rules to *embed* the second sentence in the first one. The noun phrase *the man* in the embedded sentence has been

Table 7.1 Kernel sentences and their transformations

1. KERNEL SENTENCE:	John committed the crime.
2. Negative:	John did not commit the crime.
3. Passive:	The crime was committed by John.
4. Passive-negative:	The crime was not committed by John.
5. Question:	Did John commit the crime?
6. Question-negative:	Did john not commit the crime?
7. Passive-question:	Was the crime committed by John?
8. Passive-question-negative:	Was the crime not committed by John?

replaced by *who*. The operation of embedding allows us to use tremendously complex and interrelated systems of kernels.

Chomsky's theory also suggests that the elements and rules of meaning contained in deep structures are innate and patterned into the human nervous system. He claims that we are all born linguists. From innate deep structures and exposure to the language that is spoken in our environment our nervous systems create a set of rules for the production of language. Chomsky believes that innate deep structures account for similarities in patterns of language development among different cultures. He also points out that we can learn other languages very quickly and that we can understand surface structures that we have never before encountered.

Chomsky holds that there must be inborn principles of mental organization that provide the basic structure for all cognitive processes, including perceiving, learning, and thinking. These structures and transformational rules develop naturally as a person matures. Experience and learning are also involved, but they provide information only about the specific aspects of language (e.g., phonemes and morphemes) that are needed to communicate with other people within a particular language community (Chomsky, 1968).

Chomsky's theory contrasts sharply with behavioristic theories of language development, such as Skinner's, which stresses the role of reinforcement in learning speech responses. Skinner (1957) proposes that the development of speech is determined by reinforcing behaviors from parents; children learn speech patterns because they know they will be rewarded by having their needs met. Chomsky's theory challenges this idea that language development and usage are controlled completely by environment. The resulting debate has generated a great deal of research on the process of language development. We return to this controversy as it relates to language development in Chapter 9.

Can animals learn language?

Everyone knows that animals cannot talk. In 1968 Noam Chomsky wrote, "Anyone concerned with the study of human nature and human capacities must somehow come to grips with the fact that all normal humans acquire language, whereas acquisition of even its barest rudiments is quite beyond the capacities of an otherwise intelligent ape" (1968, p. 59).

But in 1969 the foundations of psychology and psycholinguistics were rocked by reports that Allen and Beatrice Gardner of the University of Nevada

A chimp named Lucy signs "lipstick" to researcher Roger S. Fouts. (Courtesy of Dr. Roger Mellgren, Psychology Dept., University of Oklahoma.)

had trained a chimp to communicate through sign language. All previously unsuccessful language work with chimps had involved training them to vocalize words. The vocal apparatus of the chimpanzee is not physically capable of producing human speech, but chimps have fine manual dexterity. The Gardners reasoned that an attempt to teach a chimpanzee deaf sign language would be a more conclusive test of its ability to use language.

The Gardners began training Washoe, a 1-year-old female chimp, in 1966. They used virtually every known training method to get her to produce signs, including operant training and reinforcement, modeling, and actually holding her hands. During her waking hours she was constantly in the company of a human being, who communicated with her through sign language during her feeding, bathing, grooming, and other daily routines.

By the time she was 4 years of age, Washoe was using 85 different signs; by age 5 the number had increased to 160 (Fleming, 1974). In fact, she was using up to five signs in sequences that were very similar to sentences. Some of the sign combinations were her own creations and not ones she had learned from her trainers. For instance, when she was threatened by an aggressive rhesus monkey, she combined the signs for *dirty* and *monkey*. Washoe often produced as many as 150 signs during an evening's meal.

When Washoe was 4 years old, 249 of her two-sign combinations were analyzed in accordance with the semantic categories used to classify children's speech (Brown, 1973). Seventy-eight fitted into these categories. This figure is very close to those for cross-cultural studies of 2-year-old children's combinations. At present there are over a dozen chimpanzees in various laboratories around the country using sign language with varying degrees of fluency.

The training of Sarah. At about the same time that the Gardners were training Washoe to use sign language, David Premack was conducting a comparable project at the University of California, Santa Barbara. This project also involved an attempt to teach language to a chimpanzee, but the training approach was quite different. In place of sign language Premack developed a set of "word symbols," pieces of plastic in various shapes and colors with magnetic backings so that they could be used on a felt-covered metal "language board." Premack used shaping to train a chimp named Sarah to associate the word symbols with various aspects of her environment.

First, Sarah was shaped to name a prized object or food in order to receive it. Next, she was required to use symbols that signified the names of her several trainers along with symbols for desired objects. She also learned to use a symbol to refer to herself. After this she learned rather quickly a series of verbs, so that it was possible for her to develop sentence structures. Sarah was then able to communicate such sequences as "Mary [trainer]—insert—banana—bowl." She could also read and follow instructions when they were communicated with plastic symbols. (See Figure 7.14.)

As her training progressed, Sarah learned the meaning of a question mark. Once this happened her trainer could ask her questions whose answers required varying degrees of linguistic ability. Through these questions they discovered that Sarah had fully learned certain concepts. For example, when the symbol for *color* was included in a comparison question about a banana and a yellow ball, she correctly replied that they were the same. Sarah was aware of what the concept of color meant; she had learned to draw comparisons on the basis of specific concepts.

Although linguists debate whether the accomplishments of Washoe and Sarah can legitimately be compared to the use of language in human beings, there is little doubt that these animals have demonstrated linguistic accomplishments that scientists considered impossible only a decade ago. Although human beings remain the undisputed champions of the linguistic world, we are beginning to hear the footsteps of the chimpanzee behind us. It may not be long before other intelligent species, such as dolphins, also enter the race.

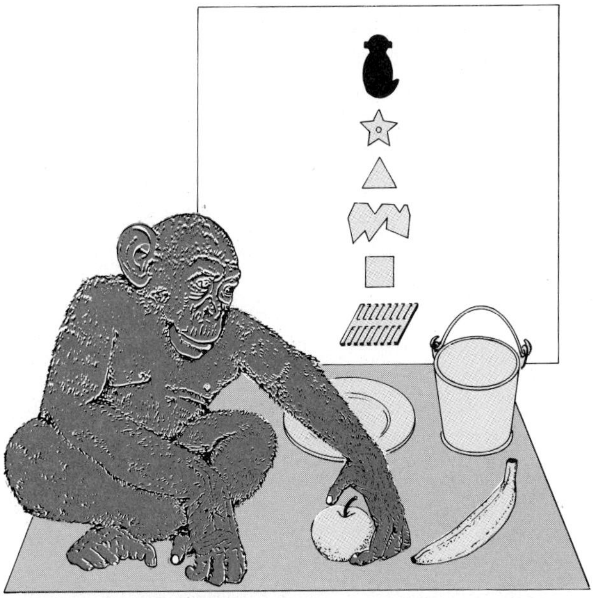

THINKING AND PROBLEM SOLVING

Language and thought are intimately related. Once we acquire language, most of our thinking makes use of it. Words, the basic units of language, and concepts, the building blocks of thought, are closely related, if not identical. Both are symbols we manipulate to create meanings.

Images and concepts

An *image* is an internal representation of sensory information that has previously been perceived. Most images are mental pictures, but any of our sensory systems can produce images; sometimes we rehear our experiences. Some individuals have images of smells, tastes, or tactile sensations. Although images are based on sensory information, our interests, motivations, and experiences can produce changes in the images we carry with us so that they are no longer perfect replicas of our original perceptions. Separated lovers sometimes find on being reunited that the images they were carrying with them were far more attractive than the stimuli they finally perceive.

A very small percentage of human beings (under 10 percent) is capable of what is known as *eidetic imagery*. These individuals can produce very clear visual images in astonishing detail. For example, one

Figure 7.14 Sarah, after reading the message "Sarah insert apple pail banana dish" on the magnetic board behind her, performed the appropriate actions. To be able to make the correct interpretation that she should put the apple in the pail and the banana in the dish (not the apple, pail, and banana in the dish) the chimpanzee had to understand sentence structure rather than just word order. In actual tests most symbols were colored. (Premack and Premack, "Teaching language to an ape." Copyright © 1963 by Scientific American, Inc. All rights reserved.)

227

Pictures such as this are used in the study of eidetic imagery. Some subjects can report a great deal of detail after seeing the picture for only 30 seconds. Look at the picture for a half minute. Can you remember how many workers are in the field and which way each one's rake is pointing? How many chimneys are on the house? Someone with eidetic imagery could answer such questions without knowing what would be asked at the time he or she looked at the picture. (Ingri D'Aulaire and Edgar Parin, *George Washington*, Doubleday, 1936.)

Concepts are a second set of symbols used in thinking. Concepts represent connections or common characteristics among two or more objects or events. They help us to reduce an overwhelming number of objects and situations to their common denominators, so that we can classify them and think of them in groups rather than individually. Elephants, sharks, and amoebas are very different in appearance and in other respects, but we still classify them together as animals. Concepts also enable us to select objects or events that have one or a few particular properties from a larger set, and to sort out the ways in which various objects and events are either similar or dissimilar to one another. Because concepts are so important in our cognitive processes, a good deal of research has been devoted to discovering the ways in which they are formed and used.

Concept formation

Concept formation involves the ability to recognize common qualities in different objects or events. Our ability to use language enables us to deal with concepts on many different levels. Some concepts involve concrete classifications, such as *human beings;* others, such as *justice*, are highly abstract. Many experiments have shown that concrete concepts are more easily acquired than abstract ones, so that they are the first to be learned. The ability to acquire increasingly abstract concepts is a sign of cognitive maturation.

Concepts can serve as bridges that link the same response to a number of different stimuli. A child who has learned the concept *dog* is likely to respond in much the same way to all the individual animals who fit within this conceptual class. If the child is knocked down or bitten by one dog, he or she may respond with fear to other dogs with much different physical characteristics.

We can form concepts in a number of ways. We attach names or labels to objects and events so that we gradually abstract out the common properties that define categories. Children form concepts by observing properties that objects in their environment, such as dogs, people, and trees, have in common.

The use of language helps us greatly in forming concepts. It enables us to communicate to others what a particular concept means, so that they do not

study found that out of 151 children who viewed a picture of 10 Indians for only a few seconds, 12 could produce an image so clear that they were able to report details as minute as the number of feathers in each Indian's headdress, as well as the different colors in a complex multicolored blanket (Haber and Haber, 1964). Eidetic imagery is much less common in American adults than in children; the reason for this difference is not clear.

All of us have wished for perfect recall at some time in our lives, especially around final exam time. But this ability is a mixed blessing. Sometimes people who have eidetic imagery have difficulty thinking abstractly (Luria, 1968). For example, if the word *tree* were mentioned to a person with eidetic imagery, that person would immediately conjure up a photographic image of a particular tree and could not abstract enough to think of the general idea of a tree.

228

have to form the concept through their own observations and experiences. We have defined many psychological concepts in this book through language. Language is particularly important for learning abstract concepts, such as *morality, goodness,* and *concept.* We also acquire new concepts through the *contexts* in which they appear. Sometimes we are able to grasp the meaning of an unfamiliar word by the way in which it is used in a sentence, or by hearing it used in a number of different contexts. Concepts are the building blocks of thought; the development and use of concepts are of critical importance in problem solving.

Problem solving

We all spend a great deal of our time in formal or informal problem solving. Consider the following example:

> Enter Michele, aged three, onto the scene. The scene involves Michele, a cookie jar, and a shelf. The cookie jar is on the shelf and the shelf is 4 feet off the ground. . . Michele, stretched to her longest (tiptoes, arms stretched, all that) is only 3 feet, 6 inches high, even giving her a few inches. Michele on the ground sees the cookie jar—goal object is now relevant—so she walks over trying the direct approach. She raises her right arm, it won't do; she raises her right arm and gets up on tiptoes, no luck; she grasps some wall molding with her left hand, raises her right arm and jumps. Almost, but no cigar. She goes to the corner of the room, brings a step stool, climbs up and gets her reward . . . : Happiness is a newly filched cookie. (Pollio, 1974, p. 120)

Trial and error. Michele's behavior illustrates the use of the trial-and-error method of problem solving. She tried a series of approaches until she found one that worked. We all often use trial and error as a way to deal with a new situation. In other cases a set of rules, such as those used in mathematics or foreign languages, can be used to solve a problem. Sometimes having solved similar situations in the past helps. At other times we may achieve a big breakthrough or have an insight that suddenly makes the solution plain. Samples of the many kinds of problems psychologists use to study problem solving are shown in Box 7.5.

BOX 7.5
Problems used in research on problem solving

These problems have been used in the scientific study of thinking and problem-solving behavior. Try to solve them if you like, but beware: Problem 4 may take an hour or more. Solutions are given below.

1. Write an English word that uses all the letters of the word *time*.
2. Try to solve this problem in your head: 69 × 8.
3. Without lifting your pencil from the paper, connect all nine dots by drawing four straight lines

    : : :
    : : :
    : : :

4.   D O N A L D
    + G E R A L D   D = 5
    ‾‾‾‾‾‾‾‾‾‾‾‾
      R O B E R T

This is a *cryptarithmetic* problem. The task is to replace the letters in this array by numerals, from 0 through 9, so that all instances of the same letter are replaced by the same numeral, different letters are replaced by different numerals, and the resulting numerical array is a correctly worked out problem in arithmetic. As an additional hint for this particular problem, the letter D is to be replaced by the numeral 5.

4. D = 5, T = 0, B = 3, E = 3, L = 9, N = 8, O = 6, G = 2, G = 1, R = 7, A = 4.

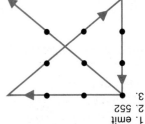

3.
2. 552
1. emit
Solutions to problems

229

BOX 7.6
Limitations of protocol analysis

Although verbal protocols can provide us with a great deal of valuable information, we must remember that they are not usually complete. In an early study of reasoning N. R. F. Maier (1931) combined an experimental situation with the use of protocols. He presented subjects with the situation illustrated here.

Two cords were hung from the ceiling of a room. Subjects were told to tie the strings together, but the strings were hung so that it was impossible to reach both of them at the same time.

Using objects scattered around the room, subjects came up with a number of solutions. One of these was of particular interest to Maier, and he devised two hints to lead subjects toward this solution.

Hint 1: The experimenter walked around the room and when he passed the cord that hung from the center, he gently put it into motion. Subjects did not know that this was a suggestion. The experimenter merely walked to the window and had to pass the cord.

Hint 2: In case Hint 1 did not work within a few minutes, subjects were handed a pair of pliers and told, "With the aid of this and no other object, you can solve the problem."

At this point Maier divided his subjects into two groups: those who claimed they used the hint and those who claimed they did not use it. Subjects who insisted that the hint did not help at all still solved

Maier's experimental problem. (Adapted from Maier, 1931. Copyright 1931 by the American Psychological Association. Reprinted by permission.)

the problem much more quickly than a control group who received no hints at all. Only 20 percent of the control group solved the problem, whereas among those who received the two hints, almost everyone solved the problem in less than a minute.

The protocols of the hint group did not mention any hints, yet, obviously, the hints would have assisted them in finding the solution. The protocol is only a partial description of the actual internal processes. It is still a powerful tool for reconstructing the events that take place during problem solving and for exploring strategies for complex problem-solving tasks.

Approaches to thinking and problem solving

Observational approaches
In order to study any phenomenon we must first try to observe it. When we study human thinking and

problem solving it is often impossible to make direct observations. As was pointed out, psychologists have tried to get around this difficulty by asking people to "think out loud" while they are solving a problem. They tape-record and transcribe verbal thought processes to obtain what is called a *verbal protocol.* One problem with this procedure is that protocols usually include only a summary of the individual's steps in reasoning. Some crucial ideas may be omitted. For an example of this see Box 7.6.

In one use of the protocol method a subject was presented with one of the problems in Box 7.5.

$$\begin{array}{l} D\ O\ N\ A\ L\ D \\ +G\ E\ R\ A\ L\ D \\ \hline R\ O\ B\ E\ R\ T \end{array} \qquad D = 5$$

The subject's verbal protocol contained 2200 words produced in 20 minutes. The protocol begins as follows:

1. There are ten different letters and each of them has one numerical value.
2. Therefore I can do—what? Looking at the 2 Ds—each D is 5; therefore T is zero. So I think I'll start by writing that problem here. I'll write 5, 5, and zero.
3. Now do I have any other Ts? No. But I have another D. That means I have a 5 over the other side.
4. Now I have two As and two Ls that are each—somewhere—and this R—three Rs.
5. Two Ls equal an R. Of course, I'm carrying a 1, which will mean that R has to be an odd number because the two Ls—any two numbers added together result in an even number, and 1 will be an odd number. So R can be 1, 3, not 5, 7, or 9.

What principles can we uncover in an analysis of this verbal protocol? First of all, we can see that the subject started off with a burst of energy and discovered that T equals zero. (See statement 2.) He then attempted to determine whether his knowledge that T is zero and D is 5 could help him anywhere else in the problem. He looked first for another T (see 3), then for another D (see 3).

Clearly, the subject attempted to reach his final goal by breaking it down into a number of smaller steps or subgoals. Unfortunately, he was incorrect in his analysis of R. To solve the problem this error must be corrected. Can you carry on the protocol to find the solution?

Algorithms versus heuristics. From the analysis of protocols we can distinguish use of two kinds of methods: algorithms and heuristics. An *algorithm* is a plan that automatically generates a correct solution. The rules for multiplication or addition might be called algorithms. If you use them properly you will always get the right answer. For example, if the distance a car travels and its speed are known, the time required for the trip can be found by using the algorithm:

$$Time = \frac{distance}{speed}$$

The difficulty in using algorithms comes in situations in which a number of possible combinations must be tried to find the best solution. For example, in a chess game an algorithm might be written to include all possible combinations of moves from an existing position to the termination of the game. If this algorithm were then used to select the one move that would lead to checkmate of the opposing king, even a high-speed computer would probably need a very long time to complete the process (Shannon, 1950).

In complex solutions the use of algorithms is not practical. In these situations *heuristics* are more useful. Heuristics are more like rules of thumb. They are search procedures that are quick and easy to use, but they do not always work. If you were in the middle of a chess game and about to make a move, usually you would resort to using a heuristic, such as (1) trying to control the four center squares; (2) making sure your king is safe; (3) trying to add a new attacker to the list of active pieces; or (4) trying to take the opponent's king farthest from its base. Choosing a move that added a new attacker to the list of active pieces would not necessarily be the best move you could make, but it could be made quickly, without working through each possible move.

Two kinds of heuristics are often found in verbal protocols—*make-a-plan* and *means-ends analyses*. A *make-a-plan* heuristic would go like this: Subjects first find a simple problem of the kind that they are to solve. They solve it and use the method as a plan to solve the more complex problem. In a *means-ends analysis* subjects first define a subgoal they hope to achieve (an *end*). They then compare that subgoal with their present state of knowledge. If there is a discrepancy or a difference between them, subjects try to find a *means* to reduce that difference.

BOX 7.7

Therapist or computer?

In 1967 Kenneth Mark Colby of Stanford University programmed a computer to act as a therapist (Colby and Enea, 1967). The program permits the computer to carry on a simple therapeutic dialogue similar to the interview a live therapist might conduct in the first sessions with a patient. Subjects sit at a teletype connected to the computer and type out anything they wish to say. The computer sends back a typewritten reply.

Look at the two interviews below and see if you can tell whether the responses come from a live therapist or from a computer.

1. First Interview (Ther = therapist; Pt = patient)

Ther: How can I help you?

Pt: I'm not sure myself. All I know is I've decided I've got to do something about myself. I've been reading some of those psychology books, and I can see myself on every page. I just think it would be a good idea for me to see a psychiatrist and get myself straightened out. Mother would die if she knew I was coming, because she doesn't believe in psychiatry. It's not that she's old-fashioned or any-thing, but she just thinks everybody has problems and the only way to solve them is by leading a clean life. Get lots of sleep, take walks, and don't worry about things, she says.

Ther: What things do you worry about?

Pt: Well, I don't exactly worry, but things upset me. Not school, I'm doing fine there. To be honest about it, I guess it's boy friends. I can't seem to hang on to one very long, and I always wind up being hurt. Then I get in a tizzy and get all upset.

Ther: What happens to you?

. . . later in the session . . .

Ther: And what else is bothering you?

Pt: I don't know how important it is, but in the last few years I've been having trouble with my mother. It seems we're always arguing about something or other. Like today, she was giving me a bad time about coming in late last night. She thinks a girl should be home and in bed by eleven o'clock. You'd think I'd committed a crime the way she carries on when I come home later. With her nagging at me on top of vomiting all night, sometimes I think I'm going crazy. Do I sound crazy?

2. Second Interview

Ther: I would like to know more about your background, especially about your family life.

For example, suppose your problem is that you have to get to Paris. As a subgoal you might figure out how to get to New York. If you were on the West Coast you would notice that it is possible to go from the West Coast to New York overland, so that your means might be "Get on a train." Once you were in New York you would need a subgoal, "Get to Paris." Of course, you would not be able to use the same means. Your new one would have to be "Get on a plane or a ship."

Simulation models

After study of human verbal protocols produced by subjects who attempt to solve a particular problem, a computer simulation model may be written. This model is a program or set of instructions delivered to an electronic computer to mirror (or simulate) the processes used by the human subjects. One of the first significant attempts to simulate complex cognitive processes took place at Carnegie-Mellon University. Allen Newell and Herbert Simon attempted to

Pt: My father and mother did not get along well.

Ther: Tell me something else you think is important about your father.

Pt: He was hard to live with because he was so domineering.

Ther: Are you like your father?

Pt: No, I am not.

Ther: In some way though you must be like your father.

Pt: He liked to fish and I do too.

Ther: Did you admire him when you were young?

Pt: I don't think so.

Ther: Why not?

Pt: Because he was too weak a person.

Ther: I see. Now tell me something else about him.

Pt: Well, he was very opinionated.

Ther: Was there much friction between you and him when you were growing up?

Pt: Yes. We fought all the time.

Ther: Perhaps you were afraid of him.

Pt: I certainly was. He used to really blow up.

Ther: Perhaps you are still fearful of older men.

Pt: Let's talk about something else.

Could you tell which interview was conducted with a live therapist and which with the computer-therapist? The first of the two interviews was an actual therapeutic interview (Colby, 1951, pp. 40–43). In the second, a computer played the role of therapist (Colby and Enea, 1967, p. 21).

develop a computer program capable of discovering and formulating a logical proof. The original model, the Logic Theorist (LT), was designed to simulate a human approach to proving mathematical theorems. Later, Newell and Simon extended their efforts and came up with the General Problem Solver, or GPS. GPS simulates means-ends analysis and other heuristics.

How well does GPS duplicate the performance of flesh-and-blood subjects involved in solving similar problems? We can answer this question by comparing protocols from subjects working on problems with a computer program's approach to the same problem. The test involves presenting a protocol to an expert to see whether the expert can tell if it came from a computer or from a person. Look at Box 7.7 and see if you can tell the source of each protocol.

The process of developing a computer simulation program forces an investigator to define rules for operation of the computer. The computer's performance will be only as good as the programmer's understanding of the ways in which human beings function.

In Colby's "therapist" program the rules are complex. The computer is programmed to recognize several hundred key words or phrases, such as *I hate, I worry,* or *my mother,* and to select a response from a group of replies designated as appropriate for that key word or phrase. The response selected might simply involve the addition of certain appropriate words to the patient's sentence. For example, when the patient says, "My mother dislikes me," the program might reply, "Why do you feel your mother dislikes you?" The computer also keeps track of key topics for use in formulating future responses. If the "patient's" statement does not contain any key words, the program steers him or her back to a previous topic. For example, if the patient says, "The weather is great today," the program might reply, "Let's go back and talk a little more about why you think your mother dislikes you."

Stages in problem solving

Researchers have found that most human problem solving occurs in a series of distinct progressive stages. Protocols are often used to study these steps. In one approach to the solution of problems the following question was posed: If there is an inoperable stomach tumor and a ray that at high intensities would destroy both healthy and diseased tissue, how can the tumor be destroyed without damaging the surrounding tissue? When this problem was presented to college students, many of them proceeded through four specific stages in their attempt to solve it. Figure 7.15 illustrates this pattern.

The first step was the statement of the problem. Students then considered three potential *general-range* hypotheses. These involved restatements of

233

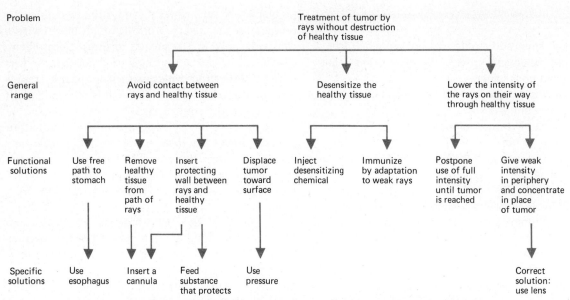

Figure 7.15 One subject's approach to solving Duncker's tumor problem. Progression through four specific stages is shown. (Adapted from Duncker, 1945.)

the problem that emphasized one or another factor that might be changed to avoid destruction of the healthy tissue. At the next stage *functional solutions* were considered. These involved implementations of the three general-range alternatives. These were all general strategies and did not name specific procedures. Finally, *specific solutions* were generated on the basis of the functional solutions. These involved specific procedures or instruments that would allow implementation of the functional solutions. As we can see, the respondent in Figure 7.15 arrived at five potential specific solutions that were then considered in terms of potential success and practicality. The correct solution then appeared with the characteristic swiftness and surety of an insight: "Use of a lens in order to focus the rays on the tumor." Actually, this solution is only correct in principle, because X-rays cannot be reflected by lenses. But given the small amount of information that subjects had, it is a very acceptable solution. Another correct solution was to use several weaker ray beams that converge on the tumor from different directions. The ray beams would be intense where they intersect at the tumor but elsewhere weak enough that they would not harm the healthy tissues.

This experiment shows that there are definite stages in the problem-solving process. Psychologists now define four stages that seem to be involved in the solution of many problems: *preparation, incubation, illumination,* and *verification.*

In the *preparation* stage we explore problems, the various elements involved in them, and the relationships among the elements. Often this exploration involves a random application, either at a mental or a physical level, of the direct and obvious possibilities of a solution.

If no solution to the problem can be found during this stage, we frequently "give up" for the moment and leave the situation to *incubate* for a period of time. We make no attempt to think about the problem during this time, but we are often delighted to find that a new approach occurs to us later when we return to the problem situation. Sometimes this is an *illumination* (or *insight* or "aha!") experience in which the solution to the problem becomes obvious. Finally, the *verification* stage is a test of the validity of the solution that appeared during the illumination phase.

234

Experimental approaches to problem solving

An early experimental approach was the string problem shown in Box 7.6. In the experimental approach various aspects of the situation are manipulated or changed and the behavior of the subject is compared under both (or several) sets of conditions. By contrast, the observational approach involves simply watching and recording subjects' behavior or asking them to describe it by means of a verbal protocol.

Functional fixedness

The problem of whether the customary use of an object interferes with its use in a novel situation is called the study of functional fixedness. In the string problem the heavy objects that could be used to make a pendulum were all tools with other uses. It was difficult for the subject to think of them in new ways.

Another experimental situation used to study the effect of functional fixedness is shown in Figure 7.16. Subjects must put two rings on a peg from a position 6 feet from the peg. In order to solve this problem, subjects must find a way to extend their reach. They can tie two short sticks together with a string; the sticks are left in an obvious place, but the string sometimes hangs by itself on a nail in the wall and sometimes is used to support a mirror. If it is hanging by itself, subjects almost always use it, but if it is supporting the mirror, they don't "think" to use it, and fail to solve the problem. Clearly, their perception of the string as "something with which to hang things" interferes with the thought of using it as "something with which to tie things together."

Mental set

We get into the habit of solving particular kinds of problems in a particular way. This means we are using a kind of *mental set*. These habits can make life much easier because we do not have to stop each time to figure the process out from the beginning. We simply pull out the familiar pattern, use it to solve the problem, and move on to the next task. Sometimes this use of patterns is less efficient in solving the problem than taking a fresh look, or if the pattern does not fit, the problem may be impossible until we look for another method of solution.

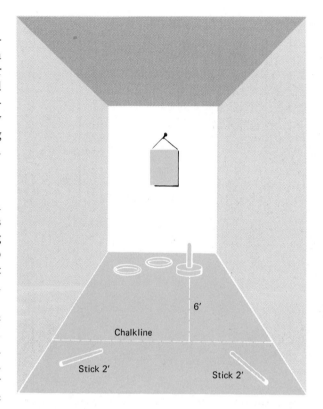

Figure 7.16 Ring and peg problem could be solved with a piece of string with which to tie the two sticks together. The only string in the room hung on a nail on the wall. When it hung there alone, every subject solved the problem. When it was used to suspend a cardboard, an old calendar or a cloudy mirror, some people failed. When the string was a hanger for functional things, such as a sign, a clear mirror or a current calendar, more than half failed. (Martin Scheerer, "Problem solving." Copyright © 1963 by Scientific American, Inc. All rights reserved.)

One kind of problem for studying mental set is the water jar problem used by A. S. Luchins. In a "water jar" experiment, subjects were given a series of problems involving three different jars—*A, B,*

235

BOX 7.8
Water jar problems

Subjects are asked to solve a series of problems.

1.	$A = 21$	$B = 127$	$C = 3$	obtain	100
2.	2	40	4		30
3.	1	27	6		14
4.	2	16	3		8
5.	7	59	12		28
6.	12	80	19		40
7.	23	49	3		20

The first six problems can be solved by the formula $B - A - 2C$. The seventh problem could be solved much more simply by using the formula $A - C$. Subjects usually used the more complicated formula unless they were given a hint about problem 7.

In a variation of this experiment it might be impossible to solve problem 7 using the same formulation. Try this example:

$A = 2, B = 27, C = 7$ obtain 14.

Subjects who had solved the earlier problems would have more difficulty solving this new problem than would subjects who had not practiced the series.

(Solution: $2C = 14$)

and *C*—and told the amount of water each would hold. Subjects had to use some combination of the three jars to obtain a specific amount of water. For example, if they were told to obtain 100 quarts, and if *A* held 21 quarts, *B* held 127 quarts, and *C* held 3 quarts, they had to determine how they could use the jars and end up with 100 quarts.

In a typical water jar experiment, subjects were shown seven problems that could all be solved in exactly the same way. The seventh problem also had a simpler solution. For example, the simplest solution

to the preceding problem is $B - A - 2C$, or $127 - 21 - 2(3) = 100$. This formula might be the easiest solution to the next five problems, but the seventh might be as follows: Given that jar *A* holds 23 quarts, jar *B* holds 49 quarts, and jar *C* holds 3 quarts, how can the jars be used to obtain 20 quarts? The expression $B - A - 2C$ works for this problem, but so does the much simpler expression $A - C$.

Luchins and others who have repeated his experiments found that over 50 percent of the subjects solved the seventh problem using the complex expression $B - A - 2C$ rather than the simpler $A - C$. Under one condition subjects were warned, "Don't be blind" before they tried to solve the seventh problem. These subjects often found the simpler solution. Sometimes a problem that could not be solved by the usual pattern was used at the end of the series. Subjects often had trouble solving a simple problem because they continued to use the old pattern. (See Box 7.8.)

Anagrams can also be used to study mental set. Look at this list:

E C A P H
E P P L A
N O L E M
H A G U L

It is easy to make assumptions that may be invalid. If the first three items are fruits, an assumption might be made that all items name fruits. Although this assumption is reasonable, in this case it is not valid. Did that invalid assumption interfere with the process of unscrambling the name of a nonfruit?

Solution: peach   apple   lemon   laugh

Many problems are made more difficult by invalid assumptions. Part of the skill of problem solving lies in taking a critical look at what is assumed. Sometimes the individual is not even aware of certain assumptions. The third problem in Box 7.5 is an example of this kind in which assumptions can make a solution harder. Subjects can solve this problem only if they realize that they can and must extend the lines beyond the dots. Unless they can break away from this stereotyped assumption they will not solve the problem.

Another kind of problem in which previously

learned behavior interferes with achieving the solution is a variation of the anagram problem. Look at the sample anagram N E L I N. These letters can be rearranged to form the English word L I N E N. Now look at the following two sets of anagrams. Try to solve those in set I, then those in set II.

Set I	Set II
tirfu	canoe
tanog	stalk
ightr	lemon
hacir	scold

You probably solved those in Group I more quickly than those in Group II. Researchers have found that it takes much longer to solve anagrams that are words to begin with. The subjects seem to associate other words to the word-anagram presented and this makes it difficult for them to seek new letter combinations.

A Psychological Frontier:
Problem solving in the real world

Students of law or medicine must learn to solve difficult and complex problems. One way they do this is by the traditional method of working closely with experts and modeling their own methods after the ways these outstanding individuals solve problems. The rapidly growing number of students in these fields means that many more experts would be needed to preserve low ratios of students to faculty. Not only is the number of experts limited, but the high costs of maintaining small classes also makes another approach necessary.

Some very bright students seem to learn these techniques even when classes are large and there is no opportunity to work closely with an expert. But what about the other students? Could problem-solving techniques help them learn the skills they need to become competent professionals? You might think that, using the protocol method, it would be easy to learn how experts think about problems. The students could learn to follow the thought pattern of the expert and the problem would be solved. Unfortunately, protocols of lawyers and physicians solving problems in their practice do not show a logical pattern a student could copy. At the University of Leyden in the Netherlands a group working on protocols of lawyers described its results this way:

. . . the results were disappointing. The most striking result was that what was said while thinking aloud created a rather chaotic and unsystematic impression. Often a person seemed to have a solution, although a provisional one, at an early stage, for which he subsequently tried to find supporting arguments. Moreover, during the reasoning process, the subject did not seem to complete one part after the other, but rather to jump wildly back and forth. . . . Our subjects seemed already to have, at an early stage, a provisional solution. . . . They seem in many instances to reason from the end to the beginning, i.e., regressively, in such a way that the hypothetical solution becomes prescriptive for the solving process. (Crombag et al., 1975, pp. 169–170)

A group working in medical education at Michigan State University has reported similar findings (Elstein et al., 1972).

Skilled practitioners seem to solve problems by combining their basic knowledge with their experience. Students, lacking experience, must solve problems in another way. At Leyden a training program was designed to teach all students to follow a rational reconstruction of the legal problem-solving process. The program guides students through the series of steps experts would follow if they solved problems in a strictly rational manner. Whether this approach will help make practice of these disciplines "a science rather than an art" remains to be seen, but early results look promising.

SUMMARY

1. Cognitive psychologists study memory, thinking, language, and problem solving. They are interested in how information, or input, is received by the senses, is retained, and then is used by the individual.

2. What is remembered can be measured by *recall* of the material, by *recognition* of it, or by the number of trials needed to *relearn* the material compared to the number of trials originally needed.

3. Until the 1960s most memory research was based on the *associationist* or S-R idea that

237

two stimuli that occur together in time become linked. *Cognitive approaches* to memory then became popular. These developed from *information theory*, advances in *brain surgery* technique, ideas borrowed from *Gestalt* theorists, and the *psychoanalytic concept of repression* or motivated forgetting.

4. One of the most popular models used to describe the memory process divides the memory system into sensory store (SS), short-term memory (STM), and long-term memory (LTM). Another model emphasizes not where information is stored but the way in which it is processed or organized.

5. Forgetting can be explained as a fading away of the *memory trace, interference* of other material, or a *failure to retrieve* the information because the correct place in the storage or memory filing system cannot be found.

6. Memory can be improved by repeating the material many times or by organizing it and fitting it into material already in the memory. One method of organization is by use of *mnemonic devices,* such as weaving words together into a story or associating each with a number, rhyme, or particular place in a mental picture.

7. Psycholinguistics is the study of the way sounds and symbols are translated into meaning and of the psychological process involved.

8. Language can be divided into units. The smallest, the vowel and consonant sounds, are called *phonemes. Morphemes* are the smallest units of meaning. In English, morphemes include whole words, prefixes, and suffixes. *Syntax* is the way morphemes are put together in meaningful phrases or sentences.

9. Language has both a *surface structure* and a *deep structure.* The surface structure describes how the words are organized. The deep structure refers to the underlying meaning. This distinction is the basis for Noam Chomsky's theory of *transformational grammar.*

10. For many years the use of language was thought to distinguish human beings from all other animals. This distinction is now less clear. Recently several chimpanzees have been taught to use symbols to communicate complex thoughts.

11. Symbols used in thinking include *images* or mental pictures and *concepts,* similarities or connections among objects or events.

12. Psychologists explain problem-solving behavior by past experience or the use of former solutions, by trial-and-error behavior, or by insight based on an understanding of the essential relations involved. To solve some problems *algorithms,* formulas, or specific rules are helpful. For complex problems *heuristics* or rules of thumb are more practical.

Suggested readings

Brown, R. *A first language.* Cambridge, Mass.: Harvard University Press, 1973. A readable book by a prominent researcher in the field of language development.

Kintsch, W. *Learning, memory and conceptual processes.* New York: John Wiley & Sons, Inc., 1970. A good summary of experimental work on memory.

Lorayne, H., & Lucas, J. *The memory book.* New York: Ballantine Books, Inc., 1974. (Paperback.) A popular guide to the use of mnemonic techniques like those described in this chapter.

Norman, P. A. *Memory and attention.* New York: John Wiley & Sons, Inc., 1969. A discussion of human information processing from a theoretical viewpoint. No previous knowledge is assumed.

Premack, A. J. *Why chimps can read.* New York: Harper & Row, Publishers, 1976. An interesting account of how a young chimp was taught to read and to communicate with humans.

Wason, P. C., & Johnson-Laird, P. M. (Eds.) *Thinking and reasoning*. Harmondsworth, England: Penguin Books, 1968. This book of readings summarizes many of the most provocative experiments on problem solving.

Young, R. K. *Human learning & memory*. Module A-6, Personalized Psychology. New York: Harper & Row, Publishers, 1975. A short (56-page) paperback that includes sections on learning, remembering, forgetting, and programmed learning.

Chapter 8

Self-control of Behavior

(Brody, Stock, Boston)

Whenever I feel afraid
I hold my head erect
And whistle a happy tune
So no one will suspect
I'm afraid. . .
The result of this deception
Is very strange to tell,
For when I fool the people I fear,
I fool myself as well.

(RODGERS AND HAMMERSTEIN,
"THE KING AND I")

Chances are, if you were raised in America, someone sang this song to you when you were very young. In fact, during the entire time you have been growing up, you have probably heard increasingly more sophisticated versions of the same message. Our bookstores are filled with hundreds of "you can do it" books. They tell us how we can overcome our problems, present a better "front" to others, and enjoy life more when we stop smoking, lose weight, study more efficiently, or learn new sexual techniques. We have a great deal of faith in our ability to control our own behavior, yet many of us find ourselves unable to behave in desired ways. Countless others suffer from emotional problems that they feel powerless to control. As a species, we have evolved from a creature almost completely at the mercy of the environment to one that has mastered many aspects of it, but one of our greatest and most elusive challenges is mastery over ourselves.

We have already seen that the external environment exerts an influence on our behavior but that its influence is in large part determined by cognitive factors within ourselves. We can also act on our environment and change it in various ways to influence the way in which it affects us. To achieve self-control we must change both our behavior and our environment. The topic of self-control illustrates the meshing of cognitive and environmental influences on behavior that have been discussed in Chapters 6 and 7.

In this chapter we examine some of the techniques that have been developed to increase self-control of behavior. We show how they have been tested and applied, and how you might make use of them in your own life.

(Rawle, Stock, Boston)

CONCEPTIONS OF SELF-CONTROL

"Willpower"

Traditionally, self-control has been viewed as the result of "willpower," an internal psychic force that allows individuals to regulate their behavior in a

241

disciplined fashion. Often the inner will is represented as a separate agent within an individual that uses reason to arrive at decisions regarding what is right and wrong. If this will is strong enough, it allows the individual to suppress his or her baser impulses and desires and to "do good" or "avoid evil."

Unfortunately, this concept of willpower can cause people to be overly pessimistic about their ability to change their behaviors, especially if their first attempts are not successful. They may simply resign themselves to the fact that they are just not "strong" enough to control their behavior and stop trying. This admission of "weakness" is also likely to lower their self-esteem and may cause them to sink into depression.

The concept of willpower is also somewhat troublesome from a scientific point of view, because the only way we can operationally define *willpower* is in terms of the behavior it is supposed to cause. For example, how do we know if individuals who want to stop smoking have willpower? If they stop or markedly decrease their smoking, of course! But *why* do they stop smoking? Because of their willpower. This kind of circular reasoning can deceive us into thinking that we have explained something when in fact we have simply used a behavior to "demonstrate" the presence of an internal state (willpower), which we use in turn to explain the behavior. This is the same kind of faulty reasoning we discussed in Chapter 5 in relation to hypnotic "trance" explanations of hypnosis.

Behaviors such as thumb sucking are often embarassing to children as they grow older. Because their self-control skills are less well developed, they sometimes have difficulty in changing such behaviors. (Wide World)

Self-control as behavior

A second approach to self-control argues that by altering environmental conditions that influence our behavior, we can gain greater control over it. This cognitive-behavioral conception of self-control views self-regulation as the result not of some internal force, such as willpower, but rather of *behaviors* people use to alter conditions around them. In other words, self-control is the product of *self-controlling behaviors*. Internal, or *covert*, responses (e.g., thoughts, images, and feelings) and external, or *overt*, responses (e.g., running or eating a banana split) may function as self-controlling behaviors. In the song from "The King and I" quoted at the opening of the chapter, "whistling a happy tune" served as a self-control behavior that not only affected the external environment (not showing fear affects how "the people I fear" will respond to me), but also served to reduce the person's own fear.

This cognitive-behavioral approach to self-control requires that we operate as our own scientists. We must seek out the conditions that seem to cause the behavior we want to increase or decrease. We attempt to identify circumstances or situations (*antecedents*) that precede the occurrence of the behavior to be changed (the *target behavior*) as well as the results (*consequences*) of the behavior. Once we identify the antecedents and consequences we may then use self-controlling behaviors to alter them and bring about the desired change. A simplified representation of this process is presented in Figure 8.1.

Self-controlling behaviors are affected by their consequences, just as other behaviors are. In order to maintain them we must reinforce them. Reinforcement may involve external rewards, such as social approval or financial and physical rewards, or it may involve self-approval and encouragement from seeing desired changes occurring in oneself. In addition, there is evidence that the perception of personal freedom is itself reinforcing. For example, children study more and work harder on homework when they are allowed to choose their own reinforcers and the requirements they must meet in order to earn them (Lovitt and Curtiss, 1969). Their response rates are higher even when the reinforcement conditions they choose are identical to those previously imposed by a teacher.

We are not truly free unless we have the option of

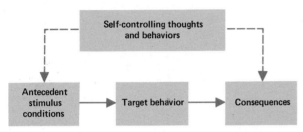

Figure 8.1 A diagram of the cognitive-behavioral self-control model. The person uses overt or covert self-controlling behaviors to change the antecedents and/or the consequences of the target behavior.

engaging in a variety of behaviors. Most of us have problem areas that limit our behavioral options, and this is perhaps the worst kind of tyranny. Self-control procedures can free us from present or past conditions that have limited our options and thereby increase our behavioral freedom. Freedom in this sense is more meaningful than the value often put on the freedom of the will.

Self-control procedures can be grouped conveniently into three categories, which involve (1) the modification of antecedent stimulus conditions; (2) the alteration of response consequences; (3) the development of coping behaviors for controlling maladaptive emotional responses. (See Table 8.1.)

An invitation to the reader
In the following pages we discuss specific ways in which self-control procedures can be used to change behaviors, as well as experimental evidence concerning their effectiveness. Some procedures are supported by a wealth of scientific evidence, others by

Table 8.1 Basic self-control procedures

I. Modifying antecedents
  A. Stimulus control procedures involving planned alterations in stimulus conditions that affect the target behavior
  B. Changing what individuals say to themselves

II. Altering response consequences
  A. Self-monitoring
  B. Self-administered reinforcement
  C. Self-punishment

III. Developing coping skills
  A. Self-desensitization

only a few case studies. Most have not been compared with other methods of behavior change. In particular, we do not yet have enough information on those instances in which the techniques are *not* effective. Nevertheless, the area of self-control is an important frontier in psychology, and the methods have a sufficiently sound theoretical and experimental basis to warrant presentation in this book.

Think of a behavior you would like to increase (e.g., studying, performing boring but necessary tasks, being more pleasant to others) and one that you would like to decrease (e.g., eating, smoking, anxiety in certain situations). The following procedures should enable you to work constructively on these problems and teach you some potentially useful self-modification techniques. Some personal or behavioral problems, however, are best dealt with in a professional therapist-client relationship. If these techniques do not work, you should not be discouraged from seeking professional help for problems that interfere significantly with your well-being.

SELF-CONTROL PROCEDURES

The flow chart in Figure 8.2 shows the basic steps for designing and implementing a self-control program.

Specify the problem
Before you can begin your program you must pinpoint the behaviors you want to change. This may be more difficult than it sounds. We tend to use abstract words such as *"lazy," "unmotivated," "hostile,"* and *"dependent"* to describe our problems. These are general, vague "trait" words that do not take into account specific behaviors and the situations in which they occur. Individuals who identify their problem as "being hostile" are *not* "hostile" in all situations, but only under certain circumstances. Such abstract terms as *hostile, dependent,* and *unmotivated* encompass a multitude of behaviors. Hostility can mean anything from giving another person a dirty look to exchanging good-natured volleys of gunfire with him. That is why abstract traits are not very helpful in specifying a problem for a self-modification program.

Statements of the problem in motivational terms are also not very helpful. They typically describe

243

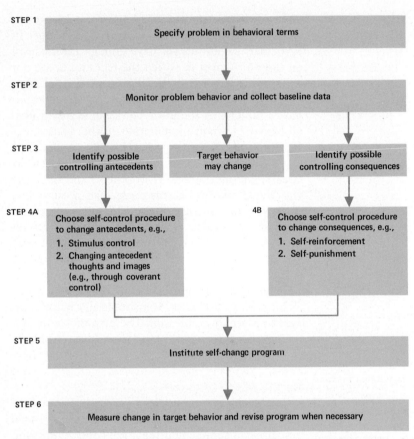

STEP 1 Specify problem in behavioral terms

STEP 2 Monitor problem behavior and collect baseline data

STEP 3 Identify possible controlling antecedents | Target behavior may change | Identify possible controlling consequences

STEP 4A Choose self-control procedure to change antecedents, e.g.,
1. Stimulus control
2. Changing antecedent thoughts and images (e.g., through coverant control)

4B Choose self-control procedure to change consequences, e.g.,
1. Self-reinforcement
2. Self-punishment

STEP 5 Institute self-change program

STEP 6 Measure change in target behavior and revise program when necessary

Figure 8.2 Flowchart showing the basic steps and options in designing a self-control program that involves modifying antecedents or consequences of behavior.

problems in terms of underlying motives rather than specific behaviors. For example, one student described her problem by saying, "I'm just not motivated to study hard." If she had said, "I don't receive enough rewards for studying to make me want to do that instead of doing something else," she would have been specifying the problem in behavioral rather than motivational terms. This would have been more helpful in focusing on the behaviors she wished to change. But this would still have been only a starting point; in order really to pinpoint the problem she would have needed to specify exactly what behaviors were involved in her studying, as well as the situations in which these behaviors did or did not occur. By doing this she might eventually have

arrived at a statement of the problem, such as, "I do not spend enough time at my desk between the hours of 7:00 P.M. and 10:00 P.M. reading and outlining my psychology textbook and trying to answer the review questions in my workbook." Then she would have specified both the target behaviors and the situations (time and place) in which she wished to make the changes.

If the problem you wish to work on seems unclear, try writing down instances in which you have exhibited the undesirable behavior. Then try to see if these situations have anything in common. If they do you will have specified one behavior-in-situation unit that constitutes a problem. If they do not then you may in fact be dealing with several situation-behavior units that you may need to approach one at a time.

Perhaps the most useful way for you to specify the problem is to observe your own behavior carefully. Rather than speculating about the problem behaviors, see how often and under what conditions they occur. Think in terms of situation-behavior relationships, and try to specify the antecedents, the precise behaviors, and their consequences. Keep a daily log to record this information. If you are *not* performing a desired behavior (e.g., studying), keep a record of what occurs when you *should* be performing it and what you do *instead of* performing it. For example, one student found that when she went to the library to study, she spent her time searching out classmates for conversations. Another found that when he studied, he spent a good percentage of his time daydreaming about other things. When he began to collect more systematic data, he discovered that he was spending only 15 to 20 percent of his "study" time actually studying.

Specify the goal

Many problems can be stated in terms of competing behaviors, one desirable, the other undesirable (e.g., studying vs. not studying; eating prudently vs. over-eating; not smoking vs. smoking; being assertive vs. being overly submissive). A general rule is that whenever possible, self-modification programs should be designed to increase positive behaviors through reinforcement rather than to decrease undesirable behaviors through punishment. As we saw in Chapter 6, reinforcement is a more effective means of changing behavior than is punishment. The negative side effects of punishment, such as avoidance learning and negative emotional arousal, can result from self-administered punishment as well as from punishment delivered by others. Moreover, simply decreasing some undesirable behavior does not guarantee that a desirable behavior will appear in its place, whereas developing a desirable alternative behavior through the use of positive reinforcement does. For example, it is better to reinforce yourself for studying than to punish yourself for not studying.

Self-monitoring

The next phase in your project is to collect baseline data on your behavior. Accurate baseline data pro-

vide valuable information about how frequently and in which situations target behaviors occur and allow you to evaluate changes when you start self-modification procedures. In addition, self-observation frequently produces changes in problem behaviors.

In order to collect baseline data you must develop a recording procedure that will enable you to keep accurate records of your behavior. First you must decide on the unit of measurement to use. This should be either the frequency with which the behavior occurs or the duration of the behavior. For example, if you wish to increase the amount of time you spend studying, it would be better to count the number of minutes you spend studying rather than to count the number of times you study (in which case a three-hour study period would have the same significance as a 30-second study period). If, on the other hand, your target behavior is smoking, it would be most useful to count the number of cigarettes smoked during a given period of time.

Whether you measure "how often" or "how long," it is essential that you define the category of behavior specifically enough that you can decide immediately whether the target behavior has occurred. For example, let us assume that you want to increase the amount of time you spend studying at your desk between 7:00 and 10:00 in the evening. You define studying as reading and outlining your textbook and answering study questions in your workbook. If you were merely to record the amount of time you spend sitting at your desk between specified hours, you would be including both study behaviors and nonstudy behaviors (daydreaming, doodling, listening to the radio). A better approach for collecting accurate data might be to keep records of the amount of time you spend at your desk *and* the amount of time you spend actually studying.

In order to keep accurate records of your behavior it is very important that you record your behaviors *as soon as they occur*. Do not trust your memory! You can carry a 3- × 5-inch card around with you easily to make recordings. Another useful device is a small golf stroke counter available at sporting goods stores. One overweight student used a counter to record the number of mouthfuls of food he consumed each day. Another student interested in improving his social relationships used a hand counter to record the number of times he said something pleasant to his acquaintances. A smoker counted the number of cigarettes he had with him in the morning and the number that remained at the end of the day.

If you wish to measure the amount of time you spend engaging in a given behavior, a stop watch may be useful. For example, you might use it to measure the amount of time you actually spend studying. The technique you use to record data will depend on the nature of the target behaviors and the situations in which you will be recording them. But whatever system you use, record *every* instance of the behavior (no excuses!) and keep written records of it from day to day.

Collecting baseline data can be a somewhat tedious or even discouraging task. After all, because you will be focusing on a problem area, you may not like what your data tell you. You may be embarrassed because you are performing some undesirable behavior very often or not performing a desirable one often enough. If this happens you may be tempted to start the self-modification procedures immediately. But you should avoid doing this. Unless you have good baseline data you will have no means of assessing change when you do begin your self-modification program. You might not notice slight positive changes in the early phases of the program, become discouraged with your apparent lack of progress, and stop the program prematurely. In addition, during the baseline period you may discover some key information about the antecedents and consequences of the target behavior that will be useful in planning your self-modification program. Finally, the baseline period will allow you to solve any problems that arise in measuring the target behaviors. If you find that collecting baseline data is so punishing that you begin to stop doing it, devise a way to reinforce yourself positively for keeping accurate records. It is wise to remember that the behaviors necessary for self-control programs (such as collecting data) can themselves be maintained through reinforcement.

How long should you collect baseline data? As long as it takes for you to get a good estimate of how frequently the target behavior occurs naturally. If the frequency or duration of the behavior does not vary greatly from day to day, a week of baseline data should be enough. If there is great variability you will need to go longer, perhaps two to three weeks. It

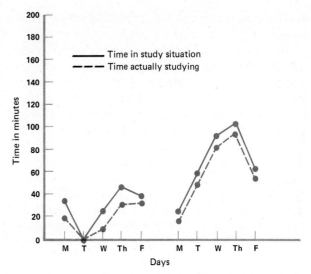

Figure 8.3 A graph used by one student in a self-control program. He graphed both the amount of time he spent in the study situation and the amount of time he spent actually studying. He measured actual study time with a stopwatch.

might be more helpful to express your baseline data as a simple daily or weekly average.

Graphing data over time

The most effective way to examine and detect changes in behavior over time is by plotting data on a graph. The behavioral data collected and graphed over a two-week period by a student on a self-modification program to increase study behaviors are shown in Figure 8.3. The measure of the target behavior is shown on the vertical axis; the time unit is entered on the horizontal axis. The student has graphed both the amount of time spent in the study situation and the amount of time spent in actual study.

MODIFYING ANTECEDENTS

Behaviors are highly influenced both by the situations in which they occur and by the conditions they create. We will first discuss self-control procedures that focus upon the antecedent conditions that stimulate behavior.

We constantly respond to stimuli in our environment, and many of our behaviors eventually come under the control of these stimuli. When response consequences are experienced under certain stimulus conditions, these stimuli come to signal the probable consequences of the behavior. These antecedents, or *discriminative stimuli*, trigger or cue off the behaviors in an almost automatic fashion. Undesirable behaviors tend to occur within a specific range of situations. Overweight people do not continually overeat; they do so in certain situations, such as while they are watching television or feeling tense. Students who have difficulty studying often find that certain cues (e.g., the presence of friends) trigger behaviors that are incompatible with studying. While you gather baseline data you should be alert to the conditions that trigger the behavior you want to change and record those conditions by making notes on your charts.

If behavior is under this kind of stimulus control, then it should be possible for an individual to increase the frequency of desirable behaviors or decrease the frequency of undesirable behaviors by changing the stimulus environment. Thus one body of self-control procedures involves systematic attempts to alter the antecedent conditions that affect the target behavior. In this section we discuss stimulus-control procedures; self-instructional responses are discussed later in the chapter.

Attending a group or class is one way of instituting stimulus control procedures. These women have placed themselves in a situation conducive to little else besides exercise. (Herwig, Stock, Boston)

Stimulus control procedures

Antecedent conditions usually involve specific aspects of an individual's physical or interpersonal environment. You may use stimulus control procedures to alter those conditions, sometimes by avoiding them. For example, if you cannot study effectively in the library because there are too many attractive members of the opposite sex, then choose a place to study by yourself. If you overeat you are probably set off by specific stimuli (e.g., favorite high-calorie foods) or specific situations (e.g., parties, restaurants). If you avoid these stimuli or situations, you may not eat as much.

In most weight control programs the first step is to remove "temptation" foods from the house. This includes snack foods and foods requiring no preparation that may trigger impulsive eating, such as bread, cheese, and canned goods. For the same reason, it is a good idea to freeze leftovers. It is also important to *narrow the range* of stimuli associated with eating,

for example, to eat in only one place in the house and keep food out of all other rooms. Some successful programs require that individuals do nothing but eat during eating periods; they cannot read, watch TV, or listen to the radio, because these are activities that can set off compulsive eating. Concentrate strongly on your eating, savor each mouthful, and put down your eating utensils until you swallow each mouthful. Take several five-minute breaks during the meal, so that you can realize that you do not necessarily have to eat when food is in front of you, and direct your attention to internal feelings of satiation. Research has shown that the eating behavior of obese individuals is controlled more by external stimuli than by internal hunger cues (see Chapter 10), so that acquiring a greater sensitivity to internal stimuli could be an important step in reducing food intake.

Stimulus control techniques can also help you modify your study behavior. Select a particular place in which you do *nothing* else but study. If you find

247

B. F. Skinner. (Wide World)

wanted to cut down on his beer drinking. He found that he downed an entire six-pack every evening while he watched television. At about 9:00 every evening he became hungry, went to the kitchen, and popped a huge bowl of heavily salted, buttered popcorn. He then drank a can of beer with the popcorn and went on to drink at least five more. In order to change this pattern he tried substituting an ice cream sundae for the popcorn. Predictably, he did not have the same urge to wash down this snack with beer. By disrupting the chain of events that normally led to drinking beer, he was able to stop drinking.

Stimulus control techniques can be very effective for self-modification programs. But they are probably most effective when they are used in conjunction with some of the following response consequence techniques.

ALTERING RESPONSE CONSEQUENCES

Although antecedent conditions stimulate and guide our behavior, the *consequences* of our behaviors determine whether we will maintain them. We have the power to arrange our own consequences, which provides us with an effective way to control our own behavior.

The consequences of self-monitoring

Often when individuals collect data on their target behavior, the behavior begins to change in the desired direction during the baseline period. In fact, the problem may even disappear completely, at least temporarily. There are several reasons for these changes. Individuals are sometimes dismayed when they begin to observe their behavior systematically and see how frequently they are performing an undesirable behavior or how seldom they are engaging in a desirable one. Recording the behaviors can become a punishment, and may cause some individuals to stop making observations. But others may become motivated to change their behavior, and any positive changes they observe will then be reinforced by self-approval. Internal reinforcement processes probably account for many of the positive changes that occur simply as a result of self-monitoring. Self-observation is also likely to make people more aware

your attention wandering, get up immediately and leave the study area, because your objective is to condition yourself to study in response to cues in that particular area. In time the study area will become a powerful discriminative stimulus. Skinner uses this technique for getting himself to write. He does all his writing at a desk in his home and keeps a running or cumulative record of the amount of time he spends doing it.

Often a target behavior is the last link in a chain of behaviors. (See the discussion of chaining in connection with the woman shoplifter described in Chapter 6, Box 6.8.) The chain of cues and behaviors that precede the target behavior serves as a string of antecedents. By breaking the chain before the target behavior, it is possible to weaken the influence of these antecedents. One student, for example,

of the antecedents of their behavior, which may alter the effects of those antecedents. For example, a habitual nail biter reported, "I took a baseline count for three weeks. The frequency of nail-biting ranged from one to eight times a day, but during the last week it's down to two times a day. I think counting the biting makes me more aware of it, and sometimes I stop where I would have gone ahead and bitten them before" (Watson and Tharp, 1971, p. 54).

Although self-observation alone may result in positive changes in behavior, its effects vary from study to study, and they are often only temporary. In many studies self-observation is combined and therefore confounded with other techniques, such as self-reward or self-punishment, so that it is impossible to know how much of the behavioral change can be attributed to self-observation. A number of studies have found no positive changes in behavior as the result of self-observation alone. Apparently, self-observation is most likely to result in long-term behavioral changes if it is used in conjunction with other procedures.

You may find it useful to post the data that you collect on your target behavior in a place where others can see them. For example, you might post a chart of changes in body weight in the bathroom. (Of course, you would not want to do this if you do not want others to know about your target behavior or if certain people might ridicule positive changes, as is sometimes the case with study behavior.) Making a commitment by posting your data publicly is likely to increase your motivation to change as well as to win you encouragement and social reinforcement for positive changes from your friends.

Self-administered reinforcement

Self-administered reinforcement is one of the most effective self-modification procedures, and it should be the cornerstone of your project. Research has shown that self-administered reinforcement has roughly the same effects on behavior as does externally administered reinforcement. In fact, it sometimes has a more positive effect on performance (Marston, 1967; Lovitt and Curtiss, 1969). An example of a weight control program based on self-administered reinforcement is described in Box 8.2.

Use of self-reinforcement procedures in a self-modification program requires that you find an ef-

fective reinforcer and that you arrange to make it available to yourself only if you engage in a desired behavior. Although the principle itself is quite simple, there are a number of practical considerations that are very important in the effective use of self-reward.

Choosing the reinforcer. If the reinforcer you choose is to be effective, it must be both controllable and potent. First, you must have complete *control* over it so that you can make it contingent on your behavior. Use a trip to Acapulco as a reinforcer only if you can provide it for yourself. It is best to avoid reinforcers that require the cooperation of other people unless you can guarantee that they will cooperate. If you must borrow money from your parents to go to Acapulco, make sure ahead of time that they want to lend it to you. Second, the reinforcer must be *potent* enough to maintain the desired behavior. Awarding yourself a penny for each 40 hours of study time is unlikely to affect your study behavior. Moreover, the reinforcer must be potent enough to override the effects of the natural reinforcers that maintain the problem behaviors.

At first, you will have to decide intuitively whether or not the reinforcer is likely to be effective. Once you actually begin to use it, you will be in a better position to assess its effectiveness. If it appears to be ineffective even when you correctly apply the other principles of self-modification, you should try another reinforcer.

Self-observation may uncover consequences that are reinforcing an undesirable behavior. One very simple and effective way to bring about a desired change is to make the reinforcer that normally maintains the undesirable behavior contingent on the desired behavior. For example, Watson and Tharp (1972) describe the case of a young man who recorded his studying behaviors, specifying how much time he spent in the library and how much time he spent actually studying there. Less than 20 percent of his time was spent in actual study; in most of the remaining time he watched girls. He concluded that girl watching was the reinforcer for not studying, and he designed a self-modification plan in which he reinforced an hour of studying alone in his room with a trip to the library, where he could then watch girls without feeling guilty. Watson

249

BOX 8.1
Self-observation and behavior change

A case study by Broden, Hall, and Mitts (1971) illustrates the positive effects that self-observation may have on a target behavior. Lisa, an eighth grader, requested help because she was doing very poorly in her history class. The school counselor made arrangements for an observer to record the amount of time Lisa spent "studying" during the class over a seven-day baseline period. *Studying* was defined as working on a task assigned by the teacher, taking lecture notes, facing the teacher, looking at a classmate who was responding to a question, or reciting when called on by the teacher. The baseline data showed that Lisa's average proportion of study time was about 30 percent. Beginning on the eighth day, Lisa was provided with a self-recording sheet and asked to indicate every few minutes with a plus or minus sign whether or not she had been studying. The external observer who had collected the baseline data continued to make observations that served as the experimental data.

The period of self-recording continued for five days, during which the average proportion of studying time increased to 80 percent. For four days beginning with the fourteenth day, Lisa was not provided with recording sheets, and the amount of study time dropped to an average of 27 percent. She was given recording sheets again during nine of the next 11 days, and the average study time rose again to 80 percent. On the two days out of 11 during which Lisa did not record her study behavior, the proportion declined to 42 and 22 percent, respectively.

After the second self-recording phase Lisa was instructed to continue recording her study behav-

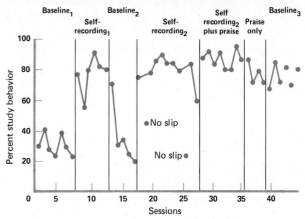

A record of Lisa's study behavior during baseline₁ (before experimental procedures); self-recording₁ (Lisa recorded study or nonstudy on slips provided by counselor); baseline₂ (self-recording slips were withdrawn); self-recording₂ (self-recording slips were reinstated); self-recording₃ plus praise (self-recording slips were continued, and teacher praise for study increased); praise only (increased teacher praise was maintained and self-recording withdrawn); and baseline₃ (teacher praise was decreased to baseline levels). (Adapted from Broden, Hall, and Mitts, 1971, p. 194. Copyright 1971 by the Society for the Experimental Analysis of Behavior, Inc.)

iors, and the teacher was told to reinforce the behaviors with praise and increased attention. This increased the average proportion of time she spent engaging in the target behaviors to 88 percent. During the final phase Lisa was told to stop the self-recording, but the teacher continued to reinforce the study behaviors over a four-day period. This decreased the proportion of study time to an average of about 80 percent. The teacher then stopped providing special reinforcement. Final baseline recording showed that Lisa was averaging about 80 percent study time, an increase of about 40 percent over the first baseline period. The data from this case study are presented above.

250

BOX 8.2

A weight control program based on self-reinforcement

In one weight control study (Mahoney, 1974) over-weight adults were classified by degree of obesity and randomly assigned to one of four groups, one of which was a no-treatment control group. Subjects in the three treatment groups were weighed on a weekly basis and recorded their own eating habits and body weight over an eight-week period. Following a two-week baseline period, subjects used different self-control procedures for the next six weeks. One group set weekly goals for weight loss and improvements in their eating habits. The other two groups used self-reward procedures. In addition to setting weekly weight loss and habit-improvement goals and monitoring themselves, members of one group rewarded themselves with money or gift certificates whenever they lost a given amount of weight, whereas members of the other self-reward goup gave themselves similar reinforcements whenever they met or exceeded their weekly goals. A two-month follow-up was conducted in order to determine the long-term effects of the self-control procedures.

After the formal study was completed the control subjects were placed into a six-week self-control program in which they rewarded themselves with money or gift certificates whenever they *both* lost weight and improved their habits.

The results of the study are presented graphically. The data show that self-monitoring alone resulted in weight loss, but that most of the loss occurred during the first week. Other findings have also shown that self-observation may cause an almost immediate change in the target behavior. But these initial weight losses were maintained over at least a 15-week period. Both self-reward strategies

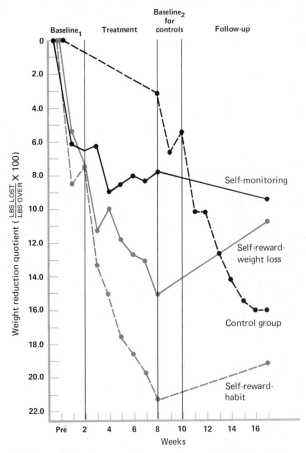

Median weight changes displayed by subjects during baseline, treatment, and follow-up phases. During weeks 11 to 17, control subjects self-rewarded achievement of both weight loss and habit improvement goals. (Adapted from Mahoney, 1974.)

resulted in greater weight loss than did self-monitoring alone, but they were more effective when they were made contingent on changes in *eating habits* than when they were given for actual *weight loss.* This points to the importance of defining goals in terms of changes in specific *behaviors.* It is also encouraging that the subjects who used self-reward to change their habits maintained their losses through follow-up.

251

and Tharp reported that this self-reinforcement strategy was successful in increasing the student's study time.

Virtually any object or activity can serve as a reinforcer, if it is both controllable and potent. In choosing a reinforcer you may find it helpful to ask yourself questions such as the following:

1. What kinds of things do you enjoy having?
2. What would be a nice present to receive?
3. What are your major hobbies? Which activities do you enjoy most?
4. What would you hate to give up?
5. What do you do to relax?
6. Which behaviors do you perform every day?
7. Are there other behaviors that you perform instead of the target behavior?

(Watson and Tharp, 1972)

By answering questions such as these it should be possible to generate a list of potential reinforcers to use in your self-modification program.

Of course, it may be difficult for you to find a reinforcer to manipulate. You may already have everything you want, or you may not have the time or financial resources to do or obtain something that you would like. In such instances it is useful to employ the *Premack principle.*

The Premack principle. Basically, the Premack principle (Premack, 1965) states that a behavior that occurs often may be used to reinforce one that occurs less frequently. You may use certain daily behaviors, such as watching television, taking a shower, talking to others, eating lunch, and so on, if you require that a lower-probability target behavior precede it. For example, if you like coffee you could make drinking coffee at the end of your meal contingent on eating less. The student who made girl watching dependent on studying was employing the Premack principle, because initially he was more likely to watch girls than to study. The frequent behavior need not be highly pleasurable in order for the Premack principle to work, but it should not be unpleasant.

In selecting a reinforcer, do not necessarily choose the most powerful one you can think of. There are likely to be times when you will not earn the reinforcer so that you should not choose one whose loss will seriously disrupt your life or punish you severely enough to endanger your self-modification program.

Contingencies and contracts. Once you have selected reinforcers you must decide how to use them to change the target behavior. It may help to draw up a contract; write and sign it yourself. The contract should specify in detail the reinforcement contingencies for each stage of your plan. You must state precisely how often or how long you must or must not perform the target behavior, and the kinds and numbers of reinforcers you will receive for specific achievements. You may change the terms during the program, but you should always be operating under a specific contract.

A young woman whose problem was extreme shyness chose greeting people in her classes as an initial target behavior. She selected watching television in the evening as her reinforcer. Her baseline data indicated that she never greeted another person unless she was greeted first. During the first phase of her program she drew up the following contract with herself: "During the school week of October 10–14, I will watch TV in the evening *only if* I have smiled and said "Hi" to one girl in one of my classes without being greeted first. I will do this only when we are walking in opposite directions so that I won't have to stop and converse with the other person. I must greet a different person each day." Although this is a very simple contract, it carefully specifies the target behavior, the situation, the reinforcer, and the contingency.

Using reinforcers effectively. In Chapter 6 we discussed the importance of the timing of reinforcement and said that immediate reinforcement is more effective than delayed reinforcement. You should try to provide immediate reinforcement for your target behavior whenever possible. This is especially true when the behavior is a strong habit you are trying to break or when it provides immediate reinforcement of its own, as does eating, drinking, or smoking.

If your reinforcer is not available immediately, you might try using tokens that can later be converted into a reinforcer. One subject carried a number of pennies in his left pocket. Whenever he performed the desired behavior, he transferred a certain number of pennies into his right pocket until he "qualified" for his weekly reinforcer, a dinner at his favorite restaurant. A point system can also be used effectively. The performance of a desired behavior is worth a specified number of points, which can later be "redeemed" for the reinforcer. Both the point values of the desired behaviors and the point cost of the reinforcer are specified in the contract. Individuals may carry a card to record points as soon as possible after they perform the behavior for immediate reinforcement. One student who wanted to increase his study time drew up a contract in which each 15-minute period of study was worth one point, and he exchanged each point for 30 minutes of TV that evening.

Another advantage of the token system is that the tokens may be linked to a great number of reinforcers rather than to only one or a few. This prevents individuals from getting tired of a reinforcer. By cataloguing a number of reinforcers in terms of their "point values," you may create your own "token economy."

One woman created the following token economy for use in her self-modification program:

15 minutes of TV	(1 point)
one coke	(2 points)
taking an afternoon nap	(4 points)
going bowling	(5 points)
reading *Playgirl* magazine	(3 points)
one beer	(3 points)
going to a movie	(6 points)
eating at my favorite restaurant	(10 points)
doing anything I want to, all day	(15 points)

The use of shaping in self-modification

Many self-modification projects are designed to acquire some new and desirable behavior or to increase a desirable behavior to a higher level. In many instances the desired behavior may never have been performed in the past and the individual may be incapable of making a behavioral change immediately. Students with poor study habits, for example, probably could not increase their study time from 23 minutes a week to 10 hours a week immediately and permanently. Likewise, overweight people probably could not acquire healthy eating habits immediately and spontaneously.

Once we decide to change our behavior in some way, we usually want to do it "all at once," but attempts to do a complete behavioral about-face al-most always fail. That is why New Year's resolutions are generally ineffective (Marlatt and Kaplan, 1972).

The most effective way to build new behaviors is through shaping, or successive approximations. Shaping starts with the behaviors a person is already able to perform and reinforces behaviors that resemble more and more closely the final desired behavior. We saw in Chapter 6 that this method is used to train animals to perform complex behaviors.

If you collect good baseline data you will know the current level of performance for your target behavior. Shaping requires that you begin at this level or *slightly* beyond it and begin to move *slowly* toward your goal, reinforcing yourself at each step. Start with a very small change and make the steps (subsequent changes) small. If you encounter difficulty, reduce the size of the steps. Through experimentation you will discover the correct pace for yourself. It is far better to move forward too slowly than to try to progress too rapidly, lest you become discouraged and abandon the project. Impatience is your greatest enemy.

Always use a shaping procedure to change study behaviors. Do not let your initial steps be influenced by how much you think you should be studying. Start slightly (10 to 15 minutes) above your current daily level and reinforce yourself when you succeed in studying for a slightly longer period of time. Successive increases should not exceed 10 to 15 minutes unless you find that you can succeed easily with larger ones.

The following shaping schedule was used by a student who wanted to increase his study time to two hours a day so that he could keep up with the reading assignments and lecture materials in his classes and stop "cramming" for tests. He tried studying in a specific area of the library, collected baseline data over a two-week period, and found that he was studying an average of five minutes a day. He then mapped out the following steps for improvement.

Baseline: Five-minute average per day.

Step 1. Increase study time to 15 minutes per day.

Step 2. Increase study time to 30 minutes per day.

Step 3. Increase study time to 40 minutes per day.

Step 4. Increase study time to 50 minutes per day.

Step 5. Increase to 60 minutes per day.

Step 6. Increase to 75 minutes per day.

Step 7. Increase to 90 minutes per day.

Step 8. Increase to 105 minutes per day.

Step 9. Increase to 120 minutes per day.

He prepared a graph to record the time he spent studying each day and kept it in one of his notebooks. He awarded himself one point for each successful period of study. Before he moved on to the next step, he had to master each step for three consecutive days.

As in most programs of this type, the student had to change the steps several times. When he reached Step 4 he had great difficulty studying for more than 45 minutes. In other words, he reached a *plateau*, and could not move beyond it. Accordingly, he changed the requirement at Step 4 from 50 minutes to 45 minutes. In a few days he was able to move up to 50 minutes without difficulty.

In addition to plateaus some individuals have trouble with *cheating*, that is, delivering the reinforcer when they have not performed the required behavior. This usually reflects a problem in the shaping procedure. It generally occurs because the target behavior is at present too difficult to perform. The easiest way to remedy cheating is to reduce the level at which you are required to perform in order to receive the reinforcer. In our impatience to change we often make the steps in the shaping procedure too large. Remember, your self-modification procedure should not be a test of your pain tolerance. The goal is to bring about gradual change while enjoying plenty of "honest" reinforcers. The way in which you arrange the reinforcement contingencies is the most critical determinant of whether this goal is achieved.

Self-administered punishment

Because of the undesirable side effects of punishment (negative emotion, avoidance learning), which we discussed in Chapter 6, punishment is theoretically less desirable as a means of changing behavior than is positive reinforcement. Self-modifi-

cation projects based exclusively on self-punishment have had low rates of success, in sharp contrast to the almost consistent success of self-reinforcement techniques.

Self-punishment that involves aversive stimulation is different from self-punishment based on the withdrawal of a positive reinforcer. Both have been used in self-modification studies with different degrees of success, but it appears that self-punishment based on the withdrawal of positive reinforcers is usually more effective.

Punishment through aversive stimulation

Self-punishment based on aversive stimulation occasionally yields spectacular results, as in a case study by Morganstern (1974). Three separate behaviors (eating candy, cookies, and doughnuts) were monitored while self-punishment was successively applied to each. The subject was an obese nonsmoker. When he ate the forbidden fattening foods, he punished himself by inhaling cigarette smoke. Figure 8.4 shows that each target behavior declined quickly when the self-punishment contingency was applied to it. The subject lost 53 pounds over a 24-week period. Fortunately, the cigarette smoke remained offensive to him over the course of the self-modification project; otherwise he might have ended up being an obese smoker.

In spite of the success achieved in the preceding study most evidence indicates that self-punishment through aversive stimulation is not consistently effective in changing behavior and the dropout rate is usually high.

Punishment through withdrawal of reinforcers

The few reports concerning the use of self-punishment through withdrawal of positive reinforcers have been somewhat more encouraging. In one case study (Axelrod et al., 1974) a subject punished himself by withdrawing reinforcers in order to cut down on his smoking. A baseline assessment indicated that he was smoking an average of about 17 cigarettes per day. He set an initial daily limit of 15 cigarettes and pledged to tear up a dollar bill for each cigarette that exceeded the limit. Using the principles of shaping, he then decreased the limit by one cigarette every five days. After 50 days the subject's rate of smoking had decreased to zero and remained there after a

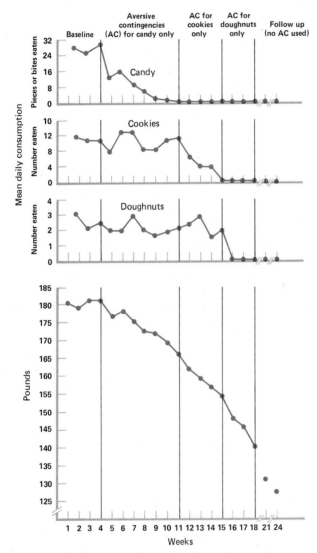

Figure 8.4 Daily consumption of candy, cookies, and doughnuts in a program using punishment by aversive stimulation. The bottom chart shows change in weight over time. (Adapted from Morganstern, 1974.)

two-year follow-up period. The subject never exceeded his daily limit during the course of the project, so that he never had to punish himself.

The relative effectiveness of self-reward, self-punishment, and a combination of the two was assessed in a recent study (Mahoney, Moura, and Wade, 1973). Self-reward subjects gave themselves money for progress in weight reduction, whereas self-pun-

ishment subjects gave up money for failure to make progress. A third group used both monetary self-reward and self-punishment. Self-punishment alone proved ineffective; after four weeks subjects in this condition had made no more progress than untreated control subjects. When self-punishment was combined with self-reward, however, it proved to be the most effective of the treatment procedures. These results are consistent with the literature on externally administered punishment in indicating that punishment is most effective when it is used in conjunction with positive reinforcement of a desired alternative behavior.

An alternative to punishment: Strengthening incompatible behaviors

Instead of reducing a behavior through punishment it is possible to strengthen a more positive behavior that is incompatible with the unwanted one. This involves positive reinforcement rather than punishment, so that it is a more effective technique. In order to find a behavior to reinforce instead of your target behavior, ask yourself the following questions:

1. Is there some directly opposite behavior that I would actually like to increase while decreasing the undesired behavior?
2. What behaviors would make it impossible for me to perform the undesirable one?
3. Is there any basically meaningless act that I could substitute for the undesirable behavior? Would it fit into the formula: I will do (the substitute behavior) instead of (the undesired behavior)?

(Watson and Tharp, 1972, p. 137)

If you select an incompatible behavior to strengthen, it is important to obtain a baseline count of it as well as of the undesirable behavior, and to continue to collect data on both throughout your project.

CONTROL OF EMOTIONAL RESPONSES THROUGH SELF-DESENSITIZATION

Self-defeating emotional responses play a central role in many problems. Do you become so tense and anxious during tests and examinations that you "go blank" or forget facts you would ordinarily know? Or are you so anxious *before* a test that you cannot study effectively? Do you fear heights or airplane travel? Are you painfully anxious in certain social situations, or so "high-strung" that you never seem able to relax? Do you become angry at other people for inappropriate reasons? Is fear or anxiety one of the antecedents to eating or losing your ability to concentrate?

If you have any of these problems then you may want to try self-desensitization. Self-desensitization involves learning a coping response (relaxation) that is incompatible with fear and anger and that may thus be used to control these emotional responses in situations that normally trigger them. Systematic desensitization has been employed by therapists treating clients for over two decades, and it has proved to be a highly effective fear reduction technique (Rimm and Masters, 1974). It has also been effectively applied to the treatment of maladaptive anger responses (Rimm, de Groot, Boord, Heiman, and Dillow, 1971). Far less research has been done to assess the effectiveness of self-applied (rather than therapist-applied) desensitization procedures, and self-desensitization is best regarded as an experimental rather than an established clinical technique. The limited data do, however, suggest that self-applied desensitization techniques can be used effectively to control maladaptive emotional responses (Kahn and Baker, 1968; Donner and Guerney, 1969).

Self-desensitization procedures involve training oneself in deep muscular relaxation and then using it to exercise control in imagined anxiety- or anger-arousing situations. The control that subjects learn in imaginary situations can be transferred to real ones to change the impact of these troublesome situations.

Relaxation training

Deep muscular relaxation is a motor skill, like bowling or tennis; it requires training and practice to master the technique. Deep muscular relaxation is a very useful skill to acquire. It has been used effectively in natural childbirth and in the treatment of insomnia, headaches, menstrual pain, back and neck pain, and other problems. In addition, it is a pleasant experience, so that you might want to learn it even if you have no need for self-desensitization.

Most relaxation training techniques involve pro-

gressive tensing and relaxation of specific muscle groups. Successful training results in a deeper than usual state of general relaxation, an ability to notice relatively small changes in muscular tension (at which point many people become aware for the first time how frequently they have been tense without realizing it), and skill in relaxing specific muscles.

Box 8.3 contains a set of relaxation-training exercises. After you have been through the exercises several times you will be able to practice them without the instructions. Initially, they will require about 30 minutes to complete, but as you master the technique, the required time will become progressively shorter and you will be capable of deeply relaxing yourself very quickly. Many individuals reach this point after about a week of practice.

It is recommended that the relaxation exercises be practiced at least once (and, if possible, twice) a day until they are mastered. Before bedtime is a good time to practice, because this will relax you prior to retiring. Practice should occur in a comfortable chair, sofa, or bed and in a relatively quiet atmosphere. It is essential that relaxation be thoroughly mastered before self-desensitization is begun.

Stimulus presentation

Although the ultimate goal of self-desensitization is self-control of emotional responses in real-life situations, the training procedure involves the use of imagined situations. The basic reason for this is that you can control what you imagine, whereas you may have little control over what occurs in an actual situation. Thus you can start with imagined situations that arouse low levels of emotion that you can easily control with the relaxation coping response. You can then learn to control your emotional responses in progressively more arousing situations. These later situations will decrease somewhat in their emotion-arousing ability as a result of mastery of the less arousing success.

The series of scenes having a common theme that a person imagines during desensitization is called a *hierarchy*. The scenes are arranged in order from the least emotionally arousing to the most arousing. The hierarchy scenes may proceed along a *time* dimension (e.g., a series of scenes leading up to a feared event in time), a *physical distance* dimension (a person afraid of heights, for example, might try to imagine being in progressively higher places), or along a *seriousness* dimension (for example, a series of scenes composed of progressively more unpleasant encounters with another person). Some hierarchies are based on combinations of these dimensions.

The following hierarchy was used by one of our students to reduce high test anxiety. It is based on a time dimension.

Scene 1. Hearing about someone else who has a test.

Scene 2. The instructor announcing a test in three weeks.

Scene 3. Instructor reminding the class that there will be a test in two weeks.

Scene 4. Overhearing classmates talk about studying for the test, which will occur in one week.

Scene 5. Instructor reminding class of what they will be tested on in two days.

Scene 6. Leaving class the day before the exam.

Scene 7. Studying the night before the exam.

Scene 8. Getting up the morning of the exam.

Scene 9. Walking toward the building where the exam will be given.

Scene 10. Walking into the testing room.

Scene 11. Instructor walking into room with tests.

Scene 12. Tests being passed out.

Scene 13. Reading the test questions.

Scene 14. Watching others finish the test.

Scene 15. Seeing a question I can't answer.

Scene 16. Instructor waiting for me to finish the test.

The following is a hierarchy of anger-inducing items constructed along a seriousness dimension. It was constructed by a young mother who wanted to reduce her anger responses to her two-year-old son. She usually reacted to him by losing her temper and screaming.

Scene 1. Billy begins to whine for a glass of milk.

Scene 2. I tell Billy to eat his food and he yells, "No!"

Scene 3. Billy throws a tantrum when I refuse to give him a cookie.

Scene 4. Billy wets his pants. (He is toilet trained.)

Scene 5. Billy has a bowel movement in his pants after telling me he doesn't have to go.

Scene 6. Billy stumbles while running and pours a glass of grape juice on the floor.

Scene 7. I tell Billy to come. He runs away.

Scene 8. While eating lunch, Billy purposely drops his plate of food from his high chair.

Scene 9. Billy throws a metal toy at his baby brother.

It is possible to use self-desensitization for several problem areas simultaneously by constructing a series of hierarchies, one for each problem area.

The self-desensitization procedure

Once you have finished relaxation training and constructed a hierarchy, you will be ready to begin self-desensitization. Put yourself into a state of deep relaxation and imagine the first (least arousing) scene in the hierarchy as vividly as possible. It is important to focus on the scene completely and not allow your imagination to "drift" to a higher scene in the hierarchy. Often the deep relaxation completely neutralizes any emotional reaction the scene might ordinarily produce. If you do feel some arousal, *continue* to imagine the scene and apply the relaxation technique until you eliminate the emotional response so that you can experience the scene while you are completely relaxed. Ordinarily, this will not require more than a few minutes. Then imagine the scene in a relaxed state for at least 30 seconds. Stop imagining the scene, concentrate totally on relaxing yourself even further, then imagine the scene vividly a second time. Again use your relaxation response to control any emotional response. This process of controlling your emotional response with the relaxation is most crucial to your training.

After you have become desensitized to the first

257

BOX 8.3
Training in relaxation

The ability to relax deeply and quickly is extremely useful for coping with stress and maladaptive emotions. It is the cornerstone of the self-desensitization technique. The following procedure should allow you to learn this important behavior within a week or less. Once you have mastered it you can use the relaxation response to cope with stress or tension as soon as you begin to feel it.

Practice these relaxation exercises at least twice a day until you master them. They will initially require about 30 minutes of practice, but as you master them the time will become shorter. It is a good idea to practice before bedtime because the exercises will help you sleep well. Use a comfortable chair, sofa, or bed in a relatively quiet atmosphere.

1. Get as comfortable as possible. Loosen any tight clothing and do not cross your legs. Take a deep breath, let it out slowly, and become as relaxed as possible.
2. Raise your arms and extend them out in front of you. Now make a fist with both hands, squeezing hard. Notice the uncomfortable tension in your hands and fingers. Hold the tension for five seconds, then let it out halfway and hold for an additional five seconds. Notice the decrease in tension but also concentrate on the tension that remains. Now let your hands relax completely. Notice how the tension and discomfort drain from your hands and are replaced by sensations of comfort and relaxation. Focus on the contrast between the tension you felt and the relaxation you now feel. Concentrate on relaxing your hands completely for 10 to 15 seconds.
3. Tense your upper arms hard for five seconds. Focus on the feeling of tension. Let the tension out halfway for an additional five seconds. Again focus on the tension that remains. Now relax

your upper arms completely for 10 to 15 seconds and focus carefully on the developing relaxation. Let your arms rest limply at your sides.
4. With your toes supported and your legs relaxed, dig the toes of your feet into the bottom of your shoes. After five seconds relax your toes halfway and hold the reduced tension for an additional five seconds. Now relax your toes completely and focus on the relaxation spreading into them. Continue relaxing your toes for 10 to 15 seconds.
5. Point your toes downward so that your feet and calves are tensed. Hold the tension hard for five seconds. Let it out halfway for an additional five

seconds, then relax your feet and calves completely for 10 to 15 seconds.

6. Extend your legs, raise them approximately 6 inches above the floor, and tense your thigh muscles. Hold the tension for five seconds, let it out halfway for an additional five seconds, then relax your thighs completely. Concentrate on totally relaxing your feet, calves, and thighs for about 30 seconds.

7. Tense your buttock muscles hard for five seconds, then let the tension out halfway for another five seconds. Finally, relax your buttocks completely and focus on the sensations of heaviness and relaxation. Concentrate again on relaxing the other muscle groups with which you have already dealt.

8. Tense your stomach muscles hard for five seconds and concentrate on the tension. Let the tension out halfway for an additional five seconds before relaxing your stomach muscles completely. Focus on the spreading relaxation until your stomach muscles are completely relaxed.

9. Press the palms of your hands together and push to tense your chest and shoulder muscles. Hold the tension for five seconds, then let it out halfway for an additional five seconds. Now relax those muscles completely and concentrate on the relaxation until they are completely loose and relaxed. Concentrate again on the muscle groups that have already been relaxed.

10. Push your shoulders back as far as possible to tense your back muscles. Let the tension out halfway after five seconds, hold the reduced tension and focus on it carefully for an additional five seconds, then relax your back and shoulder muscles completely. Focus on the spreading relaxation until these muscles are completely relaxed.

11. Keeping the muscles of your torso, arms, and legs relaxed, tense your neck muscles by bringing your head forward until your chin digs into your chest. Hold for five seconds, release the tension halfway for another five seconds, then relax your neck completely. Allow your head to hang comfortably while you focus on the relaxation developing in your neck muscles.

12. Clench your teeth and notice the tension in the muscles of your jaws. After five seconds let the tension out halfway for five seconds, then relax completely. Let your mouth relax completely with your lips slightly parted and concentrate on totally relaxing these muscles for 10 to 15 seconds.

13. Tense your tongue by pushing it up into the roof of your mouth. Hold for five seconds, let the tension out halfway, hold for an additional five seconds, then relax your tongue completely. Focus on completely relaxing the muscles of your neck, jaw, and tongue.

14. With your eyes closed, squint and rotate your eyeballs upward as if you were looking up. Hold the tension for five seconds, then release it halfway for an additional five seconds. Relax your eyes completely. Focus on the relaxation devel-

259

oping in your eyes and concentrate on relaxing your other facial muscles.

15. Wrinkle your forehead and scalp by raising your eyebrows. Hold the tension for five seconds, then release halfway for another five seconds. Relax your scalp and forehead completely, as always focusing on the developing feeling of relaxation and contrasting it with the earlier tension. Concentrate now for about a minute on relaxing all the muscles in your body.

16. Controlled breathing is one of the most important elements of the relaxation response, because you can make yourself relax by breathing correctly. Take a series of short inhalations, about one per second, until your chest is filled. Hold for about five seconds, then exhale slowly for about ten seconds while thinking silently to yourself the word *relax* or *calm*. Think or picture the word to yourself as you slowly let out your breath. Repeat this process at least five times, trying each time to deepen the state of relaxation you are experiencing.

Practice deep breathing as frequently as possible. Research has shown that it can quickly lower bodily arousal and tension. In subsequent relaxation practice sessions, try the deep-breathing exercise between each muscle group exercise to deepen the state of relaxation and to practice muscle relaxation in conjunction with the deep breathing.

After you have been through the instructions a number of times, you can replace them with a list of the muscle groups to be tensed and relaxed. You may also wish to modify the sequence of muscle groups to find the one that is best for you.

scene in the hierarchy, repeat the procedure with each of the succeeding scenes. You may have more intense emotional responses to other scenes, but you will find that these can be controlled progressively faster as you learn to reduce them with relaxation. Individuals who are well trained in this self-control procedure find that they are able to "turn off" even fairly intense emotional responses quite rapidly.

Sometimes individuals are unable to control emotional responses to given scenes. This sometimes occurs when they have not fully mastered the relaxation technique; continued practice in attaining deep relaxation leads to improvement in self-control. In addition, the steps in the hierarchy may be too large. Adding intermediate steps generally resolves the problem. If a given item arouses intense emotions you cannot control, try to pinpoint the aspect of the scene that is responsible. Then create a new scene in which this aspect is a little less intense. For example, if your first scene involved giving a speech before a very critical audience and the nature of the audience was the aspect of the scene that aroused intense anxiety, then you could create new scenes in which the critical nature of the audience was gradually increased.

Self-desensitization sessions should generally last from 30 to 40 minutes. The number of hierarchy scenes you cover within a single session will vary. Remember that you should never proceed to a new hierarchy item until you completely master the previous ones. Begin each session by repeating all the previous scenes.

Generalization to "real-life" situations

The self-desensitization procedure as it is conceived here involves acquiring self-control skills that you can use to cope with maladaptive emotional responses in many settings. Your training will be reinforced if you also practice controlling your emotional reactions with relaxation in corresponding "real-life" settings. Sometimes the problem involves situations that are more difficult to find in real life, but you should always try to apply the coping responses to actual situations.

Self-desensitization is a relatively new method, and it is unclear how effective it is in comparison with desensitization treatment administered by trained psychotherapists. You should consider it as an area for possible exploration. If you have problems with it or if you do not make any progress with it, you may want to consult a professional. This is true for all the procedures discussed in this chapter. As we said earlier, lack of success in self-modification should not discourage you from seeking professional help if the problem is serious enough to disrupt your life.

SELF-CONTROL OF COVERT BEHAVIORS

Covert behaviors are those internal, private behaviors, such as thoughts and images, that make up our "mental life." Although these behaviors cannot be observed or measured directly by another person, they have many qualities in common with *overt* or observable behaviors. Of course, covert behaviors are usually translated in one way or another into overt behaviors, so that it is often wise to work "from the inside out" in self-modification programs. A variety of methods for controlling covert mental and physiological responses were described in *The Bhagavad Gita*, written over 2000 years ago. Modern popular approaches to self-change, such as Maltz's *Psychocybernetics* (1960) and Norman Vincent Peale's *Power of Positive Thinking* (1960), emphasize the importance of controlling mental images and self-statements. Box 8.4 describes some recent research on the role of covert processes in the ability to delay gratification. The growing interest in self-control on the part of psychologists is resulting in an extension of self-control methods to the control and modification of covert as well as overt behaviors.

Covert behaviors as antecedents, target behaviors, and consequences

As we have seen, self-modification involves dealing with the complex relationships among *antecedents*, *target behaviors*, and *consequences*. Although it may not be fully obvious at first, covert mental behaviors may function in all these roles. As *antecedents* to other behaviors, they may take the form of self-instructions, plans, or images that help to stimulate and direct behavior. (See Box 8.5.) For example, individuals learning a complex skill, such as driving a car, often find it necessary to tell themselves mentally what to do while they are shifting, parking, and escaping from the scenes of accidents. Covert behaviors may also be *consequences*, such as internal self-reinforcement processes. We have already seen that behavior can be greatly influenced by individuals' self-praising or self-critical responses to their own behavior. Finally, because covert processes are behaviors, they may be influenced by antecedents and consequences, and individuals can gain significant control over their own mental and emotional re-

sponses. In other words, covert responses may function as *target behaviors* that can be modified.

In recent years researchers have been working to develop new techniques to allow individuals greater control over their covert behaviors. The work on biofeedback and control of physiological responses that we described in Chapter 6 is one example, and the self-desensitization procedure described earlier is another. In this section we describe a number of techniques designed to modify thought processes. Although relatively little systematic scientific work has been done in this important area, the data we do have are quite encouraging.

Coverant control

In 1965 Lloyd Homme, a behavioristic psychologist, wrote an influential paper in which he urged behaviorists to turn their attention to the study and modification of *coverants* (covert operants), "the operants of the mind." Homme emphasized that thoughts should be subject to the same controlling influences as are other behaviors. It should be possible, he reasoned, to increase or decrease the occurrence of certain "covert operants" (thoughts or images) through reinforcement.

Covert behaviors are often important elements in the response chains that lead up to a given behavior. For example, images and thoughts about smoking comprise an "urge to smoke." By changing these covert elements in the response chain, it should be possible to affect the final behavior, or smoking itself. Homme suggested a technique that involves weakening the coverants that lead to smoking and strengthening through reinforcement those that compete with smoking. Examples of competing coverants for smoking might be the following: "Smoking causes lung cancer"; "Smoking makes my breath stink"; "Smoking is costing me a lot of money." In addition, there is a list of positive coverants about nonsmoking: "I'll be healthier if I don't smoke"; "My food will taste better"; "Think of all the money I'll save." Table 8.2 contains lists of competing coverants for thought chains that lead to eating and not studying.

Reinforcers can be used to strengthen the thoughts that compete with the urge to smoke. Homme recommends using the Premack principle, selecting a behavior that is more likely to occur than

261

BOX 8.4
Cognitive strategies in delay of gratification

A very basic form of self-control involves passing up immediate rewards in favor of larger future rewards, or delaying gratification. For example, college students give up many pleasures and often live within very modest means in order to increase their chances for a more rewarding life after graduation.

For over a decade Walter Mischel of Stanford University has been studying the ability of children to delay gratification. He offers his subjects the choice of an immediate small reward (e.g., 10¢) or a larger reward in the future (e.g., 25¢). The child's choice serves as an objective measure of ability to delay gratification.

Recently, Mischel has been investigating the role of cognitive variables in ability to delay gratification. Although these studies were conducted with children, their results can be applied to more sophisticated situations. For example, Mischel (1974) reports that if the larger future reward is visible when children are asked to make a choice, the ability to delay gratification is *reduced*. The result is the same when the reward is not visible, but the children are told to imagine having it in the future. Apparently, both of these situations increase the children's frustrations over not actually having the reward. Making the choice becomes more painful, and the delay period seems less tolerable, so that they tend to choose the smaller but immediately available reward. When children are asked to visualize the future reward in an

abstract fashion (e.g., by imagining that candy bars are logs or that marshmallows are clouds), however, their ability to delay gratification increases. This is most likely because the abstract imagery reminds them of the conditions they must meet ("if I wait, I get the big one") without arousing their frustration as much as does an image of consuming the reward.

It appears that if we can avoid thinking about having (consuming) either the available reward or the future reward and focus instead on the abstract qualities of the future reward, we can increase our ability to delay gratification. Another strategy is to imagine having some reward that is unavailable and irrelevant to the delay of gratification situation. Mischel reports that this seems to provide some degree of gratification and also distracts individuals from the immediate discomfort of the delay.

To apply these principles, consider a situation in which you must decide whether to spend your present savings for a vacation trip in the United States (small immediate reward) or to continue to save for a summer trip to Europe (larger future reward). Mischel's findings suggest that to increase your ability to forego the immediate trip, you should not imagine how wonderful the European trip will be, for this may increase your frustration over not being able to go at this time, and prompt you to settle for the immediate reward. You might instead think about abstract features of Europe, such as the languages and cultures. Or you might visualize consuming some irrelevant and unavailable reward, such as attending a concert featuring your favorite musical performers.

Mischel's work has demonstrated the importance of cognitive factors in the delay of gratification and some of the ways in which cognitive transformations of reward stimuli can increase this form of self-control.

BOX 8.5

Aversive imagery and self-control

In the following excerpt Earl Ubell illustrates the potent influence that aversive imagery, a self-produced antecedent, has had on his eating behavior.

I used to be a big steak-and-potatoes man, capable of wolfing down a 12-ounce steak at a sitting and enjoying every mouthful. Of course, I was 30 per cent overweight, and God knows the condition of my arteries. Then I drastically reduced my consumption of animal fat and switched to fish and fowl. Not only did I begin to enjoy fish and fowl, but when I would occasionally try a 12-ounce steak, I no longer enjoyed it, nor could I finish it.

This amazing change occurred because I had found a way to change my habit of eating. The method is now scientifically demonstrated to be effective, and anyone can use it to lose weight or to change any lifestyle habit. I learned how to do it quite by accident. You can learn it by design. Let me tell you what happened to me.

When my father died of a coronary heart attack at the age of 44, he, too, was overweight by nearly 35 pounds. His diet had been extremely rich in fat, just as mine was. I had become a science reporter in the interim and wrote regularly on the effects of overeating. I understood only too well the relationship between overweight and my father's misfortune.

In the week just before my father's death, I visited him in the hospital every day, spending long hours with him. I well remember the pale, quivering face. Fear and pain swept over him like angry waves on a dark shore. On the day he died, I arrived a few minutes after his last heartbeat—mouth open, cheeks gray, appalling.

I recount that sad and terrifying moment for you because of a curious phenomenon that occurred when I began to try to lose weight eight years later. Lunchtime. A cafeteria. The salad counter. The hot table with corned beef, frankfurters, french-fried potatoes. Like an addict, I am drawn to the hot table. I actually hear the rationalization in my mind. Well, it doesn't matter today. I've been good so far . . . only 300 calories. I'll make it up at dinner. The stimuli are very strong. At the sight of the corned beef, I can actually feel my jaw working. My habit is very deep indeed.

And then an image of my father's face as I last saw it flashed before me. I am appalled. I try to turn off the picture by moving away from the hot table. I take a salad. The picture returns. I shout silently to myself: Stop! I try to think of something pleasant: my forthcoming trip to Europe, a happy afternoon with my little daughter . . . anything to get that hospital scene off the screen of my mind. But note. I ended up with the salad rather than the corned beef. And it happened day after day. (From *How to Save Your Life*, copyright © 1973 by Earl Ubell. Reprinted by permission of Harcourt Brace Jovanovich, Inc.)

Table 8.2 Competing coverants for thoughts that lead to eating and not studying

Eating	Not Studying
I hate the way I look when I'm overweight.	I'm wasting my time if I don't apply myself here at school.
It's not healthy to eat this stuff.	I'll really feel lousy if I get a low grade.
I'll sure look better when I lose weight	It's worth studying to do well on the test.
I'll be in better physical shape if I can avoid foods like these.	If I bear down now, I can enjoy myself more later on in the term.

are the new thoughts in order to reinforce their occurrence. Instead of allowing the usual coverants ("I sure could go for a cigarette") when his subjects started to feel an urge to smoke, they were told to think of an antismoking thought ("this cigarette might be the one that gives me lung cancer") followed by a pro-nonsmoking thought ("I'll save lots of money by not smoking"). They were also told to follow on these two thoughts with immediate reinforcement (coffee drinking).

Unfortunately, Homme's coverant control technique has not been thoroughly researched, and the results obtained are not always positive. In one suc-

263

cessful experimental study (Horan and Johnson, 1971) overweight subjects were asked to develop lists of negative thoughts about being overweight and positive thoughts about not being overweight. Some of them were instructed simply to think a negative-positive thought pair several times each day; others were told to reinforce such thoughts with a high-probability behavior. After eight weeks only the subjects who had used the Premack principle to reinforce the thoughts lost a significant amount of weight in comparison with members of a control group. Clearly, reinforcement is an important factor in coverant control.

A clinical application of coverant control in the treatment of severe depression was reported by Todd (1972). An important aspect of depression is the occurrence of self-critical thoughts that serve to maintain and increase the depression. The patient in Todd's case was a middle-aged woman with a history of three suicide attempts. She was told to develop a list of positive statements about herself. Initially, she could think of only six. Because smoking was a high-probability behavior for her, she was told to read one or two of the statements to herself before each time she lit up. Within one week her depression had decreased considerably and she was able to generate a list of 14 positive statements about herself. By the end of the second week, she reported feeling much better, and had thought of a total of 21 positive statements about herself. Todd attributed these changes to the strengthening of positive thoughts about herself by reinforcing them when they occurred.

Thought stopping

Another form of covert self-control involves a technique called *thought stopping*, which is used to cope with troublesome thoughts that occur repeatedly and that cause unpleasant emotional reactions, such as anxiety, depression, or anger. These are the thoughts that you "can't get out of your head," that keep you from concentrating on other things. When they are extreme and chronic, these uncontrollable thoughts are called *obsessions*. Most of us suffer from milder forms of this problem from time to time.

In clinical thought-stopping procedures, patients are asked to concentrate on the troublesome thoughts. As they do so the therapist suddenly yells,

"Stop!" The loud command interrupts the thoughts. After the procedure is repeated several times, the responsibility for yelling "Stop!" is given to the patient. (Obviously, this is not done in public.) On subsequent trials clients are told to give themselves the command in a whisper and later to subvocally tighten their vocal cords and mouth the word without actually saying it out loud. Eventually, they are able to block out unwanted thoughts with a mental command.

David Rimm and John Masters (1974) suggest a potentially useful addition to this procedure. In addition to saying "stop," subjects say something positive and reassuring to themselves in a forceful manner. For example, a young man who was obsessed with the possibility of having a "mental breakdown" was trained not only to tell himself to stop, but also to follow this instruction immediately with the covert statement "Screw it! I'm perfectly normal!" Although well-controlled experimental studies are needed to examine fully the effectiveness of thought stopping, the evidence we have at this point from clinical case studies suggests that the technique may be useful in dealing with intrusive thoughts.

Changing internal self-statements

What people say (think) to themselves in the form of self-instructions, beliefs, and evaluations of situations clearly influences their behavior. Most emotional responses, for example, are the result not of external events, but of what we covertly *tell* ourselves about the events. For example, if you respond to low grades by telling yourself that it is a catastrophe and proves that you are stupid and worthless, you will have a different emotional reaction from what you will if you tell yourself, "So what? It's not the end of the world. I'll do better next time!"

The following statement was made by a psychotherapy patient who learned to "tune in to" and change the internal sentences that were causing her emotional problems.

> Whenever I find myself getting guilty or upset, I immediately tell myself that there *must* be some silly sentence that I am saying to myself to cause this upset; and almost immediately, usually within literally a few minutes of my starting to look for it, I find this sentence . . . the sentence invariably takes the form of "Isn't it terrible that . . ." or "Wouldn't it be awful if"

And when I closely look at and question these sentences, and ask myself, *"How* is it really terrible that . . .?" or *"Why* would it actually be awful if . . .?" I always find that it isn't terrible or wouldn't be awful, and I get over being upset very quickly. In fact . . . as I keep questioning and challenging my own sentences, I begin to find that they stop coming up again and again, as they used to do before. . . . Only occasionally, now do I start to tell myself that something would be terrible or awful if it occurred, or something else is frightful because it has occurred. And on those relatively few occasions, as I just said, I can quickly go after the "terribleness" or the "awfulness" that I am dreaming up, and factually or logically reevaluate it and abolish it. I can hardly believe it, but I seem to be getting to the point, after so many years of worrying over practically everything and thinking I was a slob no matter what I did, of now finding that *nothing* is so terrible or awful, and I now seem to be recognizing this *in advance* rather than *after* I have seriously upset myself. Boy what a change that is in my life! I am really getting to be with these new attitudes, an entirely different sort of person than I was. (Ellis, 1962, pp. 31–32)

Cognitive modification. Donald Meichenbaum (1972) conducted a study with students who had high test anxiety. This is a common problem among students, and it has a negative effect on academic performance. In testing situations these students are plagued with worries about their performance, feelings of inadequacy, fear of failure, and other intense emotions. These preoccupations keep them from focusing their attention on the task at hand, and they "freeze," forget facts they already know, or make silly mistakes. Meichenbaum hypothesized that these students might learn to control their worry and to redirect their attention to the task through training involving self-instructional responses. He designed a *cognitive modification* program that included self-instructional training as part of a desensitization procedure. First, he told subjects that their test anxiety and its effects on their performance were largely the result of what they said to themselves in test-related situations. He then helped them discover their disruptive internal statements ("I don't know if I can pass this test. . . . It looks like other people know the stuff. . . . I'm blowing it. . . . I can't remember that. . . . What'll people think if I screw up this test. . . .") and to learn adaptive internal statements that would help to redirect their attention to the task ("No negative self-statements, just think rationally. . . . Just pay attention, and you can handle this. . . . Forget what others are doing. . . . Relax. . . . I'm in control. . . . Don't think about fear, just about what you have to do. . . ."). Subjects were also trained in deep muscular relaxation. During group treatment sessions they were asked to imagine test-related scenes. Whenever they began to feel anxious, they were told to imagine themselves coping with the anxiety by relaxing, stopping their disruptive self-statements, and replacing them with adaptive internal instructions that focused their attention on the task.

The cognitive modification treatment was very effective. Subjects reported large decreases in anxiety within testing situations and improved their performance significantly on a series of tasks administered under testlike conditions. More importantly, they showed significant posttreatment increases in grade point average.

The development and testing of methods designed to increase individuals' control over their own behavior is attracting the attention of a growing number of psychologists. In this chapter we have explored the major self-control techniques and have indicated ways in which you can apply these methods to your own life. We have seen that self-control is best viewed as the ability to apply overt and covert behaviors that alter the environment that affects the target behavior. We hope that the information you have received in this chapter will enhance your ability to act as your own scientist, to discover and change the conditions that affect behaviors you might want to change. The continued development and refinement of a technology of self-control promises to give a new dimension of meaning to the phrase "Power to the people."

SUMMARY

1. Traditional conceptions of behavioral self-control have emphasized the role of internal traits and attributes, such as willpower and strength of character. This conception is

contrasted with one that views self-control as *behaviors* by means of which people alter the environmental conditions affecting other behaviors. Self-control behaviors may be directed at modifying behavioral antecedents, changing response consequences, or developing emotional coping skills.

2. A critical first step in self-modification involves specification of the problem. It is important to avoid describing the problem in terms of abstract traits and motives and instead to specify the problem in terms of behaviors in situations. Once a behavioral specification occurs it is possible to define goals in terms of the changing of specific *target behaviors.*

3. *Baseline data* are those data collected before the self-modification procedures are begun. They furnish a baseline against which later changes can be evaluated. A portable data collection system is required so that the behaviors can be recorded as they occur. The data may be graphed so that changes over time can be observed.

4. Because many behaviors are under the stimulus control of the environment in which they occur, one set of self-control procedures involves changing stimulus conditions. Stimulus control procedures have been successfully used in many self-modification programs.

5. Observation of one's own behavior may itself result in positive behavioral changes. Such effects probably occur because of increased awareness of antecedent conditions and/or because of the person's self-evaluative responses, which serve as reinforcers and punishers. In addition, the presence of the recording instrument may become an antecedent stimulus for desired behaviors. Research results indicate that positive changes occurring as the result of self-observation alone are frequently only temporary. More permanent changes occur when self-observation is used in conjunction with other self-control procedures.

6. Self-administered positive reinforcement has proved to be a highly effective self-modification technique. Positive reinforcers appear to be more effective when they are made contingent on changes in specific behaviors (e.g., eating habits) rather than the attainment of certain goals (e.g., specified weight losses). In order to be effective a potential reinforcer must be *controllable* and *potent.* An important variety of positive reinforcement occurs in the use of the *Premack principle*, in which a higher-frequency behavior is used to reinforce a lower-frequency behavior. Immediate self-reinforcement is more effective than delayed reinforcement.

7. Token reinforcement systems are valuable in that they allow access to a variety of reinforcers. The reinforcement contingency should be spelled out in detail in the form of a specific contract that is written up.

8. Shaping procedures are extremely important in building up desirable behaviors. The goal of self-modification programs should be gradual rather than sudden and complete change. Two important rules are therefore (a) to start with a very small change and (b) to keep the steps small. Whenever difficulty is encountered, the size of the step should be reduced. *Plateaus* and *cheating* are two difficulties that frequently reflect problems in the shaping procedures.

9. Self-punishment has not proven to be as effective a self-modification procedure as self-reinforcement. Available evidence suggests that (a) punishment through removal of positive reinforcers is more consistently effective than punishment based on aver-

266

sive self-stimulation and (b) punishment is most effective when it is used in conjunction with positive reinforcement of an alternative behavior. It is recommended that whenever possible, the self-modification goal be to increase a desirable competing behavior through self-reinforcement procedures rather than to decrease an undesirable behavior by means of self-punishment.

10. Self-desensitization is a procedure whereby persons can gain greater self-control of emotional responses. The procedure involves training oneself in deep muscular relaxation and then using this coping response to control emotional responses to imagined and real-life problem situations.

11. Internal processes, such as thoughts, images, and feelings, are viewed as *covert behaviors*, which are subject to the same kinds of controlling influences as are other behaviors. Covert behaviors can serve as *antecedents*, *consequences*, or *target behaviors*. Homme's coverant control, the technique of thought stopping, and Meichenbaum's cognitive modification procedures are presented as examples of techniques that are being developed and studied by psychologists interested in self-control of covert behaviors.

Suggested readings

Mahoney, M. J., & Thoresen, C. E. *Self-control: Power to the person.* Monterey, Calif.: Brooks/Cole, 1974. A collection of theoretical papers and scientific reports of self-control procedures.

Thoresen, C. E., & Mahoney, M. J. *Behavioral self-control.* New York: Holt, Rinehart and Winston, Inc., 1974. A review of the principles and research evidence relating to behavioral self-control in terms of a cognitive-behavioral framework such as that used in the present chapter.

Watson, D. D., & Tharp, R. G. *Self-directed behavior: Self-modification for personal adjustment.* 2nd Edition. Monterey, Calif.: Brooks/Cole, 1977. A useful and detailed guide to the application of behavioral self-control principles in solving problems. Contains many concrete examples and suggestions.

Four

Development
and Adaptation

Chapter 9

Psychological Development

(Carroll, EPA)

Tape recordings of conversations of parents with their children's doctors might provide some illuminating insights into the psychology of human development and child rearing. The father of a 2-year-old girl told her pediatrician, "Dr. Mason, we are worried because Laura doesn't seem to want to play with other children. She doesn't run away from them but she just keeps on digging in the sand or piling up the blocks without including the other child. Do you think she's antisocial?"

The following are questions raised by two other adults about children's behavior: A grandmother said, "I'm worried about Jim. I've been trying to toilet-train him since he was 10 months old and now at 18 months he still doesn't respond. Do you think the fact that I take care of him while his mother works is harming him?" And a mother commented as she watched the doctor examine her daughter, "Karen can't seem to learn to roller skate. Her 7-year-old sister learned so quickly. Do you think it's because Karen is 4 that she's having trouble? She walks and runs well enough."

These adults are concerned about development. Understanding the regular process of development and how it is related to skills, abilities, and general behavior helps us to know what kinds of behavior are typical and possible at various ages.

The study of psychological development deals with changes in individuals over time. Interest in this topic developed later than interest in other psychological processes, such as perception or learning. In recent decades there has been an upsurge of interest in it, including a new focus on, "life span developmental psychology"—the study of developmental processes through adulthood and into old age.

Although developmental psychology properly includes the study of all living organisms, this chapter emphasizes human development, particularly during childhood.

WHY STUDY DEVELOPMENT?

Interest in development, especially human development, has grown for a number of reasons. First, psychologists who studied adults began to realize that the origins of the patterns of behavior that they saw might lie not in the previous moment or the previous week, but in the whole life history of the individual. Psychologists interested in perception realized that the study of perceptual processes had to begin with young infants. Others interested in cognitive functioning in adults began to look at the origins of different styles of thinking. Social learning theorists turned to the study of children because of their conviction that the whole reinforcement history of an individual, and all the opportunities for modeling from birth onward, had an impact on the behavior patterns of adults.

But there are other reasons for studying development, particularly early development. The rate of change early in life is much faster than it is at any other time. Early infancy, childhood, and adolescence are times when the mutual influences of biology and environment are quite easy to see and comparatively easy to study.

Finally, the study of human development has great practical importance—for parents; for courts that must decide about the placement of children; for schools, physicians, social and physical planners; and for others. For example, the research findings of developmental psychologists have been used in a number of important arguments before the Supreme Court. Using such findings, the case of *Brown* v. *Board of Education* found racially separate but equivalent educational facilities to be inherently unequal and marked the beginning of legally enforced moves toward school integration in the United States. Other findings have contributed to the current trend toward granting fathers custody of minor children in an increasing number of divorce cases. In placing students and planning curricula, schools rely not only on good judgment and past experience, but also on findings from research by educational and developmental psychologists. Physicians and psychologists are combining forces to study a wide range of physical, social, and emotional problems, such as the long-term effects of being born prematurely, of poverty, and of the aging process.

How can development be studied?

Development can be studied longitudinally, that is, by periodically measuring changes in the same individual or group as time passes, or by comparing the characteristics of groups of individuals of different ages.

There are several disadvantages in using the *longitudinal method*. Besides taking a long time, it is expensive. In addition, the period from infancy to adulthood in subjects' lives may extend beyond the life span of the investigator. Subjects might move away or die and bias the findings in unknown ways. The problems studied in infants may not be those of interest in adulthood, and measuring techniques and scientific knowledge may improve and render earlier work less valuable.

The advantage of longitudinal studies is that they study the same group of individuals throughout. This eliminates many sources of variation that might make the results less meaningful.

The *cross-sectional method* is less expensive and takes much less time than the longitudinal method. Loss of subjects during the research and changes in available methodology are not significant problems. The greatest difficulty with cross-sectional studies is the amount of variation they introduce, which may be related to other factors besides age, such as growing up in different socioeconomic environments. The years of individuals' births may make a significant difference in their lives because of historical events. For example, consider the age groups shown in Table 9.1. If the four age groups shown were studied in the 1970s, it would be difficult to separate the effects of different historical periods from differences attributable to age alone.

Measurements of such variables as attitudes would, of course, be much more affected than measurements of physiological variables. However, physiological variables could also be influenced by such factors as developments in medicine or technology or changes in pollution levels. Differences in intelligence scores among 20-year-olds, 40-year-olds, and 60-year-olds could be related to physiological changes, to differences in group education level, to changes in nutrition, or to many other factors.

The cross-sectional and longitudinal methods may be modified to capitalize on the best features of each approach. For example, a longitudinal study of limited duration (e.g., five years) may trace the development of a particular behavior or growth pattern over a period when great change is expected.

An intriguing modification of a cross-sectional approach is *age simulation* (Baltes and Goulet, 1971). This procedure attempts to discover the cause

Table 9.1 Some differences in the social environment for four age groups

	Age at Time of Event for Persons Born in			
	1900	1920	1940	1960
World War I	14–18	–	–	–
Women won right to vote	20	–	–	–
Stock market crash	29	9	–	–
Great Depression	30–40	10–20	–	–
World War II	41–45	21–25	1–5	–
Postwar boom	45–50	25–30	5–10	–
Korean War	50–53	30–33	10–13	–
Vietnam War	61–73	41–53	21–33	1–13
1970s inflationary spiral	70–	50–	30–	10–

for differences in the performance of groups of various ages by manipulating variables until the performances become comparable. For example, in a task such as dart throwing, if the scores of the older group are worse than those of the younger one, then conditions would be varied until the scores became comparable. If the room lighting were increased for the older group and this brought the scores into balance, the researchers would know that some aspects of vision were important. Or if moving the older group closer to the target improved their scores, the researchers would conclude that muscular strength was important.

Conceptions of development

The four perspectives on behavior have all led to important contributions to the study of psychological development. Interest in *biological development* was a logical outgrowth of Darwin's ideas about evolution. If it was possible that living things have changed over time, it was also possible to think of a process and pattern of development within any particular organism or species. G. Stanley Hall, the "father" of developmental psychology, was interested in development as a way of gaining insight into human behavior during earlier evolutionary periods.

Arnold Gesell, an American psychologist and physician, was struck by the regularities and consistencies in development, especially psychomotor development. He thought of child development as a genetically determined pattern that is invariant and universal and paid relatively little attention to cul-

273

tural factors. We follow the same paths of development, he thought, because each of us goes through a biologically determined process of maturation. The genetic inheritance of the individual may affect the speed of this process but not the order in which development proceeds.

The *psychoanalytic* view of development originated with Sigmund Freud and was expanded by Anna Freud, his daughter; Erik Erikson; and others. Freud was concerned with problems of interpersonal relationships, which he believed were influenced by situations or experiences occurring at particular points in an individual's development. Any interference with this process could produce difficulties in psychosocial relationships in an individual's later life. His psychoanalytic theory influenced methods of child rearing during much of the twentieth century. In recent years Erik Erikson's neopsychoanalytic point of view has been particularly influential because he stressed the importance of identifying the challenges of social development throughout the life span, as well as during childhood (Erikson, 1968). The theories of both Freud and Erikson are discussed in Chapter 13. Like the biological theorists, the psychoanalytic thinkers look at human development as a process of unfolding and maturing, but they add the idea that relationships with people are vital to development.

The *cognitive* viewpoint on development is currently popular with many psychologists. Jean Piaget is its best-known advocate; his views also stress the unfolding of the individual. Piaget has been struck by how development proceeds in regular stages in children from many cultures. Most of Piaget's work has been on the development of thinking rather than on emotions or personality. His experiments in thinking and problem solving led to a theoretical approach that, after receiving little attention for many years, has recently become a primary source of experimental ideas.

John B. Watson was one of the first psychologists to apply concepts from the field of learning to the study of child development. He was not interested in development as an unfolding process as an organism matured. The *behaviorist* view of development, which Watson first introduced, differs from the three preceding views by emphasizing that all behavior follows the laws of learning. Development, then, is a result of learning experiences rather than an internal process of the organism. This approach has had a great impact on psychological and educational thought and on social policy in the United States and elsewhere. Research on classical and operant conditioning and observational learning has shown that learning exerts an important influence throughout the life span, including infancy, where its effects have often been underestimated.

BIOLOGICAL DEVELOPMENT

Psychological development often cannot be distinguished neatly from biological development. Heredity, maturation, and the effects of hormones before birth and during later development play important roles in influencing thought and behavior.

Heredity

A basic knowledge of the mechanisms of heredity is necessary to understand the biological development of the individual. Genetics is the branch of biology concerned with heredity. Psychologists are particularly interested in *behavior genetics*, the study of the inheritance of behavioral characteristics.

Because sex cells, which carry hereditary traits to new generations, are very small, study of hereditary mechanisms could not proceed until the invention of the microscope in the seventeenth century. One popular idea that lasted well into the nineteenth century was that heredity was transmitted in the blood. Another popular theory in the nineteenth century was proposed by the French scientist Jean Baptiste Lamarck, who believed that characteristics acquired during individuals' lifetimes could be inherited by their descendents. This theory was adopted by Russian geneticist T. D. Lysenko and officially endorsed by Russian science from the 1930s until 1964, when Lysenko was officially discredited.

Present genetic theory is based on the work of Gregor Mendel, who reported on his experiments with garden peas around 1865. Although many experiments involving plant hybridization were conducted in the century before Mendel's work, no one had understood their meaning fully. Mendel showed in his work with peas that heredity did not mean a general blending of characteristics of parents in off-

274

spring, but that it was a transmitting of specific factors (genes) to offspring. These factors might be visible in children or they might simply be carried for possible transmission to another generation. All the children of one set of parents did not inherit the same characteristics. Early in the twentieth century, geneticists formulated a distinction between *genotype* and *phenotype*. *Genotype* refers to genetic materials that individuals inherit, whereas *phenotype* refers to their outward appearance and behavior.

The biological basis of human heredity

The union of two cells, the *egg* from the mother and the *sperm* from the father, is the beginning of a new individual. These two cells, like all other cells, carry within them material that forms a definite number of rodlike units called *chromosomes*. These chromosomes carry specific heredity factors, or *genes*. The cell nucleus that contains the chromosomes is made up of *deoxyribonucleic acid*, or *DNA*, in combination with protein compounds. (See Figure 9.1.)

Every cell in a normal individual contains 46 chromosomes, made up of 23 pairs. (See Figure 9.2.) The sex cells, however, the egg and sperm, have only 23 chromosomes. At conception the sex cells unite to form a new cell, which contains the full 46 chromosomes, or 23 chromosome pairs.

Because genes also occur in pairs within the chromosomes and the new individual receives one of each parent's pair of each type of gene, a human parent potentially could produce several trillion genetically different egg or sperm cells. In other words, the possible differences in both genotype and phenotype among children in the same family are enormous. The only exception to this uniqueness of the individual occurs in monozygotic twins, whose heredity is identical.

Sex determination. In most cases the two members of a chromosome pair appear almost identical in size and shape when they are viewed under a microscope. In the human male there is an exception to this rule. One pair of chromosomes has one large member, called X, and one small member, called Y. Every normal male has an XY chromosome pair. Females have an XX pair. The normal human sperm are of two types, X and Y. If a Y sperm fertilizes an egg, then the result is XY and a male will develop. If

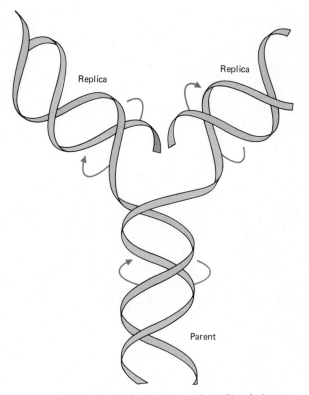

Figure 9.1 Although the importance to heredity of chromosomes and the genes they contain has been known for some time, the way in which heredity was transmitted was not understood until 1953 when James Watson and Francis Crick proposed a model of the DNA molecule like that shown here. This model makes it possible to see how the genetic code reproduces itself. The inverted ladder of the DNA molecule can "unzip" up the center and reproduce the missing halves so that each new DNA molecule contains the complete code of the original.

the egg is fertilized by an X sperm, an XX individual, or a female, will develop.

Sometimes variations in the sex chromosome pattern appear and individuals may have XO, XXY, or XYY sex chromosomes. Each of these variations produces identifiable characteristics in the individual. An XO combination, in which a female has only 45 chromosomes, is called *Turner's syndrome*. Although her external genitalia are female, her ovaries, uterus, and breasts do not develop normally, and she is almost always incapable of reproduction. In *Klinefelter's syndrome* the individual has an XXY combination and 47 chromosomes. He has external male

275

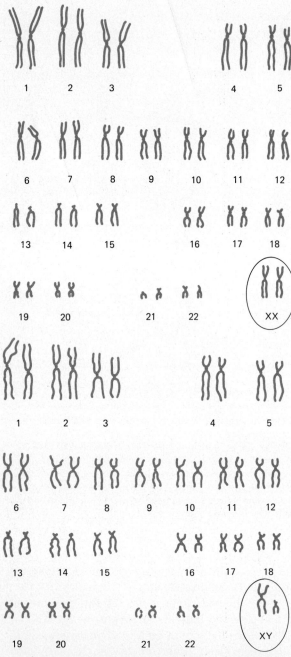

Figure 9.2 The 23 pairs of chromosomes in females (top) and males (bottom). Note the difference in the twenty-third pair, the sex chromosomes. (Liebert et al., 1974, p. 49.)

genitalia but small testes and feminized breasts and is likely to be mentally retarded. The XYY male tends to be tall and may be psychologically disturbed or mentally retarded.

Proliferation, differentiation, and growth. After the egg and sperm cells join, the development of a new individual is governed by several processes. First the cell proliferates to form more cells. Two cells form, then four, then eight, and so on until the billions of cells necessary for a human embryo are formed. As the process of proliferation of cell division proceeds, the cells also differentiate. This means that they become specialized for certain functions, such as nerve, muscle, fat, and so on. Before each division the cell grows. During this stage it manufactures new living substance as directed by the genes contained in its nucleus.

The process of inheritance
As we noted above, one gene in each pair is inherited from each parent. Some genes are *dominant;* some are *recessive.* An individual with a certain dominant gene displays the characteristic associated with that gene whether one or both genes in the same pair are dominant. If a gene is recessive the characteristic associated with it does not show unless both genes in the gene pair are recessive. If an individual has only one recessive gene in a pair its effect is masked by its dominant partner, but a recessive gene may be passed on to an individual's offspring. Certain characteristics are produced by a single gene or gene pair. However, some genes have more than one noticeable effect. A single gene may affect development in several parts of the body. (See Table 9.2.)

Sex-linked characteristics. Some hereditary characteristics are carried only by the female chromosome (the X chromosome) and are said to be sex-linked. For example, red-green color blindness and hemophilia (a tendency to hemorrhage) are sex-linked traits. The male inherits an X chromosome from the mother and a Y chromosome from the father. If he inherits one of these recessive genes from his mother he will have no matching gene from his father because only Xs carry these sex-linked characteristics. Therefore the trait will appear. Females inherit one X chromosome from each parent. The female may

What happens when a male Sardinian donkey mates with a female zebra? The staff of the animal haven where this creature was born decided that the result was a "zebroid" that resembles both parents. (UPI)

inherit the recessive characteristic from her mother but the chances are great that it will be masked by a dominant gene from the X chromosome she inherits from her father. Only if her father shows the trait (carries the recessive gene) could the female inherit the same recessive gene from both parents.

Multiple-factor inheritance. Some traits arise because of differences at more than one paired gene location along the chromosomes, so that several genes may be involved in producing particular characteristics. Variations in hair color among children in one family can be explained in this manner. Of course, this type of heredity is more difficult to study than single-factor inheritance.

Table 9.2 Some human characteristics thought to be caused by a single dominant gene (D) or by a single pair of recessive genes (R)

D or R	Trait or Characteristic	Description
D	cataract	opaqueness of lens of eye
D	Huntington's chorea	degeneration of particular brain centers
D	amyloidosis	congestive heart failure
R	albinism	lack of pigment in hair eyes, and skin
R	deaf-mutism	deafness from birth
R	microcephaly	abnormally small head

Chromosome variations. An abnormal number of chromosomes may cause other problems besides sexual abnormalities. A particular type of mental retardation, the Down syndrome (see Chapter 14), involves an extra chromosome on the twenty-first pair. In most cases if a chromosome is lost during development, the result is fatal. If only a small part is lost, the embryo may survive.

Mutation. Ordinarily, as a cell grows and divides, it reproduces perfectly. But if a mutation occurs in the egg or sperm, it is likely that the mutated gene will be passed on to future generations. If a mutation occurs in other cells of the body, then the cells that grow from it will carry the change, but the change will not be transmitted to the next generation. For example, certain individuals have flecks of brown in a blue eye. This means that most of their cells reproduced normally, and the mutation of one cell to brown affected only cells descended from that particular cell and colored only a portion of the iris. Although observable mutations in human beings occur very seldom, there are environmental factors that may increase the mutation rate. The most common of these factors is ionizing radiation, such as that from X-rays and atomic explosions.

277

Heredity of behavior

An individual's heredity is realized in the process of development through all the stages from a single cell to an embryo, infant, child, adolescent, adult, and aged person. In all these stages environmental conditions affect the ways in which the organism develops. Behavioral genetics examines the ways in which heredity and the environment have each affected an individual's traits. The ways in which geneticists study these effects are described in the following paragraphs.

Selective breeding. Geneticists often select plants and animals to breed for certain traits. For example, some rats learn to find their way to food in a maze much more quickly than other rats. One experimenter bred fast-learning rats together and slow-learning rats together (Thompson, 1954) and found that in the sixth generation, the bright rats made 100 percent fewer errors than dull or slow-learning rats.

Although we can make deductions based on these experiments about human heredity, ethical considerations do not permit the use of selective breeding as a method for studying human heredity. Two major approaches are used instead: pedigree analysis and twin studies.

Pedigree analysis. In pedigree analysis the investigator first identifies the characteristic of interest (e.g., the Down syndrome), then an individual who has it. The investigator then studies the family history and examines the traits of ancestors, descendents, and other relatives (siblings, uncles, aunts). This information may make it possible to identify a Mendelian pattern of inheritance for the defect. The information available is usually incomplete, so that this approach has some built-in difficulties. A related method is a *consanguinity study*, which contrasts the statistical probability of occurrence of the trait in close relatives, distant relatives, and the general population.

Twin studies. The method used most often in psychological research on heredity is *twin studies*. Twins are either *monozygotic* (identical, or produced from a split in the fertilized egg) or *dizygotic* (fraternal, or produced from two eggs). Although monozygotic twins share an identical heredity, dizygotic twins are no more alike than are ordinary siblings. Presumably both types of twins reared together are reared in similar environments. If the

monozygotic pairs show closer behavioral resemblances than the dizygotic pairs, these differences may be caused by heredity.

Other twin studies examine monozygotic twins separated at an early age and reared apart so that they would not have experienced the effects of a similar environment. Of course, there are only a small number of cases of identical twins reared apart, and there are other problems with this method as well. The greatest is that the placement of these twins in foster homes does not seem to be by chance; rather, it is influenced by such factors as the appraisal of the intellectual and social status of the original parents and the physical characteristics of the infants. Although many of the conclusions about the effects of heredity on development come from these studies, they must be viewed with caution.

Maturation

Maturation refers to those aspects of growth or change that are governed by internal, biological mechanisms that unfold or unravel over time. The pattern of maturation is *species-specific*; that is, each species has its own pattern of growth, controlled by its own internal mechanisms. In addition, the pattern is *sequential*. The growth of the human baby during the nine months of gestation occurs in a fixed sequence, with the limbs, eyes, mouth, internal organs, hair, and so on, each developing at a particular time. The sequence can be interrupted or interfered with by some outside force, such as a drug or a disease that affects the mother, but each normal human fetus contains within it the blueprint for this sequential pattern of growth. Much of physical development after birth is patterned as well.

Gesell pointed out that the process of change, the slow acquisition of motor skills, follows a specific pattern that appears to be the same for all human beings. For example, control of the upper part of the body develops earlier than control of the lower part of the body, and control of the trunk develops before control of the limbs. Babies develop control of the neck before the back, and of the arms before the legs. Gesell proposed that this steady progression is governed by systematic changes in the brain, the nervous system, and the muscles, and research has confirmed this idea.

The study of the maturation process has

278

important practical applications. For example, research on the growth of muscles in infants shows that the sphincter muscle, which controls defecation, is not fully developed until well into the second year of life. Until this time the muscle itself is rudimentary and is not fully connected to the nervous system. A child cannot be fully toilet trained until this muscle is under voluntary control. Mothers who insist that their 10-month-old child is toilet trained are usually kidding themselves; they have trained themselves to respond to the child's signals, but the child does not have real voluntary control. Recognition of this fact has changed the advice that doctors give to mothers about the appropriate time to try to begin toilet training. Normative charts, such as the one in Figure 9.3 can help a parent determine how a child's development compares with that of other children.

Hormones

A third source of biological influence on the developing child comes from hormones. Hormones play a vital role in sexual development throughout an individual's life, but research in this area has been sparse, and we have much left to learn. We do know that during the prenatal period the pituitary gland of a male fetus releases the male hormone *testosterone* so that the fetus will develop as a male, with male genitals. If this does not occur, then the fetus will develop as a physical female. Experiments on mon-

keys and other animals show that injecting male hormones into an animal carrying a female fetus produces female offspring with notably masculine behavior patterns. They show more rough-and-tumble play and more mounting behavior, for example, than do normal females. One study of human girls whose mothers were given a drug during pregnancy with some of the chemical properties of testosterone suggests that it may have a similar "masculinizing" effect in humans (Money and Ehrhart, 1968). We also know that both testosterone and *progesterone*, the female sex hormone, play some role in prenatal development, and a major role at puberty. It is still not entirely clear, however, what role they play during infancy and early childhood, nor is it clear to what extent sex differences in behavior can be accounted for by differences in hormonal patterning.

Stages of development

Prenatal development

The first division (*mitosis*) of a fertilized egg cell occurs about 24 hours after conception, and cell division then continues at an accelerated pace. Within a few days there are several dozen cells. Then the group of cells, called the *zygote*, travels down the Fallopian tube to the uterus and implants itself in the uterine wall about two weeks after conception. The group of cells is then an *embryo*. During the next six weeks the developing embryo continues to increase

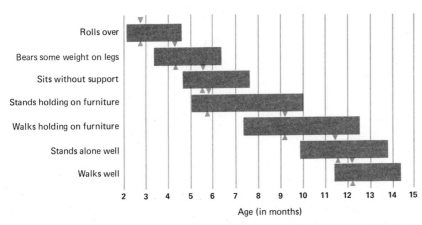

Figure 9.3 Maturation of the human infant. (From W. K. Frankenburg and J. B. Dodds, The Denver developmental screening test, *J. Pediatr.* 71:181–191, 1967.)

in size through mitosis, but it also begins to organize into distinct parts, including the placenta, the umbilical cord, and the sac of amniotic fluid.

The embryo begins to develop distinct body parts and features very early. By about eight weeks after conception it is about an inch long and has the beginnings of facial features, arms and legs, and even fingers and toes.

At about the beginning of the third month of pregnancy (about eight to nine weeks) the third phase of development, the fetal period, occurs. During the seven months of gestation period the fetus continues to grow in size and fills in the sketchy features and organs that were present in primitive form during the embryonic period. By 28 weeks (approximately seven months) the fetus has developed most of the major organ systems and may survive if it is born prematurely, although fetuses at this stage are still very small and their nervous systems are not nearly as well developed as they will be two months later.

The prenatal period has a firmly fixed sequence of development. The pattern unfolds steadily, with one step following the next in logical order. Outside influences can disrupt this pattern, however, and the impact that the disruption has depends on the time in the sequence that it occurs. Disruptions that occur early in the sequence, particularly during the embryonic period, seem to have more pervasive effects, presumably because the organism is more primitive and the outside stimulation affects more parts of the developing body.

Among the outside influences that can have an impact at this stage are drugs taken by the mother; certain diseases, such as rubella (German measles) or syphillis; deficiencies in the mother's diet, particularly a protein deficiency; and X rays or other radiation. It is important to understand, however, that not all diseases contracted by the mother have an impact on the developing embryo or fetus. The placenta is constructed in such a way that most disease organisms cannot pass through from the mother's bloodstream to the infant's.

Another potential environmental influence, and the least understood, is the mother's emotional state. It is clear that the effect, whatever it may be, is indirect. The mother's emotions affect her own body chemistry, and the change in the chemical or hor-

monal balance in her body affects the child through a change in the composition of her blood. When a mother is under stress or upset, the fetal activity rate goes up, so that some of her stress hormones may be passed through her bloodstream to the child (Sontag, 1941). The long-term effects of maternal stress are harder to pinpoint. Some research suggests that children born to mothers who were chronically stressed during pregnancy are more fussy and colicky than are children born to mothers who were calmer during pregnancy (Lakin, 1957). But one cannot be sure that it was the stress during pregnancy that caused the later colickiness, because stressed women are likely to be less confident and perhaps less capable mothers. Animal research, however, strongly supports the notion that stress and anxiety during pregnancy have some long-term effects on offspring such as increased emotionality.

Infancy and childhood

At birth a normal infant has a whole range of skills and abilities. It can hear and respond to sounds that are approximately the same pitch and loudness as a human voice (although it is not likely to respond to very high, very low, or very soft sounds). By six months, and probably much earlier, babies can also tell the location of a sound and will turn their heads to look for the source. At birth and thereafter infants are also particularly responsive to rhythmic sounds, such as heartbeatlike sounds, lullabies, cooing, and so forth.

At birth infants have a whole range of visual abilities, including a pupillary reflex (the widening and closing of the pupil in response to light variations) and a tracking response (following a moving object with the eyes). They are able to coordinate both eyes on a single spot soon after birth. They can also make some simple discriminations among smells and tastes and can respond vigorously to touch.

Motor abilities at birth are severely limited. Babies have a series of reflexes that are important for their survival, including the sucking and swallowing reflexes necessary for nursing. There is, however, little apparent voluntary control over the movements of the body. The nervous system at this early stage is not fully developed, and the connections between the brain and the muscles of arms and legs are not

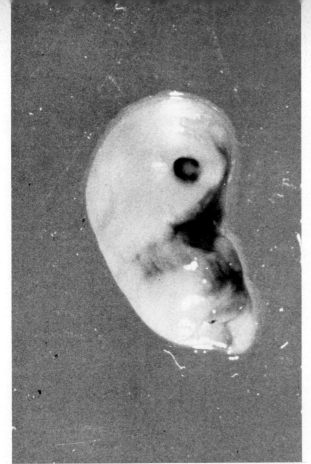

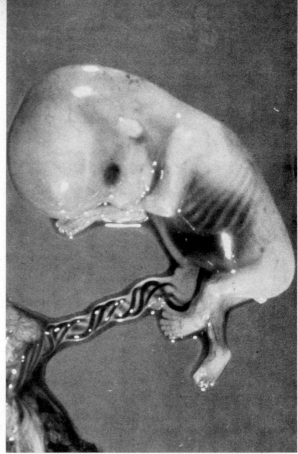

These photographs show the embryo and fetus at different stages of development. The embryonic period includes the first 2 months of pregnancy. The fetal period extends from the third month until the birth of the child. Top left: At 6 weeks the embryo can be recognized as a human being, although a strangely proportioned one. Top right: By the end of 16 weeks the fetus is about 4½ inches long. Its lips are well formed, the mouth and hands can open and close, and the fetus may show some swallowing activity. Bottom: By the end of 28 weeks the nervous, circulatory and respiratory systems are well enough developed to allow the child to live if it is born prematurely. The survival rate for children born this early is not high. (Rotker, Taurus)

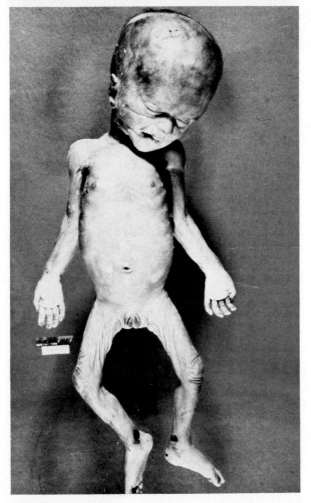

well formed. Only gradually over the first year of life, as the nerves and spinal cord acquire the necessary sheathing (myelin), is fuller voluntary control possible.

Some sex differences are present at birth or can be observed during the early years of life, but by far the majority of sex differences in behavior are not observed consistently until children are well into elementary school.

At birth girls are more physically mature than boys; their maturational timetable is perhaps four to six weeks faster than that of boys. They continue to be ahead physically through childhood, and at adolescence girls begin and end the pubertal changes earlier. Boys' bodies are also proportioned somewhat

281

differently, with a larger proportion of body weight devoted to muscle tissue in the newborn. This difference too is accentuated at adolescence, when boys develop denser muscle tissue and greater lung and heart capacity.

From conception onward girls are less susceptible to nearly every variety of stress or physical insult. More males are spontaneously aborted during the pregnancy, more males have difficulties during the birth process, more boys die during the first year of life, and more boys show up in virtually every kind of clinic or special class.

Motor skills develop regularly from birth onward. At the age of 1 month an infant can raise its chin off the mattress or floor when lying on its stomach. By 4 or 5 months of age it can roll over; by 8 months or so it can sit up and may try to stand by holding onto furniture. Children usually walk for the first time at about a year, and by 18 months most can walk well alone. By age 2 the child can run, by age 3 it can ride a tricycle, and by age 4 it can manage stairs one foot to a step, rather than going one step at a time as a younger child does.

This developmental sequence seems to be very heavily influenced by the process of maturation. The body grows, the nervous system develops more fully, the muscles develop, and the bones harden. Gradually the child can achieve greater and greater control over its body. Practice and experience, however, do make a difference. Children who are deprived of opportunities to move about regularly, as is the case in some institutions, may be severely retarded in their development of motor skills.

Obviously, while motor skills are developing there are also changes in the child's height and weight. A newborn baby is about one-third of an individual's final height, and by age 2 it is about half as tall as an adult. From age 2 to about age 11 or 12, when the "adolescent growth spurt" occurs, growth is steady and regular, but it proceeds at a slower pace than it did during infancy, and than it will during adolescence.

Of all the body's organ systems the brain and nervous system are the least fully developed at birth. The brain stem—that part of the brain that governs motor coordination, sleep and wakefulness, and attention, among other basic processes—is the most fully developed at birth. The *cortex*, the furrowed, or

convoluted part of the brain that lies above the brain stem, is present at birth but is not completely developed. (See Chapter 3.) During the first six months to two years of a child's life new connections between cells in the cortex are built up. At the same time the nerves running to and from the brain develop an important sheathing, or myelin.

Adolescence

Sometime around age 10 or 11 in girls and somewhat later in boys the pituitary gland begins to secrete larger amounts of a variety of hormones (gonadotropic hormones). These in turn trigger an increase in the output of hormones in the ovaries and testes, which promote sexual growth, and hormones from the adrenal and thyroid glands, which promote general physical growth.

In girls sharp increases in the levels of estrogen (secreted by the ovaries) begin at about age 10 to 11, when breast buds first begin to appear. These increases occur in cycles and eventually a girl begins to menstruate, usually at about age 13. At the same time she develops pubic hair and goes through the "growth spurt," with the most rapid changes in height occurring at about age 12 or 13.

In boys this process occurs two or three years later. There are noticeable increases in testosterone in the system at about age 12 or 13, accompanied by growth of the penis and testes, pubic hair, and somewhat later by a sharp spurt in height. In boys the height spurt begins later, peaks later (on the average at around age 14), and lasts longer than in girls (Tanner, 1970).

In both boys and girls there is also an increase in the length and thickness of muscle tissue at adolescence, although this change is much more marked in boys than in girls. Boys also develop larger hearts and lungs relative to their size than do girls, and a higher level of hemoglobin in their blood.

It is important to remember that all the ages given are *averages*. There is a great deal of variation among children in the timing and speed of puberty, so that the range of ages that is considered normal for any one of these changes is great.

Adulthood and aging

As a human being grows older many functions seem to slow down because of physiological changes.

There also seems to be an increased susceptibility to disease. Even though the average human life span has increased because of improved medical care, those people who do grow old do not live longer than they did in previous generations. Fewer die at an early age, but those who live into late adulthood do not live longer.

Physical changes continue throughout the life span, although after adolescence there is generally little further growth. For example, the skeleton is fully formed by the early 20s. But as age increases, chemical changes occur in the bone structure that make the bones more brittle. Collagen, one of the components of connective tissue, also changes with age. Older people may appear to shrink because of changes in the collagen in discs between their spinal vertebrae. Collagen changes are also responsible for changes in the texture and elasticity of the skin. Age seems to cause decreases in adrenal gland secretion, which result in hair loss. Sleep patterns also change with age. Spontaneous awakening during sleep increases with age. The amount of rapid eye movements (REM) and stage 4 sleep (see Chapter 5) declines (Timeros, 1972). Sensitivity in vision, hearing, smell, taste, and tactile sensations also appears to decline with age. There are central nervous system changes that may result from the loss of cells that do not replace themselves, changes in hormone levels, oxygen deficiencies caused by impaired blood circulation or changes in cell components.

Presumably, the physical changes that are part of the aging process are governed in part by maturational processes, in the same way that growth during the prenatal and early years is governed or guided by maturational "maps." It is still not clear how heredity and environment interact in the aging process. Studies of twins indicate that genetic differences play an important role, because identical or single-egg twins have more similar life spans than do fraternal, or two-egg, twins (Kallmann and Jarvik, 1959).

COGNITIVE DEVELOPMENT

The development of thinking

Behavioristic and cognitive social learning approaches

Theorists trained in the behavioristic tradition assume that the basic principles of learning—reinforcement, observational learning, and so forth—apply to the learning of complex concepts as much as they do to any other aspect of behavior. (See Box 9.1.) Early research on children's learning was intended in many ways as a demonstration: Children do learn; the same principles do apply; children can be taught complex concepts through reinforcement.

At the same time, researchers who applied these basic principles to children's learning began to discover that there were differences in the way younger and older children approached a given problem.

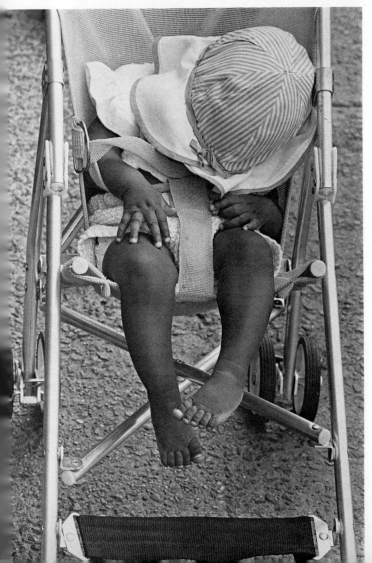

Sleep patterns change with age. (Prelutsky, Stock, Boston)

283

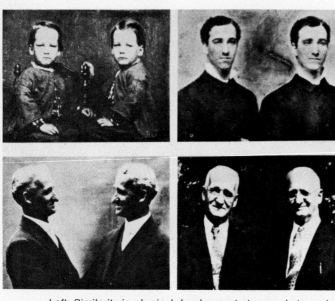

Left: Similarity in physical development at several stages in the life span is shown in these photographs of one-egg twins at the ages of 5, 20, 55, and 86 years. Right: Contrast the appearance of these fraternal twins with the highly similar appearance of the identical twins. (James E. Birren, ed., *Handbook of Aging and the Individual,* The University of Chicago Press, 1959.)

284

Older children not only learned more rapidly, but in some cases seemed to approach the task differently (Stevenson, 1972). For example, in problems involving memory, children under the age of about 5 do little or no rehearsal of the things they are supposed to recall. They appear not to use language as a *mediator* in their thinking processes at this age. But an older child of perhaps 7 or 8 will use language as a mediator quite consistently (Flavell, 1970). Children under the age of about 4 have great difficulty in learning how to solve oddity problems, in which subjects must pick the one item that is different (or "odd") out of a set of three. For this task the period from ages 4 to 7 is transitional. Earlier than this age most children are unable to learn the concept; past this age virtually all children can learn it almost immediately.

This type of observation, and many more similar observations with other tasks and problems, has led developmental psychologists with a behavioristic perspective to ask questions, such as, "What are the most salient developmental changes that occur in children's learning? Learning occurs from the time of earliest infancy and from that time on the effects of prior experience accumulate, so that the manner in which the child approaches a task at one time may not be characteristic of his performance at a later date" (Stevenson, 1972, p. 347).

This statement, which reflects ideas in many respects similar to those of Piaget, is fairly typical of those emerging from both the cognitive social learning and behavioristic perspectives in current writing. There are indications that the two theories are merging, and many behavioristic psychologists have begun to include cognitive concepts in their own theories.

Piaget's theory—a cognitive approach

A cognitive theorist and researcher who has had great impact on ideas about children's thinking is Jean Piaget. Because his views are so influential the main points of his theory are described in detail. Piaget was trained as a biologist. He turned to the study of cognitive development in children early in his professional life, convinced that it would be possible to apply basic biological principles to the process, and he has continued in this attempt over the past 50 years. He has also recorded an extraordinarily rich set of observations about children.

Like the behaviorists, Piaget thinks that children learn from experience. But the behaviorists argue that the child *reacts* to stimuli and is shaped by the reinforcement patterns, whereas Piaget views the child as the active ingredient in the process. The child examines, explores, matches, sorts, looks at, classifies, and compares experiences, objects, and events. The environment does not impinge on the child or "happen" to the child; rather, the child comes to or interacts with the environment. Piaget sees the child as an inventor or a theoretician. Each child, over the course of the first 10 or 15 years of his or her life, must rediscover basic principles of nature and devise basic theories about how the world works and how objects relate to one another.

Piaget sees the human being as a unit and assumes that there must be some common denominators in biological and mental functioning. One of these, he suggests, is the concept of *adaptation*. The human body adapts to its environment biologically; we adapt to what is available for food, and our bodies adapt food for their own uses once it has been eaten. In the same way, we adapt to the environment in the process of intellectual growth. The whole sequence of change that Piaget sees in a child's cognitive development is a gradual process of adaptation to experiences.

Piaget sees four major stages in the continuous process of growth and change in cognitive development during childhood.

The sensorimotor period. The sensorimotor period begins at birth and lasts until approximately 18 months of age. During this time children's functioning, their interactions with the environment, are at an *action* level and involve sensing and motor movement. Until the end of this period children have no fully developed internal representation of things, no mental image of the ball they may touch, no word for the ball, no way of representing it to themselves when it is not there.

Indeed, in the early months of this period children do not yet understand that things exist at all when they cannot see or feel them. The development of the concept of *object permanence* is one of the major accomplishments of this period and is not fully complete until about 18 months of age. The development of this concept is gradual. By the age of 6 months babies look for objects that have been hidden under a cloth while they are watching. But they do not keep looking for long, and if the object is hidden sequentially under a series of cloths, they look only under the first one. It is not until about 18 months of age that infants search for objects they have not actually seen being hidden.

Infants approach new experiences in whatever ways are open to them. They grasp a block if it is placed in their hands, they suck on it if it is placed near their mouths, they look at objects that come into their field of vision. Somewhat later, as they gain experience with looking and touching at the same time, they are able to coordinate information from the two senses into perhaps the first rudiments of images of objects. Throughout this process of development not only are their bodies changing through maturational processes, but they are forming a series of expectations through their experiences. New experiences constantly alter these expectations, just as repeated experiences with objects that disappear help children understand that objects still exist even when they can no longer be seen.

Through this slow process of change children eventually arrive, at about 18 months or 2 years of age, at an understanding of the constancy of objects. They also acquire the ability to represent objects and events to themselves through images or with the few words in their vocabularies.

285

The preoperational period. During the preoperational period, which lasts from about age 2 until age 7, children discover still more important things about

BOX 9.1
The role of learning in infancy and childhood

Psychologists have now shown that most basic learning processes begin during the first days or weeks of life. Classical conditioning has been demonstrated in a 4-week-old baby (Brackbill, 1962), and for some kinds of behaviors, such as sucking, conditioning may occur somewhat earlier (Lipsitt, 1963). Classical conditioning continues to play an important role in child development, particularly in the development of "irrational" emotional reactions. For example, if a child were holding a carrot when suddenly frightened by a loud noise, it could develop a fear response to the carrot. Some aspects of toilet training (and other early training) may also include

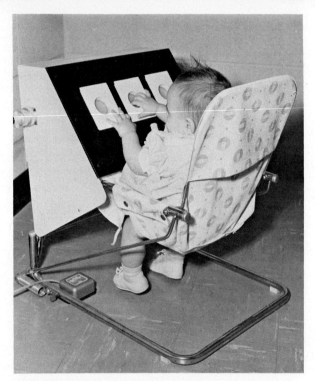

Psychologists have built ingenious apparatus to study the process of learning in infants. (Lewis L. Lipsett)

objects and events. If understanding the constancy of objects is one of the major achievements of the sensorimotor period, then understanding that objects can be classified and grouped is one of the major accomplishments of this period. In the early years of the preoperational period children group things on the basis of what can be done with them—things you can throw, things you can put in your mouth, things that mothers use, and so forth. By the end of the period children group things more systematically, often by color or shape.

Another shift during this period is a lessening of what Piaget calls *egocentrism*. Younger children are not able to anticipate how an object looks from the viewpoint of another person and fail to recognize

that another viewpoint is possible. At 2 or 3 they are locked inside their own perspective; what they experience is what exists. So, for example, if you were sitting across from a child at a table and you asked for a description of how the table looked from the child's side and then for a description of how the table looked from your side, the child would be unable to describe your view and would describe his or her view both times. Or suppose you gave the child a stick to hold with one end sharpened to a point and the other end covered with cotton, then asked the child to feel both ends and describe each feeling to you. If you held the soft end and gave the child the sharp-pointed end and asked the child what the pointed end felt like, the child would de-

classical conditioning. If a potty chair is repeatedly present when a child feels internal physiological signals for urination or defecation, then eventually merely the sight of the chair may trigger the response.

Instrumental or operant conditioning, however, is clearly of greater importance in a child's early development. There is an endless array of bits of information and behavior that may be learned or strengthened through reinforcement. The child learns that some things may be touched and that others may not; that there are some times of day when mommy pays attention and others when she does not; that eating nicely makes mommy happy, whereas throwing the chocolate pudding does not; and so forth. Some psychologists emphasize the importance of the development of secondary reinforcing properties by the mother and by other important people and events in the baby's life. Because the mother (or other major care giver) is so frequently associated with primary reinforcement—feeding—she gradually acquires some reinforcing properties of her own. From then on, what she wants or expresses approval of will be more likely to be elicited from the child. Others have suggested that physical contact

with the mother, her touching and cuddling, is innately rewarding to the child, so that there is no need for secondary reinforcement (Maccoby and Masters, 1970). In either case it is clear that human attention very rapidly (if not immediately) has reinforcing properties for the young child and that the child's behavior is controlled in part by the reinforcement contingencies around it.

Because of the variability in parents' behavior toward children, the most common pattern of reinforcement for a child to experience is some kind of partial or inconsistent reinforcement. Of course, some parents are more consistent than others, but some level of inconsistency is probably the rule rather than the exception.

Inconsistencies in reinforcement patterns make it difficult to predict behavior among children. This is not to say that the "laws of learning" do not apply, but merely that it is virtually impossible to know as much as one would need to about the specific reinforcement history of a single child.

Observational learning or modeling also occurs early in development. Children begin to imitate others very early in life, and they learn a whole range of skills and behaviors through observation.

scribe it accurately. But if you asked what your end felt like, the child would most likely say it felt sharp, just as his or her end did.

This inability to step outside of one's own perspective, or egocentrism, gradually weakens. As children enter the next, or concrete operations, period they begin to recognize that there are other points of view and can usually begin to describe things from someone else's perspective.

Concrete operational period. The third period, which runs from approximately age 7 to approximately age 12, marks a new series of events. Piaget suggests that at some time during this period children shift gears again to a still higher, more complex level of func-

tioning. They acquire a whole new set of skills, which Piaget calls operations. These involve the ability to understand that certain mental processes are reversible. For example, if two numbers are multiplied, the product can be divided by one of them to produce the other.

Children at this age can grasp the concept of conservation. They understand that objects have fundamental qualities that do not change even when their outward appearance changes. Younger children are still caught up by the outward changes, such as the change in shape of a ball of clay flattened into a pancake. Older children may realize that, "It looks different, but it's still the same amount," or that, "It's the same amount because you haven't added any-

287

This Piagetian task is a test for the ability to conserve liquids using variously shaped glasses. (Shelton, Monkmeyer)

thing or taken anything away," because they understand the operations of addition and subtraction. Or they may realize that, "This one is bigger this way, but thinner the other way, so it's the same," because they understand the fact that changes in two dimensions can complement one another.

At this age children can also grasp the concept of *serial ordering*. If you were to give a very young child a set of blocks that varied progressively in height and ask the child to put them in order, it would not be able to do it. A child in the concrete operational period could. At about age 7, children also come to understand the principle of *transitivity*; if they see, for example, that they are taller than Mary and that Mary is taller than Frank, then they understand that they are taller than Frank.

Older children grasp the principle of *class inclusion*. If you were to show children of different ages a bunch of flowers, most of which were daffodils and some of which were tulips, then ask them to name each kind and to label the whole bunch *flowers*, both preoperational and concrete operational children could perform the task. But if you were then to ask, "Are there more daffodils, or more flowers?" The younger children would say there are more daffodils—again being captured by the appearance, the fact that they see lots of daffodils—but the older

children would say there are more flowers. This is an instance of the principle of class inclusion, the notion that one class (in this case daffodils) is included in a larger class, in this case flowers, and that the included class is always smaller. Children in the concrete operational stage can also produce a *mental representation* of a series of actions, for example, drawing a map to show the route to school. A younger child might be able to lead the way to school but could not represent the route in a symbolic way.

Children in the concrete operations period (roughly grammar school age) can perform a great many complex kinds of analyses. They can group things several ways at once, they can reason inductively, they can see other people's perspectives, and they can begin to approach tasks systematically. They can begin to go beyond the surface appearance of objects or events and deal with underlying principles. But children of this age are still to some extent caught up in the concrete world. They are not yet able to think in the abstract. They can classify things in complex ways, but they must have the things before them to look at or to touch. In the next period they step back one more step from the concrete.

Formal operational period. Formal operations begin around age 11, although they begin much later for some children. During this period children become capable of *deductive* logic, or "if-then" reasoning. ("If this theory is true, then I ought to be able to observe. . . .") Most scientific logic is of this nature, and research hypotheses are very often the result of a chain of deductions from theory. Younger children, in the concrete operational period, can begin from observations and figure out some theory or system. But it is not until they are about 12 or 13 that they can reverse the process and go from the theory to something that ought to be seen, going beyond their own specific, concrete observations.

For several decades Piaget's account of cognitive development was openly discounted in the United States, where psychology had been dominated by behaviorists interested primarily in the external forces at work on a child. In the last decade or so, however, Piaget has been "discovered" by the American educational community and has had enormous influence on "open education" and related movements.

Piaget in a classroom at Geneva University, Switzerland. (Sirdofsky, EPA)

The role of individual differences

Even though there is consistency from one child to another, it is the sequence rather than the rate that seems consistent. Some children go through the process a great deal more slowly than others. Differences in richness or variety of experience may play a large role in differences of rate. Piaget talks about the environment as *aliment*, which means "food." He sees the environment as "food for thought," and the more balanced and nutritious the diet, the more rapidly and completely the child's intellectual skills grow. There is some evidence to support this idea. Children in institutions and those from poverty environments typically develop intellectual capabilities more slowly than do children from wealthier families. Investigators who have used Piaget's own tasks and problems to explore this theory have found that children from poverty backgrounds develop the concept of conservation perhaps a year later than do

middle-class children, and they develop advanced forms of classification somewhat later as well (Gaudia, 1972; Wei, Lavatelli, and Jones, 1971). But the sequence of development is highly consistent, even though the rate may vary, and this consistency of sequence has been found across cultures as well as across social class groups within our own culture (Ginsburg, 1972).

Cognitive development through the life span

Although there have been major advances in the study of thinking in childhood, psychologists have been slower to explore cognitive development later in life.

Although the pattern of results is far from clear, some research has been carried out on the cognitive abilities of older persons as reflected in their performance on intelligence tests. Scores on tests of verbal intelligence show little decline, at least up to

289

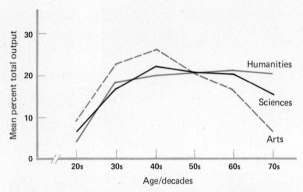

Figure 9.4 Percentage of total output as a function of age. The humanities, sciences, and arts are represented by several specific disciplines. (Data from Wayne Dennis, in Botwinick, 1967, Fig. 21.)

age 50. For superior subjects scores may even increase with age. Performance tests show greater decreases perhaps because of slowing reaction time and other central nervous system functions. Memory for newly acquired material may decline with age, but long-term memory seems largely unaffected. Total productivity for creative persons decreases after middle age, but the rate and timing of the decline differ in various disciplines. (See Figure 9.4.)

Among older individuals, those who function best intellectually tend to be those who are also in the best health. Some researchers have suggested that there is no decline in intellectual function until a *terminal drop* in intellectual function occurs in the period preceding death.

Language development
One of the most fascinating and delightful processes in human development is the acquisition of language. Over a two- or three-year period, from the age of about 18 months until the age of about 4 or $4\frac{1}{2}$, the child goes from an essentially nonlinguistic creature to one capable of communicating extraordinarily complex thoughts in understandable form. In the process, each child goes through a series of fairly clear stages.

This task is an immense one. Not only must children learn a vast number of words and the common meanings of each, but they must also learn how to put those words together into sentences, how to ask questions, how to state negatives, and so on. The precise way in which they accomplish this is not yet fully understood, but psychologists and linguists have mapped the process itself.

The sequence of language development
A baby begins to make sounds from the moment it is born. At first it makes crying sounds and little else. But within a few months it is making a few others, perhaps cooing. By 6 or 8 months of age the baby begins to put several sounds together, making what sound like syllables, such as *ba*. Very often such syllables are repeated over and over, a process that is called *babbling*. At about 1 year (give or take a few months) the baby utters its first word. Often, of course, this is not a word that appears in an adult's vocabulary; rather it is a sound or set of sounds that the child uses consistently to refer to a particular thing or event, such as *ba* to mean "bottle."

Over the next few months, from the age of 1 year to the age of about 18 months, the vocabulary grows slowly, a few words at a time. Most children have a vocabulary of about 50 words within six to eight months after they speak their first word. At the age of about 18 months to 2 years they speak their first "sentence," usually consisting of only two words. From this point on, change is very rapid. The child continues to increase its vocabulary at a rapidly accelerating pace; several hundred words may be added during each six-month period over the next few years. At the same time, the child's grammar grows rapidly, from the simplest two-word sentences, to three-word sentences, to the beginnings of questions and negations, and on to more complicated combinations.

Children seem to have a grammar all their own. They go through a stage in which they attach a *wh*-word (*why, who, where, when, what*) to the beginning of sentences, without changing the internal structure of the sentence:

"Why he play little tune?"
"Why you see seal?"
"Why it's resting now?"

This is a consistent system, but it is not one the child copies from anyone around it.

In addition, the stages in this development appear to be quite consistent from one child to the next, and even to some extent across languages. Children learning Russian, for example, appear to construct sentences with very similar grammatical features at about the same time as children learning English.

The whole process appears to be a creative one, rather than an imitative one. Very little that a child says is a direct imitation of something it has heard. Rather, it constructs its own sentences, using whatever grammatical form it has reached. There is some imitation, particularly for such remarks as *please* and *thank you*, but this constitutes a small portion of the child's language.

While the grammar is growing, the child's vocabulary and sense of the meanings of words grow too. Children's early words are of several kinds. They have words for people and objects, words about feelings and relationships (e.g., *please, no, yes, want, ouch*), and action words (e.g., *go, look, up*). What is missing in these early vocabularies is *superordinate words*. Two- to three-year-olds may have, for example, words for *cookie, grapes, milk, peas,* and other foods, but they are unlikely to have the word *food* in their vocabularies, or if they have it they are unlikely to use it in the general sense to include all the others. In this sense, then, the early vocabulary is *specific;* words tend to refer to particular objects or groups of objects (such as *chair, bed, bottle*). But even at this early age children do have a sense of classes of objects. Children with the word *chair* do use it to refer to several different chairs, rather than just one specific chair.

Explanation of language development

The intuitively obvious explanation of language development is that children are, in some sense, taught language, that they learn it through imitation of some sort. In some ways this is clearly true. Children, after all, learn the language they hear. Those growing up in the United States normally learn English. Children also learn to pronounce words in the way their parents pronounce them, and learn the specific grammar their parents use, even if it is not "proper" grammar.

But direct learning does not account for every aspect of language development. Studies of parents and children talking to one another have not revealed any significant amount of either imitation or direct teaching of language. Children do not usually imitate what they have just heard, and parents do

not usually correct the child's grammar. Parents do something called *expanding;* they change a child's simple sentence into a more complex adult sentence. (For example, "go to store" is turned into "Adam is going to the store.") However, it is not at all clear that this practice does anything to hasten the development of grammar.

Parents seem to reinforce the child's language for its "truth value" rather than for its grammatical correctness. If the child says, "I go store," the parent is likely to say, "Yes, we're going to the store," not, "No, that's not a good way of saying it," or, "We won't go to the store until you can say it properly." Parents respond, then, to the content of the child's language much more than to its form. If reinforcement were the only factor operating there would be no reason to expect that the form of the child's language would change under these conditions. But, of course, it does, regularly, and in a sequence that is highly similar from one child to another.

The fact that children's language is not the same as adult language, that it appears to have a grammar, a sense of its own, and that it changes in regular sequences is difficult to account for in any simply behavioral theory. Children do need to hear language spoken around them, and those that are talked to more do develop more quickly, but beyond that the role of both imitation and reinforcement seems to be minimal.

It is precisely because of the great regularity of the sequences in the child's developing language and the apparently "creative" aspect of the child's functioning in this area that many linguists and psychologists have approached the problem from a biological perspective. Their fundamental suggestion, which is not really yet a theory, is that children come into the world "programmed" to learn language (Chomsky, 1968). As the brain develops over the first year of the child's life, it reaches a state of readiness for language. The language that the child hears is presumably processed or analyzed in specific ways. In some sense the basic structure of language is built in, so that all children have to do is learn the specific language they hear.

Although this may seem like a very farfetched idea, there is some support of it. Human beings are "programmed" in other ways from birth. For example, when babies who are 1 or 2 days old look at such

Figure 9.5 Psychologists often study language development by observing and recording the speech of young children. In this picture, psychologist Jerome Bruner plays with a preschool child as he studies how children's speech develops and changes. (Ted Polumbaum)

figures as squares or triangles, they tend to look at the corners rather than at the figure generally or at the center. There is apparently a built-in strategy for scanning, for collecting information visually, so that there may also be a language-scanning strategy.

It is also true that languages all over the world have important basic features in common. They all have a way of making a negative and of asking questions, and they all have some relationship between a subject and a predicate. Perhaps these basic features of language are in some way built into organisms.

Some psychologists, such as Jerome Bruner, believe that even young children's interest is centered not in things but in people and speech is an essential tool in a social relationship. Children learn to speak not as a part of innate development but to relieve the stress they feel at being unable to communicate well in a social situation. (See Figure 9.5.)

SOCIALIZATION AND INTERPERSONAL RELATIONSHIPS

Socialization is the developmental process through which we fit into an organized way of life. Human animals become human beings and acquire a set of distinctive personal attributes, motives, and social behavior through learning by various methods—imitation, identification, reward, and punishment.

Although some similar patterns of development seem to occur across cultures, there are many noticeable differences. Contrast the two sets of photographs in Figure 9.6; they illustrate differences in behavior between siblings that result from different cultural emphases. It is easy to suppose that the social development of children in Western culture has been a relatively constant process for a long time. That this is not the case may be surprising. One historian's summary of these changes is illustrated by Box 9.2.

During recent decades Western culture has been heavily child oriented. It places great value on raising children well, providing them with a good education, and helping each child achieve her or his fullest potential. We see children as a separate group, unintegrated into adult society. In fact, the period of "childhood" has been steadily lengthening over the past decades, as the amount of training needed for basic jobs has increased. Until about the seventeenth century, once children were relatively mobile and independent—perhaps about the age of 7—they were expected to participate in the adult world. They spent time with adults, learned adult jobs, cared for younger siblings or neighbors, and were generally accepted into adult society. This same pattern still holds in many rural cultures. There may be a further initiation into adulthood at adolescence, but young

Figure 9.6 These photographs of children of tribes living in New Guinea (top) and Bali (bottom) were taken by anthropological researchers. They provide an example of the disparities in child behavior in societies that emphasize either affectionate or hostile sibling relationships. (Top photos by E. Richard Sorenson, courtesy National Anthropological Film Center, Smithsonian Institution. Bottom photos from G. Bateson and M. Mead, *Balinese Character,* The New York Academy of Sciences, New York, 1942.)

BOX 9.2
Modes of parent-child relations

The time periods of modes of parent-child relations reflect the adoption of different procedures by the most advanced part of the population in the most advanced countries. People in many countries still seem to be fixed in earlier historical modes. For example, we all recognize that some people still beat, kill, and sexually abuse children.

1. *Infanticidal mode* (antiquity to fourth century A.D.)

Until the fourth century A.D. the public did not consider infanticide wrong in either Greece or Rome.

Data obtained from periods as different as prehistoric times and the fourteenth century show a high ratio of males to females, which can be explained only through selective infanticide.

2. *Abandonment mode* (fourth to thirteenth century A.D.)

Christianity brought with it the idea that the child has a soul. Killing children outright then became less easy to rationalize, so that parents began to abandon their children by sending them to a wet nurse for the first years of their lives and later to a monastery or nunnery, foster family, or another household, where they became servants. This occurred even in wealthy families. Children were thought to be full of evil and to require beatings in order to be good.

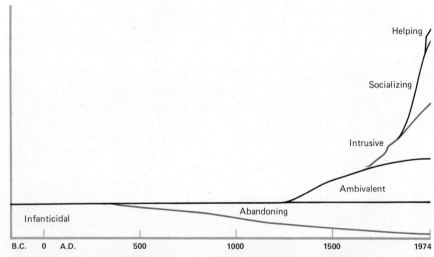

The evolution of child-rearing modes. (DeMause, 1974, p. 51.)

3. *Ambivalent mode* (fourteenth to seventeenth centuries)

In the fourteenth to seventeenth centuries the child was considered to be something like clay or plaster to be molded or beaten into shape. In the fourteenth century there was an increase in the number of treatises on child instruction. Bodily processes were influenced through the use of enemas and purges; external behavior was controlled by frequent and severe whippings and other physical punishment.

4. *Intrusive mode* (eighteenth century)

The eighteenth century marked a great change in parent-child relations. No longer were physical controls used so often. Parents tried to control their children by punishment involving threats and guilt. Toilet training was introduced and the use of enemas declined. These improvements in the level of care reduced infant mortality.

5. *Socializing mode* (nineteenth to mid-twentieth centuries)

In the nineteenth century child rearing began to emphasize training children rather than conquering them. Twentieth-century child rearing practices based on both psychoanalytic and behavioristic conceptions are examples of this approach.

6. *Helping mode* (mid-twentieth century)

In the helping mode parents and children have changed roles. The child knows best and the parents' job is to fulfill the child's needs. There is no attempt to discipline the child or to train it in "desirable" habits.

(Adapted from De Mause, 1974, pp. 50–53)

children are not set apart as a separate species, as is often true in our own society.

In reaction to the abuses of children in the factories of the nineteenth century, social reformers began to exert pressure to require education for all children. Toward the end of the century in the United States, concern about the socialization of the large number of immigrants and their children produced added pressure for universal and extended education.

The segregation by age through adolescence that has occurred in Western society is really a phenomenon of the last 100 years. The idea of adolescence was not "discovered" until the end of the nineteenth century, and not until the 1920s did the beginnings of the present youth culture emerge. There was a rapid increase in the proportion of the population that fell into the teenage–young-adult age range, and these people attended school for a much longer time, particularly in the United States. (See Figure 9.7.)

After World War II the desire for a return to normality and postwar economic prosperity produced a "baby boom" and the idea that the good life consisted of a suburban split-level house and a station wagon full of children.

During this era the child became a dominant figure in the culture. But by the late 1960s changes in women's roles, rapid inflation, and a decrease in expectations for an expanding economy shifted the emphasis away from the child again.

Psychologists have studied the process of socialization in many different areas. In this chapter we look at the effects of the socialization process in several areas of development—attachment, sex role development, and moral behavior. Another area affected by the socialization process is aggression, discussed in Chapter 2.

Attachment

The significance of early attachment

Freud and many of his followers, including Erik Erikson, Anna Freud, and Melanie Klein, emphasized the importance of the child's relationship with its mother (or other constant care giver) and tried to specify the important features this basic relationship should have in order to foster normal and healthy emotional and personal development. Much of the public interest in and concern about the effect of

BOX 9.3

A psychological frontier: The American family in transition— the impact on a child's development

American society still behaves as if most children in the United States grew up in stable, child-centered families with two parents and a mother who cares for the children while the father provides for them.

Statistics show that this stereotype is not true. The accompanying figure illustrates the rapid increase in employment for married mothers who are living with their husbands. Notice especially the sharp increase in the number of working mothers with young children. The total number of mothers employed (including single parents) is much higher. In addition, in 1974, one out of every six children under 18 years of age was living in a single-parent family (about 1 percent of these families were headed by males, the rest were headed by females; Bronfenbrenner, 1975). Most of these one-parent families were found in the low-income group and in urban areas.

American families may also be growing less child centered. Surveys show that couples who have no children rate themselves as happier than those who do. Surveys also show less interest in children as a means of self-fulfillment.

The feminist movement has contributed to the breakdown of stereotypes about the American family by giving greater acceptance to working women and to childless women.

During the rapid inflation of the early 1970s many potential parents cited the cost factor as primary in their decision about family size.

What effects do these changes in the family have on the children who live in them? What kinds of child care should be provided and by whom? How does life in a single-parent female-headed family affect a child's development? Some experts are concerned that there is already too much separation of age groups in American society. Will institutionalized child care, if that is the solution adopted, further isolate children from the "real world" of relationships? Will the lengthened period of school attendance, economic dependence, and a decrease in emphasis on family life make children's lives empty of purpose? Will they feel left out of society? Is the child of the 1980s going to live as an "expensive consumer item" for some 20 years rather than as an active part of society? How will these changes affect the course of child development?

The effect of changing family configurations on diverse dimensions of behavior was shown by Robert Zajonc (1976) in a recent investigation on Scholastic Aptitude Test scores. Between 1962 and 1975, average Scholastic Aptitude Test scores of high school seniors dropped from 490 to 450. Zajonc thought family size and configuration might be involved in this seeming decline in academic aptitude and found that:

1. Intellectual performance increases with decreasing family size.
2. When the intervals between successive births are

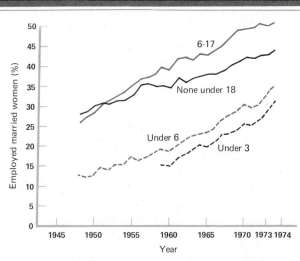

This graph shows the change in the period from 1948 to 1973 in the percent of employed married women with children. The percentages are reported separately for women with children in four different age categories. If unmarried, divorced, separated, and widowed mothers had been included, the percentages would be much higher. (Based on Bronfenbrenner, 1975, p. 440.)

relatively short, earlier-born perform better than later-born children.

3. Twins, other multiple-birth children, and the last child in a family have relatively low test scores. (When the last child born in a family is widely separated in age from other siblings, this relatively poor performance tends to disappear.)

Zajonc believes that within a family the intellectual growth of every member is dependent on that of all the others, and that the rate of this growth depends on the family configuration. In 1947, 42 percent of all births were first children. In 1962 only 27 percent were first children. By 1975 the percentage of first-borns had returned to the 1947 level. Zajonc believes that as a result of this return to high percentages of first-borns, by the 1980s Scholastic Aptitude Test scores will increase significantly.

institutional upbringing on children arose from the fear that a child who did not have a single caretaker would be deprived of the essential conditions for healthy emotional development. But despite these concerns and interests, relatively little systematic research work on early attachments was done until the past 10 or 15 years.

Attachment may be defined as the tendency of an infant during the first two years of life to be most receptive to being cared for and approached by a certain person or several persons. The infant is also less afraid of the environment while in the company of these people than when it is away from them.

At first the explanations of attachment focused on the personal experiences with the caretaker, especially on the feeding of the infant, as the reason for the development of attachment. Two lines of experimental work, that of Harry Harlow and his colleagues and that of such ethologists as Konrad Lorenz, who developed the concept of *imprinting*, suggested that this explanation was too simple.

Harlow, in a long series of experiments with infant monkeys, showed that a number of factors were related to the development of attachment. When monkeys live in the wild, a young monkey spends a great deal of time clinging to the mother as she moves about. Harlow found that the satisfaction of clinging seemed more important in building a relationship than did the satisfaction of being fed. When he reared a young monkey in a cage with two objects that served as substitute mothers—one covered with terry cloth, the other constructed only of wire mesh—the young monkey, if frightened, chose to run to the terry cloth figure, to which it could cling, instead of to the wire mesh figure, from which it was fed. (See Figure 9.8.) The clinging response, which has survival value when monkeys live freely, is still important in very different conditions.

Ethologists (zoologists who study the naturally occurring behavior of animals in natural settings) have observed attachment behavior they call *imprinting*. If during a certain crucial period of development a young animal sees a moving object, it shows attachment for the object by continuing to follow it for some time. Ordinarily, the baby animal learns to follow its mother, but ethologists have shown that if a human being or an object moves past the animal during this crucial period, imprinting on

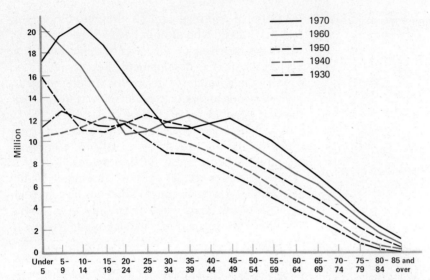

Figure 9.7 U.S. population by 5-year age groups in 1930, 1940, 1950, 1960 and 1970. This graph shows that there were more people in the 10 to 14 age group in 1970 than in any other age group in the population. In ten years these same individuals will be 20 to 24 years old, still the largest age group in the population. The number of 10 to 14 year olds in 1980 will be slightly more than 17 million compared to the more than 20 million in the group 10 years earlier. As their numbers change, the influence of teen agers on the society may change also. (Porter, 1976, p. 91.)

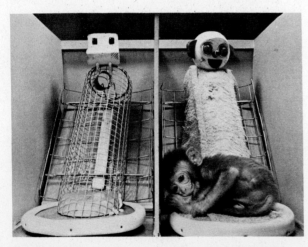

Figure 9.8 Although the young monkey receives its food from the wire mother on the left, it still runs to the cloth-covered mother on the right when a frightening event occurs. The preference for the cloth mother seems related to the clinging response that young monkeys show. (H. F. Harlow, University of Wisconsin Primate Laboratory)

this person or thing may result. The response of following the mother is a practical one that helps a young animal survive. Some psychologists think that attachment behavior in human infants has the same practical result; it helps to keep the infant near its caretaker.

In the early 1960s, two longitudinal studies of infants in two different cultures were conducted that showed a very definite developmental pattern in the growth of the attachment between mother and child that extended across cultures (Ainsworth, 1963; Schaffer and Emerson, 1964).

The first phase, from birth until approximately 6 or 7 months, was labeled *indiscriminate attachment.* The baby during this period shows many social behaviors, such as smiling, cuddling, and vocalization, but these do not seem to be directed only at the mother rather than to other family members or strangers. The child is usually happy to be picked up, but it does not seem to matter who does it. At about 6 or 7 months the pattern changes and the first *specific attachment* is formed. That is, babies begin to be selective; they smile more for the mother, cuddle more for her, hold out their arms to be picked up by her, and may reject similar approaches by strangers or semistrangers. This specific attachment may become extremely strong, and the child may cling to the mother or care giver, show great distress when she leaves, and crawl vigorously toward her when she returns. At about 8 months children ordinarily show some fear of strangers, and cry when one approaches. By about 1 year of age the single attachment begins to spread to a series of separate attachments. Infants show pleasure around several people, perhaps the father, a relative, or a frequent babysitter. The fear of strangers gradually wanes, and by 18 months most of the infants observed in these two studies showed some attachment to at least two people, often many more.

Maccoby and Feldman (1972) observed a group of children from age 2 to until they were 3 in a series of standardized situations with their mothers. The children at age 2 were more disturbed when their mothers left and were less likely to interact in a friendly way with strangers, but they would approach strangers and interact with them if their mothers were present. At age 3 these same children were friendly and outgoing toward strangers, even when their mothers were not present. Again, the patterns of behavior were very similar for an American sample and for a group of children and mothers living on a kibbutz in Israel.

Overall, then, children go from a period of diffuse attachment to a period of intense individual attachment, followed by a gradual widening of attachment and greater comfort with strangers. However, researchers studying the process of attachment have observed some individual differences along these dimensions. For example, some babies never develop a single strong attachment; they move directly from diffuse attachment to strong multiple attachment. There is some suggestion in both the Ainsworth and the Schaffer and Emerson studies that this is more likely to happen with infants who have multiple caretakers (for example, a mother and a babysitter) from very early in life.

It has been suggested that among those babies who do show strong individual attachments, some are "securely" and others "insecurely" attached, pre-

sumably because of differences in the pattern of early care. For example, Mary Ainsworth and her associates (Ainsworth, Bell, and Stayton, 1972) found that positive, apparently secure attachments—as evidenced by the child's showing pleasure at being held, following the mother, and seldom crying—occurred in families in which mothers picked up the child fairly infrequently, but when they did pick it up, held and cuddled it for a long time in an affectionate manner. These mothers apparently enjoyed holding their babies and picked them up at times other than for feeding and diapering. Mothers whose babies were more fussy about being picked up and fussier about being put down were likely to be less affectionate with their babies and were more likely to pick the baby up in a way that interfered with its activities. But before we leap to the conclusion that the mother's behavior is the sole cause of a child's secure or insecure attachment, we should note this important caution, expressed well by researcher Leon Yarrow:

> We should also recognize that environmental influences cannot be seen as a simple antecedent-consequent relationship; rather, there is an interaction between the child's characteristics and the kinds of stimulation he receives. Some characteristics of the child are more likely to elicit varied social stimulation and higher levels of responsiveness from others. For instance, alert, active infants who smile, vocalize, and make approach movements toward their mothers are apt to receive more attention than infants who are quiet and apathetic and who show little responsiveness. (Yarrow, 1972, pp. 91–92)

Several studies have found that babies are markedly different from the earliest days of life in mood, adaptability, approach-withdrawal tendencies, and intensity of reaction to stimuli. Not only do mothers bring their patterns of behavior to their interaction with infants, but infants bring their own temperamental characteristics to the relationship.

Later patterns of attachment

There is evidence that by age 3, children are more willing to be separated from their mothers and are more comfortable with strangers. Observations of children in nursery school settings confirm these conclusions and suggest that there is also a shift at

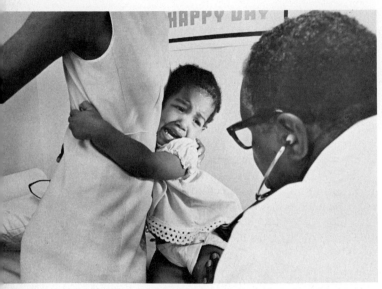

By age three children are willing to be separated from their mothers in most situations; the doctor's office may provoke a less mature response. (Higgins, Photo Researchers)

about this age toward much greater interest in relationship with peers. Children between the ages of 3 and 4 are more independent of their teachers and other adults, less clinging, more likely to seek approval than physical contact, and more likely to spend the majority of their time playing with other children. But children in this age range do differ from one another on these dimensions, and some 3- and 4-year-olds do still show a less mature pattern of seeking to be near adults.

From school age onward, children's interpersonal energies are increasingly devoted to peers rather than to adults. During the elementary school years peer groups usually consist of children of the same sex. During adolescence this trend gradually changes to one of heterosexual groups, and finally to the pairing of individual boys and girls into couples.

Sex role development

One aspect of the child's development of self-image is discovery of his or her own sex and sex role. By about age 5 or 6 children know their names, have some sense of their bodies and where they start and stop, and have some feeling for their own characteristics, abilities, and weaknesses. The development of

sexual identity plays an important part in these concepts.

There are fairly distinct developmental stages. A 3-year-old knows the labels *boy* and *girl*, and applies the correct label to himself or herself, but is probably not capable of applying these labels correctly to others. The generalization of the concepts *boy* and *girl* does not occur until about age 4. At that age children can usually classify people into male and female and can use the correct pronouns when talking to or about people. At this same age children begin to show some preference for toys stereotypic of their sex (e.g., trucks for boys, dolls for girls), but 4-year-olds do not yet realize that their boyness or girlness is a permanent feature. A child of this age is very likely to think that it will be possible to change from a boy to a girl, or vice versa, perhaps by changing clothes.

It is only at about age 5 or 6 that children typically understand the permanent nature of gender and the relationship between genital differences and gender classifications.

This developmental progression is not faster in families that permit or encourage nudity, nor is it more rapid in families in which there is extensive discussion of physical differences. However, bright children go through the whole sequence somewhat faster than do less bright children, and they arrive at a full understanding of their sexual identity perhaps a year earlier.

Behaviorists argue that children are trained directly to adopt appropriate sex roles, both through reinforcement of "correct" behaviors and through reinforcement for imitating the same-sex parent. Boys are rewarded directly with praise or attention for playing with trucks, for being a little tough, and for imitating their fathers. Girls are reinforced for imitating their mothers and for adopting appropriate female attitudes and behaviors in their play and other activities. Both sexes, the behaviorists say, learn their appropriate roles through observational learning (observing the same-sex parent and others of the same sex) and through direct reinforcement.

From the cognitive perspective, the child's understanding of his or her own sexuality is a cognitive accomplishment. *Male* and *female*, *boy* and *girl* are concepts, not unlike the concepts *big*, *little*, *happy*, *sad*, and so forth. Children during the preschool years gradually develop broadened and more consist-

300

ent concepts in all these areas as the result of repeated experiences with objects and extensive opportunity to experiment and put labels on things. Parents or others may play some role in this by providing appropriate labels for objects, but the process of developing concepts occurs inside the child. It has been suggested that the realization that maleness and femaleness are constants is equivalent to the realization, which occurs at about the same age, that objects are constant in various ways as well; this quality Piaget calls *conservation*. Only after the concepts of *male* and *female* have developed do children begin to imitate adults of the same sex.

In contrast to the cognitive view, the behaviorist sees the child's sex role identity built up slowly over many years, when the child is systematically trained to perform "male" or "female" behaviors. The concepts of *maleness* and *femaleness* presumably grow out of these experiences.

There is some research support for both views; clearly, children do imitate models, and they can be reinforced for imitating some models and not others. At the same time, it is only at about age 4 or 5 that they begin to show a preference for toys that are stereotypically acceptable for their own sex. If systematic training had begun earlier, social learning theory suggests that toy preferences should be shaped along sex role lines somewhat earlier as well, but this does not occur. However, bright children find their mature sex role earlier than do less bright children. This seems to support the cognitive view (Kohlberg and Zigler, 1967). Both social learning and cognitive theorists agree on the important role of observational learning; they differ in their opinions of the point in the sequence at which it becomes most important.

A third view of the development of sex roles has been offered by Freud and others who take a psychoanalytic perspective. Freud proposed the concept of identification to account for the development of appropriate sex roles. He suggested a series of psychosexual stages, beginning with the oral stage during earliest infancy, followed by the anal stage at about age 2, and in turn followed by the phallic stage at about age 4 or 5. It is during the phallic stage, Freud thought, that the Oedipal crisis occurs: The boy, in simple terms, desires his mother and fears his father, particularly his father's fantasized ability to castrate

"You call it 'taking out the garbage', I call it rotten sexist role playing!"
(Jacques Rupp, *The Seattle Times*)

him. The resolution of this conflict occurs through the process of identification. The boy "incorporates" the father, and tries to match his own appearance, behavior, and attitudes to his father's. By becoming as like his father (or rather, as like the internal image of his father) as he can, the boy deals with his fear and at the same time thinks he is making himself as desirable as possible to his mother.

For a girl the process is somewhat different. Current psychoanalytic interpretations of the female Oedipal crisis emphasize the girl's fear not of the mother's power, but of the loss of her mother's love. It is this fear that the girl resolves through identification with her mother.

In all views, particularly the psychoanalytic and cognitive, the period of time around age 5 or 6 is seen as crucial for the development of the child's sex role identity, and observational and experimental evidence certainly bears out this emphasis. At about this age the child discovers the permanency of gen-

301

der, and at about this age clear preferences of boyish or girlish toys and games develop. Some of the sex role concepts of both children and adults are inaccurate. These, called sex role stereotypes, are discussed in Chapter 17.

Moral development

Parents have been concerned over the centuries with their children's moral training. They expect children not only to know what is right and wrong, but also to be able to follow the rules for good or appropriate behavior. But how do children learn such rules? And how do they control the impulse to do "bad" things? Both psychoanalytic and social learning theorists have been concerned with these questions.

Cognitive theorists have approached the problem somewhat differently. They focus not on how the child learns specific rules about right and wrong, but on how the child makes a judgment about what sorts of things may be right or wrong. They are concerned with the intellectual, or cognitive, component of moral behavior.

The difference between these three aspects of moral behavior—rules, the self-control to follow those rules, and moral judgments—may be illustrated with an example. Ask a young child of about 5 or 6 the following question: "Which is worse, knocking accidentally against a table and breaking ten cups and saucers or throwing your mother's favorite cup and saucer onto the floor and breaking it because you are mad at her?" The child would have no difficulty telling you that it is worse to break ten cups and saucers than just one, because breaking more things is worse. By about age 10 or 11, children take intent into account and say that it is worse to throw down the single cup and saucer because that was on purpose and the other was an accident. In both cases the rule is the same, but the basis on which the judgment of wrongness or rightness is made changes with age.

Distinctions among rules, self-control, and judgments are important, because they help make sense out of the differences among the theoretical perspectives. Researchers and theorists from several perspectives have asked different kinds of questions and looked at different aspects of developing morality. Each, then, may have something unique to contribute to our understanding of the child's moral growth.

Psychoanalytic perspectives

In Freudian theory the identification process is seen as the major source of moral rules. In the process of "incorporating" the parent of the same sex, the child adopts the parent's rules along with attitudes and behaviors. The "parent within you," which Freud calls the *superego* (roughly equivalent to the common meaning of the word *conscience*), acts as a kind of moral judge. When children do something that conforms to their internal rules, they are pleased with themselves; when they disobey those internal rules, they feel *guilt*, which is a kind of self-punishment.

The self-control to follow the rules of the superego comes from a different part of the personality, the *ego*. As we pointed out earlier, Freud thought that the ego developed in response to the demands of the environment. In order to obtain the greatest pleasure, children must learn how to plan, organize their behavior, wait for the appropriate moment to ask, and so forth. These are all ego skills, as is the ability to *inhibit* behavior.

Freud's formulation suggests a number of hypotheses. First, children's moral rules should not change much past the age of 5 or 6, when the identification process takes place. What is thought of as right and wrong should be fixed at that age. Second, delinquents or others who behave "immorally" could have either a weak superego, a weak ego, or both. Delinquent children may have a good set of internalized rules but simply be unable to follow them, or the children may have a set of internalized rules that conflict with the rules of society. Still others may have very weak or underdeveloped superegos without a clear set of rules. Clinicians and researchers who have worked with or studied delinquents agree that there are, in fact, several types, just as one would predict from Freudian theory.

Social learning and behavioristic perspectives

Several different explanations of moral behavior have been offered by behavioristic theorists. One of these suggested that repeated punishment for a particular action eventually leads to a kind of anticipation of punishment (Mowrer, 1960). Suppose a child hits its mother several times and each time is punished for it. Eventually, the anxiety associated with the punishment would become associated with the

302

act of hitting itself. When the child thought of hitting her, it would become so anxious that it would stop the hitting action. This would be a learned avoidance reaction. In this view moral rules are merely a collection of learned avoidance reactions. More recently, it has been shown that children do indeed learn to avoid behaving badly through punishment, but the effect is greatest if the punishment occurs at the very beginning of the child's misbehavior (Aronfreed and Reber, 1965).

A different behavioristic approach to the development of moral behavior stresses that many aspects are learned through modeling. A number of studies have shown that children can learn a whole range of moral behaviors through imitation; they can observe adults regretting their own bad behavior, they can hear moral judgments being made, they can watch parents or other adults setting high standards for their own behavior, and so on.

A number of social learning researchers believe that we need not use the concept of an internalized rule to account for moral behavior. We observe that children do or do not adopt behaviors acceptable to their family or to society. These behaviors can be acquired through observational learning, in much the same way that a child learns aggression from television, or learns any other behavioral pattern.

Research on the antecedents of moral behavior suggests that children whose parents explain why something is wrong or right are likely to have children with the most consistently "moral" behavior. Parents who consistently punish wrong behavior and those that threaten withdrawal of love are not as successful in producing children who are able to resist temptation or refrain from cheating or lying (Hoffman, 1970). Although this finding does not provide direct support for the social learning view, explanations of the reasons for good behavior can be thought of as a kind of verbal modeling. Such parents may provide consistent behavioral models as well.

Cognitive perspectives

Cognitive researchers approach the whole problem from a different angle. They are not particularly interested in the specific content of a child's morality—the particular things that the child considers right and wrong—but in the ways in which its thinking about right and wrong changes with age. A

child may think that lying is "bad" and may not change its mind about this over the years from age 5 to 15, but the conception of what lying is and when it may be justifiable may change over this period of time.

Piaget's theory of development grew to a considerable extent out of a clinical method in which he talked and played at length with individual children. In the following conversation Piaget discusses lies with a 6-year-old boy:

Piaget: Do you know what a lie is?
Clai: It's when you say what isn't true.
Piaget: Is $2 + 2 = 5$ a lie?
Clai: Yes, it's a lie.
Piaget: Why?
Clai: Because it isn't right.
Piaget: Did the boy who said that $2 + 2 = 5$ know it wasn't right, or did he make a mistake?
Clai: He made a mistake.
Piaget: Then if he made a mistake, did he tell a lie or not?
Clai: Yes, he told a lie.
Piaget: A naughty one?
Clai: Not very.
Piaget: You see this gentleman (*a student*)?
Clai: Yes.
Piaget: How old do you think he is?
Clai: Thirty.
Piaget: I would say 28. (*The student says he is really 36.*)
Piaget: Have we both told a lie?
Clai: Yes, both lies.
Piaget: Naughty ones?
Clai: Not so very naughty.
Piaget: Which is the naughtiest, yours or mine, or are they both the same?
Clai: Yours is the naughtiest because the difference is biggest.
Piaget: Is it a lie, or did we just make a mistake?
Clai: We made a mistake.
Piaget: Is it a lie all the same, or not?
Clai: Yes, it's a lie.
(Piaget, 1932, p. 143)

Studies of children's moral judgments over the school age years suggest that there are, in fact, systematic changes in the child's basis for making decisions about right and wrong. One of the shifts, as mentioned earlier, is from judging wrongness by the absolute amount of harm or damage to judging it by the intention of the wrongdoer. This is a cognitive change, not a change in the context of the moral rules.

303

Another shift is from judgments based on fixed rules to judgments based on general principles. Children of 10 or 12, for example, are likely to think that if something is against the law, it is automatically wrong. Older children see laws as less absolute; they try to decide whether something is wrong on the basis of whether it violates some basic principle, such as the importance of human life.

Lawrence Kohlberg (1964) described a series of stages in the development of moral judgments that are at least partially linked to the child's general level of cognitive development. Children who progress rapidly in their cognitive growth are somewhat more likely to have a more advanced sense of moral judgment, although the link is not perfect. Kohlberg believes that there are three levels of moral development (each with sublevels):

1. *The preconventional level.* The child's moral behavior is based on the likelihood of punishment and on absolute standards laid down by authority figures.
2. *The conventional level.* Although the consequences of actions are still important, the child's moral judgments are based to an important degree on the norms and expectations of a group (family, school, neighborhood) to which he or she belongs.
3. *The postconventional level.* At this level (usually early adulthood), personal moral values come to the fore and the individual's behavior is influenced by ethical standards of his or her own.

Kohlberg's classification system has extended Piaget's concepts to an older group and makes it possible to compare levels of moral judgments among cultures. These are the kinds of problems Kohlberg presents when he studies the moral judgment of adolescents.

On the battlefield, an officer orders a retreat because of heavy enemy attack. A bridge should be blown up behind the troops before they retreat. Whoever is sent to blow up this bridge will amost certainly be killed. The officer knows this but he also knows that he is the best person to lead the retreat. What should he do?

A man's wife is almost certain to die without a certain drug. The druggist who invented the drug won't sell it to the husband except at a very high price, more than the husband can possibly pay. He will not consider the possibility of receiving part of the money later. Should the husband steal the drug to save his wife's life? (Kohlberg, 1964)

Because cognitive and social learning theorists often talk about different aspects of the problem of moral judgments, it is quite possible that both points of view are right to some extent. Children may learn specific rules about right and wrong through modeling (or perhaps through identification), but those rules may also go through the kinds of cognitive modifications Kohlberg suggests.

Social development as a lifelong process

It is important to remember that the social development process continues throughout life and affects an individual's status in society and the roles he or she plays. In young adulthood the change to an independent status and new responsibilities may be difficult and pose interpersonal problems. The roles of spouse and parent call for new ways of adapting. Adjusting to children leaving home or to the peaking of career prospects also requires change. Finally, living with the physical problems associated with age and dealing with the idea of one's own mortality requires a monumental adjustment.

Social development during childhood does not adequately prepare individuals for all the roles they may need to play in the future. If children are reared in a subgroup of society, they may not be prepared for the role demands of a larger group. Sometimes society provides additional means of social development, such as adult education or training programs. Sometimes individuals must be resocialized because their knowledge of one or more social roles is incorrect rather than incomplete. These people may be hardened criminals or simply middle-class neurotics.

SOME CONCLUDING THOUGHTS

In talking about development we have placed heavy emphasis on general trends, statements that are true for development as a whole. Of course, there are very large individual differences in the course of human development as well, in intellective functioning, social behavior, temperament, personality, and other aspects of our lives.

Early interest in developmental psychology was stimulated by the process of biological development as it related to the concept of evolution. Later, interest in intellectual development was encouraged by practical problems associated with children in an urbanized society and the expansion of public education.

One of the controversies that dominated the 1920s and 1930s that still arises from time to time concerns the ways in which environmental and biophysical factors influence behavior—the "nature-nurture" question. Thousands of studies have been conducted on different aspects of this question, but although some information has been gained, many answers remain unclear. Most researchers now acknowledge that environment interacts with heredity and they seek to study the influences of each rather than debating the question in an either-or manner. (See Chapter 14.)

At present, the major theoretical argument within the field of developmental psychology lies between the behavioristic and the cognitive perspectives. But they need not be thought of as either-or alternatives. The underlying flow of development may indeed follow consistent sequences, arising both from maturational changes and from the kind of logical step-by-step discoveries that Piaget suggests. The underlying bodily structures and the child's underlying logic, its way of approaching problems and its manner of exploring the environment, may develop sequentially. But at the same time, the child's specific behaviors, its attachment or dependency, its competence or independence, its sense of self-worth, its moral behavior may all be determined or affected by the models around it, and by specific patterns of reward and punishment it encounters. To be sure, these two perspectives do not yet live comfortably together, but over the next decades theorists and researchers in developmental psychology may find that they can be combined in helpful ways. If relevant biophysical factors can be integrated into this framework, a long step will have been taken toward a truly comprehensive developmental psychology.

SUMMARY

1. Information from the study of psychological development has been used in many practical ways: to help parents know what to expect of their children at certain ages, to aid in educational and social service planning, and to provide information for court decisions about such varying matters as racial integration and child custody.

2. Although development occurs throughout life, the most rapid development occurs early in life. At this time the relationship between biological development and the environment is easy to see. Development later in life is important too. Little is known as yet about the development process in adulthood and in later life.

3. Development can be studied by the *longitudinal method* (following the same individual or group as they develop) or by the *cross-sectional method* (comparing groups at different stages of development.)

4. Physical development is based on a combination of heredity, the maturation process, and the effect of hormones secreted by the individual. The process of development follows a regular pattern. This is true even though the environment, both before and after birth, can influence development and the rate of development can vary from one individual to another.

5. Jean Piaget's theories about the development of thinking in children are currently influencing not only cognitive theorists but behavioral theorists as well. According to Piaget, the child's cognitive development takes place in four distinct stages: the sensorimotor, the preoperational, the concrete operational, and the formal operational periods. Interaction of the child with the environment helps the child find new ways to classify ideas and to move from one stage to another.

6. Theorists disagree on the process by which children learn language. Learning by imitation seems logical but close observation shows that children do not imitate adult

305

speech but instead progress through a series of speech patterns. This regularity in language development has led to the idea that the basic structure of language is "built in" to the child and appears as it matures.

7. We fit into an organized way of life through the process of socialization. The culture in which a child is brought up is a strong force in determining the social behavior of the child as it grows. Socialization affects many areas of development, such as attachment, moral behavior, and sex role development.

8. Attachment, the tendency of an infant to be most receptive to care from one or several particular people and to turn to the same people when frightened, has been studied from several theoretical viewpoints. An understanding of its importance is necessary to make intelligent decisions about such questions as the effect of day care on young children.

9. Like other aspects of development, sex role development shows fairly distinct stages which are related to age. Each of the four theoretical views explains some aspects of sex role development, but none can deal with it best in all respects.

10. Moral sense, the concept of what behavior is "right" and what is "wrong," seems to develop in stages as the child grows older, just as do other kinds of thinking and behavior.

11. Developmental psychology emphasizes the patterns seen as children grow. Although individual characteristics and how people differ are important to all psychologists, the developmental viewpoint reminds us of the importance of the regularities and patterns of growth and change in understanding human behavior.

Suggested readings

The following three books provide reviews of research and theory concerning human development:

Bee, H. *The developing child.* New York: Harper & Row, Publishers, 1975.

Liebert, R. M., Poulos, R. W., & Strauss, G. D. *Development psychology.* Englewood Cliff, N.J.: Prentice-Hall, Inc., 1974.

Mussen, P. H., Conger, J. J., & Kagan, J. *Child development and personality.* New York: Harper & Row, Publishers, 1974.

The following books discuss particular aspects of the development process:

Dale, P. S. *Language development: Structure and function.* (2nd ed.) Hinsdale, Ill.: The Dryden Press, Inc., 1976. Offers an up-to-date review of the development of language and thought.

Kimmel, D. C. *Adulthood and aging.* New York: John Wiley & Sons, Inc., 1974. Reviews the psychological, social, and physiological aspects of the postadolescent years.

Maccoby, E. E. & Jacklin, C. N. *The psychology of sex differences.* Stanford, Calif.: Stanford University Press, 1974. This is the most comprehensive survey of sex differences available.

Stevenson, H. W. *Children's learning.* New York: Appleton-Century-Crofts, 1972. Contains an authoritative survey of the role played by learning in the development of children.

Chapter 10

Motivation, Emotion, and Stress

(Wide World)

The two students had worked hard on their experiment. When Professor Muller mentioned that one of the pieces of research required for his psychology laboratory course would be a joint project, Sheri Frank and Bob Grayson leaped at the opportunity to work together. Not only did they know and like each other, but they had talked about human memory many times and wanted to try out some of their ideas in the laboratory.

They had spent hours planning the experiment, and a still greater number running the subjects. One reason they were especially excited about the research was an offhand comment Professor Muller had made about the possibility that one or two of the projects might be good enough for presentation at the state psychological association convention. They felt sure their experiment might answer a few important questions and had given some thought to how the results could most effectively be written up.

"I can't believe we didn't get any of the results we predicted," said Bob. "Not only didn't we get what we wanted, we didn't get anything—not even a result in the opposite direction. Just a bunch of random scores."

"It hadn't occurred to me till now how high our hopes were for this project," said Sheri. "It's embarrassing, but true that we've gotten nothing. You might say we've failed."

"Even worse, Muller might say we failed," Bob thought out loud. "Wouldn't that be nice! The convention's out, but I'm not even sure how to write up the mess without seeming like a fool. It meant so much to me. Now I don't have any appetite and feel tense. My hands have felt sweaty all day. Besides that I really can't think straight enough to organize the write-up."

Sheri felt sorry for Bob. She felt terrible too, but the disaster didn't seem quite the disaster to her that it did to Bob. "Look, Muller knows that every experiment doesn't work on the first attempt. He even mentioned how many studies Skinner had to do before he got the bar in that box just right. Let's make a list of what might have produced the results we got. That way we can suggest some next steps in our report. If he thought one of them was reasonable, we might be able to do an independent project on it for him next term."

Like most human predicaments, much could be said about this situation. A few of its elements are of particular psychological interest. First of all, it seems evident that Bob and Sheri were engaged in an activity that meant a good deal to them. Inherent interest and the possibility of participating in a professional meeting, together with a desire to please their instructor, contributed to its importance. Bob and Sheri were highly motivated students.

Motivation is a general term referring to forces regulating goal-seeking behavior and the quest for incentives. A person might be motivated either because of situational demands or because of subjective values, needs, and desires. Often these two determinants combine, as in the hero who struggles feverishly to untie his sweetheart who was tied to the railroad tracks by the villain. The hero would, of course, strive mightily to save the life of anyone in such danger, but his loved one is not just anyone, so his motivation is even greater.

A calm, relaxed, and contented feeling is not characteristic of situations in which goal-seeking behavior plays an important role. The motivated individual usually shows several signs of emotion. *Emotions* are states of the person in which feelings and sentiments express themselves. Although each of us has a general impression of what emotions are, they pose difficulties for the psychological researcher. One reason for this is that emotions are private experiences and the psychologist must depend at least partly on the person's description of his or her feelings. Furthermore, individuals differ in their emotional reactions to the same situation. Both Bob and Sheri seem to have been highly motivated, but Bob seemed to react more emotionally than did Sheri. This showed up not only in what Bob said about his state of mind, but in his physiological reactions (sweaty palms) as well.

Motivational and emotional states are closely linked with a third concept, *stress*, which refers to the person's perception of a situation as demanding, challenging, and requiring some sort of response. Both Bob and Sheri experienced stress when they discovered that the experiment had yielded results that were not significant. Whereas Bob dealt with this setback in a rather emotional way and with some degree of dread, Sheri reacted in a planful, controlled manner. Although it is true that, "Where there's life, there's stress," it is also true that certain reactions to stress are more adaptive than others.

This chapter deals with the topics of motivation, emotion, and stress. Our goal is to understand human behavior better in the presence of challenges either imposed or created by us.

MOTIVATION

In the typical television courtroom drama the prosecuting attorney must attempt to establish that the defendant had a clear motive for committing the crime. In fact, the jury's conclusions as to the motivation behind the defendant's action may determine whether he or she will be convicted of murder or the much less serious charge of manslaughter.

We often use motivation to explain our own actions. For example, we might say about a successful tennis match, "I was really up for it. I really wanted to win." Or if we received a low grade in a course, we might say, "Somehow I just wasn't motivated for that course. I didn't care enough to study."

Concepts of motivation attempt to answer the question "Why?" about an action. Why do we choose one activity rather than another? Why do different people respond in different ways to the same event? Of course, we cannot really observe internal motives directly. They are constructs that we must infer on the basis of observable situations and responses.

Not all behavior can be explained in terms of motives. Much of it is better explained in terms of maturation or learning, or in terms of situational cues. Psychologists generally use motivation to describe behavior that (1) is energized and (2) has direction—that is, behavior requiring effort and seemingly directed toward attaining some goal. The nature of the goal determines the name they attach to the motive (e.g., achievement motivation, need for social approval, need for power).

Perspectives on motivation

Darwin's widely accepted theory of evolution, which hypothesizes that human beings descended from lower animals, led many nineteenth-century scientists to explain human motives as instinctual. For example, they called motherly tenderness and affection "maternal instinct" and explained exploratory behavior as the product of a "curiosity instinct."

In 1908 a British psychologist, William McDougall, published a book entitled *Social Psychology*, in which he stated that human social behavior was primarily determined by a group of instinctive tendencies. These included flight, repulsion, curiosity, fight, self-abasement, and others. McDougall believed that these instincts were inherited and that they both aroused activity and directed that activity into specific ways of satisfying the instinct. McDougall's definition of *instinct* bears similarities to our description of motivation: behavior that is energized and has direction.

The popularity of the instinct doctrine declined rapidly in the 1920s. There was little evidence to indicate that complex behavior patterns were innate. In addition, labeling a behavior as instinctive seemed to remove the need to explain it further, though there was little agreement on criteria for classifying an action as instinctive. For instance, McDougall explained war and violence by hypothesizing that there was a pugnaciousness (aggressive) instinct in human beings, but cultural anthropologists pointed out that there were a number of peaceful societies outside of the Western world. Anthropologists studying other cultures found that most behavior was not universal. We now believe that a great deal of it is learned. Although the popularity of the instinct doctrine has declined, the notion of motivation has not. We still seek to identify the causes of aroused and directed activity, but we now label them as motivations, drives, or needs instead of instincts.

Biological drive theories

Both human beings and lower animals depend on resources in the environment for survival. Animals that have been deprived of food engage in activities required to obtain nourishment. Human beings seek out food in the same way. The drive theory of motivation explains these behaviors through the principle of *homeostasis*. This is the tendency of the body to return itself to a balanced state whenever its physiological equilibrium is disturbed. When the external temperature drops, for example, the blood vessels near the skin surface contract in order to preserve

309

Hunger can be a sufficiently strong primary drive to override inhibitions and fear. (Shackman, Monkmeyer)

310 internal heat. In addition, animals seek escape from environmental conditions if they become too severe.

Deprivation of warmth, food, water, or oxygen causes a physiological need in any animal. Many psychologists believe such a need arouses a *primary*

drive. This aroused condition motivates the animal to satisfy the need, and the resulting goal-directed activity is an indication of drive. If the animal achieves its need, then the drive is reduced. Drive reduction has reinforcing properties because it follows a response that satisfies a need.

Secondary drives are drives that are not aroused by tissue deficiencies. Some theorists believe that they are learned through certain conditions associated with the reduction of primary drives. For example, the presence of people, especially parents, is associated with the reduction of many primary drives in children, such as hunger, thirst, and pain. Because of this association children acquire an affiliation motive and desire the presence of others. Drive theory states that distinctively human motives are built on primary biological drives through a learning process.

Drive theory has been influential in psychology, but it is not without its flaws and its influence has waned somewhat in recent years. It can account for much of animal behavior, which seems to be motivated primarily by biological drives, but it is not as successful in accounting for complex psychological motives in human beings that involve cognitive processes. Critics of drive theory point out that both animals and human beings occasionally seek out stimulation and arousal rather than attempt to reduce it. Boredom and inactivity can cause us to seek out "exciting" things to do, such as skydiving, mountain climbing, and auto racing. There is apparently an unlearned curiosity motive in both animals and human beings that causes them to seek out new and novel stimuli. For example, monkeys quickly learn a discrimination task when the reinforcement for a correct response is nothing more than opening a window that allows them to look outside for a few seconds. Moreover, they will work for long periods of time to solve puzzles even if there is no primary reinforcer.

Cognitive theories of motivation

Cognitive theories of motivation emphasize the role of thoughts, anticipations, imaginings of future events, and other mental processes in influencing goal-directed behavior. One influential cognitive approach to motivation is known as *Expectancy X Value theory.* It argues that the direction and inten-

(Ritscher, Stock, Boston)

sity of goal-directed behavior is jointly determined by the strength of the person's expectation that certain actions will lead to the desired goal and by the *value* of the goal for the individual. Goal-directed behavior will be strongest if the goal is highly valued and if there is a high expectation that the behavior will result in attaining it. A person who greatly values academic success and who believes that study leads to success will study harder than someone who does not have these values and expectancies.

The Expectancy X Value idea encompasses many different cognitive processes. The expectancy component includes such things as planning, anticipations, the weighing of alternatives, and the memory of previous attempts at attaining the goal. The value component includes the momentary drive or need state, the importance of the goal object, and the role of previous learning.

The psychoanalytic perspective

Freudian theory bears similarities to both the drive and cognitive positions. Freud assumed that all human motives grow out of two basic drives, called the life and death instincts. These drives operate mainly on an unconscious level and influence us in much the same way as do external sources of stimulation. They motivate the person's behavior and have the aim of drive reduction (the pleasure principle). Freud's theory of motivation also has a cognitive component because he believed that the biologically based instincts have mental representations. He stressed the roles played by imagination, thought,

and defense mechanisms in the process of need satisfaction. Mental representations provide the immediate impetus to behave in a particular way (e.g., forming a particular type of social relationship).

Because there are societal and environmental prohibitions against the direct expression of such instincts as sex and aggression, the energy from these instincts is often expressed in motives and behaviors that are more socially acceptable. Through this process of *sublimation*, a variety of "higher" motives arise out of the wellspring of *instinctual energy*. When an unacceptable or anxiety-arousing need cannot be sublimated, it may affect behavior but remain unconscious in order to protect individuals from anxiety.

Measuring motivation

All researchers who study motivation must define their terms in as objective a way as possible. Operational definitions differ, depending on the concept and type of organism under study.

Motivation is frequently defined, particularly in animal research, in terms of something done to the subject by the experimenter. For example, hunger is often defined in terms of the number of hours an animal is deprived of food. Likewise, in studies with human beings experimental conditions can be arranged so that certain motives are aroused. For example, to arouse achievement motivation, some subjects might be told that a laboratory task measures important mental abilities and that they will be given feedback about how well they have performed;

311

others might be told that the experimenter is simply evaluating some simple laboratory tasks.

In another approach to motivation the organism's behavior is used as the operational definition. In measuring hunger, for example, one could measure such responses as the amount of freely available food that an animal consumes during a fixed period of time, or the speed and vigor with which an animal works in a Skinner box. Hunger could also be defined in terms of a bodily response, such as blood sugar level. Yet another response index is the amount of aversive stimulation an animal will tolerate in order to eat. In an apparatus known as the Columbia Obstruction Box, an animal must cross an electrified grid in order to obtain a goal object. Level of motivation is inferred from the animal's willingness to cross the grid.

A convenient way to measure motivation in human subjects is through *self-reporting*. Individuals may simply be asked to rate their degree of motivation. A large number of objective tests have also been developed to measure a variety of motivational variables. Some allow investigators to assess the relative strengths of a dozen or more motives on a single scale.

Based on the psychodynamic idea that needs and motives are expressed in fantasy, a number of *projective* measures of motivation have been developed. Individuals are called on to interpret ambiguous stimuli, and it is assumed they will tend to "project" their own needs onto the stimuli. One commonly used projective technique, the Thematic Apperception Test (TAT), requires subjects to tell imaginative stories in response to a series of pictures. (The TAT is described in Chapter 14.) The content of the stories is then analyzed for evidence of a particular motive. The first of the following stories was told by the owner and founder of a thriving business. He is a self-made man, hard-driving and ambitious. The TAT-type picture shows an old and young man apparently talking to each other:

> The young fellow is trying to tell the old guy that he's being placed on early retirement for the good of the firm. The young guy has just been made a manager of the sales department and he wants to justify the faith the company had in him. The older man is a nice person—maybe too nice. He's gotten too tired to go out and hustle up the orders. The young guy is aggressive, but he hates to hurt this man who has been nice to him on many occasions. But he knows his priorities and he does it. The old man retires, gets his gold watch, and in a few years the sales manager makes Vice-President.

(Krathwohl, Stock, Boston)

This contrasting story was told by a man who works in a television repair shop. He is rather passive in dealing with other people. He likes his job because he is fascinated by anything electrical or electronic:

> This kid is confused. He doesn't know what kind of vocation would be best for him. The man he is talking to could be his father, or a friend of the family, or some kind of counselor. They have a long talk. The older man asks a lot of questions and then gives his advice. The young guy follows his advice, enters a vocation he enjoys, and years later appreciates the words of wisdom he got. So it has a happy ending.

Although the two stories differ in several ways, one very noticeable difference is in the need to achieve attributed by the first storyteller to the hero, who in both stories was seen as the younger man. We explore achievement motivation later in the chapter.

The need to achieve is socially learned and only one type of acquired motive. Because research on biologically based and socially acquired motivations often takes quite different tacks, we discuss them separately and illustrate both, beginning with biologically based motives.

Biologically based motives

In order to survive, animals must satisfy certain basic biological needs. In lower animals these needs govern most goal-directed behavior. In human beings, however, even basic physiological needs are affected by psychological and environmental learning factors.

We use hunger to illustrate a biological need that organisms must satisfy. A great deal of research has focused on the hunger drive because it is easy to manipulate by depriving animals of food. An animal that has not eaten for a period of time experiences a physiological need to eat. It engages in goal-directed behavior, such as searching the environment for food. When it finally does eat, this response satisfies the tissue need for food and reduces the hunger drive.

Hunger

Why do we eat? Is it in response to some physiological signal within our bodies that occurs when the energy from the last meal is depleted? Or is it in response to social or learned signals that indicate that this is an appropriate time to eat independent of the actual needs of the body? In human beings the best evidence is that eating usually occurs to secondary or learned cues rather than to some physiological signal. We eat according to the clock, or by habit, or because of the fact that a meal has been prepared and is ready to be eaten. It is a common observation that if an individual usually eats at 6 P.M., he feels hungry at that time. Yet if he does not eat, he may feel less hungry at 8 P.M. We probably do not recognize internal signals to eat unless we are chronically starved and have only limited energy reserves in our bodies. Nevertheless, most of the research on hunger has focused on *primary hunger*, or hunger that occurs in response to the actual needs of the animal.

One popular notion is that hunger arises from the stomach. When it is empty it contracts, and these gastric contractions are sometimes called *hunger pangs*. However, people can be hungry even if their stomachs have been removed. This is also true for almost every organ of the gastrointestinal system. It is undoubtedly the case that organ responses contribute to hunger, but it is also clear that they are not necessary.

Perhaps the most popular of the contemporary biological theories of hunger is the *glucostatic theory*. This theory is based on the fact that the amount of glucose (a major source of energy for the body) in the blood is low when we are hungry and high after a meal. The theory states that when the amount of glucose being utilized by the body is low, hunger occurs; and when it is high, satiety (feeling full) occurs. The theory asserts that there are centers within the brain that monitor the rate of glucose utilization and control eating. Although supportive evidence exists for this theory, it now appears that it only holds true in emergency situations, such as when the body is actually starved and in a need state requiring quick energy.

Much research on hunger and satiety has dealt with certain structures of the nervous system. In particular, two centers of the hypothalamus, which is located at the base of the brain, have been studied extensively. The *lateral hypothalamic nucleus* is often called the eating center because mild stimulation there elicits eating even in a sated animal and because the destruction of that area leads to a reduction of food intake persisting for up to several weeks. The *ventromedial hypothalamic nucleus* is often called the satiety center because slight electrical

313

stimulation there causes a cessation of eating, even in a hungry animal, and because its destruction leads to *hyperphagia* (overeating) and obesity. Recent evidence suggests that these areas are more concerned with the regulation of body weight than with eating. It is as if lesions in these areas simply alter the weight that the brain is trying to maintain. If the organism has already attained the new weight prior to the lesion, a change in eating behavior does not occur.

For obvious ethical reasons experiments on stimulation or destruction of brain areas in people cannot be conducted. However, some persons suffer injuries to the hypothalamus and their behavior has been observed carefully. Individuals who suffer injuries to the ventromedial hypothalamic nucleus (VMH) tend to overeat. Researchers have noted some amazing parallels between obese human beings and rats whose VMH has been destroyed. Both eat more meals and eat more rapidly than do normal animals. Both are highly sensitive to the taste of food and relatively insensitive to internal hunger cues. One possibility is that certain organisms may be destined to be fat because the hypothalamus established a particularly high level of fat tissue (Nisbett, 1972; Schachter, 1971).

Cognitive influences from the cerebral cortex also play a major role, particularly in humans. These cause variations of "hunger" as a function of time of the day, the perceived palatability of the meal, the social situation, and so on.

Choosing a diet. Although we do not know the exact mechanisms involved in choice of diet, the evidence suggests that taste and smell are important. Under normal conditions once an animal begins to eat the "right" food, the uncomfortable symptoms caused by a deficiency begin to disappear, so that animals may choose certain foods because of their effect.

It appears that human beings as well as animals can follow the "wisdom of the body" in choosing foods. In one study three newly weaned human infants were allowed to select their own diet from a wide variety of available foods (Davis, 1928). Two of them selected their meals for six months, the other for a full year. All the children gained weight normally and showed no signs of nutritional disorder. One baby who suffered from rickets at the beginning of the study cured himself by selecting large quantities of cod-liver oil, which contains the vitamin D necessary to cure rickets. Once the rickets was cured this baby showed no further interest in cod-liver oil.

The infants in this study were newly weaned and had not had time to develop food preferences. There is evidence that acquired tastes can interfere with an animal's natural ability to choose food with the nutrients it needs. We know that the diets of people are affected by the large numbers of sweetened and "empty" foods they eat as children. The average American's diet contains far more sugar and carbohydrates than he or she needs, and it is often deficient in important vitamins and protein.

Obesity. Chapter 8 described some techniques most people find helpful in trying to lose weight. Obese people have a serious weight problem that often has a strong psychological component. More Americans die from medical problems associated with excessive body weight than from any form of addiction, including alcohol, cigarettes, and drugs. Obese people not only suffer serious physical consequences, but encounter numerous social problems as well. In a society that is perhaps overly concerned with physical attractiveness and that thinks that "thin is beautiful," obese people are often ridiculed and rejected. Recent research has provided some valuable leads to understanding the physiological reasons for obesity. One hypothesis is that certain obese individuals are biologically "programmed" to be fat.

The number of fat cells in our body never changes throughout adult life. It is set relatively early during our lifetime. Overeating increases the *size* of these cells but not the *number*, and dieting reduces the size but not the number. This finding may help explain why dieting often results in only a temporary weight loss for obese individuals. They may lose weight initially but still have the same number of fat cells to fill up when they begin to overeat again. In other words, individuals with a large number of fat cells have a higher normal (for them) level of body fat than individuals with a smaller number. This level appears to be determined by two factors: genetic make-up and early eating patterns.

The hypothalamus regulates food intake in order to keep fat stores at a certain level. As was noted earlier, it is possible that the hypothalamus maintains fat tissue at a higher level for obese individuals than for normal-weight individuals of the same height and bone structure. For some individuals, then, obesity may be a normal state maintained by the hypothalamus. When obese individuals lose weight, they may experience almost constant hunger because feeding centers in the brain tell them that they are "undernourished." Research on this theory of baseline body fat is still inconclusive. At this point thin people hope it is true and fat people probably hope it is not.

Eating in response to external cues.   We eat in response to a number of different stimuli. Some of the cues to which we respond are internal, such as stomach contractions. There are also external cues, such as the passing of time and the smell or sight of food, which help govern our eating behavior. Recent research indicates that normal-weight and obese people respond to different cues. Obese people respond less to internal body stimuli and more to external cues than do normal-weight individuals.

In one experiment, Stanley Schachter manipulated the physiological state of his subjects in two ways (Schachter, Goldman, and Gordon, 1968). They were told not to eat for several hours before the experimental session. Half of them were fed when they entered the session and half continued on with an empty stomach. In addition, half were told that they would experience painful electric shocks and the other half were told they would receive painless tingles. This procedure was designed to arouse fear in the first group. Fear reactions stop stomach action and cause the release of sugar from the liver into the blood. It was presumed that fearful individuals should not feel hungry because they have a high concentration of sugar in their blood.

Schachter reasoned that if the eating behavior of obese individuals is not governed by internal cues, then they should not be affected by the two independent variables. That is, they should eat as much when their stomachs are full as when they are empty, and as much when they are frightened as when they are calm. Normal subjects, however, should eat more when their stomachs are empty than when they are full and more when they are calm than when they are frightened, because their eating is more strongly affected by internal cues.

Schachter gave the subjects a bowl of crackers and asked them to rate their taste according to several dimensions (e.g., salty, cheesy). Subjects were observed through a one-way mirror during the "taste test," so that researchers could count the number of crackers eaten. Normal-weight subjects ate considerably more crackers when their stomachs were empty than when they were full. Obese subjects were unaffected by the fullness or emptiness of their stomachs. In fact, they tended to eat slightly more when their stomachs were full than when they were empty. Moreover, high fear decreased the number of crackers normal-weight subjects ate, but had no effect on the number obese subjects ate. Overall, obese subjects did not eat more than normal-weight subjects, but they seemed to ignore internal states in regulating their eating.

Research on obesity and eating behavior is an excellent illustration of the fact that behavior involves interactions between individuals and their environment. It is likely that obesity involves a complex pattern of interpretation of and responses to selected internal and external cues. Thus even in the case of a primary tissue need, such as hunger, psychological factors play an important role. Such factors assume even greater importance in the socially learned motives to which we now turn.

Socially learned motives

Experience shapes many human motives. It might seem that it would be relatively easy to ask people for accounts of their desires, goals, wants, and needs. However, there is abundant evidence that our subjective sense of intention and purpose is often an unreliable index of our behaviors. The study of human motives poses many challenges, not the least of which is how to measure a motive.

A popular research strategy is to designate in commonsense language a type of behavior that seems to involve a significant motivational component—for example, affiliative ties with other people. Efforts are then made to develop one or more measures of the disposition to behave in accord with the motive under study. Research might be directed to the motive's sensitivity to environmental and social arousal, its role in the person's total personality configuration, and its relationship to specific aspects of behavior, such as perception, cognitive processes, or learn-

315

ing. The desired outcome of this type of research is some general statements about motivational processes. Our treatment of this topic begins with a review of the need to achieve, the human motive most widely studied by psychologists.

The achievement motive

College students are well aware, often painfully aware, of the emphasis on achievement and the fierce competition that characterizes the academic atmosphere on many campuses. Americans are internationally regarded as being preoccupied with competition and success. Not surprisingly, the need for achievement (n Ach) and its origins have received more attention than any other learned psychological motive.

Measuring need for achievement

Much of the research on achievement motivation has used a measurement technique devised by David McClelland and his associates (McClelland, Atkinson, Clark, and Lowell, 1953). Subjects are shown a series of pictures and asked to write a story in response to each of them. The story is to be organized around four questions: (1) What is happening? Who are the people? (2) What has led up to this situation? That is, what has happened in the past? (3) What is being thought? What is wanted? By whom? (4) What will happen? What will be done? The content of the stories is then analyzed by trained scorers according to a well-defined scoring system. As we noted in our discussion of achievement motivation in Chapter 1, the scoring system can be applied to virtually any kind of written or oral material. This permits great flexibility in conducting research. For example, we saw in that chapter how the scoring system was applied to assessing achievement imagery in children's stories down through the centuries and related it to economic indexes.

Need for achievement and behavior

Individuals whose stories reflect a high need for achievement are ambitious, enjoy competitive situations, and are persistent in their attempts to solve problems. Achievement motivation scores are sometimes, but not always, positively related to grades and IQ. Individuals with high achievement motivation do best in courses that they perceive as relevant to

their future careers, and they tend to seek and enter more prestigious occupations than do individuals with lower achievement motivation. They are also better able to pass up immediate gratification in order to obtain greater rewards in the future. There is some evidence that very high need for achievement is positively associated with the death rate from ulcers and hypertension. Individuals with a high need for achievement are more successful than those with a low need for achievement only in firms that are especially achievement oriented. Individuals involved in sales and marketing have the highest n Ach scores in the business community.

In experimental situations subjects with a high need for achievement generally outperform individuals with low achievement motivation when the experimenter places great stress on excellence of performance. Under relaxed conditions in which achievement motivation is apparently not aroused, high n Ach subjects do not show superiority in performance.

Laboratory and field studies suggest that the achievement motive is the product of social learning experiences associated with achievement behaviors. Individuals with a high need for achievement tend to come from families who reward achievement behavior and stress the importance of successful competition, excellent performance, and independence.

Increasing achievement motivation. Because there is a positive relationship between n Ach and various kinds of success, a number of researchers have developed programs designed to increase achievement motivation. In one study a group of college students wrote stories that were scored for n Ach and then met in a series of eight weekly sessions to discuss them (Burris, 1958). The students were directed to engage in fantasy and activities that centered on achievement. The students not only had higher n Ach scores in follow-up testing, but also increased their grade point averages for the following semester much more than did a control group of students who had not undergone the training.

In another study carried out by McClelland and David Winter (1969) an attempt was made to increase n Ach in business executives in India. The procedures involved training and practice in fanta-

BOX 10.1
A sense of project

The following account by Martin Seligman of his experience on the faculty of the University of Pennsylvania is interesting, especially because of the wide individual differences he has observed in what he calls "a sense of project."

> Every year a few straight-A, advanced undergraduates elect to do a project in my laboratory. Every year I warn each of them that laboratory work is not as glamorous as they might believe: it means coming in seven days a week for months on end; looking at endless, boring printouts of data; having equipment break down in the middle of a session. Every year, half of them give up in the middle of their experiment. They do not lack intelligence, imagination, or wit. What they have is a "Sesame Street" view of education, carried inappropriately to the college level: "If it's not titillating, exciting, colorful, I won't do it." The sense of project that is necessary for scientific discovery, as well as for any creative act, consists of an ability to tolerate failure, frustration, and,

most of all, boredom. If the discovery had been easy, colorful, and titillating, someone else, probably, would have made it already. The only real, visceral gratification comes at the end of the experiment, if at all.

> I believe that many of my "failures," through too much success, have developed insufficient coping mechanisms. Their parents and their teachers, out of a misguided sense of kindness, made things much too easy for them. If a reading list was too long and the student protested, the teacher shortened it—rather than have the students put in extra hours of work. If the teenager was picked up for vandalism, the parents bailed him out—rather than have the child find out that his actions have serious consequences. Unless a young person confronts anxiety, boredom, pain, and trouble, and masters them by his actions, he will develop an impoverished sense of his own competence. (Seligman, 1975, p. 158)

Two questions raised by Seligman's experience are the following: "What sorts of experiences and characteristics are related to the strength of a person's 'sense of project'?" and, "Can the 'sense of project' be modified, perhaps through programs like those employed in heightening need for achievement?"

---

sizing about achievement, group activities including risk taking and goal setting with achievement-related tasks, role-playing activities, and intensive discussions about the cultural demands, values, and folklore surrounding achievement motivation. These training sessions lasted for several weeks, and subjects left their work to attend them. In comparison to a group of control subjects who had not participated in the sessions, the businessmen showed greater motivation in their work during a two-year follow-up period. McClelland and Winter concluded that the program had the strongest effect on individuals who had wanted to feel more effective in their work before the program began. The program increased their confidence and gave them concrete suggestions about how they could reach their goals.

Other programs to heighten need for achievement have also been developed and their results are encouraging. The programs seem to be optimally effective when coupled with training to heighten specific

job skills. The desirability of combining skills training with a reconceptualization of one's role has in a general way been known to many parents and educators for a long time. If, for example, students have little concept of what is entailed in working toward some goal, entreaties to them to "give your all" are not meaningful. One noted researcher has described some individual differences seen in very able students. (See Box 10.1.)

The motive to avoid success

During the early studies of achievement motivation conducted in the 1950s, relatively few women put high achievement imagery into their stories. The researchers concluded that women in our culture do not have high achievement motivation and are more interested in social acceptance and approval. The great majority of later studies avoided the issue by using only male subjects.

Because social learning experiences are critical in

317

BOX 10.2
Fear of success stories

The following stories were composed in the 1960s by college women in response to the first sentence "After first-term finals, Anne finds herself at the top of her medical school class." Matina Horner used them to argue that women are motivated to avoid success.

Anne has a boyfriend Carl in the same class and they are quite serious. Anne met Carl at college and they started dating around their soph years in undergraduate school. Anne is rather upset and so is Carl. She wants him to be higher scholastically than she is. Anne will deliberately lower her academic standing next term, while she does all she subtly can to help Carl. His grades come up and Anne soon drops out of med school. They marry and he goes on in school while she raises their family.

Anne is a code name for a nonexistent person cre-

ated by a group of med students. They take turns taking exams and writing papers for her.

Anne is really happy she's on top, though Tom is higher than she—though that's as it should be. Anne doesn't mind Tom winning. Anne is talking to her counselor. Counselor says she will make a fine nurse. She will continue her med-school courses. She will study very hard and find she can and will become a good nurse.

She starts proclaiming her surprise and joy. Her fellow classmates are so disgusted with her behavior that they jump on her in a body and beat her. She is maimed for life.

Anne is an acne-faced bookworm. She runs to the bulletin board and finds she's at the top. "As usual," she smarts off. A chorus of groans is the rest of the class's reply. Anne was always praised for her initiative and study habits—mainly because these were the only things one could praise her for. She studies 12 hours a day, and lives at home to save money. She rents her books. "Well it certainly paid off. All the Friday and Saturday nights with my books, who needs dates, fun—I'll be the best woman doctor alive!" And yet, a twinge of sadness comes through—she wonders what she really has. But, as is her habit, she promptly erases the thought, and goes off reciting aloud the 231 bones in her wrist.

(Horner, 1968.)

the development of the achievement motive, it is not surprising that some women have conflicts about achievement. "Feminine" women in our culture are not supposed to be successful in certain areas. Until recently, women were rarely rewarded for competitive behavior, especially when they competed successfully with men. Their needs for achievement have often been projected onto their husbands' activities rather than directed toward their own. Women married to upwardly mobile men (those who were in higher occupational levels than their fathers) told stories that contained more achievement imagery than did women who were married to men who were not as upwardly mobile.

In 1970 psychologist Matina Horner hypothesized that many women have actually learned to fear being

successful. She developed a procedure to measure what she called "the motive to avoid success." Subjects were provided with one sentence and asked to complete a story from it. Female subjects told a story that began, "After first term finals, Anne finds herself at the top of her medical class." For male subjects the name John was substituted for Anne. Fear of success was gauged by the negative consequences that occurred to the character in the story as a result of his or her success. The stories that reflected fear of success were classified into three categories: (1) those in which the negative consequences included loss of friends or social rejection; (2) those in which the character in the story expressed doubts about his or her normality; and (3) those that involved a complete denial of the character's success. Examples of stories that reflect fear of success in women are presented in Box. 10.2.

Horner found that female subjects feared success more than did males. Sixty-five percent of the women, as compared with fewer than 10 percent of the men, had fear of success imagery in their stories. Horner also found that fear of success in women apparently has behavioral consequences. In one study college women performed a series of tasks, both alone and in competition with men. Of the women who had scored high in fear of success, 77 percent performed at a significantly higher level in the noncompetitive than in the competitive situation. Ninety-three percent of those with a low fear of success performed better when they were competing with a man.

Although some recent studies of the motive to avoid success have found differences between men and women in line with Horner's findings, others have not. One reason for this discrepancy may be that the situations that arouse particular motivations for men do not do so consistently for women. In comparing men and women with regard to achievement motivation, it is probably important to specify the type of situation to which a person might respond with a strong need for achievement or fear of success. The way in which need to avoid success (and other needs as well) is measured is a factor that should also be taken into account. Not to be neglected is the fact that men and women's motives to avoid success vary with the changing roles they play in society from one time to another. There is little doubt that women's concepts of success in the mid-1970s are quite different from those prevalent in the 1960s. Men's attitudes have also undergone significant change.

The need for power

In Chapter 8 we discussed the psychological importance of self-control, or power, over our own lives. But human beings also have an apparent need to exert control over the lives of others. Power has always been of major concern to human beings, but in the twentieth century it has become almost a cultural obsession. We have had wars, revolutions, civil strife, radical protests, racial turmoil, and political struggles that were defined in terms of power needs.

A measure of the need for power (n Power) has

Heroism may be a manifestation of a "socialized" motivation for power. It involves exercising power for the benefit of others. (Culver)

been constructed in much the same way that n Ach is measured (McClelland, 1975; Winter, 1973). Subjects are asked to write stories in response to pictures, and the stories are then analyzed for power themes. A scoring system similar in many respects to the one for scoring n Ach is used. Subjects' scores are based on the number of times they use phrases and verbal images that describe impact on or control over other people. They can involve actions that range from strong, aggressive, and forceful (ordering, threatening) to subtle and socially acceptable (helping, advising, inspiring).

McClelland (1975) suggested that there are basically two kinds of power motivation. One kind is oriented toward winning out over adversaries. Individuals with this motivation see life as a jungle in which the strongest survive by destroying or eliminating their foes. In every social interaction someone wins and someone loses. The other kind of power motive is more socialized. It involves exercising power for the benefit of others and helping to further group goals by exercising social influence. Individuals with this type of motivation may hesitate to seek power because they realize that the overt quest for power may be frowned on by society. Perhaps for this

319

BOX 10.3
The quest for power

Leaders seek to get and hold onto power for different reasons. It would be difficult to find two more contrasting national figures than Adolf Hitler, Der Führer of the Third Reich, and Mahatma Gandhi, who espoused and practiced self-sacrifice and non-violence as he led India toward independence from the British Empire.

Mahatma Gandhi and former Prime Minister of India Pandit Jawaharlal Nehru participate in a demonstration for National Week, a celebration for Indian Unity, in 1946. (UPI)

sies is affected by the amount of alcohol they drink. Drinking alcohol in small amounts increases the frequency of socialized power thoughts, whereas drinking larger amounts promotes fantasies about personalized power that often involve exploitative sexual and aggressive behavior. Other studies have shown that men who have social power fantasies tend to occupy political office, whereas those who have more personal dominance fantasies tend to drink heavily and to engage in more sexual and aggressive behavior.

Some of the behavioral characteristics of males who have a high need for power have been identified (Winter, 1973). (Unfortunately, virtually all the research conducted to date has used male subjects, and very little is known about the way in which the power motive applies to females.) Male college students with a high need for power more often hold office in organizations, write more letters to university newspapers, and frequently get elected to important university committees. Most males with a high need for power are also likely to consume a good deal of alcohol and to engage in exploitative sexual activity. They are likely to play vigorous competitive sports, or at least to watch such sports, to read such magazines as *Playboy,* and to watch adventure programs on television.

People with high power needs tend to buy material goods that are advertised as prestigious. They prefer cars with high maneuverability, "which give the driver the impression of total control over the vehicle, the road, and, presumably, other drivers. It may be that for the person with a high need for power the highly maneuverable car is the model for the whole of human society, which he then sees as a series of maneuverable machines" (Winter, 1973, p 446). People with high power needs are often skilled at manipulating other people and social situations to their own advantage. They are likely to aspire to leadership positions in business or politics so that they can exercise power both socially and professionally.

Some theories have claimed that a high power drive is a way of compensating for a sense of inferiority or powerlessness as a child. (See Figure 10.1.) More recent research suggests, however, that adults who have a high need for power had a sense of power rather than inferiority at an early age (Winter, 1973).

reason most politicians prefer to be "called" to service rather than to seek an office. (See Box 10.3.)

Many people have strong power motivations of both types. For example, one study by McClelland showed that drinking alcohol increases power fantasies in men, but that the nature of the power fanta-

*"And I hereby swear that should my quest for the secret of superstrength
be successful, I shall use this power only for good."*

Figure 10.1 (Drawing by Lorenz; © 1975 The New Yorker Magazine, Inc.)

They are often first-born sons who come from upper-middle-class families. They were rewarded and approved of by their parents when they accomplished their goals successfully and when they successfully exercised influence over various aspects of their lives.

In spite of the recent increase in research in this area we know less about power motivation than about other socially learned motives. In the coming years we may be able to expand our knowledge concerning this critically important human motive. (See Box 10.4.)

We have seen that the study of motivation is taking place on a number of fronts, ranging from the effects of food deprivation to personal motives, such as the power motive. There are wide differences of opinion about how motivation can best be conceptualized and new evidence involving biological and social learning variables influence this debate. Human beings, unique as they are, work within the limits of their bodily systems and specific sets of social conditions. As the relationships between these variables become better understood, a truly integrative psychology of motivation may emerge.

321

BOX 10.4

Power and affiliation needs: Are we headed for war?

David McClelland (1975) and his associates applied a scoring system for *n* Power and *n* Affiliation (the desire to relate to others in a friendly fashion) to samples of popular literature in different nations over the past several centuries. They then related these motivational patterns to historical events, particularly wars, and found that when the literature reflected a high need for power, one higher than the need for affiliation, there was usually a war about 15 years later. More precisely, the motivational pattern plotted at the midpoint of a decade seems to translate itself into action (either war or peace) in the decade that begins 15 years after that midpoint.

When this method of study was applied to American history during the period between 1885 and the end of World War I, the prediction of war or no war based on the relative strengths of *n* Power and *n* Affiliation was correct 12 out of 13 times (the Spanish-American War was the only exception). After World War I the lead time between the development of motivational patterns and war became drastically

shorter, dropping from about 15 years to virtually no time at all. McClelland suggests advances in technology may be responsible for this change.

McClelland also found that when a nation's popular literature reflects both a high need for affiliation and a high need for power, the need for affiliation tends to decline soon afterward. Along with this decrease in concern about the welfare of individuals, militant political and social reform movements tend to develop. These large-scale reform movements may influence national and international relationships, and appear to set the stage for war. Reform movements seem to create a climate for action that makes war more likely.

> Before reformist periods—and in recent years during them—the need for Power is high, the need for Affiliation is relatively low, and a martial spirit prevails, which leads to zealous actions to right wrongs on behalf of the oppressed. This atmosphere of righteous action has led to war so many times in the history of the United States and England that it is hard to think such consequences are accidental. (McClelland, 1975, p. 48).

Of course, the fact that motivational patterns are correlated with wars does not necessarily mean that they cause wars. But McClelland does point out a disturbing finding. He and his associates found that popular literature in the United States in the mid-1960s reflected an increase in the need for power and a decrease in the need for affiliation. If we are following a traditional pattern, then a war will break out in the not too distant future.

EMOTION

Our motives and emotions are related. Ambitious executives show emotional reactions, particularly if they think their goals are in danger of being thwarted. Persons suffering intense emotional upsets (such as the unexpected death of a loved one) may find themselves unable to pursue goals and satisfy motives that normally would be compelling ones for them.

Like the study of motivation, the study of emo-

tion requires an understanding of the intricate relationships between body, mind, and behavior. Many theories about the nature of emotions have emerged over the years, and numerous techniques have been developed to measure and influence emotional responses.

Measuring and judging emotions

Because there are a number of different levels of psychological functioning involved in emotion, the measurement method that a researcher uses depends on the study's purposes. There are three basic methods for measuring and identifying emotional reactions: (1) self-reports of emotional experience; (2) measurement of physiological responses; and (3) observation and measurement of overt behavior.

Self-report measures

Emotional experiences are private events that we cannot observe directly, so that investigators often measure emotions by simply asking individuals how or what they are feeling. This may be done through interviewing and questioning either orally or in writing.

Self-report measures may focus on a single emotion, such as fear or anger, or they may attempt to cover virtually the entire range of emotional experience. The following account was given by one student on returning from Christmas vacation:

> You want me to tell about my emotional reactions over Christmas? Well, that's hard—because they are mixed. Christmas is supposed to be a happy time. You get all those nice presents and feel goodwill towards everybody. That's true for me to some extent. I enjoyed seeing my mother and father again and I appreciated the opportunity to see many of my high school friends. But at the same time, Christmas is a sad time for me. I'm not sure why, but every Christmas I can't help being depressed by all the hypocrisy connected with much of what the ads love to call "the Christmas spirit." I wish that spirit were more longlasting and more genuine. On balance, I guess Christmas for me is more unpleasant than pleasant. In fact, the hypocrisy of it really angers and depresses me.

Physiological measures

Physiological processes play an important role in emotional reactions. Increased heart rate, dilation of the pupil of the eye, and sweating are only some of the bodily events found when these reactions occur. Instruments are available for simultaneously recording a number of physiological responses. The *polygraph*, which measures emotional responses through physiological reactions (heartbeat, blood pressure, breathing, galvanic skin response), has been used as a basis for judging whether a suspect is lying. Polygraph records are obtained first during a baseline or resting period and then following presentation of an emotionally arousing stimulus. The figure in Box 10.5

shows a typical polygraph and the record it produces as a subject is exposed to an arousing stimulus.

In modern psychophysiology laboratories, polygraphs are often used simply as monitoring instruments, and all data are transferred directly to a computer, where they are analyzed quickly and stored on magnetic tape. The computer can be programmed not only to score and analyze data, but also to present certain stimuli based on the subject's momentary physiological responses.

It has been shown that different individuals respond differently to arousing stimuli (Lacey and Lacey, 1958). Some subjects show marked changes in heart functions and only minor changes in other response systems, such as muscle tension and skin resistance. Others might show the opposite pattern. No single physiological measure is appropriate for all subjects; it is important to measure as many systems as possible. After a number of measurements for one individual, an investigator might select the most reactive system to measure emotional arousal.

Overt behavioral measures

Most of us show that we are emotionally aroused through overt behavior such as a change in intensity of our speech, stuttering, facial expressions, and bodily movements. Researchers can measure fear by asking subjects to make increasingly closer contact with a feared object, such as a snake or dog. The subjects' ability to comply with the experimenter's requests and their behavior while they are doing so are used as an index of their level of fear.

In much of our everyday life we try to gauge emotions in others through facial expressions. We are rarely called on to make judgments about emotions without knowing something about the background of the situation. In a now classic study Norman Munn (1940) found that subjects' accuracy and agreement in labeling emotions was considerably better for pictures that had a background situation than for those in which the background had been eliminated so that only the person was visible. Other studies have also shown that situational cues are of great importance in judging emotions reflected in overt behavior.

At one time psychologists assumed that the cognitive, physiological, and behavioral components of emotion formed a unitary system. Recent research,

323

BOX 10.5

The polygraph: How reliable is it as a lie detector?

"People need a license to cut your hair," says 26-year-old David, "but they don't need a license to cut off your career."

This young man suspects he lost his job because of an erroneous polygraph test. David, a college graduate, clerked at a phonograph-record store in suburban Eagle Rock until early last December, when he transferred to another branch closer to home.

Several weeks later, his employer asked him to take a polygraph test, and he readily consented. The reason soon became apparent: He was suspected of involvement in a holdup at the Eagle Rock store—at a time when he was on duty at the other outlet 19 miles away.

David was tested twice by the examiner, who then declared:

"Your participation in the robbery is obvious. Are you going to confess now, or will we have to take this matter to the police?"

"You've made a mistake," replied David. "This is crazy."

The examiner pointed to bumps on the chart. "Did you receive any of the stolen money? There's the lie detector's response. Did you help plan the robbery? Look at the jump at that answer!"

The police never questioned David, and neither did his boss. But three days later, for "economic reasons," he was fired.

Was it because of the test? David is afraid to ask.

If the polygraph operator never told the record-store company that David had flunked, he didn't want to open up a hornet's nest of questions by making a protest of innocence to the personnel manager.

"The tragedy," says David, still unemployed, "is that I'll never really know why I lost the job." (Reprinted from *U.S. News & World Report.* Copyright 1976 U.S. News & World Report, Inc.)

324 Use of the polygraph is not limited to the laboratory. Its potential as a lie detector has been recognized by the police, government, and business for a long time. There are an estimated 2000 polygraphers in the United States; only a few of them are doctoral-level scientists. Polygraphers are usually trained by law enforcement or military organizations and often lack basic knowledge of psychophysiology and psychological measurement.

Unfortunately, polygraph records are not completely reliable. For example, a suspect in a criminal investigation might "fail" (by showing heightened physiological reactivity to a question like "Did you hide the TV set after you stole it?") a lie detector test for reasons other than guilt or knowledge about a crime. Innocent people may appear guilty when doubt and fear and lack of confidence arouse the activity level of the autonomic nervous system. In fact, then, there is no such thing as a lie detector. Rather, there are diverse indicators of bodily activity that may show high, but not perfect, reliability.

This means that caution is needed when decisions about people are dependent on these indicators. All aspects of a device employed to record these indicators must be subjected to research and ethical questions involved in its use thoughtfully considered. An example of the need for this caution is Psychological Stress Evaluation, or PSE, the first competitor of the polygraph. It is based on the fact that all muscles, including those controlling the vocal cords, vibrate slightly when in use. This phenomenon is believed to be an involuntary function of the central nervous system. The PSE measures emotional and stress reactions by recording certain inaudible modulations (microtremors) in the voice. The voice can be either live or tape-recorded. The recordings made by the PSE are not dependent on the flow and ebb of body chemicals, as are those made by a polygraph. Although much research will be needed to evaluate its reliability, hundreds of the devices have been sold commercially to retail and industrial firms, private investigating firms, and government agencies. The possibilities for unethical use of the PSE are disturbing. For example, it could be used to analyze telephone conversations that are tape-recorded without knowledge of people engaged in a conversation.

A polygraph recording session. (U.S. News & World Report)

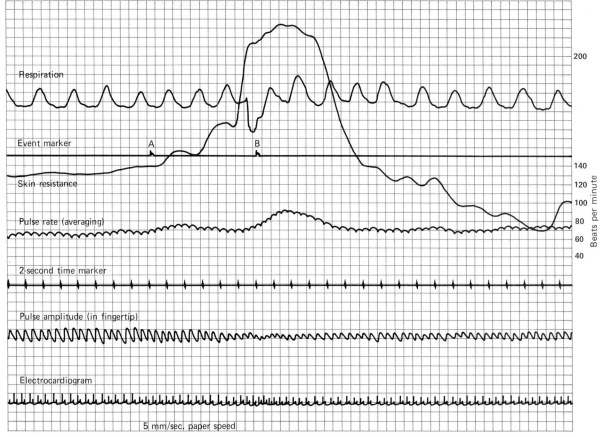

Sample of a polygraph recording. The stimulus consisted of an emotionally charged reference being whispered to the subject. At point A on the event marker line the whispered conversation began and a slight change in skin resistance occurred. As seen in the record of respiration, at the same time the pulse rate increased the pulse amplitude decreased and there was a marked decrease in skin resistance.

however, has indicated that these three systems are often unrelated to one another. For example, when individuals are confronted with an object they fear, their reports of fear, their physiological measures of it, and their overt behavioral responses may bear little relationship to one another. The fact that the emotional response systems do not necessarily function as a single unit emphasizes difficulties involved in measuring emotional reactions.

Although there are problems in defining and measuring emotions, there is evidence of a relationship between the persistence and intensity of emotions, on the one hand, and physical and mental health, on the other. In the discussion of stress that follows and in Chapter 15 we consider several facets of this relationship. In Chapter 16, which deals with treatment programs for behavioral problems, we find that learning to control and redirect one's emotions is often one path of therapeutic progress.

Components of emotion

Common sense says . . . we meet a bear, are frightened, and run; we are insulted by a rival, are angry, and strike. The hypothesis here to be defended says that this order of sequence is incorrect . . . and that the more rational statement is that we feel sorry because we cry, angry because we strike, afraid because we tremble.

This quotation is from William James (1890), an early American psychologist. Although we now tend to think that physiological responses are caused by emotions, James proposed that the perception of physiological change *is* emotion; our bodies react first, and then we feel emotion.

Carl Lange, a Danish psychologist, developed a similar theory of emotion at about the same time as James, and James's and Lange's ideas are now referred to as the James-Lange theory of emotion. Their ideas stimulated a great deal of research, and some years later a rival theory appeared.

In 1927 Walter Cannon, a physiologist and former student of James, summarized the accumulating research, most of which contradicted the James-Lange theory. The James-Lange theory implied that in order for individuals to experience different emotions, they must respond to a different pattern of physiological responses for each one. Cannon questioned whether there really were different patterns and

pointed out that internal organs are probably too insensitive for changes in them to be noticed and used as cues. In addition, Cannon noted work in which subjects are injected with adrenalin and show increases in physiological arousal. Under this condition, subjects say they feel *as if* they are angry or afraid, but they also know that in reality they are not. Cannon concluded that physiological arousal alone does not constitute a true emotional experience.

Cannon developed a theory with his student, Bard, that gave the thalamus, which consists of two groups of nerve cell nuclei inside the cerebral hemisphere, a central role in emotion. They proposed that the thalamus responded to emotionally arousing stimuli by sending messages simultaneously to the cerebral cortex and to the visceral and skeletal muscles. The thalmic messages to the cortex were responsible for the "feelings" of emotion, whereas the messages from the thalamus to the viscera and skeletal responses were responsible for physiological and overt behavioral responses.

Later research has shown that neither the James-Lange nor the Cannon-Bard theory is either completely correct or completely wrong. Emotion is not a momentary event, but an experience that takes place over a period of time. If we are in sudden danger our feelings may become noticeable immediately in response to a dangerous stimulus before we have a physiological reaction. In other instances our emotional state may be the product of a great deal of thinking about a particular situation or event. Elements of these two early theories of emotions apply under different circumstances.

Contemporary theories of emotion differ in their emphases, and there is disagreement on how they might best be integrated. These are some of the questions that are being debated at the present time:

1. Should emotions be defined as stimulus inputs? ("The child was brought up in a home that always had an emotionally charged atmosphere.")
2. Should they be defined as subjective experiences? ("He felt emotionally drained.")
3. Should they be defined as bodily states? ("His tense facial muscles showed the tension under which he was operating.")

Certain theories of emotion stress stimulus characteristics. Others stress response variables (either psychological or physiological). Still other theories treat emotion as a hypothetical concept.

Biological aspects of emotion

Neural centers and emotion. Several early theories about the role of the brain in emotional behavior hypothesized that there was a single "emotion center" in the brain, such as the thalamus. But researchers found that several areas are actually involved in emotional behavior. These areas (e.g., the hypothalamus and limbic system) produce changes in emotional behavior when they are electrically stimulated or surgically destroyed. All these areas are involved in many other functions besides emotion, and it is unlikely that there is any single "emotion center" in the brain. Researchers are now trying to discover the complex interactions that occur among many areas of the brain during an emotional reaction.

Hormonal factors in emotion. Our physiological responses to emotions are greatly influenced by the activity of the endocrine system, a series of glands that pump chemical substances called *hormones* (see Chapter 3) directly into the bloodstream. These hormones are carried by the blood to every part of the body in a relatively short period of time. The hypothalamus is the control center for the endocrine system within the brain. The pituitary gland, which is attached to the underside of the hypothalamus, secretes a variety of hormones, some of which stimulate the adrenal glands, located near the kidneys. The adrenal glands then secrete two hormones, *epinephrine* (adrenalin) and *norepinephrine* (noradrenalin). Research on these two hormones suggests that they may be related to different emotions. Studies with both human beings and animals show that epinephrine is generally associated with fear, whereas both epinephrine and norepinephrine are associated with anger. Fearful animals, such as rabbits, who survive by avoiding predators, secrete mostly epinephrine; predators, who usually attack, secrete a high amount of norepinephrine. There is also evidence that individuals who respond to stress with anger secrete high concentrations of norepinephrine, whereas those who respond with anxiety secrete relatively more epinephrine (Funk-

enstein, 1955; Funkenstein, King, and Drolette, 1957).

Physiological differentiation in emotion. Some researchers have adapted the James-Lange theory to hypothesize that different physiological response patterns are associated with different emotions. They claim that if we could perceive these patterns in others, we might know which emotions they were experiencing. In one clinical study the patient was a man whose esophagus had been so badly burned in an accident that a "window," or *fistula*, had been cut in his stomach so that food could be introduced directly into the stomach (Wolf and Wolff, 1947). Through this fistula it was possible to observe reactions in the stomach when the man was emotionally aroused. When he reported that he was angry, acid poured in, there were strong contractions, and the lining became engorged with blood. When he was fearful or anxious, there was a decrease in stomach acid and contractions, and the lining paled from a decrease in blood volume. At least in this patient, patterns associated with anger and fear seemed to be quite different.

Some years later, Albert Ax (1953) performed an experiment in which he obtained 14 different physiological measures while subjects were made angry or fearful. When he compared the physiological response patterns of the two groups, he found that they differed significantly on half of the 14 measures, but not on the other half.

Although there is limited evidence that there are different physiological patterns in anger and fear, there is no evidence that other, more subtle emotions are associated with specific response patterns. Most researchers have concluded that we cannot identify emotions purely on the basis of physiological responses, and that we must consider cognitive processes as well.

Cognition and emotion

The reason cognitive processes play a role in the study of emotions is that our interpretations of events influence how we react to them both psychologically and physiologically. Because not every perception leads to an emotional reaction, we must have some mechanism for appraising situations.

Some theories suggest that both emotional experience *and* bodily changes may follow the perception and interpretation of an object as beneficial or harmful. Emotion has motivational properties and influences the tendency to approach or withdraw from situations.

Cognitive labeling. In 1959 psychologist Stanley Schachter argued that both cognitive and physiological factors are involved in the perception of our own emotional reactions. According to Schachter, the feedback we receive from our physiological response systems tells us about the *intensity* of our emotional responses, but it does not tell us about the *quality* of the emotions (i.e., which emotions are being experienced). This information is provided through a process called *cognitive labeling.*

Once an individual experiences physiological arousal, Schachter argues, the particular emotion he or she experiences is determined by the perceived cause of arousal. Ordinarily, emotions are labeled in accordance with the situation in which they occur. "It is the cognition that determines whether the state of physiological arousal will be labeled 'anger,' 'joy,' or whatever" (Schachter, 1971, p. 2).

In an influential experiment, Schachter and Jerome Singer (1962) attempted to test this theory by manipulating both the individual's state of physiological arousal and the availability of plausible explanations for the arousal. They told subjects that they were participating in a study of the effects of a fictitious vitamin named Suproxin, then actually injected them with either epinephrine to arouse them or a placebo with no physiological effect. They gave subjects who received the epinephrine one of three different sets of instructions. They told the *epinephrine-informed group* that Suproxin sometimes had side effects, then described the expected effects of epinephrine to them. This group then had an appropriate explanation for the arousal that would occur. They told subjects in an *epinephrine-misinformed group* to expect side effects not associated with epinephrine. Subjects in the *ignorant group* were told nothing about possible side effects. Subjects in the misinformed and ignorant groups, then, had no plausible explanation for the arousal caused by the epinephrine. The placebo group served as a control and, like the epinephrine-ignorant group, was told nothing.

After receiving their injections, subjects were asked to wait in a nearby waiting room while the vitamin took effect. In the waiting room was a "plant" who had been told by the experimenters to act either angry or euphoric. If the plant was told to act angry he acted increasingly irritated with questionnaires that the subjects had been given to complete, and finally tore them up and stomped out of the room. If he was told to act euphoric, the plant acted extremely happy and played basketball with wads of wastepaper, threw paper airplanes, and enthusiastically played with a hula hoop. During the time the subjects were exposed to this plant, researchers observed their behavior from behind a one-way vision screen and noted the extent to which the subjects behaved like the plant. They also gave subjects a self-report questionnaire that asked them how irritated, angry, or annoyed they were and how happy they felt at the present time.

In general, the results conformed to Schachter's predictions. The two epinephrine groups who did not have an appropriate explanation for their arousal felt and behaved in a happy fashion when the plant acted happy, whereas the same group felt less happy when the plant acted angry. Apparently, they explained their own arousal in terms of the plant's behavior and apparent mood. Epinephrine subjects who were informed about its side effects attributed their arousal to Suproxin and did not interpret it in terms of the situation in which they found themselves. The placebo control subjects who had no physiological arousal were not susceptible to the situation either.

Another experimenter (Marshall, 1974) was unable to reproduce Schachter and Singer's results when he used more rigorous controls, so Schachter and Singer's study alone does not seem to demonstrate adequately the validity of the two-factor theory of emotion. There are several other studies, however, that do support it, and it is a widely accepted current theory of emotion.

STRESS

Although it may be exactly what is *not* needed, we often experience strong emotional reactions in situations that pose challenges, demands, and threats. In the appraisal of a situation we often ask these questions: "What does the situation mean to me?" "What

Some occupations involve many stressful activities. Police work is associated with high rates of heart disease, and depression and suicide. Some of the tension officers feel when in difficult situations may be reduced through training in stress coping procedures. (From ''Officer Stress Awareness Films,'' courtesy Harper & Row Media.)

is expected of me?" "Can I handle the situation?" "How should I approach it?" These questions are part of the problem of *stress*. Stress refers to one's perception that a given situation is personally relevant and must be dealt with in some way. When under stress we feel "on the spot." Like motivation and emotion, stress arouses the individual and influences behaviors. (See Box 10.6.)

One of the great challenges for parents is to equip their children with effective ways of handling stress. A similar challenge confronts the psychological therapist who works with persons who perceive threats in too many areas of their lives and feel unable to deal with them. Much disturbed behavior can be thought of as unrealistic ways of coping with stress and anxiety. (See Chapter 15.) In this part of the chapter we explore ideas and methods that are important in the psychological study of stress.

Biological aspects of stress

According to Hans Selye, a Canadian physiologist, stress is the nonspecific response of the body to any demand made on it (1956). He refers to these demands as *stressors*. Based on a long series of experi-

ments with animals, Selye proposed that bodily stress reactions follow a three-stage General Adaptation Syndrome (GAS). The first stage is an *alarm reaction*, which involves physiological changes generally associated with emotion: pupil dilation, heart rate increase, and GSR increase. If the stress persists the individual enters a second stage, *resistance*, during which the body recovers from the stress reaction and begins to cope with the situation. There is a decrease in output from the sympathetic nervous system, a lower rate of epinephrine secretion, and a higher than normal output from one part of the adrenal gland (the adrenal cortex) and the pituitary gland. If the stress still continues then the animal will reach a final stage of *exhaustion*, during which the adrenal glands can no longer function adequately, and the body begins to break down. (See Figure 10.2.) Selye calls this process nonspecific because the body shows the same effects regardless of the source of the stress.

Sometimes the body's defensive reactions can result in actual physical damage called a psychophysiological or psychosomatic disorder. Examples of psychosomatic disorders include high blood pressure, heart disease, asthma, and ulcers. In these diseases

329

BOX 10.6

Arousal and task performance: The Yerkes-Dodson law

Motivation, emotion, and stress all cause physiological arousal, especially at high intensities. This arousal, in turn, influences our behavioral efficiency. Low or moderate levels of arousal may increase our efficiency, whereas extremely high levels of arousal may cause us to become disorganized and inefficient.

Behavioral efficiency is also influenced by the difficulty of the task. The same high level of arousal may help us to perform a simple task, such as running, but may cause us serious problems in performing a more complex task that requires precise movements, such as threading a needle. The Yerkes-Dodson law (Yerkes and Dodson, 1908) states that there is an optimal level of arousal for the performance of any given task. This optimal level can be expected to vary from person to person. At levels of arousal above and below the optimum, performance is less efficient. That is, as arousal builds up toward the optimum, task performance increases, but at arousal levels beyond the optimum, performance begins to suffer. Second, the Yerkes-Dodson

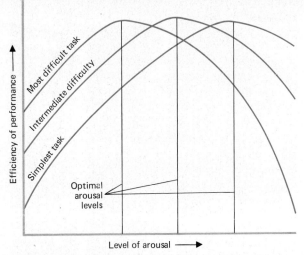

The Yerkes-Dodson law describes the relationship between arousal and performance.

law states that the more difficult the task, the lower the optimal level of arousal for performing it. For very simple tasks (e.g., running) the optimal level of arousal may be very high, whereas for tasks requiring great precision, the optimal arousal level is quite low.

These two principles are illustrated here. The relationship between arousal and performance on each task takes the form of an inverted U; the optimal level depends on the difficulty of the task.

---

strong habitual emotional reactions to stress result in bodily disorder.

Cognitive aspects of stress

We said earlier that individuals experience psychological stress when they encounter environmental conditions that they appraise as threatening. They must then engage in coping behavior designed to reduce or eliminate the threat. There are two stages in this appraisal process (Lazarus, 1968). During *primary appraisal* individuals interpret a situation as either threatening or harmless. During *secondary appraisal* they evaluate the kind of action called for

as well as the nature and potency of their resources for managing or coping with the threat or meeting the challenge. Whether and to what extent they are threatened depends on their estimate of these resources, which in turn is based largely on the flow of information from the environment and from their own experience and personal characteristics. New information can cause them to reappraise the situation either positively or negatively.

Experimental studies of cognition and stress

In a series of laboratory studies Richard Lazarus (1968) and his colleagues sought to influence experi-

emphasized the danger of the operation performed in the film, the sadism involved in it, and the pain suffered by the circumcised boys. Another emphasized that the circumcision ritual was an interesting specimen of human behavior. It had an intellectual rather than an emotional orientation. The third sound track tried to show that the native boys looked forward to circumcision and denied that it was either threatening to their health or terribly painful. No sound track accompanied the fourth showing of the film.

Figure 10.3 shows skin conductance patterns for the four experimental groups. The trauma sound track led to much higher skin conductance levels than did the other three accompaniments, and silence was more arousing than either the denial or the intellectualization of the painful experience. It appeared, then, as if the experimental sound tracks did influence subjects' cognitive appraisals of the film. Other research has shown that individual differences in personality, as well as experimental manipulations, play a role in coping with stress. Subjects characterized on the basis of psychological tests as ambitious, shrewd, confident, impulsive, forceful, and self-centered were physiologically less reactive during the subincision film than were those identi-

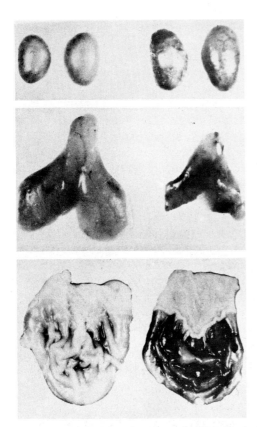

Figure 10.2 Stress and damage to bodily organs: (top) adrenal glands, (middle) thymus glands, (bottom) inner surface of the stomach. The organs on the left are those of a normal rat and those on the right of one exposed to the frustrating psychological stress of being forcefully immobilized. Note the marked enlargement and dark discoloration of the adrenals (caused by congestion and discharge of fatty-secretion granules), the intense shrinkage of the thymus, as well as the numerous blood-covered ulcers in the alarmed rat. (Reproduced with permission from *The Story of the Adaptation Syndrome* by Hans Selye. Acta Inc. Medical Publishers, 1952.)

mentally the cognitive appraisal of situations that under ordinary conditions would be at least mildly stressful. The vehicle they selected was sound tracks that accompanied films possessing certain properties.

In one experiment college students saw a film entitled "Subincision in the Arunta," which depicted crude operations on the penis and scrotum of adolescent aboriginal boys (Speisman et al., 1964). The film was shown to four groups of subjects, with a different sound track each time. One sound track

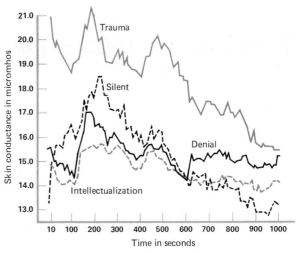

Figure 10.3 The effects of the experimental treatments on skin conductance. (Speisman et al., 1964. Copyright 1964 by the American Psychological Association.)

fied as mature, moderate, self-controlled, and responsive to the plight of others (Lazarus, 1968).

The stresses of life

Once we leave the laboratory and enter the world of everyday life we are confronted with many situations that require cognitive appraisals of possible threats (to our bodies, our self-esteem, etc.) and an ability to cope with them. Do these experiences combine in some way that has an observable effect on our lives?

Most of the research into this question during the past decade has been based on four assumptions:

1. Life changes contribute significantly to life crisis or stress.
2. These changes can be defined objectively to include both desirable and undesirable events (e.g., marriage, illness, deaths of friends or relatives) and both major and minor events (e.g., jail term and holiday).
3. The degree of adaptation needed to cope with specific life changes can be estimated from ratings by large numbers of subjects who represent the population from which research samples are drawn.
4. Life change units are additive. Many molehills may make a mountain.

Researchers sometimes ask subjects to indicate which of a series of events has occurred in their lives during a specific period of time (e.g., the last six months) and assign weights or scores to them. They then add the scores to obtain a total life change score. Box 10.7 shows one example of a life change assessment instrument. Other researchers ask subjects to prepare their own lists of events that have required significant readjustments, and even to assign their own personal "stress weights."

Although there are still many problems in measuring life stress and its relationship both to personal adjustment and disease, the information we do have seems consistent. Individuals with high stress scores describe themselves as significantly more anxious, depressed, hostile, and fatigued than those with low scores. Individuals who have experienced a great deal of stress are more likely than other people to get sick or hurt enough to require psychiatric, medical, or surgical attention. They also report higher physical

symptom intensities than respondents with low stress scores.

Life stress has been shown to be significantly correlated with traffic accidents among male drivers, especially alcoholics (Selzer and Vinokur, 1974). The possiblity that athletes who have relatively high stress levels have high injury rates has also been investigated. Steven Bramwell and his colleagues (1975) found that athletes with high life stress scores had twice the percentage of injuries as did athletes with low stress scores.

Freud may not have been entirely correct in arguing that specific types of early childhood events are correlated with maladjustments in adult personalities. But it is likely that stressful experiences leave traces that can still be seen after many years. (See Box 10.8.) One study compared the life stress histories of cancer patients with those of a noncancerous control group (LeShan, 1966). Fully 72 percent of the cancer patients had experienced a psychic trauma early in life, whereas only 10 percent of the noncancerous group had had one. (A psychic trauma was defined as an emotional relationship that involved pain and feelings of being deserted.)

Researchers have only begun to scratch the surface concerning the relationship between significant events in our lives and our physiological and psychological adjustments. Yet they have uncovered a number of leads and the area of study is growing steadily.

Work and stress

For all of us the saying "Where there's life, there's stress" seems obviously to be valid. Less obvious is the answer to the question "Is stress always undesirable?" If we found ourselves in a stress-free paradise would we have adequate motivation to accomplish tasks and experience personal growth? In any case, it is a fact that individuals differ in the extent to which they appraise situations as stressful and they react in different ways to them. The work situation illustrates this point. Some people seem to thrive under heavy work loads while others wilt under them.

Long hours, heavy work loads, unremitting responsibilites—do these sound like the attributes of an ideal job? A recent study showed that workers in occupations that entail these apparent hardships are more satisfied, less anxious, and perhaps healthier than those in less demanding jobs. In fact, boredom

BOX 10.7

Life change and stress

Thomas H. Holmes and his colleagues at the University of Washington School of Medicine have developed a scale for measuring the seriousness of changes in people's lives and related their scores to their chances of becoming ill. Life changes require adaptation that is taxing to the body. The Survey of Recent Experiences (SRE) consists of 43 different life changes that have been scaled in *life change units* for the degree of adaptation they require. Persons whose life change units over the preceding two years total more than 300 seem to be more susceptible to major changes in their health (Rahe and Holmes, 1966; Holmes and Rahe, 1967).

Survey of recent experiences

Events	Life Change Units
Death of spouse	100
Divorce	73
Marital separation	65
Jail term	63
Death of close family member	63
Personal injury or illness	53
Marriage	50
Fired at work	47
Marital reconciliation	45
Retirement	45
Change in health of family member	44
Pregnancy	40
Sex difficulties	39

Survey of recent experiences (*continued*)

Events	Life Change Units
Gain of new family member	39
Business readjustment	39
Change in financial state	38
Death of close friend	37
Change to different line of work	36
Change in number of arguments with spouse	35
Mortgage over $10,000	31
Foreclosure of mortgage or loan	30
Change in responsibilities at work	29
Son or daughter leaving home	29
Trouble with in-laws	29
Outstanding personal achievement	28
Wife begins or stops work	26
Begin or end school	26
Change in living conditions	25
Revision of personal habits	24
Trouble with boss	23
Change in work hours or conditions	20
Change in residence	20
Change in schools	20
Change in recreation	19
Change in church activities	19
Change in social activities	18
Mortgage or loan less than $10,000	17
Change in sleeping habits	16
Change in number of family get-togethers	15
Change in eating habits	15
Vacation	13
Christmas	12
Minor violations of the law	11

and lack of responsibility may be hazardous to a worker's health.

A group of researchers at the University of Michigan have found that job satisfaction had less to do with generalized working conditions, such as the average number of hours worked each week and the quantitative work load, than with more personalized factors, such as opportunities to utilize skills and participate in decision making. High job satisfaction reduces the amount of strain in the form of anxiety, depression, or irritation a worker experiences on the job and thereby reduces the likelihood of psychosomatic illness. (*Institute for Social Research Newsletter*, Spring 1975.)

For example, family physicians put in a large amount of unwanted overtime. They have one of the

333

BOX 10.8
Prisoners of war

Professor Leo Eitinger of the University of Oslo has devoted much of his career to studying the long-term consequences of having been a prisoner of war during World War II. Eitinger examined the total unselected group of 2000 Norwegian concentration camp survivors. Working with the assumption that health is not merely the absence of disease, Eitinger was interested in the general adjustment of ex-prisoners in the postwar period. He recorded the number of changes in occupation, changes of residence, changes in occupational status, and changes of job.

The ex-prisoners seemed to feel compelled to change their occupations more often than did the members of a control group. Nearly 98 percent of nonprisoners in the control group had only one residence over a long period of time, whereas the ex-prisoners moved much more, either because they were restless or because they wanted to find new jobs. Ex-prisoners were also less able to succeed at their work. One out of four had an obvious occupational decline, whereas only one out of 25 controls experienced a similar decline. One out of three ex-prisoners had to find four or more jobs during the observation period in order to continue to earn some sort of livelihood.

Eitinger recorded all sick leave taken by each person included in the sample, and each diagnosis. He also recorded how many days of that sick leave were spent in a hospital. The ex-prisoners were ill more often than the controls, and when they were ill, the ex-prisoners required hospitalization for longer periods than did hospitalized controls.

The findings showed that former prisoners of war are a highly vulnerable group. They become sick often and have a great variety of illnesses that involve almost every organic system.

largest quantitative work loads and reported that their jobs demanded high levels of mental concentration. In spite of these apparent hardships, these men reported the greatest amount of satisfaction with their jobs; low levels of anxiety, depression, and irritation; and few somatic disorders, such as difficulty in sleeping, loss of appetite, or fast heartbeat.

In contrast, assembly line workers—who do not have excessively long hours, unwanted overtime, large work loads, or particularly great demands for concentration—reported the most boredom and the greatest dissatisfaction with their work load, as well as the highest levels of anxiety, depression, irritation, and somatic disorders. This strong evidence of strain seems attributable to job insecurity, to a lack of social support from immediate superiors and other workers, and to a lack of opportunity to use individual skills and abilities or to participate in decision making.

But the researchers found that the greatest single determinant of job satisfaction is the degree of compatibility (fit) between the demands of the job and the desires of the worker. If individuals feel they want a job that differs from the one they have in terms of complexity, work load, supervisory responsibility, or overtime hours, then they will invariably be dissatisfied with their present job, no matter whether it is deficient or excessive in these factors.

Recent years have seen an increasing number of experimental attempts to "humanize" work environments and alleviate the normal stresses of low-status jobs. In some assembly plants in the United States, for example, workers have been organized into small teams that assemble a variety of components on trucks, then move them down the line to the team at the next station. These workers have more opportunities to employ varied skills and make decisions than do workers on machine-paced lines, and they have significantly lower scores on boredom, anxiety, and depression.

Unfortunately, many experiments have neglected to take individual differences into account; some have assumed that all workers on the same job are affected in the same way by stress factors, and they make unilateral changes to eliminate a problem. What constitutes a decrease in stress for some individuals may constitute an increase for others.

Diego Rivera's mural of automobile assembly line workers depicts the physical stress their jobs entail, but mental stress may be their greatest problem. The man seated below the mural seems oblivious to job stress. (Berndt, Stock, Boston)

Reactions to disaster

The research on life stress demonstrates the cumulative impact of changes that occur in our personal lives. These changes may be quite sudden as, for example, when a spouse dies in a car accident. When change occurs suddenly, violently, disruptively, and on a community basis, we describe it as *disaster*.

Disasters are special kinds of emergencies that produce observable effects on the individual and the entire social system. There are many misconceptions about disaster that research has been able to correct. More often than one might expect, people respond in a reasonably adaptive manner to disastrous happenings. (See Box 10.9.) Behavior in a disaster is influenced by several factors, including its unexpected-

ness, suddenness, intensity, and duration. The morale of the community, experience with previous emergencies, and previous training also play roles.

Most individuals adjust rapidly to the effects of disasters (earthquakes, floods, hurricanes), but about one-third of the survivors display what has been called the *disaster syndrome*. During the hours following the disaster they are dazed and wander around aimlessly. They often complain of severe psychophysiological symptoms, such as nausea, insomnia, and "the shakes."

Studies of survivors of the nuclear attacks on Hiroshima and Nagasaki showed that they had an abnormally high rate not only of cancer, but also of cardiovascular diseases. According to one hypothesis,

BOX 10.9
Nine facts about behavior in disasters

1. Mass panic, that is, headlong and terror-stricken flight, is a very rare occurrence in disasters.
2. Looting is a relatively minor problem in most disasters.
3. There are very few instances of a breakdown of moral codes.
4. Populations which have been struck by a disaster are not a dazed, helpless mass.
5. Disaster victims are seldom reduced to the level of thinking only of their personal survival.
6. Disaster-stricken people generally do not exhibit outbursts of hysteria, screaming, and weeping.
7. Emotional and physical reactions are fairly widespread following a disaster, but they tend to be temporary.
8. There is no clear evidence that disasters produce an increase in neurosis, psychosis, and other mental illnesses. However, prolonged stresses may produce or evoke psychological disturbances, especially in predisposed individuals.
9. Children generally do not cause special problems in disasters, especially if they are not separated from their parents.

(Weil, 1973, pp. 114–115)

National guardsmen help flood victims on a makeshift bridge over a river in Colorado. (UPI)

prolonged or severe stress can result in premature aging, which in turn leads to higher rates of disease than would normally be expected for particular age groups.

Coping with stress: A psychological frontier

As our knowledge of the effects of stress increases, researchers are trying to determine ways in which people can be helped to cope more effectively with stress. Some of the following methods have been useful:

1. Providing individuals with information about a potentially stressful situation *before* they actually enter it helps them to cope more effectively with it. Many surgical patients suffer unnecessarily after their operations because they are not warned that they will have considerable postsurgical pain.
2. Learning specific skills needed in stressful situations helps individuals to cope effectively. Many individuals enter dangerous situations without proper training. For example, many hiking and mountain climbing accidents are the result of poor training and preparation.

3. Individuals can be "trained" for stressful situations by going through a series of experiences graded from relatively low to relatively high in stress.
4. Observing a model who copes with stress in an effective way can help people about to enter a strange or dangerous situation.

Each of these methods for adaptive coping has an important cognitive aspect. Stressors have an impact that corresponds to an individual's estimate of how well prepared he or she is; this preparation includes not only specific skills but also thoughts. (See Box 10.10.)

Psychologists have not invented a cure-all for stress. They are, however, making progress in isolating the variables related to stressful experiences and helping people to cope with them.

SUMMARY

1. *Motivation* is a general term referring to forces regulating goal-seeking behavior. It is influenced by factors present in the situation or in the individual. It is characterized by both energy and direction. *Emotions* refer to feeling states of the individual. Emotional reactions are difficult to define and measure because they refer to internal feelings. Physiological measures can be used as a partial measure of emotion. *Stress* refers to a person's perception of a situation as being demanding and requiring a response that he or she may feel incapable of making adequately.

2. Motivation has been explained as an instinct, as a response to biological drive (primary motivation), and as a learned response to certain experiences (secondary motivation). It is often viewed as an interaction between the values the person believes in and his or her expectancy of behaving adequately enough to attain the desired goal.

3. One biological drive, hunger, has been investigated from many aspects. From one point of view hunger is defined in terms of the amount of glucose being utilized by the body. Parts of the nervous system are also related to hunger. Portions of the hypothalamus may help establish a baseline for body weight. Research on choice among food items by infants and by animals suggests that their selection of foods is in part determined by the nutritional needs of the body.

4. The eating behavior of overweight people seems to be less directed by internal stimuli, such as stomach fullness, than does the eating behavior of people of average weight.

5. Motivation affects such things as perception and learning. Social motives are related to environment and individual personality.

6. One social motive that has been extensively studied is the *need for achievement*. A quantitative scoring system has been devised to measure need for achievement in many situations. Achievement-oriented behavior seems different in men and women. The conflict many women show about achievement has been called *fear of success*. Another need that has been studied in some detail is the need for power.

7. Emotions are complex private events. They may be measured by asking individuals to describe their response to situations, obtaining physiological records, observing behavior, and combining these measures.

8. Two early theories of emotion were the James-Lange theory and the Cannon-Bard theory. The James-Lange theory says that emotion is a perception of physiological changes in the body. According to the Cannon-Bard theory, the thalamus signals both the brain and the muscles when certain stimuli are perceived. This means the feeling of emotion and its effects on the body are experienced at the same time. At pres-

337

BOX 10.10
Meeting the challenges of life-threatening stress

The concentration camp experience

A number of enlightening personal accounts of the concentration camp experience exist. They vividly portray not only some of the most shocking horrors of World War II, but also some of the survival techniques used by the camp inmates. The accounts of two inmates, Bruno Bettelheim, a psychologist (1960), and Victor Frankl, a psychiatrist (1962), are especially valuable because they make clear that cognitive and information-handling orientations of the inmates were correlated significantly with survival at places like Dachau and Buchenwald. The following true-false items are based on Bettelheim's and Frankl's descriptions of adaptive ways of coping with the concentration camp experience. Someone who receives a high score on the scale is offering self-reports similar to the kinds of thinking and problem-solving that Bettelheim and Frankl observed in themselves and other survivors.

These are true-false items based on Bettelheim's (1960) and Frankl's (1962) descriptions of adaptive cognitive responses in a concentration camp. T and F refer to true and false answers in the adaptive or coping direction:

1. When in a difficult situation I try to sit back and objectively assess what is happening.   T
2. When things get monotonous I keep my mind active by thinking about interesting topics or playing mental games.   T
3. When in strange or unfamiliar situations I often forget important, practical bits of information (such as road directions).   F
4. I might not be able to take the stress of having to spend time in jail.   F
5. In physically demanding situations I occasionally forget to pace myself.   F
6. When under stress I keep my feelings to myself and concentrate on the situation confronting me.   T
7. I believe that through careful planning, people can survive under very severe circumstances.   T
8. When treated unfairly, I can't resist complaining even though I know it won't do any good.   F
9. I would not be willing to "suffer in silence" even if speaking out exposed me to danger.   F
10. When I see how most people handle a particularly difficult problem, I follow their lead.   F
11. When things get overwhelming I tend to give up and accept my fate.   F
12. I can stay on good terms with people who are really my enemies.   T
13. I don't think clearly when surprising things happen to me.   F
14. I do not have trouble controlling my temper.   T
15. It is always better to express your emotions directly than to keep them under wraps.   F

Illustrative of item 2 is this account given by Frankl of how mental games and fantasy helped him survive the monotony and cruelty of life in a concentration camp.

I forced my thoughts to turn to another subject. Suddenly I saw myself standing on the platform of a well-lit, warm and pleasant lecture room. In front of me sat an attentive audience on comfortable upholstered seats. I was giving a lecture on the psychology of the concentration camp! All that oppressed me at that moment became objective, seen and described from the remote viewpoint of science. By this method I succeeded somehow in rising above the situation, above the sufferings of the moment, and I observed them as if they were already of the past. Both I and my troubles became the object of

338

an interesting psychoscientific study undertaken by myself. (Frankl, 1962, pp. 73–74)

The psychological stress of the cancer victim

We tend to think of bodily disorders as being only or mainly physical problems. As this newspaper story shows, this is simply not true.

The attitudes of families and friends is important to the cancer patient's well-being, said Orville Kelly, 45, a former newspaperman who is suffering from cancer.

He formed an organization two years ago called Make Today Count for advanced-cancer patients and their families. It now has 54 chapters.

"I always thought that cancer happened to somebody else, so I wasn't very well prepared," said Mr. Kelly, who was told in June, 1973, that he had lymphoma, a cancer of the lymph glands. He said he had expected to die within six months, but under drug treatments his cancer has been in remission for the past nine months.

"Following my hospitalization," he said, "I went home to await my chemotherapy treatment and I began to discover fear and depression are terrible things to live with. I gave up. I went to bed to await the inevitable. I even considered suicide as an easy way out.

"I discovered the attitudes of family, friends and relatives had changed. Old friends were uneasy around me, afraid they would say something wrong. Actually there was little they could say I hadn't already thought of several times."

He said he spoke little about his problems because he did not want to worry his family. His wife slept in another room because she did not want him to hear her crying.

"There was little communication," Mr. Kelly said. "They were trying to protect me and I was trying to protect them. It didn't work."

He said his frustrations drove him to write a newspaper article about the psychological pressures of being a cancer patient. This led to the formation of his organization.

"In sharing our problems," Mr. Kelly said, "we discovered fear, depression, rejection, sexual problems and anger were often more difficult to contend with than cancer." (Excerpt from *Washington Post* wire service story in *International Herald Tribune* April 1, 1976, p. 1)

ent, elements of both theories seem to apply in certain circumstances.

9. One current approach, *cognitive labeling,* suggests that the person perceives the intensity of emotion from a physiological response, but the particular emotions he or she experiences are determined by the situation in which the responses occur.

10. Stress has been considered a nonspecific response made by the body to demands on it. Sometimes these reactions can result in actual physical disease.

11. Sources of stress range from a variety of changes and pressures often found in life to catastrophic happenings such as a flood or earthquake. It seems likely that the effect of even minor stressful events "add up" and can cause problems if a large number occur.

12. Psychologists have found that people can be trained to cope even with great stress by developing certain skills and attitudes.

Suggested Readings

Bettelheim, B. *The Informed Heart.* New York: The Free Press, 1960. Description of author's concentration camp experiences.

Bolles, R. C. *Theory of motivation.* (2nd ed.) New York: Harper & Row Publishers, 1975. Deals with many motivational concepts, particularly as they are studied in research with animals.

Dohrenwend, B. S. & Dohrenwend, B. B. (Eds.) *Stressful life events: Their nature and effects.* New York: John Wiley & Sons, Inc., 1974. Surveys attempts to measure the effects of the stresses of life.

Lazarus, R. S. *Psychological stress and the coping process.* New York: McGraw-Hill Book Company, 1966. Contains an analysis of stress that has been influential.

McClelland, D. C. & Steele, R. S. *Human motivation: A book of readings.* Morristown, N.J.: General Learning Press, 1973. Contains articles dealing with research approaches to human motivation.

Strongman, K. T. *The psychology of emotion.* New York: John Wiley & Sons, Inc., 1973. Reviews theory and research in the area of emotion.

Weiner, B. *Theories of motivation: From mechanism to cognition.* Chicago: Markham Publishing Company, 1972. Comprehensively reviews concepts related to human motivation.

Chapter 11

Human Sexuality

(Payne, Jeroboam)

The year was 1961 and the following conclusions regarding the effects of sexually explicit books and magazines were entered into the *Congressional Record* by Senator Kenneth Keating of New York:

> Those concerned declare that no act of subversion planned by the Communist conspiracy could be more effective in shredding the Nation's moral fabric than the lethal effect of pornography. While it is not impossible that some of the material now sold is Kremlin inspired, ironically the Reds need not work too hard at this. They are aided by thousands of amoral, dollar-crazed Americans, many of them militant in defense of their constitutional rights to pander to man's baser passions and their consequent fallout: perversion and depravity. (August 29, 1961)

It was 1969 and a male teenager was being tried in the Juvenile Division of the Superior Court of California for having intercourse with his 15-year-old sister. Among the judge's remarks to the defendant were the following:

> This is one of the worst crimes that a person can commit. I just get so disgusted that I just figure what is the use? You are just an animal. You are lower than an animal. Even animals don't do that. . . . You are no particular good to anybody. We ought to send you out of the country. . . . You belong in prison for the rest of your life for doing things of this kind. You ought to commit suicide. That's what I think of people of this kind. You are lower than animals and haven't the right to live in organized society—just miserable, lousy, rotten people. . . . Maybe Hitler was right. The animals in our society probably ought to be destroyed because they have no right to live among human beings. (State of California, County of Santa Clara, September 2, 1969)

These statements represent extreme examples of the level of emotion that can be aroused around sexual issues. There is probably no other aspect of our behavior that provokes as much moral and legal controversy, as many conflicting beliefs, and as much personal conflict as sex.

It is curious and unfortunate that sex, which affects our lives so profoundly, has traditionally received insufficient attention in scientific research and higher education. But this situation is beginning to change. Society is loosening its restrictions and allowing a freer discussion of sex and an expansion of scientific research on it.

Although sex is just beginning to be recognized as a legitimate area of study, there has long been an almost obsessive interest in the subject among the general public. Newsstands and bookstores are now filled with erotic novels; "how to" books make the best-seller lists, and there is a large and highly profitable pornography industry. Advertisers use sex to sell everything from foot powder to power tools. For countless individuals sexual activity is a source of intense pleasure. But for many others it is a source of guilt and misery.

Because sexual expression is always laced with moral and legal issues, the scientific study of sexuality has been slow to evolve. Alfred Kinsey's pioneering survey studies of sexual behavior in the 1940s received strong condemnation in many segments of society, and the work of William Masters and Virginia Johnson in the 1960s also elicited cries of outrage. The so-called sexual revolution that began in the 1960s, however, brought into sharp focus many questions of great societal importance: What effects do erotic stimuli have on behavior? What are the psychological effects of varying forms of sexual expression? What are the differences in the sexual

(Magee, EPA)

BOX 11.1

Ten facts about some sexual myths

There is an extensive folklore of commonly accepted beliefs about sexual behavior within our culture. The recent increase in research on human sexuality has disclosed that many widely held beliefs have no basis in fact. Among the findings are the following:

1. There is no known aphrodisiac (sexual stimulant) that is uniformly effective in increasing sexual pleasure.
2. Penis size has no physiological relationship to sexual effectiveness or the ability to provide pleasure for a partner. A vagina can accommodate any size of penis. Penis size may affect the amount of pleasure a woman experiences, but for psychological rather than physical reasons.
3. There is no evidence that masturbation causes blindness, growth of hair on the palms, brain damage, or any other physical maladies.
4. There is no evidence that frequent sexual activity during youth causes a person to "burn out" in later years, nor that frequent sexual activity adversely affects health. In fact, frequent sexual expression in early adulthood seems to prolong the potency of elderly males.
5. There is no known physiological difference between clitoral and vaginal orgasm.
6. Sexual satisfaction is not an accurate indicator of the adequacy of a marriage in other respects.
7. An intact hymen is not proof of virginity, nor is its absence proof of intercourse.
8. Saran Wrap and similar products wrapped around the penis are neither effective contraceptives nor effective protection against venereal disease.
9. Postcoronary patients can resume sexual activity as soon as they are capable of walking several blocks or climbing several flights of stairs.
10. There is no medical reason why women should avoid sexual intercourse during menstruation. In fact, it may help relieve menstrual cramps, and many women have strong sexual desires during their periods.

attitudes, behaviors, and preferences of males and females? What are the psychological effects of birth control and abortion? What are the causes of sexual problems, such as impotence and "frigidity," and how can they be treated?

TWO APPROACHES TO THE STUDY OF SEXUALITY

Two major research strategies have provided the bulk of our knowledge about human sexual behavior. The first of these is the *descriptive approach*, directed at gathering facts about sexual behavior. What are the forms of sexual expression, and how frequently do people engage in them? What are the physiological components of the human sexual response? Survey studies constitute one form of descriptive research, and controlled observation and measurement of sexual behavior under laboratory conditions constitutes another.

The second major approach to understanding human sexuality is the *experimental approach*. This approach seeks to discover the ways in which certain variables affect sexual behavior under controlled conditions. For example, an experimenter might measure differences in the degree to which men and women are sexually aroused by particular kinds of erotic stimuli. The experimental approach is newer than the descriptive approach, but it is already providing answers to old questions about sexuality.

The descriptive and the experimental approaches

complement one another in the study of sexuality. The first step in understanding any phenomenon is to describe it carefully. But as we noted in our discussion of research methods in Chapter 1, description is not enough; scientific understanding requires that we test our explanations through prediction and control. This is possible with the experimental approach, which involves manipulating variables and studying their effects on behavior.

The descriptive approach

Survey studies

The first reports of large-scale efforts to study sexual behavior systematically did not appear until the late 1940s. These pioneering studies were carried out by Alfred Kinsey and his associates at Indiana University. The first Kinsey report, *Sexual Behavior in the Human Male* (Kinsey, Pomeroy, and Martin, 1948), presented a highly detailed statistical analysis of the sexual activities of 5300 American males ranging in age from 10 to 90. The data were collected in personal interviews that lasted about two hours, during which respondents were asked about 300 questions about their sex lives. A companion volume, *Sexual Behavior in the Human Female* (Kinsey, Pomeroy, Martin, and Gebhard, 1953), was the result of similar interviews with 5940 American women.

Although the Kinsey report remains the most comprehensive study of sexual behavior ever undertaken, it is open to a number of valid criticisms that relate to sampling and interviewing techniques. Although the sample of 11,240 people who were interviewed reflected a wide range of differences in age, educational level, occupation, religious affiliation, marital status, and so on, the sample was not representative of the population of the United States. For example, rural groups and lower educational levels were underrepresented, as were children and people over 50 years of age. All respondents were white volunteers. Kinsey was well aware of the shortcomings of his sample and was careful to point out that

More liberal social mores may account for many recent changes in sexual mores. Co-ed dorms, which are quite commonplace nowadays, would have been unthinkable fifteen years ago. (Wide World)

343

the findings did not necessarily reflect the sexual behavior of the American population.

In addition, there is considerable debate about how truthful the respondents were in reporting intimate details about their sex lives to relative strangers. There is no way to answer this question with certainty, and we must be aware of the possibility of distortions in self-reporting. It is worth noting, however, that Kinsey's findings have been supported by data collected using other methods, such as anonymous questionnaires.

Although Kinsey's data were collected a generation ago and their applicability to current sexual practices is unclear, they remain the most comprehensive source of information available. The most recent attempt to survey American sexual attitudes and behaviors was sponsored by the Playboy Foundation and was based on questionnaire data collected by a public opinion firm from 2026 men and women residing in twenty-four cities. The survey's effort to obtain a more representative sample than Kinsey's was only partially successful; about 80 percent of the individuals who were randomly selected to participate refused. Many smaller questionnaire studies have also been carried out, particularly with college students, and a fairly consistent picture of contemporary sexual behavior among young people has emerged.

Sexual standards and attitudes. Traditionally, people in the United States have believed in abstinence until marriage, with some acceptance of premarital intercourse between engaged couples or those planning to be married (Reiss, 1967). However, sexual standards have recently become much more liberal, particularly among younger prople. Studies conducted in the last decade reveal that 50 to 80 percent of college men feel that premarital intercourse is acceptable. This is especially true among students who are nonreligious and who attend eastern and western schools. Among college women, being in love is an important determinant of whether or not they feel sexual intercourse is acceptable. For example, in a study conducted at the University of Colorado (Kaats and Davis, 1970) about 70 percent of the women indicated that they would be willing to have intercourse if they were in love, but fewer than 40 percent found it acceptable if there were no affec-

tion. Recent studies have also shown that both men and women continue to share a double standard that makes premarital sex more acceptable for males than for females, particularly in relationships without love.

Sexual urges. Few studies have been conducted on how often people experience sexual urges. In one study (Kaats and Davis, 1970) 78 percent of a sample of college women and 98 percent of the men acknowledged experiencing "urges to engage in sexual intercourse," and 91 percent of the women indicated the desire to engage in "some form of sexual activity." Fifty-five percent of the women reported sexual urges weekly or more often, and of this group 90 percent were currently engaging in sexual intercourse. Awareness of sexual urges was highly related to how often the subjects were dating.

Masturbation. In Kinsey's research 58 percent of all the women in the sample reported having masturbated to orgasm at least once in their lives. The proportion was lower (32 percent) among 20-year-old college women. This percentage does not appear to have increased appreciably in recent years. Studies conducted during the past decade have consistently reported that between 30 and 40 percent of the young women surveyed have masturbated at least once. Frequent masturbation among young women is even lower, with only 8 percent in one study reporting that they masturbate weekly or more often (Kaats and Davis, 1970). The same study found that frequency of sexual urges in women was related to frequency of masturbation only among virgins, and even then the relationship was weak.

Masturbation is much more frequent among men than among women. Among the male subjects studied by Kinsey, 92 percent of all males and 96 percent of college graduates reported having masturbated to orgasm.

Petting. Heavy petting, defined as tactual stimulation of the partner's genitals, appears to have greatly increased in frequency since the Kinsey report. Among the college females in Kinsey's sample, 52 percent had engaged in heavy petting. Studies conducted with college students during the past decades have reported percentages ranging from 60 to 90 percent.

For college women, engaging in heavy petting is highly related to permissive standards for intercourse when in love and to beliefs that their girlfriends have engaged in intercourse (Kaats and Davis, 1970). Heavy petting is not restricted to love relationships; 25 percent of the women in the Kaats and Davis sample had petted heavily with two or more partners they did not love. It appears that women are far more likely to choose heavy petting than masturbation for purely sexual pleasure.

Heavy petting by males has apparently remained at a high level over the years. Kinsey reported a figure over 90 percent, and recent studies have reported percentages in the same range.

Oral-genital stimulation. A highly effective but somewhat controversial means of achieving sexual arousal and orgasm is through oral-genital contact. *Cunnilingus* refers to oral stimulation of the female genitals; *fellatio* involves oral stimulation of the male genitalia. Although some people find oral-genital contact repulsive, it is difficult to support objections on hygienic grounds if the genitalia are clean (Katchadourian and Lunde, 1975). However, in much of the English-speaking world, cunnilingus and fellatio are classified as sodomy and are punishable by law.

The practice of oral-genital stimulation seems to have become considerably more prevalent in the years since the Kinsey survey was conducted. In the Kinsey data about half the college-educated males had performed cunnilingus with their wives, but fewer than 15 percent of those with high school educations had done so. Fellatio was less frequent, with about 60 percent of the married women never having attempted it, and the rest having done so very infrequently. In the survey sponsored by the Playboy Foundation (Hunt, 1974), 80 percent of single males and females between the ages of 25 and 35, and nearly 90 percent of married persons under 25 years of age reported having engaged in oral-genital stimulation during the previous year. The largest increase occurred among individuals with lower educational levels and among women. Cunnilingus and fellatio are now being performed with about equal frequency, according to Hunt's data. The use of oral-genital stimulation declines with age to about 25 percent for both sexes beyond age 55.

(Ritscher, Stock, Boston)

Sexual intercourse. In Kinsey's national sample 48 percent of the women interviewed stated that they had engaged in premarital intercourse, and 26 percent admitted that they had engaged in extramarital sex. Approximately one-fourth of the 20- and 21-year-old college women in the sample indicated that they were not virgins. More recent studies of college women have reported premarital intercourse rates of between 35 and 72 percent. A study of 8000 first semester college freshmen and juniors yielded rates of 29 percent for freshmen and 36 percent for juniors (Groves, Rossi, and Grafstein, 1970). A more recent study (King and Sobel, 1975) reported a 72 percent figure among a sample of 371 college women. Another 10 to 20 percent of college women who are still virgins indicate that they would find premarital intercourse acceptable if they were to find the right partner (Kaats and Davis, 1970). If we assume that many of these women will be successful in their

345

quest for a love relationship, then perhaps 55 to 70 percent of unmarried college women will have had intercourse by the time they are 25 years old. This would constitute an increase over the Kinsey figure of 47 percent for college women married by age 25.

Kinsey's data showed a significantly higher rate of premarital intercourse for males (85 percent) than for females (48 percent). In addition, about half of all the married males had had extramarital sex, and about 70 percent of the total male sample acknowledged having had intercourse with prostitutes.

Almost all studies of college males have reported rates of intercourse of around 60 percent, with regional and religious variations. Males appear far more likely than females to have sexual partners whom they do not love. In the Kaats and Davis (1970) study 57 percent of the sexually experienced men had had intercourse with at least one partner they did not love, whereas this was the case for only 26 percent of the females.

The Masters and Johnson observational studies

The most extensive and sophisticated research on the physiological responses that occur during sex was conducted by William Masters and Virginia Johnson (1966). At the Reproductive Biology Research Foundation in St. Louis, volunteer subjects engaged in sexual activity to the point of orgasm while sophisticated measuring instruments monitored their bodily reactions. The study monitored about 10,000 orgasms brought about by masturbation and intercourse. Some observations of female sexual responses were made while women simulated intercourse with a transparent probe that permitted observation of the vagina.

Masters and Johnson discovered a basic four-stage pattern of sexual response for both men and women. The initial *excitement* response to sexual stimulation is vaginal lubrication in the female and penile erection in the male. This is followed in the female by nipple erection, a thickening of the vaginal walls, and a flattening and elevation of the external genitalia. In males there is a slight increase in the size and elevation of the testicles.

At the second, or *plateau* stage, sexual excitement is reflected in increased heart rate, respiration, and muscle tension. The male's testes increase in size by about 50 percent and are pulled up high in the scro-

tum. In the female the tissues surrounding the outer third of the vagina swell to reduce the diameter of the vaginal opening up to 50 percent. The clitoris retracts under the hood that covers it.

In the third stage, *orgasm*, the penis begins to throb in rhythmic contractions. Semen collects in the urethral bulb and contractions of the bulb and penis project the semen out of the penis. Muscles throughout the body contract and there is a temporary state of high physiological arousal. In females orgasm involves rhythmic muscular contractions of the outer third of the vagina and the uterus. Other muscles, such as the anal sphincter, may also contract in a rhythmic fashion.

In males orgasm is followed by the *resolution* phase in which physiological arousal rapidly decreases and the organs and tissues return to their normal condition. Females may have two or more successive orgasms before the onset of the resolution phase. (See Figure 11.1.)

The pioneering work of Masters and Johnson provided major insights into the physiological aspects of our sexual behavior. Many of their findings contradicted erroneous popular beliefs as well. For example, they found that there were no detectable physiological differences between female orgasms produced through stimulation of the clitoris and those brought about by vaginal stimulation. As we shall see in our later discussion of sexual dysfunction, they also developed a number of useful treatment techniques for certain sexual problems.

The experimental approach

In recent years more attempts have been made to study sexuality within the research laboratory. Although the experimental controls used in these studies are in many cases less rigorous than those used in some other areas of psychological research, these studies nevertheless constitute an advance in sex research because they attempt to control stimulus factors and to measure responses more precisely. We shall examine some of the research dealing with (a) stimulus factors in sexuality, (b) responses to sexual stimuli, and (c) sex differences in sexuality.

Stimulus factors in sexuality

Although our sex drive is partially attributable to biological factors, environmental stimuli appear to be

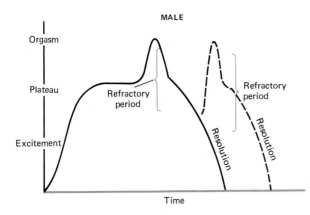

MALE

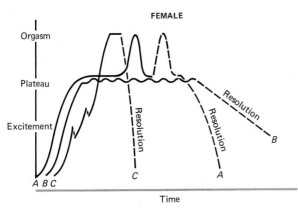

FEMALE

Figure 11.1 Male and female sexual response cycles. The solid lines indicate common patterns of response and the dotted lines indicate variations. In males there is a refractory period after one and sometimes two orgasms in which no further response is possible. Pattern B in females shows a plateau stage with no orgasm, and pattern C shows an orgasm with no preceding plateau stage. (Masters and Johnson, 1966, p. 5.)

far more important in eliciting sexual arousal and behavior in humans than in lower animals (Beach, 1969). Through social learning experiences a specific range of stimuli acquire arousing properties and influence the direction and nature of our sexual responses. Researchers are currently studying the arousal properties of various kinds of stimuli. Because ethical considerations prevent the use of "real-life" stimuli, such as nude experimenters, most of their work has used pictorial, written, or imagined stimuli.

Sexual depictions. A number of researchers have studied the arousal properties of movies and pictures containing various kinds of sexual stimuli. Subjects who view these stimuli are asked to rate the height of their sexual arousal in response to them.

Studies using photographic slides depicting various kinds of sexual activity have provided the clearest evidence of what is most and least arousing. Table 11.1 summarizes the results from four different studies of this kind. Individuals of both sexes were most aroused by pictures of petting, intercourse, and oral sex, whereas pictures involving sadism, members of one's own sex, and male homosexual behavior were rated least arousing.

We might assume that because erotic pictorial stimuli are closer to "real life" than are written descriptions, they would be more arousing. A counterargument, however, is that written stimuli give people more freedom to place themselves into the scene being described and that the more they do so, the more aroused they become. To test this hypothesis Donn Byrne and John Lamberth (1971) randomly assigned married couples at Purdue University to three experimental conditions. One group of subjects was exposed to 19 pictures depicting a variety of sexual acts; another group read 19 short mimeographed passages selected from various books to match the pictures. The third group was given short descriptions of the scenes depicted in the slides (e.g., "heterosexual intercourse, face to face, female on the bottom") and asked to imagine them as vividly as possible. The results of the experiment showed that the average sexual arousal reported by the subjects who were asked to imagine situations was twice that of subjects who saw pictures. Those who read passages from books also reported slightly more arousal than did those who saw pictures. Males and females did not differ in reported arousal level in any of the experimental conditions.

Sexual fantasies. Racquel Welch once remarked in an interview that perhaps the most erogenous zone in the body exists inside our heads. Our ability to imagine sexual stimuli has only recently begun to attract scientific attention. On a fantasy level, we can experience every imaginable sexual encounter. In a study conducted with college students (Barclay, 1973) males and females were asked to create their

347

Table 11.1 Themes presented in photographic slides that were rated most and least arousing by males and females in four studies

Male Subjects	
Most arousing themes	Least arousing themes
Sexual intercourse in various positions	Female physically hurting male
Genital petting	Male masturbating
Female engaging in oral sex with male: fellatio	Two males engaged in anal intercourse
Male engaging in oral sex with female: cunnilingus	Nude male
Female masturbating	Male in undershorts
Group oral sex	Male engaging in oral sex with male: homosexual fellatio
Male caressing female's breast	

Female subjects	
Most arousing themes	Least arousing themes
Male engaging in oral sex with female: cunnilingus	Male physically hurting female
Sexual intercourse in various positions	Male in undershorts
	Female physically hurting male
Genital petting	Two males engaged in anal intercourse
Male caressing female's breast	Clothed female
	Male engaging in oral sex with male: homosexual fellatio
	Nude female
	Nude male

From Baron, Byrne, and Griffitt, 1974, p. 477.

Inanimate objects may not necessarily cause sexual arousal, but they are often associated with what the society defines as "sex appeal." (Charles Gatewood)

own sexual fantasies and report them. There were marked sex differences in their reports. Males wrote stories similar to those in hard-core pornography, with vivid visual imagery and characters who constantly sought sexual pleasure. Females, on the other hand, often wrote stories that involved either tenderness and love or forced participation in sex.

Several recent studies have assessed the content of fantasies people have during masturbation. The results of the Playboy Foundation study, presented in Table 11.2, indicate that the most common theme for both sexes was intercourse with a person they love. Women were somewhat more likely than men to have fantasies about being forced to engage in sex and to imagine engaging in acts that they would never actually perform. Men, on the other hand, reported more themes relating to group sex and multiple partners, having intercourse with strangers, and forcing someone to engage in sex.

Hariton and Singer (1974) studied sexual fantasies reportedly experienced during intercourse by a sample of married women. The results presented in Table 11.3 indicate a wide range of themes, many involving unusual sexual behavior. Because of sample differences between the two studies, it is difficult to assess the degree of difference between masturbation fantasies and fantasies during intercourse at the present time. Many other factors related to sexual fantasies also remain to be investigated.

Love-oriented versus sex-oriented acts. It is commonly assumed that female sexual arousal is heavily dependent on affection. In pornography the only goal of the sexual encounter generally is sexual pleasure, so that many have theorized that women would not be aroused by it.

Byrne and DeNinno (1973) studied the sexual arousal of married couples in response to a relatively mild film depicting nonorgasmic petting and a highly arousing one involving petting, oral-genital stimulation, intercourse, and orgasm. Some of the viewers were told that the film was about a pair of newlyweds deeply in love, whereas others were told that the couple had just met at a dance and were motivated only by a desire for sexual pleasure. The results showed that the intercourse movie was more arousing than the petting movie. More surprisingly, however, both males and females were *more* aroused by

Table 11.2 Masturbation fantasies of males and females

	Percentage of Sample Reporting Each Type of Fantasy	
	Males	Females
Intercourse with a loved person	75	80
Intercourse with strangers	47	21
Group sex with multiple partners of the opposite sex	33	18
Forcing someone to have sex	13	3
Doing sexual things you would never do in reality	19	28
Being forced to have sex	10	19
Homosexual activities	7	11

Data from Hunt, 1974.

Table 11.3 Intercourse fantasies of married females

	Percentage of Subjects Reporting Each Type of Fantasy
Having an imaginary romantic lover	56
Reliving a sexual experience from the past	52
Doing something wicked or forbidden	49.6
Being overpowered or forced to surrender	48.9
Sex in different setting (e.g., car, motel, beach, woods)	46.8
Exciting many men	43.2
Resisting sex, becoming aroused, then surrendering	39.7
Observing sexual activities of self or others	38.3
Pretending to be another female	37.6
Sex with several males simultaneously	35.5
Feeling helpless	33.3
Imagining self as striptease dancer or harem girl	28.4
Imagining self as whore or prostitute	24.9
Being forced to expose body to seducer	19.1
Fantasies involving urination or defecation	2.1

Data from Hariton and Singer, 1974.

349

the films when they depicted individuals motivated only by desire for sexual pleasure than when they depicted a love relationship. Another study, conducted in Germany, also showed that women did not require affection in order to become aroused by sexual stimuli (Schmidt, Sigusch, and Schafer, 1973). We have here another example of the way in which cultural beliefs frequently do not survive the cutting edge of research.

Effects of erotic stimuli on behavior
Although the question of what arouses people sexually is of great interest, researchers are even more concerned about the effects of exposure to erotic stimuli on behavior. Does exposure to explicit sexual stimuli arouse uncontrollable sexual urges and result in the performance of illicit sexual behaviors? Or does exposure tend to satisfy sexual needs and reduce general sexual arousal? Answers to such questions have clear implications for making policy decisions concerning the legality and distribution of sexual materials.

Physiological responses. A number of studies have examined the effects of erotic stimuli on physiological responses. One such investigation (Howard, Reifler, and Liptzin, 1971) assessed arousal in males using a device that precisely measured the circumference of the penis. The experiment itself was designed to test the effects of repeated exposure to pornographic materials on subsequent responses to sexual stimuli. College males were exposed to pornographic movies, magazines, and stories for 90 minutes on each of 15 consecutive days. They were then shown a new erotic film while their penile responses were measured. A control group was shown the same movie without the previous exposure to the pornographic materials. The results of this study are presented in Figure 11.2. The subjects who had been exposed to the pornography showed less of a response to the new movie. Apparently the subjects had developed a degree of adaptation to erotic stimuli as a result of their previous exposure to pornographic materials.

Research results consistently show initial increases in arousal when subjects are exposed to erotic stimuli, but a decline in sexual arousal with repeated exposure. Novel stimuli or a period of time without

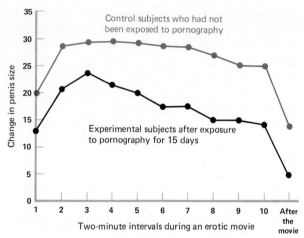

Figure 11.2 Physiological responses to a sexually explicit film by male subjects who had or had not been exposed to pornography for 15 days before the experiment. (Data from Howard, Reifler, and Liptzin, 1971, p. 118.)

exposure, however, may reawaken sensitivity to sexual stimuli.

Effects on sexual activity and sex crimes. Does exposure to sexually explicit materials cause an increase in sexual activity? Although exposure does increase sexual arousal initially and furnishes ample modeling cues, the findings of over a dozen investigations suggest that the effects of these stimuli on sexual activity are quite limited and temporary. In a study by Mann, Sidman, and Starr (1971) married couples viewed either erotic or nonerotic films over a four-week period. Researchers obtained reports of their sexual behavior during this period and over the following four weeks. Couples who saw the films reported greater sexual activity only on the nights they viewed the films. There was no increase in sexual behavior on other nights. Studies conducted with single individuals showed similar results; exposure to erotic materials resulted in only a temporary increase in heterosexual activities and/or masturbation.

There is some indication that the specific content of sexual material might influence later sexual behavior. In one study, married couples who had been

350

shown movies depicting either petting or intercourse reported on their sexual behavior in the week before and the week after their viewing. There was a greater increase in sexual behavior among those who had seen the petting movie (Byrne, Fisher, and DeNinno, 1975). Perhaps because it "left more to the imagination," it continued to affect the thoughts of viewers for a longer period of time. These findings suggest the possibility that less explicit ("R-rated") sexual stimuli may have longer-term effects on behavior than highly explicit ("X-rated") sexual stimuli. (Might we someday find that *Playboy* magazine can only be purchased in adult book stores while more exotic "adult" magazines are displayed in grocery stores?)

Of major concern to many people is the possibility that exposure to pornography may prompt some individuals to engage in sexual crimes. A number of studies have carefully investigated previous contact with pornography on the part of sexual offenders. These studies have shown that, in fact, sexual offenders have usually had less exposure to sexually explicit materials than is normal (Goldstein, Kant, Judd, Rice, and Green, 1971). One study conducted in England showed that, on the average, sexual offenders had not seen pictures depicting intercourse until they were 18 years old (Eysenck, 1972). What has not been established, however, is the effect of erotica on future sex criminals when they finally are exposed to it.

Those opposed to pornography argue that a ban on such materials would prevent them from influencing potential sex offenders. But the 1969 decision in Denmark to permit the unrestricted sale of all types of explicit sexual materials was associated with a decrease rather than an increase in sex crimes. During the first year, they decreased 30 percent, and the rate of decline has continued in subsequent years. Every class of sex crime has shown a decrease.

Although the present data are not conclusive, they provide no evidence that exposure to pornography causes sex crimes. In 1969, the Presidential Commission on Obscenity and Pornography concluded that no reliable relationship between pornography and criminal acts was found in the research it had commissioned. But even evidence that emerges from scientifically sound studies may not be accepted when it is in apparent opposition to "common

sense." For example, syndicated columnist James Kilpatrick reacted to the scientific evidence as follows:

> Some of the "empirical research" was patently absurd. Causality cannot be measured in a beaker, or plotted on a graph. In this highly subjective area of human behavior, we probably never will know precisely what motivates a man to rape or to sexual molestation. Common sense is a better guide than laboratory experiments; and common sense tells us that pornography is bound to contribute to sexual crime. (*The Seattle Times*, January 17, 1975)

Sex differences in sexuality

Stereotyped beliefs about differences in male and female sexuality abound in our culture. For example, there is a widely held assumption that women are less interested in sex than men and enjoy it less. Men supposedly have hair-trigger arousal mechanisms, whereas women are supposed to be more passive and harder to arouse. Indeed, some marriage manuals advise women to feign erotic delight in order to convince their husbands that they are fortunate enough to have a rare "sensuous woman." Finally, it is widely believed that women must be in a loving relationship in order to enjoy sex fully.

William Griffitt (1973) conducted an experiment in which he showed erotic slides to unmarried males and females and obtained ratings on their arousal and their beliefs about how members of the opposite sex would respond. There were no differences between the sexes in their self-reports of arousal, but females expected males to be much more highly aroused than males expected females to be. Moreover, females expected males to be much more aroused than males actually were! The beliefs about the opposite sex apparently reflect our cultural stereotype that men are more arousable than women, but the actual self-reports of arousal support a different conclusion.

Widely accepted popular and psychoanalytic myths about women have helped to perpetuate an image of feminine sexual inferiority. Freud proposed the term *penis envy* to describe the female's repressed desire to possess the prized male sex organ, and suggested that bearing a child (particularly a male) might be a means of compensating for the missing penis. Many physiologists shared with Freud

351

the belief that a clitoral orgasm was inferior to a vaginal orgasm, which meant that women were dependent on males for full sexual enjoyment.

These assumptions about feminine sexuality went virtually unchallenged until recent years because there was little rigorous experimental research on human sexuality. The research of Masters and Johnson (1966) provided a number of illuminating findings. First, there are no distinguishable physiological differences between clitoral and vaginal orgasms. This means that women are not dependent on men for fully erotic experiences. Second, Masters and Johnson found that, unlike men, who usually are physically capable of only one or at most two orgasms, women can enjoy sustained sexual activity and multiple orgasms. If anything, women appear to have a greater capacity for sexual enjoyment.

In our previous discussion we touched on several findings that relate to other assumptions about feminine sexuality. We found, first of all, that women seem remarkably similar to men in the degree to which they report sexual arousal when they are exposed to sexually explicit stimuli. We also saw that an affectionate or love relationship is not a precondition for females to respond with excitement to erotic stimuli. On the contrary, a study discussed earlier showed that females and males alike found films depicting sex based solely on lust more arousing than those that showed a couple who were supposedly deeply in love. Females do less frequently have sex with partners they do not love than do males, but love is not required for sexual excitement.

There are some sex differences in arousal patterns. As we would expect, men and women are aroused to different degrees by specific stimuli. For example, Byrne and Lamberth (1971) found that males were more aroused than females by slides of a clothed female, a nude female, and group oral sex, whereas females were more aroused than males by slides depicting nude and partially clothed males, male masturbation, and homosexual fellatio. It also appears that the temporal arousal pattern of males and females may differ. During a one-hour period in which various kinds of hard-core pornography were presented, men became aroused immediately, but tended to "cool off" as the session progressed, whereas women initially experienced a low level of arousal that gradually increased as time passed (Kutschinsky, 1971). It appears that the sexes have different speeds of arousal rather than different maximum arousal levels.

The differences between the sexes in sexual behaviors and attitudes in our culture do not appear to be the result of innate physiological causes. Anthropologists have studied cultures in which our traditional sex roles are reversed, where females pursue sex aggressively and males are passive and dependent (Mead, 1935).

It appears that human sexual behavior is strongly influenced by social learning factors. We learn how to respond and what to respond to with sexual excitement. For example, many American males tend to be "breast men," whereas South American men are reportedly more appreciative of buttocks. Females do not frequent hard-core pornography shops, but this is clearly not because they are unable to enjoy erotic materials. More likely, they have learned that seeking pornography is not acceptable behavior for women. However, the success currently being enjoyed by magazines that feature pictures of nude males suggests that times are changing.

The coming years promise not only an increase in our knowledge about male and female sexuality, but also continuing changes in attitudes and conventional sex roles. The need for research in the area of birth control is discussed in Box 11.2. It is hoped that future societal attitudes about sexuality will be based on scientifically sound evidence rather than on ignorance.

SEX AND AGING

Although men and women can be sexually active into their 70s and 80s, the aging process has different effects on sexual desire and responsiveness for the two sexes. The research of Masters and Johnson and others has helped to identify physiological changes that accompany aging, and research is also being focused on psychological factors that affect sexual responsiveness in older people. In a society in which people are living longer and in better health, it seems reasonable to try to identify the factors that can prolong the capacity of the elderly to enjoy sex.

Changes in male sexuality

Males reach their peak of sexual potency in their late teens, a period that corresponds with maximal secretion of the male sex hormone, testosterone. Thereafter sexual capacity gradually declines.

Men in their 20s and 30s often experience orgasm several times a day with short recovery periods. They get erections quickly, their orgasmic sensations are intense, and semen leaves the penis with considerable force. In the 30s, however, sexual urges usually become less pressing than they are in the 20s, and most men are satisfied with one or two orgasms during a lovemaking session.

Sexual pleasure usually declines for men in their 40s. They may require longer and more intense stimulation for orgasm, and orgasmic sensations that used to be intense and localized become more diffuse. By their late 40s, men may require from 8 to 24 hours after orgasm before another erection is possible. Some men in their 60s find that if they lose their erection before orgasm, they cannot regain it for 12 to 24 hours. With age the force with which semen is propelled from the body also declines. Levels of sexual tension and the incidence of masturbation both decline for men over 60.

Sexual functioning in older men may be affected by a number of factors. Masters and Johnson (1966) concluded from their research that the most important factor in maintaining sexuality is the frequency and consistency with which men have orgasms in their younger years. Whether the earlier activity is heterosexual, homosexual, or masturbatory does not seem to matter. Factors that seem to decrease sexual responsiveness in men over 40 include boredom, preoccupation with their career, fatigue, excessive eating and drinking, fear of sexual failure, and negative emotional responses brought about by their diminished sexual capacity.

The male climacteric

The point at which reproductive ability ceases is called the *climacteric*. Although the female climacteric, or menopause, need not interfere with women's ability to have orgasmic intercourse, in males it terminates the capacity to have intercourse or orgasm.

The male climacteric is caused by a drop in testosterone. It occurs in about 20 percent of men aged 48 to 58 years and in 30 to 35 percent of men aged 58 to 68. It can be treated with synthetic testosterone therapy, which usually results in a recovery of sexual potency.

Changes in female sexuality

For women sexual responsiveness tends to peak during the late 30s and early 40s (Jones, Shainberg, and Byer, 1977). Most women then experience *menopause* (an end to menstruation) and its associated hormonal changes between the ages of 46 and 50. Thereafter, there are marked changes in the sex organs and in physiological sexual responses. Clitoral responsiveness remains virtually unchanged, but the vaginal walls become thin and lose their elasticity. These changes are responsible for many of the problems associated with sex in older women, such as irritation of the vagina, urethra, and bladder. Nevertheless, postmenopausal women are completely capable of orgasmic intercourse, although vaginal lubrication takes longer, the orgasmic phase is shorter, and half as many vaginal contractions occur as with younger women. After menopause, some women experience a decline in sexual interest and capacity; others continue or even increase their orgasmic experiences. Although individual differences in hormonal changes undoubtedly play a major role in some cases, psychological factors are most important. Women who believe that their sexuality is (or should be) at an end, who suffer a loss of self-esteem because of advancing age, or who have an aging and/or unresponsive mate may very well lose interest in sex. Psychological factors that may increase sexual desire are freedom from fears of pregnancy, decreased family responsibilities as children leave home, and a desire to relive or recapture earlier sexual delights. Regular and fairly frequent intercourse is also likely to contribute to a continuing desire and capacity for sexual enjoyment.

An ever-increasing proportion of our population is over 65, yet society has been unresponsive to the sexuality of the elderly. As one elderly woman noted, "We tell the elderly that it's all over for them, that it's something to snicker at. . . . And we do this at a time of life when they're lonely" (*The New York Times*, June 28, 1974).

SEXUAL DYSFUNCTION

Everyone experiences fluctuations in sexual desire and sexual competence. Sometime in their lives most people experience situations in which they are un-

BOX 11.2

Psychological aspects of birth control: A psychological frontier

During recent years cultural factors and concerns about unchecked population growth have combined to focus increasing attention on birth control and on the practical and psychological issues surrounding it. There are only two ways to prevent childbirth: by preventing conception (contraception) or by destruction of the fetus after conception has occurred (abortion). For the first time in its history the human race has the ability to regulate birth rate through either means. But the decisions involved in birth control are deeply personal and a source of great conflict for many people. Psychological research on many aspects of birth control is badly needed, as are applications of psychological knowledge in providing counseling for individuals contemplating contraception or abortion.

The ready availability of effective birth control devices as well as changing cultural and religious beliefs has led to a greatly expanded use of contraceptives in the 1960s and 1970s. One of the strongest attitudinal and behavioral shifts toward contraception has occurred among American Roman Catholics. Studies indicate that the percentage of Catholic married couples who use contraceptives has increased from about 30 percent to over 70 percent in the period since 1955. The vast majority of Catholics are currently opposed to the Church's stand on birth control. Yet we have little sound information on how Catholics resolve their conflicting beliefs.

Although contraceptives have increased sexual freedom among many people, they do not appear to have unleashed a wave of promiscuity among the young, as many predicted. Indeed, the number of young people who engage in intercourse without contraceptive protection is quite surprising. A study of a national sample of 15- to 19-year-old girls showed that only 15 to 20 percent of the nonvirgins always used contraceptives, and a similar percentage *never* used them. The other 60 percent used them only occasionally (Zelnik and Kantner, 1973). Studies of college samples show that about 10 percent of unmarried sexually active students never use contraceptives. It appears that, especially among the young, the increases in sexual behavior that occurred during the past decade cannot be strongly attributed to the availability of contraceptives. Indeed, some young people repeatedly risk unwanted pregnancy because they feel that taking contraceptive measures "dehumanizes" sex and robs it of its spontaneity. Moreover, young women frequently distort the likelihood that they might become pregnant. One study of sexually active black and white teen-aged women found that 28 percent of the whites and 55 percent of the blacks did not believe they could become pregnant "easily" even if they did not use contraceptives (Kantner and Zelnik, 1973). In another study of unwed teenagers who suspected they were pregnant but subsequently were found not to be, 41 percent of the women continued to be sexually active without use of contraceptives even after their "close call" (Evans, Selstad, and Welcher, 1976). The striking discrepancy between knowledge about contraceptives and the use of contraceptives clearly demands further research, given the high stakes of unwanted pregnancy.

Perhaps one reason some young people do not regularly protect themselves from unwanted pregnancies through contraception is that abortions are so readily available. Through a Supereme Court decision handed down in 1973, terminating a pregnancy became a decision to be made by a woman and her physician. Although many women choose to deliver unwanted children because they find abortion personally unacceptable, many more are choosing abortion. Estimates of the percentage of women who have at least one abortion during their college years range from 10 to 20 percent.

For many people the decision concerning abortion is a momentous one, fraught with conflict. Because of the importance of the decision and its potential effects on the psychological reactions of those involved, the need for research and for competent and thoughtful counseling is being emphasized by many professionals.

Concerning psychological effects of abortion, the evidence to date (which is based largely on clinical case histories and questionnaire studies) indicates that an immediate negative response to abortion is not uncommon. Many women experience at least temporary unhappiness and guilt, but serious psychiatric complications probably occur in fewer than 10 percent of women who undergo abortions. The risk of serious psychological problems appears highest when the woman has conflicting feelings about the abortion, when she is coerced into it, or when she has already existing emotional problems (Friedman, Greenspan, and Mittleman, 1974).

Methodologically sound studies of the psychological responses of women who undergo abortions (as well as those who decide against them), including long-term follow-ups, are badly needed. In addition, an assessment of the effects of various kinds of counseling procedures on women contemplating abortions would be of great value.

The threatening shadow of unchecked population growth is steadily lengthening over the human race. Attempts to promote contraceptive practices in overpopulated countries such as India have met with limited success. Psychologists could make major contributions by studying the variables that determine adoption of contraceptive practices in such settings. Such research not only is important from a theoretical perspective, but could have practical implications for designing programs to promote sexual practices based on responsible decision making and an explicit weighing of religious, moral, and practical considerations.

able to experience or give sexual gratification through intercourse. Of course, individuals with little sexual experience often do not know enough about how to stimulate their partners or how to obtain stimulation themselves, and initial sexual encounters can be awkward and unsatisfying. These normal experiences and fluctuations become constant occurrences for some individuals and can cause extreme unhappiness, self-devaluation, and a lack of erotic gratification. *Sexual dysfunction* refers to cases in which a couple's sexual relationship is detrimentally affected by sexual difficulties experienced by the man, the woman, or both. In a high percentage of cases of dysfunction, the problem seems quite specific to sexual relationships and is not part of a general personality disorder.

Male sexual dysfunction

Among men the primary forms of sexual dysfunction are impotence and inability to delay ejaculation. Both disorders can have devastating psychological effects because for many men their concept of masculinity and even personal worth are closely linked to sexual performance.

Impotence (failure to achieve or maintain an erection) occurs in varying degrees among men of all ages. It affects about 1 in every 100 males under 35 years of age and about 1 in every 4 males over 70 years old. According to one estimate, at least half of the male population has experienced at least occasional episodes of impotence (Kaplan, 1974). Some experts distinguish between *primary impotence*, in which the male has never been able to have an erection of sufficient strength for intercourse, and *secondary impotence*, in which the impotence is restricted to certain situations or occurs in at least one-fourth of a man's attempts at intercourse (Masters and Johnson, 1970).

Impotence may result from both physical and psychological causes. Physical causes include early undiagnosed diabetes, hormonal imbalance, use of narcotics and alcohol, and aging. From a biological standpoint, men should be capable of intercourse beyond 80 years of age, but many suffer a reduction in potency as they enter middle and old age, perhaps because of psychological factors.

In many cases "performance anxiety" apparently inhibits erection. In other instances psychologi-

355

cal conflicts and guilt centering around sexuality or disturbances in the interpersonal relationship between the partners seem to play a prominent role.

The inability to delay ejaculation long enough for the woman to experience orgasm, or *premature ejaculation*, is probably the most common type of sexual dysfunction in men. Research findings indicate that three out of four men reach orgasm within two minutes of penetration (Katchadourian and Lunde, 1975). The inability to delay orgasm often results in feelings of sexual inadequacy.

As is the case with impotence, performance anxiety and tension resulting from personal conflicts seem to be important factors in many cases of premature ejaculation. It is perhaps ironic that as we become freer about sexual expression, new problems are arising for both sexes because of increasing demands to "perform" and to please one's partner. Men as well as women find themselves very concerned about "how they are doing" during intercourse. In men this not only can increase performance anxiety and stimulate ejaculation, but may also cause them to become spectators of their own actions, to lose their spontaneity and enjoyment of sex.

Female sexual dysfunction

Disturbances in sexual functioning among women are often referred to as *orgastic dysfunction*. This term applies to cases that involve pain and fear as well as to those that involve apathy and inability to respond. Problems of orgastic dysfunction, like impotence, can be either generalized or restricted to particular situations, partners, and so on. Until rather recently such problems did not receive as much attention as impotence, because a woman can have intercourse even if she is unresponsive. Moreover, the relationship between the female orgasm and sexual gratification is not totally clear. Many women who are not regularly orgasmic report that intercourse is highly pleasurable for them (Hunt, 1974).

Although there are few definitive data, the available evidence indicates that female orgasmic problems are less common than they have been in the past. In a recent survey (Hunt, 1974) 53 percent of women married 15 years or more reported that they always or nearly always reached orgasm during intercourse. The corresponding figure reported by Kinsey's group

(1953) was 45 percent. Moreover, Hunt's (1974) data indicated a decrease in the proportion of wives who never experienced orgasm from 28 percent in the Kinsey years to 15 percent.

In typical cases of orgastic dysfunction the woman may become sexually aroused but not experience orgasm. Although some women obtain great pleasure from satisfying their partners, others find sex without orgasm extremely frustrating. Another type of dysfunction involves pelvic pain at penetration, during intercourse, or afterward, which may prevent the woman from experiencing erotic pleasure. Like secondary impotence in men, orgastic dysfunction in women may be limited to particular situations or partners.

There may be a variety of psychological causes for orgastic dysfunction. Unresolved guilt and conflicts over sexual activity, anxiety and revulsion toward the sex act, and disturbances in the partners' interpersonal relationship may all take a heavy toll on female sexual responsiveness. Quite frequently sexual dysfunction is the result of a long series of learning experiences that imparted negative attitudes and emotional reactions to sex.

Treatment of sexual dysfunction

Many people carry the burden of sexual inadequacy in silent suffering. But liberalized sexual attitudes that have encouraged research on sexuality have also stimulated the development of treatment programs for victims of sexual dysfunction.

The research carried out by William Masters and Virginia Johnson resulted not only in a great expansion of our knowledge about the physiology of sex, but also in the development of a highly effective treatment program for individuals suffering from sexual dysfunction. The techniques for treatment are described in detail in Masters and Johnson's *Human Sexual Inadequacy* (1970).

The success of the Masters and Johnson approach to sexual dysfunction has stimulated the growth of sex therapy as a distinct discipline. Many reputable sex treatment clinics have opened, staffed by well-trained professionals. (Unfortunately, some individuals offering "sex therapy" are not sufficiently qualified.) Treatment is now so accessible that no individual or couple need experience the miseries of sexual dysfunction without the possibility of working to achieve more gratifying sexual experiences.

ALTERNATIVE MODES OF SEXUALITY

Of all human behaviors sex is perhaps the most controversial and the most subject to contradictory judgments. Human beings achieve sexual pleasure in countless ways, some of which are viewed by society as "healthy" or "normal" and some as "deviant" or "abnormal."

Public attitudes toward crime, drugs, and alcohol have undergone considerable change over the years, but the change in attitudes toward sexual variations has been even more dramatic. Although sexual deviations involving violence continue to evoke strong expressions of outrage, a growing segment of the population seems to accept the view that sexual activities involving consenting adults are private matters about which the public should not make judgments.

Homosexuality

Public and professional reactions to homosexual relationships between consenting adults have undergone a revolution. Not too many years ago the public reacted to homosexuality with revulsion, and mental health professionals viewed it as the symptom of an underlying personality disturbance. Today, although there is still a stigma attached to homosexuality, public attitudes are much more benign then they once were. Still, there is far from complete agreement about the social and legal status of homosexuals. In 1977 citizens in Dade County, Florida, after an emotional campaign, voted to rescind a law against housing, and job discrimination on the basis of sexual orientation.

In the United States punishment for homosexual acts between males varies widely from state to state; there are no laws against homosexual acts between females. In Arizona homosexual acts performed by males are categorized as sodomy, a crime punishable by one to five years in prison. In several states homosexuals are included in the category of sexual psychopaths and may therefore be subject to harsher penalties.

On December 14, 1973, there were several million "mentally ill" homosexuals in the United States. The most dramatic "cure" in psychiatric history occurred on December 15, 1973, when the American Psychiatric Association's board of trustees voted unani-

(Forsyth, Monkmeyer)

mously to remove homosexuality from the category of mental illness. The board introduced a new category, called "sexual orientation disturbances," which is for individuals whose sexual interests are directed primarily toward people of the same sex *and* who are either bothered by their sexual orientation or wish to change it. All other homosexuals are considered free from psychiatric disturbance. The points of view expressed in the following statements reflect the controversy that has raged over the "delisting" of homosexuality from the official psychiatric nomen-

357

clature. This is an excerpt from a statement by a group of psychiatrists in support of the board of trustees' action:

> The revision in the nomenclature does not sacrifice scientific principles in order to further the struggle for the civil rights of homosexuals. Quite the contrary: it has been the unscientific inclusion of homosexuality *per se* in a list of mental disorders which has been the main ideological justification for the denial of the civil rights to individuals whose only crime is that their sexual orientation is to members of the same sex. (*Psychiatric News*, February 6, 1974, p. 3)

Many psychiatrists did not agree with the action of the board, believing that distortions in personality cause homosexual behavior. Wardell Pomeroy, a psychotherapist and former member of Kinsey's sex

(Picatti, Jeroboam)

research group, has offered some thoughtful observations on this point:

> If my concept of homosexuality were developed from my practice, I would probably concur in thinking of it as an illness. I have seen no homosexual man or woman in that practice who was not troubled, emotionally upset, or neurotic. On the other hand, if my concept of marriage in the U.S. were based on my practice, I would have to conclude that marriages are all fraught with strife and conflict, and that heterosexuality is an illness. In my 20 years of research in the field of sex, I have seen many homosexuals who were happy, who were practicing and conscientious members of their community, and who were stable, productive, warm, relaxed, and efficient. Except for the fact that they were homosexual, they could be considered normal by any definition. (Pomeroy, 1969, p. 13)

The homosexual experience

Most homosexuals live more than one life, and the façades they present to their parents, wives, employers, and members of the gay community may be dramatically at variance with one another. "Coming out" occurs when an individual makes the decision to become immersed publicly in the homosexual subculture. A relatively high proportion of homosexual men discover the "gay world" before they are 21. For most homosexuals, coming out represents the culmination of many years of questioning and self-doubt. For some it almost takes the form of an initiation, and for others it is a gradual process of shaping their sexual orientation. (See Box 11.3.)

Research on homosexuals

The data published in 1948 by Kinsey, Pomeroy, and Martin continue to be among the most reliable on male homosexuality, considering the methodological problems associated with surveying socially condemned practices. They suggest that about 4 percent of the adult white male population of the United States is exclusively homosexual. Another 10 percent is primarily homosexual for at least three years between the ages of 16 and 65. A total of 37 percent of the white male population has at some time between adolescence and senility experienced homosexual orgasm. By age 55, according to the Kinsey et al. study, half of all white males have had some type of homosexual contact. The prevalence of homosexual experiences among women seems to be much lower

BOX 11.3

Coming out

Here are descriptions by several homosexuals of the process of coming out.

At age 20, the realization suddenly hit me. I was not going out with women, or I did not want to, and here I was going out with men and I wanted to and then I said to myself, you must be queer, and it sounded funny to me but I accepted it. (Saghir and Robins, 1973, p. 67)

We were out at sea and I had heard that one of the dental technicians was a homosexual, and he had made advances toward me, and I felt like masturbation really wouldn't solve the problem so I visited him one night. He started talking about sex and everything. I told him I had never kissed a boy before. And he asked me what would you do if a guy kissed you, and I said you mean like this and I began kissing him. Naturally he took over then. . . . There were other people on the ship that were homosexual and they talked about me. A yeoman aboard ship liked me quite a bit, was attracted to me; so he started making advances toward me, and I found him attractive, so we got together, and in a short period of time, we became lovers. He started to take me to the gay bars and explain what homosexuality was all about. He took me to gay bars when we were in port. (Dank, 1971, p. 186)

My first crush on a woman was at the age of 13. However, I was not aware of homosexuality and I was not conscious of any specific differences in my feelings compared to other girls. However, I was always dissatisfied with dating. There seemed to be something missing. I got tired of the necking and the crude advances, the scratchy beards and the lack of gentlemanly love and care. At 19 I got married to a 25-year-old man. Following the marriage, he would go out with the boys and would leave me alone. I don't think he went out with other women. Repeatedly, I would get pregnant and he would promise to stay at home, but he always broke his promises. He never took me out and I did not believe in drinking. At 24 I had been friends with a 30-year-old teacher for about a year. Once she asked me to spend the weekend with her but this was not the first time. During the year I had felt a gradual physical attraction to her and finally this culminated in a sexual contact on the weekend at her home. I felt relieved the first time it happened. I felt very satisfied sexually and emotionally. Then I started asking questions and $2\frac{1}{2}$ months later I was reading everything about it. At 26 I found out about D.O.B. (Daughters of Bilitis), a lesbian organization—through one of the books, and I started going to their meetings and discussions. I met a girl there and liked her company and she was the kind of person I hoped I would find in a man. She was good company and fun to be around and had a good character. We had a sexual relationship for 4 months after associating with her for several years. I am still married to my husband. However, we have had sex only on three occasions in the past 2 years, as I came to believe that I was a homosexual. I withdrew from him sexually. (Saghir and Robins, 1973, pp. 233–234)

(Kenyon, 1968, 1970; Kinsey, Pomeroy, Martin, and Gebhard, 1953). Kinsey et al. (1953) found only about one-half to one-third as many females as males who were, in any age period, primarily or exclusively homosexual. They estimated the cumulative proportion of female homosexual experiences to be about 28 percent.

A recent study found that 67.8 percent of a sample of homosexuals in the United States attempted to conceal their sexual orientation from heterosexuals (Weinberg and Williams, 1974). Only one-fifth were completely overt homosexuals.

Theories of homosexuality

Some homosexuals claim that any psychological problems they may have are caused mainly by excessive societal pressure to conform to arbitrary sexual norms. Many other homosexuals feel that they are neurotic and would prefer to express their sexuality in more conventional ways. As is the case for most personal issues, each case deserves individual consideration. To assume either that homosexuality is an adaptive form of sexual behavior for all those who engage in it or that it is a socially destructive force that must be eradicated completely is dangerous,

359

because there are serious gaps in our knowledge about sexuality and its psychological, physiological, and sociological dimensions.

Chromosome and endocrine studies have so far failed to identify any consistent biological differences between homosexuals and heterosexuals; there is no firm evidence to date that biological factors determine sexual orientation.

Behaviorists claim that early exposure to homosexual models or to parents who positively reinforce contacts with youngsters of the same sex and punish contacts with the opposite sex may strengthen homosexual tendencies. The pleasure that accompanies homosexual activities may be sufficiently intense to overcome feelings of anxiety or apprehension. Behavior therapy (see Chapter 6) has been used to modify sexual orientation, but as we have seen, homosexuals differ widely in the extent to which they wish to change their sexual orientation.

The psychoanalytic theory of homosexuality emphasizes the role of sexual conflicts that are rooted in childhood. It views homosexuality as the result of a sexual attachment to the parent of the same sex that is carried into adulthood. Other psychoanalytic explanations of homosexuality suggest that male homosexuals sleep with other males because female genitalia arouse infantile fears that they will be castrated, and that female homosexuals avoid males to avoid being reminded that they lack the penises that they desire on an unconscious level. There is no scientific evidence to support these speculations.

Both the psychodynamic and behavioral approaches to homosexuality deal with the relationship between previous experience and current behavior. Research on homosexuality indicates that many homosexuals have faulty, disturbed, or pathological parental relationships in childhood. However, the causal links are still not clear.

Transvestism

Transvestites are people who like to dress in the clothing of the opposite sex. Transvestites see themselves as an oppressed minority, and although they are few in number, they have achieved a certain degree of cohesiveness. They form clubs, hold conventions, and publish a magazine, *Transvestia*, for heterosexual cross dressers. Many psychiatrists see transvestism as a product of aberrant psychosexual development. Behaviorists view it as a conditioned

(Virginia Hamilton)

response that can be treated using aversion therapy, in which dressing in women's clothing can be paired with an aversive stimulus. Although the causes of transvestism remain unclear and society's response to it continues to be negative, it is encouraging that discourse among transvestites, researchers, and the public is increasing. (See Box 11.4.)

Transsexualism

Transsexuals are people who feel an intense desire and need to change their sex, including their bodies. Transsexuals often live and pass for members of the opposite sex. Many have surgery in order to have their sex organs changed and undergo hormonal treatments to acquire other physical characteristics of the opposite sex. Although the number of transsexuals is very small (one estimate is 1 per 100,000

BOX 11.4

The transvestite

The following is a male transvestite's letter to his wife after discussing with her his need to dress like a woman:

Since you have given me your permission and wonderful assistance, my love for you and my delight in our marriage have increased immeasurably. My life is now free of falsity and apprehension, and I am no longer troubled with the deep anguish that is the necessary result of such intense sublimation.

We transvestites realize that to most laymen, transvestism is regarded at worst as a confession of homosexuality, either latent or overt; at best as "sissified" or "unmanly." Knowing me, my dear, you must admit that such is not the case. The personal masculine attributes that first attracted you to me are, as you know, an integral part of my personality, just as my transvestism is. It has always been a part of me, and as such, was definitely a contributing factor toward making me into the type of man to whom you were attracted enough to marry.

For those of us so blessed (or afflicted), this urge sometimes reaches such an overpowering intensity that we feel on those occasions that we would cast aside all of life's goals and rewards for the opportunity to gratify this all-consuming hunger . . . .

You know, of course, that when I indulge in my short periods of fantasy, I am known to you and our TV friends as "Theresa," and this seems to alienate you in some obscure manner which I cannot fathom and you will not explain. It is perfectly natural if you will only see it that way. We are only make-believe girls, and we know always that we are really men, so don't worry that we are ever dissatisfied with manhood, or want to change forever into a woman. When we are dressed in feminine clothes and attain as close a resemblance as possible to a real girl, we do certainly pretend that we are girls for that short time, but it is a pretense and definitely not a reality. (Prince, 1967, pp. 80–81)

Wardell Pomeroy has given this account of a transvestite convention he attended:

Seventy-three people had gathered for the event, including nine wives and six or seven transsexuals. Their ages ranged from twenty to seventy, their social level from those with an eighth-grade education to people with advanced degrees. There were those who did it all the time. As in nudist camps, where all the conversation is about nudism, the transvestites talked only of dressing and how they looked. There was no radio or television, no newspapers, and although there was a great deal going on in the world at the moment, no one was interested. On Saturday night there was a floor show, with entertainment by the guests—some talented, others the rankest of amateurs.

The transvestites presented striking contrasts. I remember one man, a rich contractor, a big chap about six feet four and weighing 275 pounds, who looked grotesque. But to him the opportunity to dress was so important that he did not care what others might think. On the other hand, there were some who looked like beautiful girls. I filmed the whole affair for the archives of the Institute.

One morning my fellow researcher and I had a group session with the wives. One of them had not known what the affair was to be; she didn't know her husband was a transvestite until she arrived at the hotel. Horrified by the discovery, she started to hitchhike home, but was persuaded to come back. Others, however, not only knew about their husbands, but loved the arrangement. In their daily lives these women would talk about clothes with their husbands and even shop with them when they were dressed. But even these women objected if their husbands dressed in feminine nightclothes or played their role in bed. They wanted a man in bed, and liked the dressing only when it was done for the street. (Pomeroy, 1972, p. 451)

population), they have attracted a great deal of curiosity and attention during recent years.

Scientists who study transsexualism usually do so in the hope that it will shed light on the general nature and development of *gender identity* (Green and Money, 1969). Gender identity is a basic feature of personality, and refers to an individual's convictions about being either male or female, to behavior that is culturally associated with males or females, and to preference for male or female sexual partners

(Green, 1974). One's gender identity is part of the self concept and is expressed through a broad range of behaviors, attitudes, and fantasies.

Current knowledge about transsexualism is inadequate, and there is heated controversy over the use of medical methods that enable transsexuals to achieve desired bodily changes. For males these methods include removing the genitals and substituting an artificial vagina, and administering female hormones to reduce hair growth and stimulate the development of breasts.

Studies of male transsexuals have shown that they had feminine tendencies since early childhood. They often have mothers who expressed a lifelong sense of worthlessness and a desire to be men. Researchers have hypothesized that as signs of feminity appear in her son during the first few years of life, this type of mother encourages these trends and discourages behavior she interprets as masculine. The fathers of transsexuals seem to be passive, distant, and cold (Stoller, 1973). There is a need to learn more about the possible roles of psychological and biological factors in transsexualism, and about consequences—both anticipated and unanticipated— related to changes in anatomical features.

Fetishism

Fetishism, in which an inanimate object serves as a primary source of arousal and gratification, is usually ignored by the law. Most fetishists conduct their sexual activities in solitude, although in some cases they commit crimes in order to acquire articles they desire. Fetishists are almost always male, and the object of the fetish can range from the obviously erotic (an article of women's underwear) to articles with little apparent connection with sexuality (rubber boots):

> I always seem to have been fascinated by rubber boots. I cannot say exactly when the fascination first started, but I must have been very young. Their spell is almost hypnotic and should I see someone walking along with rubber boots, I become very excited and may follow the person for a great distance. I quickly get an erection under such circumstances and I might easily ejaculate. I am most excited by boots that are black and shiny and hip length. Whenever I see a picture of boots in a magazine, I become excited.
>
> I frequently dream of boots and when I do, I have a

seminal emission. Sometimes I just see a pair of boots in the dream—and I quickly have an emission. I self-stimulate myself [masturbate] frequently—I either look at a pair of boots, then, or simply allow the image of boots to come to my mind. When I am sitting alone, the thought of boots frequently comes to my mind, and I cannot control these thoughts. The sight of the boots comes to me, and I cannot fight it off. At these times, the thought and the sight of the boots makes me tense—it becomes painful, although usually the thought of the boots brings on a very pleasant feeling. I often put the boots on and look at myself in the mirror—this makes me stimulate myself. I often will take the boots to bed with me, caress them, kiss them, and ejaculate into them. (Epstein, 1965, pp. 515–516)

Very little is known about fetishism, but some learning theorists view it as the result of classical conditioning. They argue that an object acquires erotic properties because it is paired with sexual excitement and orgasm. Psychoanalytic theory, on the other hand, explains the fetish in terms of its symbolic sexual meaning, or in terms of a displacement of the sexual impulse from some forbidden object onto the object of the fetish.

There are many ways in which a person can deviate from conventional sexual norms. Not all sexual behavior is equally adaptive, socially desirable, healthy, and moral, and it is as appropriate to make judgments about sexuality as it is to make judgments about other types of behavior. However, such judgments should be made with great care. History has shown how easy it is to inflict unnecessary pain and hardship on people whose only offense is that they are different.

The psychological study of human sexual behavior, although of relatively recent origin, has already yielded a body of important information and a variety of techniques for helping individuals who have sexual problems. The study of sexual behavior is an important frontier not only because sexuality is a vital part of our lives, but also because basic psychological processes, such as learning, motivation, attitude development and change, cognition, and physiological factors are all involved in sexual behavior. The study of sexuality thus provides an opportunity to learn more about these basic processes. Sexual research seems certain to attract the attention of an increasing number or psychologists.

SUMMARY

1. Two research strategies have provided most of our scientific information about sexuality. The *descriptive* approach includes attempts to survey sexual attitudes and behavior and to describe the pattern of physiological responses that occur during sexual arousal. The survey studies of Kinsey and the laboratory research of Masters and Johnson are examples of the descriptive approach. The *experimental* approach involves attempts to manipulate variables experimentally and study their effects on sexual responses.

2. Survey studies of sexual behavior suffer from a number of methodological problems, including sampling difficulties and possible distortion in the reports given by subjects. Recent surveys indicate a liberalization of sexual standards but a still existing double standard that makes premarital sex more acceptable for men than for women. Heavy petting, oral-genital stimulation, and sexual intercourse have apparently increased among unmarried individuals, but masturbation has not.

3. Masters and Johnson measured physiological responses during thousands of male and female orgasms and discovered a four-stage pattern of sexual response consisting of *excitement*, *plateau*, *orgasm*, and *resolution*. They also found that there are no physiological differences between clitoral and vaginal orgasms.

4. Experimental studies of stimulus factors in sexual arousal and behavior have shown that imagining sexual scenes can produce a higher level of arousal than actually viewing similar scenes. Married males and females both report higher arousal when they view films that depict lustful acts than when they view the same acts supposedly occurring within a love relationship. Several studies have reported differences between men and women in the content of their sexual fantasies.

5. Studies assessing the effects of erotic stimuli on behavior suggest that repeated exposure results in a temporary adaptation to sexual stimuli. The effects of such stimuli on sexual activity seem to be limited and temporary. There is no evidence linking exposure to pornography with sex crimes.

6. Research results have discredited many widely held sexual stereotypes about men and women. Women are as readily arousable by erotic stimuli as are men, and love is not required for female sexual enjoyment. Most of the attitudinal and behavioral differences that exist between men and women appear to result from social learning rather than from innate physiological differences.

7. The aging process has different effects on the sexual motivation and behavior of men and women. Research is focusing on the psychological as well as physiological factors that affect sexual responsiveness with increasing age.

8. Sexual dysfunction occurs in both men and women. Impotence and premature ejaculation are the most common male forms, whereas orgastic dysfunction in women refers to an inability to enjoy orgasmic intercourse. Anxiety, personal conflicts around sexuality, and problems in the relationship between the partners are major psychological causes of sexual dysfunction. Masters and Johnson developed a successful treatment approach to many varieties of dysfunction.

9. Both public and professional attitudes about homosexuality have undergone a rapid change in recent years, and homosexuality has been removed from the list of psychiatric disturbances. Much remains to be learned

363

about factors that result in the development of a homosexual orientation. Transvestism, in which individuals achieve pleasure in dressing in the clothes of the opposite sex, is also poorly understood. The study of transsexuals, who feel an intense desire to change their sex, promises to provide information on the development of gender identity. In fetishism the sexual object is an object rather than another person, and both behaviorists and psychoanalysts have offered theoretical explanations for this mode of sexual expression.

Suggested readings

Green, R. (Ed.) *Human sexuality: A health practitioner's text.* Baltimore: The Williams & Wilkins Company, 1975. Nineteen authorities in the area of human sexuality discuss various aspects of the field from the point of view of the medical practitioner who deals with both normal sexuality and with sexual dysfunction.

Katchadourian, H. A. & Lunde, D. T. *Fundamentals of human sexuality.* (2nd ed.) New York, Holt, Rinehart and Winston, Inc., 1975. A comprehensive overview of human sexuality from medical, psychological, and sociological perspectives.

Wagner, N. N. (Ed.) *Perspectives on human sexuality: Psychological, social, and cultural research findings.* New York: Behavioral Publications, Inc., 1974. A series of theoretical and research articles dealing with many aspects of human sexuality.

Chapter 12
Social Psychology

(Joel Gordon)

A touch of spring was in the air during the early morning hours of March 13, 1964 as Kitty Genovese returned to her home in a middle-class area of New York City. As she left her car, a man lurking nearby followed her and then attacked with a knife. "Oh my God," she screamed, "he stabbed me! Please help me!" The brutal assault continued for over 30 minutes. Her assailant returned to stab her on three separate occasions as, mortally wounded, she screamed for help and tried to reach her home.

A murder in New York City is not particularly newsworthy. However, this one attracted national attention for one startling reason: At least 38 of her neighbors had heard her screams and witnessed the brutal slaying from their windows. Not one of them had attempted to help her. In fact, no one even called the police until after she was dead. (See Figure 12.1.)

The year was 1962, and Richard M. Nixon's political career had apparently ended. Narrowly defeated by John F. Kennedy in the presidential election two years earlier, he had lost his bid to become governor of California as well. The public viewed Nixon as an untrustworthy man having little sensitivity or warmth. As he left the podium from which he had acknowledged his defeat, he snarled at newsmen: "Well, gentlemen, you won't have Nixon to kick around anymore." Yet from the rubble of these two crushing political defeats and his tarnished personal image, Richard Nixon rose like a phoenix to become president of the United States in 1968. When in 1972 he kicked off the greatest landslide presidential victory in history, there were few hints that he would eventually fall into disgrace under the weight of the Watergate scandal.

Nixon's rise to the White House in 1968 was aided, if not determined, by one of the most costly and concerted image-building campaigns in history. In *The Selling of the Presidency, 1968*, Joe McGinniss (1969) described the methods used by professional advertising men to change Americans' attitudes toward Nixon. As a result of these carefully contrived strategies, many Americans came to perceive Nixon as a warm, caring, and competent leader, prepared to confront and solve the nation's foreign and domestic problems with courage and conviction.

Most white people can never really know what it feels like to be a member of an oppressed racial minority group. Grace Halsell, however, decided to take a special medication that temporarily turned her skin black and to live as a black person for a short time. One day she went to a Harlem hospital to have infected foot blisters treated by a white physician and wrote the following account of the incident:

"You people," he lectures me, "should bathe more often. Your feet are *dirty*." He says there is nothing

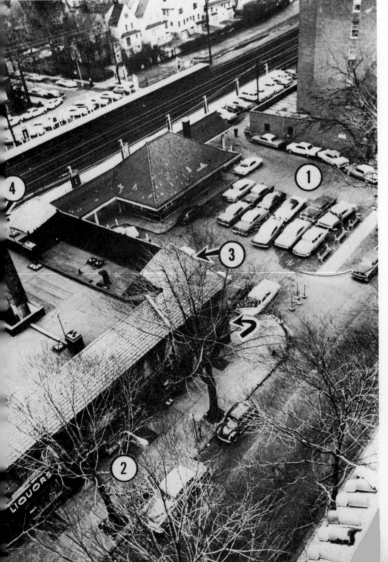

Figure 12.1 This photo shows where Kitty Genovese parked her car (1) and where her assailant attacked her with a knife on three separate occasions (2), (3), and (4). (UPI)

wrong with my feet. "Just blisters." Again he utters the stern injunction that I must bathe myself and my feet every day. He gives me no treatment or medication. I leave wondering if he talks to all "colored people" as he has talked to me, indicating that we were all dirty, somehow less than human. (Halsell, 1969, p. 76)

What are the social forces that prevented Kitty Genovese and other unfortunate victims from receiving help? Which psychological principles did the advertising experts use in changing the public's attitudes toward Richard Nixon? How do people develop attitudes such as those reflected in the white physician's conversation with the "black" patient, and what effects does such prejudice have on its victims? These are but a few of the many questions about human social behavior that we deal with in this chapter.

In a very fundamental way each of us is a social animal, embedded in an interpersonal environment that exerts influence on us from birth until death. Our lives are acted out in a world of social forces, some of which we ourselves initiate. The scientific study of these social forces—of how they are produced and of how they influence our behavior—is the focus of social psychology.

RESEARCH METHODS IN SOCIAL PSYCHOLOGY

Because human social behavior is so diverse, social psychologists study it in numerous settings and employ a variety of research methods. *Survey studies* are frequently used to obtain information about opinions and attitudes. As we saw in Chapter 11, much information has been obtained about sexual attitudes and behavior using this method.

Field studies involve observing and recording behavior in its natural settings, with no attempt being made to manipulate variables or to influence the individuals being studied. On the contrary, great care is taken to minimize the observer's effects on the observed behavior. Jane Goodall's famous studies of the social behavior of apes in their natural habitat exemplify field studies.

Sometimes fate and nature produce a unique opportunity to study the effects of a variable that is manipulated by circumstances beyond the experi-

(Wide World)

menter's control. *Natural experiments* are field studies that are carried out to coincide with the occurrence of the natural event. Later in this chapter we describe a natural experiment carried out by several social psychologists who joined a doomsday group that was predicting the end of the world on a particular date. The investigators were presented with a unique opportunity to study how the club responded to a disconfirmation of their strongly held beliefs.

Field experiments, like field studies and natural experiments, are performed in "real-life" settings. In field experiments, however, the variables of interest are manipulated by the experimenter. An example to be described later is the Robbers Cave experiment in which social psychologists manipulated conditions in a boys' camp so as to create intergroup conflict and study its effects on the social behavior of the boys.

The *laboratory experiment* offers researchers maximum control over the variables they wish to manipulate. The cost of such control is a sacrificing of the real-life quality of natural situations. Although behavior studied in the laboratory is just as "real" as any other behavior, the differences between laboratory and real-life settings raises the question of how

367

BOX 12.1

The social psychology of the research setting

The human factor in the relationship between researcher and subject can affect the data that are obtained. There is evidence, for example, that *experimenter expectancy effects* can bias the responses given by subjects. It has been shown that when experimenters expect that they will obtain certain results, they may subtly and unintentionally influence their subjects to respond in the expected manner. Such experimenter characteristics as race, sex, attractiveness, and personal mannerisms may also affect how subjects respond in experiments.

Knowledge on the part of subjects that they are being observed or studied may cause them to change their "natural" behavior patterns so as to create a desired impression. In addition, many re-

search situations contain stimuli, termed *demand characteristics,* that give subjects information about how they are expected to behave. Demand characteristics do not affect all subjects in the same way. Some are eager to be "good subjects" and make use of demand characteristics to give the experimenter the results they think he or she wants. Others may respond in the opposite fashion, and some subjects may try to ignore demand characteristics and respond "honestly."

In an attempt to create particular experimental conditions, many experimenters (particularly in social psychology) make use of deception. Some psychologists regard these deceptions as dishonest and unethical, whereas others regard them as necessary if we are to acquire important knowledge about human behavior that cannot be acquired in any other way. Aside from the ethical issue, which is an important one, widespread knowledge about deception in psychological experiments has resulted in many suspicious subjects who expect to be deceived and who approach the experiment as a duel with the experimenter. The validity of data obtained from such subjects is questionable.

---

much one can generalize laboratory research results to the "natural" environment outside the laboratory. This question is, of course, specific to each study and can be answered only by research directed at determining the degree of correspondence between laboratory findings and naturalistic events.

Wherever it is carried out, research involves a relationship between experimenter and subject, and the nature of the relationship may influence the data that are obtained. Recognition of this fact has resulted in many studies of the "social psychology" of the research setting. Some of the important methodological problems that such research has identified are discussed in Box 12.1.

Social psychology is concerned with many diverse social phenomena. Aggression and sexual behavior, which have been discussed in previous chapters, are two areas of great interest to social psychologists. In

this chapter we discuss a number of other important social psychological phenomena. We begin by considering the process of interpersonal perception. Then we examine social attitudes, including attraction and prejudice, which are both affected by and affect interpersonal perception. Social influences on attitude and behavior change are then explored. Finally, we examine the influence of group forces on the behavior of individuals.

INTERPERSONAL PERCEPTION

All our social behavior is ultimately based on our perception of other people. Most of us observe others carefully and try to understand their motives, plans, and feelings, particularly in relationship to our own. It is obviously in our best interests to do so, because accurate perceptions about others are the basis for predicting their behavior and for carrying on rewarding relationships with them.

Understanding others is, however, not an easy task. Other individuals are, like ourselves, highly complex, and they often try to disguise their true motives, feelings, and thoughts. Our impressions of them are frequently based on incomplete or even conflicting information. How do we go about sorting through information we receive from and about others to decide what is important? How do we integrate these bits of information to arrive at a unified impression of another person? How do our personal characteristics influence our social perceptions? What are the processes involved in making judgments about others and about the causes of their behavior? Answers to these questions are crucial in understanding the social world to which we respond. For this reason, research on social perception has had a long history in social psychology.

Impression formation

Solomon Asch was one of the first psychologists to study systematically the ways in which we form impressions of other people. His experimental approach was quite simple. First, he would present subjects with a short list of traits, supposedly describing a person (called the stimulus person). The subjects would first be asked to write a short personality sketch about the stimulus person based on the impressions that they had gathered from the trait list. Next, they would check on a scale the additional traits that they thought described the person. Asch found that there were two types of traits, which he termed *central* and *peripheral*. Central traits were those with a strong influence on the subject's perceptions; peripheral traits exerted very little influence.

In Asch's most famous study (1946) he read subjects one of the following lists of traits to describe a stimulus person:

1. intelligent, skillful, industrious, WARM, determined, practical, cautious
2. intelligent, skillful, industrious, COLD, determined, practical, cautious

Note that the two lists are identical except for the words *warm* and *cold*. Asch found that warm and cold were central traits. Subjects who received the

list with the word *warm* in it tended to write more favorable descriptions and to ascribe more socially desirable traits to the stimulus person than did subjects who heard the same list with the word *cold*.

Asch then repeated this study using the words *polite* and *blunt* in place of the words *warm* and *cold*. In this case sketches and the adjectives that subjects checked on the scales were quite similar, regardless of which trait list they had been given. These two experiments suggested that warm-cold was a central trait and that polite-blunt was a peripheral trait. (See Table 12.1.)

Are some traits always central? Asch thought that the centrality of a trait was relative, because it depended on the entire list of traits that were used to describe a person. A trait that is central in one group of traits might be peripheral within a different set. Asch also felt that our individual personalities determine which traits in others are most important to us. For these two reasons Asch concluded that it would be futile to search for universal groups of central and peripheral traits.

Some years later Julian Wishner (1960) proposed that we might be able to predict when a given trait will be central by relating it to the kinds of judgments that are to be made. He suggested that the centrality of a given trait is determined by how strongly subjects think it is related to the characteristics on which they rate the stimulus person. The trait *good typist* would probably be a central one if you were judging a person's abilities as a secretary but peripheral if you were deciding how well the

Table 12.1 Effects of descriptions on subjects' impressions

Other Traits Attributed	Description of Stimulus Person			
	Warm	Cold	Polite	Blunt
Sociable	77	13	71	48
Happy	90	34	75	65
Goodnatured	94	17	87	56
Wise	65	25	30	50
Generous	91	8	56	58

Effects of describing a person as either warm *vs.* cold or polite *vs.* blunt on subjects' impressions of him. The numbers reflect the percentage of subjects in each condition who attributed additional positive characteristics to the stimulus person. It is clear that warm *vs.* cold exerted a stronger influence than did polite *vs.* blunt, suggesting that it is a central trait. (Based on data from Asch, 1946.)

369

BOX 12.2
Beauty:
Only skin deep?

One of the first traits we notice about someone is his or her physical attractiveness. Does this quality influence our perception of his or her other characteristics and traits? To study this question Karen Dion, Ellen Berscheid, and Elaine Walster (1972) asked University of Minnesota students to rate a series of photographs of both males and females for physical attractiveness. Later another group was given photographs of those people that had been rated as either high, average, or low in attractiveness by the first group. They were asked to rate these people on a number of personality traits and to predict future events in their lives.

The results of the study showed that we do indeed judge a book by its cover. Subjects thought attractive people of both sexes had more socially desirable personality traits than the less attractive people. It did not seem to matter whether the subject was of the same or the opposite sex as the person in the photograph. In addition, the subjects pre-

dicted that the attractive people would have greater personal happiness, more prestigious occupations, and happier marriages than the less attractive people.

The effects of physical appearance on impressions begin to occur early in life, and they affect both children and adults. Attractive children are more popular with peers than are their less attractive counterparts as early as ages 4 to 6 (Dion, Berscheid and Walster, 1972), and adults also form more favorable impressions of attractive children. In one study women read a description of an aggressive act performed by a 7-year-old child and were asked to describe the child who committed the act. The description was accompanied by a photograph of either an attractive or an unattractive child. The attractive children were described far more favorably than were the unattractive ones. The unattractive children tended to be described as bratty, selfish, and antisocial, whereas the aggressive act of the attractive children was more likely to be viewed as a departure from their normal behavior.

Physical attractiveness appears to be a central trait within our culture. It is perhaps unfortunate that a trait over which we have only limited control should exert such a strong influence on the impressions others form of us.

(Vandermark, Stock, Boston)

What are your impressions of these people?

370

(Cole, Stock, Boston)

(Siteman, Stock, Boston)

(Albertson, Stock, Boston)

(Dietz, Stock, Boston)

(Carlson, Stock, Boston)

person would function as a ski instructor. In our culture physical attractiveness is a central trait for many people. The influence of this trait is discussed in Box 12.2.

How important are first impressions?

Many of our interpersonal relationships involve a series of interactions with others over a considerable period of time. But we do form impressions of people as soon as we meet them. How important are these early impressions compared with information we receive later?

Researchers have tested the relative importance of initial information and information we receive later by presenting subjects with conflicting pieces of information. When a judgment is made on the basis of the information received first, this is called a *primacy effect*. When the second block of information is more influential, there is a *recency effect*. Through careful experimentation, researchers have identified some of the factors that determine whether a primacy or recency effect is dominant.

One critical factor is the point at which the judgment is made. If the conflicting pieces of information are presented on the same occasion and a judgment is called for immediately, there is a strong primacy effect. People pay more attention to initial information when they are trying to form an immediate impression of someone. Once they do form this initial impression, not only do they pay less attention to subsequent information, but they also may perceive subsequent information selectively or in a distorted way so that it is consistent with their first impressions.

First impressions are not always dominant, however. Abraham Luchins (1957b) found that if subjects were warned not to make snap judgments, but rather to listen carefully to and evaluate all information, the primacy effect disappeared. He also found that if time elapsed between the points at which subjects received two conflicting pieces of information and if during that time interval the subjects worked on irrelevant tasks, such as arithmetic problems, then the judgments they made actually reflected a recency effect. The longer the time interval, the stronger was the recency effect. The subject's memory of the first block of information seemed to grow dimmer and to be replaced in memory by the later conflicting information.

The research results suggest that first impressions are most important in "one-shot" interactions, such as blind dates and job interviews. Relationships that continue over a long period of time and involve successive interactions more often reflect recency effects. But, of course, if an initial impression is sufficiently unfavorable, there may be no future interactions. How many unpleasant blind dates do you suppose might have ended in happy marriages were it not for primacy effects?

Putting it all together:
Additive and averaging models

In the course of time we can gather a considerable amount of information about another person. How do we go about combining these bits of information into a unified impression of that person?

There are two competing theories of information integration. The *additive model* states that we simply sum all the information we have about a person. For example, the judgment we make about a person's likability would be based simply on the sum of the likability of all his or her traits. The *averaging model* states that our impression of another will be based not on the sum of individual traits, but rather on the arithmetic average of our evaluation of all his or her traits.

There are a number of circumstances under which the additive and averaging models lead to different predictions. Consider the following example: You meet two different individuals, A and B. You find that they are equally sincere and warm, traits that you value very highly. Somewhat later you find that person B is also conscientious and intelligent, traits that you value, but not as highly as you do warmth and sincerity. You receive no additional information about person A. Which person will you like more, A or B? The additive model predicts that you will like B more, because you have information about more positive traits so that the sum will be greater than the one for A. The averaging model predicts the opposite, because you do not value the additional traits that you have learned about person B (intelligence and conscientiousness) as highly as you do warmth and sincerity. When you average the new information in with warmth and sincerity, they drag the average down.

The preceding situation was tested experimentally by Norman Anderson (1965). He found that person A was liked more than person B. The results of this and many subsequent experiments support the averaging model over the additive model. It seems that if you want to make the best possible impression, you should show others only your most positive traits.

Perceiver characteristics in social perception

Now that we have examined some of the ways in which people organize the information they receive about others into overall impressions, we have again learned that what we "see" is not always a mirror image of what is "out there." Our own biases and distortions can strongly affect our social perceptions. We now examine one important perceiver characteristic.

Implicit personality theories. On the basis of our own social interactions and the knowledge we gain about ourselves and others, we develop our own informal theories about "what makes people tick." These *implicit personality theories* contain our personal assumptions about the ways in which various personality traits are related to one another. For example, if you know only that another person is religious, what other traits will you ascribe to him or her? Your answer to this question reflects your "theory" about what religious people are like. And it is quite likely that your "theory" is different from the theories of others.

The role of implicit personality theories in perception was demonstrated in a study conducted with children in a summer camp (Dornbusch et al., 1965). The children were asked to describe each other in their own words, which allowed them to employ their own trait categories. The researchers then analyzed the content of the written paragraphs. They found that the descriptions that were given of any particular child were not very similar, but there was a fairly high degree of consistency in the way each child described others. In fact, the descriptions that each child wrote about other children were more similar than were the descriptions written by many children

about a particular child. Each child seemed to have his or her own cluster of traits that were used to form judgments about fellow campers.

Implicit personality theories provide a structure for perceptual information; they help us to fill in informational gaps and to arrive at a unified image of another person on whom we have incomplete information. How often have you heard such statements as, "I'm sure Roscoe's an honest person because I've seen that he's very conscientious?" This statement tells us that the perceiver's implicit personality theory links conscientiousness with honesty, but it does not provide us with reliable information about Roscoe's honesty. After all, a master criminal can be just as conscientious as a bank security guard.

Asch's theory of central and peripheral traits is related in important ways to implicit personality theory. Indeed, implicit personality theories can be viewed as collections of the central traits that individuals use in organizing their perceptions of other people.

Attribution: perceiving the causes of behavior

A major goal in perceiving other people is to understand why they behave as they do. If we can pinpoint the causes of our own and others' behavior, we increase our ability to predict and control the environment in which we must operate. The process of pinpointing these causes, or seeking an answer to the question "Why?" in relation to behavior, is called *attribution.*

Suppose you were asked to explain why a man stole a large sum of money. If you concluded that he did it because he was a basically dishonest person (as a prosecuting attorney might), you would be making a *personal* attribution. Your judgment would imply that the cause for the behavior resided within the man himself. If, however, you explained the act in terms of circumstances in the man's past and present situation, such as poor schooling, lack of employment opportunities, and exposure to bad company (as the defendant's lawyer might), you would be making a *situational* attribution. You might also choose to explain the crime in terms of a combination of personal and situational factors (e.g., this is a

373

basically dishonest person who was provided with a perfect opportunity to commit the crime).

From acts to dispositions

When we form conceptions of other people's personalities, we must rely on their overt behaviors. We may learn about these behaviors through statements they make about themselves, reports of their behavior by other people, or our own observations of them. On the basis of such information we draw inferences about their internal dispositions or personality traits. Because we seem to draw these inferences quite automatically, this might appear at first glance to be a fairly simple process. But for a variety of reasons most of us occasionally draw false inferences about what another person is really like.

First of all, much of the behavior any person exhibits is so trivial and conventional that it gives us little definitive information about personal characteristics and traits. Consider the person who sits in front of you in your psychology class. You are around that person for several hours each week, but you probably receive relatively little information about his or her personality. Second, people often attempt to project false images of themselves. If you accept all their actions at face value, you can easily make incorrect trait attributions. Finally, and perhaps most importantly, in many instances behaviors that we attribute to internal dispositions are in fact caused by external forces we either underestimate or of which we are unaware. In Milgram's research on obedience, for example (Chapter 1), we saw that almost *all* people are capable of great cruelty and insensitivity if they are acting under the orders of a strong authority figure.

People have a pronounced tendency to attribute the behaviors of other people to personal (dispositional) factors, but to attribute similar behaviors of their own to situational factors. In one study, for example, male college students were asked to state why they chose their college major and their girlfriend. Then they were asked to state the reasons they thought their best friend had selected his girlfriend and major. The subjects' answers were then coded as either situational causes (e.g., "there are great employment opportunities for chemists") or dispositional causes (e.g., "he likes to play with nitroglycerine"). Subjects made an equal number of

dispositional and situational attributions to account for their own behaviors but made three times as many dispositional as situational attributions to account for their best friend's behaviors (Nisbett, Caputo, Legant, and Maracek, 1973).

There seem to be several reasons for this difference in the way we attribute causes to our own acts and those of others. One reason is that we have different information about ourselves and others. When we are in a given situation we concentrate on the situation and are likely to view ourselves as responding to it. In perceptual terms, the situation is the figure and we are the background. When we watch someone else, however, we are likely to be concentrating more on the person than on the situation; the person is the figure and the situation is the background. We are more likely to perceive that the person's behaviors come from within and to make personal attributions. A second reason is that we observe ourselves across time and in many situations, and we know that our behavior varies somewhat according to the situation. We usually do not have this kind of information about other people, so that again we are more apt to attribute their behavior in a given situation to personal causes.

Effects of dispositional and situational attributions

The type of attribution we assign to a given behavior can markedly affect our reactions to that behavior. Because people tend to attribute their own behaviors to situational factors and explain the behaviors of others in dispositional terms, they are often more tolerant of their own misdeeds and shortcomings than they are of others'. Individuals who blame external factors for their each and every shortcoming also are unlikely to try to change their behavior.

But some people show the opposite tendency. Depressed individuals and those with low self-esteem may attribute the unfavorable outcomes in their lives to their own personal characteristics and attribute positive outcomes to situational causes or "luck." This attributional pattern is likely to perpetuate their feelings of low self-worth.

When we attribute a negative behavior to personal causes, there are a number of implications. One is that we have less reason to be optimistic about future positive change, because people are harder to change than situations. As a consequence, we and other people may be less likely to help the people whose behavior was in question. For example, if we concluded that underprivileged college students have academic problems because they are lazy and unmotivated, we might be less likely to help them than if we attributed the problems to inadequate high school preparation. Box 12.3 discusses a theory of why we sometimes blame victims for their plight.

One important consequence of social perception is the formation of attitudes toward the objects of our perceptions. As we see in the next section, however, our attitudes, once formed, influence our subsequent perceptions. Social perception and social attitudes are thus interdependent, with each affecting the other.

SOCIAL ATTITUDES

A social attitude is a relatively enduring combination of beliefs, feelings, and behavioral tendencies toward individuals, objects, or events of a social nature. As this definition implies, attitudes have three components: beliefs or knowledge (a cognitive component); feelings (an emotional component); and tendencies to respond in particular ways to the objects of the attitude (a behavioral component). Many psychologists view these three elements as critical to understanding the organization of experience and behavior.

Origins of social attitudes

Social attitudes have their origins in learning. Many of our attitudes are based on our personal experiences. For example, if you find your first course in psychology interesting and if your professor presents the material in an exciting way, then you will probably develop a positive attitude toward psychology as a topic of study.

Many attitudes are acquired from other people. Of the many social interactions in which human beings participate, those with parents are probably most important in the initial development of attitudes. Parents have control over important sources of reward and punishment, and they use their influence to establish "correct" attitudes and values in their children. Moreover, parents are the child's most im-

portant and dependable source of information about the world. The information they communicate, both knowingly and unknowingly, plays an important role in shaping attitudes.

As children grow, the number of social influences in their life increases. They begin to receive information from friends, teachers, and other relatives. Sometimes this information is consistent with the information they receive from parents; other times it is radically different, and the child may experience intense conflict as a result of the discrepancies. With the arrival of adolescence and young adulthood, peers become increasingly influential in shaping attitudes, much to the dismay of some parents. The term *reference group* refers to those social groups with whose standards and beliefs an individual identifies. A classic study by Theodore Newcomb (1963) demonstrated the influence of reference groups on attitudes.

In 1935 Newcomb conducted extensive interviews with the freshman class at Bennington College, whose student body consisted mainly of the daughters of wealthy and politically conservative New Englanders. He found that a large majority of the incoming women shared their parents' conservative attitudes but that upperclassmen and faculty tended to have extremely liberal political beliefs. Newcomb was interested in the extent to which the attitudes of the freshmen women would change as a result of their college experience. He found that political tendencies were highly correlated with popularity and prestige on campus. Those whose reference group shifted from family to upperclassmen and faculty became most liberal, whereas students who remained very attached to their families tended to remain more conservative at the cost of lower popularity and influence on campus.

Follow-up data collected by Newcomb indicated that the attitudes formed through associations with college reference groups were just as enduring as those formed by close attachments to family. In 1960 he reinterviewed the entire class of 1939. Those who had become more liberal during their college years continued to be liberal and had tended to marry extremely liberal men, whereas conservative women remained conservative and married conservative men.

The mass media can have an important influence

375

BOX 12.3

The just world: People get what they deserve

All of us seek to administer and receive justice. The American Dream, in fact, is based on a world in which people deserve what they get and get what they deserve. Yet it seems clear to most of us that this is not really the way the world operates. "Undeserving," immoral people often flourish, and good, innocent people suffer all sorts of misfortune. Sometimes, when bad things happen to innocent victims, these people are even blamed for their misfortune. Have you ever heard someone say that people who live in ghettos without heat and with rats scurrying around the floors *deserve* their fate because if they *really* wanted to, they could better themselves?

Melvin Lerner proposed the *just world hypothesis* to account for the fact that people often view victims as responsible for their own plight. We all want, he said, to believe that we live in a just world in which we will receive our due. When something bad happens to someone who seems to be a good person, it is inconsistent with our notion of a just world and therefore threatens our hopes that we will be treated justly ourselves. One way to remove the threat is to convince ourselves that victims really deserve their fate because they are not such good people after all. In a just world it is acceptable for something bad to happen to a bad person.

Lerner and Carolyn Simmons (1966) tested the just world hypothesis in an ingenious experiment.

Small groups of female subjects were told that they were in a study of emotional expression and that they would be asked to rate the emotional reactions of another subject in a learning experiment being shown over closed circuit TV. Actually, there were no other subjects, and the real subjects viewed a carefully prepared video tape. On the tape the subjects saw a learner who received painful shocks whenever she made a mistake. After a series of learning trials, the experimenter appeared. Some subjects were told that the experiment was half over and that the learner would receive another series of trials with shock. Others were told that in the next part of the experiment, the learner would receive monetary rewards for correct responses instead of shocks for mistakes. Subjects in a control group were told that the experiment was completed. Then the subjects were asked to rate the learner on a set of 20 personality traits.

Those who were told that the learner would be rewarded rated her quite favorably in comparison with the ratings of subjects in the control group. Those who believed that the victim would receive more shock rated her very unfavorably. Apparently, because they were powerless to aid the victim, the subjects needed to find a reason for her to deserve her fate and chose to perceive her as an undesirable person. In subsequent experiments it was shown that the more painful the shocks appeared to be, the more the victim was devalued by those observers who were told she would have to endure more pain.

Obviously, people do not always devalue innocent victims. But perceptual distortions such as this and others we have considered occur frequently enough to underscore the fact that perception is a product of our own creation rather than a faithful mirroring of the external world.

---

on the development of attitudes. Researchers have found that television, radio, and the press are effective to varying degrees in transmitting information, arousing emotions, and influencing actions. Thus the cognitive, emotional, and behavioral components of attitudes are all subject to varying degrees of influence from the mass media.

Our individual needs and personalities are also closely related to the attitudes we form. We appear to have a general need for *consistency* in our attitudes and beliefs. We want them to be mutually supportive and not to conflict with one another. Later in this chapter we examine an important theory about our need for consistency.

We now turn to two important social attitudes, interpersonal attraction and prejudice. Both play critical roles in the functioning of social systems, and social psychological studies of them have helped to pinpoint many of the factors that influence the formation of our social attitudes.

Interpersonal attraction

All of us evaluate the persons, things, and events that we encounter on a dimension that ranges from positive to neutral to negative. These evaluations give rise to feelings that we classify as "liking," "indifference," or "dislike." Because other individuals are an important part of our lives, they are the object of many of our evaluations. What factors determine whether we like, dislike, or love another person? Earlier, we described how physical attractiveness can affect our evaluations of others. There are additional factors which are equally or even more important.

Similarity and attraction:
Do opposites *really* attract?

How often have you heard the old saying "Opposites attract"? Many accept this as a basic law, and in fact you can probably think of instances in which people who seem very different from one another have somehow formed positive and lasting relationships. However, research has shown quite clearly that similarity, not dissimilarity, breeds attraction. People seem most attracted to others who are similar to them in a variety of ways. This is why most computer dating systems are designed to bring similar people together.

It has long been known that people who like each other tend to have similar attitudes. Much of the recent research on attitude similarity and attraction has been conducted by Donn Byrne of Purdue University and his students, using a rather simple experimental method. First, they ask subjects to indicate their attitudes on a variety of topics (e.g., the existence of God, nuclear disarmament, smoking). After they have completed the attitude scale, subjects are presented with a scale supposedly filled out by another subject but actually generated by the experimenter on the basis of each subject's responses. The experimenter can directly manipulate the amount of agreement between the two "subjects," as well as the topics on which they agree. After reading the "other

subject's" responses, subjects are asked how much they think they might like the stranger.

Byrne found that attraction is related in a linear (straight line) fashion to the proportion of similar attitudes held by the stranger. This relationship has been so consistently found that it has been possible to write an equation to predict the attraction score on the basis of the proportion of similar attitudes. Figure 12.2 shows that attraction scores predicted by the formula correspond very closely to actual attraction scores provided by research subjects. This was true not only for American college students, but also for subjects in Japan, Mexico, and India, who ranged from fourth-graders through retirees.

The similarity-attraction relationship holds for such variables as intelligence and spending habits, as well as for attitudes. In a study concerned with the effects of personality similarity, all entering college freshmen were given a personality test. Six months later, female class members were asked to name three classmates of the same sex whom they liked best and three whom they liked least. The researchers then compared 12 pairs of subjects who *liked* each other and 13 pairs who *disliked* each other. The pairs who liked each other had similar personality profiles; those who disliked each other had very different profiles (Izard, 1960).

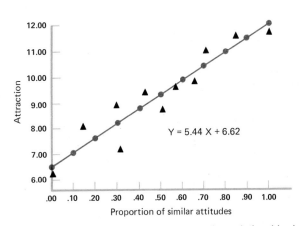

Figure 12.2 The attitude similarity–attraction relationship. In the formula, Y is the attraction score obtained on the interpersonal judgment scale and X is the proportion of similar attitudes. The triangles are data points provided by actual subjects, and the line is that predicted by the formula. (Byrne and Nelson, 1965. Copyright 1965 by the American Psychological Association. Reprinted by permission.)

Similarity and complementarity. Similarity seems to play an important part both in the early stages of a romance and in marital happiness. In one experiment married couples were asked to give both their opinions and the opinions they thought their spouses might give. The researchers found that spouses not only had similar opinions, but also that they *overestimated* the degree of similarity that actually existed (Byrne and Blaylock, 1963). A later study showed that this overestimation was especially marked for couples who indicated considerable happiness in the relationship; couples who reported marital unhappiness tended actually to underestimate similarity (Levinger and Breedlove, 1966).

But similarity does not explain everything. Certain trait pairs, such as dominance-submission and dependency-nurturance complement, or "fit" with, each other. For example, in order for one person in a couple to be dominant in some area, the other must be submissive or passive. Many psychologists have hypothesized that complementary personality traits are important determinants of successful relationships.

A. C. Kerckhoff and Keith Davis (1962) studied couples who had dated for a relatively short time (less than 18 months) and others who had dated longer than 18 months. They tested and interviewed the subjects at the beginning of the study and again seven months later to see whether each couple had moved closer to or further from a permanent relationship. Among the couples who had dated only a short time when the study began, those with similar values tended to form more permanent relationships, regardless of whether or not they had complementary personality traits. Among couples who had been together longer than 18 months at the outset, those with complementary traits had become closer, regardless of how similar their values were. This pattern led Kerchoff and Davis to suggest that there is a sequential process in relationships. Individuals initially establish relationships with others who are similar to themselves in important ways. Later these relationships become stronger if they have similar values, and finally the degree to which their personality traits complement each other influences the degree of permanence and intimacy they establish. It appears that in some instances "opposites" may indeed attract, but only if their "opposite" behaviors and traits complement each other.

Attraction responses from others

It is perhaps obvious that we should like others with whom we have interactions that are personally rewarding. But the context in which we receive indications of being liked affects their meaning and therefore their value to us. Social behaviors typically do not occur in isolation. They are usually part of an ongoing sequence of behaviors, and the reward value of a given behavior may be affected by what has gone on before it.

An experiment by Elliot Aronson and Darwyn Linder (1965) provides a prime example of the way in which a pattern of reactions can influence attraction. Each of the female subjects thought that she was working as a research assistant in the experimental situation. She was required to engage another woman (who was actually a confederate of the experimenter) in conversation on seven different occasions. After each conversation the subject overheard the other woman talking to the experimenter about her. In one condition the woman consistently said nice things about the subject; in another condition the woman consistently said unkind things about the subject. In a third ("loss") condition she said nice things the first few times, but then became increasingly unkind. And in a fourth ("gain") condition the woman initially said unkind things but gradually began to say kind and complimentary things.

When the series of interactions was over, subjects were asked to complete a questionnaire about the other woman. One question asked how much they liked the woman. The results shown in Figure 12.3 indicate that the subjects found the interaction more rewarding when the woman began with negative comments and changed to positive comments than when the comments were positive all along. Likewise, they found the condition in which they received consistently negative comments less unpleasant than the one in which the initial positive comments changed to negative ones.

There are real-life counterparts of these results. Sometimes consistent compliments or kindnesses from those who are close to us tend to lose their impact as time goes by. A wife or husband may attach little significance to a positive comment from a spouse but be quite flattered by the same compliment from a stranger. Paradoxically, this may give strangers more reward power than friends. However,

378

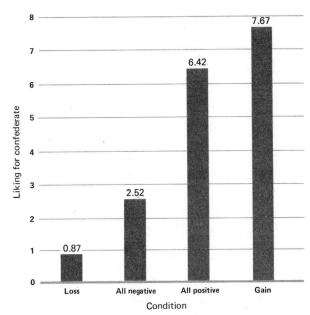

Figure 12.3 Attraction for another person who evaluated subjects positively at first and then negatively (loss), consistently evaluated them negatively or positively, or evaluated them negatively at first and later positively (gain). (From data reported by Aronson and Linder, 1965.)

criticism from loved ones is often more devastating than negative comments from strangers.

Proximity: Familiarity breeds liking, not contempt
Leon Festinger, Stanley Schachter, and Kurt Back (1950) asked married students who lived in a housing complex to indicate which couples they socialized with most frequently. The results showed that most socializing occurred with next-door neighbors and couples who lived on the same floor rather than with couples who lived a few yards further away. A more recent study among police trainees who were assigned to rooms and positions in the training sessions in alphabetic order indicated that predictions of friendship based on the alphabet were quite close to the men's actual preferences (Segal, 1974).

Of course, in these studies the subjects were similar in a number of important respects (sex, age, school, or occupational status), so that proximity promoted attraction among fairly similar persons. Proximity may be relatively less important among individuals who are not as similar.

Do people who are close to us become more at-

tractive merely because they are physically close? We see individuals who are physically closest to us most frequently, so that they become most familiar and perhaps most attractive. But this possibility directly contradicts the old saying that "familiarity breeds contempt." Which theory is closer to the truth?

Studies involving both human and nonhuman stimuli have shown that degree of familiarity is an important determinant of desirability or attractiveness. Robert Zajonc (1968) presented subjects with slides showing Chinese symbols, some of which he showed more frequently than others. When they were tested later, subjects indicated a preference for the symbols that had been shown more frequently. Zajonc also showed subjects pictures from college yearbooks. He showed each face 1, 2, 5, 10, or 25 times. He then mixed these photos with photos that the subjects had not seen, and showed them again. Degree of liking corresponded with frequency of exposure; faces seen most were liked best; those seen least often were judged least attractive. In a third experiment, unacquainted female subjects participated in a beverage-tasting experiment and were shuttled quickly from booth to booth. The shuttling was arranged so that each subject shared a booth with one of five other women various numbers of times. No talking was permitted. Subjects were then asked how much they liked each of the other five subjects. The more frequently they had shared a booth with another subject, the more they liked her (Saegert, Swap, and Zajonc, 1973). The evidence indicates, then, that familiarity may in fact breed liking rather than contempt.

Prejudice
During the course of history, prejudice has had more destructive effects on the fabric of society than any other social attitude. It is at the root of racial, ethnic, religious, and sex discrimination; destructive and bloody intergroup confrontations; and the feelings of inferiority and self-rejection that plague its victims.

Prejudice, like all other attitudes, consists of a combination of beliefs, feelings, and behavioral tendencies toward members of particular groups. Figure 12.4 shows how the components of an attitude are expressed in one variety of racial prejudice.

The foundation of prejudice is a set of beliefs based on inaccurate or incomplete information. Prejudiced individuals derive "facts" from this informa-

379

BOX 12.4
What's in a name?

Stereotyping occurs when we attribute the characteristics of a group to an individual we assume is part of that group. Stereotypes do not recognize individual differences; we simply assume that the individual possesses *all* the traits or characteristics we have previously perceived in members of that group.

Clearly, stereotyping can affect our social perceptions. Our expectations of a person's traits and characteristics influence what we actually see. We may distort or pick up only certain cues that reinforce our original stereotyped image. Gregory Razran (1950) performed a study that examined the way in which stereotypes affect perception. He asked subjects to rate pictures of young women in terms of beauty, likability, and character. Two months later, he asked the same subjects to reevaluate the same pictures, but this time he attached names to them. The names were either Jewish, Italian, Irish, or Anglo-Saxon. Subjects judged the girls with Jewish and Italian names lower in liking on the second set of ratings than on the first set and somewhat lower in beauty and character. In addition, they rated the girls with Jewish names higher on ambition. Clearly, the subjects' stereotyped images of members of these ethnic groups determined the way they perceived individuals thought to belong to the groups.

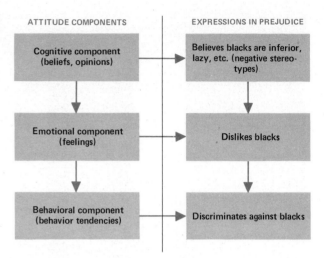

Figure 12.4 The components of an attitude as expressed in prejudice toward black people.

tion and generalize them to a group of people, a process called *stereotyping*. Stereotyping is not necessarily an undesirable process when it is based on valid generalizations, for it can be a way of simplifying and organizing the perceptual world. However, inaccurate stereotypes can blind us to individual differences and exceptions within a group.

Earlier we discussed attribution, the process of perceiving the causes of behavior. Stereotyped beliefs are often used to "explain" behavior. For example, there are widespread and uncritically accepted beliefs that men and women have distinctly different abilities. The influence that these sex role stereotypes can have on attributions has been demonstrated in several recent studies in which women succeeded in "male" occupations and tasks. In one study male college students were asked to account for the accomplishments of highly successful male and female physicians. They rated the female as less competent than the male, said that she had an easier path to success, and that she had higher motivation and drive. Apparently, they felt that a woman could not possibly have the skills required to become a successful physician, so that if she "made it," it was either because she had it easier or because she tried harder (Feldman-Summers and Kiesler, 1974). The implications of findings such as these are quite sobering: If success by members of groups who are the target of prejudice is always attributed to "luck" or to "having it easier," then these people are robbed not only of the rewards and respect they rightfully deserve, but also of the chance to change the stereotype that they are inferior.

One of the most tragic consequences of prejudice is that the targets of discrimination may themselves come to accept the stereotypes, resulting in lowered self-esteem, feelings of hopelessness, and even self-rejection. In some instances, as a defense against the negative features they perceive as part of their own

In recent years women have organized themselves to fight against the effects of being stereotyped for centuries. (Charles Gatewood)

identity, oppressed individuals may come to identify with those who oppress them. In an experiment conducted during the 1940s, black preschool children were given two dolls, one black and one white, and were asked to indicate which of the dolls "looks like you." The white doll was chosen more frequently than the black one. In another version of the same experiment, about two-thirds of a large sample

BOX 12.5

The creation of instant prejudice

A remarkable demonstration of how quickly prejudice can form and how devastating its effects can be was carried out by a third-grade schoolteacher in a small Iowa town. One day Jane Elliot announced to her students that brown-eyed people were more intelligent and better people than blue-eyed ones. She then laid down guidelines to keep the inferior blue-eyed children in their place: She told them to sit in the back of the room and to stay at the end of the line at recess and lunch; she forbade them to drink from the water fountain, which was reserved for the superior brown-eyed children. They were subjected to many other demeaning and frustrating regulations.

Within minutes, profound changes began to occur in both groups of children. The brown-eyed youngsters, according to the teacher, "became

nasty, vicious, discriminating little third graders . . . it was ghastly." They rejected the blue-eyed children, refused to play with them, and told them in many ways that they were inferior. The blue-eyed youngsters, in turn, became depressed and angry. Their academic performance dropped, and when they were asked to describe themselves, they used such words as *awful, stupid,* and *bad.*

The next day Elliot reversed the roles. The teacher said she had lied the day before and that, in truth, blue-eyed people were superior to brown-eyed ones. The children followed an almost identical pattern in reverse: blue-eyed children became the hostile ruling class who discriminated against the brown-eyed youngsters, and the latter were emotionally devastated and performed poorly in their studies.

The next day Elliot told the children that there were actually no differences between blue-eyed and brown-eyed children, and the children embraced each other in a single happy group. They had learned firsthand how arbitrary prejudice can be and how it feels to be a target of it. Elliot hoped that their experience would help them to empathize with others who are oppressed in the outside world.

of black children between the ages of 3 and 10 characterized the white doll as "good" and preferable to the black doll (Clark and Clark, 1947). More recently, however, the emergence of "black pride" has manifested itself in a marked preference by black children for the doll of their own race (Hraba and Grant, 1970).

Causes of prejudice

Prejudice has no single cause; a variety of social learning experiences and personal needs may cause it to develop. Researchers have, for the sake of discussion and experimentation, identified three basic causes: socialization and conformity; group competition and conflict; and personality factors. These three causes are not mutually exclusive and they may all be working together within any given individual.

Socialization and conformity. Prejudices usually develop on the basis of "hearsay," rather than through personal contact with the targets of the prejudice. Children of prejudiced parents, for example, may overhear negative comments from them about minorities, hear them justify discriminatory acts, and perhaps be forbidden to associate with children from minority groups. They may also receive approval from their parents when they begin expressing prejudiced attitudes similar to the parents'. It is therefore not surprising that the racial prejudices of children tend to resemble those of their parents.

Because most individuals want to "fit in" and to be accepted by important reference groups, conformity can be an important determinant of prejudice. Just as conservative Bennington girls acquired liberal attitudes because they associated with liberal reference groups, individuals who associate with preju-

diced reference groups may become more prejudiced. On the other hand, if prejudiced individuals
begin to relate to less prejudiced reference groups,
then their prejudice may decrease. One study found
that Army recruits from the Deep South became less
prejudiced toward blacks after they had associated
with less prejudiced Northerners (Pettigrew, 1961).

Group competition and conflict. Political and economic forces are often at the base of a prejudice.
Competition for power, jobs, or other resources that
are in limited supply may motivate a dominant
group to exploit or discriminate against a less powerful group in order to gain some material advantage.

There is considerable historical support for the
idea that competition breeds prejudice. Research
conducted in the 1970s showed that whites who
were just above blacks on the socioeconomic ladder
were the most highly prejudiced against them, especially if the two groups were in close competition for
jobs.

A classic field experiment on intergroup conflict
and conflict resolution was conducted at a summer
camp in Robbers Cave, Oklahoma, by Muzafer Sherif
and his associates (1961). The subjects were 22 well-
adjusted 11-year-old boys. When they arrived at the
camp the boys were divided into two groups, who
chose to call themselves the "Rattlers" and the "Eagles." The camp counselors tried to encourage group
identification and cohesiveness. The two groups
worked separately and successfully on projects that
required the members to cooperate with one another
in order to accomplish goals valued by the group
(such as improving the swimming hole).

When the Eagles and the Rattlers had become
separate and cohesive groups, the experimenters
began to pit them against each other in competitive
contests and games. As the games went on, the boys'
good sportsmanship gradually deteriorated into deep
resentment, hostility, and discriminatory practices
between the Eagles and the Rattlers. The counselors
arranged a party to reconcile the two groups, at
which they could "let bygones be bygones." Half of
the food was fresh and attractive, whereas the other
half was crushed and unappetizing. They allowed
one of the groups to arrive first, and naturally they
ate the appetizing food. The other group was furious,
and began an open conflict.

The experimenters then set out to restore harmony between the groups. They soon learned that
simple contact simply served to increase the hostility, so that they tried the same procedures they had
used to create harmony *within* the groups and forced
the boys to cooperate. The experimenters arranged
for the water supply system to fail, and the groups
had to cooperate to fix it. They told the boys about a
very exciting movie, and the groups decided to pool
their money in order to rent it. The Eagles and the
Rattlers had to cooperate again in order to tow in a
broken-down truck. Gradually the hostility and the
tendency to stereotype members of the other group
disappeared and were replaced by a spirit of friendship and cooperation.

The Robbers Cave experiment, along with others,
suggests that prejudice and intergroup hostility can
be reduced if groups are made to work toward a
common goal. This principle has been used at times
by political leaders who create crises with foreign
powers in order to unite warring domestic factions
against a common foe.

Personality factors. The wholesale murder of 6 million Jews during World War II stimulated the American Jewish Committee to launch a research project
to investigate the personal characteristics of the *authoritarian personality* (Adorno et al., 1950). The
project attempted to pinpoint the personal characteristics of individuals who establish and accept the
principles of authoritarian societies, such as the one
in Nazi Germany.

The researchers described authoritarianism as an
attitudinal system consisting of a number of interrelated antidemocratic sentiments. They characterized
authoritarians as individuals who use repressive
means to control their sexual and aggressive tendencies. Authoritarians project their "evil" sexual needs
onto others, so that they have an exaggerated concern with sexual behavior and a desire to punish
sexual "deviants." They project their hostility onto
others as well, so that they see the world as a threatening place and feel justified in expressing their
hostile impulses because they think they are punishing aggressors. They develop highly conservative attitudes and behavior patterns, and tend to submit to
authority figures with whom they strongly identify.
Authoritarians are *ethnocentric*; they identify

383

strongly with reference groups and are intolerant of "out-groups."

To measure authoritarian tendencies, Adorno and his associates developed an F (for Fascism) Scale. The F-Scale contains statements with which an authoritarian person presumably would agree, such as the following:

1. A person who has bad manners, habits, and breeding can hardly expect to get along with decent people.
2. Obedience and respect for authority are the most important virtues children should learn.
3. Most of our social problems would be solved if we could somehow get rid of the immoral, crooked, and feeble-minded people.

Scores are based on the number of times the individual agrees with such statements. Adorno and his group assumed that prejudice was a natural outgrowth of authoritarianism, because minority groups serve as a convenient target for repressed hostility and ethnocentric tendencies. Other researchers have found that scores on the F-scale are highly related to anti-Semitism, but that they are *not* strongly related to prejudice against blacks and other minority groups. Despite many attempts to do so, researchers have not succeeded in identifying a specific personality pattern that is consistently associated with prejudice against all minority groups.

Although there may not be a single "prejudiced personality," personality dynamics are an important factor in many forms of prejudice. The *scapegoat theory* of prejudice, which is an outgrowth of the frustration-aggression hypothesis (Chapter 2), argues that frustrated individuals sometimes displace their aggression onto groups that are relatively powerless. The form the aggression takes depends on what is deemed appropriate by the person's reference group.

SOCIAL INFLUENCES ON ATTITUDES AND BEHAVIOR

People are manipulators. Each of us tries to influence the behavior of others, and they, in turn, try to influence ours. If we want a person to like us, then we behave in likable ways. If we want sympathy, help, submission, or a fight, we behave in ways that are likely to produce these reactions. The world of social interaction can be viewed as a constant exchange of attempts at social influence and a constant series of responses to these attempts. Of course, sometimes these attempts are made by groups rather than by single individuals, and they may be subtle or even unconscious. In order to examine various forms of social interaction from this perspective, we must acquire a vocabulary for it by looking first at typical responses to these attempts.

Three responses to social influence

Social psychologist Herbert Kelman (1961) has grouped responses to attempts at social influence into three classes: *compliance*, *identification*, and *internalization*. His theory also specifies the kinds of motivation underlying each type of response and the degree of permanence it is likely to have.

Compliance

Compliance refers to responses that are made solely in order to obtain a reward or to avoid punishment. It is quite possible to make a man "willingly" hand over his wallet if you point a gun at him. You might "agree" with someone's opinion in order to be liked and approved by that person, even though you privately disagree with him, or her.

Solomon Asch (1958) performed a classic series of studies on compliance behavior in the laboratory. Subjects were seated at a table with six other "subjects" who were actually confederates of the experimenter. The subjects had to make a series of rather simple perceptual judgments. On each trial they were shown a card with three vertical lines of different lengths and asked to indicate which of the three lines was the same length as a line drawn on another card. The situation was arranged so that the real subject always announced his or her judgment next to last. The correct response was quite obvious, and on most of the trials, the confederates each made the correct judgment. On some trials, however, they all chose the same wrong line. Under these circumstances the real subjects also chose the wrong line about one-third of the time. About 74 percent of them conformed on at least one trial. The six confederates seemed to exert a striking degree of social influence on the subjects.

Asch conducted additional studies that showed

384

that if even one of the confederates made the correct judgment, then very little conformity (only about 6 percent of judgments) occurred on the part of the subjects. Moreover, other research has shown that even if one of the confederates makes a judgment that is even more *erroneous* than those of the others, subjects are still more likely to make a correct judgment than they are if all six confederates make the same incorrect judgment (Allen and Levine, 1971).

Of course, Stanley Milgram's studies of obedience to authority (described in Chapter 1) are a classic example of the tendency to conform under pressure. A high proportion of subjects administered what they thought were extremely high levels of shock to another person under the orders of an authority figure, despite the fact that they protested the orders verbally.

As we might expect, compliance is not necessarily a very enduring change. Typically, the compliance occurs only when the potential reinforcing or punishing agent is watching, and only as long as that person or group controls important rewards or punishments. How often have you heard people mutter how glad they will be when they can quit their job and tell that (expletive deleted) boss what they *really* think of him? Likewise, prisoners of war are often pressured into making public propaganda statements that they repudiate as soon as they are released.

Identification

The second major type of response to social influence, *identification*, is brought about by an individual's desire to be like another person or to be identified with a particular group. Children, for example, may copy behavior and express attitudes voiced by their parents, heroes, or peers. There is often identification among individuals in particular occupations and they adopt similar attitudes and behaviors.

Identification, like compliance, is prompted by a relationship with another person or a group and it is not necessarily internally satisfying for the individual. Although the individual may actually believe that the attitude or behavior he or she adopts is correct (which is not necessarily true for compliance), he or she will probably maintain it only as long as the relationship with the source of influence remains satisfying. If another person or group that

has conflicting attitudes or behavior patterns becomes more important, then the individual will probably change his or her attitudes and behavior.

Internalization

Internalization is the most permanent and deeply rooted response to social influence. Individuals respond to outside influences because their characteristic behavior or attitudes are consistent with the individual's own value system. The motivation for internalization is a desire to believe and act correctly. For example, individuals with liberal political attitudes are likely to support civil rights legislation because they have a basic belief in equal opportunity for all. Internalized attitudes and behaviors become independent of the source of influence and they do not change easily.

In all three kinds of responses the way in which the individual views the source of influence is the key factor. In compliance the source of influence has the *power* to provide rewards or punishments for the individual. In identification the source is *attractive* to the individual. In identification the individual must view the source as *credible and trustworthy*, because the individual's underlying motivation is the desire to be correct.

A given behavior or attitude can be the result of either compliance, identification, or internalization. It is also true that a behavior or attitude can be originally acquired through one type of response to influence and maintained by another. For example, students who are forced to study math in order to pass a required math course may find math so interesting and challenging once they begin to master it that they decide to become math majors. Here we have gone from compliance to internalization. Or perhaps a syndicate hit man may suddenly decide that killing is wrong, but continue to engage in his unsavory profession because he knows that he will be liquidated if he quits the mob. In this instance a behavior originally resulting from internalization is now maintained through compliance.

Attitude change

Many social influence attempts are designed to change attitudes. Advertisers try to induce a positive attitude toward their products. Politicians try to project an image that promotes positive attitudes

BOX 12.6

The delicate art of persuading terrorists

In increasing numbers in recent years, innocent people have been swept up at gunpoint and held hostage by terrorists and psychologically disturbed individuals to give force to their demands. These incidents have stimulated the development of a new police specialist who is trained to apply the psychological principles of persuasion to bring about the release of hostages and the bloodless surrender of the criminal.

Several important principles have been adopted by police for dealing with the captors of hostages:

1. *Analyze your adversary.* Police try to find out as much as possible about the psychological characteristics of the captor in the hope of finding areas they can exploit and arguments that will strike a responsive chord.
2. *Buy time and establish trust.* Police attempt to es-

tablish communication with the terrorist and develop trust through a "we're in this together" approach. They emphasize to their adversary that they and other people "understand" how he feels and why he is acting as he is. Buying time often stimulates the captor to reconsider if he is *really* willing to die rather than surrender and it gives him time to establish a comradeship with his hostages. The passing hours or days frequently result in a growing unwillingness to kill or to be killed and a willingness to "work things out" with one or more trusted policemen.

3. *Negotiate.* Time is usually bought through painstaking negotiations aimed at convincing hostage-takers that they can have what they want without dying. This is accomplished by simply listening, by allowing the captors to publicize their grievances, or by granting modest concessions and minor compromises over such issues as food, cigarettes, etc.

By their attempts to increase their credibility and present persuasive counter-arguments to individuals holding hostages, police are attempting to apply sound psychological principles in an arena where the stakes are life and death.

---

toward them and their viewpoints. Government leaders try to gain support for the decisions they make. During the Vietnam War an expensive and intensive program of "Vietnamization" was undertaken in an attempt to change attitudes of the South Vietnamese and foster commitment to fight against Communism. A great deal of effort and money is invested in attempts to change attitudes because most people assume that the cognitive and emotional components of attitudes strongly influence behavior.

Persuasion

By far the most common technique used to change attitudes is simple persuasion. However, "simple" persuasion is really not simple at all. There are innumerable approaches to persuading others and the processes involved are so complex that, in spite of

several decades of research and hundreds of studies, we do not yet fully understand them.

A number of factors have been studied in relation to persuasive communications, including the characteristics of communicators and the form and content of the communications. But these factors interact with one another in complex ways, so that researchers have been forced to study them in combination with one another as well as individually.

Characteristics of the communicator. In the 1950s a Yale research group that included Carl Hovland, Irving Janis, and Harold Kelley (1953) began to study systematically the role of the communicator in the process of persuasion. They identified *credibility* as a critical communicator characteristic. This characteristic has two major components, *expertness* and *trustworthiness*. The most effective persuader is one who has expertise in the area he is talking about and who appears to be presenting the "truth" in as unbiased a manner as possible. Nixon's image builders operated on these assumptions. During the 1968 presidential campaign they concentrated on increasing his credibility among potential voters. One of their most effective ploys was a series of staged question-and-answer programs in which Nixon "spontaneously" gave knowledgeable and lucid (but carefully rehearsed) answers to questions from carefully selected panels designed to represent all segments of the viewing public. The shows were highly successful in presenting Nixon as a warm, knowledgeable, and trustworthy candidate.

The Yale group's research did indicate that credible communicators can produce greater changes in attitude than can communicators with low credibility. But this advantage decreases over time. As Figure 12.5 shows, there is both a *decrease* in attitude change produced by the high credibility source and an *increase* in change produced by the low credibility communicator. This change over time is called a

sleeper effect (Hovland and Weiss, 1951). Apparently, as time goes by, people stop linking the message with its source, so that whatever change occurs must be produced by the message alone. However, if people are reminded of the source of the message when they are tested, then the credibility effects are maintained over time (Kelman and Hovland, 1953).

The source of a communication can also affect the meaning it conveys. Consider the following statement: "A little rebellion now and then is a good thing; it is needed to prevent political stagnation." What meaning would this statement convey if it were made by a conservative spokesman such as Ronald Regan? Would the meaning be different if the statement were attributed to Karl Marx? If respondents do not trust the communicator, they may change the meaning of an otherwise credible message to make it less believable.

Characteristics of the communication. When trying to persuade someone, is it more effective to present only one side of the issue, or is it better to present the opposition's arguments as well and then try to refute them? The relative effectiveness of the two approaches seems to depend on the initial attitude of the audience toward the position stated in the message and its awareness that there are two reasonable sides to the issue. *One-sided* arguments are most effective for those who agree with the message or who are ignorant of the other side of the issue, because they do not raise any new doubts. But *two-sided* messages are more effective with individuals who disagree with the position or who are aware that there is another side to the issue. These people are likely to perceive a one-sided argument as biased, and to construct counterarguments against it. Two-sided arguments that acknowledge and refute the arguments against their position seem more fair and discourage a negative audience from formulating arguments to bolster its own position.

Is it best to state the conclusion of an argument or to let an audience draw the conclusion by itself? Research indicates that there is usually more attitude change when a speaker draws explicit conclusions. However, there is some indication that it may be more effective not to draw explicit conclusions if the audience is both intelligent enough to arrive at the correct conclusion and motivated enough to

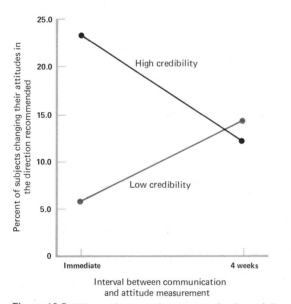

Figure 12.5 Effects of persuasive communications delivered by high and low credibility sources. Although high-credibility sources produced more immediate attitude change, this difference disappeared after a period of four weeks, indicating a "sleeper effect." (Based on data from Hovland and Weiss, 1951.)

387

make the effort required to do so (Linder and Worchel, 1970).

Some attempts to change our attitudes and behaviors are specifically designed to arouse fear. We are told that smoking will increase our chances of developing lung cancer and that speeding will increase our chances of never developing anything again. We are warned that if we do not stop polluting our atmosphere, we will destroy our habitat. Some of Nixon's 1968 campaign commercials featured still pictures of wars and race riots followed by the written words, "This time, vote like your whole world depends on it. Nixon." In 1972 a McGovern advertisement pictured a nuclear explosion. How effective are fear appeals such as these?

An early experiment (Janis and Feshbach, 1953) indicated that strong fear appeals actually produced *less* attitude change than weak ones. However, more recent studies have consistently shown the opposite to be true. For example, one investigation compared the effects of high-fear and low-fear appeals on changes in both attitudes and behaviors related to dental hygiene. One group of subjects was shown pictures of decayed teeth and diseased gums; another was shown less frightening materials, such as plastic teeth, charts, and graphs. Subjects who saw

the frightening materials reported more anxiety and a greater desire to change their dental practices immediately after receiving the appeal than did the low-fear group.

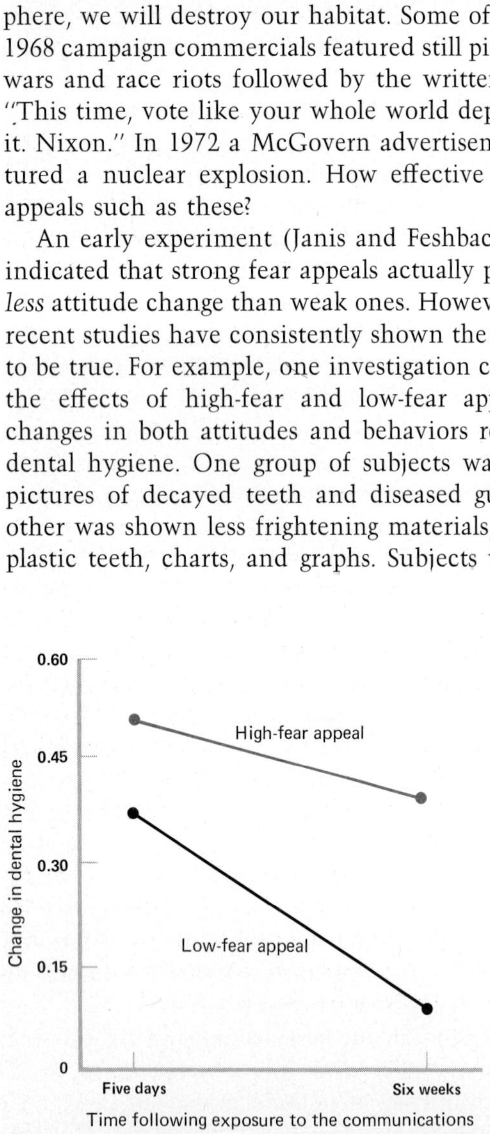

But were these reactions translated into better dental hygiene practices? In order to answer this important question subjects were called back to the laboratory on two occasions (five days and six weeks after the experiment) and chewed disclosing wafers, which stain uncleaned areas of the teeth red. This provided a direct indication of how well they were taking care of their teeth.

Figure 12.6 shows that the high-fear appeal resulted in greater and more permanent changes in dental hygiene. Arousing a realistic level of fear and providing clear behavioral guidelines for reducing the cause of the fear can be an effective way to change behavior. If the message is too frightening and if people are not given guidelines to help them reduce the cause of the fear, they may reduce their anxiety instead by denying the message or the credibility of the communicator. It is unlikely that attitude or behavior change will occur under these circumstances.

"Inoculation" against persuasive communications. William McGuire has suggested that it is possible to "inoculate" individuals against attempts to change their attitudes by presenting weak arguments against their position and then refuting them. McGuire argued that this technique stimulates people to think up additional refutations of their own. If they are presented only with one-sided arguments favoring their position, he claimed, people develop little resistance to persuasive attacks.

To test this theory, subjects were given one-sided and two-sided "inoculations" against attacks on widely shared beliefs that are rarely challenged, such as "most forms of mental illness are not contagious" (McGuire and Papageorgis, 1961). Each subject was presented with three beliefs, two of which were preceded by inoculations. One inoculation consisted of four arguments in support of the belief. The second consisted of four arguments against the belief that were then refuted. The third belief was simply presented by itself.

Two days later, each subject received three messages, one attacking each of the beliefs. After the

Figure 12.6 The effects of high- and low-fear appeals on dental hygiene behaviors. Subjects exposed to high-fear warnings brushed their teeth more carefully than did those who saw low-fear warnings. (Based on data from Evans et al., 1970.)

attacks the researchers measured the subjects' beliefs about each of the three truisms. The results showed quite clearly that the second type of inoculation was most effective in preventing attitude change. Attitudes toward the belief that had received the one-sided supportive defense changed nearly as much as the attitudes toward the belief that had not been defended at all.

Exposing individuals to counterarguments that are then refuted appears to strengthen their attitudes and to make them highly resistant to change. Parents or governments who do not permit exposure to opposing viewpoints tend to foster attitudes that are as rigid as glass but that are just as easily shattered if they are finally hit with convincing counterarguments.

Changing attitudes by changing behaviors

Researchers have found that under certain circumstances, if individuals are forced to change their ordinary behavior, they may change their attitudes as well.

Role playing and attitude change. Role playing can be an effective way to encourage attitude change. In one experiment, highly prejudiced whites were asked to play the role of a black person. They developed more favorable attitudes toward blacks as a result (Culbertson, 1957). In a more recent study, Clore and Jeffery (1972) used role playing to influence people's attitudes toward the handicapped. They placed a group of individuals in wheelchairs and asked them to imagine that they had been in an accident that had left them permanently paralyzed. The subjects were then sent on a 25-minute wheelchair trip across the University of Illinois campus to the student union and back. Compared with a control group that did not role-play, the role players developed more positive attitudes toward the handicapped, expressed a greater willingness to tour the campus with a handicapped student, and felt that more funds should be directed toward campus facilities for the handicapped. Apparently, role playing can increase *empathy* and enable subjects to experience what it *feels* like to be a member of an underprivileged or minority group.

Role playing can also increase the effectiveness of fear communications. In one study (Janis and Mann, 1965), female cigarette smokers role-played the part of a medical patient who was told that she had lung cancer. The smoking habits of these women, as well as those of a control group who simply listened to a tape of one of the role-playing sessions, were then monitored during an 18-month period. Both groups cut down on their smoking, but the subjects who had role-played cut down more. Evidently they had become more convinced of the dangers of smoking by personally "experiencing" its possible consequences.

Finally, role playing may bring about changes in attitude by making opposing viewpoints and arguments more convincing and reasonable. Several studies have shown that when subjects deliver speeches that advocate positions opposite to their own, their attitudes actually shift in the direction of the speech they have given. This principle of *counterattitudinal advocacy* is occasionally used by mediators in labor disputes. They ask company executives and labor leaders to switch roles for a time so that each group can understand the problems and goals of the other.

Compliance, attitude change, and cognitive dissonance theory. As we discussed earlier, compliance is a response to social influence that is based solely on external reward and punishment. We also saw that in most instances, compliance does not lead to internal change. There is, however, a notable exception to this rule. When an individual complies in order to receive a reward that seems *insufficient* to justify the behavior, then there may be a change of attitude.

Consider the following experiment: Subjects work on an extremely dull and boring task (e.g., packing thread spools into a box, dumping them out, repacking them, etc.) for a considerable period of time while an experimenter records their performance. At the end of the experiment subjects are asked, but not required, to tell another subject who is waiting to begin the experiment that the tasks are interesting. Some subjects are offered $1 to do this, whereas others are offered $20. After the subjects meet with and lie to the next participant in the experiment, they are asked to evaluate the experiment and how enjoyable the task was. The question is, "Which group of subjects, the $1 group or the $20 group, will evaluate the task most favorably?" If you think the

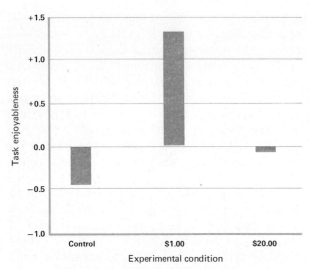

Figure 12.7 Effects of compliance on attitudes toward a boring task. Subjects given a small reward to tell another that a dull task was enjoyable evaluated the task more favorably than did subjects given a large reward to lie. (Based on data from Festinger and Carlsmith, 1959.)

$20 group will because they received more reward for doing so, you are wrong. As Figure 12.7 shows, when this experiment was actually performed, the $1 group rated the task as far more enjoyable than did the $20 group (Festinger and Carlsmith, 1959).

Leon Festinger explained this result in terms of his theory of *cognitive dissonance*. The theory deals with relationships among cognitions, the bits of information individuals have about themselves, their attitudes, their behavior, and their environment. Festinger believes that individuals strive for psychological consistency among cognitions that are related to one another. For example, they try to make cognitions about their behaviors consistent with cognitions about their attitudes. If two cognitions are psychologically inconsistent (e.g., "I am a brilliant person" and "I just flunked out of school again"), then an unpleasant state of tension, or *dissonance*, results. In order to reduce this tension individuals either change one of the cognitions or add more cognitions to explain the inconsistency.

In the preceding experiment both groups of subjects presumably viewed themselves as basically moral people. They also knew that they told another person that a boring task was enjoyable (i.e., they lied). These two cognitions were inconsistent, and were likely to produce dissonance. However, individuals in the $20 group could justify their behavior in terms of the large reward they received ("After all, who wouldn't tell a little lie for $20?"), so that they had little reason to change their attitude toward the task. The subjects who lied for only $1 could not justify their behavior for the same reason. But there was a way out for them: If they were to decide that the task was enjoyable after all, then they would no longer have to think that they told a lie and the dissonance would be removed.

Elliot Aronson and Judson Mills (1959) performed another experiment inspired by dissonance theory. They noted that a person's commitment to membership in certain groups, such as fraternities, clubs, and military units, often becomes much stronger if they must undergo severe initiation rites. They hypothesized that the justification for this might be verbalized as, "If I had to work that hard to get in, it must be a great organization." The investigators suggested that this is a dissonance-reducing attempt to justify what they have gone through to get into the organization.

To test this suggestion experimentally, Aronson and Mills gave female students who wanted to join a group to study the psychology of sex an "embarrassment test" that was either mild or severe. The severe test required the subjects to read aloud to the male experimenter 12 obscene words and 2 vivid sexual passages. The mild test required that subjects read aloud five sexual but nonobscene words. Following this initiation, subjects were allowed to listen to a tape of one of the psychology group's discussions, an extremely boring conversation about animals. Subjects then filled out a questionnaire that asked them to evaluate the interest value of the discussion. As dissonance theory would predict, the group that took the severe test evaluated the group discussion far more positively than did the group that took the mild test. Apparently, they reduced the dissonance between what they had gone through to get into the group and the apparent value of the group by adopting a high opinion of the group.

Studies have shown quite clearly that attitude change can occur as a result of compliance *if* compliance is obtained with a weak inducement. Strong rewards and severe threats may be more successful in

This individual seems to have a personal commitment to noncompliant behavior. (Herwig, Stock, Boston)

encouraging compliance, but they do not often produce changes in attitude. Perceived *free choice* fosters dissonance. If individuals are forced into behaving a certain way, then they will attribute the difference between their attitude and their behavior to external demands. Dissonance is also greater when individuals make a *personal commitment* to a behavior. For example, performing a behavior in public requires more of a commitment than performing it privately or anonymously.

Clearly, the causal connection between attitudes and behavior is a two-way street. The cognitive and affective components of attitudes can give rise to behaviors, but they can also be affected by the behaviors that we engage in. (See Box 12.7.)

GROUP DYNAMICS

The groups that influence our behavior vary in size, function, and importance. Some are groups to which we actually belong (membership groups); others are groups with which we identify or compare ourselves (reference groups). What kinds of social influences do these groups exert on our attitudes and behavior? In this final section we examine this question.

Social roles and norms

Within any social system particular members occupy particular positions and carry out particular functions; even animal societies have distinctive roles. In human society everyone plays a number of social roles. We are, in various situations, friends, workers, sons or daughters, and perhaps parents. Each of these roles requires a somewhat different set of behaviors. For any individual some of these roles are more satisfying than others.

Every role has particular *norms*, or behavioral rules, associated with it. These norms specify proper behavior both for the individual and for others who relate to that individual. Often the attitudes and behavior of others toward an individual are deter-

391

BOX 12.7
When prophecy fails

There are times when psychologists have the opportunity to test predictions based on their theories in unique, "real-life" situations. An opportunity to conduct a natural experiment occurred for Leon Festinger and his colleagues (Festinger, Riecken, and Schachter, 1956) as they were developing cognitive dissonance theory in the mid-1950s. Festinger and his colleagues discovered a cultist group in Minneapolis organized around a clairvoyant, Mrs. Keech, who prophesied the destruction of much of the United States by a cataclysmic flood on a specific date. Mrs. Keech claimed that the prophesy was a message sent from the planet Clarion by superior beings called Guardians, and that she had received it through automatic writing. She had attracted a small but dedicated group of believers who, despite ridicule and criticism, had quit their jobs, given away their property, or dropped out of college. These believers, she said, would be picked up by a flying saucer from the planet Clarion on the eve of the predicted disaster.

When Festinger and his colleagues heard about the group, they joined it in order to study the behavior of group members. They attended lengthy seances during which messages were received from the Guardians, and they dictated their observations onto tapes after each meeting. On the basis of dissonance theory, they predicted that when the prophesied disaster did not occur, the group members would show an *increase* in their convictions and proselytizing activities. If they could convince others that their beliefs were correct, the researchers reasoned, then the dissonance between the prophecy and the fact that the flood did not occur would not seem quite as great.

On the eve of the predicted disaster the group waited to be picked up at midnight by a flying saucer. When it did not appear the group spent five hours in agonizing tension as the believers tried to maintain their faith. Then a message arrived from the Guardians: Because this small group had such great faith, God had decided to spare the world.

The group received the glad tidings without question and felt a great urgency to share the news with others. By 6:00 A.M. they had contacted all newspapers and wire services to announce the message. For several days the group called press conferences to announce new messages received by Mrs. Keech and showed a startling degree of commitment to their mission. Although Mrs. Keech could not make very accurate predictions from her messages, the researchers could make them quite well using dissonance theory.

---

mined more by social position and role than by individual personality traits. Even when people are placed into roles that are not necessarily consistent with their personalities, they often become intensely involved in those roles and behave accordingly. We have already seen that role playing can have a powerful effect on attitudes.

The powerful effect of roles on behavior was dramatically demonstrated in a mock prison study conducted at Stanford University (Zimbardo, Haney, Banks, and Jaffe, 1973). The subjects were male college students who had volunteered in order to earn $15 per day. They were first interviewed and given a battery of psychological tests to ensure that they did not show any signs of pathology, and that they did not have any criminal records. When they were asked to indicate a preference for the role of prisoner or guard, they all chose prisoner. None entered the study with an excessive desire to control others. The "prison" (complete with "yard," cells, and "the hole" for solitary confinement) had been constructed in the basement of the psychology building, and the experiment was conducted after the summer session, when the building was used very little. The experiment was to continue for 14 days.

Subjects were randomly assigned to prisoner or

BOX 12.8

Behavioral contagion: Mass hysteria in a quiet town

As the following news story illustrates, group processes can result in a spread or contagion of behavior among group members.

Berry is a quiet town of about 1,000 people in the soybean and cotton growing area of northwestern Alabama. Its one-story, 15-room elementary school draws the children of farmers and factory workers from 20 miles around. Not much exciting about that.

Rather commonplace, that is, except for the week that Berry Elementary School went beserk. For seven days in May, a frightening "epidemic" sent a third of its 400 pupils, and even a few teachers, into a frenzy of scratching, fainting, vomiting, numbness, crying and screaming.

Ambulances carried more than 70 children, 20 of them unconscious, to the country hospital in nearby Fayette on Friday, May 11, when the strange malady first struck. Frantic parents arrived to take home their children, some of whom had scratched themselves bloody, convinced along with school and local authorities that some disease or toxic substance or perhaps a swarm of biting insects was to blame.

When on the following Tuesday and Friday two smaller outbreaks occurred, the school was closed 10 days early for summer vacation. All told, 105 pupils and three teachers fell ill the first Friday, and 32, some of them repeaters, the next week.

The Berry hysteria has been pieced together by U.S. Public Health Service medical intelligence officer Dr. Richard J. Levine and others who investigated the incident.

It began, they say, when a fifth-grade girl, who had had a skin rash for about a week, began scratching so vigorously that her teacher asked her to sit in the hall. During the 10:30 A.M. class break, the girl's classmates gathered around her in the hall and they, too, began scratching furiously. They ran to a restroom to wash off whatever was causing the itch, where they "infected" others.

The epidemic spread rapidly, class by class. Teachers vainly tried to ease the itching by applying alcohol, but many children had scratched their skin raw and the alcohol only stung them more, adding to the panic that set in.

There was one strange aspect to the spread of the illness, notes Mrs. Elaine P. Campbell, a psychologist from the University of Alabama School of Medicine. The pupils didn't get sick, she notes, unless they actually saw someone else with the symptoms.

Interestingly, first and second graders, as well as two classes of "special" students, who were segregated from the other classes and thus didn't see the others during the outbreak, didn't fall victim to it.

By one o'clock, with students retching, complaining of burning eyes and throats, numbness, chest pains, and general weakness—and with several pupils fainting—the principal rang the fire alarm and ordered the building evacuated. (Reprinted with permission of *The Wall Street Journal*, © Dow Jones & Company, Inc. 1973. All rights reserved.)

guard roles. Guards were instructed to maintain law and order, to take no nonsense from prisoners, and not to use physical violence (instructions similar to those given to "real" prison guards). The guards almost immediately assumed an authoritarian attitude toward the prisoners and soon appeared to relish their duties. Their behaviors ranged from tough but fair to sadistically cruel. When the experiment was terminated after only six days because several of the prisoners had emotional breakdowns, only the prisoners were glad it was over.

Initially, the prisoners were actually arrested by Palo Alto police, then searched, handcuffed, and hauled to the police station for booking and fingerprinting. They were taken to the "Stanford County Prison," where they were stripped naked, deloused, and given a smock-type uniform to wear. This experience, which the prisoners had not expected, was designed to lend an aura of reality to the experiment. It undoubtedly aroused feelings of resentment and hostility on the part of the prisoners. In fact, the prisoners staged an early rebellion, which was speed-

393

ily crushed by guards. This only served to increase the hostility of the prisoners, which in turn brought out more aggression in the guards. In this vicious circle the guards became increasingly cruel and the prisoners became increasingly distrustful, self-deprecating, depressed, and helpless. The guards stretched routine ten-minute lineups into hour-hour ordeals, filled with verbal assault and abuse. They refused to allow the prisoners restroom privileges during the night and forced them to use containers in the cells. The resulting stench gave the prisoners a real justification for self-deprecation and the guards a rationale for abusive and contemptuous treatment.

There are numerous reasons that might explain the guards' hostile behaviors. Their learned role expectations concerning appropriate prisoner-guard relationships played an important part. The role requirements may have altered or counteracted any sense of individual responsibility the guards may have had to be humane. In addition, as in real prisons, there were aggressive and masochistic cues: Guards were provided with billy clubs, handcuffs, and keys; prisoners wore stocking caps, had chains on their ankles, and were placed behind bars. Prisoners were referred to by number, and all guards had to be called "Mr. Correctional Officer." Both prisoners and guards wore uniforms, and the guards wore reflecting glasses that prevented eye contact. The guards were removed from the public eye and from the possibility of public disapproval—only they and the prisoners would know of their actions. (They were unaware that their behavior was being monitored by the experimenters.)

One of the student guards recalled, "I was surprised at myself. . . . I made them call each other names and clean the toilets out with their bare hands. I practically considered the prisoners cattle, and I kept thinking: I have to watch out for them in case they try something" (p. 42). The director of the study later observed, "It was remarkable how readily we all slipped into our roles, temporarily gave up our identities, and allowed these assigned roles and the social forces in the situation to guide, shape and eventually to control our freedom of thought and action" (p. 46).

Of course, we cannot conclude from the results of this study that the students who played the guards would behave the same way if they were *really*

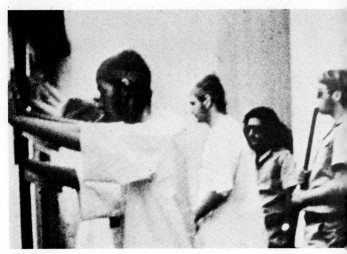

A prison lineup during the Stanford prison experiment. (Philip G. Zimbardo)

working as prison guards. They were hired to play the role of prison guards, and we do not know the extent to which they became immersed in that role. It is quite clear, however, that playing the role profoundly affected their behavior.

Group influences on problem solving

Traditionally, people have formed groups to solve problems involving survival and security, the performance of particular tasks, or emotional and social needs. Psychologists have studied the ways in which groups approach and solve problems and have devised numerous ways to gauge their effectiveness.

Individual versus group productivity

Are group efforts really more effective than any one member of that group would be working alone? Groups may be able to perform physical tasks that would be virtually impossible for a single person. A number of studies have shown that groups also develop more adequate intellectual solutions than do individuals. This is because in a group there are more opportunities for errors to correct themselves, and if the problem is complicated there is a greater chance that at least one person will have the skills needed to solve it. In some situations, however, groups are not more effective than individuals. They tend to work much more slowly, and their processes may actually interfere with the activities of a very gifted individual (Kelley and Thibaut, 1969).

Groups are usually more effective than individuals in performing tasks or solving problems that can be subdivided easily. On *unitary* tasks, which cannot be subdivided, a group usually performs at the level of its most gifted member if the task is simple and the solution is obvious to all once that member proposes it. If a unitary task requires a high degree of organization and an orderly progression through a large number of steps (e.g., writing a term paper) an individual may function more effectively than a group.

Predictably, groups that consist of highly competent individuals have been found to be more effective than groups composed of individuals with lower abilities. Beyond this, however, there are few clear patterns. One variable that has been carefully investigated is similarity among group members. Whether similar or dissimilar groups function more effectively depends on the nature of the task and the characteristics on which group members are either alike or different. A group composed of similar individuals might be expected to be more cohesive, but similarity can also produce "blind spots" in relation to a task that would not exist in a more varied group. An example of this is seen in the phenomenon known as "groupthink." (See Box 12.9).

Group decision making

Because many important decisions are made in group settings, social psychologists have considerable interest in the processes that influence group decision making.

Generally the group majority determines the final decision, but under certain circumstances a minority may prevail. This usually occurs when the minority takes a firm and uncompromising stand, thereby casting doubt on the correctness of the majority's viewpoint and creating conflict within the group. In attempting to resolve the conflict, the majority generally places pressure on the minority to conform. But if the minority remains firm their ideas may be incorporated or even adopted.

The risky shift. Many decisions carry with them an element of risk. A fairly consistent research finding has been that groups make decisions that are more risky than do individuals who are not in a group. Further, when individuals who have indicated how much risk they would be willing to accept in making a given decision are brought together into a group and asked to arrive at a decision that is acceptable to all members of the group, the group consensus is usually found to be riskier than the average of the individual decisions made earlier. This phenomenon is known as the *risky shift*.

Three concepts that have been used to explain the risky shift are *diffusion of responsibility*, *risk as value*, and *group polarization*. Diffusion of responsibility refers to the fact that when a group decision is made, no individual group member feels completely responsible for the consequences of the decision. This causes the individuals to act in a riskier manner than they would individually.

The *risk as value* explanation of the risky shift assumes that taking risks is admired in our society. In a group situation everyone wants to feel that he or she is at least as risky as other people, if not more so. This may cause people to increase their level of risk during the group discussion because it is the socially desirable "gutsy" thing to do.

Finally, it has been suggested that group discussion moves a group toward a more extreme version of the position they originally held. If the original position was a somewhat risky one (as is usually the case because of risk as value), then group decision making will result in a risky shift; if the initial position was conservative, then it will become more conservative following group discussion. Consistent with this *polarization* hypothesis is evidence of a "conservative shift" when original positions of group members are conservative (Fraser, Gouge, and Billig, 1971).

Leadership

Sooner or later in almost any group one or more individuals begin to exert more influence than other group members and to direct the activities of the group. The quality of these leaders is a major determinant of the group's efficiency and morale. A number of approaches have been taken to studying leadership.

Trait approaches

One of the oldest leadership theories holds that

BOX 12.9

Groupthink

The phenomenon that social psychologists have labeled *groupthink* can drastically reduce a group's effectiveness in planning and problem solving. Groupthink tends to occur under stressful conditions in highly cohesive groups that are so committed to reaching a consensus that each member suspends his or her sense of critical judgment. In the interest of remaining loyal they stick with the policies and courses of action to which the group has already committed itself even when it becomes obvious that they are not working out well and there are obvious alternatives. They are ready to believe any proposal advanced by the leader or the majority of the group. Any group member who expresses reservations about the group's policies is faced with immediate and direct pressure to "stop rocking the boat." Extremely intelligent people can be forced to stop thinking independently, to stop weighing alternatives, to abandon their consideration of moral principles, and to ignore all the other elements involved in careful decisions.

By analyzing the formulation of critical policy decisions such as the decision to escalate the war in Vietnam and the decision to invade the Bay of Pigs in 1960, Irving Janis (1972) identified a number of characteristics of groupthink:

Invulnerability and moral self-image. The members of the group believe that their plan is bound to succeed, no matter what the risk. This illusion of invulnerability is bolstered by a belief in the righteousness of their cause, so that individual members never bother to question the morality of the group's decisions.

Rationale. Victims of groupthink ignore warnings and construct elaborate rationalizations in order to discount them, along with any other evidence that is inconsistent with their plans. These rationalizations commit them to decisions that they have made in the past.

Stereotypes of the opposition. Group members think of the opposition in simplistic terms and stereotypes. They usually view their adversaries as evil, weak, and stupid. They are the good guys, and their adversaries the bad guys.

Conformity pressure. There is great pressure to conform to group norms. To raise doubts or suggest alternatives is to be disloyal.

Self-censorship and illusion of unanimity. In response to the strong pressures to conform in a groupthink situation, group members begin to censor their own doubts and objections to their chosen course of action. As a result, there is an illusion of unanimity within the group that reinforces all the other groupthink processes.

Mindguards. Within most groups undergoing groupthink there are self-appointed "mindguards," individuals who suppress the discussion of information that is inconsistent with the group's decisions.

Can groupthink be counteracted or prevented? Janis suggested that leaders should regularly encourage and reward critical thinking and even disagreement among group members. Several outside policy-planning and evaluation groups with different leaders should be set up to prevent the formation of an insulated ingroup. Outside experts should be invited to each meeting and encouraged to question group policy. At each stage of the group's deliberations members should be encouraged to state any doubts they might have, and the group should review alternative courses of action.

effective leaders have certain unique traits that qualify them for leadership roles. Hundreds of studies have been designed to pinpoint these traits.

Two major assumptions underlying the "great-person" theory have received little support from research. The first is that leaders are unique or have unique backgrounds that make them different from followers. However, most individuals who are rated as good leaders are *also* rated as good followers by their peers, which suggests that leaders are not really unique in many ways (Hollander and Webb, 1955). The second assumption is that leadership is a general attribute that gives an individual the ability to lead in all situations. In fact, however, research shows that different group members are likely to emerge as leaders in situations in which they have the skills or knowledge necessary to lead the group toward a goal.

Although there does not appear to be a unique cluster of "leader" traits, there are certain traits associated with the tendency to assume leadership. These are high intelligence, talkativeness, large physical size, and the ability to gain respect from other group members. However, the relationship between these traits and leadership is not strong, and trait theories cannot fully account for everyone who becomes a leader. Attention has therefore shifted from investigating the traits of leaders to examining the effectiveness of various styles of leadership.

Leadership styles

During the 1950s several important studies were conducted to observe and classify leadership behaviors. Two major classes of leader behaviors emerged. One class, which was labeled *initiating and directing*, is oriented toward organization and task accomplishment; the second, labeled *consideration*, refers to behaviors aimed at increasing morale, motivation, and group satisfaction. These two types of behaviors are usually expressed by two different individuals within the group. In other words, groups tend to have one leader, the *task specialist*, whose efforts are directed toward getting the job done, and a *socioemotional* leader, whose chief concern is to create an enjoyable and satisfying group atmosphere (Bales and Slater, 1955). These two leadership styles appear to exist within many different kinds of groups, including families. A study of families in 56 societies showed that most families contain a task specialist (usually the father) and a socioemotional leader (usually the mother) (Zelditch, 1955).

Fiedler's contingency model. At present a very influential theory of leadership is the *contingency model* developed by Fred E. Fiedler of the University of Washington. Fiedler argues that the effectiveness of task-oriented and group-oriented leadership styles is dependent or *contingent* on the favorability of the leadership situation. A highly favorable leadership situation is one in which the leader's relationship with the members is very good, the task is clear and well defined, and the leader's power to direct the group is acknowledged and accepted by the members. An unfavorable situation is one in which the group dislikes or is not willing to follow the leader, the task is uncertain or ambiguous, and the group members question the leader's right to power.

The contingency model stresses that the effectiveness of a leader is affected both by the style of leadership and by how favorable the situation is. Fiedler maintains that task-oriented leaders are most effective when conditions are either highly favorable or highly unfavorable. In a highly favorable situation the relationship between the leader and the members is already good, so that the leader can concentrate on completing the task. In a highly unfavorable situation there is confusion and ambiguity, so that the group needs the structure and task orientation. Group-oriented leaders, says Fiedler, should function most effectively in moderately favorable situations that are somewhat defined and in which the leader's member-oriented approach can increase group satisfaction and morale. Fiedler's predictions have been confirmed in experiments with groups ranging from tank crews to store managers. The contingency model, unlike the great-person theory, takes both the characteristics of the leaders and the leadership situation into account. We have here another example of how individual and situational influences interact to affect behavior.

Group factors in helping behavior

The murder of Kitty Genovese in the presence of 38 passive witnesses shocked the entire nation. Columnists, clergymen, and political leaders fashioned editorials, sermons, and speeches around what appeared to be an example of shocking apathy and insensitivity to human suffering and helplessness.

Do people simply not care? Is "bystander apathy" an unfortunate but inevitable byproduct of modern life? Interviews conducted with witnesses to the Kitty Genovese murder showed that most of them, far from being apathetic, were concerned, even horrified. Then why had they not helped? Answers to this question indicated that some of the bystanders interpreted the assault as a "lovers' quarrel." Others thought that someone else either was on the way to

397

This is not an unusual sight in big cities; long-time residents seem to become conditioned against responding to many forms of human distress. (Joel Gordon)

aid the victim or had at least called the police. Still others feared for their own safety.

The publicity surrounding this and other instances of "bystander apathy" prompted a number of psychologists to study the social conditions that inhibit helping behavior.

Three factors that affect helping

Suppose that as you walk along a city street, an elderly man ahead of you staggers and then slumps to the sidewalk. You wonder what is wrong with him. Is he sick? Drunk? Having a heart attack? Setting you up for a mugging? As you try to figure out what is happening, you look around to see if you are alone or if there are others nearby. If others are around, you look to see how they are reacting. Do they seem

concerned? You might say to yourself, "Well, whatever, keep cool. Don't make a fool of yourself by acting panicky. There are others around. They don't seem concerned, so it mustn't be anything too serious. Besides, if you don't help, someone else will. It's not your responsibility." This monologue captures the essence of three important group processes involved in bystander intervention:

Social comparison. Because many emergency situations are quite ambiguous, if others are present we compare their reactions with our own to determine how much concern the situation warrants. But in our culture it is fashionable to "stay cool," so that we may mistakenly interpret an emergency as a matter of little concern.

Evaluation apprehension. Moreover, most of us are concerned about the impression we make on others. We do not want to appear foolish by trying to help in an inappropriate situation.

Diffusion of responsibility. Of course, when we are the only bystander present, then the total responsibility for action falls on us. But if others are also present, the total responsibility is spread or diffused throughout the group so that no one person has to think that he or she is totally responsible.

Safety in numbers?

These factors suggest that if there is more than one bystander in an emergency, then a victim is less likely to receive help than he or she would be if there were only one bystander. The presence of others may give false social comparison cues, arouse anxiety about acting inappropriately, or reduce feelings of personal responsibility.

The factor of diffusion of responsibility was studied in an ingenious experiment in which John Darley and Bibb Latané (1968) exposed subjects to a fake emergency in the laboratory. The subjects were in an experiment that involved discussion of their experiences and difficulties in college. They were told that in order to maintain anonymity and encourage freedom of expression, each would be situated in a research cubicle by himself or herself and would communicate with others through an intercom system. When a light went on near the subject's microphone, he or she was to make a contribution to the discussion. Some subjects thought they were conversing with only one other subject. Others thought the group included either three or five others. Actually, the other participants were phantom voices on a tape recording prepared by the experimenter.

During the comments made by the first phantom subject he confided that he occasionally suffered from severe epileptic seizures that caused him anxiety and embarrassment. When it became the epileptic's turn to speak again, he said only a few words before he began to gasp and stammer that he was having a problem. His voice became louder and more incoherent. He gasped, gurgled, muttered, "Gonna die," and then became silent.

The experimenters were interested in whether, and how quickly, subjects in the various experimental conditions would leave their cubicles to report the epileptic's condition to the experimenter. Subjects who thought that they were alone with the epileptic responded quickly: 85 percent of them reported the incident before the victim had finished speaking; the remaining 15 percent reported it shortly afterward. But subjects who thought that others had also heard the epileptic victim responded less frequently and more slowly: 62 percent of those in the three-person groups and 31 percent of those in the 6-person groups reported before the epileptic stopped speaking; 15 percent and 38 percent, respectively, did not report at all. Other laboratory studies have also found individuals are more likely to help if they think they are the only available helper.

A lady in distress

In another experiment, designed to study the role of social comparison, a male subject was seated at a table across from another man (a confederate of the researchers) to complete a series of experimental forms. Suddenly the attractive female experimenter put her hand to her head, moaned softly, and staggered to the doorway of an adjoining room. She lurched inside and there was a loud crash as she fell and upset a table, sending objects clattering across the floor. Then there was silence, except for occasional gasps and moans.

For half the subjects the confederate appeared to be totally unconcerned and returned nonchalantly to filling out his forms. For the others he showed great concern and alarm (but made no move actually to help). The researchers found that the confederate's response to the situation had a profound effect on the subjects' behavior. When he showed a lack of concern only 13 percent of the subjects went to help the experimenter within three minutes. When he showed alarm 60 percent of the subjects helped (Smith, Vanderbilt, and Callen, 1973). It should be noted that evaluation apprehension as well as social comparison may have influenced these results, because it is obviously more risky to intervene in the presence of another bystander who seems to feel that intervention is not appropriate. The more ambiguous the emergency situation, the more important social

399

comparison and evaluation apprehension could conceivably become in influencing helping behavior.

The social context influences our behaviors in many ways. All too often we underestimate the power of the social forces to which we are exposed. These forces interact with the personal characteristics of the individual in complex ways, many of which are not yet understood. Although humans have been social animals from the beginning, discovering the many ways in which the social systems we create influence our actions constitutes an important frontier of psychology. Constructive solutions to social problems will surely involve the application of social psychological principles. Some of these applications are discussed in Chapters 17 and 18.

SUMMARY

1. Social psychology is the study of how individual and group behavior is influenced by social forces. The major methods used to study social behavior are survey studies, field studies, natural experiments, and laboratory experiments.

2. Impression formation studies have shown that people frequently form global impressions of another on the basis of knowledge of only one or a few *central traits*. The centrality of a given trait depends on how strongly it is related to the nature of the judgment that is to be made. It appears that we average our evaluation of others' traits to arrive at a global impression of them. Researchers have also studied the conditions that determine whether initial information (primacy effect) or more recent information (recency effect) will more strongly affect our judgments.

3. Among the perceiver characteristics that affect social perception are implicit personality theories.

4. *Attribution* is the process whereby we perceive the causes of behavior. The extent to which we attribute a given behavior to personal or situational factors can have profound implications for how we respond to that behavior. There is a general tendency for individuals to attribute their own behavior to situational causes, while attributing others' behavior to personal (dispositional) causes. Behaviors that deviate markedly from social norms or that are performed in private are especially likely to be attributed to dispositional causes. The *just world hypothesis* holds that we sometimes modify our impressions of others to be consistent with good or bad things that happen to them.

5. Attitudes have three components: beliefs or knowledge (a cognitive component); feelings (an affective component); and behavioral tendencies. They are based on social learning experiences. Reference groups with which we identify have a strong influence on attitude development.

6. A number of factors have been found to be important determinants of interpersonal attraction. Similarity has been shown in many studies to be positively related to attraction. In long-term relationships, such as marriages, complementarity becomes important. We also tend to like those who provide us with rewarding outcomes, those with whom we come in contact frequently, and those who are physically attractive.

7. Prejudice is a social attitude based on stereotypes that obscure individual differences. It has no single cause, but socialization experiences and conformity to attitudes of prejudiced reference groups is often a major determinant. Group competition and conflict also can increase prejudice. Although no specific personality pattern consistently associated with prejudice against all minority groups has been found, personality dy-

namics may enter into many forms of prejudice.

8. Three responses to social influence attempts are compliance, identification, and internalization. Compliance is based on the power of the source of influence, identification on the source's attractiveness, and internalization on the source's credibility and trustworthiness.

9. Persuasion is the most common approach to changing attitudes. A characteristic of the communicator that enhances persuasiveness is *credibility*. Credibility effects tend to dissipate over time—a *sleeper effect*. The relative effectiveness of one-sided and two-sided arguments depends on characteristics of the audience. Usually there is more attitude change when explicit conclusions are drawn by the communicator, but if the audience is intelligent and motivated enough to draw its own conclusion, not drawing an explicit conclusion may be effective. Fear-arousing communications are an effective means of persuasion if the level of fear aroused is not excessive and if clear behavioral guidelines are given.

10. Individuals can be *inoculated* against future persuasive communications by presenting them with weak arguments against their position that can be easily refuted.

11. Attitudes can be changed by changing behaviors. Role playing can bring about attitude change by increasing empathy, by increasing the effectiveness of fear communications, and by making opposing viewpoints more convincing. Attitudes may also change when an individual complies in order to receive a reward that seems insufficient to justify the behavior. *Freedom* and *commitment* enhance this effect. Festinger's *theory of cognitive dissonance* explains this phenomenon as a product of a need to maintain consistency between cognitions about attitudes and behaviors.

12. The norms associated with social roles have a strong influence on behavior. Norms specify how individuals occupying particular positions in a social system are expected to behave and how others are expected to behave toward them.

13. A number of factors influence whether individuals or groups will perform a task more efficiently. Groups are typically more effective than individuals on tasks that can be easily subdivided. Beyond this, such variables as group cohesiveness and group composition are related to productivity in complex ways. *Groupthink* causes individuals to suspend their critical judgment in favor of group consensus. Group decisions often show a *risky shift*.

14. Trait approaches have not proved successful in accounting for the emergence of individuals as leaders. Attention has therefore shifted to examining various leadership styles. Leaders tend to be *task specialists* or *socioemotional* leaders. Fiedler's *contingency model* views leadership effectiveness as a joint function of leadership style and the favorability of the leadership position.

15. Bystander intervention in emergencies is affected by several social factors, including social comparison processes, evaluation apprehension, and diffusion of responsibility. These factors can reduce the likelihood that individuals will intervene when others are present.

Suggested readings

Aronson, E. *The social animal* (2nd ed.) San Francisco: W. H. Freeman and Co. Publishers, 1976. A highly readable social psychology text written primarily for the nonpsychologist that covers a variety of important areas of research in social psychology.

401

The following are general textbooks in social psychology which survey the major theories and research findings in the field. All the topics discussed in this chapter are covered in greater detail by these books, as are additional topics we did not have sufficient space to cover.

Worchel, S., & Cooper, J. *Understanding social psychology.* Homewood, Ill.: Dorsey Press, 1976.

Baron, R. A., & Byrne, D. *Social psychology: Understanding human interaction.* (2nd ed.) Boston: Allyn & Bacon, Inc., 1977.
Berkowitz, L. *A survey of social psychology.* Hinsdale, Ill.: The Dryden Press, Inc., 1975.

Five

Personality and Psychological Assessment

Chapter 13

Personality: Understanding the Individual

(George Gardner)

The young couple walked slowly through the park, oblivious to the droplets of rain that were beginning to fall. They had come to this park often in the past, and many memories of a budding romance still lingered among its trees and along its paths. A year ago, before they each went away to separate colleges, they would have been walking hand in hand. Now they walked several feet apart.

Jane spoke first. "Tom, it's just not right with us since we've gotten back from school. We used to be so compatible, but now it seems as if we can't agree on anything. I don't feel as if I've changed much, but you seem like a different person. Your personality is so different from what is was."

They walked in silence for several minutes before Tom spoke. "I still love you, Jane, and I do want to work out our problems. But I guess my personality has changed a lot. In fact, sometimes I wonder who I really am these days. Since getting away from home, I've had lots of experiences in college that have changed how I feel about things and how I relate to people. I guess I feel that I'm growing in a lot of ways, but some of the changes I see make me feel as if I'm adrift, searching for the real me."

Perhaps you have occasionally experienced feelings like Tom's. But most of the time you probably feel more like Jane—that there is a core of self-identity that remains relatively constant over time. The concept of personality is relevant to both consistency and change in behavior. Sudden environmental experiences or changes in status (e.g., the sudden popularity experienced by Farah Fawcett-Majors) may or may not result in personality change, depending on the individual. Personality lies at the heart of our attempts to know and to understand ourselves and other individuals.

Few, if any, topics in psychology have received as much attention as has personality. As an area of inquiry, personality has attracted many theorists and researchers who have devoted their careers to expanding knowledge about the factors that produce the individual identities we possess. In this chapter we focus on and evaluate some of the major conceptions of personality that have arisen in the quest for understanding of the individual.

WHAT IS PERSONALITY?

Many students are drawn to psychology by their desire to learn more about personality functioning. Perhaps the same is true of you. But individuals who begin to study personality theories are sometimes perplexed by the diversity of viewpoints that exist about the nature of personality: "it seems hard to believe that all the theorists are talking about the same creature, who is now angelic and now depraved, now a black-box robot shaped by reinforcers and now a shaper of his own destiny, now devious . . . and now hardheadedly oriented to solid reality" (Stone and Church, 1968).

An analysis of what personality is, and what it is not, may help us to account for the many different conceptions of personality that we will encounter in this chapter.

Because it is a noun, the term *personality* is used in our speech as if it were a *thing*, something that people *have*. We speak of *the* personality, *her* personality, and so on, as if it had real and concrete existence. But personality is not a thing. It has no existence apart from behavior. Personality is a concept, or *construct*, that arises from certain types of

Farah Fawcett-Majors. (Wide World)

406

behaviors. For example, when we say someone has a "good" personality or a "lousy" one, we mean that the person customarily behaves in ways that are either pleasing or displeasing to *us*.

Once we realize that personality exists only as a construct drawn from observable behaviors, we are ready to consider why we have invented the concept of personality and the kinds of behaviors it encompasses.

Individual differences and individual consistency

If everyone behaved in exactly the same fashion, not only would it be a dull world, but there would be no need for such a concept as personality. But even when individuals are put in highly controlled environments, there are observable differences in their behaviors. The concept of personality is part of our attempt to account for those differences. In addition, individuals seem to show some degree of *consistency* in their behavior as they move from situation to situation. They seem to have predispositions to behave in certain ways so that their behavior is somewhat predictable even under changing circumstances. From this perceived consistency comes the notion of *personality traits*, which describe an individual's characteristic ways of responding to his or her world.

Inferring personality from behavior

The behaviors that are viewed as reflecting an individual's personality seem to have a number of characteristics. In a thoughtful analysis of the concept of personality, psychologist Leon Levy (1971) identified three key characteristics.

First, the behavior serves as a *component of identity*. That is, it helps to establish the personal identity of the individual as distinct from others. Joe's eye color tells us nothing about his personal identity, but the fact that he frequently "blows up" at others does.

Second, the cause of the behavior is seen as residing within the individual rather than in the immediate situation; it has a *perceived internal cause*. When a behavior is clearly caused by environmental factors, it gives us little information about what a person is like. If an individual stands up and cheers wildly during an exciting football game, the behavior

is less likely to be viewed as a reflection of his or her personality than if the same behavior occurs during a funeral service.

Third, behaviors that reflect personality are viewed as having *organization and structure*. When the behaviors of the individual seem to "fit together" in a meaningful fashion, we find it convenient to attribute them to a "personality" that guides and directs behavior. Much of the work in analyzing an individual's personality involves explaining how the behaviors that serve as components of identity and that appear to have internal causes "fit together" and are organized to pursue goals and satisfy needs.

All three of the preceding criteria involve perceptions of the individual's behavior. These perceptions may vary according to the behaviors being observed, the situation in which the person is behaving, and the personal characteristics of the observer.

All the preceding points lead to the following conclusion: *Personality is a product of our perceptions of behavior rather than something existing within the person being observed.* Viewing personality as a product of perception helps us to understand why there can be so many different theories of personality and eliminates the question of which theory of personality is *true*. There can be as many different conceptions of personality as there are personality theorists. In fact, personality theories can be viewed as specific outgrowths of the general perspectives on behavior described in Chapter 2.

Personality theories and their functions

A theory consists of a system of constructs and a series of generalizations or propositions that specify the ways in which the constructs are related to one another. Personality itself is a construct, and the components of personality theories are constructs as well. In the following pages we discuss a number of constructs from personality theories, such as id, ego, superego, anxiety, personal constructs, expectancies, and the self. It is important to remember that all these constructs were invented by theorists to explain behavior and its causes.

As we discussed in Chapter 1, a construct cannot be scientifically useful unless it can be *operationally defined* in terms of observable situations or behaviors. That is, theorists must tell us how to define and measure the observable events to which their constructs refer. For example, a construct such as anxiety may be operationally defined and measured in terms of measures of physiological arousal, responses on paper-and-pencil tests designed to measure anxiety, or such actions as trembling and stammering. These are all observable behaviors. When constructs within theories cannot be operationally defined, it is impossible to test empirically whether or not they are related to one another as the theory says they are. Unfortunately, many personality theories contain constructs that cannot be operationally defined, and this severely limits their scientific usefulness.

A theory is scientifically *useful* to the extent that it (1) provides a comprehensive framework into which already known facts can be incorporated; (2) allows us to predict future events with some precision; and (3) stimulates the discovery of new knowledge. After considering the various personality theories, we evaluate them briefly in terms of these three scientific standards.

Because the field of personality is an extremely broad one, the four perspectives presented throughout the book (biological, psychoanalytic, cognitive, and behavioristic) have all focused upon the phenomenon of human individuality.

Recent attempts to explore the biological basis of personality have focused on genetic and neurological bases for individual differences. We know that intelligence is partially determined by inherited characteristics, and this topic will be explored in greater detail in Chapter 14. There is also evidence that differences in such characteristics as activity level, emotionality, and social introversion-extraversion are in part genetically determined. The chief evidence for this is the finding that identical twins are more similar in such characteristics than are fraternal twins, who are not genetically identical (Buss and Plomin, 1975).

Biological influences such as brain disorders, hormonal changes and drugs can bring about dramatic changes in personality. We have noted some specific examples in Chapters 2, 3, and 5, and we shall examine the therapeutic use of drugs and electroshock therapy in Chapter 16. Many psychologists feel that the most dramatic future breakthroughs in understanding and controlling personality development and change will emerge from the biological perspec-

tive. In the meantime, however, most psychologists still focus on psychological rather than biological conditions in their research on personality, and the most currently influential systematic theories of personality are products of the psychoanalytic, cognitive, and behavioristic perspectives. It is to these theories that we now turn.

SIGMUND FREUD'S PSYCHOANALYTIC THEORY

On the basis of his intensive experiences as a therapist and his often agonizing analysis of himself, Sigmund Freud developed a theory of personality development and functioning and a method of treatment for personality disturbances. He based his theory on careful clinical observations and constantly sought to expand it. Freud formulated hypotheses about cases and tested them by making predictions about what should happen in therapy. He constantly revised and modified his ideas as he gathered new "data," and he never viewed his theory as a finished product (although some of his disciples did). In his own way Freud was very much a scientist, and few theories have had as great an impact as his.

Psychic energy and mental events

Freud's conception of personality as an energy system was based on the hydraulic models of nineteenth-century physics. Psychic energy, or *libido*, is generated by instinctual drives and constantly presses for discharge. Equilibrium in the psychic energy level is maintained by discharging impulses in either a direct or indirect fashion. For example, a buildup of energy from sexual instincts may be discharged either directly as sexual behavior or indirectly through such diverse behaviors as sexual fantasies, farming, or creative activities.

Mental events may be *conscious*, *preconscious*, or *unconscious*. Freud considered the conscious, preconscious, and unconscious to be actual areas of the mind. The conscious mind consists of mental events of which we are presently aware; the preconscious is an area that contains memories, thoughts, feelings, and images of which we are not now aware but which can potentially be recalled, such as a friend's telephone number, a date learned in history class, and memories of earlier experiences.

The conscious and preconscious areas of the mind are tiny in comparison with the unconscious, a dynamic body of wishes, feelings, and impulses beyond our awareness. It is only when the impulses from the unconscious are discharged in one way or another, such as in dreams, neurotic symptoms, or overt behavior, that the unconscious reveals itself.

The structure of personality

Freud divided the personality into three structures: id, ego, and superego. These three structures interact intimately with one another, but each has its own separate characteristics. (See Figure 13.1.)

The *id* is the innermost core of the personality, and the only structure present at birth. It contains the instincts, which makes it the ultimate source of all psychic energy. Freud described the id as "a chaos, a cauldron of seething excitations" (Freud, 1964, p. 73). The id exists within the unconscious mind, and because it has no direct contact with reality, it functions in a totally irrational manner, in accordance with the *pleasure principle*. When the demands of the instincts increase tension, the id seeks immediate gratification or pleasure, regardless of rational considerations or environmental realities.

Because it has no contact with reality the id cannot directly satisfy its needs by obtaining desired

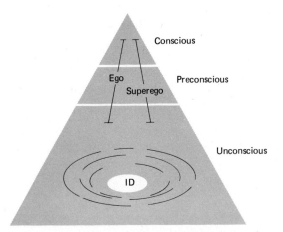

Figure 13.1 Relation of the id, ego, and superego to the conscious, preconscious, and unconscious areas of the mind.

BOX 13.1
Carl Jung and the collective unconscious

Carl Jung, a friend and associate of Freud's before he broke away and developed his own theory, expanded Freud's notion of the unconscious in a unique direction. Jung believed that, in addition to a *personal unconscious*, which corresponds with Freud's preconscious and unconscious and is unique to each individual, humans possess a *collective unconscious*, which consists of memories accumulated throughout the history of the human race. The contents of the collective unconscious are *archetypes*, mythological images or predispositions to characteristic thoughts that are reflected in such universal concepts as God, the wise old man, the young potent hero, rebirth (resurrection), and evil spirits. Jung believed that the archetypes, which express themselves only symbolically, reflect all of the knowledge and wisdom gained by our ancestors. He devoted much of his life to the study of archetype expressions in primitive societies, mythology, alchemy, and dreams.

Jung viewed the unconscious as a source of wisdom and a guide to achieving unity and wholeness. The focus of his system of *analytical psychology* became the study of the unconscious, and its method involved helping people to become more receptive to their dreams as reflections of archetypical wisdom and as guides to living.

effects from the environment. Therefore in the course of development the *ego* develops out of the id. The ego is in direct contact with reality, and it works to satisfy the demands of the id while ensuring the survival of the individual in society. It is devoted to reason, considerations of safety, and realistic evaluation of the environment so that it can mediate suc-

409

BOX 13.2
A Freudian slip?

Among the indicators of unconscious content hypothesized by Freud are so-called slips of the tongue. Psychoanalysts believe that the true meaning of a person's communications may be expressed in verbal slips. For example, while talking about her family during a therapy session, a young woman stated, "My *sin's* name is Tommy." Further questioning by the analyst revealed that the woman believed Tommy was the product of a brief affair she had had several years earlier.

In January, 1975, while he was being seriously criticized for failing to deal more decisively with a lagging economy, President Gerald Ford gave a talk at a meeting of college athletic directors. In noting the similarities between the job of athletic director and president, Ford said, "We both buy aspirin by the six pack and we both have a certain lack of *performance* in our jobs" [italics ours]. According to an Associated Press report, the prepared text had read "permanence in our jobs."

cessfully between the demands of the id and those of the external world. Because the ego is an outgrowth of the id, it receives all its energy and power from the id, and never becomes totally independent of it.

The ego functions primarily at a conscious level, and it operates according to the *reality principle*. It tests reality to decide when and under what conditions impulses can safely be discharged and needs satisfied. Whereas the id demands immediate gratification, the ego strives to delay gratification until conditions are appropriate. Its logical decision-making function has led to its nickname, "executive of the personality."

The third and last personality structure to develop is the *superego*. This is the moral arm of the personality. It contains the traditional values and ideals of the society communicated to the child by its parents and other representatives of society. This communi-

cation occurs chiefly through their use of rewards and punishments that teach the child what is "right" and what is "wrong." With the development of the superego, self-control is substituted for external control.

Like the ego, the superego strives to control the instincts of the id. However, like the id, it is irrational. Whereas the ego simply tries to postpone instinctual gratification until conditions are safe and appropriate, the superego, in its blind quest for perfection, tries to block gratification permanently, particularly of those sexual and aggressive impulses that are condemned by society. For the superego, moralistic goals take precedence over realistic ones, regardless of the potential cost to the individual.

Personality dynamics
The dynamics of personality involve a continuing struggle between id instincts struggling for release and counterforces generated by the ego and superego to contain the instincts. Observable behavior is the product of this continuing struggle.

Conflict and anxiety
As the "executive of the personality," the ego is squarely in the eye of the storm. It must satisfy the instinctual needs of the id in a world that has the power to produce pain and increase tension as well as to reduce tension and provide need satisfaction. When the ego is confronted with id impulses that threaten to get out of control or with dangers from the environment, the result is *anxiety*, an increase in tension that serves as a danger signal to the ego and motivates it to deal with the danger at hand. In many instances the anxiety can be reduced through realistic coping behaviors directed toward the real world. However, when realistic strategies are ineffective in reducing anxiety, the ego may resort to another line of defense, one that involves the denial or distortion of reality. These are *defense mechanisms*, constructed by the ego to ward off anxiety and to allow the release of instincts in disguised forms that will not conflict with conditions in the external world or with the prohibitions of the superego.

The defense mechanisms
The defense mechanisms are one aspect of ego functioning that occurs at an unconscious level. People

410

are usually unaware that they are using self-deception to ward off anxiety. Defense mechanisms may
be mobilized in response to either external or internal sources of threat.

The most primitive defense for dealing with
external threat is *denial*, in which the individual
blocks out disturbing realities by simply refusing to
acknowledge them. Peter Bourne (1970) described
extensive use of this mechanism by soldiers in Vietnam. Some of the men refused to acknowledge their
vulnerability and actually convinced themselves that
they were invincible. One Green Beret insisted he
was under divine protection and bolstered his belief
by riding a bicycle 20 miles along Viet Cong-con-
trolled jungle roads in order to receive daily confession and communion from a Vietnamese priest who
could not speak English. Less extreme forms of denial
are seen in individuals who refuse to acknowledge
criticism or who fail to perceive that they make
others unhappy or angry.

The most basic defense against internal threat is
repression. This is an active process in which the ego
uses some of its energy to prevent anxiety-arousing
memories, feelings, and impulses from entering consciousness. Repression is the primary means the ego
uses to "keep the lid on the id." It is the foundation
on which all other defenses against internal threat
are built. The other defenses all involve repression
plus some other means of preventing awareness of
the disturbing material, in some instances allowing
the release of impulses in disguised form.

Projection involves repressing some undesirable
impulse or characteristic and attributing it to someone else. For example, if the awareness of hostile
impulses in yourself would be anxiety arousing, then
you might project your own hostile feelings onto
others and perceive them as hostile instead. Then
you could consider any hostile behavior on your
own part as an appropriate response to their hostility.
In one study conducted with college students, fraternity members were asked to rate themselves and
their fraternity brothers on a series of undesirable
traits. Individuals who were seen by others as having
a strong undesirable trait but whose ratings of themselves indicated that they were not aware of that trait
tended to assign the trait to others to a far greater
extent than did subjects who did not follow the same
high-possession–low-awareness pattern (Sears, 1936).

The defense mechanism of *displacement* involves
repressing an undesirable impulse toward a feared or
forbidden target and directing the same impulse
toward a substitute target. The target of displaced
impulses is likely to wonder, "Now what did I do to
deserve *that?*" The displacement of aggression is
thought by some theorists to be one possible cause of
prejudice.

Sublimation involves channeling an undesirable
impulse into another form that is socially desirable.
A forbidden sexual impulse, for example, may be
expressed as artistic or creative behavior. Freudians
view most scientific and cultural achievements as
the products of sublimated sexual impulses.

Reaction formation involves repressing an undesirable impulse and expressing its opposite in an
exaggerated form. Several "psychological" novelists
have been fascinated by the effects of this defense
mechanism. Sinclair Lewis wrote a famous novel
entitled *Elmer Gantry*, in which a man protects
himself from his own "sinful" impulses by becoming
a fire-breathing, hellfire-and-brimstone evangelist.
Another instance of reaction formation is presented
in Box 13.3.

Displacement, sublimation, and reaction formation all allow the release of instinctual energy while
preventing awareness of the anxiety-arousing impulse. Repression alone would not permit such a
release, so that these defense mechanisms serve an
additional adaptive function by reducing the
amount of energy the ego must devote to controlling
the id.

Two defense mechanisms, *rationalization* and
intellectualization, involve extensive use of the ego's
higher mental processes. In rationalization a distortion occurs in which a "good" reason is substituted
for the "true" reason for an anxiety-arousing experience or behavior. An aspiring athlete who fails to
make the team may attribute his failure to not being
given a fair tryout. A student who does poorly on an
exam for which she studies hard may blame the
professor for asking "trick" questions or for not emphasizing important points.

Intellectualization is a slightly more involved
process in which a person protects himself or herself
from anxiety by dealing with an emotionally charged
situation in a highly intellectual, abstract manner.
The emotional element is "split off" and repressed.

411

BOX 13.3

Reaction formation

The operation of reaction formation is revealed by the exaggerated nature of the "opposite" behavior and by occasional "slips" that reveal the true underlying impulses. Consider the following excerpts from a letter sent to a researcher by a "humane" individual protesting the use of animals as subjects in research on alcoholism:

> Instead of torturing helpless little cats why not torture the drunks or better yet exert your would-be noble effort toward getting a bill passed to exterminate the drunks. They are not any good to anyone or themselves and are just a drain on the public, having to pull them off the street, jail them, then they have to be fed while there and it's against the law to feed them arsenic so there they are . . . . My greatest wish is that you have brought home to you a torture that will be a thousand fold greater than what you have, and are doing to the little animals. . . . If you are an example of what a noted psychiatrist should be I'm glad I am just an ordinary human being without a letter after my name. I'd rather be just myself with a clear conscience, knowing I have not hurt any living creature, and can sleep without seeing frightened, terrified dying cats—because I know they must die after you have finished with them. No punishment is too great for you and I hope I live to read about your mangled body and long suffering before you finally die—and I'll laugh long and loud. (Masserman, 1961, p. 38)

Medical personnel sometimes use this defense to develop a "clinical" approach to their suffering patients, with whom they cannot afford to become too emotionally involved if they are to function effectively. Some individuals are so out of touch with their feelings that they deal with almost every aspect of life at a "head" level. It becomes impossible for them to become emotionally involved in almost anything. (See Box 13.4.)

It is important to remember that defense mechanisms are constructs applied to certain behaviors. Labeling a given behavior as rationalization, displacement, or reaction formation may be useful from a descriptive point of view, but it does not in itself explain the causes of the behavior. A complete understanding requires an identification of the underlying needs that motivate an individual to rely on the defense mechanism.

Everyone uses these defense mechanisms to some degree in daily living. Only individuals who use them to such an excessive degree that they abandon more realistic approaches to dealing with problems are considered to be maladjusted.

Psychosexual development

Freud's theory of personality development placed tremendous emphasis on the effects of experiences that occur during the first five years of life. During this period children pass through a number of distinctive *psychosexual stages* during which their *libido* is focused on particular pleasure-giving, or *erogenous,* zones in the body. These regions become the source of new pleasures and new conflicts. Freud believed that pleasure is focused successively on the mouth, anus, and genitals, which results in *oral, anal,* and *phallic* psychosexual stages within the first five years of life. The individual then enters a *latency* period, which lasts until adolescence, when the sexual impulses are once again activated. If all has gone well to this point, the individual reaches the mature, *genital* stage.

What happens to children during the psychosexual stages helps to mold their adult personality. If they are unsuccessful in resolving psychosexual conflicts at a given stage or if they are severely deprived or overindulged, then they may become *fixated.* Fixation is an arresting of psychosexual development and the development of a character structure built around the unresolved difficulties of a given stage. Moreover, if the individual encounters severe difficulties later in life, he or she may *regress* to an earlier and more satisfying stage.

The oral stage

During the first year of life the mouth is the primary source of pleasure for an infant. At this time the child is totally dependent on its mother, and must adjust its demands according to her availability. Fixation at or regression to the oral stage may result in extreme dependency, an excessive concern with "intake" in the form of acquiring possessions or knowledge, or extreme gullibility (a willingness to "swallow" anything).

The anal stage

During the second year of life, children begin to derive pleasure from expelling feces. Toilet training usually begins at about this time, and the child's experience with this first societal attempt to regulate an instinctual impulse may have decisive effects on the development of its personality. Freud believed that repressive and punitive toilet training methods may cause children to hold back their feces and become constipated. This response may later generalize to other behaviors, so that the child develops an obstinate and stingy, *anal-retentive* character. Or the child may vent rage by expelling feces at the most inopportune times, which may lead to *anal-expulsive* characteristics, such as disorderliness, temper tantrums, cruelty, and destructiveness.

If the mother encourages the child to have a bowel movement and then praises the child extravagantly for it, the child may come to prize its "productions" and, according to Freud, this may form the basis for later productivity and creativity.

The phallic stage

During the third through the fifth years of life, libido becomes focused on the genitals, and the child begins to derive great pleasure from masturbatory exploration. This is also the stage during which the *Oedipus complex* occurs. According to Freud, both male and female children want to possess the parent of the opposite sex in a sexual way and to do away with the other parent. However, boys fear castration by their fathers as punishment for their incestuous impulses and wish to see their fathers dead. Gradually, in order to reduce his *castration anxiety*, and also to achieve vicarious sexual gratification through his rival, the little boy identifies with the father and tries to be like him. This identification leads to the development of the superego, which internalizes the father's (and society's) prohibitions against incest and homicide. After age 5 the Oedipus complex is repressed in boys, but it continues to exert a strong influence throughout their lives.

During the phallic stage, according to Freud, little girls develop *penis envy* when they discover that they lack what Freud considered the more desirable male sex organ. A girl holds her mother responsible for her castrated condition and transfers some of her love for her mother to her father, because she desires to share his penis with him. Freud suggested that the lack of a penis is partially compensated for when the woman later has a child, particularly if it is a male child.

Unlike the male's complex, the female's Oedipus complex is not repressed, because she has no castration anxiety, but it does undergo some modifications because of real barriers to possessing her father. Freud would agree wholeheartedly with the message behind the words to the song, ". . . but my heart belongs to Daddy."

Latency and genital stages

At the end of the phallic stage a *latency* period occurs during which overt sexuality and memories of infantile sexuality are repressed. During this period of about six years there is considerable social development centered around same-sex peer relationships. With the onset of puberty sexual impulses toward the opposite sex return, but in a new form. Earlier the individual chose love objects only because they provided pleasure. In adolescence some of this *narcissistic* love is normally channeled into a nonselfish and altruistic love. In well-socialized adults the sexuality of earlier psychosexual stages becomes fused into a mature, genital love, and the individual is then capable of genuine caring and adult sexual satisfaction.

Freud's ideas about psychosexual development are undoubtedly the most controversial aspect of this theory. Although many theorists agree that childhood experiences are very important in the development of personality, many of them reject Freud's assertions about childhood sexuality. Indeed, many of the theories we consider in the remainder of this chapter were stimulated by opposition to Freud's theory.

Contributions and evaluation

Psychoanalytic theory has had a profound impact on the field of personality. Freud's most notable contributions were his recognition of the influence of

413

BOX 13.4
Intellectualization

The loss of contact with feelings that intellectualization can foster is illustrated in the following letter from a troubled student:

> Long ago I lost touch with my body—my brain became separated from my body and started commanding it. My body turned into just a machine for transporting my brain around from place to place to talk unfeelingly and analytically with other detached brains. I was glad it was a big and efficient machine—but I thought it was the inferior part of me, and that my brain should be in charge and call the tune for my feelings, letting the "positive" ones out and keeping the "negative" ones tucked in. . . .

> But now I feel lost in that head, out of phase with people—and somehow I want to reach them and my own guts—to know what I really feel, and stop all those precious intellectual games—to really live and not just to exist—So what do I do now? (Mischel, 1971, p. 101).

unconscious motives and conflicts on behavior and his emphasis on the importance of childhood experiences in personality development.

Freud's emphasis on unconscious determinants of behavior influenced the development of personality measures known as *projective techniques*. Projective tests present the subject with ambiguous stimuli, such as inkblots, and require that the subject interpret the stimulus. It is assumed that the subject needs to project his or her own needs, wishes, or conflicts into the stimulus in order to arrive at an interpretation of it. Projective tests are discussed in Chapter 14.

Many attempts have been made to demonstrate Freud's defense mechanisms experimentally. As an example, let us consider an experiment dealing with repression (D'Zurilla, 1965). Subjects from an experimental and a control group were shown a list of 20 words and then tested for recall. The groups did not differ in recall. Next the subjects were given an

inkblot test said to measure "latent homosexual tendencies." At this point an attempt was made to induce "repression" of the memorized words by introducing threat into the experimental situation. Subjects in the experimental group were told that their responses to the inkblots indicated the presence of homosexual tendencies. The control group subjects were told that there was no evidence of homosexuality in their responses. Both groups were again administered the recall test, and this time the experimental group recalled fewer words than the nonthreatened control group, suggesting a threat-induced repression effect. The investigator then tried to remove the repression effect by telling the experimental group that the inkblot test really was not a measure of homosexual tendencies. Following this revelation, which was designed to remove the threat that presumably induced the repression, the last recall test was administered. The experimental group now performed as well as on the test as did the control group.

Although these results would appear to support the concept of repression, some non-Freudian psychologists have pointed out that there are other possible explanations for the results. For example, the "repression" effect may be due not to an unconscious blocking out of the words because they were part of a threatening situation, but simply to the fact that thinking about their "latent homosexuality" may have competed with the attempts of the experimental group to recall the words. When interviewed, many of the subjects indicated that they were indeed preoccupied and worried about their "homosexual tendencies." A problem that plagues many experimental studies of defense mechanisms is that their results can be explained in other ways. This does not mean that these defensive processes do not exist, but it has been difficult to provide clear-cut experimental demonstrations of them.

Freud's theory of personality evolved largely from his experiences in treating psychiatric patients, and it has had a major role in attempts to understand and treat behavior disorders. We discuss these contributions in Chapters 15 and 16.

Although it has had a powerful influence in psychology, psychiatry, and other fields, psychoanalytic theory has been criticized on scientific grounds. Many of Freud's constructs are ambiguous and dif-

414

ficult to operationally define and measure. How, for example, can we measure the strength of an individual's id impulses and defenses? Moreover, because very different (even opposite) behaviors can result from the same impulse, it is difficult to make specific behavioral predictions. If, for example, we make a prediction from psychoanalytic theory that an individual will behave aggressively and the subject behaves instead in a loving manner, is the theory wrong, or is the aggression being masked by the defense mechanism of reaction formation? The difficulties in operationally defining psychoanalytic constructs and in making clear-cut behavioral predictions means that many aspects of psychoanalytic theory are untestable, and this detracts greatly from its scientific usefulness. Despite its limitations as a scientific theory, however, psychoanalysis has stimulated much research and theorizing in such diverse areas as child development, cultural anthropology, and psychotherapy.

NEOANALYTIC THEORIES

As we noted earlier, Freud's psychoanalytic theory made one of its greatest scientific contributions by arousing storms of controversy. Many of his own followers eventually came to feel that he emphasized infantile sexuality at the expense of other important determinants of personality. Two criticisms in particular stimulated the development of *neoanalytic* theories that incorporated many of Freud's basic ideas but that departed from psychoanalytic theory in important ways. One criticism was that social and cultural factors were not given a sufficiently important role in the development and dynamics of personality. Alfred Adler's theory of individual psychology was founded on this criticism. The second criticism was that Freud overemphasized the events of childhood as determinants of adult personality. Although neoanalytic theorists agreed that childhood experiences are important, some of them felt that personality development continues throughout the entire life span as individuals confront problems that are specific to particular stages in their lives. Erik Erikson's theory of psychosocial development expanded Freud's developmental stages across the entire life span.

Alfred Adler's individual psychology

In contrast to Freud's assumption that behavior is motivated by inborn sexual and aggressive instincts, Alfred Adler insisted that humans are inherently social beings, motivated by social urges. Adler's conception of human nature was much more optimistic than was Freud's, for he viewed humans as creatures who relate to others, cooperate with them, and place general social welfare above selfish personal interests.

Freud argued that individuals were *pushed* by forces and counterforces over which they have little control, but Adler felt that they were *pulled* by their individually developed goals. As creative, choosing, and self-determined decision makers, people chart their own destinies. He argued that life is full of potential risks, and each of us must choose how much we will risk in order to become all that we can

Figure 13.2 Alfred Adler (1870–1937) was, like Freud, a Viennese psychiatrist. He was originally a follower of Freud's and was at one time president of the Vienna Psychoanalytic Society. However, his views began to diverge sharply from Freud's over the issue of infantile sexuality and the importance of social motives. In 1911 he broke with Freud and established a movement known as *individual psychology.* (Courtesy of the Adler family.)

be. Adler viewed the maladjusted person not as "sick," but "discouraged," afraid to risk changes in thinking patterns and behavior. Adler emphasized conscious determinants of behavior, although he did acknowledge the existence of unconscious phenomena.

Inferiority, striving for superiority, and social interest

Adler believed that striving for superiority is an innate drive, an expression of life itself. By superiority he did not mean social distinction or a preeminent position in society. He meant something much broader: a striving for perfection and self-actualization, a "great upward drive" manifested by each person in his or her own way. Adler believed that neurotic individuals strive for egoistic or selfish goals, such as power, fame, and self-love, whereas well-adjusted individuals strive for societal goals.

Striving for superiority is motivated by feelings of *inferiority*, which arise from conscious or unconscious recognition of physical, psychological, or social imperfections. Because, according to Adler, all of us are constantly striving for self-perfection, to feel inferior is to be human. However, some people refuse to accept inferiority as a condition of human existence, become discouraged, and develop rigid and maladaptive ways of trying to overcompensate for their inadequacies. Adler referred to this as the *inferiority complex*, a term that has become a part of our everyday language.

Because we are social creatures embedded in a society from the first day of our lives, striving for superiority normally becomes socialized and is expressed as attitudes and behaviors that reflect the goal of helping to create a better society. This striving is called *social interest*. Selfish personal goals become secondary to social goals in well-adjusted individuals, and striving to improve society compensates for individual inferiorities. "Social interest is the true and inevitable compensation for all the natural weaknesses of individual human beings" (Adler, 1959, p. 31).

The life-style

As children grow they develop out of their subjective experiences a *life-style*, a set of convictions about themselves and the world. The life-style is a kind of "cognitive map" of an individual's reality. It contains four basic classes of convictions (Mosak and Dreikurs, 1973):

1. The self-concept: the individual's convictions about who he or she is.
2. The self-ideal: convictions about what the individual should be in order to be a worthwhile person.
3. The world-picture: convictions about the world, other individuals, etc.
4. The ethical convictions, or moral beliefs.

It is clear that Adler's definition of *life-style* has a cognitive orientation. His use of the term differs somewhat from its conventional use as a description of the behaviors that characterize an individual's pattern of living.

Adler believed that people could be changed for the better by creating social conditions that would result in the development of realistic and adaptive life-styles. He therefore attached great importance to training parents in effective child-rearing techniques and to the early education of children. He was a strong believer in what we refer to today as "preventive mental health."

Erik Erikson's psychosocial theory

Erik Erikson (1963) developed a theory that, like Adler's, emphasizes the importance of social factors in personality development and functioning. Like Freud, Erikson postulated a number of stages in personality development. However, he referred to them as *psychosocial* rather than psychosexual stages to emphasize his belief that social problems encountered at various periods in development are more important than are those caused by biological instincts. He also argued that personality development continued through life and was not determined entirely in childhood.

Development involves a series of eight stages through which we pass during the course of our lives. As we grow up, we engage in a widening range of human relationships. In each of Erikson's stages we are confronted with a basic crisis that has two possible outcomes, one positive, the other negative. How well we resolve the problems facing us at each stage determines how adequately we will be prepared to deal with the psychosocial crises of later stages.

Figure 13.3 Erik Erikson (b.1902; second from right) was teaching in a small private school in Vienna when he became acquainted with the Freud family and went into analysis with Anna Freud, Sigmund's daughter. The analysis led to his enrolling at the Vienna Psychoanalytic Society and becoming an analyst. In 1933 Erikson came to the United States as Boston's first child psychoanalyst. (Clemens, Kalischer)

Table 13.1 Erickson's eight stages of psychosocial development

Stage and age	Psychosocial crisis
I. Oral-sensory (1st year of life)	Basic trust vs. basic mistrust
II. Muscular-anal (2nd year)	Autonomy vs. shame, doubt
III. Locomotor-genital (3rd through 5th year)	Initiative vs. guilt
IV. Latency (6th year to start of puberty)	Industry vs. inferiority
V. Puberty and adolescence	Identity vs. role confusion
VI. Early adulthood	Intimacy vs. isolation
VII. Young and middle adulthood	Generativity vs. self-absorption
VIII. Mature adulthood	Integrity vs. despair

Based on Erikson (1963) and modified from original.

The eight stages and the crisis that occurs at each are shown in Table 13.1.

Psychosocial stages

Stage 1: Oral-sensory. During the first year of life, we are totally dependent on our parents. The adequacy with which our needs are met and the amount of love and attention we receive determine whether we develop *basic trust* or *basic mistrust* in the world. Those who develop basic trust carry into later stages a faith in the world and in themselves. Healthy personality development is built on the foundation of basic trust. This stage corresponds to Freud's oral stage.

Stage 2: Muscular-anal. The second critical stage occurs in about the second year of life; at stake is the attainment of *autonomy*. Children who have developed basic trust become ready to separate themselves from their parents and to exercise their individual-ity. Erikson views many of the rebellious behaviors of the "terrible twos" as a manifestation of these attempts to establish individuality. Children whose parents do not allow them to become autonomous, or who make harsh, unreasonable demands during toilet training tend to develop *shame and doubt* about their abilities and later lack the courage to be independent individuals. This stage corresponds to Freud's anal stage.

Stage 3: Locomotor-genital. During the third to sixth year, children begin to develop an exploratory curiosity about their world. They want to know the "whys" and "hows" of things around them. Their curiosity also leads them to explore their bodies, and they become attracted to the parent of the opposite sex. If they are allowed their freedom and if they receive answers to their questions, they develop a sense of *initiative*. If they are held back or punished, they develop *guilt* about their desires and suppress their basic curiosity. This stage corresponds to Freud's phallic stage.

Stage 4: Latency. During the period from age 6 to puberty, children are in school and the critical issue becomes the development of *industry* versus *inferiority*. Children who are able to achieve and experience a sense of pride in being able to master tasks

417

During Erikson's locomotor-genital stage, children develop curiosity about many aspects of their environment, including the human body. (George Gardner)

and reach their goals develop industry. If they fail repeatedly or do not receive encouragement for trying, they develop feelings of inferiority. During this stage children identify with what they do: "If I *do* good, I *am* good." This stage corresponds to Freud's latency stage.

Stage 5: Adolescence. One of the most critical life periods is adolescence, when the issue becomes the establishment of a personal *identity* versus *role confusion*. Even if an individual has developed trust, autonomy, initiative, and industry during earlier stages, this period can be fraught with conflict, turmoil, and anxiety. Preferred roles and actions change rapidly, and adolescents often rebel against authority figures who they see as preventing them from discovering and being what they want to be.

418   If adolescents are given freedom and encouragement to find themselves, then they can resolve their confusion through experimentation and by discovering values, attitudes, and roles that "feel right." This process often continues in their 20s.

Stage 6: Young adulthood. The issue during early adulthood becomes one of *intimacy* versus *isolation*. Young people who have developed basic trust, autonomy, initiative, industry, and a stable identity are prepared to take the emotional risks involved in establishing intimate relationships. Those who have not developed these qualities often feel vulnerable and afraid to get close to others. They may live unhappy lives devoid of intimate relationships.

Stage 7: Adulthood. In middle adulthood the issue becomes one of *generativity* versus *stagnation*. It is quite possible for people who have passed satisfactorily through the first stages to settle into a life of complacency and stagnation. Continued growth requires that people commit themselves to working for the next generation and for society as a whole. Parenthood and a positive role in society provide continued stimulation and a sense of mission in life.

Stage 8: Maturity. When they reach maturity people come to grips with the issue of *integrity* versus *despair*. Despair grows out of the feeling that "it's too late now." But individuals who have dealt successfully with the crises of the first seven stages can look back with a sense of peace and fulfillment as they live out their lives.

Erikson's theory has had a strong influence on psychoanalytic thought and developmental psychology. By expanding on Freud's developmental stages and by analyzing the social and role requirements that accompany maturation, Erikson has stimulated interest in personality development across the entire life span.

Contributions and evaluation

The neoanalytic theories expanded on the ideas of Freud, but they emphasized the influence of social rather than biological (instinctual) factors in shaping personality. Both Adler and Erikson rejected Freud's emphasis on sexual and aggressive instincts, as well as his notion that psychosexual development during childhood was the major determinant of adult personality. As a result, there emerged a more positive and optimistic conception of human nature than that presented by psychoanalytic theory. Adler proposed that humans have an innate potential to cooperate and work for the social good, whereas Erikson

Individuals who reach Erikson's psychological stage of maturity can continue to contribute to society and enrich their own lives by sharing their knowledge and experiences with younger generations. (Copyright, Seattle Times Co.)

emphasized the evolving nature of personality across the life span.

Like Freud, Adler and Erikson were therapists, and their theories were developed primarily on the basis of their clinical observations and philosophical beliefs. Like Freud's theory, their theories suffer scientifically from vaguely defined constructs and problems in behavioral prediction and testability. Although they have directly stimulated a small body of research, they are perhaps more important for the role they have played in focusing attention on social variables and developmental aspects of personality across the life span.

Adler's theory of personality contributed to the development of an approach to psychotherapy that is gaining in popularity among therapists. We describe his therapeutic approach in Chapter 16.

COGNITIVE THEORIES

Cognitive and perceptual processes occupy a central position in a number of personality theories. The way in which we subjectively experience and inter-

pret both our environment and our own behavior plays a crucial role in our personal adjustment. *Phenomenological* theories focus on the role of the momentary subjective experiences of the individual.

Out of our experiences we develop a conception of who we are as persons and what we can expect of the world in which we live. The theories of George Kelly and Carl Rogers focus on somewhat different aspects of this process. Kelly emphasizes the way in which we cognitively sort out and understand the objects of our experience, whereas Rogers attaches great importance to the development and role of the self-concept.

George Kelly's theory of personal constructs

A theory developed by George Kelly is the clearest example of a purely cognitive perspective on personality. According to Kelly, our primary goal is to make sense out of our world, to find personal meaning in it. In order to do this we try to explain and understand the events of our lives, and we test our understanding in the same way scientists test theirs: We attempt to anticipate, to predict. We do not react so much to the past as we do to the present and future, reaching out for mastery and control.

Kelly's primary interest was in the manner in which we construct our reality by sorting the persons and events in our lives into categories. Kelly termed these categories *personal constructs*.

Personal constructs

All perception involves categorizing. Even if we see something we have never seen before, we categorize it as "something we have never seen before." From birth on, stimuli are categorized, given meaning, and reacted to in terms of the categories into which they are placed. Every person has his or her own pattern of preferred categories or personal constructs. By understanding these constructs, the rules an individual uses to assign events to categories, and his or her hypotheses about how the categories relate to one another, Kelly believed that we can understand the individual's psychological world. Personal constructs, like scientific constructs, must have operational definitions or *referents*. For example, what does a person mean when he or she uses the category *obnoxious?* What kinds of behaviors fit into that construct? We

Figure 13.4 George Kelly (1905–1966) was an innovative and creative psychologist who spent many productive years on the faculty at Ohio State University. Like Freud, Adler, and Erikson, Kelly was a clinician whose theory was highly influenced by his observations of psychotherapy clients. (Ohio State University)

need either examples of behaviors that the individual would label as obnoxious or a statement of the individual's criteria for *obnoxious* in order to understand the personal meaning of the construct.

The same event can be categorized, or perceived, in entirely different ways by different individuals. For example, suppose that two lovers break up. One observer may construe the event as "simple incompatibility"; another may think that one person was "jilted" by the other; another might describe the breakup as the "result of parental meddling"; another might call it "a terrible development"; and a fifth might see it as "a blessing in disguise."

Rather than evaluating alternative constructions according to whether or not they are "true" (which we cannot know), Kelly preferred to examine the consequences of construing in particular ways. If an individual categorizes himself as "a worthless failure," Kelly would try to discover the implications for the individual's life in construing himself in that way. If the construction is not *convenient* (that is, if it leads to bad outcomes or predictions), then the task is to find a better alternative (for example, "I am a person who hasn't made it yet, but who can if I keep trying"). Kelly saw psychotherapy as a way of demonstrating to clients that their constructions are hypotheses rather than facts. Once clients realize this they can be encouraged to test their constructs so that the maladaptive ones can be replaced by more useful ones.

Kelly noted that people are capable of enacting many different roles and engaging in continuous change. Because behavior is the result of an individual's construction of a situation, playing a new role requires that we first temporarily adopt a new construct viewpoint. For example, if you were asked to role-play Adolph Hitler for a day, you would have to try to view the situations you encountered that day through Hitler's eyes.

Kelly applied this principle in a therapy technique called *fixed-role therapy*. In order to help clients experiment with new viewpoints and behaviors, the therapist writes role descriptions for clients that differ from their typical view of themselves. For example, a shy person might be asked to play a more confident and assertive role for two or three days, to think and act like a confident person. The therapist then asks the client to practice the fixed role within the therapy situation to be certain that he or she has a command of the required behaviors and the view of the world that confident individuals would have. By trying out a new role, clients may gain an appreciation of the ways in which different constructions and behaviors lead to more satisfying life outcomes.

Carl Rogers' self theory

Carl Rogers' theory of personality emphasizes the individual's unique moment-to-moment reality. All behavior is a response to reality as we perceive it, and because no one else can directly know our percep-

The self

Rogers theorized that as children interact with their environment, a portion of their perceptual or "phenomenal" field gradually becomes differentiated as the *self*. The self, or self-concept, is an "organized, consistent, conceptual gestalt composed of perceptions of the characteristics of the 'I' or 'me' and the perceptions of the relationships of the 'I' or 'me' to others and to various aspects of life, together with the values attached to these perceptions" (Rogers, 1959, p. 200).

Once the self-concept is formed, there is a tendency to maintain it. Experiences (including one's own behaviors) that are inconsistent with the self-concept constitute *threat*. Well-adjusted individuals can respond to threat adaptively by modifying their self-concept so that the experience fits or is *congruent* with the self; other individuals may deny or distort the experience to remove the incongruence between it and their self-concept.

For example, suppose a young man's self-esteem requires that every woman find him irresistible. He meets a young woman whom he finds very attractive but who shows a total lack of interest in him. This incongruence between his self-concept and experience would produce threat. He could react adaptively by acknowledging that he is not irresistible to all women after all and modify his self-concept accordingly. On the other hand, he might resolve the incongruence by denying or distorting reality. He might deny her lack of interest: "She's just playing hard to get." Or he might distort the situation: "If she doesn't go for me, she must be crazy. Thank heaven I found that out before she fell hopelessly in love with me."

At the other extreme, consider a young man with low self-esteem who believes that he is totally unattractive to women. If an attractive woman were to show obvious romantic interest in him, he too would feel the incongruence between his self-concept and the experience. In order to reduce the resulting threat, he might deny or distort the woman's interest in him ("She just feels sorry for me, and I don't want pity") or sabotage the relationship to remove the threat. As many psychotherapists have noted, it is often as difficult for people with negative self-concepts to accept success as it is for those with unrealistically positive self-concepts to accept failure.

Figure 13.5 Carl Rogers (b.1902) has been a leader in the "human potential movement" and an eloquent spokesman for the humanistic movement within psychology. His theory of personality and psychotherapy has had a major impact not only within the field of psychology, but also within other fields such as education and social work. (Anthony de Gesu)

tions, we each have potentially the most complete information about ourselves. He viewed behavior not as a response to external stimuli, but as "the goal-directed attempt of the organism to satisfy its needs as experienced, in the field as perceived" (Rogers, 1951, p. 491).

Basic to Rogers is his faith in the self-directing capacity of the individual. He believes that human beings have an innate tendency toward *self-actualization*, which, when released, causes them to strive for personal perfection.

Rogers' conception of human nature is an optimistic and positive one, far different from Freud's conception of humans as basically irrational beings driven by destructive impulses. It is also drastically different from the behavioristic conception of human beings as the pawns of external forces. Rogers felt that the forces that direct behavior are within us, and when societal conditions do not distort them, they direct us toward positive growth.

"I can't say I like the looks of that bunch."

Figure 13.6 According to Rogers, we tend to behave in ways which are congruent with our self-concept. (Drawing by Dana Fradon; © 1971 The New Yorker Magazine, Inc.)

The more rigid and inflexible an individual's self-concept, the less open he or she will be to accepting incongruous experiences and the more maladjusted he or she will become. If there is a significant degree of incongruence between self and experience, the defenses used to deny and distort reality may collapse, and the individual may experience extreme anxiety, and a disorganization of the self-concept. (See Figure 13.7.)

The fully functioning person

Rogers has worked with individuals who fall everywhere along the continuum from adjustment to maladjustment. In recent years he has become more involved in working with relatively well-adjusted individuals who want to grow into what he defines as *fully functioning persons* (1959; 1961).

Fully functioning persons do not hide behind "masks" or adopt artificial roles. They fulfill themselves in their own way, refusing to accept uncriti-

cally parental and cultural conditions of worth. They can accept inner and outer experiences as they are, without modifying them defensively to suit a rigid self-concept. They have no fear of behaving spontaneously, freely, and creatively.

Finally, fully functioning individuals make their own evaluations and decisions. They feel a sense of inner freedom, self-determination, and choice in the direction of their growth.

The theory of Abraham Maslow, who, like Rogers, emphasized the concept of self-actualization, is discussed in Box 13.5.

Contributions and evaluation

The theories of Kelly and Rogers have made a number of important contributions. Both theorists emphasized the importance of cognitive and perceptual processes that cannot be directly observed, and both were totally committed to developing a scientifically sound theory capable of generating testable hypothe-

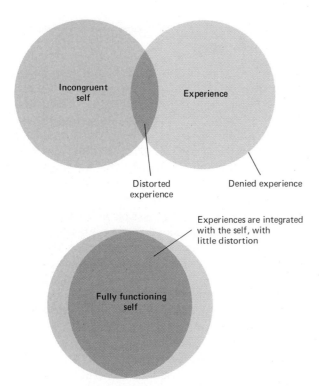

Distorted experience

Denied experience

Experiences are integrated with the self, with little distortion

Incongruent self

Experience

Fully functioning self

Figure 13.7 Adjustment in Rogers' theory is defined in terms of the degree of congruence between self-concept and experience. Maladjustment is caused by incongruities between self and experience (top figure), whereas well adjusted or "fully functioning" individuals integrate experiences into the self (lower figure). (Adapted from Rogers, 1951, p. 527.)

ses. Both were research-oriented clinical psychologists who developed influential approaches to psychotherapy. We briefly described Kelly's fixed-role therapy earlier. Rogers' approach, known as client-centered therapy, is described in Chapter 16. Rogers has also made major contributions to the research literature in psychotherapy.

Because phenomenological approaches emphasize the conscious subjective experiences of the individual, they deal with behavioral determinants that are clearly very important. However, critics of this approach argue that this perspective is too limited in scope. They feel that past experiences and influences that the individual is not aware of at the moment are also likely to be important.

A second criticism frequently directed toward the phenomenological approach is that it relies almost completely on the individual's self-reports. The assumption that individuals are both able and willing to describe their private experiences has been seriously challenged by research showing that self-reports are often systematically distorted because of a lack of insight or attempts to create a desired impression. Critics fear that using self-report as the primary means of studying personality may lead to erroneous conclusions.

Finally, some critics regard certain important constructs within phenomenological theories as having little scientific value. An example is Rogers' notion of the self-actualizing tendency. Critics argue that it is impossible to define operationally an individual's actualizing tendency except in terms of the behavior it supposedly produces. Under such conditions it is very difficult to make behavioral predictions with any degree of precision.

LEARNING APPROACHES TO PERSONALITY

The psychology of learning has had a pervasive influence within American psychology, and this influence has extended to the area of personality. Most of our behaviors, and particularly those that fall within the realm of personality, are acquired through learning. Approaches to personality based on learning regard personality as a set of learned behaviors and attempt to specify the conditions under which particular patterns of behavior are developed, maintained, and changed.

Behavioristic approaches to personality differ in the extent to which they restrict their attention to externally observable events. The most rigorously behavioristic conception of personality is the approach inspired by B. F. Skinner. Skinnerians reject any reference to unobservable processes occurring within the individual. They regard internal "personality" processes as "explanatory fictions" that deflect attention from the true causes of behavior, which to them reside in the external environment and in the past learning history of the individual. The Skinnerian approach is thus concerned with establishing empirical relationships between observable *stimuli* and *responses*. An operant approach to personality

423

BOX 13.5

Abraham Maslow's theory of self-actualization

Abraham Maslow, a leader in the humanistic movement in psychology, developed an influential theory of motivation that had self-actualization as its "highest" need. Maslow described a hierarchy of needs arranged in terms of the degree to which satisfaction of each is a prerequisite to the search for satisfaction of the next. That is to say, "lower" needs in the hierarchy must be relatively satisfied before individuals can try to satisfy "higher" ones. In Maslow's need hierarchy, the most basic ("lowest") needs are basic *physiological* ones, followed by *safety, belongingness and love, esteem, understanding and knowledge, aesthetic,* and *self-actualization needs.* By self-actualization Maslow meant self-fulfillment and complete realization of one's potential. He felt that

few people actually attain this highest goal of human existence.

Maslow spent many years studying the characteristics of people whom he considered to be self-actualized. Included among those whose lives were studied were Abraham Lincoln, William James, Albert Einstein, Eleanor Roosevelt, and Thomas Jefferson. Maslow also studied college students who seemed exceptionally self-fulfilled.

The characteristics that Maslow attributed to self-actualized persons included self-acceptance, an ability to perceive reality without defensive distortion or "blind spots," spontaneity in thought and behavior, a good sense of humor, creativity, an abiding concern for the welfare of the human race, a deep appreciation of the basic experiences of life, and an ability to establish deeply intimate and satisfying relations with a few people.

Like Rogers, Maslow emphasized the self-directing capacity of the individual and the potential for positive growth. He and Rogers arrived at very similar descriptions of the fully functioning, or self-actualized, person.

---

involves careful and precise measurement of the individual subject's behavior as it is affected by observable environmental conditions. Skinnerians believe that their approach is more likely to isolate the variables that cause behavior to develop and change than is an approach that attributes behavior to the internal workings of an unobservable "personality."

A more recent behavioristic approach that is attracting many adherents is *cognitive social learning theory.* Although it also focuses on environmental causes of behavior, this approach differs from the Skinnerian position in that it emphasizes the importance of cognitive processes that mediate between stimulus and response. Cognitive social learning theorists like Albert Bandura believe that humans are more than passive responders to external stimuli and that there is a need to understand how individuals cognitively process information from the environment.

Because the cognitive social learning approach has been, by virtue of its willingness to consider cognitive processes, more important than the Skinnerian approach in stimulating theoretical and empirical advances in personality, we elaborate on it in the discussion to follow.

Social learning and personality

Individual differences in behavior are explained by cognitive social learning theorists in terms of the learning experiences that we encounter in the course of our development. We have already discussed in Chapter 6 the major learning processes involved in social learning, so that a brief summary is sufficient here.

Some of our behavior patterns are learned through directly experienced rewards, nonrewards, and punishments. But many others are learned through the use of complex cognitive processes that allow us to

424

code and store in memory our observations of others' behaviors and the consequences that follow. In other words, we often learn complex social behaviors through *observational* or *vicarious* learning.

There is an important distinction between *learning* and *performing* observed behaviors. Observation alone is sufficient for learning, but whether or not observers subsequently perform a behavior depends on the consequences the model experiences and observers' expectations about the consequences they would experience were they to perform the behavior.

The individual either maintains or changes learned behaviors as a result of their consequences. Rewards and punishments may be either external or self-administered. Social learning theorists place strong emphasis on the importance of self-reinforcement processes. In some cases powerful self-administered consequences may override external consequences, as when a behavior that is unrewarded or even punished by others is maintained by self-approval or self-praise.

A critical issue:
How consistent is "personality"?

When we considered the concept of personality earlier in this chapter, we pointed out that people seem to retain certain characteristic behaviors as they move from situation to situation. This observed consistency in behavior allows us to ascribe personality "traits" to them. We all "see" this consistency, but is it really there?

Over 50 years ago Hartshorne and May (1928) conducted a classic investigation in which thousands of children were exposed to a variety of situations in which they could lie, steal, and cheat. Although there was a high degree of consistency in the children's self-reported opinions and attitudes about moral issues, there was much less consistency in their behavioral "honesty" from situation to situation. The less similar the various situations were, the less consistency there was in behavior.

Research on personality traits as diverse as anxiety, self-control, dependence, aggression, and even punctuality has shown that inconsistency across different situations appears to be the rule rather than the exception, particularly when different behavioral measures of the trait in question are used. What people say about themselves may not correspond to

Winning a beauty contest constitutes social reinforcement for behaviors as well as appearance. (Beckwith Studios)

the way they behave, and their behavior in one situation may be very different from behavior in another.

On the basis of such findings, some psychologists have begun to question the usefulness of the concept of personality traits. Although there is consistency in intellectual variables and cognitive abilities related to intelligence, there is little evidence of other kinds of behavioral consistency across situations. Some

425

BOX 13.6

A psychological frontier: Whence the consistency we perceive?

Why are we able to see "personality traits" in other people if there is little evidence that they actually exist? Researchers have suggested a number of possible reasons (Bem and Allen, 1974; Jones and Nisbett, 1971):

1. Perhaps we perceive consistency that "isn't there." We usually see acquaintances in a limited number of situations, and our presence may serve as a stimulus for their behavior. They may behave quite differently when we are not there. Another possible factor is that when we observe other people, we generally pay more attention to their behavior than to the background situation. We are therefore more likely to attribute the behavior we see to the person we are watching than to situational causes and to view "internal" causal factors as determinants of their behavior in other situations that we do not see. Also, it is the case that there *is* consistency in such characteristics as intellectual skills, verbal behavior, and physical appearance. We may generalize from these observed consistencies to other behaviors that are not as consistent. Finally,

there are well over 20,000 trait or traitlike terms in our vocabulary. We use many of these terms in the personal constructs through which we perceive our surroundings, so that we "force" our observations into our trait constructs.

2. A second possibility is that there actually is more consistency in behavior than our research data show. Traditionally, research has compared groups of subjects on the same trait in different situations. Suppose that for some (perhaps even most) subjects, the trait being measured were not important or central to their personality? We might expect to find little behavioral consistency for such individuals. It is possible that a given person will be consistent for some traits but not for others, depending on how important the trait is to the individual's functioning.

Recently Bem and Allen (1974) asked subjects to rate their own cross-situational consistency on a series of traits. They found that individuals who identified themselves as consistent on a particular trait did in fact behave more consistently across situations than did those who identified themselves as highly variable. This suggests that cross-situational consistency may itself be a measurable variable and that it is possible to predict which traits will be consistent across situations for a given individual. The issue of consistency versus situational specificity in behavior may depend on the trait in question and its importance to the particular person being studied. Thus the issue of consistency in personality is not yet settled, and it promises to occupy the attention of personality psychologists for some time to come.

---

possible reasons for the discrepancy between our perception of consistency and the research results are discussed in Box 13.6.

Personality as a situation-person interaction

Behavior always involves an individual interacting with the environment. An adequate conception of personality must take into account both situational and individual factors. Social learning theorists have recently begun to move in this direction.

Situational variables. When we enter a given situation our behavior is influenced by the specific characteristics of the situation, our cognitive appraisal of it, and the consequences that we have experienced in similar situations, either directly or through observation of others.

The fact that most social behaviors are not uniformly rewarded across different situations may be responsible for the inconsistency that occurs in behavior. We learn to discriminate between situations

Parties are situations in which individuals may behave in ways that seem inconsistent with their everyday behavior. Individuals who usually seem self-assured may behave as if they were shy and introverted in response to the intense social pressures of a party and vice versa. (Sitemann, Stock, Boston)

in terms of the outcomes that a given behavior is likely to produce. If the same behavior is rewarded in many different situations, then we tend to generalize the behavior and perform it in all those situations (i.e., it becomes a "stable trait"). Individuals who are consistently rewarded in a variety of situations for "standing up for their rights" will develop a general quality of "assertiveness." But those who are rewarded for assertive behavior in some situations and punished in others learn to discriminate between situations in which they can afford to be assertive and those in which they cannot, and they show less cross-situational consistency in assertiveness.

Person variables. When we behave within a given situation we are responding to that situation as we perceive it. In this sense we respond to a *psychological* rather than to a *physical* situation. Cognitive social learning theorists have recently begun to focus their attention on individual difference variables that determine the ways in which individuals cognitively construct and give "meaning" to situations. Walter Mischel (1973) has suggested five such variables:

1. *Cognitive and behavioral construction competencies.* These refer to the individuals' ability to

427

generate adaptive, skillful cognitions and behaviors that have beneficial consequences. This includes such skills as knowing how to plan, how to solve problems, and how to behave adaptively. These skills are related to intelligence, mental maturity, and competence.

2. *Encoding strategies and personal constructs.* Different individuals can encode, categorize, and selectively attend to situations in different ways that influence the ways in which they behave. Mischel, as did Kelly, emphasizes the importance of understanding the cognitive categories into which we "sort" reality.

3. *Stimulus-outcome and behavior-outcome expectancies.* Individuals behave in accordance with what they expect will happen under particular circumstances. *Stimulus-outcome expectancies* refer to their anticipations of what will occur when certain "signs" or discriminative cues are present in a situation. For example, if another person approaches you with an angry expression on his face, you may anticipate a negative social interaction. *Behavior-outcome expectancies* refer to anticipated outcomes of particular behaviors. You respond to the angry-looking person after you decide which possible approach you *expect* will work best in helping you achieve your immediate goal.

4. *Subjective values of outcomes.* A given outcome may be highly reinforcing for one person and very punishing for another. These values are determined by an individual's past experiences in a variety of situations.

5. *Self-regulatory systems and plans.* These refer to an individual's self-imposed standards for self-reinforcement or self-punishment. They also include the person's plans or behavioral intentions.

Until recently individual difference variables were virtually ignored, and the focus was on the processes that affect behavior rather than on the psychological products of those factors. Mischel's recent attempt to specify person variables that influence the ways in which an individual responds to situations is a major step toward making the cognitive social learning approach a more comprehensive theory of personality.

Contributions and evaluation

The behavioristic perspective has made many important contributions to the study of personality. Learning approaches have been especially valuable in specifying learning processes whereby behaviors are acquired and changed. Principles of learning derived from experimental research with both animals and humans have been applied in many therapeutic settings with impressive results. (See Chapters 6 and 16.)

Learning approaches have also contributed to the area of personality assessment. The emphasis of Skinnerians on the observation and measurement of behavior in response to specific stimulus conditions has stimulated the development of *behavioral assessment* procedures that have proved very useful. These procedures are described in Chapter 14.

Because learning approaches to personality tend to remain at or close to the level of observable behavior, it is easier to derive testable predictions from them than from some of the theories we discussed earlier. Many critics maintain, however, that the greater scientific precision of behavioristic approaches is gained at the expense of a consideration of factors (e.g., unconscious dynamics) that other theorists believe to be important determinants of behavior. They believe that learning approaches present a vastly oversimplified conception of personality.

Other criticisms have also been leveled against the behavioristic approach. Some critics are skeptical about generalizing the results of animal learning studies to humans because they believe that different processes may be involved. This consideration has helped to stimulate the development of cognitive learning approaches. Another criticism especially relevant to the area of personality is that external factors are overemphasized at the expense of individual differences that may affect responses to the external factors.

AN APPRAISAL OF PERSONALITY THEORIES

Now that a variety of theoretical approaches to the understanding of personality have been considered, let us briefly evaluate their adequacy as scientific theories in terms of the three criteria discussed earlier in the chapter.

First, a theory should help us understand facts we already know. Most of the theorists we have considered constructed their theories with this goal in mind. Many were psychotherapists and their theories were attempts to make sense out of their clinical observations of individuals struggling with the problems of living. By and large, the theories are successful in explaining behavior. Almost any behavior can be "understood" in terms of any of the theories. But we must ask what kind of understanding we have achieved. Because all the theories can account for just about everything on an after-the-fact basis, how can we distinguish among them in terms of their relative validity?

This brings us to the second criterion for a useful theory, its ability to predict successfully. If all the theories can explain a behavior once it has occurred, perhaps a more rigorous test of their value is their ability to *predict* behavior. Most of these theories were not constructed for making predictions, and most do not predict terribly well. In fact, as we have seen, it is extremely difficult to generate testable predictions from some of them because many of their constructs cannot be operationally defined in an agreed upon way. For example, because of the many interlocking constructs in psychoanalytic theory, it would be most difficult to predict precisely the conditions under which a given behavior would occur (although we could easily explain anything that happened once it occurred). The behavioristic approach has perhaps the greatest predictive ability because it concentrates most on observable phenomena. But the ultimate predictive power of the social learning approach will probably depend on how successful psychologists are in developing reliable measures of such cognitive person variables as those suggested by Mischel. Situational variables alone are not enough to ensure predictive precision.

The third measure of a scientifically useful theory is its capacity to stimulate and generate research that leads to the acquisition of new knowledge. Most of the theories have stimulated considerable research, but in many instances the studies did not constitute adequate tests of the theories. Not surprisingly, theories whose constructs can be operationally defined and measured are most likely to stimulate sound research.

Personality theories of the future will probably not attempt to explain all of human behavior within one grand framework. The current trend is toward the development of "mini-theories" that focus on specific areas of behavior and attempt to specify controlling variables. These more precise theories will not be as much fun to read, nor will they provide us with as many rich insights into the meaning of human existence. But they should lead to more precise predictions of behavior, to more direct ways to control the conditions that affect our lives, and to greater understanding of human individuality.

SUMMARY

1. The concept of personality arises from observations of individual differences and individual consistencies in behavior. Personality itself does not exist; it is a concept or construct used in reference to certain behaviors. The term *personality* is applied to behaviors that are perceived as components of identity, as internally caused, and as having organization and structure. Because all these conditions are perceptual in nature, it is concluded that personality exists in the eye of the observer rather than within the person being described.

2. Personality theories consist of a system of constructs and a series of propositions that specify how the constructs are related to one another. In order to be scientifically useful, a theory's constructs must be capable of operational definition. Theories have three basic functions: (a) to organize existing knowledge; (b) to allow prediction of future events; and (c) to stimulate the discovery of new knowledge.

3. Freud's psychoanalytic theory views personality as an energy system. Personality dy-

429

namics involve modifications and exchanges of energy within this system. Mental events may be *conscious, preconscious,* or *unconscious* in nature. Freud divided the personality into three structures: *id, ego,* and *superego.* The id is the innermost core of the personality. It contains the instincts and is thus the ultimate source of all psychic energy. The id is irrational and seeks immediate instinctual gratification on the basis of the *pleasure principle.* The ego operates on the *reality principle,* which requires it to test reality and to mediate between the demands of the id, the superego, and reality. The superego is the moral arm of the personality. It represents the acquired moral standards and values of the society in which the person lives.

4. The dynamics of Freudian personality functioning involve a continuous conflict between impulses of the id and counterforces of the ego and superego. When dangerous id impulses threaten to get out of control or when danger from the environment threatens, the result is *anxiety.* In order to deal with threat, the ego develops *defense mechanisms* that are used to ward off anxiety and to permit instinctual gratification in disguised forms.

5. Freud held that personality development involves a series of *psychosexual stages* during which psychic energy is focused on various body parts. The *oral, anal,* and *phallic* stages, which occur during the first five years of life, are considered to be of great importance in terms of future personality functioning. During the phallic stage the *Oedipus complex* occurs, and the resolution of this conflict is important in the development of the superego and sex role behavior.

6. Neoanalytic theories incorporated many of Freud's basic ideas but stressed the importance of social rather than sexual determinants of personality development and functioning. Alfred Adler emphasized *social interest,* a tendency to strive for the perfection of society. Of central importance in Adler's theory is the life-style, a set of convictions about oneself and the world that develops out of experience. Erik Erikson expanded on Freud's developmental stages. He proposed eight psychosocial stages that extend across the life span. At each stage the individual is forced to deal with a basic crisis that has a positive or negative outcome.

7. Phenomenological theories emphasize the subjective experiences of the individual and thus deal with perceptual and cognitive processes. The theories of George Kelly and Carl Rogers represent this viewpoint. Kelly viewed people as scientists whose major goal is to understand, predict, and control their world. His cognitive theory emphasizes the way in which people mentally create their own reality by means of the personal constructs they use to categorize the events and persons in their world. Carl Rogers' theory postulates an innate tendency toward self-actualization. Central importance is attached to the role of the self. Experiences that are incongruous with the established self-concept produce threat and may result in a denial or distortion of reality. Rogers has described a number of characteristics of the fully functioning person.

8. Learning approaches conceive of personality as a set of learned behaviors and attempt to specify the conditions under which particular patterns of behavior are developed, maintained, and changed. The Skinnerian approach restricts its attention to externally observable stimuli and responses, whereas cognitive social learning theory also considers internal cognitive processes. The usefulness of trait conceptions of personality is questioned on the basis of research results

showing that behavior is often not consistent across situations. The role of observational learning in complex social behavior is emphasized. Personality functioning is viewed as a situation-person interaction, and Mischel has proposed a set of cognitive "person" variables that influence responses to situations.

9. Most personality theories are better at explaining past behavior than they are at predicting future behavior. Many of them were not constructed with prediction and testability as their goal, and many constructs are incapable of operational definition. The trend today is away from all-encompassing theories of personality and toward the construction of miniature theories that focus on specific areas of human behavior. These smaller but more precise theories are likely to result in the maximum scientific yield at the present stage of development of the field of personality.

Suggested readings

Byrne, D. *An introduction to personality: Research, theory and application.* (2nd ed.). Englewood Cliffs, N.J.: Prentice-Hall, Inc., 1974. This book deals primarily with a review of research in personality which is derived from various personality theories.

Hall, C. S., & Lindzey, G. *Theories of personality.* (2nd ed.). New York: John Wiley & Sons, Inc., 1970. A classic textbook that describes and evaluates the major theories of personality.

Mischel, W. *Introduction to personality.* (2nd ed.) New York: Holt, Rinehart and Winston, Inc., 1976. A general introduction to theory and research in personality primarily from a cognitive social learning perspective.

Munroe, R. L. *Schools of psychoanalytic thought.* New York: Holt, Rinehart and Winston, Inc., 1955. A comprehensive description of Freud's psychoanalytic theory and of neoanalytic theories of personality.

Chapter 14

Psychological Assessment: Intelligence and Personality

Four seniors sat in the high school cafeteria tentatively exploring the contents of their brown bags, but their attention was directed elsewhere. They had just received the results of college entrance examinations they had taken seven weeks earlier. Ellen French had gotten very high scores, Phil Crane and Jack Cransky had gotten average scores, and Harriet Fallon had scored below the average level of students admitted to the state university.

Phil was the first to speak. "I don't know whether to feel good or bad because I'm average. And what does average mean? I wish I knew." "Well, I know what average means," said Harriet. "It means that if you are below it your college choices become limited. It doesn't seem fair to me. My grade point average is way above average. What should I think—have I been overachieving all this time? Or is that high-prestige test underestimating my real abilities?"

Ellen seemed embarrassed and didn't know what to say at first. Then she commented cautiously, "I'm sorry, Harriet; I really am—we all know that I'm better than you in some things and you are better than I am in others. For example, you've got a knack with foreign languages I'll never have. We all know these tests don't tell the whole story—and that's okay with me except that our careers and futures may be influenced by mistakes in the way we're classified."

Jack picked up quickly on Ellen's last point, "Just thinking about it in general, I can accept the fact that each of us is unique and that any measure of whatever it is that is unique or characteristic about us can't be perfect. Actually, I think that test pegged me about right. I'm not dumb, and I'm better in math and science than in English. And that's pretty much what the test showed. But I'd like to know more about where tests come from, who thinks them up, and exactly what is known about them."

Like these students, you have probably felt at times as if the course of your life were being determined by your performance on tests about which you knew very little. This chapter describes some of the background and the development of various widely used measures, and, it is hoped, will provide you with a better understanding of the tests you have taken and those you must face in the future. Although psychologists are not the only specialists who develop, use, and evaluate tests (educators and personnel workers, for example, are also deeply involved in the broad field often referred to as assessment), they have been among the most important contributors to theory and research. In this chapter we direct our attention toward some of the problems that have concerned them. Most of these problems relate to the fact that different individuals have widely different abilities, attitudes, interests, and preferences, as well as physical characteristics. Psychologists have been especially interested in measuring individual differences in the areas of intelligence and personality, and this chapter will focus on these two important areas of human variation.

THE CHARACTERISTICS OF TESTS

The field of assessment is concerned with individual differences and their relationship to human behavior. Psychiatrists in need of information about clients' problems, personnel managers who want to

(Zimbel, Monkmeyer)

BOX 14.1

Correlation

The reliability and validity of tests are most often and most conveniently reported in terms of *correlation coefficients,* which express the degree of relationship between two variable measures (for example, IQs obtained on the same test taken at different times, or IQs and grade point averages). A correlation coefficient (designated r) can range from $+1.00$ to -1.00. A positive correlation between IQ and grade point average indicates that people with high IQs also have high grades. A negative correlation between IQ and grade point means that high IQs are associated with low grades, and vice versa. A correlation of $r = +1.00$ means that there is a perfect positive $(+)$ relationship between two sets of scores. A correlation of $r = -1.00$ designates a perfect negative $(-)$ relationship between two variables. A cor-

relation of $r = .00$ means that there is no statistical relationship between two sets of scores. Therefore a correlation of $-.60$ indicates a stronger relationship than does one of $+.40$.

A correlation of $r = 1.00$ is rarely obtained between two variables, but the closer the correlation coefficient is to 1.00, the stronger the relationship. On most tests reliability coefficients of $+.70$ or above are considered acceptable. Our best intelligence measures have reliability coefficients of more than $+.90$. Validity coefficients are seldom as high as reliability coefficients. A test is generally considered to have high validity if its scores correlate $+.60$ with the criterion measure.

The degree of correlation between two variables determines our ability to predict one from the other. The more highly two variables are correlated, the more accurately we are able to predict one of them if we know the other. If we know that scores on a given test are highly correlated (either positively or negatively) with job performance, we can use test scores to predict how well individuals will perform

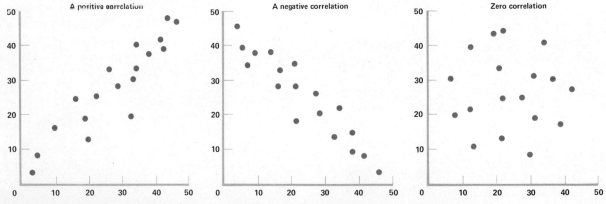

Graphic plots of three correlations. These hypothetical examples assume in each case that a group of subjects took two tests and the tester wished to determine the relationship between the tests.

on the job. The higher the correlation coefficient, the greater the test's validity. This is the assumption underlying college entrance examinations, screening tests, and the variables used by insurance companies to establish premiums and insurability limits.

A correlation between two variables does not mean one causes the other. But two factors do not need to be related in a definite causal manner in order to make them useful for prediction. It is useful to know simply that two factors are correlated (e.g., smoking and lung cancer). Some researchers who work in applied settings do not attempt to establish causal relationships to achieve scientific understanding; they only attempt to predict one event on the basis of another.

The graphic plots of three correlations shown here assume that a group of subjects took two tests and the tester wished to determine the relationship between the tests.

The correlational method allows us to study relationships between variables that we cannot or do not wish to manipulate. It can also provide valuable leads to be followed up in experimental research that does involve manipulating and controlling variables so that we can study their causal effects on behavior directly.

Sometimes our ability to predict a particular aspect of behavior increases if we take more than one predictor variable into account. For example, we might best predict future college performance if we took into account not only college entrance examination scores, but also measures of other potentially important factors, such as IQ, interest, motivation, difficulty of high school curriculum, and freedom from emotional problems. If we can quantify these factors we can mathematically derive an equation that combines all the scores on these factors in the way that best predicts future performance.

know something about job applicants, teachers troubled about students who seem "slow" in class, and researchers trying to predict creativity are all concerned with individual differences. They may use various approaches to carry out assessments, but the goal in each instance is to obtain *reliable* and *valid* measures.

Reliability

We know that measurements are subject to error, so that any single score may not represent an individual's "true" score. The smaller the measurement error, the more reliable the data. For example, if you step on your bathroom scale several times and it registers the same weight each time, your scale is a reliable instrument. If you get different weights each time, your scale is unreliable.

There are several different ways to assess reliability. *Test-retest reliability* is measured by administering a test to the same subjects on two occasions and correlating the two sets of scores. This correlation is a measure of the stability of the scores over a period of time. (See Box 14.1.) In *split-half reliability* the items of a test are "split" into two sets (this can be done at random or by taking either odd-numbered or even-numbered items) and a correlation coefficient is computed between the subjects' scores on the two halves. Using this method, *parallel forms* of a test can be constructed that can be used interchangeably, although the items on one form are not the same as the items on the other. For example, there could be two college entrance examination forms, each composed of items with the same range of difficulty and each designed to produce the same score for any given individual.

Another type of reliability is important when measures are derived from observers' ratings. *Inter-observer reliability* refers to the level of agreement between two or more observers who are rating the same behaviors.

Validity

Validity has to do with the degree to which a test measures what it is supposed to measure or accomplishes the purpose for which it is intended. Validity can be estimated in several ways. For example, some *criterion*—an event, condition, or outcome—can be compared with the results of a measuring device to test the device's validity. Academic performance or grade point average might be used as a criterion to evaluate the validity of a college entrance examination.

Sampling

A potential user needs facts about the samples used to develop a test. In *representative sampling*, all the major groups in the population are proportionally represented in the sample. This is the procedure used by most public opinion polling firms. In *random sampling*, the probability of each person in the population being included in the sample is independent of whether or not any other member is selected. Therefore chance plays a greater role in random than in representative sampling, particularly when the sample is not large. In both representative and random sampling, the test constructor must try to avoid collecting a sample that is biased (e.g., in relation to sex, socioeconomic status, or region of the country sampled). The failure to include racial minorities in the normative samples of several widely used intelligence tests has limited their usefulness.

Standardization

If the same test administered to different individuals is supposed to measure the same things, it is important that every test be administered in exactly the same way. A *standardized* test is one for which the instructions, administration procedures, materials, and scoring procedures are so explicit that it can be administered at virtually any time and in any place with comparable results. Standardization also involves the development of *norms* for interpreting scores. The test is administered to a large sample of people who under optimal conditions are representative of the population for whom the test will be used. There is often an attempt to obtain proportional representation of subgroups by sex, race, or age. The distribution of scores for the norm group serves as a standard against which any individual's score can be compared and interpreted.

Percentile scores are a useful way to rank an individual's performance. Percentile rank indicates what percentage of the group scored above and below a given person. One who scores in the middle of a distribution is at the 50th percentile. A person who scores at the 65th percentile is higher than 65 per-

cent (and lower than 35 percent) of those in the norm group.

INTELLIGENCE TESTS

Intelligence tests became at the turn of the century the first widely recognized psychological assessment tool, ancestors of today's college entrance examinations and other qualifying examinations.

Interest in measuring intelligence arose during the latter part of the nineteenth century. At that time testers relied heavily on sensory tests and other discrimination tasks. The English naturalist and mathematician Sir Francis Galton (1822–1911) tried to evaluate intelligence by measuring such variables as reaction time, the ability to discriminate between weights, sensitivity to pain, and the ability to differentiate among tones.

The Binet tests

While Galton's work was attracting much attention, Alfred Binet, a French psychologist, questioned the relationship between sensorimotor responses and understanding of intellectual functioning. He developed a series of tests that were noticeably different from those previously used to measure intelligence. He tried to measure reasoning, the ability to understand and follow directions, and the exercise of judgment. Although he did not stop measuring sensorimotor tasks, he deemphasized their role in constructing his intelligence tests. (See Box 14.2.) Some of the tasks included in the 1916 intelligence scale developed by Binet and Theodore Simon, another French psychologist, were recognizing objects in a picture, discriminating lines rapidly, completing sentences, defining simple words, repeating digits, and recalling seen objects.

Binet's work must be viewed within the context of a growing concern early in this century over questions about teaching methods and the proper placement of children in school classes. There was particularly strong interest in developing criteria for placing retarded children in special education programs. The rapid adoption of Binet's approach to intellectual assessment for this and other purposes led to numerous revisions, translations, and other versions of his original test. In the United States,

BOX 14.2

The contribution of Alfred Binet

Alfred Binet (1857–1911) not only helped to establish the field of intelligence testing, but also had a significant impact on the development of child psychology, education, and the study of mental retardation. A significant portion of Binet's early career was devoted to experimental psychology. This work gave him invaluable research experience and helped him realize that individual differences must be explored systematically before one can define laws that apply to all people.

Another factor in Binet's development was his role as a parent. He made careful observations of his two daughters, Alice and Madelaine, and reported not only on the way they learned to walk, but also on the way their personalities grew. Binet became very curious about developmental changes in particular ordinary daily activities and in the mental abilities characterizing particular ages. Initially, he defined intelligence in terms of perception and seemed to envision it as something very vague and general rather than as specific faculty or function.

As his interest in age and related behavioral changes grew, Binet began to explore a variety of individual difference variables. He constructed questionnaires to measure children's fears, lying, anger, and other characteristics. He was also drawn to problems concerning mental fatigue, the proper age to begin teaching reading, achievement tests, vision, and the proper posture for writing. He speculated about the nature of intelligence and began to see

Alfred Binet (1857–1911). (Culver)

the mental test as an incomplete, constantly evolving mechanism for making behavioral observations. He recognized that with changes in teaching methods, changes in memory, judgment, and reasoning would occur. He recognized also the role that personality, health, and attitudes played in both test scores and daily functioning.

Binet's professional career was a relatively short one, lasting only 30 years. At the time of his death he was still seeking to understand the human mind and personality. Among the giants in psychology, there are few equal to Alfred Binet in curiosity, inventiveness, and achievement.

Lewis Terman of Stanford University was instrumental in developing English versions of the Binet tests. Over the years, Terman not only revised the tests but also improved the sampling procedures used to gather normative data on them (Terman, 1916; Terman and Merrill, 1937, 1960). In 1972 a new set of norms was obtained.

The Stanford-Binet scales are the products of many years of effort by Terman and his associates. Binet defined the intelligence quotient (IQ) as mental age (MA; a mental age value is assigned to each item, then the mental ages for all items passed are added together) divided by chronological age (CA), and multiplied by 100. For Binet, IQ =

437

(MA/CA) × 100. (An IQ of 100 indicates that an individual is average for his or her age group.) In 1960 tables became available that permitted direct computation of IQ without this formula.

The use of Binet tests has declined, in part because the tasks on the Binet scales do not provide sufficiently reliable analyses of mental abilities in several areas (e.g., imaginative problem solving or word associations). But perhaps the most important reason for the decline in the use of the Binet scales is that they were designed primarily for work with children. Although they are still generally regarded as valuable tools for this purpose, other tests that are versatile and easier to administer have replaced them, especially at the adolescent and adult levels.

The Wechsler tests

The major competitor of the Stanford-Binet test in the United States is the set of scales originally developed in the 1930s by David Wechsler. He stressed

A subject being administered the Block Design Subtest of the Wechsler Adult Intelligence Scale. (The Psychological Corporation)

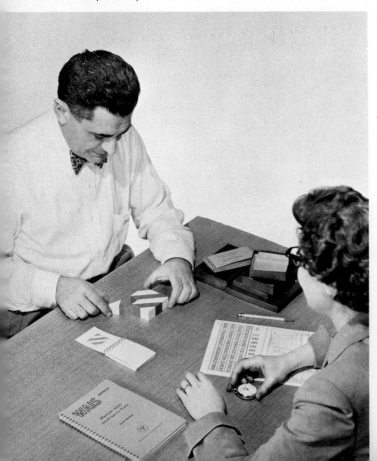

that intelligence is simply a concept or construct that cannot be touched or seen:

> Unfortunately, the problem with which psychologists are concerned in defining intelligence is quite different from that which the physicist deals with when he defines amperes, farads, and watts, or the biologist when he classifies living things as plants and animals. The difficulty involved is similar to what the physicist encounters when asked to state what he means by life. The fact is that energy and life are not tangible entities but limiting constructs. You cannot touch them or see them under a microscope even though you are able to describe them. We know them by their effects or properties. The same is true of general intelligence. It is not a material fact but an abstract construct. What we can reasonably expect of any attempt at definition is only a sufficiently clear and broad connotation as to what it comprehends. Mind you, not what it is but what it involves and eventually, what it distinguishes. (Wechsler, 1958, p. 4)

Wechsler thought Binet-type tests were deficient because they produced only a single score. Intelligence, he believed, could better be measured as a group of abilities. A revision of Wechsler's original work, the *Wechsler Adult Intelligence Scale* (WAIS), consists of 11 subtests, 6 of which are verbal and 5 of which are nonverbal. In addition to being able to add up points for the entire test, one can also score each of the subtests separately. This permits scorers to analyze *patterns* of subtest scores. Three IQs are obtained with Wechsler-type scales: a Verbal IQ, which reflects level of attainment on subtests dealing with general information, attention and rote memory, comprehension, ability to think in abstract terms, and arithmetic; a Performance IQ, which reflects level of attainment on tasks requiring the solution of tasks such as puzzles, the substitution of symbols for digits, and the reproduction, with blocks, of designs (see Box 14.3); and a Full-Scale IQ, the total score. Wechsler's adult intelligence scales were so successful that in 1949 the *Wechsler Intelligence Scale for Children* (WISC) was introduced. In 1967 the *Wechsler Preschool and Primary Scale of Intelligence* (WPPSI) was published. The Wechsler tests are today the most widely used individually administered tests for intelligence.

For both Wechsler and Binet the IQ was simply a convenient way of summarizing a person's level of attainment on a given test relative to a norm group.

BOX 14.3
Wechsler performance tests

The following items are similar to those included in one version of Wechsler performance measures. In picture arrangement (a) the task is to place the pictures in logical order. In object assembly (b) subjects must assemble the pieces to form an object. In each picture completion item (c) there is an omitted detail or feature that the subject must name. The digit symbol subtest (d) requires that the subject learn a code.

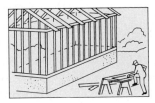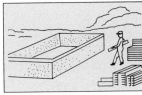

a. Picture arrangement

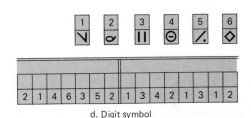

b. Object assembly c. Picture completion d. Digit symbol

Table 14.1 indicates the percentages in the population that fall within certain IQ ranges on the Stanford-Binet. It is important to realize that scores on different intelligence tests (e.g., the Stanford-Binet and one of Wechsler's tests) while positively correlated are not interchangeable because of different methods of test construction and different norm groups.

The Binet and Wechsler tests are widely used as measures of intelligence, but there are many other tests available designed to fit a variety of needs. For example, special nonverbal performance tests have been developed to measure intellectual functioning among the deaf, persons with certain types of neurological damage, and those who do not speak English. Various group tests measuring abilities and attitudes are available for mass testing. These tests do not permit the tester to observe the behavior of an individual directly, but they do provide a convenient method for obtaining test scores. Group tests are used to estimate students' ability levels, to make

Table 14.1 Percentages of population in various Stanford-Binet IQ ranges

IQ	Percentage in Groups	Characterization
Above 139	1	Very superior
120–139	11	Superior
110–119	18	High average
90–109	46	Average
80–89	15	Low average
70–79	6	Borderline
Below 70	3	Mentally retarded
	100	

439

decisions regarding the admission of college students, to select employees, and in research to divide subjects into groups of equal ability in order to compare different methods of instruction or to study the effects of motivation.

Social issues in intelligence testing

Major decisions are often based on tests of general and specific abilities. The label *mentally retarded* may be attached to children in part on the basis of their scores on a standardized intelligence test. Whether or not an individual is considered to be college material may be determined by his or her scores on a general ability test. In several European countries the scores received by 10- and 11-year-old children determine whether or not they can realistically hope ever to enter a university. (See Box 14.4.)

Despite advances in constructing and standardizing intelligence tests, they are still controversial, primarily because they play such an influential role in many decisions, and there is a lack of agreement about the definition of intelligence. Controversy also centers around important social issues.

The issue of culture bias

It is difficult to compare the intellectual performance of various groups of people because their experiences and cultural surroundings vary. Although some researchers have tried to develop "culture-free" tests to avoid discriminating against those who are not from their own middle-class background, they found that it was impossible to separate cultural experience from skills and abilities. When the content of many items was modified to deemphasize certain kinds of information and skills, the usefulness of the tests as predicting devices seriously declined. The emphasis then shifted to "culture-fair" tests that would minimize cultural influences in various ways and still serve as valuable predictors. One way to make a text "culture-fair" is to select items that involve objects or concepts that span all socioeconomic groups. For example, in a question about similarities, instead of asking:

Which is most similar to *xylophone?*
violin, tuba, drum, marimba, piano

the question could ask:

This is a popular method of fishing in Fiji. If a child from Fiji were asked a question about fishing on a standardized American Intelligence test, he or she might be totally baffled by the response choices. (Hatton, Woodfin Camp)

Which is most similar to *bus?*
car, truck, airplane, trailer

The second question would be a better measure of reasoning ability among all groups of urban children because more of them would be more familiar with all the basic concepts than with the concepts in the first questions.

Another way to make a test more culture-fair is to remove the effect of certain factors that the test is not intended to measure, such as past experience. For example, if a task involves using blocks to copy designs from a card, subjects who see a number of demonstrations and have practice trials may be able to perform as well as those whose backgrounds included training in this area.

We tend to think of culture bias as a problem most common to industrialized countries with minority populations. But in fact the problem is even more acute in the Third World nations. The number of educational opportunities in these countries is severely limited by the economy, and cultural and academic backgrounds vary much more among individuals than they do in the United States (Drenth, 1975).

Interpreting the IQ

The first intelligence tests were devised to predict academic success and to permit children with similar abilities to be grouped together. Unfortunately, this system had its problems. There were children who had tested poorly and were placed in the "slow" group in school, although in fact their intelligence was well above average. There were disadvantaged children whose academic potential seemed limited because there was little intellectual stimulation in the home. Intelligence tests provided reliable, but not perfect, information about an individual's general ability level at the time of testing. But they did not explain why someone had a low IQ score or whether the score would increase if certain environmental or educational changes were made. Figure 14.1 shows the scores obtained by three subjects in a longitudinal study of intellectual development. The wide variability at age 2 is not surprising because intelligence tests constructed for very young children are much less reliable than those for older groups, and they also measure mostly nonverbal skills. Although

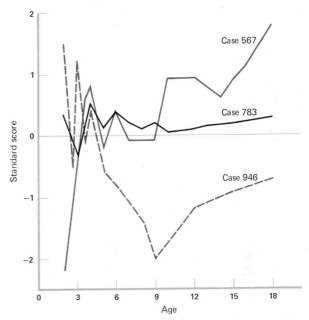

Figure 14.1 Records made by three children on successive mental tests. (From Honzik et al., 1948.)

the IQs of all subjects are nearly equal at 4 years of age, they become increasingly diverse over the years. Case studies of individuals with pronounced changes in IQ suggest that the changes tend to be associated with significant changes in opportunities to learn and in an individual's personal life.

IQ tests differ in content, scoring, and other ways that affect the interpretation of their scores. Scores on intelligence tests might better be regarded as descriptive indexes rather than as explanatory concepts. An IQ is an expression of an individual's ability level at one particular time, in relation to norms for other individuals of the same age. We have seen that IQs are not fixed and unchanging, and that they measure a variety of abilities. In some instances they reflect to a significant degree the personality of the individual tested. (See Box 14.5.)

An individual's relative ability tends to increase with age for functions valued by the culture or subculture, and to decrease with age for functions not valued by the culture. Most intelligence tests are actually measures of scholastic aptitude. Because the skills taught in the educational system are of basic importance in our culture, the IQ is also an effective

441

BOX 14.4
Tests and suicides in West German children

Dozens of West German children have committed suicide as a result of anxiety over the implications of relatively poor performance on written tests and in school courses. The following article describes the general problem that exists.

> The heart of the problem appears to lie in West Germany's punishing system of preselection for higher education. As early as age 10, a child faces a grueling series of written tests that determine whether he can prepare for university admission at a "gymnasium," or whether he must settle for a general education and confront the ever-tighter job market in his late teens. Today, both options are increasingly bleak. There are now 120,000 under-18s out of school and jobless—and the number is growing. Moreover, chances of getting into a university with anything short of top marks are perilously slim. As a result, 9-year-olds regularly put in up to ten hours of classwork and preparation a day. "School is awful," says one Hamburg 11-year-old. "My head hurts all the time." (*Newsweek*, International Edition, March 8, 1976, p. 16)

predictor of performance in many occupations and other activities in adult life. However, there are certain important abilities that intelligence tests have never tried to measure (e.g., the ability to survive in an urban ghetto).

Some school districts have banned IQ tests completely on the grounds that labeling a child as unintelligent creates a terrible stigma that is practically impossible to overcome. Intelligence tests have been misused at times and some people have been harmed by them. But these are problems of application rather than problems with the tests themselves.

Poor performance on tests of intellectual ability

may be caused by a variety of factors, including personality. Jerome Kagan of Harvard University has investigated one factor: the tendency to respond to problems without reflecting on alternative possibilities. *Reflective* children weigh the relative merits of alternative responses; *impulsive* children do not. Differences in these qualities have been observed as early as 2 years of age. Whether we view the tendency to be either reflective or impulsive as a component of intelligence or as a personality trait that influences intelligent behavior, it is clear that this tendency, as well as other aspects of personality, should be integrated into research on intelligence.

When they are used correctly intelligence tests can be valuable in identifying strengths and weaknesses in verbal facility, ability to handle quantitative relationships, and various kinds of problem-solving skills. Nevertheless, there is a need for more research on the construction of intelligence tests, their standardization, and the criteria they use. Research is also needed on how such factors as the atmosphere in the testing situation and the subject's socioeconomic level influence performance. But perhaps the greatest need is for new information about the nature of intelligence, a topic to which we now turn

THE NATURE OF INTELLIGENCE

The study of intelligence is one area in which technological progress seems to have outstripped theory. Sometimes scores on intelligence tests correlate with such criteria as progress in school and ability to perform certain types of tasks. But what, exactly, do these tests measure? What is intelligence? When we describe one person as more intelligent than another, what do we mean?

According to one theory, intelligence is an innate capacity, which is transmitted through the genes. A second theory argues that intelligence is primarily the product of cultural exposure and conditioning. A third theory defines intelligence simply by the scores obtained on intelligence tests.

Some theorists believe that there is one dominating intellectual trait (a general, or "g," factor) that determines ability in all areas. Others believe that different kinds of problems or situations require

BOX 14.5

The Process of intelligent thinking: A psychological frontier

Research such as that dealing with the tendency to be reflective and thoughtful or impulsive underscores the fact that a score on a test is merely an end product, the outcome of a complex chain of events. Psychologists are trying to assess not only that end product but also the steps that come before it. In order to do this they must first determine what those steps are.

From the work on reflectiveness and impulsiveness we know that impulsive responses to problems are often incorrect. In addition, some individuals seem to lack the ability to think critically because their attention is directed to extraneous thoughts; others do not pay enough attention to all the facts mentioned in the problem. Some have a poor memory for facts after they have read them; others have difficulty relating the problem to knowledge that might be useful in helping them find a solution. Some cannot plan well, so that their thought patterns are muddled.

Many of these problems can be corrected through training and mental exercises. Psychologists are working to move from simply assessing intelligence and aptitude to developing bases for rational educational planning using the results from intelligence testing (Whimbey and Whimbey, 1975).

Woody Allen, noted humorist, actor, and director, is also a fine clarinet player who performs often in a New York night club. Do these many talents reflect a "g" factor or distinctive abilities? (Harris, Photo Trends)

reasonable; in fact, the debate as to whether there is one factor that determines intelligence in all areas or whether there are many factors is centuries old. There are solid arguments to support both positions.

There is an interesting international difference concerning theories of intelligence. English psychologists prefer the concept of general intelligence whereas American researchers prefer the theory that there are multiple abilities with more or less equal status and influence. For example, in the 1930s the American L. L. Thurstone (1938) developed a battery of tests to measure seven "primary mental abilities:"

Spatial ability
Perceptual speed
Numerical ability
Verbal meaning
Memory
Verbal fluency
Inductive reasoning

separate, distinctive kinds of intelligence. Still others argue that both general intelligence and specific abilities must be employed in varying degrees for various tasks. (See Box 14.6.) All these possibilities seem

BOX 14.6

A knock on the head

Liam Hudson is one of England's leading psychologists who works in the area of intelligence. In his autobiographical book *The Cult of the Fact* Hudson tells the following anecdote to illustrate the multifaceted nature of intellectual ability.

> My concern with intelligence has an identifiable if inauspicious source; in a knock on the head I received, or thought I received, whilst playing rugby in the army during my National Service. This knock resulted in loss of memory and persistent headaches; and the latter I carried with me to Oxford. On failing my first examination there I was put through the screening procedures devised by the local mental hospital for the university's mentally disturbed students. My intelligence was tested. I completed the Thematic Apperception Test and the Minnesota Multiphasic Personality Inventory, and my physique was measured in various ways. Gradually, the headaches disappeared of their own accord; I passed my examination at second attempt; and was left with an odd item of information about myself: that I possessed a bias of intelligence in marked degree. Tactfully, the psychologist at the Warneford Hospital told me that my facility with words was "rather below average" for an Oxford undergraduate; but that I was good with shapes and patterns. (Hudson, 1972, pp. 57–58)

More recently, J. P. Guilford (1967) of the University of Southern California developed an intellect model that classified abilities according to content (whether they are figural, symbolic [involving letters, numbers, words], or semantic [involving meaningful ideas]); the basic psychological operations they involve (cognition, memory, evaluation, original or analytical thought); and their products, the forms of information they produce (such as a set of relationships, transformations, classes, or systems). Figure 14.2 is a schematic picture of Guilford's model. Although the reader need not be concerned

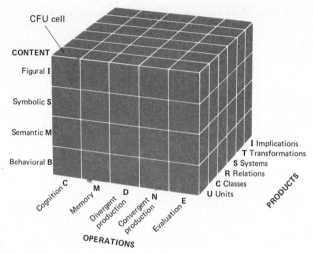

Figure 14.2 Guilford's model of intellect. (Based on Guilford, 1967, p. 63.)

with the details of the model, Guilford's model does reflect the complex nature of intellectual abilities. He and his associates have been working for more than 25 years to measure a large number of specific abilities included within the structure of the model. For example, a test designed to measure the ability represented by cell CMR would test the semantic ability to sense relations between words. A test to measure the behavioral ability represented by cell CBR would include items that display pictures of faces, gestures, postures.

Heredity and environmental influences

One controversy in psychology that has generated much research and few hard conclusions deals with the relative roles of heredity and environment in intelligence. There is some evidence that heredity does affect intelligence. For example, studies of identical twins reared in different environments show that their IQs are highly similar. The IQs of members of the same family, even if living apart, are also more similar than those of unrelated people, although the relationship is not as close as that between identical twins.

During the past ten years the controversy has been heightened by the difficulties of such social programs as Head Start, which were designed to improve the school performance of children from socioeconomically disadvantaged backgrounds.

Mental retardation

Most experts define mental retardation as a level of intellectual functioning that is significantly below the average. Although most people perform poorly on occasion because they are anxious, preoccupied, or sleepy, it is clear that they could perform better under more favorable circumstances. Mentally retarded individuals, however, function at a low level that does not appear to be attributable to such fac-

A child afflicted with Down syndrome. Such children are considered capable of learning at a much slower rate than normal children. (Lebo, Jeroboam)

tors. Mental retardation is usually evident early in life, when a child cannot pass developmental hurdles that most children pass.

About 3 percent of the population of the United States is mentally retarded. The following are the five levels of retardation listed by the American Association on Mental Deficiency and the IQ ranges roughly associated with them:

1. Borderline mental retardation, IQ 68–83
2. Mild mental retardation, IQ 52–67
3. Moderate mental retardation, IQ 36–51
4. Severe mental retardation, IQ 20–35
5. Profound mental retardation, IQ under 20

Intelligence does not necessarily correspond to social effectiveness. Some individuals test very low but still have the skills they need to live within the community. However, if individuals both test low and seem socially incompetent, then they are usually considered mentally retarded. Of course, this classification is most reliable when both their intellectual and social development appear to have been retarded since early childhood.

The determinants of mental retardation

The determinants of almost any type of complex behavior are likely to be complex. Yet the question of causation in the case of mental retardation is often posed in either-or terms: Is retardation caused by physiological defect or by the effects of environmental forces on a developing individual? In certain cases specific causes can be isolated. In others gross environmental defects seem to be a cause. But in a large number of instances no single cause can be identified. Just as the term *psychosis* is a broad concept that encompasses a variety of different bizarre response patterns, so also is *mental retardation* a term that encompasses a variety of behavioral deficiencies.

Biological factors. One rather common type of retardation is caused by a chromosomal abnormality. The problem is known as the Down syndrome, or mongolism. There are several characteristic physical symptoms for this syndrome, including very delicate skin, a protruding belly, and smaller than normal hands and feet. The eyes slant up and outward, the face is broad and flattened, and instead of the whorls found on the fingerprints there are loops. Most of

445

these individuals have IQs below 50. They are often extremely placid, cheerful, and cooperative. The Down syndrome is difficult to diagnose in infants but it becomes increasingly more recognizable in older children. The life expectancy of this group is short. A high percentage of them are born to mothers over 40 years of age. In 1959, French geneticist Jerome Lejeune and his co-workers discovered that these children have 47 rather than the usual 46 chromosomes. At present, Down syndrome patients comprise about 10 percent of the patients in institutions for the retarded.

Social and cultural factors. The overwhelming majority of mentally retarded individuals do not have detectable biological defects and come from society's lowest socioeconomic groups. One estimate is that the frequency of mental retardation among the poor is between 10 and 30 percent, whereas the frequency is less than 3 percent among the general population. However, the picture is not the same for all types of retardation. The severely retarded are normally distributed among all social classes, but the mildly retarded are predominantly from the lower social classes.

Poverty may contribute to the causes of mental retardation that we have already mentioned. Poor women are less likely to receive adequate medical attention and nutrition during pregnancy and birth than wealthier ones. Complications during pregnancy, birth injuries, premature births, and malnutrition have all been linked to retardation. More recently a host of other conditions that are often associated with poverty have been correlated with intellectual and social performance. These conditions include overcrowding, lack of stimulation and encouragement, unattended emotional problems, and an atmosphere of defeat. We do not yet know precisely how or whether these conditions affect intellectual development, but experiments with animals have shown that the environment can influence physical characteristics, such as the actual weight of the cerebral cortex.

Attitudes toward the retarded, as well as methods for treatment and care, have changed over the years. Public schools are currently expanding their programs for the retarded with the hope of preventing institutionalization. Psychotherapy has been used to

446

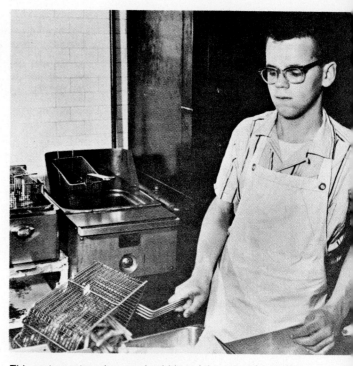

This restaurant worker received his training when he participated in a special community-based program for retarded persons judged to be potentially employable. (Tacoma Goodwill Industries)

encourage self-development in some retarded individuals, but the use of learning principles, particularly those of operant conditioning, seems to be especially effective with large numbers of retarded individuals.

Racial differences in intelligence

In 1969 and 1973 psychologist Arthur Jensen concluded that there was a genetic basis for the difficulties that black children had in school:

In view of all the most relevant evidence which I have examined, the most tenable hypothesis, in my judgment, is that genetic, as well as environmental, differences are involved in the average disparity between American Negroes and whites in intelligence and educability, as here defined. All the major facts would seem to be comprehended quite well by the hypothesis that something between one-half and three-fourths of the average IQ difference between American Negroes and whites is attributable to genetic factors, and the remainder to environmental factors and their interaction with the genetic differences. (Jensen, 1969, p. 363)

Jensen's conclusions, backed by H. J. Eysenk (1971), a prominent British psychologist, caused great shock waves on both sides of the Atlantic. Here was a view that seemed to lend support to the prejudice reformers and liberals had been trying to remove. Some feared this theory would be used as an excuse to stop efforts to improve social conditions and educational programs.

Among those rejecting the theory was William S. Schoenfeld, who made the following comments in a presidential address to the Eastern Psychological Association:

It must be clear that our culture's pocketful of assumptions and attitudes is far removed from the realities of experience that have made the child what he is as he stands before a school psychologist, offering a sample of his present behavior and awaiting assignment to a class. How did he get there? How many influences have shaped his test performance? Or the difference between his performance and another child's? Since tests are inventories of behavior, are they not built up in any individual by the operation of laws of learning, the laws of behavior acquisition? Even as an inventory, a test's adequacy for evaluating an individual depends on how well the laws of learning were applied when he was exposed—if he was exposed—to the stimulus materials and the behaviors the test draws from. Our rush into deductions about his "intelligence" and about "limits" on his learning may be more symptomatic of our own history than of the child's.

. . . The idea of "race differences in intelligence" is nonsense. Nonsense in the framing of the question, nonsense in the populations tested, nonsense in the instrument used, nonsense in the "intelligence" that is postulated. The theme is pure fabrication, an example of spinning a discussion out of nothing but linguistically open categories and cultural fantasies. To me it appears that we ought to stop reacting to the idea of intelligence differences. (Schoenfeld, 1974, pp. 30, 32)

One of the problems in discussing racial differences in intelligence is the fact that race is not a purely biological concept. Although the members of different racial groups may have very different appearances, differences in gene structure are in most cases relatively small. There are variations among human populations in the frequency of gene-based diseases and also in the frequency of various protein and blood group genes. It is therefore possible that there could be differences in the frequency of one or several genes that affect intellectual performance. Certainly the field is a legitimate one for research. However, it is one thing to point out what is conceivable and quite another to assume that particular racial differences, independent of environmental factors, actually exist.

John Loehlin and his colleagues (Loehlin et al., 1975) took a middle position in this controversy and suggested that observed average differences in the scores of members of different U.S. racial-ethnic groups are a reflection of three important factors: inadequacies and biases in the tests themselves, differences in environmental conditions among groups, and genetic differences among groups. These three factors are not necessarily independent, and may interact. Moreover, the factors may have different degrees of importance for different groups. Most importantly, the differences among individuals *within* racial-ethnic (and socioeconomic) groups are much greater than the average differences *between* such groups.

Those who accept this position are trying to gather more information and to implement new programs in those areas we can change: testing and environmental conditions. They are trying to devise effective educational programs, to determine the ages at which children should begin these programs, and to assess the need to continue special educational programs throughout a child's educational career for certain groups of children. They feel that there is a crucial need to foster intellectual and socioeconomic advances among disadvantaged groups.

Sex differences

Another issue in the heredity versus environment controversy is sex differences. The distributions of scores for males and females on intelligence tests are not identical. There is a wider range of scores among men than among women. Girls and women tend to score higher on verbal tests and usually do better than boys and men on tests that involve short-term memory, speed, and deftness. Boys and men score higher in arithmetic and on tests that involve vis-

447

ual-spatial skills. Research is needed to determine whether these differences have a biological basis or whether they are the product of sex role training.

Intelligence and creativity

Concepts of intelligence refer to mental abilities and individual differences related to them. Can the standard concepts of intelligence account for the abilities of an Einstein, a Beethoven, or a Van Gogh? Are "giftedness" and "creativity" different from ordinary intelligence? Some theorists argue that creativity can be accounted for in terms of a given set of intellective abilities; others insist that it involves very special mechanisms.

At one time psychologists were fascinated by the concept of creative genius. Lewis Terman, who developed Binet's original work into the Stanford-Binet intelligence test, defined genius by the presence of a very high IQ. In 1950 Guilford suggested that creativity and intelligence are far from the same thing and urged scientific study of creative thought. Since 1950 research on creativity has grown rapidly, although there is still little agreement about the definition of creativity.

Although she hardly ever used the word *creativity* in her writings, Ann Roe's (1952, 1953) studies of exceptionally able and productive people helped to stimulate current thinking about intelligence and creativity. She worked with small groups of middle-aged male scientists cited by their peers as outstanding in their respective fields. She interviewed these men, recorded their life histories, and gave them intelligence and personality tests. Some scored high on tests of verbal, mathematical, and spatial relations abilities, but many did only as well as, or worse than, the average of a sample of graduate students. Roe's research showed that these eminent scientists were strongly motivated to achieve in situations that called for independence in thought and action, but unlike less creative individuals, they did not strive for achievement in settings in which conformity was expected or required.

Unfortunately, Roe did not use suitable control groups in her studies. We cannot conclude, for example, that the independence displayed by so many of her subjects is characteristic only of eminent scientists; it might be an attribute of most research scientists, regardless of their achievements.

Years later, Donald MacKinnon (1962, 1967) performed a series of studies to pick up where Roe had left off. In his best-known study he compared three groups of male architects whose levels of creativity, as rated by their peers, were quite different. Like Roe, MacKinnon found that the creative architects were independent thinkers and tended to be self-sufficient. He concluded that, given the minimal level of intelligence required to master a body of knowledge, nonintellectual factors, such as personality, determine whether or not an individual will perform creatively. (See Box 14.7.)

MacKinnon's work, along with the work of Roe and others, has shown that intelligence tests alone are not effective in identifying individuals who are capable of making innovative contributions.

Divergent thinking and brainstorming

Many researchers have approached the study of creativity by attempting to analyze the thought patterns that give rise to creative ideas. One such pattern is *divergent thinking*, or generating a number of possible solutions to a problem. The Unusual Uses test measures the capacity for divergent thinking. It asks individuals to list as many uses as they can think of for some commonplace item, such as an empty tin can or a brick. Some researchers argue that tests that measure divergent thinking measure different capacities from conventional tests of mental ability. Although this is probably partly true, there may also be considerable overlap.

One important factor in divergent thinking seems to be the individual's willingness to lower his or her threshold for ideas worth considering. In this sense divergent thinkers are conceptually less inhibited than other people. *Brainstorming* is a group procedure for problem solving that is aimed at lowering this threshold for all people.

Brainstorming groups usually consist of from five to ten people. Group members are encouraged to suspend judgments about their ideas and an effort is made to instill them with a spirit of enthusiasm so that they will spark ideas in others. No evaluation of any kind is permitted, so that the emphasis is on generating ideas and not on defending and criticizing them.

Brainstorming has at times been criticized as a shallow, even questionable, way of generating origi-

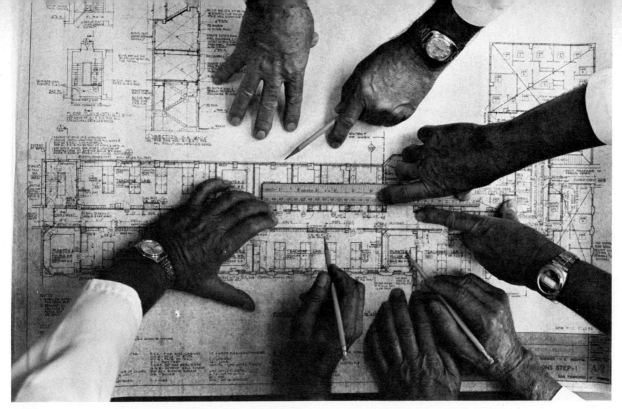

Brainstorming can be used at many points in the development of a project. (Powers, Jeroboam)

nal ideas. Yet it merits study because very little is known about which conditions are especially conducive to originality. Although originality cannot be equated with productivity, usefulness, or excellence, stimulating original ideas may very well lead to practical ends.

PERSONALITY ASSESSMENT

As we have seen, intelligence tests do not tell the whole story about an individual. Many procedures are used today, often in combination, in the search for a well-rounded picture of any individual.

Personality refers to the collection of attributes, dispositions, and tendencies that makes up a single individual. Personality assessors seek to make accurate, useful statements about these characteristics. Some assessment instruments have grown out of researchers' intuitive ideas about the major determinants of behavior; others have grown out of available empirical information (e.g., test items that seem to be reliable and valid). Some assessments may be quite impersonal and may not even require direct observation of the individual under study. For example, those that concern an individual's childhood experiences and medical and educational histories do not require direct contact.

Usually when researchers develop a procedure such as a test, they have in mind certain methods for assessing its validity or usefulness. Tests are often constructed to answer specific practical questions. For example, the personnel department of an insurance company might find a test that could predict the success of insurance salespeople very useful. The test might be given to salespeople already employed by the company, and the scores could then be compared with the amount of insurance they sold during a particular time period. The amount of insurance would serve as a criterion or standard for judging the effectiveness of the insurance salespeople. If the test were valid, high scorers would sell the most insurance. Correlations could be made between test scores and other criteria as well in order to assess the test's validity. Validity, in this instance, would be judged in accordance with whether a test did the job that had been assigned to it.

A researcher may have a very clear idea of what is to be measured, such as the amount of insurance an individual has sold, how long an individual might be expected to live, or how resistant an individual is to communicable diseases. In such a case the procedure for defining an individual difference variable, determining its reliability, and judging its validity by correlating it with criteria is relatively uncomplicated.

Often the characteristic measured is believed to influence behavior in a range of situations. In this case the test would be designed to measure a *construct*, a general personality characteristic (e.g., submissiveness). Whereas an insurance company might be interested primarily in the sales records of its sales

449

BOX 14.7

Conditions for creativity

There is reason to believe that a high level of intelligence is only one of the ingredients of creativity. A driving force, an urge to create, along with total absorption in a particular idea or problem also play important roles. What role do environmental conditions (living arrangements, social relationships, etc.) play in encouraging or stifling creative achievements?

Here is Mozart's description of the process of musical composition:

When I am, as it were, completely myself, entirely alone, and of good cheer—say, travelling in a carriage, or walking after a good meal, or during the night when I cannot sleep; it is on such occasions that my ideas flow best and most abundantly. *Whence* and *how* they come, I know not; nor can I force them.

. . .

When I proceed to write down my ideas, I take out of the bag of my memory, if I may use that phrase, what has been previously collected into it in the way I have mentioned. For this reason the committing to paper is done quickly enough, for everything is, as I have said before, already finished; and it rarely differs on paper from what it was in my imagination. (E. Holmes, *The Life of Mozart,* including his correspondence. London: Chapman & Hall, 1878, as quoted in Pickering, 1974, pp. 273–274)

Henri Poincaré (1854–1912) was one of the greatest mathematicians of modern times. This is his account of his solution to a problem concerning what are known as Fuchsian functions:

For fifteen days I strove to prove that there could not be any functions. I was then very ignorant; every day I seated myself at my work table, stayed an hour or two, tried a great number of combinations and reached no results. One evening, contrary to my custom, I drank black coffee and could not sleep. Ideas rose in crowds; I felt them collide until pairs interlocked, so to speak, making a stable combination. By the next morning I had established the existence of a class of Fuchsian functions, those which come from the hypergeometric series; I had only to write out the results, which took but a few hours. (Poincaré, 1924)

personnel, a psychologist who studies a personality characteristic must observe behavior in a wide variety of situations. The process of integrating observations pertaining to the characteristic is called *construct validation.* Researchers construct hypotheses about test behavior and verify them using objective procedures, such as experiments. Box 14.8 illustrates the development of a personality test and the assessment of its construct validity.

There are several ways of measuring personality, ranging from asking the person to describe himself or herself, to giving tests, to making behavioral observations. We now take up some of these methods.

The interview

Interviews are designed for gathering information in a conversational setting. They are used for diagnostic, therapeutic, and research purposes, and inter-

viewing techniques range from informal interchanges to well-organized series of specific questions designed to elicit specific responses. *Diagnostic interviews* are designed to gather information about problems or complaints (See Box 14.9.) On the basis of the interviewee's verbal and nonverbal behavior, the interviewer draws conclusions about the problem. *Therapeutic interviews* are designed to allow patients to talk about problems they would normally keep to themselves so that the therapist and patient can work together to solve them. *Research interviews* are often designed to gather specific pieces of information needed to test an hypothesis. This information might relate to the interviewee's family, recreational interests, opinions, and attitudes.

Good interviewers do not limit their attention to what the interviewee says. In the course of an interview they note the interviewee's general appearance

Kamikaze (suicide mission) pilots were carefully selected by the Japanese military during World War II. The American military often used personality assessment procedures to select persons for dangerous, stressful assignments. (UPI)

BOX 14.8

Assessing submissiveness: An example of construct validity

Suppose for a moment that you were an investigator who hypothesized that submissiveness is a tendency to yield to the will and suggestion of others. How would you go about testing the hypothesis? First, you would have to assume that there is a variable that determines individual differences in the tendency to be submissive. You would try to construct a test or index of the variable so that you could place subjects on a submissiveness scale. There are several types of tests that you might construct: true-false, multiple choice, projective. For example, you might test for submissiveness by asking persons to rate how much they yield to the will of others in different types of situations. Whichever type you selected, you would have to do some trial-and-error exploration. You would have to make sure that the test was reliable and that it could be administered under standardized conditions.

Your next major task would be to validate the construct underlying the test: your original hypothesis about submissiveness. One way to do this would be to conduct experiments in which you expected individuals who are high and low in submissiveness

to behave differently. In comparing performances under these conditions, you would have to demonstrate that the differences could not be attributed to such variables as intelligence or sex. You would do this by comparing the behavior not only of subjects with different submissiveness scores, but also of subjects who differed on other variables, such as intelligence and sex.

No single experiment would establish the construct validity of your test. However, if the test did predict the subjects' behavior accurately in a variety of situations, then you would know that your construct did have some degree of validity. If individuals with high scores on the submissiveness test conformed more than low scorers under social pressure, if they followed orders more willingly, and if they objected less frequently to insults directed toward them, you would have made an encouraging start on the construct validation of your test.

Of course, you could not reasonably expect your submissiveness scale to be accurate for every situation that might involve submissive behavior. High scorers might be very submissive in certain situations (those involving bosses), slightly submissive in others (those involving peers), and perhaps even dominant under certain conditions (those involving marriage partners). Individuals with the same submissiveness scores who differ in intelligence or socioeconomic status might also behave in different ways in different situations. It is hoped that in testing the construct validity of your scale, you could increase your knowledge of the specific ways in which personality variables and situational variables interact to influence behaviors.

---

and grooming, voice and speech patterns, content of his or her thoughts, and his or her facial expressions and posture.

They must recognize and note all the reactions they have not anticipated. Experienced interviewers are skilled at observing behaviors that interviewees either believe they are hiding successfully or that they are unaware of themselves. The following record of an interview demonstrates this skill.

During the interview she held her small son on her lap. The child began to play with his genitals. The mother, without looking directly at the child, moved his hand away and held it securely for a while. . . . Later in the interview the mother was asked what she ordinarily did when the child played with himself? She replied that he never did this—he was a very "good" boy. She was evidently entirely unconscious of what had transpired in the very presence of the interviewer. (Maccoby and Maccoby, 1954, p. 484)

BOX 14.9

Excerpt from a diagnostic interview

The following is an excerpt from a diagnostic interview between a clinical psychologist and a 38-year-old woman. Note the psychologist's efforts to gauge how depressed the client is and whether she has considered suicide (psychologist = P, client = C).

P: You said earlier that since your father died in 1957 you haven't been happy at all. Could you tell me more about that?

C: Well, there's not much to tell. I was very close to him and I keep thinking of all the nice things I could have done for him—and with him—that I never did. That's hard to live with. If I could only stop thinking about "What might have been." (*pause*)

P: How sad, how blue do you feel?

C: Right this minute I don't feel so depressed—but at times, at times I wonder what life is all about and what the purpose of my life is. I also wonder about why, if I'm so upset about things I didn't do for my father, why I'm not nicer to my mother. Actually, I feel very angry towards her sometimes. I wonder why?

P: When you are experiencing depression, what is it like? What goes on?

C: A lot of the time my mind is blank. Not much is happening. I'm of course terribly sad. One thought that recurs is the question: why should I live? (*pause*)

P: Where does that question lead you?

C: Well, the idea of taking my life has occurred to me—but I always reject it. While I'm unhappy and see no purpose in life now, I guess in the back of my mind I've got the hope or wish or fantasy that things might get better some time.

Experienced interviewers must bear in mind that the person being interviewed either may not understand or may resist the purpose behind the interview. Interviewees state facts, opinions, and attitudes; and in some cases they distort facts and lie. They may behave in a variety of ways—sigh, gesture, avert their eyes, tap their feet, and smile or grimace at the interviewer. Interviewers can extract and use only a small percentage of this information.

In addition, interviewees may be defensive and hesitate to discuss personal opinions, attitudes, and concerns openly. Interviewers must estimate the degree to which the interviewees' desire to place themselves in a socially desirable light may invalidate some or all of their responses.

Content analysis of interview data

Making order out of spontaneous responses in interviews can be a complicated task, and some researchers have given up on trying to quantify these data. But although it may not be possible to quantify all the emotional overtones in verbal communications, it is possible to categorize and count many factors in a response. The categories used in a particular content analysis depend upon the researcher's interests and ingenuity. They should be ones that can be used with high agreement (reliability) by content analyzers.

Edward Murray (1954) wanted to find out if the scores from a content analysis of verbal expression reflected changes in a patient's behavior during psychotherapy. Murray chose the case of a young college graduate who sought help because of a fear that he might die while he was asleep. Murray hypothesized that the patient's problem was the result of a strong, consciously experienced anxiety that was in turn related to strong hostile tendencies and inadequate defenses. Murray studied two verbal categories: hostile statements and defensive statements. For each therapy session he tabulated the frequencies of hostile expressions that the patient made about important others, such as his mother, his aunt, and the therapist. He also tabulated the frequency of statements in which the patient used intellectualization and preoccupation with health as defenses, statements in which he expressed his views concerning philosophy, current events, and his body. Figure 14.3 shows the frequency of hostile and defensive state-

453

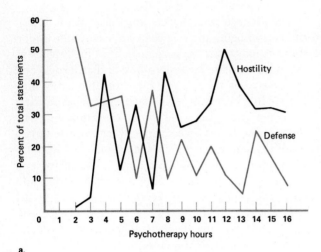

a.

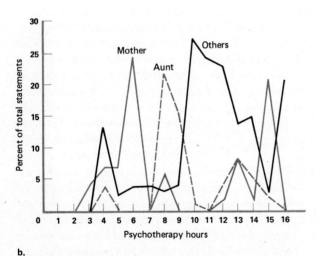

b.

Figure 14.3 (a) Percentage of hostile and defensive statements throughout therapy of a young college graduate. (b) Hostile statements toward mother, aunt, and others made by a young college graduate during therapy. It seems clear that he changed the target for his hostility considerably as therapy proceeded. (After Murray, 1954. Copyright 1954 by the American Psychological Association. Reprinted by permission.)

ments over 16 sessions. The curves show that the hostility statements increased and that the defensive statements decreased. Murray hypothesized that as therapy proceeded, the patient found that he could deal more comfortably and directly with his hostility and be less rigidly defensive.

Content analysis need not be limited to oral self-reports or to data gathered in formal interviews. It may be used to quantify statements made in written documents, casual conversations, or public speeches.

Personality tests

The development of personality tests was stimulated by a number of considerations, both practical and theoretical. On the practical side, testing is more economical than interviewing. In addition, because test items are the same for each person who takes the test, it is possible to develop scoring systems for quantifying data easily. This in turn permits the development of norms and the assessment of reliability and validity.

Personality theories have also provided a powerful impetus for the development of tests. Tests provide ways to define operationally and to measure the concepts involved in a theory.

Rating scales

On a rating scale, subjects are presented with a stimulus (a concept, a person, a situation) to which they must respond by selecting one of a number of phrases to describe the item. A rating scale is similar to a multiple-choice item except that the options on the rating scale represent degrees of a particular characteristic rather than completely different characteristics. Rating scales are convenient and economical ways of obtaining reactions to a stimulus, whether the rater is oneself or someone else. Examples of rating scales used for specific purposes are shown in Table 14.2.

A scale may consist of a set of ordered categories with numbers; it may be a series of adjectives, phrases, or statements arranged in a sequence that corresponds to different degrees of what is being rated. It might be a line whose end points are labeled with two numbers (e.g., 0–100 or 0–10) on which the rater estimates a degree or amount, often with respect to some reference group. For example, if a psychiatric patient is judged to be average on a certain trait in comparison to a reference group consisting of chronic schizophrenics and is to be rated on a scale with numerical indices ranging from 0 to 10, then a rating of 5 would probably be appropriate. As

Table 14.2 Examples of rating scales

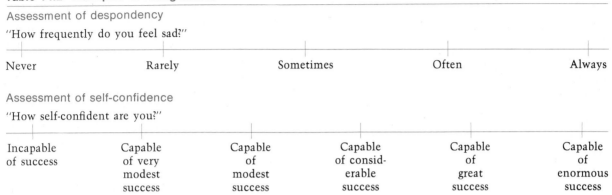

Assessment of despondency

"How frequently do you feel sad?"

Never	Rarely	Sometimes	Often	Always

Assessment of self-confidence

"How self-confident are you?"

Incapable of success	Capable of very modest success	Capable of modest success	Capable of consid-erable success	Capable of great success	Capable of enormous success

this example shows, rating scales can be used either for self-characterizations or for characterizations of others.

As does any method, rating scales have their difficulties, and attempts have been made to overcome them. Perhaps the biggest problem is a *halo effect*. This refers to a favorable rating on a specific characteristic that is made primarily because the rater likes the person he or she is rating. Some raters want to say only nice things about people and others use only the midrange on the scale.

There are some safeguards against these problems. One is to word rating scale items clearly. The degree of ambiguity in the items and the way in which the rating scales are labeled affect ratings. Providing clear directions to raters, training them in the use of rating scales, and ensuring that the concepts behind the scales are unambiguous can greatly increase the accuracy and reliability of the scales. Researchers should also know something about the individuals who perform the rating scale task. For example, they should know how well the rater knows the person who is being rated. The more information the rater has about the subject, either through personal acquaintance or through information provided by the researcher, the more accurate the rating will be.

Questionnaires and inventories

In the early part of this century educators, clinicians, personnel workers, and psychologists found that scores obtained by individuals on intelligence tests

were of practical value in counseling and planning and in predicting behavior. However, because it was clear that intelligence test scores alone did not account for individual differences in behavior, it also seemed worthwhile to attempt measurements of personal characteristics other than intelligence.

In World War I large numbers of recruits flooded into the armed forces, and it was clear that some kind of selection procedure was needed to identify men whose personality problems might be detrimental to the war effort. It seemed equally clear that it would not be possible to interview each recruit. Instead a psychologist named Robert Woodworth developed a personality inventory that could be administered to large groups of recruits. Woodworth's Personal Data Sheet consisted of printed statements relating to various behavioral problems. Subjects responded *yes* or *no* to such items as the following:

Have you ever been afraid of going insane?
Does it make you uneasy to cross a bridge over a river?
Do you ever walk in your sleep?

Subjects whose responses indicated that they might have psychological problems could then be interviewed personally. Thousands of recruits were rejected for active duty at least partly on the basis of their responses on the Personal Data Sheet, and the test was hailed as a great success.

Most of the paper-and-pencil inventories after World War I focused on the identification of personal problems. Few people questioned their validity.

455

Test constructors seemed to be concerned only with the apparent or *face validity* of their instruments. Because instruments labeled as "tests of adjustment" contained items that their authors believed indicated maladjustment, everyone assumed that they measured maladjustment. However, it is clear that tests such as the Personal Data Sheet could easily be faked, depending on the subject's motivations.

Often subjects' responses to items in which they were asked to describe themselves were summarized in terms of overall score, as if only one characteristic were being measured. It has become clear in recent years that the meaning of *maladjustment* is not immediately obvious, and furthermore that individual differences in personality are too complex to be summarized into a single score. There is now a strong trend in the direction of *multidimensional* rather then unidimensional self-report measures. However, for research purposes and when the goal may be something other than a comprehensive personality description, unidimensional measures play a useful role.

The Minnesota Multiphasic Personality Inventory. The Minnesota Multiphasic Personality Inventory, or MMPI, was originally designed to provide an objective basis for classifying different types of psychiatric patients. It consists of 566 statements to be answered *true*, *false*, or *cannot say*. (*Cannot say* means that the subject is undecided about the truth of the statement.) The items (16 of which are repeats) are so varied in content that it is not easy to generalize about them. Some are concerned with attitudinal and emotional reactions, others relate to overt behavior and symptoms, and still others refer to aspects of the subject's past life. The following sample items suggest the diversity of MMPI statements:

1. I believe there is a God.
2. I would rather win than lose a game.
3. I am worried about sex matters.
4. I believe I am being plotted against.
5. I believe in obeying the law.
6. Everything smells the same.

456

After the subject has taken the MMPI, the responses are scored in relation to a number of keys. These scores are then plotted on a graph or profile sheet that reflects the degree to which the individual deviates from the norm.

Although many scales have been added over the years, the original MMPI consisted of nine clinical scales. By scoring these nine groups of items it is possible to determine the similarity of an individual's responses to the responses of patients used to construct groups. A high score on any given scale indicates that the individual's responses to its items are similar to those of the particular type of patient whose responses were used to construct the scale. The following are the MMPI's nine clinical scales and their abbreviations:

1. Hypochondriasis (Hs).
2. Depression (D).
3. Hysteria (Hy).
4. Psychopathic deviate (Pd).
5. Masculinity-femininity (Mf).
6. Paranoia (Pa).
7. Psychasthenia (Pt).
8. Schizophrenia (Sc).
9. Hypomania (Ma).

Most of the MMPI scales were developed by means of the *empirical approach* to test construction. In the empirical approach a large and comprehensive collection of self-report statements or items is administered to people who are known to differ in important ways. Researchers then determine whether certain items in the pool successfully discriminate between the different groups of people. Discriminating items are retained to form the scale, whereas items which are not answered differently by the groups being compared are discarded.

The method used to develop the Schizophrenia scale of the MMPI illustrates the empirical approach. Two groups of subjects were used in developing the Schizophrenia scale. The normal subjects were visitors to the University of Minnesota Hospital (nonpatients), college students, medical personnel, nonpsychiatric patients, and members of other groups that appeared to have no major behavioral deviations. The test results of these normal subjects were compared with those of patients diagnosed as schizophrenic. Only those patients about whose diagnosis there was a substantial agreement among psychiatrists were included in the tested group. The researchers then determined whether the subjects diagnosed as schizophrenic responded to each MMPI item differently from normal subjects. Those items on which schizophrenics differed from normals as well as from other psychiatric groups were used for the Schizophrenia scale. A high score on the scale indicates that an individual responded to these items in a manner similar to that of the schizophrenics in the original group.

On the basis of findings gathered over several decades, MMPI users believe that its scales are valuable not only for categorizing patients, but also for comprehensive personality descriptions. Furthermore, they think that even though the MMPI was constructed for use in clinical situations, it may be valuable for describing the characteristics of individuals who do not display overt symptoms. It is used widely as a screening device in industrial and military settings, and in student counseling as well as in clinical practice.

In addition to clinical scales, the MMPI has scales designed to measure the tendencies to lie, "fake good," and place oneself in a socially desirable light, all of which are capable of affecting MMPI scores. The responses of the individual who responds with *true* to such items as the following may be somewhat suspect:

I read the editorials in the newspaper every day.

I never get upset.

I am always kind and thoughtful.

The score on one of these validity scales, the K scale, is used to adjust the scores obtained on several of the clinical scales. A high score on the K scale of defensiveness can result in a substantial increase in clinical scale scores.

Projective techniques

Personality questionnaires such as the MMPI are convenient and easy to score, but they do not leave individuals with very many alternative ways of responding. Projective techniques have much looser structures than questionnaires, involve stimuli that are relatively unclear and ambiguous, and give subjects a wider range of possible responses to those stimuli. (See Box 14.10.) They are more difficult to score and interpret.

Historically, projective techniques have been used to study unconscious processes, and they are used most often by psychodynamically oriented psychologists. Remember that Freud stressed the importance of free association and believed that individuals would more fully reveal themselves and their unconscious thoughts in ambiguous situations than in those in which they have a very clear idea of what is expected of them. Projective techniques attempt to provide individuals with stimulus situations that are relatively ambiguous and that give few cues concerning the appropriateness of possible responses to them. Projective techniques allow subjects to "project" their own feelings and conflicts.

The Rorschach inkblots. Hermann Rorschach's preoccupation with inkblots grew out of his use of free association in work as a psychotherapist. He viewed responses to ambiguous stimuli as a diagnostic tool for studying unconscious processes, just as Freud used free association in his work as a therapeutic device.

There are ten Rorschach inkblots. Subjects are shown each one and asked, "What does this look like? What might it be?" Examiners write responses down verbatim. (See Figure 14.4.) They also carefully note subjects' behavior during testing—gestures, mannerisms, attitudes. They categorize and score responses to the inkblots in terms of the types of things to which they refer (e.g., animals, human movement, tiny details) and the correspondence between the responses and the objective characteristics of the inkblots.

Much research has been conducted on the relationship between Rorschach responses and behavior, and many of the studies have not been able to demonstrate consistent relationships. Nevertheless, Rorschach tests continue to be among the most widely used personality instruments. There is no simple explanation for this state of affairs. Clinical psychologists, who are among the prime users of psychological tests, know about the discouraging results in the literature, but they continue to put the Rorschach

457

BOX 14.10

The diversity of projective techniques

Almost any stimulus that is ambiguous can be used for projective testing. The following two types of stimuli, incomplete sentences and individual words, illustrate the approach of projective techniques.

The Sentence Completion Method

The subject's task in a sentence completion test is to complete unfinished sentences. These are examples of sentence stems that subjects are asked to complete, together with sample responses.

Compared to others, I . . .
 am pretty ordinary.
 often get very angry.
 don't like to be pushed around.

My mother . . .
 the less said about her the better.
 has done a lot for me.
 has influenced me in many ways, some good,
  some bad.

Try constructing a set of sentence stems and obtain completions from both close friends and class members whom you do not know very well. See if your relationship to the subject affects the sentence completions you obtain.

Word Association Test

The word association test was a precursor of the sentence completion test. It was administered by presenting stimulus words to which subjects responded with the first word that came to mind. In addition to categorizing the subjects' response words, the test measured their reaction times and emotional reactions.

The following table presents words that have been used in eliciting free associations, together with some of the responses given to them:

Word	Associations
table	chair, word, eat, gamble
mother	father, relative, dead, woman
student	study, flunk, dorm, class
war	peace, death, win, lose

Word associations are influenced by the situation in which they are obtained. These influences can be studied from an experimental standpoint. Try making a list of stimulus words, then do the following:

1. Compare free associations before and after meals.
2. Compare the associations of men and women.
3. Compare the associations of children and adults.
4. Compare the effects of different instructions on the associations given. For example, compare "Assume you are a psychologically troubled person and tell me the first word that comes to mind" with "Assume you are Jimmy Carter. . . ." and "Assume you are Elton John. . . ."

test near the top of their list of assessment techniques. They still feel that it helps them in personality evaluation.

It appears that although empirical investigations of Rorschach scoring categories have produced few stable and consistent findings, the test is considered to be valuable in the hands of trained users. Further inquiry is needed into the relationships among the perception of ambiguous stimuli, attitudes and motivations, and behavior.

Thematic Apperception Test. The Thematic Apperception Test (TAT) was developed in the 1930s by Henry Murray of Harvard University. It consists of 30 pictures, including one blank card. (Usually no more than 20 cards are presented in a single test.)

Figure 14.4 Rorschach inkblot. Inkblots can be made by spilling ink (one color or several) on a piece of paper and folding the paper in half while the ink is still wet. Try making several inkblots and compare your own perceptual reactions to them with the reactions of other people. (Granger)

The pictures were obtained from a variety of sources—paintings, drawings, and illustrations from magazines. Although they are more ambiguous than are most photographs, they have much more structure than inkblots. Subjects are told to tell a story about each card, to describe what is going on in the scene depicted on the card, what the characters are thinking and feeling, and what the outcome of the situation will be. (See Figure 14.5.) Both TAT and Rorschach responses can be analyzed using the content analysis procedure mentioned earlier in this chapter.

Descriptions of personality written on the basis of the TAT usually deal with such topics as

1. The subject's behavior in the testing situation.
2. Characteristics of the subject's words or phrases.
3. The kinds of fantasies the subject talks about.
4. The personal relationships depicted in the stories.

5. The conscious and unconscious needs of the individual.
6. The individual's perception of the environment.
7. The emotional tone of the stories.
8. The outcomes of the stories.
9. Common themes that run through the stories.
10. The degree to which the stories reflect control over impulses and contact with reality.

Researchers use TAT responses as both dependent and independent variables. When they use them as independent variables, researchers compare the be-

Figure 14.5 A picture similar to those used in the Thematic Apperception Test. Select from magazines, newspapers, and books a group of pictures that are vague and ambiguous but that seem to reflect particular motivations and needs. Then compare the responses of different individuals to these stimuli. How can you categorize the responses? (Reprinted by permission of the publishers from Henry A. Murray, *Thematic Apperception Test*, Cambridge, Mass.: Harvard University Press, Copyright © 1943 by the President and Fellows of Harvard College; renewed 1971 by Henry A. Murray.)

459

havior in other situations of individuals who respond in different ways to the TAT. For example, they see whether people who tell TAT stories with strongly aggressive themes behave more aggressively in social situations than do those whose stories are not especially aggressive. We have seen in Chapters 1 and 10 how TAT-like pictures have been used to obtain fantasy measures of achievement, affiliation, and power motives, which are then related to other behaviors of interest. When TAT responses are used as dependent variables, efforts are made to influence the stories told by means of experimental conditions. For example, the TATs of hungry subjects and those of subjects who had just eaten might be compared.

A concluding comment concerning personality tests. Personality tests present subjects with particular problem-solving tasks. Whatever the problems, solutions arrived at by subjects are not simply a function of personal characteristics and abilities. Behavior on a test may also be affected by attitudes toward the task and by nontest stimuli in the testing situation, such as the way the tester dresses and behaves, or by such things as a recent argument with a close friend or a headache.

Whatever the nature of an assessment situation, the data require interpretation. Whereas some kinds of data processing may be carried out in impersonal ways (even with a computer) the complex data of human behavior usually calls for judgment and sensitivity on the part of a psychological interpreter. This is true even in the case of rigorously constructed tests, such as intelligence tests. The psychologist's integration of his or her observations of the subject's behavior with the subject's answers may lead to conclusions that could not be obtained from a set of answers and test scores.

Clearly, awareness of these interacting factors is not an end point, but rather a prelude to increased sophistication in personality assessment.

BEHAVIORAL ASSESSMENT

Interviewers often try to piece together the meaning behind what an interviewee says, but behavioral assessors may accept sampled behavior at face value. They usually try to carry out assessments in situations that resemble everyday life experiences or in situations that are actually causing problems for the individual. Behavioral assessors direct their attention to known facts and environmental conditions in the lives of individuals rather than to unconscious motivations, complexes, and intrapsychic tensions.

Behavioral assessment procedures provide reliable information about how frequently certain classes of responses occur, as well as the conditions under which they occur. By observing and recording in different situations (at school, home, the playground), it becomes possible to classify the stimulus situations that give rise to specific types of behavior. Behavioral assessors do not simply say that "Jerry is disruptive" or "Mary isn't achieving up to her potential in arithmetic." Instead, they try to answer such questions as "What does Jerry *do* that causes disruption and what events precede and follow his disruptive behavior?" and "How many long division problems can Mary do in ten minutes?" Once they identify a specific type of response, the next question is, "How often and under what conditions does it occur?"

Historically, behavioral assessment developed within a clinical context. For that reason it has been closely linked with the processes of modifying problem behavior. However, there is no reason why behavioral assessment should be limited to responses that pose problems or reflect personal deficiencies. For example, it might be very useful to conduct a behavioral assessment of highly successful college students to see which aspects of their day-to-day behavior seem to correlate with success.

Behavioral assessment requires an accurate description of an individual's response repertory. Assessors must be trained to be totally unresponsive to those they observe. If they were to react to the behavior of the individual being assessed so that their own behavior was influenced, then they would obtain a distorted picture of the typical response. It is also necessary to allow a sufficiently long baseline period so that the individual can become used to the presence of an observer. Finally, observers must prepare a list of categories of behavior to be observed in advance so that their data are acceptable and understandable to others.

As we saw in Chapter 8, using behavioral assessment techniques in our daily lives may be helpful in

460

BOX 14.11
Behavioral assessment of a famous coach

John Wooden is regarded by many as the greatest basketball coach of all time. Before he retired in 1975, he coached the UCLA basketball team to ten national championships in 12 years. It is unlikely that his brilliant coaching record will ever be matched.

What does a successful coach like Wooden actually do during his practice sessions? To answer this question, psychologists Roland G. Tharp and Ronald Gallimore (1976) used behavioral assessment tech-

niques to study Wooden's coaching behaviors. By carefully observing him during eight practice sessions, the psychologists found that they could code virtually all of Wooden's behaviors into ten response categories.

Having developed the behavioral coding system, Tharp and Gallimore then observed Wooden during more than 30 hours of practice sessions and coded a total of 2,326 of his behaviors. The results of the behavioral assessment are presented in the accompanying table.

It would be interesting to do a similar assessment of less successful coaches to see how they differ. But the behavioral assessment of Wooden has wider educational implications, since Wooden is known as a great teacher. Tharp and Gallimore are applying what they learned from this assessment to other educational programs.

Code	Category	Description	Percent of Total Communications
I	Instructions	Verbal statements about what to do or how to do it	50.3
H	Hustles	Verbal statements to activate or intensify previously instructed behavior	12.7
M+	Modeling-positive	A demonstration of how to perform	2.8
M−	Modeling-negative	A demonstration of how *not* to perform	1.6
V+	Praises	Verbal compliments, encouragements	6.9
V−	Scolds	Verbal statements of displeasure	6.6
NV+	Nonverbal reward	Nonverbal compliments or encouragements (Smiles, pats, jokes)	1.2
NV−	Nonverbal punishment	This infrequent category included only scowls, gestures of despair, and temporary removal of a player from scrimmage, usually to shoot free throws by himself	trace
W	Scold/reinstruction	A combination category: a single verbal behavior which refers to a specific act, contains a clear scold, and reasserts a previously instructed behavior; e.g., "How many times do I have to tell you to follow through with your head when shooting?"	8.0
O	Other	Any behavior not falling into the above categories	2.4
X	Uncodeable	The behavior could not be clearly heard or seen	6.6

identifying specific problem areas. For example, a couple that has been fighting continually might find that their often vaguely defined tension and anger can be broken down in a way that permits them to change their behavior. For example, the wife might realize that her husband's failure to ask, "Did you have a good day?" when he comes home in the evening makes her feel that he does not care about her. If the husband knew this he could do and say things to show that he is interested and does care about her.

In this chapter we have examined some of the ways in which psychologists have sought to measure personal attributes and to use the measurements in various ways. As we have seen, these efforts have not gone without controversy. However, given the considerable progress during the short history of the assessment field, there is reason to be optimistic that these gaps will be narrowed in the years to come.

SUMMARY

1. In any assessment or measuring procedure the goal is to obtain *reliable* and *valid* measures. On a reliable test someone could expect to have a similar score if he or she took the test again at another time. Validity refers to whether a test measures what it is claimed to measure.

2. A test is more useful if it is standardized. This means that the way in which the instructions are given and the test is administered and scored are clearly defined so that the test can be used in exactly the same way each time it is given. Standardized tests also have *norms* by which to interpret the scores. The norms are developed by testing a group of people similar to those for whom the test will be used so that the frequency of each score can be determined.

3. The first intelligence tests that measured a wide number of types of intellectual func-

tioning were developed by Alfred Binet. Binet defined the intelligence quotient as mental age as determined by the test score divided by chronological age and then multiplied by 100 (IQ = (MA/CA) × 100). His tests were later modified and better standardized by Lewis Terman at Stanford University. Although widely used for many years, these Stanford-Binet tests are now less often used than other intelligence tests that provide scores in several areas.

4. The Wechsler intelligence tests, which now include three scales (preschool, school age, and adult), are based on the idea that intelligence is best measured as a group of abilities. Among individually administered intelligence tests the Wechsler tests are the most widely used today.

5. Many characteristics of a person influence his or her intelligence test score. Special tests have been constructed for special purposes, such as testing blind persons or those who do not speak the language well. People not from the same middle-class group as the test constructors (e.g., those from minority groups) may score low because the test asks for information common in middle-class culture but perhaps not common among other groups. Personality factors such as impulsiveness in response can also cause low test scores. One area of disagreement is whether, if they are modified to take these differences into account, tests are still as effective in predicting performance.

6. The question of what intelligence "is" or how it should be defined has never been finally answered. Some theorists believe in a general trait of intelligence that determines ability in all areas, whereas others believe in the existence of separate and not necessarily related kinds of intelligence. The idea that both general intelligence and specific abilities exist in each person is a popular one.

7. How much of intelligence is inherited and how much is due to environmental factors has been debated for many years and never settled. This issue and its implications are currently a topic of hot debate among psychologists and others.

8. Creative ability may be different from intelligence. Studies of eminent scientists have shown that many are not more intelligent than other scientists but do show greater independent thinking.

9. Mental retardation affects about 3 percent of the U.S. population. Some individuals' test scores are in the retarded range, but because they are socially competent they are able to get along fairly well in society. In some cases the cause of mental retardation can be a clearly seen biological defect, but most of the time no biological defects are detectable.

10. Most personality tests measure *constructs*, general personality characteristics that affect behavior in a variety of situations.

11. Personality is measured in many ways: by interviews, rating scales, questionnaires and inventories, projective tests, and behavioral inventories.

12. The Minnesota Multiphasic Personality Inventory (MMPI) is one of the most widely used paper-and-pencil personality tests. It was constructed by selecting items that were answered differently by different groups of psychiatric patients and also differently by the patients and nonpatient control groups.

The test scores form a profile or pattern and not only can indicate the possibility of psychiatric disturbance, but can be used to give a comprehensive personality description.

13. Projective tests give the individual many more options for response than more structured tests do. Projective tests include many kinds, from sentence completion and word association tests to those using inkblots and ambiguous pictures. The Rorschach inkblot test and the Thematic Apperception Test are two of the most important projective tests.

14. Behavioral assessment is a technique of carefully observing certain classes of responses and the situations in which they occur. This information can then be used to understand and modify specific behaviors.

Suggested readings

Anastasi, A. *Psychological testing.* (4th ed.) New York: Macmillan Publishing Co., Inc., 1976. A thorough and authoritative survey of all aspects of psychological assessment.

Loehlin, J. C., Lindzey, G., & Spuhler, J. N. *Race differences in intelligence.* San Francisco: W. H. Freeman and Co. Publishers, 1975. An analysis of racial, genetic, and environmental factors that bear on intelligence and its assessment.

Mischel, W. *Introduction to personality.* (2nd ed.) New York: Holt, Rinehart and Winston, Inc., 1976.

Sarason, I. G. *Personality: An objective approach.* (2nd ed.) New York: John Wiley & Sons, Inc., 1972. This text and that by Mischel are two general surveys of the field of personality that contain descriptions and discussions of the major approaches to personality assessment.

Whimbey, A. E., & Whimbey, L. S. *Intelligence can be taught,* New York: E. P. Dutton & Co., Inc., 1975. Describes methods of accelerating development of skills and raising intelligence testing scores.

Six

Personal and Social Problems

Chapter 15

Behavior Disorders

(Culver)

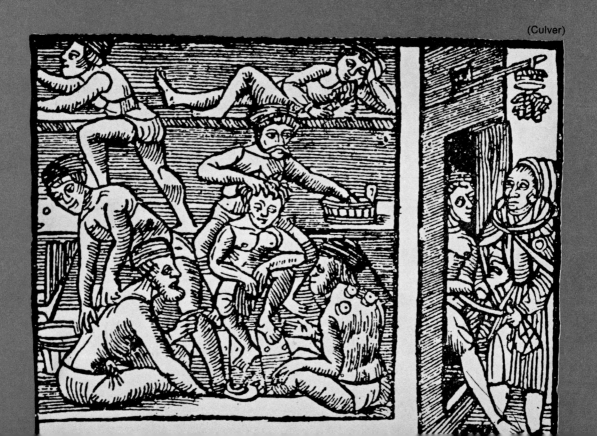

The dream was over and Al Castle lay in bed, his sweaty pajamas clinging to his body. The dream, which he had had many times, was full of the terror and rage he felt as a boy when the tough kids in the neighborhood would taunt him about his "nutty" father. The terror came partly from the fact that he resembled his father in many ways. "Maybe I'll go crazy, too." His rage was directed at the kids and his father. He wanted to tear the taunting toughs to shreds—only they were too big, too tough, and too well organized; and he hated his father because he had to defend his father's reputation when his father was crazy. Often he couldn't even go to work. It was really his father's problem, not his—wasn't it?

Al Castle is 41 years old. He is married, has a son and daughter, and has a good job in a large multinational company. He has had his nightmares in Ottawa, Tokyo, and London, among other places. At the office and in his travels he is usually cheerful, cooperative, and pleasant. People other than family members rarely see him when he is depressed. Outsiders do not know that he wakes up at 5 A.M. and does not go back to sleep, must force himself to get up, take a shower, and drive to work. He is never sure he'll make it to the office.

"Depression is a nightmare. I feel like Dr. Jekyll and Mr. Hyde. At the office, I smile at the secretaries. At home I tell my kids jokes. Then I slam my bedroom door and sweat and pray I can get through another day. That's the way it must have been with my father. Sometimes I think it might be best for everybody if I just turned the steering wheel a little too much to the left and ended it all."

Al Castle might or might not make an attempt to end his life. His problems and unhappiness easily evoke our concern and sympathy, perhaps partly because each of us may at least occasionally experience troubling personal preoccupations and unhappiness. In this chapter we examine problems of living that usually require some type of professional help.

A word of caution! Virtually everyone who has ever studied the behavior disorders has seen something of himself or herself in that subject matter. In clinical training programs there is even a widely recognized condition called intern's disease, the major symptom of which is seeing yourself as afflicted with the clinical problems you study. Fortu-

nately, this "disease" disappears in a reasonable period of time when the student realizes that most clinical conditions are exaggerations of the worries, emotions, and preoccupations experienced by all people. So if you see something of yourself in the pages that follow, it does not mean you are abnormal. It simply means you are a human being adapting to the experiences of life.

We spend every waking minute of every day adapting to the changing conditions of life. All of us experience worry and anxiety when we are confronted by events that require new adjustments. We are influenced, often in major ways, by events in the world around us. Still, most of us manage to live reasonably satisfying and effective lives. But some individuals are not able to "roll with the punches." They live their lives in fear and anger, unable to relate meaningfully to others, lacking the skills needed for satisfying social relationships. Others are able to work, function in the community, and lead independent lives, but only with great unhappiness and anxiety. Another sizable group of individuals can adjust adequately throughout most of their lives, but their behavior deteriorates significantly during periods marked by high degrees of psychological stress or physical change. Some of these behavior disorders seem to occur independent of environmental conditions. They may be caused by any of a variety of biological defects, and they vary a great deal in severity.

We are not concerned with mild eccentricities, unusual beliefs and attitudes, and unconventional tastes in this chapter. We examine instead behavior that is considered socially deviant, that poses major personal problems over time. There are two general categories for classifying social deviations. First, certain members of social groups may not "get the message." They may fail to understand the rules, norms, and values of their society. In many nonliterate and folk societies these common notions are quite clear. In modern, complex societies they are not as easy to perceive. Second, although individuals may be aware of group standards, they may reject them in favor of more personalized, idiosyncratic norms and values.

Behavior that is defined as abnormal, either by the individual or by society, often causes serious adjustment problems. (See Box 15.1.) This chapter describes that behavior, and Chapter 16 describes various ways of treating it.

HISTORICAL BACKGROUND OF ABNORMAL PSYCHOLOGY

Like many modern theorists, a number of ancient scholars, including Hippocrates (450–337 B.C.) and Plato (429–348 B.C.), believed that extreme mental deviations should be viewed as natural disorders for which rational treatments could be developed. By the Middle Ages these attitudes had been suppressed, and superstitious, anti-intellectual attitudes became popular. Belief in mysticism and witchcraft was widespread, and even religion was mingled with elements of magic and alchemy. With the social upheavals associated with the Renaissance, belief in ideas such as "possession by the devil" declined. There was a rise in humanism and scientific inquiry, and interest in the objective study of behavior. But even as late as the sixteenth century, the attitudes of both laymen and professionals toward mental disorder were quite backward. The "therapies" were unwholesome punishments, and social institutions did not keep pace with the creativity of individual thinkers.

Treatment for abnormal behavior over the ages has covered a wide range of techniques. At one extreme there were drastic medical and surgical methods; purging and bleeding were used extensively, and the ancients (as well as many moderns) used various types of drugs and cranial operations. At the other extreme were incantations and exhortations, flogging and cold-water shock. For centuries deviants received capital punishment, as in the worldwide witch prosecutions.

The witchcraft of the middle ages

There was a time when witches existed, not only in the popular imagination, but also in public laws. These laws defined witch's crimes for judges and prosecutors who sentenced the "guilty" creatures to torture, burning, and hanging.

In the Middle Ages the witch concept was firmly implanted in the network of cultural practices and beliefs. Witches and witchfinders formed an inter-

Belief in witches and witchcraft is still very much alive in many cultures. Here witchdoctors from a village in West Africa pose with tribal dancers. (Clardun, Monkmeyer)

locking system. Witchcraft is not just a phenomenon of the past. Modern anthropologists continue to study it in Africa and other places. Their studies have shown that "witches" are often helpless, unhappy people whose personalities hold no trace of the evil powers they are supposed to possess.

At this comfortable distance from the Middle Ages, we tend to call our "witches" hysterical, obsessed, or schizophrenic. We can also consider a diagnosis for the witchfinders, obsessed with ferreting out evidence of witchery, searching for anesthetic areas in a witch's private parts. Taken together, these players enacted a weird and ghastly scene, a kind of absurd black comedy. Today we no longer use such concepts as "pacts with the devil." Instead we speak of unconscious impulses, genetic defects, and learned behavior. Although some present-day ideas may better enable us to understand and control behavior, a few may very sell serve—as widely held cultural beliefs have in the past—to mask and conceal reality.

The reform movement

By the nineteenth century those who had been la-

469

BOX 15.1

Adjusting to the abnormal

The challenge of nonadjustment as a way of life concerned Rabbi Abraham Heschel. . . . Before his death in 1972, he told a story. Once upon a time in a distant kingdom, it happened that after the grain crop had been harvested and stored, it was discovered to be poison. Anyone who ate it went insane. The king and his advisors immediately took counsel as to what should be done. Clearly, not enough food was available from other sources to sustain the population. There was no choice but to eat the grain. Very well, the king said, let us eat it. But at the same time we must feed a few people on a different diet so that there will be among us some who remember we are insane. (Colman McCarthy, *Newsweek,* January 13, 1975, p. 11)

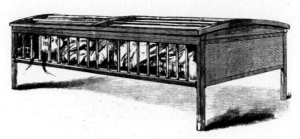

Figure 15.1 The crib was an early "therapy" for violent patients. (Bettmann Archive)

attention to neighboring states, then to the West and the South. Her efforts resulted in the construction of special hospitals for mental patients in more than 15 states and Canada; throughout the nation methods of treatment improved. She aroused a new and lasting interest in the problem of mental illness both in the United States and Europe.

Modern approaches

Over the past century there have been numerous theories concerning the relationships among mental and physical disorders, disturbed behavior, and therapeutic methods. Nonpunitive mental hospitals developed in part from a gradual acceptance of the idea that moving the mentally ill from a poor home and community environment to a sympathetic asylum would help them to heal. But more recent studies seem to indicate that prolonged separation from the community may not be helpful, and may even have undesirable effects. More and more effort is being made to deal with behavioral problems on a preventive basis as early as possible and outside of large institutional settings.

beled in former times as being "possessed by the devil" became the "insane." Among scientists there was a growing curiosity about natural events. Most writers who studied what was called "moral insanity" felt obliged to back up their arguments with data about clinical cases rather than with religious statements. There was a new acceptance of humanitarian ideas, and many people recognized the need for reforming social institutions. Reformers argued that many forms of maladaptive behavior reflected a mental *illness.* They began a vigorous movement to establish protective asylums for the mentally ill.

One of the leaders of this movement was Dorothea Dix, a Boston schoolteacher. Her career as a reformer began in 1841, when she accepted an invitation to teach a Sunday School class in an East Cambridge (Massachusetts) jail. There the sight of the insane thrown into prison with criminals stirred her deeply. In the next 18 months she visited every place in Massachusetts where the mentally ill were confined, and she revealed the shocking conditions in a report to the state legislature in 1843. When the state set about making improvements, she turned her

All serious students of abnormal behavior agree on one point: We must study behavioral disorders rationally, and continue to question popular beliefs. This means that we must be open to alternative explanations of events. What is mental illness? Who defines its diagnosis and treatment? Has anyone the right to call himself or herself mentally ill? Has a clinician the right to call anyone mentally ill? Psychiatrist Thomas Szasz (1974) contended that mental illness is a myth; it is a label, a concept, not a physical state. When individuals are labeled as mentally ill, he claimed, there are a number of serious

New programs for the mentally disturbed and the mentally handicapped emphasize self-care so that individuals can function effectively in their own homes. (Kubota, Magnum)

social consequences. They are shut out socially and may lose their civil rights if they are hospitalized involuntarily. What is usually referred to as mental illness Szasz views as a primarily moral problem. Essentially, society tells certain individuals that their behavior is wrong, but that they are not personally responsible for it; therefore they have little to say about the methods society chooses for modifying it. Soon after Szasz made his opinions public, the commissioner of the New York State Department of Mental Hygiene demanded that he be dismissed from his faculty position. Szasz continues to argue that labeling people as mentally ill should not relieve them of a sense of personal responsibility and make it easy for society to violate their rights.

Today many personal problems are brought voluntarily to the attention of clinical workers, such as psychiatrists, psychologists, and social workers. These problems range from worries and tensions that are quite private and relatively minor to seriously deranged thought and bizarre behavior. When the behavior is extreme, professionals consider hospitalizing their clients. Under certain circumstances the hospitalization may be involuntary. A judicial decision is made to commit the individual against his or her will if there is evidence that he or she is a potential danger to self or others.

Advances in humanistic thought and scientific method have had positive effects on the ways in which behavior disorders are handled, but two questions remain to be answered. One of these is conceptual: How should we think about these disorders? Is diagnosing a neurosis or a psychosis comparable to diagnosing an ulcer or pneumonia? Or are they the product of a failure to follow societal norms? The second question has to do with the clinican's diag-

471

nostic judgments. There is a large body of evidence that indicates that clinicians are often unable to agree about diagnostic labels to attach to clients and decisions as to how to treat them. Both the conceptual question of how maladaptive behavior should be interpreted and the problem of making reliable clinical judgments are among the issues most often discussed by clinicians and researchers.

Mental health professionals

A *psychiatrist* is a physician with postgraduate training and experience in treating emotional disorders. Psychiatrists have legal responsibility in commitment procedures and in supervising the operation of mental hospitals. Because they are M.D.'s psychiatrists can prescribe drugs and electric shock therapy. A *clinical psychologist* is a psychologist with a graduate degree, usually a Ph.D., who specializes in treating many of the same sorts of emotional disorders that psychiatrists treat. But clinical psychologists are trained to diagnose and treat personality problems that are not medical. They are also specialists in the use of personality and intelligence tests, and in planning and conducting research. A *psychiatric social worker* holds a graduate degree in social work and is trained to work with families, social agencies, or other community resources to help solve clinical problems. Psychiatric social workers are especially concerned about the links among disturbed individuals and their families, social environments, and work environments.

The activities of psychiatrists, clinical psychologists, and social workers overlap (e.g., all three are trained to do psychotherapy and counseling) and they often collaborate closely in treating disturbed individuals. (See Box 15.2.) In addition to clinical workers, researchers with diverse backgrounds, including research psychologists, physiologists, sociologists, and anthropologists, are concerned about behavior disorders.

VARIETIES OF DISORDERED EXPERIENCE

472

The personal problems that people experience vary in seriousness and include an almost overwhelming variety of behavioral symptoms. Some problems are vague; others are quite specific. Some are acute and quickly overcome; others last a lifetime. Some have physiological causes; others seem to be the product of living in undesirable social environments. Certain types of problems occur at particular periods of life (e.g., in early childhood, adolescence, or old age); others can occur at any time. In the following pages we review some of the major behavior disorders, then consider contemporary theories as to how they should be treated.

The neuroses

At one time the term *neurosis* implied a severe disorder. Today, however, it refers to disorders involving a wide range of problems and anxiety arising from an individual's unsuccessful attempt to deal with inner conflicts and stress. These attempts at problem solving tend to be repetitive and to fail. Neurotic behavior results more from the individuals' perceptions of situations than from the situations themselves. For example, neurotics often see themselves as being rejected by others when there is no objective basis for drawing such a conclusion. Neurosis impairs an individual's overall judgment, the ability to retain a healthy contact with reality, and the capacity to relate effectively to others.

Individuals who have fundamental doubts about their own competence and merit and who do not believe that their environment is basically friendly and accepting are diagnosed as neurotic. The major types of neurosis are:

1. *Anxiety neurosis:* persistent, unfocused tension and apprehensiveness.
2. *Phobic neurosis:* irrational and highly specific fears.
3. *Dissociative neurosis:* repeated alterations in states of consciousness.
4. *Hysterical neurosis:* bodily symptoms in the absence of any observable physiological disturbance.
5. *Obsessive-compulsive neurosis:* persistent, irrational, often anxiety-provoking thoughts (obsessions) and/or uncontrollable repetitive actions (compulsions).
6. *Depressive neurosis:* self-devaluation, apprehension, and a continually pessimistic outlook.

Any given case may include features characteristic of several of these categories. The diagnostic categories are used for convenience and to make communication easier among clinical workers. They are abstractions based on observations of behavior. Those who work with neurotics and others suffering from psychological dysfunctions often have a great deal of trouble deciding on the most important features of a case. Clients who seek help rarely recognize which aspects of their own behavior and thought are most important and which aspects of their environment are most in need of change.

Anxiety neurosis

Individuals with an anxiety neurosis feel apprehensive and fearful far more than do most people. Anxiety is a nonspecific fear that is not connected with definite situations or objects. In some cases anxiety may develop into panic. The following case concerns a 35-year-old mathematician with a 15-year history of heart palpitations and faintness.

His chief complaints were that at any time and without warning, he might suddenly feel he was about to faint and fall down, or tremble and experience palpitations, and if standing would cringe and clutch at the nearest wall or chair. If he was driving a car at the time he would pull up at the curbside and wait for the feelings to pass off before he resumed his journey. If it occurred during sexual intercourse with his wife he would immediately separate from her. If it happened while he was lecturing his thoughts became distracted, he could not concentrate and he found it difficult to continue. . . . Between attacks the patient did not feel completely well, and a slight tremulousness persisted. The attacks could come on at any time of day or night. The patient felt that he lacked energy but was not depressed. He denied that he experienced fear, anxiety, or panic during his attacks. (Marks and Lader, 1973, p. 11)

Phobic neurosis

Phobic individuals have extremely strong and highly specific fears (e.g., fear of syphilis, dirt, high places) in situations that pose no real dangers. In some cases, a number of these fears may be present simultaneously. The following describes a phobia experienced by a college student:

For several months prior to coming to the student mental health center, Ronald H., an 18-year-old freshman at a midwestern university, had noticed that each time he left his dormitory room and headed toward his classes he experienced a feeling of panic. He could not understand this since he was reasonably pleased and satisfied with his classes and professors. "It would get so bad at times," he told his freshmen advisor, "that I thought I would collapse on the way to class. It was a frightening feeling and I began to be afraid to leave the dorm." Even after he returned to the dormitory, he would be unable to face anyone for hours or to concentrate on his homework. But if he remained in his own room, or not too far from it, he felt reasonably comfortable. He had experienced similar fear reactions, although not as intensely, since about the age of 13. He also reported other fears, such as becoming contaminated by syphilis and growing prematurely bald. Both of the latter fears were sufficiently intense and persistent to cause him to compulsively scrub his hands, genitals, and head until these parts became red, and sometimes even bled. In addition, he touched doorknobs only reluctantly, never drank water from a public fountain, and only used the toilet in his home or on the dormitory floor. (Kleinmuntz, 1974, pp. 168–169)

Dissociative neurosis

Individuals with dissociative neuroses may behave as if they are in a stupor and they may lose their memories. They seem to have no sense of personal identity; they may seem to "freeze," they may sleepwalk, or they may lose touch with reality. They might run away from stressful environments, take up residence elsewhere, and be unable to remember their past. This reaction is known as a *fugue* state.

Samuel O., a graduate student, impoverished and far from home, was invited to dinner at the home of an instructor whom he had known when they were socio-economic equals in another town. He accepted the invitation because he was lonely and hungry, but he regretted it almost at once because his clothes were shabby. He thought, in retrospect, that the instructor had seemed condescending. That evening he left his rooming house in plenty of time for the dinner, but he failed to show up at the instructor's home. Two days later he was picked up by the police in a neighboring state. He could remember vaguely having ridden a freight train, talking with strangers, and sharing their food; but he had no idea who he was, where he had come from, or where he was going. The contents of his pockets identified him and he was fetched by relatives.

Later on, this young man was able to remember the events leading up to the fugue and something of what went on during it. He had started for the instructor's

473

BOX 15.2
The mental health team

A Psychiatrist in Private Practice

I see all kinds, from people with minor problems who think they are major to those for whom everybody would agree the problem is really a shattering one. . . . I'm in private practice and share a suite of offices with three other psychiatrists and a clinical psychologist. We talk about cases and new journal articles at sack lunches and mini-staff meetings we have twice a week.

I have two kinds of cases—those in which I play primarily the role of pill-pusher, giving tranquilizers to people who can't afford to, don't want, or don't need lengthy psychotherapy. The drugs really work, but I find they are not quite as effective as the drug ads in the psychiatry journals imply. The other kind of case is the one that requires psychotherapy.

My psychotherapy isn't of one particular school. I guess I'm more Freudian than anything else, but the development of behavior therapy by the psychologists really intrigues me. I use those methods more and more. I also do some group work. One of my colleagues occasionally joins me as co-therapist in the groups.

A Clinical Psychologist in a
Community Mental Program

I'm a member of a team that serves 70,000 people in a big section of the city. My work is mainly in the outpatient clinic for children. The kids come for a variety of reasons—they are doing poorly at school, they are annoying neighbors, their parents are worried that they are "crazy."

A major part of my job is just listening. I have to filter the real problems from nonsense or misinformation. It's not easy to listen attentively and it's even harder to keep yourself from quickly coming to decisions about what the problem is. Unfortunately, most human difficulties, particularly those occurring in families, are complicated—each of the family members seems to have his or her own gripe or inadequacy.

I use a variety of techniques in my work. I interview, test, do a lot of family therapy, and spend a lot of time on the phone talking to people who are involved in the case in one way or another. For example, this morning I saw a 14-year-old girl who thinks she is pregnant and doesn't know how to tell her parents. I spoke with a doctor in the Health Department, a school social worker, and a worker in a storefront clinic that is part of the county's mental health program. I didn't call the girl's mother. The girl wasn't ready for that and, anyway, I hope she will do that herself.

A Psychiatric Social Worker at a Mental Hospital

My job is to forge new links between the patient in the hospital and the life he or she should want to return to as soon as possible.

I don't just sit in my office. I spend a lot of time on the ward talking to patients who are part of my caseload and their doctors. Sometimes family members see me here, sometimes I see them at their homes. I also contact people like employees, friends—even real estate agents when there is a housing problem.

I don't just do what the textbooks say should be done. I'm a problem solver and as I've gotten more experience I've also gotten more confidence in myself.

When I came here I was really quite anti-hospital. I saw mental hospitals as snake pits. I don't feel that way anymore. Most hospitals, including this one, are more bad than good, but I do see that some people need an institution to help them because they are just not in contact with reality or because they have no place to go.

474

house while still in strong conflict over the condescension, and afraid to express what he felt and call the dinner off. On his way he was held up at a grade crossing by a slowly moving freight train. He had a sudden impulse to board the train and get away. When he acted on this impulse he apparently became am-

nesic. He retained enough . . . integration, however, to be able to carry through complex coordinations, to converse with others, and to get food. Nonetheless, he was much less in contact with people than anyone suspected until the police began to question him. (Easton, 1959, pp. 505–513)

Hysterical neurosis

Hysterical patients have physical symptoms without any observable physiological disorder. These symptoms usually involve parts of the body that are under voluntary control. Blindness, deafness, and paralysis may result from a hysterical reaction.

Because of their dramatic and persistent symptoms, hysterical patients are often hospitalized for observation, X rays, and a variety of medical and surgical procedures. Box 15.4 illustrates the markedly increased surgery rate in hysterical individuals. Hysterical individuals have a number of common characteristics: susceptibility to suggestion, excitability, emotional instability, and a tendency to overreact to unusual situations. Individuals who display these characteristics but do not have any of the usual physical symptoms of hysterical neurosis are labeled as *hysterical personalities*. From time to time there have been outbreaks of group hysteria among people who live or work together.

Obsessive-compulsive neurosis

In this neurosis ideas and actions occur repetitively and seemingly without reason (e.g., an individual cannot stop thinking about a particular word, or repeatedly washes his or her hands). Obsessive-compulsive individuals are literally tyrannized by their own thoughts and actions. For example, if someone asked an obsessive-compulsive to find an English word that rhymes with *orange* (there is no word that does), he or she might be unable to stop searching for a word. Compulsive individuals feel compelled to perform particular actions or series of actions again and again (e.g., stepping on cracks in the sidewalk). The possibilities for obsessive thoughts and compulsive acts are practically unlimited.

If obsessive-compulsive individuals do not perform their rituals they experience intense anxiety. When the rituals or thoughts begin to interfere with important parts of daily life, they become significant problems that require professional attention. A psychoanalyst wrote this description of the obsessional patient:

> The obsessional lives in a world of painstaking efforts to be exactly right. He cannot tolerate being wrong and, for him, there must be a right in every matter and nuance. He does not drive a new Ford. He drives one

that is 3—no, 3½ months old now, with 6,000 miles on it, more or less, which he bought at a pretty good price; well, maybe he could have gotten a better deal if he had shopped around more; but he had a number of pressing matters and he really didn't have the time . . . etc.

> He is no Hemingway. He cannot tell or live a straight story. One might call obsessionalism a disease of adjectives, contrasted with the hysteric who suffers a disease of adverbs. The hysteric is "horribly" upset, "abysmally" depressed, "completely" exhausted, "fantastically" interested, and eats in "divine" restaurants, pointing to a preoccupation with a world of affect. The obsessional's preoccupation with accuracy of fact is part of his goal to bury affect, not to praise it, in pursuit of an anxiety-free existence, and the maintenance of a fragile sense of self-esteem via the expression of power over realities. . . . The obsessional's is a world of description, never action or emotion. His is a world of objectification or reification, a static dehumanized world, not one of process and vitality. His perception of the world is that, if he can only get it exactly right, he will be in control and a correct state will follow. Since this does not correspond to the real world of ceaseless change and endless becoming, action is often preceded by a period of agonizing and then an eruption, often in an impulsive fashion. (Schimel, 1974, pp. 95–96)

Depressive neurosis

It is difficult to diagnose a neurotic depression. Often the symptoms are very close to those of psychotic depressions and involve significant distortions of reality. These distortions often take the form of delusions, or beliefs that clearly do not conform to reality.

Neurotic depressives constantly feel guilty and have very little regard for themselves. Neurotic depressions often take place following the loss of a loved one or a cherished possession. The following case shows how depressed individuals punish themselves because of flaws they think they have and transgressions they think they have committed.

A fifty-two-year-old executive complained of constipation and abdominal pains. His physician noted his downcast and pessimistic demeanor and discovered that, although not seriously incapacitated, he had been staying home from work, remaining for the most part in bed and responding to his family's concern about him with unaccustomed irritability. At first he could

BOX 15.3

A case of multiple personality: The Three Faces of Eve

Multiple personality is a rare, dramatic type of dissociative reaction. Two or more separate and markedly different personalities can apparently coexist within the same individual. Multiple personality is usually interpreted as an attempt to escape from frustration and unhappiness. The classic case of *The Three Faces of Eve* illustrates the phenomenon of multiple personality:

[Description of Eve White] She did not at first appear to be an unusual or a particularly interesting patient. This neat, colorless young woman was . . . twenty-five years of age. . . . Demure and poised, she sat with her feet close together, speaking clearly but in soft, low tones. This superlatively calm, utterly self-controlled little figure of propriety showed no suggestion of anything that the layman might think of as nervousness. Her hands lay still on the arms of her chair as she spoke. . . . She was not undernourished but seemed somehow very delicate, the reticent, meticulous manner suggesting a physical fragility. . . . Her personal problems were complicated and serious, but by no means extraordinary.

[Description of how Eve White suddenly changed to Eve Black] The brooding look in her eyes became almost a stare. Eve seemed momentarily dazed. Suddenly her posture began to change. Her body slowly stiffened until she sat rigidly erect. An alien, inexplicable expression then came over her face. This was suddenly erased into utter blankness. The lines of her countenance seemed to shift in a barely visible, slow, rippling transformation. . . . Closing her eyes, she winced as she put her hands to her temples, pressed hard, and twisted them as if to combat sudden pain. . . . Then the hands lightly dropped. . . . A pair of blue eyes popped open. . . . There was a quick reckless smile. In a bright unfamiliar voice that sparkled, the woman said, "Hi there, Doc!"

With a soft and surprisingly intimate syllable of laughter, she crossed her legs, carelessly swirling her skirts in the process. She unhurriedly smoothed the hem down over her knees in a manner that was playful and somehow just a little provocative. . . . The demure and constrained posture of Eve White had melted into buoyant response.

[Description of Jane] Sometime after the returning of the headaches and blackouts, with Eve White's maladjustment still growing worse generally, a very early recollection was being discussed with her. The incident focused about a painful injury she had sustained when scalded by water from a washpot. As she spoke her eyes closed sleepily. . . . After remaining in this sleep, or trance, for perhaps two minutes, her eyes opened. . . . Slowly, with an unknown but curiously impressive voice and with immeasurable poise, she said, "Who are you?"

From the first moment it was vividly apparent that this was neither Eve White nor Eve Black. . . . This new woman showed herself ever more plainly and in all respects to be another entity. . . . She showed no evidence of Eve Black's obvious faults and inadequacies. . . . She also impressed us as being far more mature, more vivid, more boldly capable, and more interesting than Eve White. . . .

This third personality called herself Jane, for no particular reason she could give. . . . In her, early appeared the potential or the promise of something far more of woman and of life than might be expected from the two Eves with their faults and weaknesses eliminated and all assets combined. (Thigpen and Cleckley, 1957. Copyright 1957 by the American Psychological Association. Reprinted by permission.)

Eve was portrayed by Joanne Woodward in a movie entitled *The Three Faces of Eve*. (Culver)

not think of any recent change in his life circumstances, but he finally remarked, "I did hire a new secretary six weeks ago." He acknowledged that he had developed sexual feeling for his new secretary and that he found these feelings frightening and unacceptable. "After all, she's young enough to be my daughter."

He recalled that in twenty-nine years of a happy marriage, there had been one extramarital episode. Twenty years earlier, he had had sexual intercourse with a fellow employee on one occasion. He had felt guilty and had broken off the relationship without really coming to grips with his feelings about it, and ever since then he had tried to forget it. Although he had not acted on his feelings toward his new secretary, he nevertheless felt he deserved punishment because he had transgressed in the past. (Daniels, 1962, p. 436)

Understanding neurotic behavior

Although there is no standard explanation for the preceding types of neuroses, we do have a number of clues as to their causes. There are several competing theories that incorporate different sets of these clues, based on different basic models of human behavior.

The observations and theories of Sigmund Freud have had an enormous impact on the way in which the dynamics of neuroses are characterized. Freud's idea of unconscious motivation, especially with regard to sexual desires, hostility, and the avoidance of anxiety, has become a central feature of most *psychodynamic* orientations to behavior disorders. Building on this idea, Freud came to see neurotic patterns of life as the ultimate consequence of defensive inhibitions learned early in childhood as a means of avoiding the dangers, real or fancied, that attend meeting parental expectations and discipline.

Many clinicians view neurotic behavior in a psychodynamic framework, within which the major causes are inner conflict, anxiety, and unconscious motivations. A distinctive characteristic of neurotic anxiety is that alarms are frequently sounded when there are no adequate causes. Neurotics suffer from inner fear of imaginary danger, from inner turmoil. They may suddenly be overwhelmed by intense anxiety, even in the quiet, confined space of their own living room.

Psychodynamic theorists argue that these individuals have inadequate defenses. All of us struggle with internal pressures and fears, but most of us manage to "put a lid" on them; neurotics cannot do this. They often perceive themselves as unable to cope with environmental pressures, separation, or the anticipation of separation or abandonment by people important to them. From a psychodynamic viewpoint, they feel severely threatened by their own repressed antisocial impulses. They overreact to threats or to the anticipation of disapproval, and to withdrawal of love. Their anxiety is usually free-floating, that is, not tied to any particular situation. It may fasten itself to certain situations, but usually without any understanding on the part of the individual. Neurotic symptoms are self-defeating attempts to cope with a high anxiety level. Sometimes these attempts are successful in helping the individual to "keep up a good front." (See Figure 15.2.)

Psychodynamic theorists believe that we cannot take behavior we see at face value. Rather, we must examine the dynamics that underlie it. On the other hand, behaviorists, such as B. F. Skinner, believe that neurosis can be explained by looking at observable behavior. Therapists, they say, must pay careful attention to stimuli and the patient's responses to

Figure 15.2 Snoopy may or may not be neurotic, but the "raging turmoil" he refers to is characteristic of neurotics. (Schulz, 1965, © United Feature Syndicate, Inc.)

BOX 15.4

Potential for polysurgery in a hysterical personality

50 hysteria patients   50 healthy controls

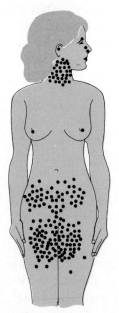 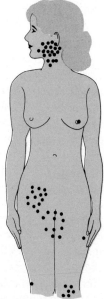

● = 1 operation

Comparison of number and location of major surgical procedures in 50 hysteria patients and 50 healthy control subjects. By weight, it can be calculated that the mass of organs removed in hysteria patients is more than three times that in control subjects. (From *Psychiatric Diagnosis* by Robert A. Woodruff, Donald W. Goodwin, and Samuel B. Guze. Copyright © 1974 by Oxford University Press, Inc. Reprinted by permission.)

A clinical psychologist relates the following account of his experience with a teenage girl with an hysterical personality. This case illustrates the hysteric's potential for polysurgery or unnecessary surgery.

Several years ago, I treated a 15-year-old girl we'll call Susan _____ who had been referred by a physician because of severe abdominal pains for which no physical cause could be found. She had had the pains for six years and had gone from doctor to doctor seeking a cure. I gave her a battery of personality tests, and the results indicated a person who denied, repressed, and avoided negative feelings, especially those involving resentment and anger. Her MMPI profile (see Chapter 14) indicated an hysterical personality type. These results were consistent with my clinical impressions. She was vivacious and extremely likeable—as many hysterics are—but she was also extremely resistant to treatment. There were some really bad things going on between her and her mother, but she could never deal with them. She steadfastly denied feelings of anger toward a woman who made *me* mad just hearing about the way she behaved. One day, Susan came for her appointment moaning in pain. She collapsed in my office complaining of terrible pains in her right side. I had a medical intern examine her, and she had all the symptoms of a ruptured appendix. They rushed her up to surgery and operated immediately. To their amazement, they found nothing wrong with her appendix, and they could find no other cause for her symptoms.

Shortly afterwards Susan dropped out of therapy, claiming that she had no psychological problems. I often think about her and wonder how many more operations she might have had, given her symptoms. I hope she resolves her problems before she runs out of parts.

The psychologist made his diagnosis of hysterical personality partly on the basis of Susan's responses to the Hysteria scale of the MMPI.

Hysteria (Hy) scale items

The items of the Hy scale involve physical complaints and denial of negative feelings. (T and F refer to true and false responses; T means the subject agrees with the statement, F indicates disagreement.)

- I seldom worry about my health (F)
- I have few or no pains (F)
- I feel tired a good deal of the time (T)
- Once in a while I think of things too bad to talk about (F)
- I think most people would lie to get ahead (F)
- I sometimes feel resentful if I don't get my way (F)

them. (See Box 15.5.) Like the behavioristic approach, the cognitive-behavioral approach stresses the importance of identifying stimuli and responses, but it also recognizes that behavior changes when individuals think about and develop insight into their problems. Cognitive-behaviorists interpret neurotic behavior as a product of unrealistic thinking, undesirable learning experiences, and unproductive problem-solving strategies. As therapists, they seek to teach clients more realistic and effective ways of thinking about and responding to problematic situations.

Like psychodynamic theorists, cognitive-behaviorists are concerned with the inner life. They, however, are prone to focus more on conscious than on unconscious mental events to help clients solve the current problems they face (e.g., overcoming a phobia), and not to explore early childhood experiences. They rely heavily on conditioning and learning programs that facilitate improved ways of experiencing situations and planning action.

Researchers have not been able to discover any direct physiological cause for most neurotic conditions, but it is difficult to deny the possibility that many of the conditions we presently regard as *functional* disorders (having no physiological cause) are somehow related to physical defects.

There is some evidence that heredity plays a role in neurosis. One study found a statistically significant link between generations in anxiety neurosis, but little or no generational link in hysterical neurosis (Miner, 1973). Heredity interacts in complex ways with environmental forces. If neurosis runs in a family, it is difficult to say with any certainty whether it is caused by genes transmitted from parent to child or by the parents' methods for raising children, or both.

Neurotics have been treated successfully with various drugs as well as with psychotherapy. The many psychiatrists who prescribe tranquilizers report that they help reduce tension. Their effects vary with their chemical composition, and dosage schedules vary among different patients. Despite intensive research by clinical investigators, there is little information by which doctors can predict which anti-anxiety drug will be the most beneficial in a given case. They adjust the dosage in accordance with the amount of anxiety the patient is experiencing and with his or her ability to tolerate side effects. Most

clinical conditions that require the use of tranquilizers improve within a few days or weeks. Medication is then reduced as the patient's anxiety subsides. Many psychodynamically oriented therapists use tranquilizers as a means of lowering patients' anxiety levels, so that they can explore their inner feelings more easily.

Psychophysiological disorders

The relationship between psychological states and physical illness has long puzzled and intrigued doctors, scientists, and laymen. Hysterical neurosis often results in physical symptoms, but there is no actual tissue damage or structural change. *Psychophysiological disorders*, however, do involve tissue damage and physiological changes. Psychosomatic medicine, as the field of medicine concerned with psychophysiological disorders was originally called, is relatively young, and there are many gaps in our knowledge.

Stomach ulcers and high blood pressure are examples of "traditional" psychophysiological disorders. But what about the psychological factors that seem to hasten or slow death in terminally ill people whose conditions are not regarded as psychosomatic? Mark Twain was born on November 30, 1835, when Halley's comet lit up the sky and he died, as he predicted—when it reappeared on April 21, 1910. There are many terminally ill persons who manage to stay alive until an important event, such as a birthday or anniversary. Three of the first four presidents of the United States died on July 4. Many people living today have expressed the desire to "be around" when we enter the twenty-first century. One of the tantalizing aspects of the field of psychophysiological disorders is the light it might ultimately shed on the psychological side of physical illness and even death.

The concept of psychophysiological disorders arose in connection with the study of a group of diseases or conditions, such as migraine headaches, for which there was no clearly established physiological cause. Psychological factors seem to play a major role in the following diseases:

1. Cardiovascular disorders, such as hypertension and high blood pressure.
2. Respiratory disorders, such as hiccoughs and asthma.
3. Skin disorders, such as dermatitis and eczema.

BOX 15.5

Freudian and behavioral interpretation of a phobia

The case of Little Hans, reported in 1909, is one of the most famous illustrations of a phobic neurosis. When he was 5 years old, Hans refused to go out into the street because he was afraid of horses. He was especially afraid that they would bite him. His father, a physician, discussed the case with Freud, who interpreted the horse as a symbol of Hans's hatred and fear of his father. Hans harbored aggressive fantasies and thoughts toward his father, he said, because his father was Han's only rival for his mother's love. He was "a little Oedipus who wanted to have his father 'out of the way,' to get rid of him so that he might be alone with his handsome mother and sleep with her" (Freud, 1950, p. 253).

At the same time, however, Hans also loved his father. To resolve his Oedipal conflict, Hans repressed his love for his mother. He continued to love his father, and to displace his hatred for him onto horses, which he could avoid more easily than he could his father. Freud hypothesized that Hans focused on horses because his father had often played "horsie" with him. Horses' bridles reminded him of his father's dark moustache. In his fantasies

Hans expected his father to punish him for his hostility. This expectation was also displaced into the fear that horses would bite him. Freud maintained that Little Hans was suffering from a classic conflict, in which he felt both love and hatred for the same person. Hans was treated by his father with Freud's advice. He recovered from his phobia and was able to cope with his conflict in a more effective way.

In the 1960s a number of writers (Wolpe and Rachman, 1960; Bandura, 1969) took another look at the case of Little Hans. They argued that external cues elicited and controlled Han's phobic responses, that his behavior was not simply an incidental vehicle for feelings and fantasies. They noticed that there were three major elements that seemed to be present whenever Hans had a phobic response: (1) a large horse, (2) a heavily loaded transport vehicle, and (3) a high travel speed for the horse and vehicle. Freud's description of the case stated that Hans was more frightened of large than of small horses, more frightened of rapidly moving vehicles than of empty ones. Hans became quite fearful when a horse-drawn vehicle made a turn. He was also afraid of railways and locomotives, which were similar in many ways to the transport vehicles. The behaviorists claimed that these stimuli, and not displaced anger for his father, were the cause of Little Hans's reactions. Freud also noted that Hans became afraid of horses after he was frightened by an accident involving a horse. The behaviorists argued that Little Hans underwent a classical conditioning process when he saw the accident, so that he continued to respond with great fear to horses.

---

4. Gastrointestinal disorders, such as peptic ulcers, constipation, and colitis.

5. Musculoskeletal disorders, such as muscle cramps and backaches.

6. Genitourinary disorders, such as some types of menstrual disturbances.

Medical specialists do not assume that these conditions always have a psychological connection. Fur-

thermore, even when they do think that physical disorders might have psychological bases, they still use medical treatment to provide relief for physical pain and symptoms. Psychophysiological disorders seem to be caused by the same emotional states that are associated with neurosis—anxiety and anger. If individuals continue in these states with great intensity, they may even produce structural changes in their own organs.

Understanding psychophysiological disorders

Psychophysiological disorders have been interpreted in a number of ways. According to one view, they are biological responses to symbolic threats or stress, analogous to animals' adaptive responses to physical stress such as prolonged cold. Psychodynamic theorists suggest that individuals who are prone to psychosomatic disorders cannot cope with stress and anxiety, react in a neurotic way, and for some reason develop somatic reaction patterns. They feel that psychotherapy is the most effective long-term approach to these disorders.

Conditioning may account for the strength of some physiological responses. For example, attention from others might reinforce particular bodily responses so that the individual would tend to repeat them. Recent research indicates that bodily responses that we have always defined as involuntary can actually be controlled through operant conditioning. (See Chapter 6.) Furthermore, counterconditioning techniques have been used to treat some psychophysiological disorders. For example, deep relaxation has been paired with stimuli graded for their likelihood of causing asthmatic attacks. The training caused a significant reduction in the frequency of wheezing attacks (Moore, 1965).

Both classical and operant conditioning can be involved in asthmatic reactions. An allergen (such as dust, pollen) may serve as an unconditioned stimulus for a wheezing response, but if the presence of the allergen is associated with certain stimuli or situations, then the wheezing response may become classically conditioned to such situations, and occur in the absence of the allergen. Once established, the wheezing response could be maintained and strengthened in an operant fashion through reinforcement (e.g., attention from others).

Some patients have been taught to use their thought processes constructively to deal with various types of heart and circulatory difficulties. For example, individuals can learn to control high blood pressure by watching a machine that gives continuous visual feedback on blood pressure. Whenever the machine indicates that the pressure is rising, they try to think relaxing thoughts or to make their muscles go limp. Whenever pressure falls a little, they try to remember what it was they were imagining or feeling when the drop occurred, so that they can repeat that thought or emotion in the future. This training technique involves cognitive-behavioral principles. It is particularly effective with individuals who for one reason or another cannot use the drugs that are usually used to control circulatory or digestive problems. This technology will probably be used widely in the future to help individuals with other problems gain voluntary control over many of their physiological responses.

Researchers will also continue to study the relationships between individuals' perceptions and thought processes and their physiological reactions. We already know that cognitive appraisals strongly affect our physiological responses to stress and pain. By modifying these appraisals it may be possible to modify our responses as well.

Environmental and cultural factors often interact with an individual's biological state to cause physical disorders. For example, studies show that the pace of life is correlated with coronary heart disease. Cross-cultural studies show significant differences in the incidence of some psychophysiological disorders. Medical treatment can relieve psychophysiological symptoms that are as painful and potentially harmful as those of any "real" illness. But the same factors that cause illness—personal and environmental stress, physiological defects and tendencies—also determine whether or not an individual can be completely "cured."

There are two basic principles involved in considering psychophysiological disorders. The first is that of *individual response stereotyping*. This means that each individual responds autonomically to a variety of different stress situations in a particular stereotyped way. Some individuals may have consistently strong cardiac responses to stressors; others may have strong gastrointestinal responses. The second principle is that of *stimulus-response specificity*. This means that psychologically based physiological reactions may occur only in response to very specific stimulus situations that constitute problem areas for the individuals.

Intense or continuous life stress can reveal weaknesses in an individual's "carrying capacity" (whether it is an aging dockworker's capacity to carry loads or a new widow's ability to carry and cope with interpersonal adjustments). Sometimes a

481

BOX 15.6

Type A personality

Is there a heart attack-prone personality? Friedman and Rosenman (1974), two heart specialists, have concluded that a heart attack-prone personality exists. These people, called Type A's, are prone to operate under high pressure and to be hard-driving and demanding of themselves and others. They are believed to run inordinate risks of having heart attacks. Further research is needed on the personality of the heart attack-prone person and on the ways in which cardiac risks can be reduced. The characteristics that are hypothesized to typify the Type A person include the following:

(Joel Gordon)

1. Talking rapidly and at times explosively.
2. Moving, walking, and eating rapidly.
3. Becoming unduly irritated at delay (e.g., waiting in line).
4. Attempting to schedule more and more in less and less time.
5. Feeling vaguely guilty while relaxing.
6. Trying to do two things at once.

Heart disease is a product of the interaction among behavior patterns, environmental demands, and dietary factors. But as more becomes known about the Type A personality, it may be necessary to conclude that our typically American, hectic, go-getter pace carries with it a high burden of tension and anxiety and risk of death at an early age. It may also lead to questions of a developmental nature, such as the impact of parental modeling of Type A behavior on children.

crisis reveals a latent and slowly developing constitutional weakness. If an individual smokes heavily, eats poorly, and works too hard for 30 years, a long-developing coronary condition may suddenly appear during an emergency. (See Box 15.6.)

We must be careful, however, about linking certain personality traits to particular psychophysiological disorders. Clinicians should not forget that too much exercise, cold weather, and exhaustion, together with other biochemical, genetic, and impersonal factors can also cause coronary problems, independent of the personality of the patient.

Psychosis

A psychosis is a disorder that involves major intellectual and/or emotional distortions, often accompanied by delusions and hallucinations. Psychoses often require hospitalization. They include the most serious forms of maladaptive behavior, and most psychotic individuals have little or no insight into the nature or severity of their disorder. Table 15.1 compares the characteristics of individuals with neuroses and psychophysiological disorders with characteristics of psychotics.

Schizophrenia

This first-person account describes the kind of retreat from reality that characterizes the most common psychosis: schizophrenia. This disorder takes a great toll in human suffering—particularly among adolescents and young adults.

> What I do want to explain, if I can, is the exaggerated state of awareness in which I lived before, during, and after my acute illness. At first it was as if parts of my

Table 15.1 Comparison of characteristics of neurotics and psychophysiologically disturbed with those of psychotics

Neurotic and Psychophysiologically Disturbed	Psychotic
Frequently talk about symptoms and do not accept their condition. Talk about how healthy they used to be and anticipate the day that they will return to their normal selves.	Often deny that there is anything wrong with them and tend to accept their disorder as inevitable. If someone calls attention to their unusual behavior, they will defend it. They live their psychoses.
Do not lose contact with reality. If anything, they seem to be unable to ignore reality.	Have frequent losses of contact with reality or have a shaky sense of reality. Often substitute fantasy for reality.
Have a sound orientation toward people, places, and time.	Orientation is often poor or entirely gone.
Complain about "falling apart," but rarely do.	Behavior may be disorganized by their disorder, and life-style is chaotic or verges on the chaotic.
Continue to function socially and on the job.	May harm themselves or others. Often require close care or hospitalization. Close relatives are among the first to insist that the psychotic individuals seek help because they are often the victims of their strange behavior.
Chances of responding to treatment and being able to function effectively are favorable.	May benefit from treatment (sometimes recovery is spontaneous), but "cure" is often temporary.

brain "awoke" which had been dormant, and I became interested in a wide assortment of people, events, places, and ideas which normally would make no impression on me. Not knowing that I was ill, I made no attempt to understand what was happening, but felt that there was some overwhelming significance in all this, produced either by God or Satan, and I felt that I was duty-bound to ponder on each of these new interests, and the more I pondered, the worse it became. The walk of a stranger on the street could be a "sign" to me which I must interpret. Every face in the windows of a passing streetcar would be engraved on my mind, all of them concentrating on me and trying to pass me some sort of message. Now, many years later, I can appreciate what had happened. Each of us is capable of coping with a large number of stimuli invading or being through any one of the senses . . . it is obvious that we would be incapable of carrying on any of our daily activities if even one hundredth of all these available stimuli invaded us at once. So the mind must have a filter which functions without our conscious thought, sorting stimuli and allowing only those which are relevant to the situation in hand to disturb consciousness. And this filter must be working at maximum efficiency at all times, particularly when we require a high degree of concentration. What had happened to me in Toronto was a breakdown in the filter . . . new significance in people and places was not particularly unpleasant, though it got badly in the way of my work, but the significance of the real or imagined feelings of people was very painful. . . . In this state, delusions can very easily take root and begin to grow. . . . By the time I was admitted to the hospital I had reached a state of "wakefulness" when the brilliance of light on a window sill or the color of blue in the sky would be so important it could make me cry. I had very little ability to sort the relevant from the irrelevant. The filter had broken down. Completely unrelated events became intricately connected in my mind. (Boisen, 1952)

Schizophrenia encompasses a group of behavioral patterns characterized by a loss of contact with reality, blunting of the emotions, and a disturbance in thinking. The resulting behavior is often so bizarre that the individual must be hospitalized. Schizophrenics often have delusions and hallucinations. A *delusion* is an incorrect belief about an object or event that an individual maintains even in the face of clear evidence to the contrary. A *hallucination* is a sensory perception that takes place in the absence

of an external stimulus. Hallucinations are usually visual ("seeing things"), but they may occur for other senses as well.

Schizophrenia is a complicated issue. The behavioral problems that it causes are much more severe and incapacitating than any of those previously described, and the presence of schizophrenics in a community can cause serious social difficulties. It is also a fairly common problem. Over 800,000 schizophrenic patients are treated yearly at some type of mental health facility.

Schizophrenics are often unable to communicate in a coherent way with others, and their thought patterns are confused. Figure 15.3 contains a series of drawings by Louis Wain, an English artist who suffered a schizophrenic breakdown in middle life. His drawings reflect the breakdown of the artist's thought patterns and contact with reality.

Schizophrenics think in extremely concrete terms. A schizophrenic might interpret the saying "A stitch in time saves nine" as "I should sew nine buttons on my coat," giving overly personalized and concrete meaning to a common proverb. Schizophrenics may also *overinclude*. Their thoughts and verbal behavior are filled with irrelevancies and it is difficult to make sense out of their stream of talk. Language seems to become a means of self-expression rather than a means of communication. Their thought processes seem like programs run in a computer constructed with unreliable components.

Aside from this confusion in thought, schizophrenics have difficulty communicating because their emotional responses are usually inappropriate. They frequently appear to be indifferent and totally apathetic. This is the result of a blunting of the emotions and of an arbitrary dissociation of feeling from verbal expression. The term *schizophrenic* literally means "split personality." This does not mean that schizophrenics have two separate personalities; it means that there is a separation between cognition and emotion. One schizophrenic talked about his child's death with a broad smile on his face. Another reacted with rage to a simple question about how he slept last night. Doctors observe the degree of emotional blunting and inappropriatness of emotional reactions to gauge the severity of a psychosis (Chapman and Chapman, 1973). Box 15.7 contains a group of first-person accounts of schizophrenic experiences.

484

We still do not know exactly what schizophrenia is. Is it a manifestation of a physical illness? A learned maladaptive behavior? A communication disorder? A way of life? Although many researchers have been investigating these and other questions for years, schizophrenia remains a severe clinical and social problem.

Researchers have, however, identified a number of characteristic clinical symptoms. It is unlikely that *all* the following features would be present in a given case, but most cases include several of them:

1. Delusions and hallucinations.
2. Hearing voices.
3. Feeling of being controlled by others.
4. Highly idiosyncratic language.
5. Inappropriate expressions of emotion (or no expression whatsoever).
6. Apathy.
7. Bizarre behavior.
8. Social isolation.
9. Poor occupational or academic performance.

There are four major types of schizophrenia: catatonic, paranoid, hebephrenic, and simple.

Catatonic schizophrenia. Disturbance in motor activity is the major symptom of catatonic schizophrenics. They may be immobile, with muscles that are rigid and inflexible, or they may be extremely agitated. Some catatonic schizophrenics have *waxy flexibility;* if their arm or leg is placed in one position, they will leave it there indefinitely until someone moves it again. Agitated catatonics move about a great deal and talk and shout almost continuously. They can be extremely dangerous to others.

Paranoid schizophrenia. Paranoid schizophrenia seems to be a primarily cognitive disorder, characterized by delusions and extreme suspiciousness. In some cases there may be dramatic shifts in the content of the delusions and hallucinations; for example, delusions of persecution may suddenly change to delusions of grandeur (from "They are out to get me" to "I am God"). But certain intellectual functions may be unaffected by these delusions. Paul Morphy, an American chess champion in the 1800s, developed paranoid schizophrenia in his mid-20s and

Figure 15.3 Four portraits by the artist Louis Wain of his cat. The portraits reflect the growing disorder in his thought. (Wide World)

was hospitalized for years, yet he remained a chess master.

Hebephrenic schizophrenia. Hebephrenic schizophrenia involves some of the most bizarre psychotic behavior. Hebephrenics have delusions and hallucinations (particularly visual hallucinations), make

485

BOX 15.7

The schizophrenic experience: First-person accounts

Schizophrenic experiences are so powerful that they leave indelible marks on an individual's life:

> Living with schizophrenia can be living in hell, because it sets one so far apart from the trend of life followed by the majority of persons today, but seen from another angle it can be really living, for it seems to thrive on art and education, it seems to lead to a deeper understanding of people, and it's an exacting life, like being an explorer in a territory where no one else has ever been. I am often glad that illness caused my mind to "awaken" eleven years ago, but there are other times when I almost wish that it would go back to sleep.

The schizophrenic's thinking is disorganized, fragmented, and confused:

> My concentration is very poor. I jump from one thing to another. If I am talking to someone, they only need to cross their legs or scratch their heads and I am distracted and forget what I was saying.
>
> Half the time I am talking about one thing and thinking about half a dozen other things at the same time. It must look queer to people when I laugh about something that has got nothing to do with what I am talking about, but they don't know what's going on inside and how much of it is running around in my head. You see, I might be talking about something quite serious to you and other things come into my head at the same time that are funny and makes me laugh. If I could only concentrate on one thing at a time I wouldn't look half so silly.
>
> My thoughts get all jumbled up. . . . People listening to me get more lost than I do.

The schizophrenic feels isolated from others:

> I felt all this tumult of madness—all this stark, lonely living which is worse than death—and the pain, futility and hopelessness of it all—and the endlessness, the eternity.
>
> (*Schizophrenia: Is There an Answer?*, NIMH, 1972)

strange grimaces and gestures, and giggle for no apparent reason.

Simple schizophrenia. Perhaps the least conspicuous and most common of all psychoses is simple schizophrenia. Many simple schizophrenics never receive clinical attention. The major feature of this disorder is a gradual withdrawal from contact with other people, usually without hallucinations or delusions. The onset is gradual; individuals show decreasing interest in people and things around them, initiative, and ambition. Simple schizophrenia typically appears some time during or after puberty; from then on there is a progressive decline in the individual's attempts at social interaction. Simple and hebephrenic schizophrenics are generally the most resistant to therapeutic efforts.

Understanding schizophrenia

The psychodynamic perspective. Psychodynamic theorists argue that schizophrenics' irrational thoughts and bizarre behavior are caused by urges and ideas that are usually unconscious. These thoughts break through to awareness and cause a generalized fear of the world. According to the psychodynamic perspective, this fearfulness is also related to profoundly frustrating interpersonal relationships during the early years of life and to a lack of emotional ties to people. Schizophrenics seem to go through life with no expectation of support or warmth from their social environment, and they regard other people as dangerous and threatening.

As fear of people causes them to lose contact with the environment, schizophrenics struggle to provide

486

a new environment to which they can adjust. The pseudocommunity, a device usually attributed to paranoia, is also applicable to most varieties of schizophrenic reactions. A *pseudocommunity* is a reconstruction of reality peopled by both real and imagined individuals. The purpose of the schizophrenic's pseudocommunity is not so much to come to terms with reality as to establish a world that will minimize the experience of anxiety. Schizophrenia is usually described as a thought disorder that has two basic aspects. One is the failure to think and communicate in conventional terms because of social isolation; the other is the use of unrealistic thought as a defense against anxiety.

One psychodynamic view of schizophrenia that especially stresses social relationships is offered by Laing (1969). Laing sees the schizophrenic psychosis as a normal reaction to an abnormal situation. It is not a disease but the product of deteriorated social relationships. The environment of the schizophrenic is so bad that he or she has to invent special strategies to live in an otherwise unlivable situation. Laing considers the family the most salient feature of the environment for most people. The preschizophrenic copes with an undesirable environment by denying its pathological features. The flowering of the psychosis takes place when the defense of denial is abandoned. The psychosis appears as madness only to those who are unaware of the environment that gave rise to it. Laing's views have become popular in recent years, but as yet a sizable body of research has not grown out of them. However, there is strong support for the importance Laing attaches to the family environment.

The behavioristic perspective. Behavioristic explanations of schizophrenia argue that both unusual inner motivations and peculiar ways of thinking and problem solving can be learned. They assume that behavior changes gradually in response to specific events. They argue that the distinctive feature of schizophrenia is the extinction or lack of development of conventional responses to social stimuli. They also argue that schizophrenics acquire a highly personalized set of responses in basically the same way as other people develop conventional responses.

Like normal individuals, schizophrenics are sensitive to reinforcement contingencies. They can acquire responses that help reduce or remove pain and punishment. They learn to avoid painful electric shocks, and hungry schizophrenics will perform instrumental responses in order to obtain food.

In order to modify schizophrenic behavior it is necessary to modify reinforcement contingencies. This may require a drastic overhaul of the patient's environment. The responses that reinforce bizarre behavior (usually unwittingly) must either be altered drastically or be eliminated.

The cognitive-behavioral perspective. A growing body of research and clinical observation suggests that schizophrenia can be viewed as a disorder of attention. Schizophrenics seem to attend to inappropriate or irrelevant stimuli, so that they then respond in an inappropriate or irrelevant manner. They suffer from a cognitive disorder that involves a distortion of reality. Some cognitive theorists think that this disorder might be corrected through retraining. We do not have any proof for this idea, nor do we know why the cognitive failure occurs. Is it due to social or biological causes? It is possible that as we gather more data on how schizophrenics process information, we will obtain more basic knowledge about the disorder and perhaps develop better methods of treatment.

The biological perspective. Too often arguments about the basis for schizophrenia have degenerated into an either-or confrontation—either it is caused by some biological or some environmental factor. Because outer and inner world factors operate simultaneously, it is difficult to estimate their relative contributions. Although biochemical, neurological, and other physical factors in schizophrenia have been explored, it is usually not possible to tell whether these abnormalities are the *causes* of schizophrenia, the *results* of psychological or physiological changes caused by schizophrenia, or the result of living for a long time in an institutionalized environment. It is possible that biochemical changes can be caused by the lack of activity, the diet (especially vitamin deficiency), or drugs administered in institutions.

Some researchers have hypothesized that schizophrenics have an abnormality that involves the substance *serotonin*. Serotonin is found in many parts of the body and seems to play a role in regulating the

487

emotions. Researchers have found that certain drugs that produce psychotic-like symptoms, notably LSD, seem to block the effects of serotonin. However, various kinds of evidence, including personal accounts of normal people who have taken LSD, suggest that the reactions of individuals under the influence of this drug and the behavior of schizophrenics are not identical, although they are similar in many ways. It is important that researchers find the basis for the similarities that do exist so that they can pinpoint the chemical substances involved.

Many researchers have concentrated on *neurotransmitters*, which convey messages in the brain. Some study the effects of drugs believed to influence the way in which neurotransmitters function. Certain drugs (the phenothiazines) have antipsychotic effects, whereas certain stimulants (the amphetamines) seem to produce schizophrenic-like psychoses. Although this research has not yet provided the "answer" to the riddle of schizophrenia, progress is being made in clarifying the relationships between certain drugs and behavior and between these drugs and neurotransmission.

At the present time the *dopamine hypothesis* is playing a major role in stimulating biological research into the relationship between neurotransmission and schizophrenia. According to this hypothesis, drugs such as the phenothiazines block the action of dopamine, one of several brain chemicals involved in the transmission of nerve impulses. Some researchers suspect that an excess of dopamine in the brain or an increased sensitivity of nerve cells to dopamine might be involved. This might account for the schizophrenics' appearance of being flooded by environmental stimuli and their inability to attend to all of them. Evidence consistent with this suspicion suggests that (1) amphetamines can increase dopamine activity and (2) antischizophrenic drugs block the action of dopamine.

A number of researchers have speculated that schizophrenia may be hereditary. They have studied the behavior of schizophrenics and members of their families using a measure called a *concordance rate*. This is the probability or risk that one of a pair of closely related individuals in a population will show a particular characteristic, if the other individual has the characteristic. In the general population the incidence of schizophrenia has been estimated to be from 1 to 2 percent. For half-siblings the figure is about 7 percent, and for full siblings it is between 10 and 15 percent. The concordance rates are higher for identical twins than for fraternal twins. For children with one schizophrenic parent the percentage is between 10 and 15 percent, but if both parents are schizophrenic, the risk for their children ranges between 40 and 68 percent.

A different but valuable approach to evaluating hereditary factors in schizophrenia is the *cross-fostering study*, which involves a comparison of at least three groups:

1. Children of schizophrenics adopted by normal parents.
2. Children of normal parents adopted by schizophrenic parents.
3. Children of normal parents adopted by normal parents.

There is a greater percentage of psychiatric disorders among children of schizophrenics adopted by normal parents than among children in the other two groups (Wender et al., 1974). Some researchers have concluded therefore that genetic factors may contribute to schizophrenia but that adoptive family characteristics do not. They believe that there are specific genetic factors underlying schizophrenia, whereas environmental factors are highly specific and highly individualized.

Despite the hereditary threads found in the cloth of schizophrenia, it is not clear exactly what the inherited tendency or predisposition means. Environmental, biochemical, and other factors also seem to play significant roles in the disorder, but their impacts, both individually and combined, must be explored carefully before we can draw any firm conclusions.

A disproportionate number of schizophrenics come from lower socioeconomic strata. Although poverty itself is not a direct cause of schizophrenia, conditions associated with poverty may be involved in the development of the disorder.

High-risk studies. One group of researchers has concentrated on studying individuals with a high risk of schizophrenia, such as those with a schizophrenic mother. In behavioral terms, the stimulus situation

488

created by a schizophrenic mother should interfere with a child's ability to learn adaptive responses. By studying these high-risk individuals from earliest childhood, investigators hope to identify biochemical, physiological, or life-history characteristics that distinguish them, even before the disorder appears, from normal control subjects and other individuals who do not develop maladaptive behavior. The accumulated findings of high-risk studies might aid in the development of preventive intervention programs. Because these studies are relatively new, there is no long-term evidence available yet.

A long-term investigation of high-risk children is being conducted by Sarnoff Mednick and his colleagues (1970, 1971). The subjects are 207 children of mothers with histories of chronic and severe schizophrenia (high-risk) and matched controls (low-risk). Although the incidence of schizophrenia in the control group has been low, 27 high-risk children needed psychiatric care by 1971. Comparisons among the 27 "sick" subjects, the high-risk subjects who did not breakdown, and low-risk controls revealed a number of significant findings. The 27 "sick" individuals had been more disruptive and aggressive in the classroom than had the other children in the study. Although its exact significance is not clear, it is noteworthy that 70 percent of the mothers of the "sick" group had suffered one or more serious pregnancy or delivery complications—more than double the percentage for the mothers of the other subjects in the study. The fact that both mothers' psychiatric histories and their complications with pregnancy or delivery were related to the incidence of "sick" cases indicated to the researchers that they should be wary of simple, single-factor explanations of schizophrenia (Mednick et al., 1974).

Researchers who conduct high-risk studies recognize that psychological disturbance in a parent does not necessarily lead to a heightened incidence of behavior disorders among children. (See Box 15.8.) Personality disturbances among mothers seemed to have a greater effect on the child's adjustment than did disturbances among fathers (Garmezy, 1974). Table 15.2 summarizes the results of a study of the parental characteristics of the offspring of psychiatrically disturbed parents. There were greater disturbances among children whose mothers were disturbed, had high anxiety and somatic symptoms, and some-

Table 15.2 Significant differences between disturbed parents with disturbed children (hospitalized for neurotic or behavioral disorders) and those with healthy children.

Psychiatrically Disturbed Parents with Disturbed Children (n = 48)	Psychiatrically Disturbed Parents with Healthy Children (n = 69)
Most often the mother	Most often the father
High anxiety	Anxiety was not high
Somatic symptoms	No somatic symptoms
Diagnosis of personality disturbance	Did not have diagnosis of personality disturbance
Symptoms directly involved child	Symptoms did not involve child
Overtly hostile to child; i.e., open attacks	Not overtly hostile to child
Had sick spouse (30%)	Did not have sick spouse
Long-lasting disorder	Disorder not long-lasting

Adapted from Rutter, 1966.

how implicated the child in their problems. One investigation showed that in families in which both parents had experienced severe psychological disorders, children were much more likely to be disturbed than were children from families in which only one of the parents had disorders (Mednick, 1973). More comparisons of this kind are needed before we can draw any clear conclusions about the influence of disturbed parents.

Affective disorders

Affective disorders are major mood disturbances of psychotic proportions. There are three main types: depressive reactions, manic reactions, and instances in which these occur alternately. Depressed individuals are lethargic, pessimistic, and self-degrading. Unless it is discernible that an individual is having delusions, or unless his behavior is seriously out of line, it may be difficult to distinguish between neurotic and psychotic depressives. Manic individuals are hyperactive, optimistic, and overconfident. Some individuals are alternately manic and depressive.

Psychotic depression differs from neurotic depression in several ways. Psychotic depressives show more maladaptive behavior; they seem to be extremely sad and are more apt to require hospitalization. Whereas neurotic depression is often precipi-

489

BOX 15.8
The invulnerables

The personalities of some high-risk children seem to be unscathed by their unfortunate backgrounds.

Michael, age 10, has a schizophrenic mother who has been in and out of institutions, a father who is in prison and an older sister who lives in a home for the mentally retarded.

Since the day he was born, he has known nothing but poverty, chaos and a fragmented life. It would not have been surprising if Michael should have turned out to be a truant, delinquent, schizophrenic or worse.

Yet his teachers describe him as charming, bright, a good student, a natural leader and loved by everyone in the school.

Even with suicide, death in the family, alcoholism—boys like Michael emerge. They exist not just in the ghetto and inner town but in suburbia as well. They are what University of Minnesota psychologist Norman Garmezy calls "invulnerables."

These are children who thrive despite genetic, psychological or environmental disadvantages, and

Dr. Garmezy, who has just begun to study the phenomenon, believes there are more of them around than is realized.

Eleanor Roosevelt apparently was one such invulnerable child, according to Dr. Vernon Devine of the Garmezy team. Her childhood was one of great stress. She was painfully shy. Her father was a charming, alcoholic wastrel she adored from afar and her mother an aloof presence who found her homely. When both parents died, she was raised by her grandmother in cold and splendid isolation.

So, perhaps, was Patrick Moynihan—the ex-U.S. ambassador to the United Nations. His father abandoned the family, he grew up in East Harlem, worked as a longshoreman and spent his adolescence shining shoes, hawking newspapers and tending bar in his mother's saloon in New York City.

The reason invulnerables haven't been noticed before is that nobody was looking for them. In addition, invulnerability is a complicated, subtle concept. Psychology traditionally has followed the medical model, which focuses on pathology or illness, and not on what makes people well.

(Copyright, 1976,
Los Angeles Times.
Reprinted by permission.)

tated by a current or recent experience, such as the death of a loved one or the loss of a job, there is no recognizable event or immediate personal conflict that serves to bring on a psychotic depression.

An individual in a manic state has a very high energy output and may sing, shout, whistle, play pranks, and generally act like a clown. Compared with the depressions, mania is a rare disorder, and it appears to be decreasing. The following case describes a dentist with a history of hospitalization for manic episodes. He had also had periods of depression, but had not been depressed enough to require hospitalization:

Robert B., 56 years old, was a dentist who for most of his 25 years of dental practice provided rather well for his wife and three daughters. Mrs. B reported that there had been times when Robert displayed behavior similar to that which preceded his hospitalization, but that this was the worst she had ever seen.

About two weeks prior to hospitalization, the patient awoke one morning with the idea that he was the most gifted dental surgeon in his tri-state area; his mission then was to provide service for as many persons as possible so that they could benefit from his talents. Consequently, he decided to enlarge his 2-chair practice to a 20-chair one, and his plan was to reconstruct his two dental offices into 20 booths so that he could simultaneously attend to as many patients. That very day he drew up the plans for this arrangement and telephoned a number of remodelers and invited them to submit bids for the work. He also ordered the additional necessary dental equipment.

Toward the end of that day he became irritated with the "interminable delays" and, after he attended to his last patient, rolled up his sleeves and began to knock down the walls of his dental offices. When he discovered that he couldn't manage this chore with the sledge hammer he had purchased for this purpose earlier, he became frustrated and proceeded to smash his more destructible tools, washbasins, and X-ray

490

equipment. He justified this behavior in his own mind by saying, "This junk is not suitable for the likes of me; it'll have to be replaced anyway."

He did not tell any of his family about these goings-on for about a week, and his wife started to get frantic telephone calls from patients whom he had turned away from his office. During this time, also, his wife realized something was "upsetting him" because he looked "haggard, wild-eyed, and run-down." He was in perpetual motion and his speech was "overexcited." That evening Robert's wife mentioned the phone calls and his condition and she was subjected to a 15-minute tirade of "ranting and raving." She said later that the only reason he stopped shouting was because he became hoarse and barely audible.

After several more days of "mad goings-on," according to Mrs. B., she telephoned two of her married daughters for help and told them that their father was completely unreasonable and that he was beyond her ability to reach him. Her daughters, who lived within several minutes drive, then visited their parents one evening and brought along their husbands. It turned out that bringing their spouses along was a fortunate happenstance because the father, after bragging about his sexual prowess, made aggressive advances toward his daughters. When his sons-in-law attempted to curtail this behavior, Robert assaulted them with a chair and had to be physically subdued. The police were then called and he was admitted to the hospital several hours later.

During the interview with Robert, it was apparent that he was hyperactive and overwrought. He could not sit in his chair; instead he paced the office floor like a caged animal. Throughout his pacing he talked constantly about his frustrated plans and how his wife and two favorite daughters double-crossed him. It was also learned that this was not the first episode of this sort and that he had a history of three prior hospitalizations.

He responded well to lithium treatment (a promising development in drug therapy with manic individuals) and was discharged within several weeks of admission to the hospital. (Kleinmuntz, 1974, p 234)

Emotions in psychotics not only are more intense, but are also somewhat different from normal emotions. Instead of being responses to the common frustrations and successes of everyday life, some of them are so inappropriate that clinicians may attribute them to biological changes. These emotional reactions are accompanied by changes in perception, thought, belief, and action. Often manic or depressed individuals must be hospitalized to protect them and those about them from the consequences of their actions. Depressed patients are high suicide risks and require vigilant supervision.

Suicide. Depressed individuals, whether they are neurotic, psychotic, diagnosed in some other way, or not diagnosed at all, may not stop with self-condemnation. They may move from thoughts to action. Because there is a danger of suicide, depressed individuals are often hospitalized promptly as a precautionary measure.

Clinicians try to find the quickest way to lift the depression. The two most common methods are somatic-electroconvulsive therapy and antidepressant drugs. Even psychiatrists with a psychodynamic viewpoint use these approaches (especially the drugs, which are so convenient) because they are effective.

The best indication that a depressed person might attempt suicide is an announcement of an intention to do it. People who talk about committing suicide may in fact do so; few people commit suicide without warning. Another danger signal is an unsuccessful suicide attempt in the past. Lack of emotional expressiveness, extreme preoccupation, and socially inappropriate behavior are all warning signals. Recovered or improved depressed individuals are higher than average suicide risks. Ernest Hemingway committed suicide by shooting himself after he was released from a hospital following a period of depression. Box 15.9 lists 11 facts and presents comparative statistics about suicide.

Understanding affective disorders

Although there are numerous theories about the causes of depressive and manic reactions, there is no single widely accepted theory about their origins. Different theoretical positions have stimulated inquiry along particular lines, and each has contributed a few pieces of the puzzle. But it is not clear how the entire puzzle fits together.

According to the psychodynamic position, many, if not all, psychotic depressions are reactions to events that are symbolically significant. The event need not be one that all individuals would consider a grievous loss. Rather, it is given that interpretation by the affected individual. An important difference between neurotic and psychotic depression is that in

491

BOX 15.9
Suicide

How serious is the problem of suicide?

Since 1900 the annual suicide rate for the United States has fluctuated between approximately 9 and 15 cases per 100,000 people. As the accompanying figures show, there is a considerable range in suicide rates among countries. The figures for West Berlin and San Francisco are included for purposes of comparison and because they are very high. In general, official statistics do not reflect all the actual suicides.

Suicide death rates per 100,000 for five countries, West Berlin, and San Francisco

Place	Suicide Rate
West Berlin	42.7
San Francisco	29.6
Belgium	15.5
France	15.3
U.S.A.	10.7
Greece	3.6
Mexico	1.6

Based on Barraclough, 1973, and Seiden, 1967.

Eleven Facts About Suicide That Have Been Supported by Research

1. Men tend to complete suicide, whereas women tend to attempt suicide.
2. For whites, middle and old age are the most common times for suicides; blacks tend to commit suicide in their 20s.
3. Cultural factors influence the suicide rate.
4. There is no evidence that any one drug works directly to cause suicide.
5. People who threaten or attempt suicide are more likely than others actually to commit suicide.
6. Suicidal people generally have disturbed social relationships.
7. Psychological tests are not good predictors of suicide, but behavioral indicators (such as sleep patterns) may be.
8. Suicidal people tend to be rigid in their thinking and to think in extremes.
9. Economic depression seems to increase the suicide rate, whereas war seems to decrease it.
10. Phases of the moon and the activity of sunspots do not affect the suicide rate.
11. Suicide is more common among individuals who have a history of psychological disturbances.

(Adapted from Lester and Lester, 1971, p. 167)

the former the impact of the precipitating incident seems understandable to most people, whereas in the latter the reaction is out of proportion to the loss suffered. For most of us the death of a pet would be a sad occurrence, but it would not arouse an excessive mourning response.

Why does the psychotically depressed person react with such irrational grief? Most psychodynamic formulations focus on the history of relationships between the person and the figure he or she was most dependent on as a child, usually the mother. Thus a historical antecedent of psychotic depressions is a disturbance in early childhood relationships. The disturbance might be actual loss of a parental figure or a feared or fantasied loss. Because of its anxiety-provoking quality, the early loss is pushed out of awareness. Nevertheless, it exerts its influence and culminates in actual depression when set off by a symbolically significant event.

Learning theorists have characteristically viewed mania and depression in stimulus-response terms. Depression involves a marked decrease in responsiveness to stimulus conditions in the environment, a manic reaction involves a great increase in the strength of responses. According to learning theory, depression is a reaction to an event that involves severe loss of reinforcement, for example, the death of a loved one or a job loss. An individual's history of reinforcement is a powerful factor in shaping his or her self-perception and perception of others. If self-debasing attitudes are reinforced and if the individual observes models who express similar attitudes, he or she may acquire the ideas typically expressed by depressives. Similarly, the reinforcement—subtle and obvious—of manic behavior and the observation of manic models might contribute to the acquisition of manic tendencies.

Martin Seligman's (1975) concept of *learned helplessness* (described in Chapter 1) argues that depression is the result of an individual's perception that he or she is powerless to change the environment. This perception is learned. The concept of learned helplessness grew out of animal experiments that demonstrated that subjects given unavoidable electric shocks later stop trying to escape even when they can. In Seligman's research, dogs were placed in a harness and given electric shocks that they could not avoid or escape. Later they were placed in a shuttlebox avoidance learning situation. (See Chapter 6.) Animals that had been given the earlier inescapable shock made little attempt to escape the shock in the shuttlebox. They seemed to be "resigned" to experiencing pain. If human depression is in fact the product of learned helplessness—the expectation that painful events cannot be avoided—then there may be ways to "unlearn" depressive responses.

There are bodily consequences of manic excitement and depression that have definite implications for medical management. The bodies of manic individuals cannot endure their dervishlike activity for too long, and the psychomotor retardation of depressives affects the functioning of several of their bodily systems. Many researchers have hypothesized that severe swings in mood are caused by biophysical factors (endocrine imbalances, for example). One idea is that disturbances in mood are caused by an unstable state in the central nervous system. It has even been suggested that certain individuals' insatiable dependency needs may have some sort of hereditary or constitutional basis.

As we saw in connection with schizophrenia, the fact that both genetic and learning variables are interwoven within the family makes it difficult to decide on the course of the disorder. At present, it appears that genetic factors do play a significant role in certain types of disorders, but their precise character must still be clarified.

The scope of behavior disorders

We have described four groups of behavior disorders: the neuroses, psychophysiological disorders, and two types of psychoses—schizophrenia and affective disorders. They are but examples (although important ones) of the diverse conditions that researchers and clinicians deal. Each of these conditions can be approached from different perspectives that influence the work of researchers and clinicians.

It is important to remember that the behavior disorders include a wide range of problems arising from the interplay of many factors. The problems may be major or minor; they may be *acute* (come to the fore suddenly) or *chronic* (of long standing); they may involve disabilities in intellectual functioning, inability to work, high levels of personal dissatisfaction, or a combination of these difficulties. They may come about because of learning in connection with unfortunate interpersonal situations, defective bodily functioning, or significant social problems, or because of a combination of these factors. Diagnostic categories, such as neurosis and schizophrenia, are tools for research, record keeping, and easy communication among professional workers. They should not be used as a set of blinders to block out reality. Diagnostic categories have changed and will continue to change as we acquire new knowledge and develop new perspectives.

SUMMARY

1. Ideas about abnormal behavior and its causes have changed through time. Beginning in the nineteenth century, a more humanitarian approach replaced the sometimes brutal treatment of disturbed persons that had been characteristic since the Middle Ages. One current emphasis in treating those with behavior disorders is the attempt to keep these people in the community rather than isolated in large institutions.

2. Three groups of professionals specialize in treating emotional disorders—psychiatrists, psychologists, and psychiatric social workers. Although some of their activities over-

493

lap, each group has certain professional responsibilities not shared by the others and may emphasize different aspects of treatment.

3. Three major categories of behavior disorders are the *neuroses*, the *psychophysiological disorders*, and the *psychoses*.

4. *Neuroses* are disorders involving anxiety and distorted perceptions of reality. They impair individuals' overall judgment and capacity to relate effectively to others. Although neuroses can be classified by certain prominent symptoms, most neurotics' behavior includes several kinds of these symptoms. Neurosis in general and sometimes a specific neurosis can be explained from a number of different theoretical positions. Treatment based on each theoretical position is helpful in some cases.

5. *Psychophysiological disorders* not only have physical symptoms but also involve tissue damage and physiological changes. These disorders seem to be caused by anxiety and anger, the same emotional states that may lead to neurosis. Two concepts are basic in understanding psychophysiological disorders. When individuals respond to a specific situation or particular problem area with a particular physiological reaction, this is called *stimulus response specificity*. When a particular individual responds to many stressful situations in a characteristic way (e. g., by strong cardiac responses or gastrointestinal responses), this is called *individual response stereotyping*.

6. *Psychoses* are disorders that involve major intellectual or emotional distortions that are often accompanied by *delusions* or *hallucinations*.

494

7. Schizophrenia is the name given to a group of behaviors best described by loss of reality, blunting of emotions, and thinking disturbance. The four major types of schizophrenia are catatonic, paranoid, hebephrenic, and simple. Schizophrenics' behavior often is so bizarre that they must be hospitalized, although some schizophrenics (especially those diagnosed as simple schizophrenics) live marginal lives in the community.

8. Both environmental and biochemical factors seem to play a role in producing schizophrenia. Schizophrenia is more frequent among the poor. Children of schizophrenic parents are more likely than others to develop schizophrenia, whether they live with their parents or with others. Some drugs produce schizophrenic-like behavior in normal individuals, whereas other drugs cause a decrease in the symptoms of some schizophrenics.

9. *Affective disorders* are mood disturbances. Depressive reactions are the most common type. The group also includes manic reactions and alternating states that show manic behavior at some times and depression at others. Both heredity and the environment influence the occurrence of affective disorders.

10. *Learned helplessness* is a concept of depression as a reaction to a situation where an individual feels powerless to cause change.

Suggested readings

Bower, M. B., Jr. *Retreat from sanity: The structure of emerging psychosis.* Baltimore: Penquin Books, Inc., 1974. An analysis of psychotic thought that contains many provocative examples.

Coleman, J. C. *Abnormal psychology and modern life.* (5th ed.) Glenview, Ill.: Scott, Foresman and Company, 1976. Contains comprehensive reviews of behavioral disorders.

Kaplan, B. (Ed.) *The inner world of mental illness.* New York: Harper & Row, Publishers, 1964. Contains first-person accounts of behavior disorders.

Sarason, I. G. *Abnormal psychology: The problem of maladaptive behavior.* (2nd ed.) Englewood Cliffs, N.J.: Prentice-Hall, Inc., 1976. Contains comprehensive reviews of behavior disorders.

Seligman, M. E. P. *Helplessness: On depression, development, and death.* San Francisco: W. H. Freeman and Co. Publishers, 1975. Presents a theory intended to integrate laboratory and clinical information about depression.

Chapter 16

Therapeutic Behavior Change

(Preuss, Jeroboam)

Harry and Mary Lawson were both at home when the call came. From the University Counseling Center the psychologist, Dr. Carlson, told Mrs. Lawson that their son Rod was at the center, having been brought there by a friend. Dr. Carlson said that Rod was more than unhappy, he was anxious and somewhat depressed; and that the friend had told her that Rod stayed in his room in the dorm virtually all the time. He had not been to classes in a week. Apparently, Rod had been increasingly fearful of meeting people, even friends, and of having to talk with them. She felt Rod needed help; Rod apparently now felt that way too, because he had given her permission to call his parents.

As they drove to the university the Lawson's, when they were not silently sharing the shock of the phone call, talked about Rod, themselves, and what to do. "I can't say it comes as a complete shock," Mr. Lawson said. "Rod has always been a quiet, thoughtful kid. I've always wished he would tell me a little about what was going on inside. I guess it's my fault that we couldn't talk."

After a pause, Mrs. Lawson responded. "I know how you feel. I feel that way myself. But what we have to do now is think about the present and future—Rod's present and future, and ours too. When we get there we'll have to talk to Rod and his friend and to Dr. Carlson. She said she would be happy to help us consider alternatives. She seemed to think he needed some kind of counseling or psychotherapy."

We described important types of maladaptive behavior in the last chapter. This chapter deals with the topic of therapeutic behavior change. What can be done to help people like Rod—and perhaps his parents—cope more effectively with life? What are the options open to the therapist who seeks to bring about this improvement?

The history of therapeutic efforts in psychological matters is a short one. For many centuries deviant individuals were despised, subjected more often to torture than therapy. As attitudes toward mentally troubled persons became more benign, therapeutic methods grew out of various theories of causation. For example, Franz Anton Mesmer (1734–1815) believed that all illnesses could be cured by the equalization of a magnetic field that filled the universe. He claimed that there were both individual and group

forms of what he called animal magnetism. Mesmer's pretensions ultimately were exposed as trickery, but his ideas have carried over to some of today's behavior-influencing techniques, such as hypnosis, that depend on the effects of suggestion. (See Chapter 5.)

Modern approaches to behavior change stress the need to establish scientific validity for therapeutic methods. This goal is often a distant one because of the intricacies of most psychological problems. However, widespread acceptance of this goal, together with the increasing sophistication of researchers, holds promise of accelerating progress in achieving therapeutic behavior change.

There are four broad therapeutic approaches to the behavior disorders. As we have seen, the *psychodynamic approach* seeks to modify behavior through the client's acquisition of self-insight. Psychoanalysis exemplifies this orientation, as do other psychotherapeutic and counseling methods we discuss in this chapter. The *behavioral approach* views disordered behavior as a product of conditioning. It has grown out of laboratory studies of learning and is used to help clients overcome specific behavioral deficits directly rather than through psychodynamic explorations. The *cognitive-behavioral* position bears much in common with the behavioral viewpoint, but it stresses the acquisition of patterns of thought as well as overt behavior. The *biological approach* has produced a number of useful therapies, the most notable of which perhaps are the drugs that reduce anxiety and mental confusion. It is based on the idea that behavior is a product of biophysical states and structures. These approaches are not mutually exclusive; in fact, clinical workers often employ combinations of methods derived from them in treating their clients.

PSYCHOTHERAPIES

Psychotherapy takes place in a personal setting. It involves a professional worker and an individual who wants to find a way of dealing with emotional problems. Psychotherapists try to help their patients bring their anxieties and conflicts into the open so that they can determine where they came from, what effect they have, and how to deal with them.

Psychotherapy is not a standardized clinical tool. There are wide differences in emphases and methods even among therapists who share a common theoretical framework. Because it is expensive and may be slow, psychotherapy, and especially psychoanalysis, has been a privilege that only those with time and money could afford. In recent years efforts have been made to extend psychotherapy and counseling to disturbed individuals from lower socioeconomic backgrounds. Psychotherapists may disagree about some of their assumptions and clinical tactics, but most of them agree that self-understanding is an important step toward personal happiness and effectiveness.

Psychoanalysis

The first formal technique of psychotherapy was psychoanalysis as invented by Sigmund Freud. To use Freud's expression, it is a "talking therapy." It tries to free patients to think more positively about themselves and to develop without being stifled by their past. Freud asked his clients to lie on a couch so that they would not see the analyst and would feel less inhibited about revealing their inner lives.

Psychoanalysis concentrates on dreams, fantasies, and other material from the unconscious that patients reveal through free association. The analyst then tries to help patients integrate this psychic material into their everyday lives, to develop new insights into their behavior, and to develop more flexible ways to cope with anxiety. (See Box 16.1.)

The therapeutic relationship

The therapeutic relationship, the way in which the patient and therapist relate to each other, is the major vehicle for achieving therapeutic change in psychoanalysis. As patients talk about their lives and recall their pasts, they displace patterns of feelings and behavior that they originally experienced with significant figures in their earlier life (parents, brothers, or sisters) onto individuals in their current life, including the therapist. This displacement is called *transference*. In *positive transference* patients feel a great deal of trust in and affection for the therapist. In *negative transference* they feel hostile and resistive. Either or both types of transference reactions may be excessive because of the patients' irrational needs and perceptions. *Countertransference* refers to

(Powers, Jeroboam)

the therapist's emotional reactions to his or her patients. Psychoanalysts undergo their own training analysis so that they will have enough insight into themselves to reduce countertransference that could interfere with their patients' progress.

The following excerpt illustrates a number of features of psychoanalytic sessions. The analyst (A) encourages the patient (P) to free-associate and the patient shows strong transference reactions. The pa-

497

BOX 16.1

The acquisition of insight

The following excerpt illustrates the way in which fantasies can be examined to pinpoint sources of anxiety and to help relieve the anxiety.

A 26-year-old patient reported that he was feeling rejected by his fiancee although she had done nothing to justify his reaction. He then reported that the feeling had started the previous day when he had been at a picnic with his fiancee and his best friend. Although his fiancee and his friend had been attentive to him, he felt uncomfortable. He then recalled that during the picnic he had experienced the following daydream. "Jane [his fiancee] and Bob [his friend] began to look at each other in a loving way. They passed signals back and forth of getting rid of me. They arranged to get together later that night. I got the old feeling of being rejected—wanting to be in but out and not wanted. They sneaked off at night and necked and had sex. Then they told me about it and I gave her up although I felt a deep loss at the same time." After having experienced this fantasy, he had felt rejected by his fiancee even though in reality she continued to be very affectionate to him.

After recounting the fantasy in the therapeutic hour, the patient had a stream of associations. "I feel sad and low, almost as though she actually was unfaithful. Bob reminds me of competing with my brother. I was always second fiddle to him . . . he was always better than me. Everybody liked him more than me."

The patient was then able to view his unpleasant reaction at the picnic as analogous to his early pattern of expecting to be pushed to one side by his brother. He visualized Bob's displacing him as his brother had previously triumphed over him. It became clear to him that his current reactions of jealousy and vulnerability were not justified on the basis of the reality situation. With this realization, his feelings of estrangement from his fiancee disappeared. (Beck, 1970, pp. 6–7)

tient has just expressed concern about a mental block:

A: What comes to your mind about the hesitation in your thinking.

P: I have a sense of fright about my feelings toward you. . . . I was hoping that you could do my analysis (*Elaborates.*) Then . . . I felt as if I had found someone who cared and that somehow I would get a relationship here even though I know that that's ridiculous and that I'm just a patient. . . .

A Try to pursue what comes to your mind about this.

P: . . . I have the feeling that you'll be mad at me if I don't say something, and so I just can't say anything. But the longer the silence lasts the worse it gets.

A: What comes to your mind about the idea that I would be mad at you?

P: I think the way Mr. Harris [a former therapist] used to react if I didn't say anything. It also makes me think of my father and the way he would say "jump" and I'd have to jump or else he would call me "stupid."—I have a sense of hostility about it. I know when I'm feeling love but I don't know when I'm being hostile. And it scares me most to show my hostile feelings. But I wonder if maybe I have that turned around.

A: What comes to your mind?

P: Maybe I'm really afraid to show my love feelings. I have quite a bit of hostility that I'm aware of, and it's like my mother's. She takes it out on sales people. Last night I dreamed that I was going to do this but then I ran back to Harris instead of to you. Somehow I felt so sorry for you. In the dream I thought "I'm so sorry that I didn't go to him and when I didn't he cried." But then in the dream I said to myself, "You're not the first one and he's probably been hurt before."

A: Dreams are frequently useful in analysis, but we use them in a special way. After you've told me the dream itself, try to take each of the elements in the dream as it occurred and see what your associations are to each part.

P: The man in the dream somehow reminded me of a boy that I used to go with. He got upset when I left him but he also got over it almost immediately. Somehow there was a feeling of many women being in the dream and that reminds me of my father and all of his affairs.

A: What are the details of your thoughts about the boy that you went with?

P: That was really the worst time in my life and I turned into a terrible person. He was a horrible boy and he came from a very bad family but I would cling to him just as I clung to my life. I had lost all of my feeling of security when we moved to Springfield and so I grasped the nearest straw that I could find. I did lose that security that I had. (Dewald, 1972, pp. 22–23)

Both the patient and the therapist analyze the behavior that arises during therapeutic sessions. Often when individuals are confronted with an interpretation of their actions that is anxiety provoking, they try not to acknowledge it and appear surprised and confused. They may become irritated with the therapist, and in an effort to protect themselves, think of an acceptable explanation. Psychoanalytic therapy is especially aimed at helping individuals place their fears and motivations in perspective and to observe their own behavior. (See Box 16.2.) Many contemporary forms of psychotherapy rely heavily on principles derived from psychoanalytic ideas. (See Chapter 13.)

Client-centered therapy

Carl Rogers is a psychodynamic theorist who developed an approach to psychotherapy quite different from that of Freud and his followers. He too believed in using interpersonal dialogue as a means of intrapsychic exploration but described the therapist as an objective, restrained counselor who permits clients to come to grips with their own problems and allows all the attention to be focused on the client. Client-centered clinicians concentrate on the client's immediate experiences. In one of his major books, *Client-Centered Therapy* (1951), Rogers says that the job of the counselor is to try to assume the client's internal frame of reference or perspective, to see the world as the client sees it, and to communicate empathy and understanding of what the client is experiencing.

Rogerian therapists neither provide interpretations nor give advice. Rather, they try to create an environment in which clients can reorganize their subjective world. This reorganization is needed because maladjusted, anxious individuals may be threatened by the incongruity between their self-concept and their experiences. In order to reduce the threat, they may distort or deny experiences that are inconsistent with their self-concept. Whereas Freud considered psychotherapy a technical, rational, and orderly procedure, Rogers looks on it as an exploration, a self-actualizing experience. The Rogerian therapist tries to help clients understand their own internal frame of reference in an accepting and nonthreatening atmosphere. During this process clients explore their problems and learn to accept themselves. This is an excerpt from a client-centered therapy session. Note how the therapist tries to *reflect* the client's statements and how decision-making responsibility is placed on the client.

C: I've never said this before to anyone—but I've thought for such a long time—This is a terrible thing to say, but if I could just—well (*short, bitter laugh; pause*), if I could just find some glorious cause that I could give my life for I would be happy. I cannot be the kind of a person I want to be. I guess maybe I haven't the guts—or the strength—to kill myself—and if someone else would relieve me of the responsibility—or I would be in an accident—I—I—just don't want to live.

T: At the present time things look so black to you that you can't see much point in living—

C: Yes—I wish I'd never started this therapy. I was happy when I was living in my dream world. There I could be the kind of person I wanted to be—But now—There is such a wide, wide gap—between my ideal—and what I am. I wish people hated me. I try to make them hate me. Because then I could turn away from them and could blame them—but no—It is all in my hands—Here is my life—and I either accept the fact that I am absolutely worthless—or I fight whatever it is that holds me in this terrible conflict. And I suppose if I accepted the fact that I am worthless, then I could go away someplace—and get a little room someplace—get a mechanical job someplace—and retreat clear back to the security of my dream world where I could do things, have clever friends, be a pretty wonderful sort of person—

T: It's really a tough struggle—digging into this like you are—and at times the shelter of your dream world looks more attractive and comfortable.

C: My dream world or suicide.

T: Your dream world or something more permanent than dreams—

C: Yes. (*A long pause. Complete change of voice.*) So I don't see why I should waste your time—coming in twice a week—I'm not worth it—What do you think?

T: It's up to you, Gil—It isn't wasting my time—I'd be glad to see you—whenever you want to come—but it's how you feel about it—if you don't want to come twice a week—or if you do want to come twice a week?—once a week?—It's up to you. (*Long pause.*)

C: You're not going to suggest that I come in oftener?

499

BOX 16.2

A famous patient's impressions of his psychoanalysis

Though we might envision Supreme Court justices as extraordinary human beings, even they can fall prey to the kinds of physical and mental problems that bother the rest of us. The following autobiographical account describes the unique contribution of psychoanalyst George Draper to the personal development of former Supreme Court Justice William O. Douglas.

> My problem was migraine headaches, which threatened to ruin my career. I had gone to several New York specialists, paying the last one six hundred dollars. . . . "It is the imponderable that causes such illness," said Draper. Draper eventually psychoanalyzed me and helped me discover and understand the stresses and strains that produced the headaches. Once I faced up to them, the migraines disappeared. . . . The hours with George Draper were scintillating. He was strong in intuition, insight, and gentleness. . . .
>
> I never met a more daring intellect than Draper's, and I never knew anyone whose insight into other humans was more revealing and sympathetic. He was a great physician in the largest sense of the word.
>
> In sum, the main seminal influence in my life was Dr. George Draper. He did not, of course, know about law, and perhaps if he had been a lawyer he would have taken quite a different position on issues over the years than I. He was, however, a seminal influence because having discovered that I had been launched in life as a package of fears, he tried to convince me that all fears were illusory. (Douglas, 1974, pp. 177–182)

500

You're not alarmed and think I ought to come in—every day—until I get out of this?

T: I believe you are able to make your own decision. I'll see you whenever you want to come.

(Rogers, 1951, pp. 46–47)

Rational-emotive therapy

Rational-emotive psychotherapy, developed by Albert Ellis, is one of the more intriguing newer forms of individual psychotherapy. It represents a departure from the more traditional approaches because it is based more on cognitive than psychodynamic principles. Ellis believes madadaptive behavior is caused by thoughts (irrational ideas) acquired in the course of growing up. He contends that all effective psychotherapists, whether or not they realize it, function as teachers for their clients. They help their clients to review, perceive, and rethink their lives in order to modify unrealistic and illogical thoughts and emotions and ultimately to change their behavior. The rational-emotive therapist teaches the client to challenge irrational thoughts and to replace them with thoughts more in accord with reality that do not arouse anxiety. In a sense, the therapist teaches the client to talk to himself or herself. For example, it may be important for a particular client to say silently, "I shouldn't expect everybody to be nice to me."

In rational-emotive therapy the clinician may devote significant portions of a session to explaining and demonstrating productive thinking, to persuading the client to think and behave in more effective ways, and to discussing homework assignments, such as devising ways of behaving more assertively with co-workers or family members without alienating them (Ellis, 1962, 1970). Box 16.3 contains an excerpt from one session of rational-emotive therapy.

Group therapy

Group methods, of which there are many, are more economical than individual ones and permit some people to solve their personal problems within realistic social contexts. Some advocates of group therapy believe that it is more effective than individual therapy.

A group can provide individuals with an opportunity to observe the way other members handle the topics and problems that arise during each session. Group therapy for some can be a testing ground for new approaches to interpersonal relationships. For others the most significant aspect of the group may be the members' relationship to the therapist. In group therapy each member has the attention of the therapist for only short periods. Group therapists

This therapy group uses videotapes so that individuals can examine and evaluate their own behavior in a group situation at one step removed from the actual interactions. (Karales, Peter Arnold)

attempt to help group members learn to share an authority figure as well as their feelings. (See Box 16.4.) Individuals who are unable to express their ideas and emotions with others may not benefit as much from group therapy as they would from individual treatment.

As with individual psychotherapy, the clinician's goals and methods vary, depending on the client's problems. In some groups the emphasis is mainly on the client's acquisition of insight; in others the stress is on gaining the ability to express feelings openly and appropriately; and in still others it is on learning new, more appropriate, ways of behaving. Evaluating group therapy is even more complicated than individual psychotherapy because each client is part of a small society. The effects of group composition on each individual needs considerable study.

The diversity of approaches to psychotherapy

There are many therapeutic approaches and we have described only a few of the most influential ones. Therapeutic interventions differ widely in their assumptions, aims, and tactics. The following list gives some idea of just how wide this diversity is. It includes venerable approaches, such as the Adlerian, and recent developments, such as primal therapy, about which little is known.

Adlerian therapy

Adlerian therapy was founded by Alfred Adler, who rejected the Freudian emphasis on the role of sexuality. (See Chapter 13.) Adler believed that disturbed individuals are discouraged individuals. Either they never developed their courage or they lost it so that

501

BOX 16.3

Experiencing rational-emotive therapy

Excerpt from a rational-emotive therapy session

T: What are you really afraid of in regard to marrying?

C: Of rejection, it would seem. Of being left alone once again, after I had built up high hopes of remaining together with a man forever, as I did with my ex-fiance.

T: That's a surface explanation that really doesn't explain anything. First of all, you are constantly getting rejected, the way you are going on now, because you pick men who aren't marriageable or whom you refuse to wed. Therefore, your hopes of a prolonged, intense involvement are perpetually being dashed—rejected. Secondly, you are really rejecting yourself, all the time. For you are assuming that if you did get refused by some man, just as you once did, you couldn't possibly stand it—weakling that you are! This is a complete vote of nonconfidence in yourself. *You* are therefore truly refusing to accept yourself as you are. *You* are demanding that you be perfectly safe.

C: But isn't it better to be safe than hurt?

T: You mean, isn't it better to have never loved and never lost?

C: O.K. But if losing is so dreadful, *isn't* that better?

T: But why should losing be so dreadful?

C: Oh, loneliness. Not ever getting what you want.

T: But aren't you lonely *this* way? And do you *now* get what you want?

C: No, I don't. But I also don't get what I very much *don't* want.

T: Partly. But not as much as you think.

C: What do you mean?

T: I first of all mean what you mean, that you do not like to get rejected—and who the hell does?—and that you are avoiding this dislikeable event by not trying to get accepted. But I mean, secondly, that what you really dislike most about being rejected is not the refusal itself—since that merely gets you what you have when you do not try for acceptance; namely, being alone—but the belief that *this* kind of loneliness makes you a slob, a worthless person.

C: Oh, but I *do* dislike, and dislike very much, the refusal itself. I *hate* to be refused and then have to be by myself.

T: Partly. But suppose you won one of the males you desired and he died, and you lost him *that* way. Would that make you feel as badly as if you won him, he were still alive, and he *then* rejected you?

C: No, I guess it wouldn't.

T: Ah! You see what I'm getting at?

C: That it's not really the loss of the man that I'm concerned about, but his rejection of me.

(Ellis, 1973, pp. 47–48)

they could not meet the demands of life and social responsibilities. Two equals, the therapist and the client, work together to encourage the client to have faith in his or herself, to trust, and to love. The ultimate goal of psychotherapy is to awaken clients' social interest so that they can become happy, willing contributors to society.

The Alderian therapist constantly reminds clients that they are themselves responsible for their own behavior and its outcomes. Therapists use a variety of commonsense techniques, such as role playing and giving "homework" assignments.

The following case history illustrates the growth one highly disturbed individual experienced when he was guided by two Adlerian therapists to behave as a responsible social being.

BOX 16.4

The experience of group therapy: Client and therapist perspectives

A client's view

My first reaction was, "Why should I tell these people anything about myself? It's none of their business." What I found was that some of them felt exactly as I did. In principle, the idea of working out your problems in a group appealed to everybody. Still, we held back, thinking, I guess, that only the therapist could help us with our problems.

Then something happened. Not all group members were silent, fearful, and worried about their privacy. Two members decided—or so it seemed—to take over the group. They didn't shut up, compared their neuroses with each other, asked the therapist to comment on their comments, and pretty much ignored the other members of the group. It didn't take too long for some of us silent partners to ask ourselves the question, "Am I paying my money to listen to these guys' problems?" Someone actually came out and asked that question. Well, from that point on, we began working as a group, each of us having to decide when our ideas needed attention, how we might help other group members, and why we reacted to the seven other members in such different ways.

What made the group tick was our leader. He was an experienced group therapist who asked questions, sometimes answered them, made observations and interpretations, encouraged the shy and retiring people, and main-

tained enough control of the direction of each session so that each learned not only about our motivations and feelings, but how we affect others, as well.

Two therapists' views

Irv and Louise (the therapists) both felt considerable strain in the meeting. We felt caught between our feelings of wanting to continue more with Dinah, but also being very much aware of Al's obvious hurting in the meeting. Therefore, even at the risk of Dinah's feeling that we were deserting her, we felt strongly about bringing in Al before the end of the meeting.

We felt very much in a bind with Seymour. He was silent during the meeting. We felt very much that we wanted to bring him into the group and help him talk, especially since we knew that the reason he had dropped out of his previous group was because of his feeling that people were uninterested in what he had to say. On the other hand, today we decided to resist the desire to bring him in because we knew that by continually bringing Seymour into the group, we are infantalizing him, and sooner or later it will be much better if he were able to do it by himself.

Irv had a definite feeling of dissatisfaction with his own behavior in the meeting today. He felt he dominated things too much, that he was too active, too directive. No doubt this is due in large part to his feeling of guilt at having missed the previous two meetings and wanting to make up for it today by giving as much as possible.

Louise wondered whether the fact that Sarah was leaving the group was only due to her new work schedule or whether she was leaving the group because in fact she was considerably improved. It is striking that Louise said this only a few seconds before Irv was going to say it. The therapists are always looking for reassurances about their patients feeling better.

(Yalom, 1975, p. 444)

Problem. When the patient entered treatment, he had taken to bed and spent almost all of his time there because he felt too weak to get up. His wife had to be constantly at his side or he would panic. Once she was encouraged by a friend to attend the opera alone. The patient wished her a good time and then told her, "When you return, I shall be dead." His secretary was forced into conducting his successful business. Everyone was forced into "the emperor's service." The price

he paid for this service was intense suffering in the form of depression, obsessive-compulsive behavior, phobic behavior, especially agoraphobia, divorce from the social world, somatic symptoms, and invalidism.

Treatment. The patient was seen in multiple psychotherapy by Drs. A and B but both therapists were not present at each interview. It seemed to us from the patient's behavior that he probably had been raised as a pampered child, and that he was using "illness" to

503

tyrannize the world, and to gain exemption from the life tasks. If these guesses were correct, then we anticipated he would attempt to remain "sick," would resist giving up drugs and would demand special attention from his therapists. As part of the treatment strategy the therapists decided to wean him from medication, to give him no special attention, and not to be manipulated by him. Since he had undergone analysis over a period of more than three decades, the therapists felt he could probably produce a better analysis of his problems than they could. For this reason, interpretation was kept at a minimum. The treatment plan envisaged a tactical and strategic rather than interpretive approach. Some excerpts from the early part of treatment are reproduced below:

March 22. Telephones to say he must be hospitalized. Wife left him (untrue) and secretary left him (It turns out she went to lunch). Would B come to his office to see him? B asks him to keep appointment in B's office. Patient races about office upset. "I'm sweating water and blood." When B remains calm, patient takes out bottle of Thorazine and threatens to take all. Next he climbs up on radiator, opens window (17th floor), jumps back and says, "No, it's too high."

"You don't help me. Why can't I have an injection?" Then he informs B that B is soothing influence on him. "I wish I could spend the whole day with you." He speaks softly to patient and patient speaks quietly. Patient asks for advice about what to do this weekend. B gives antisuggestion and tells him to try to worry as much as he can. He is surprised and dismisses it as "bad advice."

April 2. Has habit of sticking finger down throat and vomiting. Threatens to do so when enters office today. B tells patient about the logical consequences of his act—he will have to mop up. Patient withdraws finger. "If you would leave me alone, I'd fall asleep so fast." B leaves him alone. Patient angrily declaims, "Why do you let me sleep?"

April 9. Too weak even to telephone therapist. If wife goes on vacation, he will kill himself. How can he survive with no one to tell him to eat, to go to bed, to get up? "All I do is vomit and sleep." B suggests that he tyrannizes her as he did his mother and sister. He opens window and inquires, "Shall I jump?" B recognizes this as an attempt to intimidate rather than a serious threat and responds, "Suit yourself." Patient closes window and accuses. "You don't care, either." Asks whether he can see A next time and before receiving answer, says, "I don't want him anyway." Follows this with, "I want to go to the state hospital. Can you get me a private room?" At end of interview

falls to knees and sobs, "Help me! Help me to be a human being."

April 12. Enters, falls to knees, encircles therapist's knees, whimpers, "Help me!" So depressed. If only he could end it all. B gives him Adler's suggestion to do one thing each day which would give someone pleasure. Patient admits behaving better. Stopped annoying secretary and let her go home early because of bad weather. Agitation stops.

As therapy continued, his discussion of symptoms was superseded by discussion of realistic concerns. Resistance waned. When he entered treatment he perceived himself as a good person who behaved badly because he was "sick." During therapy he saw through his pretenses and settled for being "a bad guy." However, once he understood his tyranny and was able to accept it, he had the opportunity to ask himself how he preferred to live his life—usefully or uselessly. . . . After resolving the issue of his tyranny, therapy moved on to his other "basic mistakes," one at a time. The frequency of interviews was decreased and termination was by mutual agreement. (Mosak and Dreikurs, 1973, pp. 70–73. Reproduced by permission of the publisher, F. E. Peacock Publishers, Inc., Itasca, Illinois.)

Family therapy

Family therapy is a specialized group approach whose advantages have been recognized increasingly during recent years. It is employed when the problems of one or more family members seem interrelated. The therapist encourages the family members to deal with their attitudes and feelings toward one another *as a group.* Family therapists differ in their theoretical orientations (e.g., psychoanalytic, client-centered) but agree on the importance of helping family members solve problems through group therapy.

In the following account Anthony Davids describes the use of family therapy in one clinical setting, Bradley Hospital, Providence, Rhode Island.

Psychology interns are regularly assigned families for therapy, and to me it is still a rather impressive sight to see a trainee going into his or her office with a father, mother, siblings, and a child-patient from our residential treatment program to conduct a therapy session. To accomplish this goal of interacting with all family members at once, these trainees often have to schedule their appointments in the evening or on Saturday when parents and siblings who attend school are available. In the quiet of the evening, I can sometimes hear loud voices emanating from behind the therapist's closed door, with babies crying, parents shouting, siblings arguing, and the therapist trying to inject his comments, opinions, and impressions into the proceedings. I am sure that much of the time, family interactions with the therapist proceed much more orderly and serenely. And I am certain that psychology trainees are learning a great deal more about childhood psychopathology, and treatment of it, from these *in vivo* family observations than they would from talking alone with their individual child-patient and then hearing the parents' side of the picture from a social worker's report of casework sessions with the child's mother and/or father. (Davids, 1975, p. 812)

Transactional analysis

Transactional analysis is another group therapy whose participants frequently have something in common; for example, they might be married couples. Transactional analysts emphasize the need for group members to gain insight into the social roles they seek out and play and the defensive quality of many aspects of their role playing. Openness to one's own feelings and those of others is a goal of transactional analysis.

The leader of a transactional analysis (TA) group focuses on *transactions*, the basic units of social relationships. The TA therapy process involves examining important transactions in which one person does something to another and the other person does something in return. Basic to the TA approach is the belief that a person can choose to change. Transactional analysis was originated by Eric Berne (1964) and popularized through the book by Thomas Harris, *I'm OK—You're OK* (1967).

Gestalt therapy

Gestalt therapy also emphasizes the need for insight into one's defenses. It is usually carried out in a group setting with stress placed on expressing (often through role playing) pent-up feelings and emotions. Individuals when they are on the "hot seat" receive feedback from group members (clients as well as therapists) about how their behavior affects others.

Gestalt therapy was largely created by Frederick S. Perls (1969), a physician who had studied psychoanalysis. He believed that once feelings were expressed they would wane in intensity and that the only way to get rid of anxiety was through emotional discharge. Perls contended that the therapist, rather than trying to reconstruct clients' histories of relationships with others, should stress the client's immediate moment-to-moment experiences as each session progresses. The goal of Gestalt therapy is for the client to discharge emotions in acceptable ways that do not hurt others.

Primal therapy

Primal therapy shares with Gestalt therapy the idea that bottled-up feelings cause behavior disorders. It is based on the idea that tension and pain associated with the frustration of "primal needs" in early life (e.g., frustrations created by lack of love and warmth) causes maladaptive behavior. To correct maladaptive behavior it is necessary to reexperience the intense feelings felt at the time the "primal needs" were not met. Primal therapists seek to weaken their clients' defenses so that these emotions can be expressed and handled more effectively.

T-groups

T-groups (also referred to as training, sensitivity, and encounter groups) were originally developed more as training than as therapeutic activities. T-groups emphasize feedback among participants with an emphasis on social relationships in the here and now. Members are urged to participate emotionally in the group and observe themselves and the group objectively. They are encouraged to reexamine many assumptions about themselves and their relationships to others.

T-group leaders try to foster an atmosphere in which many common props, social conventions, status symbols, and ordinary procedural rules are eliminated from the T-group. Various training exercises are used to heighten self-awareness of one's effects on others. The T-group procedure has been directed largely to the "normal" person. Although it may attract many individuals with emotional problems, this is incidental to the primary purpose of improving the functioning of an already adequate individual.

At the beginning of this section we noted that psychotherapeutic methods differ widely in their assumptions, goals, and procedures. They differ also in the degree to which they have been evaluated in a scientific manner. There is a need for more objective information about all the therapies. However, its

505

In recent years, various new therapies have become popular. One of these is depicted in this sensory awareness session, based on the premise that relaxing the body is the best way to achieve better psychological adjustment. Unfortunately, too often these new approaches have not been evaluated scientifically. (Fusco, Magnum)

Psychodrama is another new therapy that encourages patients to "act out" or concretize their feelings in order to rid themselves of negative emotions. (Zimbel, Monkmeyer)

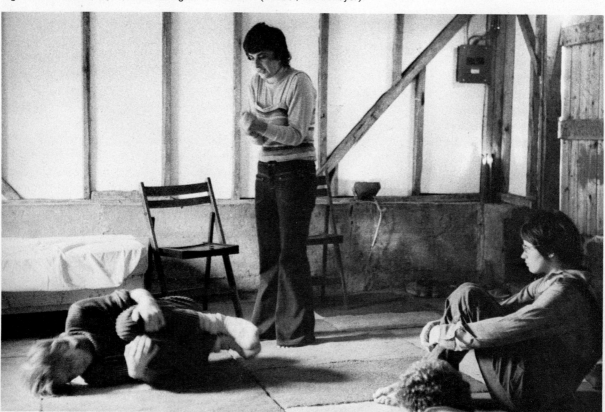

lack is particularly striking in many of the very recent methods (e.g., the Gestalt, transactional, and primal approaches). Relatively little is known concerning either the short- or long-term effects. The number of therapies has grown to such an extent that the borders among them are in many cases quite vague. As a consequence, members of the public experience difficulty in deciding whether to participate in them and what to expect.

BEHAVIORAL THERAPIES

Different psychodynamic therapies have different theoretical underpinnings and tactics, but they are all "talking" therapies. Behavioral therapies, which grew out of theories of learning, instead rely on action, conditioning, and methods for increasing or decreasing the strength of specific types of response. As we have seen in earlier chapters, there are two main behavioral approaches: the radical behavioristic approach, which deals only with identifiable stimulus-response connections, and the cognitive-behavioral approach, which, although it requires an objective definition of stimuli and responses, is also concerned with thought as it influences action. Let us examine the therapies that have grown out of these approaches.

Operant conditioning

Chapter 6 showed us that in operant conditioning, response consequences are manipulated in order to increase or decrease target behaviors. For example, a rat placed in a Skinner box for the first time will not press the bar very often. But if a pellet of food falls into a nearby dish after each bar press, the rat will begin to press the bar more often. If the rat were punished for every bar press, it would cut down on that response.

Reinforcement seems to be a factor in a number of major and minor disorders, including defects in speech and verbal expression. Many speech problems stem from psychological rather than physical causes. In stuttering, individuals repeat syllables or words and cannot make their speech flow smoothly. About 1 percent of the general population stutters, half of whom are children. Almost all stuttering begins before 10 years of age, and a great many stutterers are identified or labeled by the age of 5.

Stuttering often develops when parents begin to assume that their children should have learned to speak well. This happens at about 3 years of age. If the parents respond critically when their children have difficulty speaking, they may arouse conflict, anxiety, frustration, and anger, which cause the children to stutter.

If stuttering is the result of reinforcement, as behaviorists maintain, then direct manipulation of reinforcement contingencies can help reduce and eliminate it. In one experiment a patient was given an electric shock whenever he stuttered (Martin, 1968). His stuttering grew much less frequent as the shocks continued.

Although psychodynamically oriented therapists try to piece together a concept of the personality and the motivations underlying a patient's behavior, behavior therapists direct their attention primarily to the behavior itself and features of the environment that reinforce it. In this case the causes of stuttering were ignored and the therapist concentrated on "curing" only his stuttering behavior. Had a psychodynamically oriented therapist been handling the case, he or she would have focused on thoughts and feelings in order to help the patient to stop stuttering.

Operant conditioning principles have been used therapeutically with individuals, as in the cases of stuttering and hysterical neurosis, and with groups (e.g., in hospital wards). In the latter case, reinforcers (cigarettes, money, opportunities to leave the institution) are given for improvements in social behavior and effective work habits. In one such program a *token economy* was instituted by Theodoro Ayllon and Nathan Azrin (1965) at Anna State Hospital in Illinois on a psychiatric ward containing severely disturbed women, most of whom had been hospitalized for many years. The experimenters first decided to reinforce those behaviors necessary for effective day-to-day functioning, such as self-management, satisfactory work performance, and conventional social behaviors. The patients could earn a specified number of tokens for each behavior. The tokens were redeemable for such privileges as choice of bedroom, rental of a room divider for increased privacy, freedom to leave the ward or to be escorted to a nearby town, recreational opportunities, rental of a private television set, and purchase of such commissary items as personal grooming aids and reading

507

BOX 16.5

The A-B-A-B experimental design

Investigators who use operant conditioning procedures to change behavior often work with one person at a time. How can they determine whether the conditioning procedures cause whatever change occurs? One way to test the effect of the procedures is to use an A-B-A-B experimental design.

The A-B-A-B design consists of obtaining a precontingency or base-line measure of the target behaviors (A), instituting the reinforcement contingency procedures (B), removing the contingency so that the conditions which were present during the baseline period are reinstated (A), and, finally, reintroducing the phase B contingency (B). This repeated-measures design is a very powerful method for isolating the conditions which control behavior.

This design was used in operant therapy with a 19-year-old man admitted to a hospital with com-

Mean number of steps taken and mean distance walked as a function of instructions and reinforcement. (From Hersen et al., 1972, p. 721. Reprinted by permission of author and publisher.)

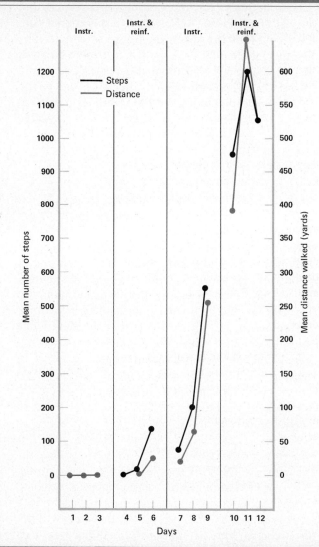

materials. Because the tokens could be exchanged for such a wide variety of desired commodities, they retained their effectiveness over time.

Ayllon and Azrin's token economy was highly effective in modifying social and work behaviors. In order to demonstrate that the tokens had a positive effect because they were serving as conditioned positive reinforcers, the investigators distributed them for a time without requiring that the patients per-

form the desired behaviors. Within a week all the patients had stopped working. When the researchers again made the tokens contingent on performance, patients resumed working almost immediately.

Classical conditioning

In classical conditioning a conditioned stimulus signals the appearance of an unconditioned stimulus. (See Chapter 6.) An unconditioned stimulus arouses

plaints of pain in the lower back, both legs and hips, and great difficulty in walking, sitting, and standing. After exhaustive medical study it was concluded that his symptoms were unrelated to physical causes and the case was diagnosed as an hysterical neurosis.

The operant therapy was begun by arranging visits by a young assistant to the patient's room three times daily. During these visits she spent approximately ten minutes talking to the patient about topics unrelated to his psychiatric disorder. During an initial three-day period she encouraged him to walk but provided him with no reinforcement for doing so. During the next three-day sequence she instructed the patient to walk and reinforced him when this happened. Reinforcement consisted of comments such as "Good," "That's great," "You're doing fine," accompanied by attention, friendliness, and smiling. Reinforcements were not given during the following three-day period and were reinstituted during the final three days of the experimental therapeutic program.

The graph summarizes the results of the program. During the instruction period alone there was no increase in walking. Addition of reinforcement resulted in increased walking. Contrary to what might be expected, improvement continued during the period of omission of reinforcements. Uncontrolled and unscheduled reinforcement by other patients may have contributed to continued improvement during this period. Greatest improvement occurred during the final phase of the program.

an involuntary or semivoluntary response. Researchers have created chronic abnormal emotional states in animals by subjecting them to inescapable conflicts and punishments and to situations in which they are forced to decide between competing alternatives that are difficult to discriminate (e.g., circles and ellipses that are very similar). The resulting *experimental neuroses* may cause hyperirritability, tenseness and restlessness during the experiment,

inhibited motor reactions, changes in sleeping patterns, respiratory and cardiac changes, changes in urination and defecation patterns in the laboratory, and social and emotional changes.

As we saw in Chapter 15, behaviorists theorize that many human preferences and needs are the product of classical conditioning. They believe that destructive or abnormal needs can be corrected through application of specific conditioning procedures. One area where this idea has been applied clinically is sexual deviations.

Oswald (1962) described the case of a fetishist, a person for whom a particular inanimate object stimulates sexual excitement. Both the client and his wife were concerned over his need to have his wife wear rubberized garments in bed in order for him to become sexually excited. Oswald used counterconditioning to eliminate the arousal properties of the stimulus. He gave the client nausea-inducing drugs repeatedly while he showed him rubberized clothes. In a 21-month follow-up, Oswald recorded the following observations:

> He feels quite indifferent to rubberized clothes and finds it hard to believe how he could ever have had this interest in them. His career has prospered extremely well by his own efforts and talents, and his wife confirms that they are normal and happy in their general and sexual life. (Bandura, 1969, p. 523)

Systematic desensitization

As we saw in Chapter 8, systematic desensitization involves both learning and cognitive processes. This technique is used most widely with individuals who suffer from specific fears and phobias.

From a behavioral perspective, systematic desensitization is a "deconditioning" process. It progressively reduces the strength of a fear reaction because the individual experiences the fear-arousing stimuli in a relaxed state. It also involves a cognitive process because the individual visualizes anxiety-arousing images, or *thinks* about a stimulus rather than actually confronting it.

Systematic desensitization has also been used to correct stuttering; stutterers were taught to relax while they thought about progressively more anxiety-provoking situations (Boudreau and Jeffrey, 1973). They named the following situations as being particularly distressing:

509

Talking to strangers.

Reading in class.

Talking in public, class, and parties.

Talking to family.

Asking questions in class.

Answering the telephone.

Figure 16.1 shows the results of a comparison between two groups of stutterers—those who received desensitization training and those who did not. The experimental (desensitization) group showed a significant decline in stuttering. Although similar results have been reported for treatment of a variety of behavioral problems, a number of questions remain to be answered, including why desensitization works. Several factors seem to be involved. Anxiety may be reduced primarily through a relaxation and deconditioning process. However, another factor is that the person undergoing desensitization has learned a new coping skill: how to use self-instructions to bring about relaxation. Yet another possibility is that muscle relaxation activates an antianxiety mechanism within the brain and external stimuli lose their ability to evoke anxiety. Regardless of which theoretical explanation is most valid, systematic desensitization is often a highly successful clinical technique and merits further scientific study.

Modeling

Observing a model reacting to a situation can provide important clues as to how to cope adaptively with that situation. Modeling is particularly effective with children. It has been used to treat a variety of problems, including intense fears of snakes or dogs, for example. Fearful individuals who watch a model perform the behavior they fear (e.g., petting a dog) without suffering any adverse consequences reduce their efforts to avoid that behavior. As we saw in Chapter 6, modeling approaches can also be used to strengthen socially appropriate behavior among individuals whose behavior is maladaptive.

Assertiveness training

Individuals who allow others to manipulate them too easily usually lack self-confidence and may not know how to react assertively in certain types of situations. Modeling plays an important role in assertiveness training: Frightened individuals can observe another person saying no or standing up for his or her rights without being obnoxious or annoying. In the following example a therapist served as a model for his client, a male college student who had difficulty making dates with girls. The client began by pretending to ask for a date over the telephone:

Client: By the way (*pause*), I don't suppose you want to go out Saturday night?

Therapist: Up to actually asking for the date you were very good. However, if I were the girl, I think I might have been a bit offended when you said, "By the way." It's like asking her out is pretty casual. Also, the way you phrased the question, you are kind of suggesting to her that she doesn't want to go out with you. Pretend for the moment I'm you. Now, how does this sound: There is a movie at the Varsity Theater this Saturday that I want to see. If you don't have other plans, I'd like very much to take you.

Client: That sounded good. Like you were sure of yourself and like the girl, too.

Therapist: Why don't you try it.

Client: You know that movie at the Varsity? Well, I'd like to go, and I'd like to take you Saturday, if you don't have anything better to do.

Therapist: Well, that certainly was better. Your tone of voice was especially good. But the last line, "if you don't have anything better to do" sounds like you don't think you have much to offer. Why not run through it one more time.

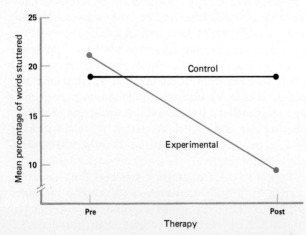

Figure 16.1 Percentage of words stuttered by experimental and control groups. (Boudreau and Jeffrey, 1973, p. 210.)

Client: I'd like to see the show at the Varsity, Saturday, and if you haven't made other plans, I'd like to take you.

Therapist: Much better. Excellent, in fact. You were confident, forceful, and sincere. (Rimm and Masters, 1974, p. 94)

By rehearsing alternative approaches to social behavior and receiving reinforcement from the therapist, clients learn to handle stressful situations more effectively. The first step in assertiveness training is to encourage self-assertion. Later, the training involves a more detailed systematic procedure, including breaking down the problem situation into a series of more manageable segments. Each segment has a practical orientation and is well rehearsed before the client attempts an integrated behavior pattern. Assertiveness training, like many newer types of therapy, involves a number of components, one of which is cognitive preparation for situations in everyday life.

The way in which we view ourselves, interpret events, and analyze problems influences our behavior in a wide variety of situations. The cognitive-behavioral perspective has contributed to the development of programs for strengthening the skills we need for effective and rewarding social functioning.

BIOLOGICAL THERAPIES

Galen, a physician in ancient Greece, attributed what today would be labeled hysterical neurosis to a malformation of the ovaries. Benjamin Rush, a physician in the early nineteenth century, believed that the cause of madness lay primarily in the blood vessels of the brain. Today well-trained clinicians understand that the biological laws governing our lives have a great deal of bearing on our psychological functioning. Biological research and theory have had an increasing influence on our study of different types of behavior disorders and in devising useful methods for treatment.

Of course, physicians who have sought physiological causes for maladaptive behavior have also sought physiological cures. At one time, many hoped that psychosurgery would prove a quick and easy therapy for disturbed behavior. During the 1930s brain operations, such as lobotomies, which sever the connec-tions between the prefrontal cerebral tissues and the thalamus, were performed frequently, especially on "hopeless" institutionalized patients. Unfortunately, the positive effects of these operations were overestimated during this period. We now know that a significant number of people do not respond well to them. Some become listless and confused; many are reduced to an essentially vegetative level of existence. These operations are rarely performed in clinical practice today. At present, there are two main physiological approaches to maladaptive behavior: *shock therapies* and *drug therapies.*

Electroshock

The most widely used of the shock methods is *electroshock therapy* (EST). Two electrodes are placed on either side of the patient's head, mouth pads are inserted behind his or her incisors, and a controlled current is applied for a fraction of a second. Each electric shock produces a convulsion followed by a brief period of coma. *Insulin coma treatment* is another shock method. It produces a coma, with or without convulsions, through an injection of insulin into the muscles. The use of insulin shock is declining because it involves medical complications and side effects.

What is the theoretical basis for the use of electroshock treatment? Although more than 50 theories have been suggested, we do not have a proven explanation for its effectiveness. Through observation, researchers have found that it is clinically effective for certain disorders. (It is not at all effective for neurotics.) In some cases the results are dramatic—a person who has been in a deep depression for months may become cheerful and active within days. A series of as few as 6 or as many as 50 shocks may be needed to produce significant improvement. Less dramatic, but still encouraging, improvement has been reported for schizophrenics, especially those whose psychotic behavior is relatively recent (generally less than a year old). In some cases delusions and hallucinations disappear completely, patients become more cooperative, and they are soon capable of living in the community. Relapses are common, however. Many therapists combine shock treatments with psychotherapy. They believe that EST diminishes the capacity to feel anxious and makes it easier for patients to explore and discuss their inner selves.

511

The use of EST has declined over the past decade. Individuals in poor physical condition may risk medical complications as a result of EST convulsions. Most patients experience some memory loss for varying periods of time. Moreover, the muscular contractions may cause fractures and dislocations, although muscle relaxant drugs are now used to minimize the risk.

Drug therapies

The increased use of drug therapies during the past 20 years has caused a decrease in the use of EST, psychosurgery, and other physiological approaches. Unlike surgical and shock techniques, drugs are used widely for mild as well as severe clinical cases.

Psychopharmacology is the study of the effects of drugs on behavior. It requires the skills of chemists, physiologists, and psychologists and is a rapidly growing area of investigation. Researchers have known for many years that chemicals influence behavior. Narcotics reduce pain; sedatives, such as barbiturates, reduce anxiety and induce sleep; stimulants, such as caffeine, relieve depression. But only during recent years have chemicals been used extensively to treat almost the entire range of behavior disorders. More than 200 million prescriptions are filled in the United States each year for drugs that affect moods, thought, and behavior.

Antianxiety drugs

Surveys have shown that more than 15 percent of Americans between the ages of 18 and 74 use antianxiety tranquilizing drugs. Between 15 and 20 percent of the patients who visit physicians are the "worried well." Some physicians routinely prescribe antianxiety drugs for them; about 90 percent of these prescriptions are written by general practitioners. The substances they prescribe are designed to reduce anxiety as much as possible but not to reduce patients' other mental capabilities. Intensive studies of drug effects on animals are carried out prior to beginning research on humans. (See Box 16.6.)

Antipsychotic drugs

Antianxiety drugs are often described as "minor" tranquilizers, in contrast to "major" tranquilizers used to treat more severely disturbed patients. If patients are hallucinating or have delusions, the drug

chlorpromazine may reduce these symptoms. If patients are withdrawn this drug makes them more active. If they are wildly excited it tends to calm them. Many patients who respond well to antipsychotic drugs relapse if they stop taking their medication. (In a few cases these drugs have dangerous side effects, so they must be used with caution.) Few schizophrenic patients now living in the United States and Europe have not received antipsychotic drugs at some time.

Antidepressant drugs

Antianxiety drugs frequently do not help depressed people and many physicians prescribe antidepressants instead. Iproniazid was one of the earliest antidepressants. It was originally used in studies of tubercular patients and researchers discovered accidentally that it energized patients who took it. Today nearly three-quarters of all depressed patients respond positively to one of a large number of antidepressant drugs. Unfortunately, there may be a lag of as long as four weeks between the time the patient starts taking an antidepressant and the time he or she shows any changes in behavior. Antidepressants have reduced the use of electric shock as a treatment for depression.

HOSPITALIZATION

Although certain programs and "therapies" have been widely recognized as ineffective and perhaps even harmful, many are still being used. Hundreds of individuals are hospitalized without sufficient reason, often against their will. Certain cases, however, require some form of hospitalization because they need 24-hour care, they must be observed, or there is some other reason.

Approximately two-thirds of the patients in public mental hospitals are considered chronic cases. Depending on the hospital, between 20 and 75 percent of the admissions and readmissions never leave. When individuals threaten to harm either themselves or others, friends or relatives may try to commit them. The laws and procedures for involuntary commitment have aroused controversy among both clinicians and the general public. Some argue that the practice should be abolished; others feel that

512

BOX 16.6

Drugs and the weaving of spider webs

Photograph of a web built by an adult female spider in a 5 × 50 cm aluminum frame. Note the spider in the hub, surrounded by a ring-shaped free zone. (Peter M. Witt)

After receiving an antianxiety drug, spiders always built relatively small, regular webs. (Peter M. Witt)

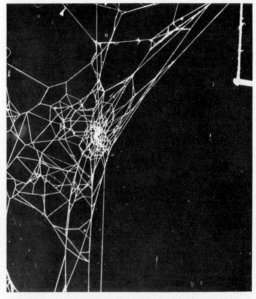

The web of an adult female spider that had received a relatively high dose of a stimulant, d-amphetamine. Note the remnants of a hub, the few irregular and frequently interrupted radii, and the irregular spiral. Twenty-four hours later this same spider built a small, irregular, but closer to normal web. The web structure was completely normal several days later. (Peter M. Witt)

Mental hospitals are often barren, depressing environments. Individuals who are hospitalized against their will lose their civil rights and may find it difficult to obtain a release. (Maynard, Stock, Boston)

individual who is being committed must be present at the hearing; in others he or she need not be. Commitments can be for specific periods of time or for an indefinite period. In some states psychiatrists play the key role in commitment decisions. In others physicians who are not psychiatrists may play dominant roles. Approximately 250,000 patients are committed every year.

Involuntarily hospitalized individuals lose their civil rights. They cannot vote, marry, obtain a divorce, or enter into contracts. Unfortunately, the rights of many individuals have also been abused both during the commitment decision process and within the hospital.

The following remarks by Judge Joseph Schneider of the Circuit Court of Cook County, Illinois, make it clear that socioeconomic factors play a very significant role in commitment proceedings.

> In my court in Chicago the majority of the people subjected to commitment proceedings are the poor. Rarely is the sanction of the court used to impose mental treatment on the middle or upper classes. Mental illness is not exclusively a disease of the poor, but alternatives to hospitalization and adequate treatment resources are available to those who can afford to pay. Resistance to treatment by the poor is not always the equivalent of lack of insight or motivation or of impaired judgment. Too often the objection to treatment is an accurate perception that the "treatment" offered is either inadequate or nonexistent. (Schneider, 1972, p. 1061)

Because of insufficient funds and lack of trained personnel, state hospitals are often little more than custodial institutions in which the amount of patient contact with professional therapists is pitifully small. In fact, some individuals do need a friendly, protective institutional setting in order to begin solving their personal problems. It is not clear how the society can provide this type of setting for large numbers of people. Objective research is needed to compare the effectiveness of different institutions and mental hospitals that are organized in different ways.

There is also a need to develop alternatives to hospitalization. In a number of studies, hospitalized individuals have been discharged to a halfway house, a specially created institution in which they participate in planning and decision making as residents

society must protect itself from potentially dangerous individuals.

All 50 states have commitment laws. The process involves a petition, a hearing, and a decision as to where to place the individual. The hearing usually takes place in court, but in one state a county commissioner hears the case, and in another the head of the hospital listens to the petition. In some states the

rather than as patients. Theoretically, the effectiveness of these community living arrangements can be gauged by comparing patients sent to them with those discharged into the regular community. There seems to be a need for permanent facilities to house those individuals who are unable to accept the greater social responsibilities of living completely on the "outside" but who are capable of living outside the confines of a hospital.

EVALUATING THERAPY

Unfortunately, in some cases therapists and clients have very different opinions concerning the client's progress in therapy. A thorough assessment of improvement in therapy actually should include data from a number of sources: the client; the therapist; people who know the client well, such as family members and friends; and independent observers who watch the client's behavior.

Evaluating the outcome of therapies requires that many factors be considered. For example, in some cases there is *spontaneous remission*—the client is greatly improved but the improvement seems unrelated to therapeutic efforts. In other cases improvement when it occurs seems more related to the personal attributes of the therapist than to the type of therapy he or she practices. Another factor that often contributes to a therapeutic effect is the fact that the therapist showed a sincere interest in the client and aroused a sense of hope about the present and future. Research into these factors is being conducted throughout the world.

Though it may never be possible to develop a single index to measure the effects of therapy, it should be possible to study the relationships among a number of variables involved in success. The assessment process is related to another important issue. If therapy is effective, what makes it work? How do different methods of therapy affect the behavior of clinicians, and ultimately of their patients? Does it make a difference whether therapists agree or disagree about theoretical orientations and views? Are differences in effectiveness related to the therapist's personal characteristics and style of social interaction more than to their views about the process of therapy?

Both the expectations of the therapist and the expectations of the client are known to influence the effectiveness of therapy (Goldstein, 1973). Their expectations about the *rate* at which the client should improve and how *much* he or she should improve are often markedly different.

Just as with parents, therapists who are indecisive and lack confidence in their abilities seem to communicate this to patients. Patients who are resistant to modifying their behavior seem to communicate this resistance to their therapists. Moreover, there are many other attitudinal factors besides expectations, and the psychotherapeutic process is always highly complex. In some instances gaining insight into one's motivations may represent a major step forward in therapy. In other instances clients must be able to behave differently.

Group therapy is also quite difficult to evaluate because of the sheer numbers of people and attitudes involved. Valid studies must use control groups with which the therapy groups can be compared. The groups should be as similar or equal as possible at the outset. Even social psychological factors must be controlled. If the staff on a ward of a mental hospital believes that its program is a significant therapeutic innovation, their behavior with the patients might be influenced by this belief. Their enthusiasm might, by *itself*, have an effect on the patients in their care. There is evidence that an *enthusiastic* attitude does have an effect on people in a great variety of situations, including hospitals, schools, and private consulting rooms.

As described in Chapter 4, *placebos*, or inactive substances that have no pharmacological effect, may also cause noticeable improvement in patients. Physicians know that their attitude when they prescribe given medicines can influence their patients' reactions. The behavior of suggestible patients might show great improvement if they are given a drug that is presented as a "wonder drug," even though it may be chemically inactive.

It is important to realize that the objective study of therapeutic situations is often extremely difficult. Clinicians can neither arbitrarily assign patients to untreated control groups nor select for treatment only those patients who fit their research needs. Teams of researchers and clinical specialists must work together to compile information in order to

BOX 16.7

Judge or panhandler: whose judgment was faulty?

Four months ago, when police tried to arrest Robert Friedman for begging for dimes in front of a downtown bus station, he pleaded:

"Don't take me in. I'm not broke. I didn't know this was a crime." And he opened a brief case he was carrying that contained $24,087 in small bills.

A few days later, he was committed to Chicago-Read Mental Health Center by a judge who said he was protecting Friedman from thugs who might be after his cash.

Today, Friedman, 42, has seen half his life savings eaten away by hospital fees and doctors' bills for treatment ordered by the court and by the $800-a-month payments the state says it costs to keep him at the mental facility he fought to stay out of. He was even ordered to pay the fees for the lawyer who argued that he be committed.

Edward J. Benett, a lawyer who has taken on Friedman's case for no fee, said he fears the case is a "frighteningly common" one of persons ordered to spend the rest of their lives unheard from because they are eccentric, though sane.

Benett said it goes beyond a recent United States Supreme Court decision which held that mental patients cannot be committed involuntarily without treatment if they pose no threat to society. Benett says that in Friedman's case the treatment itself may be illegal.

"He [Friedman] worked since he was 11 and was a very good clerk-typist and stenographer who at one time took shorthand at 100 words a minute," Benett said. "He lived frugally his entire life and saved every penny he made. He wore old clothes, lived in a $80-a-month hotel, ate day-old bread and fruit.

"His only obsession in life was saving money, unfortunately. If he didn't have that money when he was panhandling, he'd be a free man today."

Benett, a law professor at DePaul University, has appealed the commitment order of Circuit Judge Lawrence L. Genesen.

Judge Genesen himself said after Friedman was committed, "I wonder what my decision would have been if he wasn't carrying $24,000 around . . . if he only had a quarter instead of $24,000, my interpretation of his judgment might have been somewhat different."

Benett said Friedman's condition has deteriorated, and added, "He was committed on the possibility he would be mugged, beaten and mobbed and instead, he's locked up, filled with drugs and his money is taken gradually instead of in one clean sweep."

(*The Seattle Times*, August 1, 1975)

understand the process of behavior change.

Many clinical workers, on the basis of their experience, believe that psychotherapy is effective with certain types of patients. Many patients feel they have been helped by psychotherapy. Of course, psychotherapists who are professionally committed to practicing psychotherapy may unconsciously be too optimistic about the fruits of their labor, and patients who have spent a large amount of money on psychotherapy may push themselves to feel they have made a wise expenditure.

Considering the mental health needs of the population, we may assume that the practice of psychotherapy and other therapeutic methods will continue. But research to determine the ways in which they are effective and the ways in which they should be improved must be conducted at the same time. An important current concern is how most effectively to convey to the public generally and individual clients in particular one reality of therapy, the fact that it does not always work. As more data become available a more meaningful dialogue between clinical workers and potential clients should become possible.

BOX 16.8

Roadblocks to research on the effects of therapy

These observations by Jerome Frank provide some of the reasons why we know less than we would like to know about what therapy does to clients.

Psychotherapy has become a major, lucrative American industry catering to the needs of millions of consumers. It is crowded with entrepreneurs, each of whom proclaims the unique virtues of his product while largely ignoring those of his rivals, and backs his claims with speculative pronouncements supported by a few case reports. Solidly based objective information as to the nature and efficacy of the product is, by contrast, sadly lacking. This is partly because of the intrinsic difficulty of the subject matter—human beings are highly complex and do not readily submit themselves to the discipline required to maintain a research design and patients are interested only in getting help, not in satisfying the needs of research. Another obstacle is the understandable reluctance of psychotherapists to cooperate in projects that would subject their claims to impartial examination. Most have spent much time and effort to master their particular method, and both their economic security and self-esteem, therefore, depend on its therapeutic efficacy. In the words of Confucius: "A wise man does not examine the source of his well-being." (Frank, 1974, p. 325)

SUMMARY

1. There are several general therapeutic approaches to the behavior disorders and many clinical workers select combinations of these methods that seem most appropriate in particular cases. The therapeutic approaches are related to the theoretical perspectives discussed throughout this book. They include psychotherapies, behavioral therapies that are derived from behaviorism and from learning theories and biological therapies such as drugs and electric shock.

2. In *psychoanalysis* the way the patient and therapist relate to each other is central to the therapeutic process. The patient displaces patterns of feelings and behavior from the past into current relationships, particularly the therapeutic situation. This is called *transference*.

3. In *client-centered therapy* the therapist functions as an objective counselor who focuses all attention on the client and the client's exploration of his or her problems.

4. *Rational-emotive therapy* puts emphasis on cognitive principles. The client is helped to recognize which of his or her thoughts are irrational and to replace them with more realistic thoughts.

5. In *group therapy* a number of clients who may or may not have the same type of problem meet together with the therapist. With the help of the therapist the group members learn about their reactions to other people and others' reactions to them. There are many types of group therapies based on a variety of theoretical positions.

6. *Behavioral therapies* use techniques ranging from shock or other aversive stimulation to positive reinforcers, such as tokens that may be exchanged for desired privileges or objects. They differ from the "talking therapies" in that they rely on action, conditioning, and other methods for increasing or decreasing certain kinds of responses. Some behavioral therapies deal only with stimulus-response connections, whereas others incorporate a cognitive element.

517

7. The most commonly used *biological therapies* for both mild and severe clinical cases involve the use of drugs. Antianxiety and antidepressent drugs are widely used in the United States and other countries. The use of electric shock for depression has declined, as has psychosurgery for some kinds of psychosis.

8. The effectiveness of psychotherapy is difficult to measure for many reasons, and researchers are seeking improved methods to evaluate it.

Suggested readings

Most of the suggested readings for Chapter 15 also deal with therapy, what goes on in it, and its effects on clients.

Bergin, A. E. & Garfield, S. L. *Handbook of psychotherapy and behavior change.* New York: John Wiley & Sons, Inc., 1971. Provides a comprehensive review of research on psychological therapies.

Dewald, P. A. *The psychoanalytic process: A case illustration* New York: Basic Books, Inc., Publishers, 1972. Contains a session-by-session account of an entire psychoanalysis.

Kanfer, F. H. & Goldstein, A. P. (Eds.) *Helping people change.* Elmsford, N.Y.: Pergamon Press, Inc., 1975. Describes many recent developments in work on behavior change.

Korchin, S. J. *Modern clinical psychology.* New York: Basic Books, Inc., Publishers, 1976. Deals extensively with the diverse facets of modern clinical psychological practice.

Lazarus, A. A. *Multimodal behavior therapy.* New York: Springer-Verlag New York, Inc., 1976. Reviews behavioral and cognitive-behavioral approaches.

Goldfried, M. R. & Davison, G. C. *Clinical behavior therapy.* New York: Holt, Rinehart and Winston, Inc., 1976. Reviews behavioral and cognitive-behavioral approaches.

Rimm, D. C. & Masters, J. C. *Behavior therapy: Techniques and empirical findings.* New York: Academic Press, 1974. Comprehensively reviews therapeutic methods that have grown out of learning research and theory.

Yalom, I. D., & Elkin, G. *Every day gets a little closer: A twice-told therapy.* New York: Basic Books, Inc., Publishers, 1974. Contains views of psychotherapy from the points of view of one client and her therapist.

Chapter 17

Psychology and the Problems of Society

(Chih, Peter Arnold)

The following excerpt from a newspaper article shows that it may be difficult to make a psychological adjustment to a situation very different from the one in which we expect to find ourselves.

Rebel U.S. Youth of 1960s—Nearing Age of 30— Dogged by Disillusion

The rebellious, idealistic generation of adolescents that reached maturity in the 1960s is now approaching 30. For many, according to the psychiatrists and mental health counselors, the trip into adult life is being dogged by disillusionment and depression.

Many young Americans who matured during the 1960s when many traditional standards of morality came under challenge have glided easily into adulthood, they say. Many never joined the rebellion. Others have assimilated easily into the system they once rebelled against, while still others pursue alternative life styles.

But according to dozens of specialists who counsel young people, interviewed in 14 cities across the country, large numbers of men and women who grew up in the 1960s are now experiencing a malaise of frustrations, anxiety and depression.

The malaise, they say, is reflected in an increase in the number of persons in their late twenties and early thirties receiving psychiatric help; by a rise in suicides and alcoholism in this age group, and a boom in the popularity of certain charismatic religious movements, astrology and pop psychology cults.

Many who "dropped out" are said to be depressed about the difficulties they are now having in trying to enter a competitive job market at a time of economic retrenchment, while others, with little work experience and accustomed to having parents pay their bills, are having difficulty coping with the responsibilities of a job, especially work they regard as unglamorous or not socially "meaningful."

"They are threatened by the future," Dr. Edward Stanbrook, chairman of the Department of Human Behavior at the University of California School of Medicine, observed about the adolescents of the 1960s. "They see the possibility of not having jobs, not having a lot of things their parents and grandparents took for granted. They see the possibility of not having an adequate role in society."

"The values that worked for their parents are not holding today, so they don't have the same values to hold them on their journey. They feel alone," said Dr. William Ackerly, a staff psychiatrist at Metropolitan State Hospital in Waltham, Mass.

A behaviorist sees a pattern of alienation among many in this generation, a force that he says brings young people into his office to tell him: "I've got a good job, I'm successful and I want to kill myself. Life doesn't mean anything."

"People spent the sixties trying to get closer to each other, getting to learn intimacy, shedding their hangups, finding that it's okay to be authentic, to let it all hang out, as the jargon goes," he said. "But now they find that somehow, something is missing—that it didn't do the trick." . . .

Several psychiatrists reported that some young persons appeared to be emotionally burned out. While still young, they experienced things forbidden to other generations—drugs, many sexual partners, a freedom to experiment in many ways—and now have a sense of emptiness that they've "already done everything," it was said.

"The women's movement has caused a lot of anxiety among both males and females," said Dr. Felix Ocko, a Berkeley, Calif., psychiatrist. "Many men don't know how to handle the more aggressive women. And although women are more aggressive, many don't know what they want, what their role should be, how they should fit in, how much femininity they'll lose by pursuing a professional career."

Although many people in their twenties are said to have no problems coping with sexual permissiveness, several psychiatrists said pressure to perform has caused higher rates of impotence among men and depression among some women who feel they are being used. . . . (*International Herald Tribune,* February 19, 1976. ⓒ 1976 by The New York Times Company. Reprinted by permission.)

520 WHAT KINDS OF SOCIAL PROBLEMS DO PSYCHOLOGISTS STUDY?

Psychologists are making an increasing effort to go beyond restricted laboratory experiments in order to study a whole range of complex social situations. This chapter explores three very different types of social problems: how to adapt to rapid change; how to implement social equality; and how to deal with behavior that conflicts with social norms.

Rapid change

We live in a period of rapid social and economic changes that create problems in personal adjustment. Conventional rules of conduct change from time to time, sometimes very rapidly. Even when social changes recur or occur slowly, they may cause problems. The generation gap between parents and children is not peculiar to our era. When change comes rapidly, adjustment may be even more difficult. Furthermore, people who appear to conform to new demands may have problems adjusting after their intense emotional involvement has passed and their situation has changed, as the preceding news account shows.

Social equity

Throughout history certain groups have either been given or have assumed power over others. In the period since World War II, however, pressure for equal treatment and opportunity has mounted. But what constitutes equal treatment? Is it simply lack of discrimination? Does it include measures to help people who have been disadvantaged in the past overcome those disadvantages so that they can compete more successfully?

The issue of social equity embraces many factors—income and educational differences, cultural backgrounds and values, opportunities for jobs and housing. What role, then, can psychologists play in the search for social equity?

Deviation from social norms

Individuals who deviate from social norms in ways that are harmful to others, such as adult criminals and juvenile delinquents, also constitute a serious social problem. Psychologists approach criminal behavior from a number of perspectives, including a search for its causes and for ways of reducing it. They play a particularly valuable role in analyzing the effects of society's most common response to crime: punishment.

Because community problems (e.g., social change, social equity, and deviation from social norms) involve characteristics of the individual in interaction with the community, psychologists must have a broad perspective in selecting variables for study. This chapter describes the contributions of psychol-

ogists to a specific social problem in each of the preceding areas.

RAPID CHANGE: THE ROLE OF WOMEN

The pace of change in the modern world is accelerating. The future is becoming less predictable and sometimes even difficult to imagine. (See Box 17.1.) The philosopher Alfred North Whitehead describes the effects of these changes as follows:

> The point is that in the past the time span of important change was considerably longer than that of a single human life. Thus mankind was trained to adapt itself to fixed conditions. Today this time span is considerably shorter than that of human life, and accordingly one's training must prepare individuals to face a novelty of conditions. (Whitehead, 1967, p. 13)

Writer Alvin Toffler described the same phenomenon as *future shock* (Toffler, 1970). In his best-selling book by that name he defines future shock as the "dizzying disorientation brought on by the premature arrival of the future" (p. 13). Toffler suggests that "the malaise, the mass neurosis, emotionality, and free floating violence already apparent in contemporary life" (p. 13) merely hint at the problems people will have in the future unless they learn to cope with this phenomenon. Rapid advances in technology and the explosion of knowledge are two of the causes for this "future shock." These factors have been responsible for many rapid changes in values and behavior that social psychologists label as *social change*. One stimulus to social change is the social movement, a group of people with a sense of common purpose pursuing specific objectives.

Social movements and social change

The study of social movements is interesting in itself, but psychologists are particularly concerned with how the changes brought about by these movements affect individuals, both those who seek change and those who try to maintain the status quo.

The characteristics of a social movement have been summarized by social psychologist Muzafer Sherif in this way:

1. A social movement is a pattern of attempts at change which develops in stages over a period of time.

521

BOX 17.1

Coping with economic change

Until quite recently most highly trained professionals did not have to worry about finding a job. When rapid economic changes undermined their job security and expectations, many of these people experienced severe psychological symptoms.

U.S. Scientists report effect of economy on mental health

A New York City couple in their late 30s have seen the income from their jointly operated beauty salon drop by half in the last two years because of the recession.

As a result, according to a caseworker at Jewish Family Services in Manhattan, the husband has become cold and withdrawn, the wife is increasingly critical of him and both parents have been harder on their four children. Their son, 12, is having disciplinary problems in school for the first time and has been threatened with expulsion. . . .

These persons and hundreds more with similar problems have been flooding community mental health clinics and counseling services throughout the New York area and thousands more have turned to similar agencies all over the country. They are victims of the recession but casualties of a type rarely reported before.

While it is all too obvious that loss of a job or of income produces economic hardship, it is much less generally recognized that economic stress produces widespread mental and physical illness as well. For many individuals, apparently, hard times mean not only meatless meals and foreclosed mortgages, but also self-doubt, depression, alcoholism, sexual problems, marital discord and even psychosomatic illness.

According to many mental health workers, those most affected with these problems are frequently not the poor, who are accustomed to belt tightening, but middle-class individuals who have never had to cope with economic uncertainty before. Middle-aged professional men, whose whole notion of their own self-worth is often centered on their working identity, seem to be particularly hard hit by economic downturns.

"You have a terrible choice when you're unemployed," said a political science professor who went without a job for a year after he failed to get tenure at his university.

"You either have to go out and hustle yourself every single day or just vegetate," he explained. "You feel a real temptation to isolate yourself—to stay out of touch with your friends. You don't want them to see how depressed or what a failure you are." (*International Herald Tribune*, April 21, 1976. © 1976 by The New York Times Company. Reprinted by permission.)

Unemployment may pose a more significant threat to professionals who have never expected to be unemployed than to hourly workers for whom joblessness is a realistic expectation.

(Shelton, Monkmeyer)

2. A social movement is started by interaction among people who are concerned with the relative deprivation or unequal treatment of some group.
3. A social movement is carried on both by those who feel deprived and by others who sympathize with them.
4. A social movement develops a platform or ideology and therefore must have some organization.
5. The purpose of a social movement is to bring about change.
6. Efforts toward change include both measures to publicize the problem and desired changes (slogans, rallies, attempts to persuade decision makers) and more active measures (strikes, boycotts, and riots). (Sherif, 1970)

Such social movements as the civil rights movement and the student movement exerted a powerful influence during the 1960s in the United States. There were movements in both industrialized and developing countries across the world. The fast-rising feminist movement had an initial spurt after World War I, when U.S. women won the vote; gathered momentum again in the mid-1960s; and appears to be a dominant movement at present.

Feminism as a social movement

Social and economic conditions are important in shaping women's roles within any given culture. In the preindustrial United States, for example, men and women often shared economic responsibility in home-based occupations, such as farming, shopkeeping, or the production of home-crafted goods. The industrial revolution brought about a drastic change in the lower-class woman's role, moving her place of work from the home to the factory. (See Figure 17.1.) In fact, the popular notion of woman as exclusively a homemaker and mother is more myth than reality. This sex role stereotype applied only to married middle-class women who could afford to play it. For many others it was a goal, not a reality.

The women's movement received a powerful shot in the arm in the United States during the 1960s. First, the word *sex* was included in the categories protected against discrimination in the Civil Rights Act of 1964. (Ironically, it had been added in an attempt to defeat the bill.) Next, Betty Friedan's book *The Feminine Mystique* attacked the female stereotype, and pointed out the frustration and unhappiness it caused, especially for many well-educated women. When NOW, the National Organization of Women, was founded with Friedan as its first presi-

Figure 17.1 Factory work for women became very common during the nineteenth century. This scene shows women making matches around 1889. (Culver)

dent, the movement finally established an organized base.

There were a number of other factors that had changed the situation of women by the 1960s. The availability of reliable contraceptive devices made it possible to limit family size. There was an increase in the number of women who had more than a high school education, and products ranging from automatic washing machines to TV dinners were developed to help reduce house work. The inflationary period of the late 1960s and early 1970s also changed the financial situation of many families and made it more necessary to have a second wage earner in order to maintain a comfortable standard of living. Changes in attitudes toward divorce produced many single-parent families, usually headed by women.

Women as workers

Between 1950 and 1973 there was a one-third increase in the participation of women in the labor force. Women who never married have always been those most likely to work, but the gap is closing between them and women who have been or are

523

Women are playing much more important roles in the labor force, with greater numbers in both traditional and nontraditional jobs. (Top, George Gardner; bottom, Shelton, Monkmeyer)

married. Participation in the labor force for women who were never married rose 13 percent, whereas that for married women living with their husbands rose over 80 percent. The percentage of working

married women with preschool children increased from 12 percent in 1950 to 33 percent in 1974.

Women workers continue to be clustered in service jobs (40 percent), manufacturing (20 percent), and trade (20 percent), just as they were 35 years ago. In 1970, 54 percent of all female professionals were elementary school teachers or registered nurses. Now women are beginning to make inroads into high-status professions. The percentage of women lawyers increased from 2.5 in 1940 to 4.9 percent in 1970. In medicine the percentage of women rose from 6.5 in 1960 to 9.3 in 1970. Increases in the number of women students in professional schools should result in increases in these percentages in the future.

The working woman and the family

When a woman becomes a paid worker, how does it affect her family? There is very little scientific data about this issue. Statistics do show a rising divorce rate and a rapid increase in single-parent families headed by women. But whether or how these changes are related to a change in the role of women is still unclear.

There has been some research, however, on the effects of working mothers on the children in the family. The information available is incomplete, but certain conclusions have been supported in a general way by available data.

Mothers who are satisfied with their roles, whether or not they work, seem to have the most well-adjusted children. The quality of the relationship and its intensity are more important in the child's development than is the constant presence of the mother. (See Figure 17.2.) Preschool children who are cared for by others do not show less attachment to their mothers than do children whose mothers provide their daily care. A *quality* child care situation does not seem to harm the mental development of preschoolers. Middle-class school-aged children appear to be unaffected if their mothers work, but children from a lower socioeconomic class may have more adjustment problems if their mothers work full time. Academic achievement seems to suffer for boys with working mothers, but not for girls.

Children's career aspirations and their ideas also seem to be affected by whether or not they have a working mother. Children whose mothers work have

Figure 17.2 Psychological data suggest that the quality of the interaction between mother and child is more important than the amount of time they spend together. Mothers who are satisfied with their own lives, whether they work or not, usually have the best-adjusted children. (Holland, Stock, Boston)

cause they were caught between traditional male and female roles (Grossack and Gardner, 1970).

Opposition to role change by members of the group. A 1975 survey (Epstein, 1975, p. 14) found the percentages of men and women who supported the women's liberation movement were almost the same: 63 and 60 percent, respectively. Opposition to the Equal Rights Ammendment to the U.S. Constitution, which would specifically prevent discrimination because of sex, has been led by a woman and supported by a coalition of women's groups. Why do women object to the ERA? Many still seem to consider the care of the family as a woman's greatest responsibility. Some also express a fear that their husbands will no longer be "safe" if they work with women in equal positions. Psychologists offer another explanation. Some women who oppose equality, they say, may feel frightened by new roles and the changes they imply. They might believe that they are unable to compete. These women, psychologists say, may also be the victims of a *self-fulfilling prophecy*. They adopt the unfavorable assumptions others hold about their group in order to rationalize their lower status.

A psychological look at sex roles

The impact of changes in the role of women in society on the women themselves has become a topic of great interest to psychologists. Questions raised by research on women have implications for most fields of psychological inquiry. Do men and women differ in such attributes as intelligence, aptitudes, psychophysiological responses, and personality characteristics? If they do differ, what is the nature of the differences? Are sex role stereotypes learned? Is much therapeutic work based on theories that make incorrect assumptions about sexual differences? How are children affected by such changes as the use of day care rather than maternal care in early life?

Male-female differences in children's skills and personalities

In an exhaustive review of psychological research on sex differences in children, Eleanor Maccoby and Carolyn Jacklin found that there were only a few consistent differences between the sexes (Maccoby and Jacklin, 1974). Girls had greater verbal ability than boys, boys had greater visual-spatial ability and

higher career aspirations than do children whose mothers are not employed. Children of employed mothers also see fewer differences in sex roles for men and women.

The stress of role change

When individuals try to adopt new roles, they are often forced to live for at least a period of time as members of two conflicting groups. Often they are not accepted by either of the groups, yet they are forced to function in both, and to carry a double set of responsibilities. A woman who decides to combine a career with motherhood may find that she is expected to fulfill both roles completely, which places great physical demands on her. Many husbands, even if they support their wife's choice to work, may not be willing to take on more of the household chores. Working wives may meet with disapproval from more traditional members of their community who argue that a working woman cannot be a "good mother." Such wives may develop guilt feelings about their role, particularly if they are not working out of economic necessity. In one survey 28 percent of the working wives who were questioned said they would like to be men, perhaps be-

BOX 17.2
Role conflict among women athletes

Individuals who try to fill two roles may find that the demands of those roles conflict in ways that can be resolved only by giving up success in at least one of them. This article illustrates one such conflict in women who both wish to excel in athletics and also want to maintain a stereotyped woman's role.

Looks don't always mix with gold medal swims

America's women swimmers will have to stop trying to win beauty contests and swimming meets at the same time. If they want to win like the American men, they will have to look more like them.

Four years ago, female swimmers from the United States won eight gold medals at the Munich Olympic Games. Their counterparts from East Germany didn't win any gold medals.

The pendulum of power swung radically to the East Germans at the Olympic pool here. They won 11 gold medals in 13 events, while the American women averted their first gold medal shutout in 24 years by winning the last event of the competition Sunday, the 400-meter freestyle relay.

But their euphoria from that world record-setting victory doesn't obscure the facts. If winning is the name of the game at the Olympics, the East German women are playing the game all by themselves.

According to Dr. Rudolf Schramme, the East German coach, the secret is that East Germany's women and men use the same training program, including a heavy reliance on weightlifting.

"Without comprehensive weight training, no swimmer will reach peak results in modern swimming." Dr. Schramme said. "There is no difference in our country in respect to training boys and girls.

"We have given the same load to the girls as we have to the boys."

But the women from the United States resist extensive weight training. They argue that the result of East Germany's non-differentiated training program is non-differentiated sexes.

"We're put on this earth to be women," said Wendy Boglioli of the U.S. team. "If we did build muscle mass, we'd be right up there with them (the East Germans).

"Personally, I don't want to look like a man."

Schramme objects to that line of attack. "If you put our girls and the Americans in a row," he says, "I would like to see someone pick out the ones who aren't girls.

"I think our girls look nice like other girls."

But if you lined up the two groups of swimmers, you would have no trouble separating Americans from East Germans. The East Germans are much larger in the shoulders, the obvious result of an extensive weightlifting program.

American society places a great deal of pressure on its women to be feminine-looking. That's why the cosmetics industry is a multi-million-dollar business.

"Women athletes in the United States are looked down on," said Rod Strachan, an American male swimmer and gold medalist. "The trouble with the girls on our team is that they're more interested in femininity than in being athletes.

"You have to be more concerned with building yourself up than in your femininity. Some of the East German women are quite a bit bigger than some of the men on our team." (*International Herald Tribune*, August 28, 1976. By permission of the Associated Press.)

---

mathematical ability than girls; and boys were more aggressive than girls.

Although these few differences seem to appear consistently in experimental work, their causes remain unclear. Are they caused by genetic differences, are they caused by the socialization process or shaping of responses that seem appropriate to the child's sex, or are they the result of a child's imitation of the behavior of others of his or her sex? It is likely that the differences are caused by all three of these factors.

Maccoby and Jacklin concluded that "biological factors have been most clearly implicated in aggression and visual-spatial ability" (p. 360). They do not say that aggressive behavior is not learned, but that "boys are biologically more prepared to learn it"

(p. 361). Their conclusion about visual-spatial ability is based on evidence of a sex-linked gene that affects it. Again, learning is also important in determining the final level of skill.

The following popular *sex role stereotypes* were not confirmed by the research data analyzed by Maccoby and Jacklin:

1. Girls are more "social" than boys.
2. Girls are more "suggestible" than boys.
3. Girls have lower self-esteem.
4. Girls are better at rote learning and simple repetitive tasks, boys at tasks that require higher-level cognitive processing and inhibition of previously learned responses.
5. Girls lack achievement motivation.
6. Girls are auditory, boys visual.
   (Maccoby and Jacklin, 1974, pp. 349–351)

A number of other stereotypes were not supported, but there was no conclusive evidence that they did not exist. These included sex differences in tactile sensitivity, dominance, fear, timidity and anxiety, activity level, competitiveness, dominance, compliance, and nurturance. One major conclusion from this careful and complete survey is that there are many popular beliefs about the psychological characteristics of sex differences that have little or no basis in fact.

Sex roles—stereotypes

How do children learn sex role stereotypes? The women's movement lays much of the blame on learning materials and the mass media. For example, books for young children as well as books for adults link particular behaviors with males or females. (See Box 17.3.) Movies and television programs also tend to show both men and women in stereotyped roles. Our language itself contains many common terms that reflect certain sex role expectations. For example, *chairman*, *policeman*, and *fireman* imply that these jobs are filled by men. Children also learn what behaviors are "appropriate" by observing those around them, especially parents and teachers. Figure 17.3 shows a male performing what is often thought of as a woman's work. If parents share household responsibilities do their children's expectations about male and female behavior change? Psychological research is needed to answer such questions be-

Figure 17.3 As more women enter the labor market, men are beginning to share work formerly reserved for housewives. Such chore sharing is more common among couples with higher education and income levels. (Charles Gatewood)

cause the problem is complicated. The results of opinion surveys often differ from observable behavior. Surveys taken in Finland showed that public opinion between 1960 and 1970 had moved toward favoring equality in sex roles. However, the great majority of both men and women still preferred male superiors on the job, and at least half the males questioned still believed household tasks should be left to women (Haavio-Mannila, 1972). In the U.S.S.R. women have long been officially regarded as equal, but they still face much of the discrimination that women face in other countries. (See Box 17.4.)

Fear of success

Some women with high ability perform poorly in situations in which they should have been able to succeed, and their behavior is different from men's behavior in the same situation. Matina Horner introduced the concept of *fear of success* to explain this difference (Horner, 1972). The motive to avoid success, she hypothesized, is more characteristic of women than of men. It is especially characteristic of high-achievement-oriented, high-ability women who aspire to and are capable of success. Horner meas-

527

BOX 17.3

Sex role stereotypes in children's picture books

(a)

The preschool years are important in the development of sex role concepts for young children. By kindergarten, children learn to make sex role distinctions and identify with masculine and feminine roles.

Children may learn what behavior is appropriate for males or females through picture books, which describe males and females quite differently (Weitzman, 1972). Most children's books, even those published in the recent past, are about boys, men, and male animals. When women appear they often have insignificant roles, anonymous and inconspicuous. Boys are shown as active and adventuresome, girls as passive and immobile. Girls are more likely to be shown inside the house than boys, usually in traditional feminine roles pleasing their fathers and brothers. Women, if they are shown at all, are usually identified only as wives or mothers. Not one book in a study of award-winning picture books showed a woman in a job or profession. In contrast, men were shown in varied and interesting occupations: storekeepers, kings, fighters, judges, and adventurers. Illustrations are often more effective than words in conveying a message.

(b)

In (*a*) the female is pictured helplessly screaming while a brave male retrieves her purse from the thief. The next illustration (*b*) also carries human stereotypes to the animal world. The female plays the traditional housewife role while the two males relax. Recently some illustrators have begun to depart from such stereotypes. Illustration (*c*) shows a male and female working together at a traditional male job. Contrast the family scene in (*d*) with that in (*b*). Here both parents are shown involved with their children and the father has assumed the role of infant caretaker. (*a*: From *Shrewbettina's Birthday* by John S. Goodall, copyright ©

1970 by John S. Goodall. Reproduced by permission of Harcourt Brace Jovanovich, Inc. *b*: From *Sylvester and the Magic Pebble* by William Steig. Copyright © 1969 by William Steig. Reprinted by permission of Simon and Schuster, Inc. *c*: From *Pop Corn and Ma Goodness* by Edna Mitchell Preston, illustrated by Robert Andrew Parker. Illustrations copyright © 1969 by Robert Andrew Parker. Reproduced by permission of The Viking Press. *d*: From *The Quitting Deal* by Tobi Tobias, illustrated by Trina Schart Hyman. Illustrations copyright © 1975 by Trina Schart Hyman. Reproduced by permission of The Viking Press.)

ured this motive by analyzing stories that her subjects told to complete one of the following leads: "After first term finals, Anne finds herself at the top of her medical school class," or, "After first term finals, John finds himself at the top of his medical school class." (See Chapter 10.)

In one study she found that 65 percent of the women told *avoidance of success* stories for the "Anne" form, whereas 90 percent of the men told *success* stories for the "John" form (Horner, 1970).

Horner's work stimulated a great deal of argument and research. There seem to be sex differences in achievement behavior, but the reasons may be more complicated than Horner's theory—that some high-ability women are motivated to perform poorly when they compete with men because they fear that success will make them less acceptable. At least one study shows that men may not have opinions about women that women think they do. This means that women have a stereotyped view of stereotypes about women. Clearly, it will take much effort to sort out all the psychological considerations in this complex set of beliefs.

(c)

(d)

Women and psychotherapy

Feminist leaders have questioned the helpfulness of traditional psychoanalytic treatment for women who are striking out in new directions. Freud's theories were formulated at a time when women's lives and expectations were quite different from what they are today. A woman, according to Freud, was destined to be dependent on and envious of men because she did not have a penis. In addition, a therapist's own expectations about women's roles may affect his or her view of a patient.

In one study clinicians were asked to select terms describing healthy males, healthy females, and healthy persons of an unspecified sex. Their descriptions of healthy females were quite different from the descriptions for the other two categories (Broverman et al., 1970). They usually described healthy women as less healthy than people in the other two groups. For example, they viewed healthy women as more passive than healthy men. Therapists such as these might make women patients who have conflicts about asserting themselves feel unfeminine if they express a desire to assume a more active role. Both male and female clinicians had sex role stereo-

and others. For example, feminists have written detailed essays based on the data of Masters and Johnson (1966) to challenge the distinction that Freud drew between clitoral and vaginal orgasms.

Statistical data on sex differences

The data on first admissions to mental hospitals, psychiatric treatment in general hospitals, psychiatric outpatient clinics and private outpatient care, psychiatric problems seen in general medical practice, and data gathered from community surveys, all indicate that more women than men seek help for psychological problems (Gove and Tudor, 1973). This represents a change from the pre-World War II era when men were admitted to mental hospitals more often than women.

The rates for many physical illnesses are higher for men than for women, and women live longer than men on the average. Suicide is more common among men than among women, but the number of suicide *attempts*, at least in urban communities, is higher among women than among men. The number of suicides among females has increased considerably in recent years, but the number among males has not. Men traditionally have a much higher incidence of arrests for criminal behavior than women, and juvenile delinquents are overwhelmingly male. But recent statistics show a significant increase in crimes committed by females at both the juvenile and the adult level. Between 1960 and 1973 the increase in the rate of arrests among women (277.9 percent) was three times greater than the rate of increase for men (87.9 percent) according to the FBI's uniform crime reports. Of course, because the initial number of women was small compared to the initial number of men, these percentages appear much more dramatic than the actual increase in the number of cases. Although it is not clear what all these increases imply, they seem to reflect the fact that women are in a transitional state and that they are having difficulty adjusting to or defining their roles in society.

This brief look at the changing roles of women has illustrated some of the problems that may accompany rapid social change. Past experience is often of little help in solving new problems. But psychologists can help make change bearable by studying the exact ways in which individuals react to change in order to help them adapt effectively to new situations.

Although there is an increasing number of women entering local forces, police officers are still thought of as "policemen." (Harrison, DPI)

530   types that could influence the way in which they viewed their patients and the treatment they provided.

Research on the physiology of sex has also raised questions about the validity of the theories of Freud

SOCIAL EQUITY

The skills, ambitions, and habits of the middle class have shaped most customs, policies, and institutions in the United States as well as in other Western countries. After World War II an increasing number of people in the United States became concerned about discrimination against individuals because of their race, social class, or sex. A particular concern was the difficulty that disadvantaged children were experiencing in the public schools. The history of this concern provides an excellent example of the way in which psychologists build on one another's work to seek solutions to large societal problems.

Compensatory education

It has been clear for many years that children from poor or lower-class homes often do not perform well in school. Is this poor performance attributable to a lack of intellectual stimulation in the home, to teaching methods and expectations that are especially geared to middle-class children, or to some combination of these factors? Early programs designed to remedy the situation were based on the assumption that these children were missing some important experiences and lacked training in some important skills. If these factors could be supplied before the children entered school, educators reasoned, then the school experience might be changed from a negative to a positive one.

Head Start

During the 1960s early education programs, such as Project Head Start, were initiated to help prepare 3- and 4-year-old lower-income children, many of whom were members of racial minority groups, for entry into school. One problem in setting up these programs was that there were no patterns to follow. Psychologists had traditionally looked at childhood in terms of what children could do at a variety of ages. They did not know a great deal about the ways in which very young children learned and how they could be taught most effectively. There were many nursery schools for middle-class children, however, and these were a convenient model for Head Start programs. Early programs stressed social relationships and creative play for preschoolers. But nursery schools, which were originally developed to free

middle-class children from mother-dominated environments, did not always seem suitable for children whose homes were quite different. These children often had working mothers, a great deal of unsupervised contact with their friends, and little learning-oriented stimulation. Some of the programs faced this problem by emphasizing structured learning. Children were drilled on such skills as shape and color identification and matching, and elementary mathematical concepts. Training in following the directions of the teacher was also an important part of these programs.

Although enthusiasm for the Head Start programs was high and information on child development was used in planning them, the results of these programs have not been outstanding (Bronfenbrenner, 1974). Evaluations showed that they could raise children's IQ scores while they were involved in the programs, but these gains decreased when the children entered regular school classes, and they disappeared as time passed. Programs that stressed verbal and cognitive training produced more change than those that attempted general enrichment. The children who showed the least improvement and the most rapid decline were those from the most deprived economic and social backgrounds. These results convinced many psychologists that efforts to improve school performance for economically and socially deprived children must begin during the first three years of a child's life.

Changing the infant's environment

Experimenters began to study the effects of a change in environment on young children. In one such experiment Rick Heber of the University of Wisconsin and his colleagues carried out an intervention study in a ghetto slum neighborhood that had a high proportion of mentally retarded children. The subjects were 40 children whose mothers had IQs of 75 or less. The control group received no special treatment, but the experimental group received a program involving special teachers (nonprofessional or paraprofessional), most of whom lived in the same neighborhood as the children. Children in the experimental group became subjects at 3 months of age and the assigned teachers were in charge of the children for most of their waking day, 5 days a week, until 12 to 15 months of age. In addition, the chil-

531

BOX 17.4

Soviet women are equal by law but not by custom

Soviet women not liberated despite professional roles

They are bulldozer drivers and ditch diggers, doctors and judges, and occasionally even jet pilots and ship captains—but are Soviet women liberated?

Not very. According to official statistics and the observations of some women themselves, they have gained access to many professions, but prominence in few. Whatever rank they do attain disappears after working hours as they take on household chores that are extremely burdensome here without the easy shopping or labor-saving devices found in the West.

"When I leave my office and go into a store," a woman physician lamented, "and then walk down the street with two heavy shopping bags, I look like any woman—nothing special."

Soviet society has remained insulated from the consciousness-raising forces of feminism that have emerged in the West. As a result, the attitudes of both men and women here are replete with assumptions of woman's intellectual inferiority and emotional frailty, as well as of her obligation to keep a home without expecting much help from her husband.

These are such pervasive views that they are accepted unquestioningly, even by outspoken Soviet dissidents who often take great risks in fighting for funda-

mental human rights, but who react blankly when the question of women's equality is raised.

"A woman can never make a great mathematician," a leading dissident remarked recently.

He cited his wife's struggle for days over a computer problem that he then solved for her in an evening.

In some respects, women's job problems here parallel those in the United States. Women rarely reach the upper echelons of power, either in politics or in institutions and professions, where they dominate the lower ranks, the jobs they get are generally those that pay less.

For example, about 71 per cent of the secondary school teachers in the Soviet Union are women, but 72 per cent of the school principals are men. Similarly, while 70 per cent of the country's doctors are women, the heads of hospitals and other medical facilities are usually men.

Explaining the high proportion of women in the medical profession, a scientist said, "Men don't want it because the pay is low."

The Soviet Union has boasted about the alleged equality of its women ever since the day of Lenin, who declared in 1919 that "except for Soviet Russia, there is not a single country in the world in which there is complete equality between men and women." The Stalinist Constitution contains an article on the equality of the sexes much the same as the Equal Rights Amendment sought by U.S. feminists.

The myth here is bolstered by tokenism. The only woman to fly in space, Valentina Tereshkova, was a Soviet cosmonaut, Aeroflot, the Soviet airline, has a few women pilots.

Some Soviet women say they would like nothing more than to stay home with their families. But they are

dren's mothers were instructed in homemaking and child care techniques.

The teacher who was assigned to an infant was responsible for his total care, including: feeding and bathing, cuddling and soothing, reporting and recording general health as well as organizing his learning environment and implementing the educational program. Within the context of the educational program, the teacher was expected to follow and expand upon a prescribed set of activities. Her job was to make these activities interesting, exciting, and varied within the limits of

the child's general routine; viz, eating, sleeping and activity. She was also required to "objectively" evaluate and report the child's progress, pointing out areas of apparent difficulty. (Heber et al., 1972, p. 353)

After this phase of the project had been completed, children in the experimental group participated in a program of group activities designed to provide intellectual and social stimulation. Intelligence tests were administered throughout the study. Figure 17.4 presents the findings, which show that

encouraged to work by a labor-short economy, by the inadequate earnings of their husbands, by the norms and patterns of a society that expects a contribution by each citizen.

Today, 51.5 per cent of the workers are women meaning that almost all able women work.

A recent Soviet survey of 1,000 Moscow women showed 91 per cent working to earn extra money for a household. But 70 per cent said they would not quit even if their husbands alone earned as much as both did at the time. So money is not the only motivation.

"At work I feel like a full human being," said a woman scientist. "At home I feel like a slave."

It is common to go into the home of Moscow intellectuals and discover that the woman is a professional with her own career and accustomed to having her view respected.

Yet it is rare to see Soviet men doing housework. Yuri Ryurikov, a Soviet sociologist, estimated that men spent 15 to 20 hours a week on housework and women spent 40 hours. He attributed the tenfold increase in divorces during the last 25 years partly to the double burden of women and their frustrated expectations that men will take a new attitude toward them.

The government, in need of workers, goes to lengths to enable women to hold jobs. An extensive system of nurseries and day-care facilities is provided for pre-school children.

But the double burden of job and household is held responsible in part for driving the birth rate down to a point where government officials worry that it is too low to provide the necessary workers of the next generation. (*International Herald Tribune*, August 13, 1976. © 1976 by The New York Times Company. Reprinted by permission.)

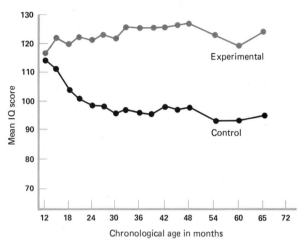

Figure 17.4 Mean IQ performance with increasing age for the experimental and control group. (Heber et al., 1972.)

the infant stimulation program improved the intellectual test performance of the children in the experimental group. This study was severely criticized by Page (1972), who doubted whether the experimental and control groups were originally similar, and who questioned whether the results were valid because the children were "trained" on tasks similar to those used in later tests. Follow-up questioning several years later showed that the children continued to perform well on tests and in school.

Parent training

Some researchers have chosen to work with parents rather than with children in order to improve the children's learning skills. In one program, mothers of infants 14 to 26 months of age spent two hours per week for an entire year in group sessions that involved the discussion of problems, role playing, and demonstrations of the use of educational toys (Badger, 1971, 1972). This technique produced significant changes in the children's IQ scores. Whether these changes will be sustained throughout their childhood is not yet clear.

Another program that has consistently produced improvements in IQ scores is the Mother-Child Home Program (MCHP) created by Phyllis Levenstein (Levenstein and Sunley, 1968; Levenstein, 1976; Horn, 1975). Mothers and children were visited at home frequently over a period of several months, beginning when the child was about 2 years old. Trained social workers served as "toy demonstrators," who brought gifts of toys and books to the children and showed the mothers how they could be used to stimulate the children's verbal development. The toys for the control group were not selected specifically to develop verbal ability, and the mothers were encouraged to be absent during the toy demonstrator's visit. The children in the experimental

533

BOX 17.5
Public opinion concerning crime

Representative surveys provide some idea of public sentiment concerning various aspects of the crime problem. The following are results from several surveys:

1. Two-thirds of the public believe that the system of law enforcement in the United States does not work to discourage people from commiting crimes.
2. Four-fifths believe that police should be tougher in dealing with crime and lawlessness.
3. Sixty percent of women and 30 percent of the men are afraid to walk alone at night.
4. Three-fifths blame society rather than individuals for crime and lawlessness.
5. Three-quarters believe the courts are too lenient with criminals.
6. Over half favor the death penalty for individuals convicted of murder.

(Based on Hindelang et. al, 1976)

groups improved their IQs far more than did those in the control groups.

Follow-up questioning when the children were in first grade showed that they had sustained their gains and had started first grade with normal achievement tests (Levenstein, 1973). This program has now been carried on for a number of years with continued success. Early contact with deprived children and training of their mothers may be one way to prevent low achievement in school.

Extension of early education
The Head Start program created great interest in learning during early childhood, and psychologists began to work on new techniques to prepare young children for school. The "pressure cooker" approach developed by Bereiter and Englemann (1966) focused on developing those skills that are tested in school

readiness exams. It involved learning to recognize letters and numerals, pronounce words clearly, and master the names and characteristics of objects. Even breaks or recess periods were used for teaching activities. The underlying theory of this approach was that children from poverty-stricken homes had to work hard and intensively to make up for lost time in their intellectual development.

The Behavioral Analysis program developed by Donald Bushell (1970) also focused on academic skills, but used teachers as behavior modifiers. Children received tokens and praise immediately when they showed improvement. Parents sometimes served as teacher aids, so that they also learned to use positive reinforcement procedures. Modified versions of these programs and others like them have been used in a federal program called "Follow-Through" for grades 1 through 3. In a summary of findings from 137 Follow-Through schools and 117 comparison schools, students in the programs stressing academic skills showed the largest gains on achievement tests (Becker, 1974.)

Early compensatory education— Does it work?
The Head Start program did not meet its original goals, but it has had important effects. When the program began, little was known about how to motivate and teach young children. The program began by trying dramatically and quickly to change children's school performance through brief exposures to group stimulation, and it failed, dismally. The program's lack of success, however, stimulated research on learning processes in young children and new techniques for teaching. It is too early to say whether these techniques will change children's school achievement over a long period of time, but the results suggest that if the new techniques include support from family members and emphasize particular skills, then young children can make permanent gains.

DEVIATION FROM SOCIAL NORMS: ADULT AND JUVENILE CRIME

Not all forms of deviancy pose a threat to society, but criminal behavior and juvenile delinquency have

534

far-reaching and serious effects on the community. Psychodynamic theory views criminal acts as manifestations of unconscious conflicts and impulses. Behavioral theory views them as the result of a failure in social learning. The causes of the failure range from undesirable experiences within the family to associations with peers who reinforce antisocial behavior to social disorganization, such as that found in urban slums. Theorists with a biological perspective have suggested the possibility that biological factors, such as chromosomal abnormalities, may contribute to criminal behavior.

About 10 million serious crimes are committed in the United States each year. One-third to one-half of all serious crimes may never be reported, so that the true figure is probably far higher. Since the beginning of the 1960s the number of violent crimes, such as rape, murder, robbery, and assault, has increased ten times faster than the U.S. population. Although crime rates in other countries are not as high as those reported in the United States, the rate of criminal activity is increasing worldwide. The increase is particularly striking in the rich and developed countries of North America, Europe, and Asia.

Public opinion polls show that crime is high on the list of public concern. (See Box 17.5.) Although a majority see society as a causal factor in crime, the public seems to be concentrating on ways to deter or punish criminals rather than on social change.

What contribution can psychologists make to the problems of crime? First, they can objectively examine causal factors. Why do some individuals commit crimes and others with very similar backgrounds do not commit them? Psychologists can also try to devise effective ways to prevent criminal behavior. Finally, they can help in the rehabilitation of individuals with a history of criminal behavior. Great efforts have been made in each of these areas, and the resulting mass of data and impressions has revealed all the complexities of the problem, but not useful answers. What do we know about the psychology of criminal behavior? A good place to start is with the youngest of criminals: juvenile delinquents.

Juvenile delinquency

Youths under 18 years of age whose behavior is not acceptable to society are called juvenile delinquents. Most "developed" societies now have special rules for dealing with these youthful offenders.

At least half of all individuals arrested in the United States each year are between 11 and 17 years old. At least one in every nine children is referred to juvenile court for an act of delinquency before his or her eighteenth birthday, and perhaps one-third of all delinquency cases involve repeaters. One recent study found that one of every three boys born in 1945 who lived in Philadelphia between the ages of 10 and 18 was arrested at least once. For black youths the ratio was one in two. (See Box 17.6.)

What "makes" a delinquent?

At least three factors have been identified that contribute to delinquency: individual pathology or personality defects; family background; and association with delinquent peers.

Individual pathology

Individual pathology accounts for the smallest group of delinquents. It has been estimated that around 1 percent have some identifiable brain or nervous system pathology that makes them unable to control their behavior. Control may improve as they grow older. Another small group, not more than 5 percent, have low intelligence. These delinquents may have difficulty understanding which kinds of behavior society classifies as right and which as wrong. Early researchers believed that as many as 50 percent of all delinquents were retarded. But current data suggest that there is little difference in intellectual level between delinquent and nondelinquent groups.

Delinquents do not fit into a single personality pattern. Probably 6 to 10 percent might be classified as *neurotic* or *psychotic*. (See Chapter 15.) Many of these individuals do not follow typical delinquent patterns. Neurotics may confine their delinquent activities to one type of crime, such as shoplifting, voyeurism (the peeping Tom), or arson. They typically carry on their activities alone rather than with friends. Psychotics, particularly those who appear overcontrolled, sometimes have outbursts of extreme aggressiveness. (See Chapter 13.)

A relatively small but troublesome group of delinquents are psychopaths who have several distinguishing traits. They seem unable to form meaningful emotional relationships with others and seemingly cannot learn through experience. Their

535

BOX 17.6

A thorough look at male juvenile delinquency in Philadelphia

Who are juvenile delinquents and what kinds of offenses do they commit? In an effort to answer this question Wolfgang, Figlio, and Sellin identified all boys born in 1945 who lived in Philadelphia during the period between their tenth and eighteenth birthdays. By using school and court records they were able to describe many features that characterized delinquents and nondelinquents living in a large city. Of the 9945 boys in the group, 3475 had a recorded police contact. By the time these 3475 boys were 17 they had committed 10,214 delinquent acts. The table shows the types of offenses they committed. One-time offenders committed 1613 delinquent acts and 8601 offenses were committed by 1862 recidivists, or repeaters.

behavior is often characterized by senseless acts of destruction or violence. They tend to be unstable, rebellious, and impulsive. Delinquents who have records of multiple arrests are often classified as psychopaths (Ganzer and Sarason, 1973).

Family pathology

A very high percentage of delinquents come from multiproblem families. In a classic study of delinquent boys, Sheldon and Eleanor Glueck (1950) found that home atmosphere and parent-child relations were the most crucial factors in predicting delinquency.

The Gluecks found in their study of matched pairs of 500 delinquent and nondelinquent boys that the differences between the families of boys in the two groups were striking. The boys were matched in intelligence and ethnic origins, and all lived in underprivileged areas. The Gluecks found that the delinquent boys were more likely to come from families with histories of mental illness, alcoholism, and criminality. These families were more likely to contain a single parent or stepparent and fewer wage earners than were the families of nondelinquents living in the same neighborhood. The Gluecks found that there was greater emotional deprivation and lax or inconsistent discipline among the delinquents' families. Although some conclusions from the study have been questioned, the high incidence of problems in families of delinquents has been verified by many later studies. (See Box 17.7.)

Association with delinquent peers

A young person who spends time with delinquent companions is very likely to become delinquent as well. Delinquents acting as groups account for the great majority of crimes. Their personalities and psychological problems seem to be much the same as those of nondelinquents, and it might be said that they simply imitate their friends and associates. This explanation is not enough, however, because many other young people reared in the same surroundings do not become delinquent. Some evidence suggests that susceptibility to delinquency is increased by weak family ties. Although minority groups have traditionally produced a disproportionate number of delinquents, some minority groups with tight family structures, such as Chinese-Americans, have traditionally produced only a very small number of delinquents.

Urban society as a producer of delinquents

Urban societies emphasize competition. Many children are poorly equipped to compete because they do not have the proper academic and vocational skills, because they have not developed good work habits.

536

Types and total number of offenses

Type of offense by race of delinquents

Offense	Nonwhites		Whites		Total	
	N	Rate per 1000 Cohort Subjects	N	Rate per 1000 Cohort Subjects	N	Rate per 1000 Cohort Subjects
Homicide	14	4.8	0	0	14	1.4
Rape	38	13.1	6	.9	44	4.4
Robbery	173	59.6	20	2.8	193	19.4
Aggravated assault	181	62.4	39	5.5	220	22.1
Burglary	394	135.8	248	35.2	642	64.6
Larceny	802	276.4	387	54.9	1189	119.6
Auto theft	187	64.4	239	33.9	426	42.8
Other assaults	365	125.8	172	24.4	537	54.0
Forgery and counterfeiting	4	1.4	1	.1	5	.5
Fraud and embezzlement	1	.3	3	.4	4	.4
Stolen property	23	7.9	7	1.0	30	3.0
Weapons	212	73.1	58	8.2	270	27.1
Prostitution	1	.3	2	.3	3	.3
Sex offenses	84	28.9	63	8.9	147	14.8
Narcotics	0	0	1	.1	1	.1
Liquor law violations	108	37.2	165	23.4	273	27.5
Drunkenness	117	40.3	102	14.5	219	22.0
Disorderly conduct	851	293.2	883	125.4	1734	174.4
Vagrancy	15	5.2	6	.9	21	2.1
Gambling	49	16.9	40	5.7	89	8.9
Road violations	0	0	4	.6	4	.4
Other traffic violations	12	4.1	25	3.5	37	3.7
All other offenses	2123	731.6	1974	280.3	4097	412.0
Hospital cases	0	0	1	.1	1	.1
Investigations	0	0	9	1.3	9	.9
Minor disturbance	1	.3	0	0	1	.1
Missing persons	1	.3	2	.3	3	.3
Reports affecting other city departments	0	0	1	.1	1	.1
Total	5756	1983.5	4458	633.0	10,214	1027.0

Adapted from Wolfgang et al., pp. 68–69.

In one study (MacCandless, Parsons, and Roberts, 1972), institutionalized teenage male delinquents read on the average at a fourth-grade level and were academically retarded in all subjects. Some teenagers cope with poor skills by dropping out of society or drifting from one unsatisfactory job to another. Some react by joining a gang as a way to gain status and to feel they are part of a group. Juveniles who are poorly equipped to deal with industrialized society often feel frustrated, confused, and hopeless. In addition, the growth of the youth culture seems to have emphasized the "apartness" of the teenage period and lengthened the time in which young people are unable or not expected to become integrated into the adult world. There has been a great increase in leisure time for many young people, and they spend many more years separated from everyone but their peers.

BOX 17.7

A family of delinquents

Many delinquents come from multiproblem families, and many commit not one, but a whole series of delinquent acts. This news report illustrates an extreme case.

192 arrests in Seattle family with 7 boys

Crime has been a way of life for a Seattle family with seven boys, accounting for 192 arrests in the last nine years, according to a police count.

"I hope to God we've turned the corner because I'll tell you, mister, I can't take much more," the mother of the boys, who range in age from 11 to 20, told Detective Stephen Heard, who is assigned full-time to the family. Under juvenile offender laws, the family cannot be identified.

There have been 39 arrests for burglary, 23 for larceny, 16 for property damage, 12 for robbery, 5 for assault, 4 for auto theft, 3 for narcotics, 2 for carrying a concealed weapon and miscellaneous crimes ranging from shoplifting to trespassing to disturbing the peace or refusing to pay a cab fare.

The police said it is the worst case of a repeating crime pattern under a single roof in the city.

One son, a 27-year-old dope addict, was killed by a shotgun blast in Los Angeles and another died at the age of 23 when he "ran into a knife," the mother said.

But the oldest, she said, has not been in trouble since being released from a Louisiana prison about a year ago.

She said her three daughters have not been in serious trouble, either, but all three grandchildren who live with her—a 12-year-old girl and boys, 8 and 9—have been arrested for burglary.

The mother, 48, has been married three times. She said her first husband was shot to death in New Orleans, her second husband got a divorce and her third husband died three years ago of cancer.

When Sam (not his real name) was 6, he and five of his brothers broke into a school and caused $1,500 in damage. Sam, now 11, has been arrested six times for burglary.

Another son, 13, has been arrested 30 times. A 15-year-old has 31 arrests and a 16-year-old has 40 arrests.

A 17-year-old was released from Cedar Creek Youth Camp July 10. The next night he was picked up in a stolen car, for arrest No. 52.

Richard, 18, is in the state penitentiary serving up to 20 years for robbery and assault. He has 29 arrests. David, 20, has 31 arrests. He's awaiting sentencing for burglary and possession of drugs. (*International Herald Tribune*, August 9, 1976. By permission of the Associated Press.)

The feeling of anonymity which comes with living in a large and changing community also plays a part in the increase in delinquency. There is likely to be less family influence as families of two, or of one parent and a few children, become more common, and extended families of grandparents, aunts, uncles and cousins are scattered over wide geographical areas. A lack of sense of belonging may be brought on in part by greater opportunities for social and geographical movement.

Adult crime

While many juvenile delinquents continue their careers of crime into adulthood, many stop committing crimes as they mature. Among adults, the crime rate falls off dramatically after age 25. Twenty-five percent of all arrests for serious crimes occur in the 18–25 year old group, and 50 percent in the 11–17 age group, so that three-quarters of those arrested for serious crimes are under 25.

Types of criminal behavior

Criminals can be divided into several groups with different psychological characteristics. Occasional criminals do not think of themselves as criminals, and, in fact, their behavior may be governed largely by opportunity. Habitual but petty criminals may have long criminal records for minor crimes, and they are often easily caught. Conventional, or social-ized, criminals are those who have continued from delinquency into adult crime. Professional criminals commit highly specialized crimes.

Two other areas of criminal activity are *white-collar crime* and *organized crime*, carried out by groups of professional criminals. White-collar crime may be defined as illegal activity carried out by one or more individuals in connection with their busi-ness or occupation. It includes individual activities by professionals, such as fee splitting by physicians or lawyers, embezzlement by employees who have access to corporation funds, and organized illegal activities by the management of a corporation. Those who commit such crimes usually do not consider themselves criminals. The frequency of these crimes has been explained as learned behavior that can be rationalized in a situation in which the group may consider such behavior normal. White-collar crimi-nals are less often sentenced to prison or prosecuted than are other offenders. This may contribute to their conception of themselves as respectable citi-zens. One unique approach to the prevention of such crimes by lower-level employees is described in Box 17.8.

Organized crime refers to large-scale rackets or crime syndicates which usually rely on political cor-ruption for protection from the law. They may oper-ate in such fields as gambling, prostitution, and drug sales. Eighty percent of cities with populations of over 1 million are believed by police to have such organized crime, according to one survey (Task Force Report: Organized Crime, 1967).

Seventy percent of those jailed in the United States are convicted of crimes against property, such as robbery, burglary, and embezzlement. The psy-chological causes of such crimes may be different from those related to crimes against persons. Those crimes that include assault, rape, assault with intent to kill, and homicide often appear to be bizarre or idiosyncratic rather than an expression of needs or social goals that might explain at least certain crimes against property. For example, 50 percent of all mur-ders are committed by a friend or relative of the victim. These murders are usually impulsive, and often take place in stressful situations. In the United States easy access to firearms makes it easy to com-mit crimes of aggression and violence. As we dis-

Shoplifters are more often petty criminals than conventional or professional criminals. Because such large numbers of people are potential offenders, stores which attract crowds of shoppers have begun to install electronic monitoring de-vices. (Dietz, Stock, Boston)

cussed in Chapter 2, the cultural glorification of violence and aggressive behavior through the mass media may stimulate both individual and group aggression.

There are marked differences among social groups and nations in the frequency of violent crimes. The United States has a very high homicide rate (over 6 per 100,000 population on an annual basis). The comparable rates in Canada, Australia, and New Zealand are less than one-fourth of this figure. The rates in England, Sweden, Norway, and other Euro-pean countries are eight or more times lower than

BOX 17.8
Hired thieves are paid to get caught

There are crooks for hire these days who get caught for a price.

They steal without worrying about jail. In fact, they aren't punished at all and their best customers are the companies who have theft problems.

Firms who suspect normally hardworking employees of filling their own pockets with company loot turn to THEFT.

The people at THEFT specialize in crooks. For a fee described as moderate they'll loan you one in any size, shape and age you choose.

A thief is "hired" with as much fanfare as any other new employee, he spends a few days blending into the regular work force, then is caught stealing. With a great deal of shouting and screaming, he gets fired and the other employees get the message.

"Our people are prepared to take as much scolding and humiliation as the employer may see fit to use," said Rae Wilder, founder and director of THEFT (The Honest Employees Fooling Thieves) which she operates out of her home in Bayshore, L.I.

"Hire someone to fire," is the firm's motto.

"The idea is that it's much better for the employer to fire an undercover employee for stealing and get the message across that way rather than lose an otherwise valuable employee.

"Say you discover that an employee you've had for 20 years is doing some stealing from your supplies or inventory. You can reprimand that person, but he'll just get belligerent. With our system, you can show him you mean business and still not lose his experience," Miss Wilder said.

Most of the "thieves" Miss Wilder lines up are unemployed actors.

(*The Seattle Times*, July 23, 1974)

that in the United States. These large differences have understandably led to speculation about the underlying causes of homicide.

Prevention of crime and rehabilitation of criminals

Although certain adult criminals as well as certain juvenile delinquents can be distinguished by particular physical or psychological characteristics, psychological research has not yet succeeded in showing that most criminals can be distinguished from noncriminals psychologically. Eysenck (1975) argued that a hereditary factor was involved, and supported his theory with data from studies of identical and fraternal twins. His summary of existing studies showed that if one twin was in prison, it was four times as likely that the other twin would also be in prison if the twins were identical than it would be if they were fraternal (Eysenck, 1975, p. 146). The data were provocative, but more evidence is needed to substantiate Eysenck's theory.

Some investigators have reported a relationship between the abnormal XYY chromosomal arrangement sometimes found in men and criminal behavior (see Chapter 3), but the nature and extent of this relationship is unclear. Several studies have linked abnormal brain wave patterns measured by the electroencephalogram (EEG) with criminal behavior, especially psychopathic behavior. Because of the large margin of error in recording and interpreting EEG records, these findings are only suggestive. Social variables, such as poor living conditions, criminal behavior in parents and peers, poverty, and poor education, can be used as predictors of the probability of criminal behavior on a group basis. However, although factors such as these are associated with an increased likelihood of criminal behavior, many individuals reared under such conditions do not become criminals.

Because we do not know exactly how criminals and noncriminals differ and because different types of criminals seem to have different characteristics, the question of crime prevention and rehabilitation is a complex one. From a psychological standpoint, criminal behavior might be decreased by either of two general methods: (1) being punished or (2) learning alternate, noncriminal responses. If individuals are punished for criminal behavior, they should be less likely to repeat it. If they do not know how to behave in a socially acceptable fashion, then they may be able to learn such behavior. If their behavior stems from a neurotic or psychotic disorder, then therapeutic treatment might be helpful. The high percentage of criminals who commit crimes after they are released from prison has discredited the idea that imprisonment is a solution to the problem of crime. It seems likely that for many criminals, prison serves as an efficient training ground for learning new criminal skills. The idea of rehabilitation, or "retraining" an individual to fit into society, either within an institutional or prison setting or as an alternative to imprisonment, has been popular for at least the last quarter century. Many efforts at rehabilitation have seemed effective in experimental or pilot settings, but as yet none have been adopted on a large scale.

Juvenile rehabilitation

Presumably, young people should be prime candidates for rehabilitation. They are still in the process of developing, and their habits should be less deeply ingrained than are those of adults. The juvenile court movement, which removed young people from the formal legal system, was based on this idea.

Unfortunately, juvenile courts have not been very successful in rehabilitating delinquent youths, in stemming the tide of juvenile criminality, or in obtaining justice or compassion for child offenders. One reason for their lack of effectiveness is that there are few scientifically tested methods of rehabilitation appropriate for juveniles. Another is that juvenile court officials have limited funds and resources available to them.

Partly as a result of disillusionment with the juvenile justice system, there has been a growing deinstitutionalization movement during recent years. Deinstitutionalization programs such as the first one established in Massachusetts are trying to empty facilities in which juvenile delinquents are isolated from the community and place the youths in potentially rehabilitative settings within the community. These deinstitutionalization experiments are still very new, and they must be evaluated carefully before we can know whether it is realistic or possible to treat all offenders outside of institutions.

Formal education is a major part of the rehabilitation program at Deer Island, an institution for young delinquents. (Wolinsky, Stock, Boston)

BOX 17.9

Achievement Place

Achievement Place, a community-based, family-type treatment center, was founded in 1967, when citizens of Lawrence, Kansas, were seeking an alternative to sending delinquency-prone boys with serious problems to the state industrial school.

The program was developed by psychologists at the University of Kansas and backed by a committee of citizens. The supervisors for the youths are a trained couple who live with the six to eight boys or girls in a remodeled house in a residential neighborhood. The program emphasizes the "active give-and-take process "between the teaching parents and the youths. It is the responsibility of the teaching parents to correct problem behavior and teach the youths new ways of handling themselves and working with other people" (Fields, p. 4).

The teaching parents try to build a relationship with each of the youths. They teach them alternate ways of interacting with others and techniques for solving everyday problems.

One of the methods they use to motivate the youths is a token economy or point system. (See Chapter 6.) It is flexible, so that it can be tailored to the individual's particular problems. The way in which the point system was used early in the program was termed "a disaster" by one of the psychologists because it was too rigid and gave too little attention to human relationships. He went on to say, "A kid should not simply get points for doing well in school; he should also receive the regard and affection of the teaching parents" (Fields, p. 4).

As the youths gain greater self-control, they advance to a merit system in which no points are given or taken away. When they have made this step successfully, they begin to spend more time at home.

Stays at Achievement Place usually range from four months to two years. Andy, who is thirteen years old, is a typical resident:

> Andy looks for trouble. He got caught a couple of times for shoplifting. He's the kind of a kid that drives teachers up the blackboard, always in fights, causing chaos in the class, a kid who has trouble keeping friends. When Andy spent his first weekend at home after coming to Achievement Place, he described it this way.

> I had to take one of these point cards to my ol' lady to fill out. Man, I thought, bein' home's gonna be as bad as bein' here now, some crummy rules for everything. I mean, my mom had to write down if I had a bath, if I helped her out with the housework, what time I went out and came home. Why don't you go join the police force, I tol' her. That first weekend I stayed out until four o'clock to be with my friends. And then, naturally I lost so many points when I came back to Achievement Place that I had to work really hard all week to earn enough to get home again, and that next weekend I didn't blow it. (Fields, 1976, p. 7)

The schools are also involved in the program at Achievment Place. Teachers have cards to fill out daily. At first they found it an extra burden, but when they saw that the students really were changing their behavior, they became enthusiastic about the program. The principal of one school said that he saw remarkable changes in program participants, and cited Andy as an example:

> He was always getting into fights with other kids. There was nothing he wouldn't quarrel about. But now his grades are up, he has established one good friend in the class and has a fresh interest in sports. When he first came here it was my feeling that he shouldn't be allowed to attend public school because his behavior was so disruptive. (Fields, 1976, p. 9)

As with adults, it is more desirable to prevent delinquency among children than to try to rehabilitate them. One promising project has been set up to socialize predelinquent boys in Achievement Place, a homelike setting (Philips et al., 1971; Fixsen, Phillips, and Wolf, 1973). Achievement Place is a group home for 12- to 14-year-old boys who have committed minor offenses (thefts, truancy) and seem to be on the road to more serious crimes. The houseparents use operant learning principles, identifying target behaviors and using token reinforcement systems to strengthen pro-social tendencies. They emphasize social conduct and academic qualities as well as self-care.

The boys receive points for their achievements that they can use to obtain permission to go downtown, stay up past bedtime, play games, and watch television. Points can be either earned or lost. The token economy has been successful in modifying aggressive behavior and in improving tidiness, homework preparation, grammar, and punctuality.

The program has grown to include more than 50 homes modeled after the original Achievement Place. Houseparents are trained in special courses developed at the University of Kansas. They learn techniques for building relationships and ways to help youths develop alternative ways of interacting as well as how to use the token economy reinforcement program.

Many delinquents have poor academic skills and low expectations for the future. They anticipate failure along the normal paths of life, and their delinquency is often an attempt to find another route to success. These youths are more pessimistic than others about their chances of finishing high school. The ones who are most pessimistic commit nearly three times as many delinquent acts as those who feel their chances of success are "good" or "very good." Delinquent youths often expect to hold jobs with low wages and little prestige when they become adults. Some programs designed to prevent delinquency concentrate on improving basic academic skills in the hopes that they can bolster the young person's self-esteem as well as his or her chances for employment.

Adult rehabilitation

Adults as well as juveniles who are confined in conventional prisons seem to develop negative feelings toward society and to acquire new antisocial skills and attitudes from more experienced criminals. For these reasons community-based systems in which the criminals may be allowed to work in the community and return to custody in the evening, or even to be paroled full time under court supervision, have become increasingly popular.

Both individual and group psychotherapy have also been tried inside and outside prisons. In addition, prisons are now built to house fewer inmates and without traditional cell blocks in order to provide a more humane setting for prisoners.

An interesting experiment is being conducted at the Tillberga Prison in Sweden. Prisoners at this institution earn as much as $300 a month working in two factories at the prison, which was erected in 1963. There are no prison walls, only a wire fence. The prisoners have their own rooms with their own lock, for which they have the key. Relatives are allowed to visit for a maximum of six hours each Sunday. Mail is never censored, and if prisoners meet certain standards, they are permitted one free weekend from Friday to Sunday each month. With the money they earn they must pay the prison for food on working days. Prisoners report that they feel an increased sense of self-worth at Tillberga, and prisoners at other institutions are clamoring to be transferred there.

CHALLENGES IN THE PSYCHOLOGICAL STUDY OF SOCIAL PROBLEMS

Psychologists face both ethical and practical problems in investigating the process of social change and specific social problems such as crime. This is especially true if they are interested not only in describing and understanding the social change process, but also in actually helping to bring about specific changes (e.g., in rehabilitating criminals).

Research in field settings, such as prisons or day-care centers, entails several problems. For example, it is more difficult to make objective observations in these settings than it is in the laboratory. Experimental approaches to field studies are very costly and usually require a large staff and a long period of time. Experiments that transform social problems into laboratory exercises often lead to confusing or misleading results because they ignore a whole group of factors that may influence outcomes in actual situations.

Ethical problems are just as difficult. Most attempts at social change imply judgments as to what is desirable and what is not. For example, home visitors in preschool programs taught low-income

BOX 17.10

A psychological frontier: treatment of criminals

Two hotly debated issues that relate to the criminal justice system are natural concerns for psychologists: (1) punishment versus rehabilitation and (2) the effect of certain punishment on behavior.

Punishment versus rehabilitation

The prison system in the United States is placing increasing emphasis on rehabilitation; critics argue that punishment would be more effective in lowering the crime rate. A number of studies have shown, however, that criminals who are given mild sentences or parole are less likely to commit another crime than individuals given longer sentences. Because the severity of a sentence is usually determined partially by predictions about the offender's future behavior, the meaning of this finding is not clear.

Certainty of punishment

If a conviction carries a mandatory sentence, will a prospective criminal be less likely to commit a crime than if he or she thinks there is a good chance of probation or a suspended sentence? States that have passed laws calling for severe sentences have found that in many cases the jury is unwilling to convict the individual if they feel the penalty is too

"Let me see now! Shall I give you the minimum or the maximum?"

There are many questions about the effects of punishment, and sometimes legal, psychological, and economic considerations are in conflict. The law gives a judge great freedom in deciding a sentence. Should judges sentence prisoners by evaluating the likelihood they will commit another crime, in accordance with the seriousness of the crime for which they were convicted, or by evaluating the cost to society of keeping them in prison or letting them go free almost at once? More to the point in our context, what role should psychologists play in helping to answer these questions? (Drawing by Handelsman; © 1976 The New Yorker Magazine, Inc.)

severe. Revisionists have argued that punishment for an offense is necessary before meaningful rehabilitation can begin, and they suggest mandatory punishment laws that specify less severe punishments.

mothers to behave more like their middle-class counterparts. Although middle-class behavior may lead to success in school, the mothers were taught to accept a set of values that they may not have shared.

In this chapter we have tried to show that social problems raise many questions of interest to psy-

chologists. Why has past research provided so few answers to these questions? How can researchers meet high experimental standards in field situations? How should they deal with the ethical issues involved in social change? The wide variety of considerations that relate to social change make it an intriguing frontier for psychologists.

SUMMARY

1. Contemporary psychologists are making an increasing effort to study problems in complex real-life settings and to apply psychological knowledge to the solution of social problems.

2. Rapid social or economic change may cause problems of adjustment. Individuals' expectations may be drastically changed in a short period and old ways of reacting to the environment may no longer be effective. Psychologists study the effects of change on the individual and are trying to develop ways of coping effectively with the stresses it produces.

3. A social movement is an organized attempt to bring about change that develops over a period of time and usually includes both those who feel deprived and others who sympathize with them. Social movements typically try to produce change by publicity and education of the public and by active measures, such as strikes and boycotts.

4. Changes in the role of women have produced a need for better information in such areas as the effects on the family of a working wife-mother, the effects of day care on young children, and the stresses of role change and conflicting expectations on the woman herself.

5. *Self-fulfilling prophecy* is the term used for self-hatred often shown by individuals who are discriminated against by others.

6. Psychological research is needed to clarify which ideas about differences in behavior and ability between males and females are sex role stereotypes (unjustified assumptions) and which are reflections of genetic or social factors.

7. Compensatory education was an important social issue in the 1960s. It was based on the idea that some children had missed important early experiences and intellectual stimulation. If these could be supplied in the preschool years, it was assumed that the children would be more likely to succeed in school later on. Such programs as Head Start produced mixed results and showed the importance of greater knowledge about the many factors involved in early school failure. Two approaches that have produced results are training the parents of young children and working with the infants themselves.

8. Although deviation from social norms may be desirable or at least acceptable, deviation that causes difficulties for society, such as criminal behavior, receives the most attention. Psychologists can contribute to solving the problem of crime by looking at causal factors, effective ways of preventing criminal behavior, and methods of rehabilitation of criminal offenders. As yet final answers have not been provided in any of these areas.

9. Factors contributing to delinquency (crime by those under 18) include (a) individual pathology or personality defects; (b) family background; and (c) association with delinquent peers. The feeling of anonymity that seems to come from living in large cities, the importance of the youth culture, and the large amounts of leisure time for teenagers all may be factors in delinquency.

10. Adult criminals can be divided into several groups that may differ in psychological characteristics: occasional, habitual but petty, socialized, professional, white-collar, and those belonging to organized groups.

11. Because at present most criminals cannot be psychologically distinguished from non-

545

criminals and different types of criminals may have different characteristics, prevention of crime and criminal rehabilitation are difficult and complex topics.

Suggested readings

Hunt, J. McV. Reflections on a decade of early education. *Journal of Abnormal Child Psychology*, 1975, 3, 275–330. This article summarizes compensatory programs for young children beginning with the Project Head Start. The author, who has been involved with the planning of these programs from the beginning, evaluates the attempts and how well public expectations have been met.

Hyde, J. S. & Rosenberg, B. G. *Half the human experience: The psychology of women.* Lexington, Mass.: D. C. Heath & Company, 1976. (Paperback.) A summary of current viewpoints about the psychology of women written from the feminist viewpoint.

Kaplan, A. G., & Bean, J. G. *Beyond sex role stereotypes.* Boston: Little, Brown and Company, 1976. A collection of articles designed for a course on the psychology of women. The authors emphasize the current revision and expansion of sex roles and their political and personal consequences.

Maccoby, E. E., & Jacklin, C. *The psychology of sex differences.* Stanford, Calif.: Stanford University Press, 1974. A detailed summary and analysis of research on sex differences in children.

Menninger, K. *The crime of punishment.* New York: The Viking Press, 1966. Menninger raises questions about the effectiveness of our penal system and suggests changes.

Toffler, A. *Future shock.* New York: Random House, Inc., 1970. An influential book whose name became a household term. Toffler draws attention to the effects of rapid change.

Wilson, J. O. *Thinking about crime.* New York: Basic Books, Inc., Publishers, 1975. The author suggests that no important changes in the amount of crime will come about unless we examine and change some of our ideas about human nature.

Wolfgang, M. Figlio, R. M. & Sellen, T. *Delinquency in a birth cohort.* Chicago: University of Chicago Press, 1974. This study of an entire group of boys born in the same year and living in Philadelphia during their adolescence is an interesting example of a comprehensive research study.

Chapter 18

Environmental Psychology

(UPI)

Alice Wilson had not seen Ted and Nancy Harris for over half a year. When they walked into her living room Alice was startled by the change in Ted's appearance. It seemed to Alice that he had aged a decade in the months since they had last met.

She had heard from Tony about Ted's attitude toward the new company headquarters, but she had not fully appreciated what life in the headquarters had done to Ted. Although Tony was quite negative about the building, his tension level had remained about the same—perhaps because he spent about half his time visiting branch offices. But Ted, as the head of the Accounting Department, was in the building all the time.

During dinner Ted described the activities of two friends who had recently retired. After dinner he began talking about his own retirement.

> I guess thinking about retirement at 54 may seem a bit premature, but I've been giving it a lot of thought recently. I may seem silly to think about quitting early just because the company has a new headquarters, but that's probably the root cause of how I feel. I'd be the first to agree that the old building was a relic—too small, very inefficient. But, at least, I had an office to myself. If I wanted to think something out I could go in there and do it. If I had to tell one of the junior accountants that he wasn't working hard enough I could invite him into the office and we could talk about it. But now it seems we're too advanced for antiquated ideas like that. Those architects really did a job on that new building. Our floor has 70 desks and only a few are separated by huge plants. Those give you a real sense of privacy.

Tony understood everything Ted said. He had that feeling too. For him it wasn't so much that he needed a lot of privacy, but it was certainly distracting having some of the 70 pairs of eyes on you all the time. He was glad he had to be out of the office so often.

Later in the evening, Ted commented: "I know early retirement has to be thought through carefully. I'm going to wait a while before making a decision. Who knows, I might even learn to like all that togetherness on the sixth floor. I hope they saved enough on the office walls they left out to make up for the cost of the time all those eyes spend watching everybody else."

How could this problem have been avoided? No doubt the architects who planned the building thought about the environment for the workers along with their concerns about meeting specifications of the building owners, the governmental building codes, and the constraints of the budget. Where did it all go wrong? Or perhaps the problem lies not in the design of the building but in the people. Should they have been more adaptable? Environmental psychologists look at both these questions and many more.

The environment in which we live and work has many effects on all of us. Some of these effects may be generally the same for everyone, such as those from high levels of air pollution, unsanitary living conditions, or insufficient food and fuel. Other changes may have greatly different effects on different individuals. Ted's reaction to the new office building may or may not have been shared by his fellow workers. Some of them may have found the change easier to adapt to than Ted did. The designers of the building no doubt thought that their decision would improve working conditions.

In this case they seem to have been wrong. Many beliefs we hold about our surroundings are based on opinions that have not been tested. For example, does living in a densely populated area have a negative effect on the inhabitants? Or are other factors more important than this density? We have little information about people's reaction to many aspects of the environment. This information seems particularly important today. Technological advances have made possible changes in the environment that would have been inconceivable a short time ago. In addition, the rapid growth of the world's population together with a rise in living standards has many implications for the environment. How can the earth's limited resources be best used to create a livable world? Many ideas have been advanced on what makes for livability, but the opinions far outweigh facts.

One of the results of these present and prospective changes in living conditions has been an interest in what aspects of the environment actually affect individuals, and how. One group that is looking at these problems is made up of environmental psychologists. They look for answers to such questions as the following:

1. Does pollution of the environment by chemicals or increased noise have a negative effect on individuals' functioning or happiness?

548

2. How can working and living places in large cities best be designed to satisfy people's needs and desires?
3. Which aspects of environmental change help people; which hurt them?
4. What individual characteristics determine how a person will react to negative environmental change.
5. What conditions or skills help people learn to adjust to an unsatisfactory environment?

CROWDING

Just over three centuries ago the population of the entire world was estimated at 500 million people. By 1850 it was estimated at 1 billion; by 1970 well over 3 billion people inhabited the earth. Although publicity about the population crisis and improved birth control may slow the rate of growth, it is still predicted that by the end of the century the population may again double itself to more than 6 billion people. (See Figure 18.1)

One of the results of the world's population growth and its increasing industrialization is crowding. If human beings were scattered uniformly over the land areas of the earth, each person would have 10 acres to spread out on. For many reasons, however, people have congregated in groups. Since 1900 this trend has been rapidly accelerating. (See Figure 18.2.) In 1970 over 70 percent of the U.S. popula-

Figure 18.2 People sometimes must endure crowded conditions for practical reasons, such as getting home from work. Does such crowding have a lasting effect on them? (Aoki, Monkmeyer)

tion lived in or around urban areas. Canada, with a small population inhabiting a large land area, is even more urbanized than the United States. In addition, 40 percent of its urban population is clustered in only seven metropolitan areas. Other Western countries are also chiefly urban, ranging from 55 percent in the USSR to 75 percent in England, Scotland, and Wales. Most Third World countries are still chiefly rural, yet they contain many of the world's largest cities.

This urban trend causes crowding together of the population. Most contemporary theorists feel that crowding does seem to have negative effects on social and personal behavior. One national commission (Kerner Commission Report, 1968) identified crowded ghetto conditions as one of the most important causal factors in the urban riots of 1967. Popular writers argue that crowded living conditions are a primary cause of psychological problems among city dwellers. (See Figure 18.3.) Although many professional planners also argue that crowding is bad, at least one observer questions their conclusions. (See Box 18.1.)

Basically, there have been four types of research on crowding: animal studies, correlational surveys

549

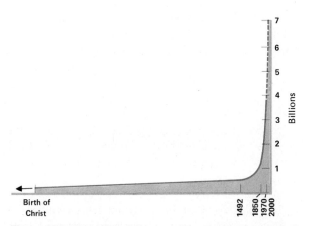

Figure 18.1 World Population growth, actual and projected. (Hartley, 1972, p. 5.)

Figure 18.3 This picture of São Paulo, Brazil, illustrates that the trend toward urban living occurs all over the world. Many of the world's largest cities are in South America or Asia. By the year 2000 it is expected that 60 percent of Brazilians will live in urban areas. (Wide World)

either completely withdrawn and disinterested in sex or increasingly hyperactive. Eventually they stopped making distinctions between male or female partners. Instances of extreme aggression and total passivity, unsuccessful births, destruction of nests, and inadequate performance of nest-building functions were observed under the high-density living conditions.

Other studies of animals living under crowded conditions have reported disrupted social relations and reproductive processes, as well as the development of certain physiological pathologies. Mice respond to increases in population density by increasing their emotional arousal and by developing abnormal variations in the weight of their organs (Christian, 1959; Thiessen, 1966). Monkeys that were kept in zoos under crowded conditions behaved more aggressively and attacked their companions (Russell and Russell, 1968).

using census data, experiments on the human use of space, and experimental studies directly concerned with the causal effects of crowding on human behavior. Because different researchers have tended to use different approaches to study the same phenomenon, there are often inconsistencies in the patterns of findings.

Animal studies

Although ethical considerations prevent researchers from manipulating human living conditions directly to study the effects of extreme crowding, researchers do create extremely crowded animal colonies to observe animal behavior. Calhoun (1962) built an ideal environment for rats, supplying them with food, water, and nesting materials. As the rats multiplied, Calhoun was able to study how the animals adapted to increasingly crowded living conditions. At first the population grew as he had expected, but then it stabilized itself at about 150 adults. If the growth pattern of the early period had been consistent, Calhoun would have expected over 5000 living rats at the end of his 27 months of observation. The reason for stabilization was an extraordinarily high rate of infant mortality. Normal maternal patterns were disrupted and few young survived. Male rats became

Figure 18.4 Picture of the experimental mouse universe. Sixteen cells made up the living space for the mouse colony. (National Institute of Mental Health)

Another study, this time in a natural setting, involved a group of deer stranded on a small island in Chesapeake Bay (Christian, Flyger, and Davis, 1960). With adequate resources at their disposal the deer were left free to breed uninterrupted. The population increased until the density was approximately one deer per acre. At that point the mortality rate increased dramatically for no obvious reason. Autopsies performed on dead animals revealed a variety of extreme endocrinological disorders, apparently the result of stress from the overcrowded conditions. Symptoms included greatly enlarged (by almost 50 percent) adrenal glands and reproductive dysfunctions.

Apparently, the deer were producing abnormally large amounts of adrenalin, which is usually produced when an animal is aroused. The mere presence of "too many" other animals seemed to arouse the animals almost constantly and drive them to an early death. Robert Ardrey (1966) has suggested that animals require a certain amount of space. When this space is violated by other animals of the same species, an instinctive aggressive response is triggered that causes the animal to drive off the intruders. This idea accounts for the extreme aggression observed in rats and monkeys, and the heightened arousal of the deer in Chesapeake Bay living under crowded conditions.

It is extremely unwise, however, to apply the results of experiments designed to test the effects of crowding on animals directly to human life.

Correlational studies

Several studies of human beings in natural settings have attempted to correlate indexes of population density with indicators of social health, such as mortality rates, fertility rates, juvenile delinquency, and admissions to mental hospitals. As an example of one such study, indexes of social pathology in Chicago were developed (Galle et al., 1972) to match as closely as possible the disorders exhibited by Calhoun's rats. There was a significant correlation between density and the occurrence of socially undesirable behaviors. Although certain social pathologies occurred together with crowded living conditions, this type of study could not demonstrate that these pathologies were caused by crowding. There were socioeconomic differences between those living in

the high-density neighborhoods and other comparison groups that may also have accounted for some of the effects the investigators observed. In field studies it is extremely difficult, if not impossible, to control for socioeconomic variables that may interact with effects caused by crowded conditions (Lawrence, 1974).

Cross-cultural studies seem to argue against the idea that there is a causal connection between crowding and increased human social problems. Schmitt studied the relationships between density and various social problems in Honolulu (1966) and Hong Kong (1963). In the Honolulu study, he substantiated the finding that there is a positive correlation between highly dense living conditions and frequent social problems. In the Hong Kong study, however, he failed to find any significant correlation between crowding and social problems. In another cross-cultural study, Lester (1970) examined the effects on the frequency of suicides of high-density living conditions in Edinburgh, Scotland, and Buffalo, New York. In Edinburgh suicide was more frequent in crowded areas of the city; this was not true in the Buffalo population.

Laboratory studies using human subjects

Laboratory studies that simulate either crowded or noncrowded conditions typically have reported that there were no noticeable differences in the variables they measured. The ability to perform simple tasks (Freedman, Klevansky, and Ehrlich, 1971), aggressive behavior or feelings (Freedman et al., 1972; Loo, 1972), and friendliness among group members (Keating and Snowball, 1974) were not noticeably different under crowded and noncrowded conditions. Men and women may respond differently to crowding when groups of a single sex are used. Men show increased negativity in personal relations and become more competitive. Women become more cooperative in crowded situations (Freedman, 1975).

Smith and Haythorn (1972) studied men who were kept in groups in either very small or rather large isolation chambers for periods of up to 20 days. Men in the small room displayed less hostile and aggressive behavior than those in the larger, less crowded rooms. The investigators concluded that when they are pushed to do it, people can adapt to crowded conditions with no noticeable negative ef-

551

BOX 18.1

What is a slum?

Ideas about what makes a desirable living area are often not verified by empirical data. Yet these ideas may affect many decisions and produce much environmental change.

The district called the North End in Boston is an old, low-rent area merging into the heavy industry of the waterfront, and it is officially considered Boston's worst slum and civic shame. It embodies attributes which all enlightened people know are evil because so many wise men have said they are evil. Not only is the North End bumped right up against industry, but worse still it has all kinds of working places and commerce mingled in the greatest complexity with its residences. It has the highest concentration of dwelling units, on the land that is used for dwelling units, of any part of Boston, and indeed one of the highest concentrations to be found in any American city. It has little parkland. Children play in the streets. Instead of super-blocks, or even decently large blocks, it has very small blocks; in planning parlance it is "badly cut up with wasteful streets." Its buildings are old. Everything conceivable is presumably wrong with the North End. In orthodox planning terms, it is a three-dimensional textbook of "megalopolis" in the last stages of depravity. The North End is thus a recurring assignment for Massachusetts Institute of Technology and Harvard planning and architectural students, who now and again pursue, under the guidance of their teachers, the paper exercise of converting it into super-blocks and park promenades, wiping away its non-conforming uses, transforming it to an ideal of order and gentility so simple it could be engraved on the head of a pin.

Twenty years ago, when I first happened to see the North End, its buildings—town houses of different kinds and sizes converted to flats, and four- or five-story tenements built to house the flood of immigrants first from Ireland, then from Eastern Europe, and finally from Sicily—were badly overcrowded, and the general effect was of a district taking a terrible physical beating and certainly desperately poor.

When I saw the North End again in 1959, I was amazed at the change. Dozens and dozens of buildings had been rehabilitated. Instead of mattresses against the

(Charles Gatewood)

windows there were venetian blinds and glimpses of fresh paint. Many of the small, converted houses now had only one or two families in them instead of the old crowded three or four. Mingled all among the buildings for living were an incredible number of splendid food stores, as well as such enterprises as upholstery making, metal working, carpentry, food processing. The streets were alive with children playing, people shopping, people strolling, people talking. Had it not been a cold January day, there would surely have been people sitting. I had seen a lot of Boston in the past couple of days, most of it sorely distressing, and this struck me, with re-

552

lief, as the healthiest place in the city. But I could not imagine where the money had come from for the rehabilitation, because it is almost impossible today to get any appreciable mortgage money in districts of American cities that are not either high-rent, or else imitations of suburbs. To find out, I went into a bar and restaurant (where an animated conversation about fishing was in progress) and called a Boston planner I know.

"Why in the world are you down in the North End?" he said. "Money? Why, no money or work has gone into the North End. Nothing's going on down there. Eventually, yes, but not yet. That's a slum!"

"It doesn't seem like a slum to me," I said.

"Why, that's the worst slum in the city. It has two hundred and seventy-five dwelling units to the net acre! I hate to admit we have anything like that in Boston, but it's a fact."

"Do you have any other figures on it?" I asked.

"Yes, funny thing. It has among the lowest delinquency, disease, and infant mortality rates in the city. It also has the lowest ratio of rent to income in the city. Boy, are those people getting bargains. Let's see . . . the child population is just about average for the city, on the nose. The death rate is low, 8.8 per thousand, against the average city rate of 11.2. The TB death-rate is very low, less than one per ten thousand, can't understand it, it's lower even than Brookline's. In the old days the North End used to be the city's worst spot for tuberculosis, but all that has changed. Well, they must be strong people. Of course it's a terrible slum."

"You should have more slums like this," I said, "Don't tell me there are plans to wipe this out. You ought to be down here learning as much as you can from it.

"I know how you feel," he said. "I often go down there myself just to walk around the streets and feel that wonderful, cheerful streetlife. Say, what you ought to do, you ought to come back and go down in the summer if you think it' fun now. You'd be crazy about it in summer. But of course we have to rebuild it eventually. We've got to get those people off the streets."

Here was a curious thing. My friend's instincts told him the North End was a good place, and his social statistics confirmed it. But everything he had learned as a physical planner about what is good for people and good for city neighborhoods, everything that made him an expert, told him the North End has to be a bad place. (Jacobs, 1965, pp. 18–20)

fects on their behavior. In light of these findings, some psychologists have argued that although our instincts seem to tell us that crowding exerts a negative influence on human behavior and underlies innumerable social problems, in fact crowding does not necessarily exert either a positive or negative effect on human behavior.

The effects of crowding on subjects may be studied not only while they are in a crowded room but later, in uncrowded situations. In one study, subjects were not affected by crowding either in their performance on a proofreading task designed to test their concentration or in their ability to tolerate frustrations as long as they remained in the crowded conditions (Sherrod, 1974). When subjects were asked to work under uncrowded conditions during the second hour of the experiment, Sherrod found that those who were crowded in the first hour could not tolerate as much frustration as subjects who were not crowded. These findings suggest that although people may be able to tolerate highly dense situations for a period of time, in the long run crowding affects their behavior negatively, just as noise does.

Experiments on the use of space

One problem that is closely related to the concept of crowding is the way in which we actually use the space around us, or our *personal space*. A number of theorists have argued that we each have our own portable territory, much like the territory that animals mark out for themselves. Robert Sommer (1969), a leading researcher in this area, used the example of a person seated alone on the end of a bench in a city park to illustrate this concept. What would happen if another person were to approach the bench, and instead of sitting at the opposite end from the occupant, sat in the middle of the bench. The initial occupant would change posture, and in general would show obvious signs of discomfort. Finally, he or she would probably leave the bench soon afterward.

Anthropologist Edward T. Hall (1959; 1966) has developed a method for studying the ways in which people use personal space, called *proxemics*. Hall found that people expect to keep various distances between themselves and others, depending on the nature of the interaction between them. *Intimate distance*, between lovers, mothers and children, or

553

Personal distances vary among cultures. Certain cultures maintain social-consultive distance for contacts which might require only casual-personal distance in others. (Burri, Magnum)

others who are close to one another, ranges from full contact to 18 inches apart. *Casual-personal* distance is from 18 to 48 inches. *Social-consultive distance,* for most business and formal contact is between 4 and 12 feet. *Public distance* for public speakers, extends from 12 feet to the maximum distance across which the voice will carry (Hall, 1964). Most of us seem to maintain these distances unconsciously in our interpersonal encounters. We grow aware of the space we need for a specific interaction only if the visual space is violated, as with the person on the park bench.

Personal space requirements seem to be different for different cultures and population subgroups. For example, Watson and Graves (1966) asked Arab and American subjects to come to their laboratory to participate in group discussions. While the groups engaged in conversations on a variety of topics the investigators unobtrusively measured the distances they maintained. As was predicted, the Arabs positioned themselves closer to one another, touched each other more, and leaned toward each other more than the Americans.

Subgroups within cultures also seem to have different spatial needs. Several studies have compared the space needs of subjects with pathological symptoms to those of a more normal population. These studies have reported that the pathological groups seem to need more personal space than the comparison groups. One investigator who studied violent prisoners (Kinzel, 1970) concluded that violent behavior may be one sign of a disturbance in the use of personal space. In different kinds of situations different distances seem natural to the individual. A closer approach may cause discomfort.

Robert Sommer (1969) has examined the human need for territoriality in various settings, such as libraries, mental hospitals, and student cafeterias. Where would you sit if you wanted to communicate that a table in the library was yours and you did not want any intruders? In one experiment (Félipe and Sommer, 1966–1967) Sommer asked a female researcher to walk into a library and then choose a chair that was either next to an unsuspecting subject's chair, one or two chairs away, or directly across from it. The researcher stayed in this position for 30 minutes and compared the time it took for the subject to move with that of another person sitting in the library. When the researcher sat in the next chair, by the end of 30 minutes, 70 percent of the subjects removed themselves, whereas only 15 percent of the controls left. When the researcher sat near or across from the subjects, 25 percent removed themselves, compared to 15 percent of the control

often deal with excessive stimulation by withdrawing physically, by becoming aloof toward others, or by giving less attention to low-priority items. These behaviors may be adaptive and allow them to feel more comfortable in the stimulating environment. Experimental results suggest that such conditions may cause physical changes, such as those found in animal glands, or may mean lowered tolerance to frustration after individuals leave the stimulating situation. *Behavioral constraint* is another interpretation of behavior in crowded conditions. This view concentrates on the idea that crowding makes people feel their freedom in behavior threatened or eliminated. Sommer's idea of personal space, discussed earlier, which established boundaries for comfortable interaction, is an example of this viewpoint. The third approach is the *ecological* model, which is

An airport waiting room. Individuals who are waiting by themselves clearly need more territory than those who have companions. (Beckwith Studios)

These vendors in Kuwait are discussing the price and sale of pigeons. As a rule, personal distances are much smaller in Arab countries than in America. (Barbey, Magnum)

subjects. These results seem to indicate that even in impersonal social situations, there are certain spatial and territorial rules.

Theoretical perspectives on crowding

Experimental results from crowding studies have been explained in several ways. The *overload model* presumes that individuals receive more stimulation from the environment than they can tolerate. They

Although the train is crowded, the experience of overcrowding is more intense and unpleasant because of "overmanning"; there are more passengers than seats. (Greenberg, DPI)

particularly concerned with the "behavior setting," a unit with cyclical patterns of activity and defined boundaries. (See discussion of Roger Barker's work later in this chapter.) Examples of behavior settings are a classroom, a shopping center, or the kitchen of a restaurant. It has been observed that the relation of the number of people present to the facilities available determines the number of roles each individual will fill. For example, a greater percentage of students in a small school take part in student life and participate in a wider variety of activities than participate in such activities in a large school. From this

556

kind of observation came the idea of *overmanning* as a critical part of the perception of crowding (Wicker, 1973). Overmanning means that if the number of persons exceeds the facilities or jobs available, the situation will be perceived as crowded. If two sewing machines are available and three people are asked to complete a sewing task or if four dictionaries are provided for five students who are asked to define words, they are likely to perceive the situation as crowded.

Is crowding detrimental?

Research on the effects of crowding on human beings has not given clear answers to the question of whether crowding has negative effects on individuals. One effort to explain why experimental evidence on crowding gives conflicting results is the *density-intensity hypothesis* advanced by Jonathan Freedman (1975). Freedman believes that crowding in itself does not have negative effects. Crowding does, however, make the other people present become more important factors in an individual's reaction to a situation. A person's positive or negative reactions to a situation are intensified under crowded conditions. According to this theory, a cocktail party is much more pleasant to a party lover when the room is full than when the participants are scattered in groups over a large room. Sometimes people create their own crowd at such a party by clustering together in one small area—the kitchen, for instance—and thus heightening their feelings of enjoyment.

Crowding also makes the outcome of a situation more important. In one study (Gochman, 1976), students who were crowded together described the situation as crowded only under certain conditions. If they were unable to attain their goals (being unable to register for desired courses) or if their expectations of a situation, either positive or negative, were not confirmed, students tended to report feeling crowded; those who had been successful or had attained their expectations, however, did not feel crowded.

Many field investigations on such topics as the effects of crowding on family aggression, health, reproduction, and child development have failed to show that increased density contributes to pathology. One of the difficulties in assessing such findings is lack of knowledge of what aspects of crowding, as

Table 18.1 Summary of theoretical perspectives of crowding

Model	Definition of crowding	Emotional reactions likely to appear	Ways of adapting to the situation
Stimulus overload	too much stimulation for comfort	1. confusion 2. fatigue	1. escape from situation by leaving it or withdrawing psychologically 2. change in physical structure of environment by using partitions, room dividers, etc.
Behavioral constraint	reduced freedom of behavior	1. negative emotion 2. feeling one is being infringed upon	1. leave situation 2. improve situation by improving relationship with others or coordinating activities
Ecological	scarcity of resources	1. worry over lack of adequate resources 2. feelings of competition for available resources	1. collective defense of resources 2. increased feelings of territoriality 3. exclusion of nongroup members

Adapted from Stokols, 1974. By permission of the publisher, Sage Publications, Inc.

it normally occurs, may be detrimental. Should residential crowding be defined as number of persons per room in living accommodations, number of living units per building, or number of individuals per square mile? Does crowding exist if the individual defines the situation as crowded or if people complain about the interference of others in their activities? Does crowding always mean an imbalance between people and resources? What characteristics of the individual make the perception of crowding more likely? Until these and similar questions can be better specified, research on this vital topic may continue to yield conflicting results.

PLANNING AND BUILDING FOR PEOPLE IN GROUPS

When people live together in large groups, the cooperation of planners, architects, and environmental psychologists becomes more necessary, because organization of activities and structures becomes more important.

Architectural determinism

Behind the work of many planners and architects is the idea of *architectural determinism*. This idea that the design of buildings and other spaces affects the behavior of the people who inhabit them is an old one. It springs from the behavioristic view of the relationship between the stimulus (the structure of the environment) and the human response. Although some aspects of the environment may affect behavior, research indicates that such statements of relationship must be cautious and carefully qualified.

The idea of architectural determinism was given a boost by the work of psychologist Leon Festinger and his associates (1950), who studied the group structure and friendship patterns of married students living in a Massachusetts Institute of Technology housing project. As was noted in Chapter 12, Festinger found that students' friendships were formed with those who lived nearby. These friendships became the basis of communication and social organization within the project. The location of the housing unit, whether it was in a central or isolated location, and the way it faced affected the friendships made by the occupants. Friendships were most frequent between next-door neighbors and less frequent between couples two houses apart. The frequency of friendships continued to decrease with distance between house entries, until it was rare to find a friendship between couples living four or five houses apart. Although Festinger pointed out that these results were found in a homogeneous group and that this fact might be important, his qualifica-

557

BOX 18.2

Furniture arrangement counts too

Psychologist Robert Sommer was asked for help in determining what was wrong with the furnishings of a state hospital ward. Several thousand dollars had just been spent to improve one large room where the patients congregated. There were new curtains, a new tile floor, and new chairs with brightly colored seats. The hospital had received an improvement award based on photographs of the new furnishings. But somehow this new setting did not seem to change the withdrawn behavior of the elderly women patients. Sommer spent several weeks sitting in the ward and observing the patients.

> There was no denying that it was the best furnished ward in the hospital; as such it was regarded as somewhat of a model to be seen by visitors on tour. It took several weeks of sitting and watching before I could sort figure from ground, and see what *was not* happening as

well as what was. With as many as 50 ladies in the large room, there were rarely more than one or two brief conversations. The ladies sat side-by-side in their new chrome chairs against the newly painted walls, and exercised the options of gazing down at the newly tiled floor or looking up at the new fluorescent lights. They were like strangers in a train station waiting for a train that never came. This shoulder-to-shoulder arrangement was unsuitable for sustained conversation even for me. To talk to neighbors, I had to turn in my chair and pivot my head 90 degrees.

After reviewing the various possibilities, we decided that the ladies would be more likely to converse if, instead of sitting shoulder to shoulder, they faced one another. Our initial view, which was modified later, was that the people should be pointed toward one another (like projectiles) in order to maximize conversation. We also felt that the large open areas should be broken into smaller spaces, so that each person could select one or two others with whom to interact. Partitions might have served our purpose, but we decided to start with small tables placed around the ward.

We found that in the new arrangement, both brief and sustained interactions almost doubled. Also, there was a remarkable increase in the amount of reading. Before the study was begun, very few magazines were seen in the dayroom despite the fact that large quantities were purchased for the patients or donated each

---

tion was overlooked by many who took up the idea of architectural determinism.

The arrangement of living quarters within a building may also make a difference in the pattern of social interactions of those who live there. Two types of military barracks, with either closed or open cubicles, were used in another study of social interaction patterns. The men in the closed cubicles had more interaction with each other and less with men from "outside" than did those who lived in open cubicles (Blake et al., 1956). In this experiment, as in Festinger's, the group studied was homogeneous (i.e., all were members of the armed forces).

The redesign of rooms and buildings has also been influenced by the idea that the physical aspects of the room and the arrangement of furniture make a difference in the behavior of those who use the area.

One of the first psychologists to study these effects was Robert Sommer. (See Box 18.2)

Although these examples show that architecture or design elements may affect behavior patterns, it is important to remember that many other things are involved in determining behavior and social or work relationships. The imperfect understanding of these complex relationships is clearly shown by the effects of some urban redevelopment projects on the residents of an area or the whole city.

Urban housing from a psychological perspective

Beginning in the 1930s in the United States and other Western nations, massive redevelopment projects were aimed at removing substandard housing and replacing it with huge projects usually in high

month. One reason for this was that there was no place to store magazines when they were not in use. If a magazine were to be placed on the floor, a nurse was likely to consider this untidy and remove it. The tables now provided places where printed materials could be left without fear of their immediate disappearance. Patients had formerly hoarded magazines, carrying them around in bundles or keeping them under mattresses where they would not be taken away. The same hoarding, which had been a sensible reaction considering the circumstances, appeared when we first laid out magazines on the tables. The first week we supplied 20 magazines a day, which disappeared as rapidly as we put them out. Later, when the ladies found that the magazines were brought to the ward regularly and could be left on the tables safely, hoarding decreased. (Sommer, 1976, pp. 381–386)

Sommer points out that the new arrangement prompted other changes. The patient's use of the tables caused the ward physician to arrange regular visits by an occupational therapist. The result was an increase in craft work and greater interaction among the patients. The final result of the change in furniture arrangement was a complex of social interactions, not just the original shifting of chairs and the addition of tables.

tower blocks. Whole areas of cities were leveled and rebuilt. Somehow this gutting and rebuilding seemed to create new problems rather than eliminate old ones. Jane Jacobs, a writer on architectural topics, describes the situation this way:

There is a wistful myth that if only we had enough money to spend—the figure is usually put at a hundred billion dollars—we could wipe out all our slums in ten years, reverse decay in the great, dull, grey belts that were yesterday's and the day before yesterday's suburbs, anchor the wandering middle class and its wandering tax money, and even solve the traffic problem.

But look what we have built with the first several billions: low-income projects that become worse centres of delinquency, vandalism, and general social hopelessness than the slums they were supposed to replace; middle-income housing projects which are

truly marvels of dullness and regimentation, sealed against any buoyancy or vitality of city life; luxury housing projects that mitigate their inanity, or try to, with a vapid vulgarity; cultural centres that are unable to support a good bookstore; civic centres that are avoided by everyone but bums, who have fewer choices of loitering place than others; commercial centres that are lack-lustre imitations of standardized suburban chain-store shopping; promenades that go from no place to nowhere and have no promenaders; expressways that eviscerate great cities. This is not the rebuilding of cities. This is the sacking of cities. (Jacobs 1965, pp. 13–14)

The reasons for the failure of many projects are complex. Some failures were based more on economics or politics than on psychological factors. Two psychological factors are important. First, the *psychological consequences* of the plan may create difficulties for the tenants. Projects are usually set up in a separate block. This separateness may make it more difficult for project inhabitants to become part of the community. The lack of shops or businesses within the project means that it does not draw in other people whose presence would make the grounds a safer place because of the many people using them. Social interaction within the project may be made more difficult by a lack of space for public use.

The project may have been designed without taking account of the *psychological requirements* of the prospective tenants. They, or people like them, may

Research has shown that furniture and spatial arrangements do affect work performance. Personnel in this aircraft company office have little spatial or visual privacy, but they do have easy access to others with whom they consult. (Hopker, Woodfin Camp)

"This city is going to hell! That used to be a parking lot."

Figure 18.5 One problem planners face is that the needs and desires of different groups may be in conflict. (Drawing by B. Tobey; © 1975 The New Yorker Magazine, Inc.)

never have been asked what features are important to them in an area that is to be their home. For example, studies in England have shown that mothers with young children believe that they need a housing situation that makes it possible for them to watch their children's outside play. Tenants also want means of controlling entry to the building and stairways and elevators that are not so isolated by their design that they are unsafe to use. Such preferences of tenants may be based on real needs. One study of families who lived in apartments showed 57 percent more illness than occurred in comparable families who lived in houses (Fanning, 1967). Differences in health were especially great in children under 10, women 20 to 29, and women over 40. The children and younger women from the apartments had far more respiratory disorders than their counterparts in individual houses. Both age groups of women from the apartments had a much higher incidence of neurotic complaints than did comparable women housed in separate houses. The most striking contrast between the two groups was the lack of communication between families living in apartments compared to those in houses. Similar results in other studies has led to the conclusion that the way in which apartment buildings are constructed often prevents contact with neighbors and thus restricts social life.

When residents of American public housing developments were interviewed, they often expressed satisfaction with their individual apartments but extreme dissatisfaction with the project as a whole (Yancey, 1971). This unhappiness with their surroundings seemed based in part on the uncontrolled or nondefensible space in the project, such as the stair wells and elevators. (See Box 18.3.) The concept of *defensible space* was originated by Oscar Newman (1972), an architect who believes that architects can design buildings that make public space defensible. By this he means designs that extend residents' feelings of ownership and responsibility outside their own doors. One way to accomplish this is to make it easy for residents to keep the area under constant visual surveillance and to feel that, along with their neighbors, they share responsibility for what occurs there. This is what happens on a small town main street, where merchants in small shops know all the inhabitants and can survey the street outside during lulls in their business activity. In limited trials Newman's idea seems to work.

Isolation of tenants in large projects from the services and social interactions of city life is one of the causes for dissatisfaction in large projects. Yet large projects are still being constructed. In Amsterdam, the Netherlands, a number of large blocks of new luxury apartments have become "white elephants." Vacancy rates were high until the Dutch government began to use the buildings for subsidized rentals for the poor. Why, in a city with a tight housing supply, were these apartments so unattractive? They were isolated. Transportation and shopping facilities were poor. The massive scale of the high-rise project produced negative feelings even in a country of high population density where people are accustomed to apartment living.

Breaking of sociopsychological ties
Large projects have another disadvantage. They usually require destruction and clearing of existing structures, often longtime homes of individuals and business. Even if these return to the project after its completion the psychological ties of the old neighborhood may have died in the interval. Many of the businesses in the surrounding area, deprived of their usual customers by the land clearing, may not be

Recent housing projects' attempts to provide a complete environment for residents may have unforeseen side-effects. Although these children have a pleasant place to play, they may feel isolated from other children in the community. (Charles Gatewood)

BOX 18.3

A housing horror story

Pruitt-Igoe, a housing project in St. Louis, may be the ultimate housing project horror story. The complex consisted of 36 11-story rectangular buildings set in parallel rows. Each building contained 70 dwelling units. Built in 1954, much of the complex has already been torn down. Its demolition is pictured at the beginning of the chapter. Why was it demolished? No one wanted to live there. Vacancy rates were high. Vandalism, theft, and petty crime made the complex exorbitantly expensive to maintain and police. Yet when the plans for the complex were first published they were commended by a leading architectural journal. What went wrong?

Housing projects often are problem areas, but Pruitt-Igoe was outstanding for its problems.

A five-year study and 60,000 pages of interview data gave sociologist Lee Rainwater and his associates a good idea of the problem (Rainwater, 1966; Yancey, 1971). The same quality that had caused the praise of original design—the lack of public space—seemed most important in Pruitt-Igoe's quick fall into disease and death. This lack of public space, although cost-efficient, made social relationships among the tenants more difficult. Although tenants may not form close relationships, they derive a feeling of safety from some social interaction. The other architectural feature that caused tenants to feel unsafe was the design of the stairwells and elevators. In some cases these were isolated from the apartments by a small anteroom that made observation difficult. This, together with lack of control over entry to the stairwells, gave tenants' fear of assault or rape a realistic base.

---

able to survive until tenants return. The massive redevelopment of New York City involved demolishing the centers of many established neighborhoods for throughways or other public construction. This and the development of huge housing complexes that grouped together and isolated the poor and the middle class have been blamed for some of the problems of the city (Epstein, 1976; Caro, 1975).

The problems of large-scale clearance have begun to be officially recognized. The government of the Philippines had planned to demolish a shanty town in Manila and rebuild it. After study of the effects of demolishing the squatters' homes and moving the inhabitants 30 kilometers away while the area was redeveloped with high-rise flats, the government decided instead to improve sanitary facilities, build schools, and at the same time provide cheap credit to the inhabitants to improve their homes. The most important ingredient in the scheme, the financing, was provided by the World Bank, which also recognized possible benefits of the new plan (Power, 1976). Will this new approach to urban restoration, a huge field study, prove psychologically as well as financially healthier? Such projects will be important test cases for environmental psychologists.

Urban working conditions

The *social design* of institutional spaces, such as offices, schools, and psychiatric hospitals, has been studied intensively. Social design reflects the psychological concern that considerations of health, efficiency, and perhaps even esthetic criteria, are not enough in constructing such buildings and designing their interiors. Factors of privacy and social interchange must also be taken into account. Many studies have shown that office design, especially the use of either cubicles or an open plan, affects the interaction of workers. Whether promoting interaction is desirable from either the point of view of the workers or the management is a complex question. In one study, employee complaints of visual distraction, noise, and loss of privacy followed the switch to an open plan. Positive changes were noted in group sociability (Brookes and Kaplan, 1972). Motivation of workers seems to vary little with differences in office plan. Perhaps the huge scale of most office

Perhaps even more enlightening than the observations of Rainwater and his group is this comment from an urban design consultant who expresses his frustrations as follows:

> The irrelevance of Dr. Rainwater's sociological insights must be apparent to any American housing designer. In a system which almost perfectly insulates him from the needs of lower class families, the social content of housing is the least of the designer's worries. Public housing architects are driven to satisfy the cost limits, the fixation on maintenance, and the bureaucratic routines of local housing authorities and the federal agency. They must conform to the usually gentle, unarticulated American disposition to keep down the poor. At the same time, architects must achieve professional self-realization through the approval of their artistic peers; others count for little. Taken together, these demands so frequently overload their problem-solving capacities, as well as their interests, that designers have little energy left for considering the fine points of behavior-space relationships in lower class life. (Montgomery, 1966, p. 31)

buildings and the way they limit options in human behavior are more important factors than interior design variations. (See Box 18.4.)

Techniques for measuring the effects of buildings and neighborhoods

Some techniques used to study the effects of such environments as buildings and neighborhoods are used in many other types of psychological studies. These techniques include correlational studies and laboratory experiments that examine effects of particular variables in the situation. Some environmental psychologists have also devised other techniques for studying issues related to the environment.

Observational techniques

Among the pioneers who have formulated techniques for studying environmental issues are Roger Barker and his colleagues at the Midwest Psychological Field Station in Oskaloosa, Kansas. Barker's main objective has been to determine the relationships between patterns of behavior in a behavior setting and the structural properties of that setting. By *be-*

havior setting Barker means the milieu within which the behavior occurs. A doctor's office, a cemetery, and a classroom are behavior settings.

Barker thinks that behavior is best studied in everyday, natural environments and uses a special *observational technique* to pursue his study of "ecological psychology." Over a period of 24 years, Barker and his colleagues made innumerable detailed observations of most aspects of daily life in a small Kansas community they have named "Midwest." Barker does not set out to establish any causal relationships; rather, he seeks to describe behavior in natural settings. He is basically interested in identifying those "discriminable phenomena external to an individual's behavior" (Barker, 1968, p. 14) that may have a bearing upon it. Barker's observers carefully recorded the actual number of people-hours spent in various behavioral settings from Burgess Beauty Shop to the Kindergarten Sunday School Class. Table 18.2 reflects the time spent by residents of the town "Midwest" and the total time spent by residents and nonresidents in each of the various behavioral settings during 1963–1964. In addition, the figures can be broken down to reflect the average number of people present, the average amount of time spent in each setting, and the sex and age of the people in the setting. This elaborate and detailed recording technique is designed to provide investigators with an accurate record of how every part of the physical environment of the town of Oskaloosa is used.

One of the most famous of Barker's studies used this detailed observational technique to study the behavioral patterns of children who attended small and large schools. In this study Barker and Gump (1964) found that because smaller schools provide more opportunities for student participation, students who attend smaller schools are more actively involved than are students who attend larger schools. Because inactive students tend to drop out of school more than do active ones, the size of the school setting may be a critical variable in controlling the dropout rate.

Simulation techniques

A second type of methodology used by environmental psychologists is the *simulation technique* for evaluating an environment. Researchers present to subjects in the laboratory a scale model or some other accurate representation of an environmental

BOX 18.4
The modern skyscraper

The following account of the World Trade Center in New York and the Sears Tower in Chicago demonstrates that "modern" does not necessarily mean "best"—or at least not "best" in terms of human values. In recent years environmental psychologists have begun to explore our living, educational, and work environments using new criteria for evaluating them.

The recent completion of New York's World Trade Center and Chicago's Sears Tower has loosed a flood of complaints about working in the huge skyscrapers. "You're a number here, not a person. You're just not in control of your life," says George Bragman, president of Anchor Business Forms, who is so burned up by the computerized World Trade Center environment that he is moving out. In fact, the 25,000 workers in the twin 110-story World Trade Center towers uniformly complain about not being able to open the windows or turn the lights off and on. To turn the computerized lights on before 7 A.M. and after 11 P.M., WTC workers must give 24 hours' notice and pay for overtime use. At the Sears Tower, computerized temperatures may vary up to 20 degrees. When the sun streams through the bronze-tinted glass windows the 16,500 employees swelter; on a cloudy day, they freeze.

Elevators, too, are a source of misery. At lunchtime, it can take fifteen minutes to reach street level, so many workers eat at their desk. To leave the WTC, most employees have to use two elevators—sometimes going up to go down—and at rush hours the crowds are as bad as in the New York subway.

Fire, of course, is a constant fear of most high-rise workers, and a blaze last week at the World Trade Center only increased anxiety. The Trade Center has no sprinkler system, and it would take an estimated three hours to evacuate the building entirely. . . .

To be sure, some high-rises, like Chicago's 95-story Hancock building, have managed to create humane environments within their vast spaces. Apartment dwellers have access to laundry facilities every third floor, as well as a supermarket, a swimming pool and even a Bonwit

The Sears Tower in Chicago. The partially demolished building in the foreground was the Pennsylvania Railway Station. (Lejeune, Stock, Boston)

Teller store. Since the Hancock converted 49 floors to condominiums two years ago, it has maintained a 95 percent occupancy, while at the World Trade Center almost one-quarter of the office space is unoccupied. Defenders of the skyscrapers point out that even the airplane was once considered bizarre and dehumanizing. But adapting to the high-rise way of life will clearly not be easy. "There are some things people just shouldn't have to adjust to," says one WTC employee, "and this building is one of them." (Copyright 1975 by Newsweek, Inc. All rights reserved. Reprinted by permission.)

Table 18.2 Behavior setting occupancy times (OT), 1963–1964 (total number of hours people of Midwest and visitors spent in these behavior settings during 1963–1964)

Behavior Setting	Midwest Residents OT	Resident and nonresident total OT
Elementary school third grade academic subjects	7,280	18,430
Burgess beauty shop	12,750	15,750
Elementary lower school lunchroom	10,103	15,500
Chaco garage and service station	9,542	14,000
Blanchard hardware store	6,822	8,322
High school, a team football game	2,710	7,467
Presbyterian church worship service	4,015	5,918
Keith barber shop	1,540	4,290
Rotary club meeting	2,083	2,341
Presbyterian church funeral	320	605
Halloween dance	150	213
Methodist church kindergarten Sunday school class	111	146

Adapted from Barker, 1968, p. 49.

setting that investigators wish to evaluate. By measuring the reactions of subjects to the representational models, researchers try to determine how people would react to the real environment they represent. This research provides investigators with a shortcut in their attempt to anticipate reactions to environmental settings that are still in the planning stages.

Winkel and Sasanoff (1966) presented a simulated museum environment to subjects in a laboratory using multiple photographic slides. The researchers observed the patterns of movement and time the subjects spent observing the several exhibits in the laboratory and those of visitors who slowly worked their way through the halls of the real museum. When they compared the reactions of the real visitors to those of the experimental subjects, they found a striking correspondence between the two sets of reactions. Obviously, the more closely the representation can simulate the actual environment, the more confident investigators can be that the simulated responses accurately reflect responses in the real setting.

Cognitive mapping

A research method that is becoming popular with both environmental psychologists and urban planners is *cognitive mapping*. Kevin Lynch is the pioneer of this method, which is used to determine the ways in which individuals perceive their unique physical world. In his pilot studies in Boston, Los Angeles, and Jersey City, Lynch (1960) discovered that in the descriptions of their cities inhabitants use five key elements to structure their images of the cities: (1) *paths*, which provide access from one part of the city to another; (2) *edges*, which define boundaries of the cities; (3) *nodes*, which are points in the cities marking major means of changing from one activity to another (e.g., bus and railroad terminals); (4) *major landmarks*, such as public buildings and parks; and (5) *districts*, which are major distinctive areas of the cities. Lynch proposed that these are the focal points around which people structure their images of cities.

In another study (Lynch and Rivkin, 1959), subjects walked around a block in Boston. After the walk they were asked to describe what they had seen during the tour. In analyzing the descriptions of these walks investigators looked for obvious similarities to see which environmental marks people used to structure their images of the city block. They made frequent references to open spaces, suggesting that people were particularly interested in the unexpected elements they encountered during the stroll. The researchers concluded that cognitive mapping may be not only a valuable research tool, but also a strong pedagogical device to awaken citizens' interest in their cities, to sharpen their critical abilities, and ultimately to increase their pleasure in well-planned environments.

POLLUTION

Ever since groups of people first gathered and remained in one place for any length of time, pollution has been a problem. Human beings pollute simply by their presence. Other types of pollution occur naturally, such as pollution of the atmosphere by sandstorms or forest fires or the pollution of a river by soils eroded from the surrounding land. Pollution as a problem is related to the concentration of pollutants in a limited area. Many problems of pollution may be solved by technology, such as by filters to remove noxious gases from industrial smoke or biological processes to break down and recycle garbage and solid wastes. What role can the psychologist play?

First, the psychological effects of various pollutants can be studied to help document whether they are harmful or merely not desirable. Some levels of pollution may not be physically harmful but may make life more stressful and perhaps less psychologically healthful for the individual. Second, psychological research should help gather data on ways human beings can adapt to polluted conditions. Third, psychologists can provide information on what the attitude of the public is toward the pollution and which factors are most important in maintaining this attitude. This kind of information is essential, for example, in any campaign to arouse public action against harmful pollutants.

Air pollution

Most of the studies concerning pollution conducted by psychologists have tried to measure the extent to which people are aware of and feel threatened by an increasingly polluted world. The threat of pollution seems to be recognized more and more by respondents to attitude surveys. In 1965 only 28 percent of a national sample viewed air pollution as a serious problem. By 1970 the percentage had increased to 70 percent (Swan, 1972). This awareness of the problems posed by pollution is related to the respondents' demographic characteristics. A Boulder, Colorado,

survey (Tognacci et al., 1972) found that the more wealthy and well-educated people were, the more they feared the threat of pollution. In a Los Angeles study, 11 percent of those interviewed planned to move within the next year because of air pollution. Those who were satisfied with their neighborhood appeared to deny the reality of high pollution level and perceived less pollution than those who were dissatisfied (Hohm, 1976).

Virtually every city with a population over 50,000 has an air pollution problem. Because in 1970 over 70 percent of the population in the United States lived in or near large urban areas, about three-fourths of the population is faced with problems related to polluted air.

Although the relationship between physical maladies such as chronic bronchitis, or emphysema and air pollution has been clearly established (Ford, 1970), we still know very little about the effect of environmental pollutants on human behavior. Immediately following the Los Angeles riots in the late 1960s, *The New York Times* expressed the opinion that the summer heat and smog in Los Angeles were responsible for the chaos in Watts (Sears and McConahay, 1973). Although there is some evidence to suggest that heat may cause aggressive behavior, there is no evidence that links smog to violence.

Noise pollution

Although smog seems to be an obvious pollutant in the environment, another environmental irritant of our society, noise, has been more extensively studied by psychologists. Noise can be defined as any sound that is unwanted and that produces unwanted effects. It is continuously present, but it is seldom noticed unless it is extreme or out of place in certain situations.

Noise is often described by its sound intensity, measured in units called *decibels*. These are logarithmic units, so that, for example, a change in level from 10 decibels to 20 decibels or 30 to 40 decibels represents an increase of 10 times in sound intensity. A sound of 80 decibels is annoying. Steady exposure to 90-decibel sound can cause permanent loss of hearing. A quiet room may have a noise level of from 30 to 40 decibels, whereas the level in a noisy room may range from 50 to 60 decibels. In Tokyo and

Table 18.3 Typical sound levels and human response

Sound Level*	Response	Industrial	Community or Outdoor	Home or Indoor
140		carrier deck operation (140)		
130	painfully loud			
120	uncomfortably loud	oxygen torch (121)		
110		riveting machine (110)		rock and roll band (108–114)
100	very loud	farm tractor (98) newspaper press (97)	jet flyover 1000 ft (103) off-road motorcycle (105) power lawnmower (96) heavy truck (95)	
90	hearing damage (8-hour exposure)		medium helicopter (88) sports car (87) city bus (85)	inside subway car 35 mph (95)
80	annoying	lathe (81) tabulating (80)	passenger car 75 mph (77)	food blender (88) garbage disposal (80) clothes washer (78)
70	moderately loud			TV audio (70) vacuum cleaner (70)
60			near freeway auto traffic (64)	room air conditioner (50–68) conversation (60)
50	quiet		light traffic 100 ft (50)	
40				
30	very quiet			
20				
10	barely audible			
0	threshold of hearing			

*Measured in decibels at typical operator-listener distance from the source. Data from U.S. Environmental Protection Agency, U.S. Department of Transportation, and Cohen, 1969.

Kyoto there are noise meters posted on busy corners that report the noise levels on large lighted signs. The readings are often well above 90 decibels.

Although the effects of noise on human behavior are just beginning to be documented, it is known that the noise levels in American residential districts have increased about 16 decibels between 1954 and 1967 (Solomon, 1970). How much noise humans can tolerate before showing obvious maladaptive behavior remains a subject for psychologists to investigate. There is some evidence that annoyance and irritability result from noise and that these may cause subjective discomfort and lead to increased interpersonal conflicts. Individual differences exist in noise tolerance, perhaps related to a personal need for social relationships (Elliot, 1971). Figure 18.6 shows that the relationship between a sound and the reaction of the individual to it is affected by many variables.

In many community studies noise is defined by its perceived level (PNdB). Surveys show that annoyance with noise is related to such things as

1. Feelings about preventability of the noise.
2. The kind of activity engaged in.
3. The general attitude of the individual toward the environment.
4. Beliefs about the effects of noise on health.

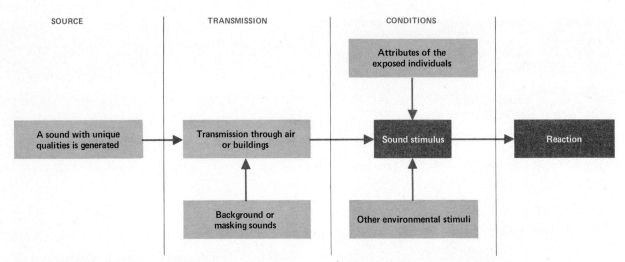

SOURCE   TRANSMISSION   CONDITIONS

Figure 18.6 How a sound is perceived and the kinds of responses it is likely to elicit are affected by a number of variables. The noise can be modified by the way it is transmitted, other sounds present, other aspects of the environment, and characteristics of the individuals hearing the sound. (Adapted from Goldsmith and Jansson, 1973, p. 786.)

5. The association of noise with frightening situations. (Shepherd, 1975)

About 30 percent of respondents in a survey conducted among residents of Detroit and Los Angeles reported that they were regularly disturbed by noise at home or at work (Cameron, Robertson, and Zaks, 1972). As you read try to listen to the noise in your environment. Do you hear the hum of your roommate's electric typewriter, or the beat of music from your own radio? Does the whirring of the dormitory elevator or the jackhammer of the street crew outside your window intrude into your environment? Does the noise affect your ability to concentrate? Does it determine your behavior?

Human beings react physiologically to noise. The electrical conductivity of the skin and the flow of blood are both affected by loud noise. The changes in these measures disappear quickly as the noise continues and adaptation occurs. But what about other kinds of adaptation? Are the effects of noise as transitory on behavior and emotional response or mood?

David Glass and Jerome Singer (1972) conducted a series of studies to assess the effects of noise on both physiological and psychological responses. Sub-

jects were exposed to 108 decibels of noise for nine seconds per minute over a period of 23 to 25 minutes. The experimenters noticed physiological signs of stress to the initial bursts of noise but the subjects seemed to adapt as the experiments progressed. If subjects believed that they could predict or control the noise, they seemed to be less physiologically aroused by the initial blasts than subjects who were unable to predict or control the noise. Subjects usually did not show any decrease in their ability to complete assigned tasks under noisy conditions. The tasks ranged from relatively simple ones such as selecting all the words in a list that contained the letter "a", to complex ones such as solving difficult mathematical problems. However, subjects who were exposed to noise during the initial tasks did not perform as well and became frustrated more easily on tasks after the noise was removed than did subjects who were not exposed to noise. This finding parallels the Sherrod findings on crowding discussed earlier in this chapter. More research is needed to determine all the long-range effects of noise upon performance. For example, one experiment shows that if individuals who are exposed to noise are asked to solve problems, they show a lack of persist-

Noise pollution from airplanes and big machinery can be a major problem in metropolitan areas. Citizens' groups have been organized to move transport and industrial facilities away from residential areas. (Saidel, Stock, Boston)

ence on frustrating tasks in the period after the noise exposure (Wohlwill et al., 1976).

While subjects performed simple and complex tasks equally well under noise and no-noise conditions, Finkelman and Glass (1970) reported that subjects who were requested to perform two tasks simultaneously under noisy conditions could do well on the primary task but could not do as well on the secondary task as subjects who performed both tasks under quiet conditions. Although this situation may seem contrived, many people must perform several tasks while exposed to noise in their daily lives. Jet pilots must guide their planes, monitor dials, and watch runways while their attendants give them verbal directions. Building engineers must monitor numerous safety dials while steam boilers and gas furnaces roar away. Truck and taxi drivers in huge cities such as New York or Tokyo must weave through jungles of traffic to the tune of honking horns and racing engines, often talking as they go.

LIVING UNDER ADVERSE CONDITIONS

As population pressure mounts, desirable living areas become scarcer. People tend to inhabit more areas previously considered marginal or inhospitable. The search for new sources of minerals and other natural materials often results in the establishment of living places in desolate areas or those with extreme weather conditions. For example, workers on oil rigs at sea or on the Alaska pipeline must live in special situations that not even adequate shelter, heat, and food make acceptable.

569

BOX 18.5

A friendly place to live in a hostile environment

The Pilbara district of northwestern Australia's outback is a sort of hell. There is barely enough vegetation on the stony hills and sere plains to support the area's population of wild donkeys, kangaroos, and emus; only rock pythons, death adders and hoards of stinging insects seem to have adapted comfortably to the climatic extremes: Winds that reach velocities of 140 m.p.h., dust storms that swirl out of the nearby Great Sandy Desert, noonday temperatures as high as 180 degrees F. For human beings it is as hostile a place as any in the world.

But man has come to the Pilbara, drawn by the region's immense iron ore reserves and the increasing global demand for the metal. For most miners the aim is to make money quickly and get out. But in one community the situation is different. Shay Gap, a tiny (pop. 862), two-year-old town 120 miles inland from Port Hedland on the Indian Ocean, is proving that even the harshest environment can be tamed.

Shay Gap was founded for sound business reasons. Officials of Goldsworthy Mining Ltd., aware that high wages alone could not keep needed workers in the Pilbara for long, decided to build a community that would make life in the outback more tolerable. Their Perth-based architect, Lawrence Howroyd, 45, quickly realized that merely air-conditioning the houses and sealing the windows to keep out dust and insects would not be enough. In the Pilbara, he explains, "the environment throws up all kinds of stresses to which people are not accustomed—the heat, the isolation, fear of children's being in the sun, the effect of the sun on women's complexions."

Howroyd turned to the world's desert areas for useful precedents and found two in the ancient settlements of the Middle East. To overcome the feeling of being surrounded by hostile nature, the Arabs built walls around their cities. To get relief from the fierce sun, they had crowded their houses close together so that one shaded another. Howroyd followed, and updated, those principles. He situated Shay Gap in a semicircle that not only

Australia's Shay Gap. (Australian Information Service)

lends a sense of protective enclosure but also provides late-afternoon shade. Similarly, the town's prefabricated houses are tightly clustered in groups, so that they cast shade on their neighbors or on a central play area for children.

Howroyd also wanted to create a sense of community. He laid out narrow, shaded walkways instead of broad streets through most of the town. By thus squeezing out cars, which are parked on Shay Gap's perimeter, he forced people to meet whenever they go outside. Indeed, says resident Mrs. Jill Nicholls: "A greeting is not just a wave as you drive past. It's a stop and a chat." As a result of all the careful planning, life in Shay Gap is pleasant, employee turnover is low, and Goldsworthy Mining is satisfied that the town is worth every cent of its $10 million construction cost.

Planners and architects now see the town as a model full of lessons for similar developments, even those far from the Pilbara region. Howroyd's next projects may be in the very places where he found his original inspiration. Government agencies in Saudi Arabia, Bahrain and Iran, seeking better ways to plan their new desert cities, want the Australian architect to re-establish in their lands the concept of a protective town with narrow streets, people in constant contact and no cars. (Reprinted by permission from *Time,* The Weekly Newsmagazine; Copyright Time Inc. 1975.)

One task of the environmental psychologist is to determine how human beings can best adapt to sometimes difficult living conditions. First, psychologists must determine how people are affected by such variables as climate, temperature extremes, and isolation.

Box 18.5 describes a successful attempt to deal with a hostile environment. Knowledge of the attitudes, emotional reactions, and social needs of the population was necessary to make Shay Gap livable. Simply using technology to control interior temperature would not have been enough. The environmental psychologist tries to provide basic knowledge to help make such projects succeed.

Climatic temperature

Although scientists claim that climates have shaped the pattern of human history, what psychologists know through empirical studies of the relationship of climate or even temperature to behavior is limited. There is some evidence that suicides, homicides, and admissions to mental hospitals are posi-

tively correlated with increases in climatic temperatures (Cerbas, 1970). Whether these behaviors increase because of temperature fluctuation or for other reasons, either related or unrelated to temperature increase, is still unknown. The relationship between violence and temperature variations has also been explored. Goranson and King (1970) have charted the mean daily temperatures for each of the 12 days preceding and the 6 days following outbreaks of violence in the 17 American cities that experienced severe riots during the past decade. Temperatures seemed to rise sharply on the day of the outbreak and to reach a peak after the first day of rioting. The riots seemed to last longer when the high temperatures lasted longer, and the temperature peak was higher for longer and more severe riots. (See Fig. 18.7.) Although such correlational data do not prove that there is a causal relationship between rioting and temperature increases, they do suggest that climatic conditions may be a factor in civil unrest.

Although experimenters cannot manipulate the

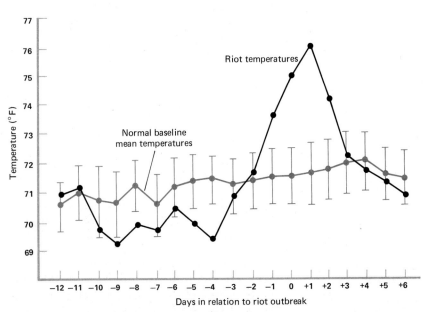

Figure 18.7 Normal (nonriot year) temperatures and riot year (1967) average daily mean temperatures preceding, during, and following riots. (Goranson and King, 1970)

571

temperature of an entire environment, they can control temperatures in experimental rooms and record changes in behavior as the temperatures change. William Griffitt and Russell Veitch (1971) found that subjects judged strangers more negatively in temperatures of 93.5° F. than in a more normal temperature of 73.4° F., which suggests that interpersonal relationships might be more negative when temperatures are unusually high. Such laboratory findings do give indirect support to the speculation that aggressive, antisocial behaviors such as rioting may break out more easily during heat waves than during normal times.

Room temperature

In a less extreme example of the psychological effects of temperature, what are the factors that make a room seem a comfortable temperature to an individual? The "just right" temperature may be much more a matter of preferences of a particular culture than a natural dictate of the human body. Interior temperatures may vary as much as 10° among Western countries. Contrast the customary 62° F. in English homes with the 72° F. of the American household. When Australian airmen, who come from a warm climate, were trained in Canada during World War II, they did not suffer from the cold as might be expected. Instead their main complaint was the "overheated" condition of their barracks (Rapoport and Watson, 1972).

THE FIELD OF ENVIRONMENTAL PSYCHOLOGY: A PSYCHOLOGICAL FRONTIER

How the physical environment (including the air we breathe, the buildings in which we live and work, and the climate of our surroundings) influences human behavior is the central question of environmental psychology. The field itself is only a decade old. Not until the early 1970s was the term used to describe a particular psychological subspecialty. The first extensive review of the literature was not published until 1973. The American Psychological Association set up its initial Task Force on Environment and Behavior in 1974. Textbooks with such titles as *Environmental Psychology* are just beginning to appear.

Environmental psychologists usually function in multidisciplinary settings, working together with planners, architects, sociologists, economists, and others. Particularly in their work with the decision makers and planners, psychologists are concerned with questions about the desirable and undesirable aspects of planned environments. The problems they study are complex and often difficult to encompass within the laboratory. A great deal of misinformation and assumed knowledge exists that must be investigated and debunked if necessary.

We are living in a period of environmental change caused by the greatly increased technology that enables people to alter the environment more radically than ever before and by the increased competition for space and materials caused by the explosive population growth of the last several decades. It is important to know what factors actually affect the psychological comfort of people's lives so that scarce resources can be used to cope with real rather than imagined problems. In addition, techniques of adapting to psychological discomfort need investigation to help people deal with existing changes in life-styles in the most effective way.

We have not said much in this chapter about the traditional theories of psychology, such as those of learning and psychodynamics. Although these orientations may have great potential in guiding the exploration of environmental psychology, for the present most workers in the field are directing their energies to uncovering facts about the environment's effects. This is a big job. The entire field of environmental psychology is one of the exciting frontiers in the study of behavior.

SUMMARY

1. Environmental psychologists study the effects of changes in living conditions on behavior. They are interested in how the individual characteristics of people and animals affect their ability to adapt to a changing and possibly less desirable environment. The conditions or skills needed for adaptation are of particular interest.

2. One area of special interest to environmental psychologists is *crowding*. Both biological and behavioral changes occur when organisms live in crowded surroundings.

3. Density of population and frequency of social problems are not always related in a way most of us would predict. Laboratory and field investigations are conducted to shed light on these relationships.

4. Researchers have concluded from laboratory studies that when humans must do so they can adapt well to a crowded situation. However, they may show greater frustration in subsequent behavior than people who have not been crowded.

5. *Personal space* refers to the amount of space or distance from others that an individual needs in order to feel at ease. These requirements vary in different cultures and cultural subgroups and between people whose relationships differ. *Territoriality* refers to the amount of territory that a person or animal thinks of as his or her own.

6. *Architectural determinism* is the idea that the design of buildings affects the behavior of people who live in them. Sometimes even the placement of furniture will alter the behavior of people who use a room.

7. Many large housing developments have not provided satisfactory homes for their tenants. The design of the buildings, the size of the projects, and the characteristics of the surrounding area all seem to contribute to this dissatisfaction. Specific characteristics of housing seem to affect both the physical and emotional health of the tenants as well.

8. In addition to many of the usual experimental techniques, new techniques have been created to study problems in the environment. These include detailed *observational techniques, simulation techniques* that duplicate the essential features of environmental settings using models, and *cognitive mapping*, which extracts key elements from people's descriptions of a city or district.

9. The effects on behavior of air and noise pollution are of interest to environmental psychologists. The recognition of air pollution as a problem is related to a person's general satisfaction with his or her living place. Annoyance with noise is related to several beliefs and attitudes as well as to differences in individual noise sensitivity.

10. Hot temperatures are sometimes associated with an increase in aggressive behavior.

11. The field of environmental psychology is so new that it is still oriented more toward measuring and listing the effects of the environment than toward building general theories.

Suggested Readings

Freedman, J. *Crowding and behavior*. New York: The Viking Press, 1975. Presents data and speculations on crowding, emotional reactivity, and how people handle various types of situations.

Glass, D. & Singer, J. *Urban stress: Experiments on noise and social stressors*. New York: Academic Press, 1973. Considers the role played by noise in creating stressful situations and the ways people react to this stress.

Ittelson, W. H., Proshansky, H. M., Rivlin, L. G. & Winkel, G. H. *An introduction to environmental psychology*. New York: Holt, Rinehart and Winston, Inc., 1974. Provides an overview of the field with special emphasis on the topics of architectural design.

Mercer, C. *Living in cities*. Harmondsworth, England: Penguin Books, 1975. Reviews the environmental psychology literature with special emphasis on crowding and architectural determinism.

Sommer, Robert. *Personal space*. Englewood Cliffs, N.J.: Prentice-Hall, Inc., 1969. Contains information and ideas about the space needs of people.

Glossary

absolute threshold—The amount of energy a stimulus must exert before we can detect its presence. When the level is below absolute threshold, there is no sensation; when it is above the threshold a stimulus can be sensed and experienced. For research purposes the absolute threshold is defined as the stimulus intensity at which a stimulus can be detected 50 percent of the time.

accommodation—The process by which the lens of the eye changes shape in accordance with the distance of the object being viewed.

acetylcholine (ACh)—A chemical transmitter substance secreted into the synapse that combines with a receptor chemical in the membrane of the dendrite or soma of the receiving cell. The chemical reaction that results makes possible firing of the receiving neuron.

action potential—The change in cell polarity that takes place during the passage of a nerve impulse. The membrane becomes permeable to sodium and sodium ions flow into the interior of the cell.

acupuncture—Ancient Chinese medical procedure involving the insertion of long, fine needles into precise points on the skin to relieve various illnesses.

additive model—A theory of information integration that says that one person's judgment of another is based simply on the sum of reactions to all the information about that person.

adrenal cortex—The outer portion of each adrenal gland. It secretes about 50 different hormones that regulate many metabolic processes, the functioning of the reproductive organs, and the balancing of sodium and potassium in the body fluids that surround the neurons and other cells of the body.

adrenal gland—One of a pair of endocrine glands, one situated over each kidney. Its two main parts are the adrenal cortex and the adrenal medulla.

adrenal medulla—A portion of the adrenal glands that secretes two very important hormones, epinephrine (adrenalin) and norepinephrine (noradrenalin), which are believed to be neural transmitter substances within the nervous system. In emergencies it is activated by the sympathetic branch of the autonomic nervous system.

affective disorder—A major mood disturbance, often of psychotic proportions. There are three main types: depressive and manic reactions and instances in which these occur alternatively.

afferent neurons—Those nerves that carry messages from the periphery of the body and the internal organs to the spinal cord and brain. Also called *sensory neurons.*

age simulation—A modification of the cross-sectional technique used in studying development, which attempts to discover the causes for differences in groups of various ages by manipulating variables until the performances become comparable.

aggression—Any behavior intended to harm or injure another. The term does not include the emotions that may underly the behavior.

alarm reaction—The first stage of the general adaptation syndrome, proposed by Selye to explain bodily stress reactions. This stage involves physiological changes generally associated with emotions, such as pupil dilation, heart rate increase, and GSR increase.

algorithm—A method of problem solving that will automatically generate a correct solution. If used properly the results will always be the right answer. Examples of algorithms are rules for multiplication or addition or such formulas as time = distance ÷ speed.

alpha rhythm—The brain wave pattern of 8 to 12 cycles per second characteristic of humans in a relaxed waking state.

alternating state—A type of affective disorder characterized by manic reactions at some times and depressive reactions at others.

amnesia—A loss of memory either partial or total. At some later time what has been forgotten may be remembered without relearning. Sometimes amnesia occurs when people cannot face the reality of their own behavior or the situation in which they find themselves.

amphetamine—A type of stimulant sold under such trade names as Benzedrine, Dexadrine, and Methadrine, and popularly known as speed, uppers, and bennies. Used in moderation, these appear to have no harmful effects. However, at higher dosages psychological dependence develops. There does not appear to be a physical dependence. Use of large quantities of the drugs can cause heart failure, cerebral hemorrhage, brain damage, or paranoid delusions.

anal stage—The second stage of psychosexual development as described by Freud. It begins at about age 2. In this stage the anal area becomes more strongly associated with sexual gratification than the oral area.

analytical psychology—The system of psychodynamic psychology originated by Carl Jung. The focus was the study of the unconscious with a particular emphasis on the use of dreams as reflections of inherited wisdom and as guides to living.

antianxiety drugs (tranquilizing drugs)—Substances prescribed to reduce anxiety but not to reduce other mental capabilities of patients.

antidepressant drugs—Often used instead of electroshock as a treatment for depression. Iproniazid is an example. Three-quarters of all depressed patients respond positively to one of these drugs.

antipsychotic drugs—Such drugs as chlorpromazine often prescribed for patients who are hallucinating, have delusions, or are extremely withdrawn or highly excited. Frequently used in the treatment of schizophrenia. Many patients relapse if they stop taking this medication.

anxiety—An unpleasant emotional state accompanied both by physiological arousal and by cognitive elements, such as a sense of impending disaster. Different from fear in that it is a general response rather than a response to a specific object or situation.

anxiety neurosis—A persistent unfocused tension and apprehensiveness.

archetypes—Mythological images or predispositions to characteristic thoughts that are reflected in such universal concepts as God, the wisdom of the old, the young and potent hero, resurrection, and evil spirits. A term used by Jung for the contents of the collective unconscious.

architectural determinism—The idea that the design of buildings and other spaces affects the behavior of the people who inhabit them.

Asch conformity situation—An experimental setup in which a subject and several confederates of the experi-

menter are each asked to make a rather simple perceptual judgment. It is usually found that the confederates seem to exert a striking degree of social influence on the subject.

assertiveness training—A method of training individuals to react more assertively in certain kinds of situations. Modeling and role-playing techniques are often used.

association areas—Those areas of the cerebral cortex that do not have sensory or motor functions. These areas, which include the majority of the cortex, are involved in perception, language, and thought.

attachment—The tendency of an infant during the first two years of life to be most receptive to being cared for and approached by a certain person or persons. In the company of this person or persons the infant is also less afraid of a strange environment.

attribution—The process of pinpointing the cause of behavior or answering the question "Why?" in relation to behavior.

authoritarian personality—An attitudinal system consisting of a number of interrelated antidemocratic sentiments. Describes personal characteristics of individuals who establish and accept the principles of authoritarian society, such as that of Nazi Germany. Authoritarian tendencies are measured by the California F scale.

autonomic nervous system—A division of the peripheral nervous system that directs the activity of the glands and internal organs of the body. It is especially important in emotional behavior.

averaging model—A theory of information integration that states that the impression of another will be based not on the sum of individual's traits but rather on the arithmetic average of the evaluation of all his or her traits.

avoidance conditioning—A learning procedure in which the subject learns to make a response when a warning signal occurs and thereby avoids an aversive stimulus.

axon—An extension from one side of the cell body that conducts electrical impulses away from the cell body to other neurons, muscles, or glands.

barbiturate—A highly addictive chemical depressant or sedative. Nembutal, Seconal, and phenobarbital are examples.

baseline body fat theory—The idea that the hypothalamus maintains fat tissue at a higher level for obese individuals than for normal-weight individuals because these individuals have a larger number of fat cells in their body than average.

behavior genetics—The study of the inheritance of behavioral characteristics.

behavior setting—A term used by Roger Barker in his ecological psychology. A unit with cyclical patterns of activity and defined boundaries. Examples might be a classroom, a shopping center, or the kitchen of a restaurant.

behavioral assessment—A technique of systematically observing certain classes of responses and the situations in which they occur. This information can then be used to understand and to modify specific behaviors.

behavioral constraint—A term used in environmental psychology to describe the idea that crowding makes people feel their freedom of behavior is threatened or eliminated.

behavioristic perspective—A view that behavior results from an organism's interactions with its environment. The belief that human beings are basically reactors and that the factors controlling human behavior reside in the external environment rather than within the individual. Behavior is determined by how the individual has been conditioned previously and the stimuli within his or her immediate environment.

binocular cue—Depth perception cue that requires the use of both eyes. Includes retinal disparity and convergence.

biofeedback—A process by which an individual can be made continuously aware of his or her own physiological responses. Uses precise measuring of physiological events and converts the electronic signals these produce into visual or auditory feedback. It has been used to train people to control voluntarily physiological responses that are involved in stress reactions and physical and psychosomatic problems.

biological perspective—The view of human behavior that emphasizes biological factors, such as brain processes and genetic determinants.

blind spot—The point in the retina of the eye in which there is no vision and where the optic nerve exits from the eye.

brain stem—The portion of the brain between the spinal cord and the cerebellum made up of the pons and the medulla. Contains many ascending and descending fibers that connect the higher and lower levels of the central nervous system.

brainstorming—A group procedure for problem solving aimed at lowering the threshold for divergent thinking for all people participating.

California F scale—A test intended to measure authoritarian tendencies. Developed in a project that attempted to pinpoint personal characteristics of individuals who establish and accept the principles of authoritarian societies, such as that of Nazi Germany.

Cannon-Bard theory of emotion—The idea that the thalamus responds to emotion-arousing stimuli by sending messages simultaneously to the cerebral cortex and to the visceral and skeletal muscles. Messages to the cortex are responsible for the "feelings" of emotion and the messages to the visceral and skeletal muscles for the physiological and overt behavior responses.

castration anxiety—According to Freud, the fear that boys feel because of their incestuous impulses toward their mothers and their wish to see their fathers dead.

catatonic schizophrenia—A type of psychosis characterized by disturbance in motor activity. Individuals may be immobile, with muscles rigid and inflexible, or may be extremely agitated. Some have waxy flexibility, so that if an arm or leg is placed in some position, they

will leave it there indefinitely until someone moves it again.

catharsis—The reduction of emotions or impulses through either indirect or direct expression, often verbally or through fantasy.

central nervous system—One of the two major divisions of the nervous system that includes all the neurons in the brain and spinal cord and is the integrating center for all behavior and bodily functions.

central traits—A term used by Solomon Asch to describe those traits that strongly influence an individual's impression of another person.

cerebellum—an area of the hindbrain that controls the coordination of motor movement.

cerebral hemispheres—The largest part of the human brain consisting of outer gray cortex composed primarily of neuron cell bodies and unmyelinated fibers and an internal white core, composed primarily of myelinated fibers.

cerebrum—The portion of the brain consisting of the two cerebral hemispheres. These constitute the bulk of brain in man and other higher animals.

chemical transfer of memory—A controversial experimental finding in which animals are trained to perform a task and then chemical extracts are injected into other animals who were never trained for the task. The injected animals reportedly learn the task more quickly than animals not given the extract.

chromosome—A rodlike unit carrying specific hereditary factors or genes that is contained in the cell nucleus.

chunk—In the study of memory, sensory stimulation that can be recognized as one unit. Multistore theorists think that about seven chunks can be retained in short-term memory at one time.

ciliary muscle—The muscle that acts on the lens of the eye to adjust its shape for viewing at various distances.

circadian rhythm—Cyclical changes in body temperature, blood pressure, blood plasma volume, hormonal secretions into the bloodstream, and other body processes that occur in humans and other mammals during periods of about 24 hours.

clairvoyance—A type of extrasensory perception that refers to the nonsensory perception of external objects or events.

class inclusion, principle of—A term used by Piaget to describe the idea that if one class is included in another class, the included class is the smaller of the two.

classical conditioning—A technique originated by Pavlov that produces learning by pairing a neutral stimulus with a stimulus that already evokes a response. The neutral stimulus will eventually evoke the same response when presented alone.

client-centered therapy—A type of psychotherapy developed by Carl Rogers in which the therapist neither provides interpretations nor gives advice, but tries to create an environment in which clients can reorganize their subjective world. Clients are helped to understand their own internal frame of reference by exploring their

577

problems and learning to accept themselves.

climacteric—The point at which reproductive ability ceases.

clinical psychology—The field of psychology concerned with diagnosis and treatment of psychological disturbances. Research on personality, psychological tests, and deviant behavior is also performed by clinical psychologists.

clitoris—An extremely sensitive part of the female external genitalia. In the female the analogue of the penis.

closure, law of—Gestalt perceptual law that states that when there are open edges or gaps in a figure, the individual tends to fill them in to make the stimulus complete.

cocaine—A stimulant derived from the coco plant. Once used widely as a local anesthetic. A white or colorless crystaline powder that is either inhaled or injected and may induce euphoria, excitation, anxiety, a sense of increased muscular strength, talkativeness, and liveliness. Overdoses can depress breathing and heart functions so that users die. Users may develop a strong psychological dependence, although there is no evidence that they become physically dependent.

cochlea—Coiled tubes filled with fluid in the inner ear that contain the organs of Corti, the tiny hair cells that transform sound vibrations into nerve impulses.

cognitive dissonance—The state of tension resulting from the experience by the individual of two cognitions that are psychologically inconsistent. In order to reduce the tension, the individual will either change one of the cognitions or add more cognitions to explain the inconsistency. The term was first used by Leon Festinger.

cognitive labeling—A term used by Stanley Schachter to indicate that the particular emotion experienced by individuals is determined by perceived cause of arousal. The different information received from the physiological responses tells about the intensity of emotional response, but not about the quality.

cognitive mapping—A research method first used by environmental planner Kevin Lynch. Investigators look for obvious similarities to determine which environmental marks people use to structure images of their environment in subjects' descriptions of their environment.

cognitive modification treatment—A procedure in which subjects learn to control and change self-instructional statements that affect their feelings and behavior.

cognitive perspective—The study of the individual's thoughts, understandings, interpretations, and ideas about the environment. This point of view emphasizes the ways in which individuals process, evaluate, and respond to stimuli.

cognitive psychology—The area of psychology concerned with the organization of memory, thinking, language, and problem solving. Cognitive psychologists study the processes by which persons acquire knowledge or become aware of it.

cognitive social learning theory—A combination of behaviorist and cognitive principles that looks for causes of behavior not only in the external environment but also within the individual. Also emphasizes that people can learn by observing the behaviors of others and storing this information in their memories. This view assumes that individuals are capable of regulating their own behavior by self-administered response consequences, such as self-approval or self-reproach.

collective unconscious—A term used by Jung for the part of the human unconscious that consists of memories accumulated throughout the history of the human race. Contains archetypes or mythological images or predispositions to certain thoughts that are reflected in universal concepts, such as God, resurrection, and evil spirits.

Columbia obstruction box—A piece of laboratory equipment used to measure motivation. The box contains an electrified grid that the animal must cross in order to obtain the goal object.

compensatory education—Special programs designed to improve the poor performance of particular groups in school situations. Methods include supplying important experiences that these individuals may lack, and providing training for basic skills. Most often the programs are aimed at the preschool child. Head Start is an example of one such program.

compliance—A term used by social psychologist Herbert Kelman to describe one type of response to social influence. Compliance refers to responses that are made solely in order to obtain a reward or avoid punishment.

compulsion—Persistent and often uncontrollable repetitive action.

concept formation—The ability to recognize common qualities in different objects or events.

concepts—Symbols used in thinking that represent connections or common characteristics among two or more objects or events.

concordance rate—A measure used by researchers studying hereditary characteristics. The probability or risk that one of a pair of individuals in a population will show a particular characteristic if the other individual has the characteristic.

concrete operations period—A term used by Piaget for the third of the four major stages in the continuous process of growth and change in cognitive development during childhood. It runs from about age 7 to age 12. In this period children acquire a whole new set of skills called operations, which involve the ability to understand that certain mental processes are reversible.

conditioned response (CR)—In classical conditioning, the response that is eventually evoked by the conditioned stimulus. Although based on the unconditioned response the CR is generally not identical with it in all respects.

conditioned stimulus (CS)—In the classical conditioning situation, the neutral stimulus that, as a result of being paired with the unconditioned stimulus, becomes capable of evoking a conditioned response.

cones—Structures within the retina of the eye that are the color receptors. They function only at relatively high levels of illumination.

conformity—The expression of attitudes, needs, or values similar to those of the predominant group.

confounding—The mixing of two or more variables in an experiment so that it is impossible to know for certain which variable produces the effect.

consanguinity study—A method of studying inheritance that contrasts the statistical probability of occurrence of a trait in close relatives, distant relatives, and the general population.

conscious—The psychoanalytic term describing the mental events of which we are presently aware.

conservation, principle of—The term used by Piaget for the concept that objects have fundamental qualities that do not change even when their outward appearances change. For example, a ball of clay flattened into a pancake still contains the same amount of clay.

construct—A word or concept that represents a nonmaterial idea or concept rather than a thing. Examples are aggression, stress, learning.

construct validation—The process of integrating observations pertaining to a particular researcher's hypothesis about the behavior and verifying them using objective procedures such as experiments.

continuity, law of—Gestalt perceptual law that states that the individual tends to see shapes, lines, and angles following the same direction established by previous elements.

continuous reinforcement—A procedure used in operant conditioning in which there is reinforcement after every response.

contraception—A means of preventing pregnancy from occurring.

control group—A group of subjects in an experiment that experiences all the same conditions as those of the experimental group except for the condition under investigation.

conventional level—The second in a series of three stages of development of moral judgment described by Lawrence Kohlberg. At this level the child's moral judgments are based to an important degree on the norms and expectations of a group to which he or she belongs, rather than just on the consequences of action.

corpus callosum—A large band of fibers that connects the two hemispheres of the brain and allows them to function as a single unit.

correlation coefficient—A statistical measure that expresses the degree of relationship between two variables. It can range from +1.00 to −1.00. A positive correlation indicates that high scorers on one of the variables also have high scores on the other. A negative correlation indicates that high scorers on one variable have low scores on the other. The correlation of .00 means there is no statistical relationship between two sets of scores.

correlational studies—A way of determining the degree of correspondence between two sets of paired measurements. Correlational studies cannot establish a cause-and-effect relationship.

cortex—The outer layer of an organ. When used alone the term refers to the furrowed or convoluted part of the brain that lies above the brain stem and covers the cerebrum and cerebellum.

counseling psychology—The area of psychology that deals with aptitude and vocational testing and counseling.

counterattitudinal advocacy—A procedure in which individuals are asked to deliver persuasive communications in support of a position opposite to their own.

countertransference—In psychoanalysis, the therapist's irrational emotional reaction to his or her patients.

coverants—A term used by Lloyd Homme as a contraction of covert operants, by which he meant thoughts or images that could be increased or decreased in occurrence through reinforcement just as other operant responses are.

covert behaviors—Internal processes, such as thoughts, images, and feelings, considered by cognitive psychologists to be subject to the same kinds of controlling influences as are other behaviors.

criterion—The outcome, such as a set of scores, that can be compared with the results of a measuring device to test the device's validity. Grade point average in college might be used as a criterion to evaluate the validity of a college entrance examination.

cross-cultural studies—A comparison of behaviors that occur in one culture with those of one or more other cultures.

cross-fostering study—A method of evaluating effect of hereditary versus environmental factors in various behavior disorders. It involves the comparison of at least three groups: (1) children of parents in the group to be studied who were adopted by normal parents; (2) children of normal parents adopted by parents in the group to be studied; and (3) children of normal parents adopted by normal parents.

cross-sectional method—A technique of studying development by comparing the characteristics of groups of individuals of different ages.

crowding—A major area of study in environmental psychology that explores the effects on the individual of various population densities.

culture-fair test—A test designed to minimize cultural influences in various ways and still serve as a useful predictor.

cunnilingus—Oral stimulation of the female genitals.

decay theory—A type of theory of memory based on the memory trace idea. The memory trace is thought to decay or vanish after a period of time.

decibel—Logarithmic unit used to measure noise. For example, a change in level from 10 decibels to 20 decibels represents an increase of ten times in sound intensity. Ninety-decibel sound can cause permanent loss of hearing.

deep structure—A linguistic term that refers to the underlying meaning of a spoken or written sentence. The meanings that make up deep structure are stored as concepts and rules in long-term memory.

defense mechanism (ego defense)—A psychoanalytic term for various kinds of psychic operations that are used by the ego to prevent awareness of anxiety-evoking or unpleasant stimuli. These stimuli may come from the id, the superego, or the external world.

defensible space—A concept originated by architect Oscar Newman. The extension of residents' feeling of ownership and responsibility outside their own doors.

deinstitutionalization—Movement to remove many inmates from large, isolated institutions to more rehabilitative settings within the community. Has been used for juvenile delinquents, adult criminals, and patients with psychological disorders. The value of this approach has not yet been clearly established.

delusion—An incorrect belief about an object or event that an individual maintains even in the face of clear evidence to the contrary.

demand characteristics—Stimuli that exist in many research situations that give subjects information about how they are expected to behave. Subjects may not all be affected in the same way by these stimuli.

dendrite—One of many small fibers that extend from the soma or cell body and receive electrical messages from adjacent cells that are then conducted to the cell body.

denial—In psychoanalytic theory, the most primitive of the defense mechanisms. Used for dealing with external threat by blocking out disturbing realities and simply refusing to acknowledge them.

density-intensity hypothesis—The idea that a person's positive or negative reactions to a situation are intensified under crowded conditions. Jonathan Freedman's explanation of why experimental evidence on crowding gives conflicting results.

deoxyribonucleic acid (DNA)—A chemical compound, characterized by large molecules, that occurs in the cell nucleus and is important in the transmission of heredity. The DNA molecule can unzip up the center and reproduce the missing halves so that each new molecule contains the complete genetic code contained in the original.

dependent variable—In an experiment, the behavior that is measured to determine any changes caused by manipulation of the independent variable.

depressant—A chemical substance that decreases the general level of activity in the central nervous system. Alcohol and such barbiturates as Nembutal, Seconal, and phenobarbital are examples.

depressive neurosis—A neurotic condition characterized by self-devaluation and apprehension and a continually pessimistic outlook.

depressive reaction—One of the major mood disturbances or affective disorders, characterized by feelings of inadequacy and hopelessness accompanied by lessened activity.

desensitization—A therapeutic technique highly effective in fear reduction in which the individual is exposed to a graded series of fear-producing stimuli until they lose their power to elicit anxiety.

determinism, assumption of—the idea that nature operates according to a set of laws and that these laws can be discovered.

developmental psychology—The branch of psychology concerned with growth and development of the organism from before birth through old age.

differentiation—A process by which cells become specialized for a certain function, such as nerve, muscle, fat.

discrimination—The ability to detect differences between stimuli.

displacement—The psychoanalytic defense mechanism in which the undesirable impulse is directed away from the forbidden target to a substitute target. Kicking the dog after being criticized by the boss is an example.

dispositional factors—Relatively unchangeable characteristics or traits within the individual.

dissociative reaction—Neurotic reaction characterized by a splitting off of a group of mental processes that function independently of the rest. Examples are amnesia; somnambulism, or sleep walking; and automatic writing.

dizygotic—Referring to fraternal twins produced from two fertilized eggs present in the uterus at the same time. These twins have no closer hereditary relationship than do any other siblings.

dominance hierarchy—A characteristic form of social organization that includes a definite power structure in which every individual is in a dominant or submissive position in relationship to the others.

dominant characteristic—A hereditary characteristic associated with a certain dominant gene that will occur whether one or both genes in the gene pair are dominant.

dopamine—One of several chemicals in the brain involved in the transmission of nerve impulses.

dopamine hypothesis—the idea that an excess of dopamine in the brain or increased sensitivity of nerve cells to dopamine might be involved in schizophrenia.

Down syndrome (Mongolism)—A rather common type of retardation caused by a chromosomal abnormality. There are several characteristic physical symptoms, including delicate skin, a protruding belly, and smaller than normal hands and feet. The eyes slant up and outward, the face is broad and flat, and the fingerprints are loops rather than whorls.

dream work—The process by which the latent dream content is transformed for defensive purposes into the manifest dream content.

eardrum—A moveable membrane that vibrates in response to sound waves.

echoic store—The sensory store for auditory information.

ecological psychology—The term used to describe the work of Roger Barker and his associates in determining the relationship between patterns of behavior in a behavior setting and structural properties of that setting.

ecology—An area of scientific interest concerned with the interrelationship of organisms and their physical environment.

educational psychology—The branch of psychology concerned with all aspects of the educational process. This includes learning, classroom instruction, vocational counseling, and the testing of abilities and attitudes.

efferent neurons—those nerves that transmit impulses from the brain and spinal cord to the muscles and organs of the body. Also called motor neurons.

ego—The psychoanalytic term for the part of the psyche that is conscious and is most closely in touch with reality. It functions as an integrating mechanism for the impulses from the id and the directives from the super-ego to make them conform to the demands of external reality.

egocentrism—A term used by Piaget to indicate that young children are not able to differentiate between their own point of view and that of others.

eidetic imagery—the ability to produce very clear visual images in great detail.

elaborative rehearsal—The process of repeating material with the intent to remember it permanently and to fit it into the memory system.

electrical stimulation of the brain (ESB)—The process of implanting tiny electrodes in various areas of the brain to which mild electrical stimulation is delivered. This can bring about marked changes in behavior.

electroencephalograph (EEG)—A record of the electrical activity of the brain obtained by attaching recording electrodes to the scalp. The EEG records the simultaneous activity of millions of neurons.

electroshock therapy—Sometimes used in the treatment of mental disorders, particularly depression. Electrodes are placed on either side of the patient's head and a controlled current is applied for a fraction of a second. This produces a convulsion followed by a brief period of coma.

elicited behavior—A term used to refer to behavior that naturally occurs in the presence of a particular stimulus.

emitted behavior—A term used in operant conditioning to describe the situation in which the organism chooses when to respond in a situation that contains many stimuli, rather than responding at a particular time to a particular stimulus as in classical conditioning.

emotion—A state in which feelings and sentiments are experienced by the individual.

empathic inference—Piaget's term for the process of carefully observing how children approach problems and then attempting to infer how they must have experienced the situation in order to respond as they did.

empathy—The ability to experience the same emotions that are felt by another person.

empirical—Information obtained through observation and experimentation.

encoding—Changing sensory input into a form in which the information can be processed by the memory system and registered in memory.

endocrine system—The system of the body composed of the glands that secrete hormones. These chemicals act to regulate metabolism and coordinate various body processes and are associated with emotion.

environmental psychology—The branch of psychology that deals with the psychological effect on the individual of his or her environment or surroundings. Environmental psychologists attempt to test many ideas about what aspects of environmental change are psychologically harmful to individuals and how changes in the environment affect individuals' behavior.

epinephrine—A hormone secreted by the adrenal glands. Secretion is associated with fear and anger.

episodic memory—A person's mental record of personal life experiences.

erotic—Tending to arouse sexual interest.

escape conditioning—A learning process whereby a subject learns to escape from an aversive stimulus. The escape response is strengthened by negative reinforcement.

ethologist—A scientist who studies the unfolding of behavior as it occurs while the animals are in their natural habitat.

expectancy × value theory—A cognitive approach to motivation that says that the direction and intensity of goal-directed behavior are jointly determined by the strength of the person's expectation that certain actions will lead to the desired goal and by the value of the goal for the individual.

experimental neurosis—A chronic abnormal emotional state produced in an animal by subjecting it to inescapable conflicts and punishment. Behaviors produced may include hyperirritability, tenseness, inhibited motor reactions, changes in sleeping patterns, respiratory and cardiac changes, and social and emotional changes.

experimenter expectancy effect—An experimental result that may be obtained in part because the experimenter expects it and may unintentionally influence the subject's response in the expected manner.

exteroceptors—Specialized receptors that respond to environmental stimulation outside the body. The eye and the ear are examples.

extinction—A reduction in response. The weakening and eventual disappearance of a learned behavior as a result of nonreinforcement.

extrasensory perception (ESP)—The perception of nonphysical stimuli. Basic types that have been studied are clairvoyance, telepathy, precognition, and psychokinesis.

face validity—The appearance of being valid. Test items that seem to be good measures of a particular characteristic on a common sense basis.

factor analysis—A sophisticated statistical technique that permits a researcher to reduce a large number of measures to a small number of clusters or factors. It identifies the clusters of behavior that are highly correlated with one another.

family therapy—A specialized type of group therapy employed when the problems of one or more family members seem interrelated. The therapist encourages family members to deal with their attitudes and feelings toward one another as a group.

fellatio—Oral stimulation of the male genitals.

fetishism—Sexual pleasure derived primarily from an inanimate object.

fetishist—A person for whom certain inanimate objects stimulate sexual excitement.

field experiment—Like a field study or natural experiment, a field experiment is performed in a "real-life" setting. However, in field experiments the variables of interest are manipulated by the experimenter.

field study—An investigative technique that involves observing and recording behavior in its natural setting with no attempt to manipulate variables or to influence individuals being studied.

fixation—Psychoanalytic idea that psychosexual development may be arrested or stopped at a particular point and a character structure built around the unresolved difficulties of that stage.

fixed-role therapy—A technique originated by George Kelly in which therapists write role descriptions for clients that differ from their typical view of themselves and ask them to play these roles for limited periods of time.

fixed schedule reinforcement—A procedure used in operant conditioning under partial reinforcement when the reinforcement always occurs after a fixed number of responses or a fixed time interval.

flooding—Clinical treatment used for phobic disorders. Extinction is forced by preventing avoidance responses and exposing individuals to the conditioned stimulus they fear in the absence of the unconditioned stimulus with which it was originally paired.

forebrain—The foremost of the three major divisions of the brain, including the cerebrum, thalamus, and hypothalamus.

formal operational period—A term used by Piaget for the fourth major stage in the continual process of growth and change in cognitive development. It usually begins around age 11. In this period children become capable of deductive logic (if-then reasoning).

fovea—A small central region in the retina of the eye that contains only cones.

free recall—A technique used in verbal learning in which subjects are asked to reproduce material they have previously learned. The material recalled may be in any order.

free will—The idea that an individual's behavior is carried out by his or her choice or will rather than being determined by external factors.

frigidity—The inability of a woman to achieve orgasm through sexual intercourse.

frontal lobe—One of the four lobes of the cerebral hemi-

spheres. It controls speech and skeletal-motor functions.

frustration-aggression hypothesis—The hypothesis that frustration (defined as the blocking of goal-directed behavior) produces a tendency to respond aggressively.

functional disorder—A disorder without a known or organic base and apparently caused primarily by psychological and social factors.

functional fixedness—A situation often found in problem-solving tasks where the customary use of an object interferes with its use in a novel situation.

galvanic skin response (GSR)—A measure of the drop in electrical resistance of the skin caused by the activity of the sweat glands when an individual becomes emotionally aroused.

ganglion—Large groups of neuron cell bodies that cluster together outside the brain and spinal cord.

gate control theory of pain—This theory of Ronald Melzack states that the aversive stimuli received through free nerve endings activates both large-diameter and small-diameter sensory fibers. Thin fibers carry the pain impulses. A neural mechanism in the spinal cord acts like a gate that can increase or decrease the flow of nerve impulses of pain receptors all over the body to the central nervous system. The degree to which the gate increases or decreases this flow is determined by the relative amounts of activity in the thick and thin fibers.

gender identity—The individual's conviction of being either male or female. It is a part of the self-concept expressed through a broad range of behaviors, attitudes, and fantasies.

gene—The unit of hereditary transmission contained within the chromosome. Each chromosome contains many genes. These occur in pairs and the new individual receives one of each parent's pair of each type of gene.

general adaptation syndrome (GAS)—Three-state cycle of bodily stress reactions as described by Hans Selye. The first stage, an alarm reacton, involves physiological changes generally associated with emotion; the second stage, resistance, the time when the body recovers from the stress reaction and begins to cope with the situation. At this time there is a decrease in the output from the sympathetic nervous system, a lower rate of epinephrine secretion and a higher than normal output from the adrenal cortex and the pituitary glands. If the stress continues, the final stage—exhaustion—is reached, during which the adrenal gland can no longer function and the body begins to break down.

generalization—In conditioning, the occurrence of the conditioned response not only to the original conditioned stimulus but also to stimuli that are similar to it.

genotype—A term used by geneticists to refer to the genetic material that people inherit.

Gestalt laws of perception—Includes the laws of similarity, proximity, closure, and continuity.

Gestalt psychology—The view that stresses the form, pattern, or configuration of the stimulus as a whole.

Gestalt psychologists believe that principles of perceptual organization are built into our nervous system.

Gestalt theory—A theory of perception that has as its center the organized whole or gestalt. The basic premise of gestalt psychology is that the "whole is greater than the sum of its parts."

glia—Fatty cells making up a large portion of the brain that support neurons and hold them in place. They may modify electrical and chemical activity of neurons.

glucostatic theory—One of the most popular contemporary biological theories of hunger. It states that when the amount of glucose being utilized by the body is low, hunger occurs; and when it is high, satiation occurs. Centers in the brain monitor the rate of glucose utilization and control eating. This theory seems to hold true only in emergency situations when the body is actually starved.

great person theory—One of the oldest leadership theories, which says that effectve leaders have certain unique traits that qualify them for the leadership role.

group dynamics—Refers to the kind of social influences that groups exert on their members' attitudes and behavior.

groupthink—An example of how group pressures can influence decision making. Unanimity of commitment to a course of action, which tends to occur under stressful conditions in highly cohesive groups. The group member who expresses reservations about the group's policy is faced with immediate and direct pressure to conform. The process causes even extremely intelligent people to ignore all the elements of careful decision making.

halfway house—A specially created institution that provides a protective and supportive environment for discharged hospital patients who are not yet ready to live independently. Residents typically participate in planning and decision making.

hallucination—A sensory perception that takes place in the absence of an external stimulus.

hallucinogenic drug—This group includes LSD, mescaline, psilocybin, and marijuana. They are usually taken orally and may produce a dream- or trancelike state. They usually distort or intensify sense perception and blur the boundaries between fact and fantasy. They are apparently not physically addictive, but psychological dependence may develop.

halo effect—The tendency of a rater to give a favorable rating on a specific characteristic primarily because the rater likes the person he or she is rating.

hebephrenic schizophrenia—A type of psychosis involving bizarre psychotic behavior, including delusions, hallucinations, grimmacing, and giggling.

heuristic—A method of problem solving characterized by quick and easy search procedures similar to rules of thumb. They can be used to make approximations of the answers to problems. In complex problems heuristics may be more useful than algorithms.

hindbrain—The portion of the brain that includes the medulla, pons, and cerebellum.

homeostasis—The tendency of the body to return itself to a balanced state whenever its physiological equilibrium is disturbed.

hormones—Chemicals secreted by the glands in the endocrine system. These chemical messengers convey information from one area of the body to another through the bloodstream.

hyperphagia—Uncontrollable overeating.

hypnagogic—The term describing the intermediate state between wakefulness and sleep.

hypnopomic—The term describing the intermediate state between sleep and full wakefulness.

hypnosis—An artificially induced state characterized by exaggerated suggestibility.

hypothalamus—A part of the forebrain, it consists of a group of small nuclei lying at the base of the brain above the roof of the mouth. Known to be involved in sexual behavior, temperature regulation, sleeping, eating, aggression, and emotional behavior.

hypothesis—A predictive statement used to explain a relationship between two or more events. A hypothesis must be checked by comparing its predictions with already known facts or by testing them with new research. The results may reject or support the hypothesis but cannot conclusively prove it.

hysterical neurosis—Psychological disturbance characterized by bodily symptoms in the absence of any observable physiological disturbance.

hysterical personality—Individuals who have characteristics in common, such as susceptibility to suggestion, excitability, emotional instability, and tendency to overreact in unusual situations, but do not have any of the usual physical symptoms of hysterical neurosis.

iconic store—The sensory store for visual information.

id—The psychoanalytic term for that part of the psyche in which all instinctual impulses and repressed mental contents are stored. The true unconscious.

identification—A process by which an individual may change his or her attitudes or behavior because of a desire to be like another person or to be identified with a particular group.

illusion—A false perception of a stimulus that is actually present.

image—An internal representation of sensory information that has previously been perceived. The majority of images are mental pictures.

implicit personality theories—Personal assumptions an individual makes about the ways in which various personality traits are related to one another.

impotence (psychic)—The inability of a male to perform sexual intercourse even though the genital organs are intact and sexual desire is present.

imprinting—A species specific form of learning that occurs within a limited period of time early in life and is virtually unmodifiable thereafter. For example, ducklings will learn to follow any object (including the

583

mother) that is consistently present within 11 to 18 hours after birth.

incorporation—The Freudian idea that the child tries to match its own appearance, behavior, and attitudes to those of the like-sexed parent by becoming as much like this parent as possible, or rather, to the child's internal image of that parent. In this way the child deals with a fear generated by the Oedipus complex.

independent variable—The variable or factor in the experiment that is manipulated by the experimenter.

individual psychology—Movement established by Alfred Adler because of his differences with Freud over infantile sexuality and the importance of social motives.

individual response stereotyping—The situation in which a particular individual responds to many different stressful situations in a characteristic way, for example, by strong cardiac responses or gastrointestinal responses. (Contrast with *stimulus-response specificity*.)

industrial psychology—A branch of psychology concerned with applying psychological principles to work situations and problems arising in the industrial field. These include selection and training of workers, conditions of work, and other personnel problems.

inferiority complex—A term originated by Alfred Adler for feelings of inferiority that arise from a sense of imperfection or incompletion in any part of a person's life. These result in rigid and maladaptive attempts to overcome the imperfection.

information—Data gained from one or several kinds of sensory input.

information processing—An approach to the study of cognitive behavior that analyzes the steps in acquiring and using information. Computer programs are often used as models of information processing.

information theory—A mathematical analysis of communications that deals quantitatively with message transmission. Information theory is the basis of computer science as we know it today.

inner ear—The internal portion of the ear that contains the vestibular apparatus and the cochlea. The receptors of the cochlea transform sound vibrations to nerve impulses. The inner ear also contains semicircular canals that, together with the vestibular sacs, control the sense of equilibrium.

innoculation—A term used by McGuire to describe a process for preventing attitude change. It involves exposing individuals to counterarguments, which are then refuted.

insight—The sudden perception of the solution to a problem. In psychotherapy, the discovery of therapeutically important material by the client.

instinct—A general term for natural or inborn behavior. Some complex adaptive responses may be based on instinct. Some kinds of instinctual behavior do not appear until certain stages of development are reached. Also refers specifically to McDougal's idea that social behavior is primarily determined by a group of instinctive tendencies that both arouse activity and direct that

activity in specific ways to satisfy the instincts. Popularity of this doctrine declined rapidly in the 1920s.

instrumental conditioning—The strengthening of behavior by the presentation of a reinforcing stimulus when the response occurs but not otherwise. Also called *operant conditioning*.

insulin coma treatment—A type of shock therapy sometimes used in the treatment of depression. A coma with or without convulsions is produced through an injection of insulin into the muscles.

intellectualization—Psychoanalytic term for the defense mechanism that functions by breaking the bond between symbols and their emotional charges or by isolating them from each other. An emotional situation is dealt with in a highly abstract manner.

intelligence quotient (IQ)—Originally defined by Alfred Binet as mental age (MA) divided by chronological age (CA) multiplied by 100 (IQ = (MA/CA) × 100). An IQ of 100 indicates an individual is average for his or her age group. IQ scores are now available from many intelligence tests, usually by consulting tables.

interference theory—A theory of memory that assumes that people forget things because other things block the items they try to remember. There are two kinds of interference: proactive and retroactive.

internalization—A response to social influence in which an individual acquires and accepts as his or her own attitudes consistent with the individual's own value system. The individual's underlying motivation is the desire to be correct.

interneurons—Nerves that perform a connective or associative function within the nervous system.

interobserver reliability—The level of agreement between two or more observers rating the same behaviors.

interoceptive conditioning—A classical conditioning phenomenon in which the conditioned stimulus is inside the body rather than outside it. The conditioned stimulus might be pressure applied to the intestine or other internal organs.

interoceptors—Specialized receptors of stimulation that respond to events inside the body (e.g., pressure-sensitive receptors within the stomach).

interpersonal attraction—The feelings, ranging from liking to indifference to dislike, that result from an individual's evaluation of other persons.

interval reinforcement—In operant conditioning, a kind of partial reinforcement schedule in which a period of time must elapse between reinforcements.

intrinsic nuclei—A portion of the forebrain that appears to play an important part in the regulation of spontaneous electrical activity in the cortex and in the control of such processes as sleep and attention.

introspection—Observation and report of one's inner experience. A method by which early psychologists attempted to study human consciousness. A specific stimulus was presented to which subjects were asked to report their internal experiences in great detail.

James-Lange theory of emotion—The idea that one's

experience of emotion is really the experience of the bodily changes following the perception of the emotional stimulus. That is, we're afraid because we run away, rather than running away because we are afraid.

just noticeable difference (jnd, or differential threshold)—The smallest difference people can perceive between two stimuli.

just world hypothesis—The idea proposed by Melvin Lerner that we wish to believe that we live in a just world in which everyone receives the treatment he or she deserves. That is, victims really deserve their fate because they are not such good people after all.

kernel—In transformational grammar, the term that refers to the meaning of the sentence. A kernel sentence is a simple declarative one. The basic structure of the kernel sentence can be transformed into other surface structures that also represent the same kernel.

kinesthesis—The sense of position and movement in the body from nerve endings in the muscles and joints.

Klinefelter's syndrome—A condition in which the individual has 47 chromosomes, the extra one occurring in pair 23, which then has an XXY combination. The individual will have male external genitalia but with small testes and feminized breasts and is likely to be mentally retarded.

Lamarckianism—The theory of evolution involving the transmission of acquired characteristics to an individual's descendents.

latency stage—The fourth in a series of psychosexual stages described by Freud. It begins at about age 6 and is characterized by dormancy of the sexual instinct.

latent dream content—Psychoanalytic term for the true psychological meaning of the dream.

law of effect—The principle that an individual tends to repeat behaviors that have produced positive outcomes and not to repeat those that produce neutral or negative outcomes. This principle is a cornerstone of operant conditioning.

learned helplessness—A concept originated by Martin Seligman to refer to a learned belief that one has no control over aversive stimuli from the environment.

learning—A change in potential behavior that occurs as the result of experience. There are three major types of learning: classical conditioning, instrumental or operant conditioning, and observational learning.

lens—The elastic structure within the eye that changes shape in accordance with the distance of the object being viewed. It becomes thinner when distant objects are viewed and thicker to view nearby objects.

lesioning—A technique for studying the function of particular parts of the brain by destroying tissue.

libido—In psychoanalytic theory, the psychic energy that is generated by instinctual drives and that constantly presses for discharge.

limbic system—A portion of the forebrain that consists of a number of structures lying deep inside the cerebral hemispheres around the central core of the brain. It has many neural interconnections with the hypothalamus.

It seems to be involved in organizing the activities needed to satisfy the basic motivational and emotional needs regulated by the hypothalamus.

linguistic determinism—The idea that people's language determines the ways in which they perceive and think about their world. Also called *linguistic relativity* or *Whorfian hypothesis*.

linguistic relativity—The idea that people's language determines the ways in which they perceive and think about their world. Also called *linguistic determinism* or the *Whorfian hypothesis*.

locomotor-genital stage—The third of Erik Erikson's eight stages of psychosocial development. It occurs in the third through fifth year. At this time the child develops initiative or develops guilt over its desires. This corresponds to Freud's phallic stage.

longitudinal method—A technique of studying development by periodically measuring changes in the same individual or a group as time passes.

long-term memory—According to one theory, it is one of the three major parts of the memory system. It has a huge capacity to hold information. It retains the information either indefinitely or for a long period of time.

lysergic acid diethylamide (LSD-25)—One of the most potent of the hallucinogenic drugs. A small dose can produce an 8- to 16-hour "trip," during which many perceptual distortions occur. After the trip is over users may suffer acute anxiety or depression, or even short- or long-term psychosis. LSD does not produce physical dependence but may produce psychological dependence.

maintenance rehearsal—The process of keeping material available in memory for immediate use by constantly repeating it without intending to remember it.

make-a-plan analysis—A kind of heuristic problem-solving device in which subjects first find a simple problem of the kind they are to solve, then solve it and use the method as a plan to solve a more complex problem.

manic reaction—One of the affective disorders or major mood disturbances, sometimes of psychotic proportions, which is characterized by high uncontrolled excitement.

manifest dream content—A psychoanalytic term that describes the story or symbol the dreamer reports.

mantra—A word on which practitioners of transcendental meditation concentrate their attention during the meditation process.

marijuana—A hallucinogenic drug derived from the hemp plant that affects the user's mood and thought patterns. It is usually either smoked in a cigarette or eaten when mixed with food. While under the influence of marijuana an individual's ability to make decisions may be affected. Some research has suggested that heavy use produces dangerous side effects, such as chromosomal damage and hormonal changes.

mass hysteria—The group process that results in the spread or contagion of panic among group members.

maturation—Those aspects of growth or change governed

585

by internal biological mechanisms that unfold or unravel over time.

mean—The statistical term for the arithmetic average computed by summing all the scores and dividing by the total number of scores.

means-end analysis—A kind of heuristic problem-solving device in which subjects first define a subgoal that they hope to achieve (an "end"). They then compare that subgoal with their present state of knowledge and if there is a discrepancy between them try to find the means to reduce the difference.

measure of central tendency—A single score that characterizes the level of performance of a group. The most commonly used measures of central tendency are the mean, median, and mode.

median—If all scores are arranged in order from lowest to highest, the median is the point that cuts the distribution in half. Half the score lie above and half below it.

mediating processes—The covert or internal processes that intervene between stimulus and response.

medulla—A portion of the brain stem that plays a vital role in bodily functions, such as heart rate and respiration. It also contains all the sensory and motor nerve tracts coming up from the spinal cord and descending from the brain. At this level the tracks cross, so that the left side of the brain receives sensory input from and exerts motor control over the right side of the body, and vice versa.

memory cue—A concept used in the interference theory of forgetting. Based on the idea that nothing is forgotten but that the individual may not always be able to find the correct place in his or her mental filing system to guarantee retrieval; that is, the proper memory cue is not always available.

memory trace—A presumed physiological change in the nervous system that occurs during learing. The basis of the decay theory of memory.

menopause—The female climacteric. The period of natural ending of menstruation.

mental retardation—A level of intellectual functioning that is significantly below the average. It is usually evident early in life. About 3 percent of the population of the United States is mentally retarded.

mesmerism—A hypnotic technique developed by a Viennese physician Anton Mesmer that attempted to cure patients through magnetic forces radiated from the planets.

methadone—A substance pharmacologically similar to other opiates that is used in the treatment of narcotic addiction. It apparently blocks off the ordinary effects of morphinelike drugs by competing at receptor sites located in the central nervous system, where the drugs have their effects.

methodology—The set of ground rules and techniques for scientific exploration.

midbrain—The portion of the brain lying just above the hindbrain and containing a number of important sensory and motor nuclei and also many sensory and motor pathways.

middle ear—A portion of the ear that includes three small bones called, hammer, anvil, and stirrup. These bones pass the vibration of the eardrum along to the oval window, the boundary between the middle and inner ear.

mindguards—The individuals within groups undergoing groupthink who suppress the discussion of information inconsistent with the group's decision.

Minnesota Multiphasic Personality Inventory (MMPI)—A test consisting of 566 statements to be answered true, false, or cannot say. The items are varied in content and were obtained by finding items that patients with different psychiatric diagnoses responded to in different ways. The original test consisted of nine clinical scales, although others have been derived over the years.

mnemonic devices—Techniques for organizing information so that it can be remembered easily. Rhyming systems and peg words are examples of mnemonic devices.

mode—A statistical measure reflecting the score obtained by the largest number of individuals.

modeling—A term used to describe observational learning. The process whereby behavior is learned simply by observing others' behavior. Whether the learned behavior will be performed depends on a number of factors, including the consequences observed in the original modeling situation.

monocular depth cue—Cues used in perceiving depth that require only one eye. These include linear perspective, decreasing size, height of the horizontal plane, texture, clarity, and interposition of other objects.

monozygotic—Two individuals produced from a single fertilized egg. They are genetically identical.

morpheme—The smallest units of meaning in a given language. English morphemes include whole words, prefixes, and suffixes. There are over 100,000 English morphemes.

motivation—A general term referring to forces regulating goal-seeking behavior. Motivation may come from situational demands or subjective values, needs, and desires, or a combination of the two.

motive to avoid success—The idea originated by Matina Horner that many women have actually learned to fear being successful. She devised a procedure to measure this motive.

multple-factor inheritance—Occurs when several genes are involved in producing a particular characteristic. Variations in hair color among the children in one family are an example.

multiple personality—A rare dramatic type of dissociative reaction in which two or more separate and markedly different personalities coexist within the same individual.

multistore models—Theories of memory that presume that long- and short-term memory processes differ.

muscular-anal stage—The second of Erik Erikson's eight

stages of psychosocial behavior. It occurs in the second year of life and corresponds to Freud's anal stage. It is the period when autonomy is developed or shame and doubt about ability are developed.

mutation—A change that occurs when a cell grows and divides and does not reproduce itself perfectly. If the mutation occurs in an egg or sperm, it is likely the gene will be passed on in future generations. If it occurs in other cells of the body, then the cells that grow from that cell will carry the change, but the change will not be transmitted to the next generation. Such environmental factors as ionizing radiation may increase the mutation rate.

myelin—The sheath of fatty tissue that covers the axons of many neurons. The sheath serves to increase speed of neural transmission.

narcissism—Extreme self-love. The psychoanalytic term for excessive preoccupation with oneself and one's own concerns.

narcotic analgesics—Substances that act on the central and autonomic nervous system and are used therapeutically to ease pain. Examples are opium, morphine, and heroin. Tolerance for and physiological and psychological dependence on narcotic analgesics develop quickly.

narrative chaining—The mnemonic device of weaving words into a story to increase recall.

natural experiment—A field study carried out to coincide with the occurrence of a natural event.

natural selection—A term used by Darwin to explain his idea that as new species evolve over time any inheritable characteristic that increases the likelihood of survival will be maintained in the species. Those characteristics that do not improve chances for survival will be eliminated over time.

need for achievement (n Ach)—A human motive often reflected in the content of stories written by subjects in response to certain standard pictures. A human motive measured by content-analyzing stories written in response to pictorial stimuli.

need for affiliation (n Affiliation)—A measure devised by McClelland to measure the desire to relate to others in a friendly fashion.

need for power (n Power)—A measure devised by McClelland to measure an individual's need to exert control over the lives of others. He divided power motivation into two kinds: (1) oriented toward winning over adversaries; (2) a socially acceptable helping or inspiring type motive.

negative reinforcement—In operant conditioning, anything that will serve to increase the behavior that results in its removal. Not to be confused with punishment.

neoanalytic—Ideas based on Freud's theory but that depart from it in important ways, for example, by including a more important role for social and cultural factors. Alfred Adler and Erik Erikson are two examples of neoanalytic theorists.

neuron—A nerve cell. It consists of three main parts: the soma, dendrites, and an axon.

neurosis—A functional personality disorder, usually mild, not accompanied by a severe behavior impairment or disorganization requiring hospitalization. The term refers to disorders involving a wide range of problems and the anxiety arising from an individuals unsuccessful attempts to deal with the inner conflicts and stress.

noise—Any sound that is unwanted and that produces unwanted effects.

nonreversal shift—A type of experiment in which subjects are required to choose one of each of several pairs of objects. They are reinforced for choosing those objects that correspond to a particular dimension, such as color or size; then they are required to choose on the basis of a previously irrelevant dimension. If they had previously been rewarded for choosing black squares after the nonreversal shift, they might be rewarded for choosing large squares instead.

nonsense syllable—A meaningless combination of letters, often a vowel between two consonants, used in verbal learning research.

norepinephrine—A hormone produced by the adrenal medulla that functions as a synaptic transmitter and thus allows nerve impulses to pass from one neuron to the next. Norepinephrine is found in high concentrations in brain structures, and many drugs that influence mood and emotions have an effect on brain levels of norepinephrine. Norepinephrine also produces physiological arousal.

normal distribution—A frequency distribution in the shape of a symmetrical or bell-shaped curve that satisfies certain mathematical conditions deduced from the theory of probability.

norms—The distribution of scores obtained when the test is administered to a large sample of people who are representative of the population for whom the test will be used. These serve as a standard against which any individual score can be compared and interpreted. Also refers to rules of behavior that exist in a particular group.

observational learning—The process by which behavior is influenced by observation of others' behavior and its consequences.

obsession—Persistent, irrational, often anxiety-provoking thoughts.

obsessive-compulsive neurosis—Characterized by persistent irrational, often anxiety-provoking thoughts (obsessions) and/or uncontrollable repetitive actions (compulsions).

occipital lobe—One of the four lobes into which each cerebral hemisphere of the brain is divided. It lies at the rear of the brain and contains the visual reception area.

Oedipus complex—Freud's term for the wish of a child for the elimination of the same-sexed parent and the possession of the opposite-sexed parent.

operant conditioning—The strengthening of behavior by the presentation of a reinforcing stimulus when the response occurs but not otherwise. Also called *instrumental conditioning*.

operant therapy—A type of behavior therapy based on the principles of operant conditioning.

operational definition—The description or specification of a concept in terms of some observable event that can be measured.

operations—A term used by Piaget to define a whole new set of skills acquired by children during the concrete operations period from ages 7 to 12. It involves the ability to understand that certain mental processes are reversible. For example, if two numbers are multiplied, the product can be divided by one of them to produce the other.

opponent-process theory—A theory of color vision based on Hering's theory that there are three types of cones, one for red/green, one for blue/yellow, and one for black/white reception. Each type of receptor can respond in one of two ways, and its specific response determines which of the two colors is sensed.

optic chiasma—The point in which the optic nerves cross after leaving the eye.

oral-sensory stage—The first of Erik Erikson's eight stages of psychosocial development. Occurs during the first year of life and is the basis for the individual's development of either a basic trust or a basic mistrust of the world. Corresponds with Freud's oral stage.

oral stage—The first in a series of psychosexual stages as described by Freud. It occurs in earliest infancy. The sucking response first associated with feeding becomes involved in the obtaining of pleasure that is not completely nutritional in nature. Indiscriminate sucking by infants is typical oral stage behavior.

organs of Corti—The thousands of tiny hair cells in the inner ear that are the actual sound receptors of the body. Their movement sets off the electrical potential that results in nerve impulses being sent to the brain through the auditory nerve.

orgastic dysfunction—Disturbances in sexual functioning among women that may involve pain and fear as well as apathy and inability to respond.

overload model—A concept used in environmental psychology. It presumes that individuals receive more stimulation from the environment than they can tolerate. They deal with this by withdrawing, becoming aloof, or giving less attention to low-priority items.

overmanning—A term used in environmental psychology to indicate that when the number of persons exceeds the facilities or jobs available, the situation will be perceived as crowded.

parallel forms—Different sets of test questions that can be used interchangeably and that have the same predictive characteristics.

paranoid schizophrenia—A type of psychosis characterized by delusions and extreme suspiciousness. Certain intellectual functions may be unaffected by the delusions.

parietal lobe—One of the four divisions of each cerebral hemisphere. It lies behind the frontal lobe and contains the body sense area.

partial reinforcement—A procedure used in operant conditioning in which not all responses are followed by reinforcement.

pedigree analysis—A technique for studying heredity in which the investigator first identifies the characteristic of interest and an individual who has it. The investigator then studies the family history and examines the traits of ancestors, descendants, and other relatives, such as siblings, uncles, and aunts. This information may make it possible to identify a Mendelian pattern of inheritance for the defect.

penis envy—In Freudian theory, a development during the phallic stage in females when they discover that they lack what Freud considered the more desirable male sex organ. A girl transfers some of her love of her mother to her father as a way of sharing his penis with him.

percentile score—Indicates what percent of the group scored above and below a given point.

perception—The interpretation of sensation by the individual into subjective experience.

perceptual constancy—The phenomenon that although the particular sensory stimuli for objects may change, our recognition and perception of the objects do not change. We have no difficulty recognizing familiar objects from a variety of angles and distances and under different kinds of lights.

perceptual defense—A proposed attentional filtering process that serves a defensive function and protects the individual from perceiving threatening stimuli.

peripheral nervous system—One of the two major divisions of the nervous system that is made up of all neurons connecting the central nervous system with the muscles, glands, and sensory receptors. This system may be further subdivided in the somatic nervous system and the autonomic nervous system.

peripheral traits—A term used by Solomon Asch to describe traits that exert very little influence on one individual's impression of another.

personal constructs—Categories used by George Kelly to describe the manner in which individuals construct reality by sorting out persons and events in their lives. They are the rules an individual uses to assign events to categories, and his or her ideas about how the categories relate to each other.

personal space—The idea that each individual has his or her own portable territory marked out much like the territoriality seen in animals. Robert Sommer is a leading researcher in this area.

personality—The collection of attributes, dispositions, and tendencies that make up a single individual.

personality trait—An individual's characteristic way of responding to the world.

phallic stage—The third in the stages of psychosexual development described by Freud. It begins at about age 4 and peaks at 5 or 6. In this stage the genitals gradually replace the anal zone as a major location of sexual pleasure. The Oedipal crisis occurs during the phallic stage.

phenomenology—The theory that behavior is determined by the way an individual perceives reality at any particular time and not by the reality as experienced by others or as described in objective terms.

phenotype—A term used by geneticists to refer to the outward appearance and behavior of the individual.

phobic neurosis—Irrational and highly specific fears.

phoneme—The linguistic term for the smallest units of sound. These are the vowel and consonant sounds that are recognized in any given language. The English language as 45 phonemes.

physiological psychology—The branch of psychology that studies neurological, genetic, and hormonal bases of behavior and also the effect of drugs on the body and on behavior.

pituitary gland—One of the endocrine glands. Also called the *master gland* because several of its hormones stimulate other glands. The pituitary gland has a close relationship with the hypothalamus and responds to certain hormones secreted by it.

placebo—substances, such as sugar pills, that have no curative power. Sometimes prescribed for patients whose complaints seem to have no physical cause.

pleasure principle—The Freudian idea that the organism is impelled toward immediate impulsive action and gratification of need independently of all other considerations. Freud thought this was the principle guiding the individual in early life and that it continued as a guiding principle of the unconscious.

polarization hypothesis—In group decision making, the idea that if the initial position of group members was conservative it will become more conservative after the discussion or if the original position was a somewhat risky one the final group decision will be more risky.

polygraph—Instrument that measures emotional responses through various physiological reactions, such as heart rate, blood pressure, breathing, and galvanic skin response. Often used as a basis for deciding whether a subject is lying.

pons—The portion of the brain stem that lies just above the medulla. Contains many ascending and descending fibers that connect the higher and lower levels of the central nervous system, and also nuclei that carry sensory information to the brain from the sense organs in the head and that are involved in respiration.

population—The group from which an experimenter selects or samples subjects for study. The assumption is made that the sampled subjects have the same characteristics as the rest of the population.

pornography—Material that aims to arouse the viewer or reader sexually and that is characterized by obscenity.

positive reinforcement—Any stimulus or event that increases the likelihood of behavior on which it is made contingent.

post-conventional level—The third of three stages of development of moral judgment as described by Lawrence Kohlberg. At this level, which occurs in early adulthood, personal values become prominent in the individual's behavior.

precognition—A type of extrasensory perception involving the perception of future events.

preconscious—The psychoanalytic term describing an area of the mind that contains memories, thoughts, feelings, and images of which the individual is not now aware but that can potentialy be recalled.

preconventional level—The first of three stages of development of moral judgment described by Lawrence Kohlberg. At this level the child's moral behavior is based on the likelihood of punishment and or absolute standards laid down by authority figures.

prefrontal lobotomy—A brain operation in which the connections between the prefrontal cerebral tissues and the thalamus are severed. Performed frequently during the 1930s, now rarely because of the significant number of patients who did not respond well.

prejudice—A set of beliefs based on inaccurate or incomplete information. These beliefs and the feelings and behavioral tendencies that accompany them are directed toward members of particular groups.

Premack principle—States that behavior that occurs often may be used to reinforce behavior that occurs less frequently. Frequent behavior need not be highly pleasurable but it should not be unpleasant.

preoperational period—The term used by Piaget for the second of the four major stages in the continuous process of growth and change in cognitive development during childhood. It lasts from about age 2 to age 7. A major accomplishment of the period is the understanding that objects can be classified and grouped.

primacy effect—Describes a situation in which information received first has the greatest effect on an individual's behavior.

primal therapy—A type of psychotherapy based on the idea that tension and pain associated with the frustration of "primal needs" in early life cause maladaptive behavior. To correct this behavior it is necessary to reexperience the intense feelings felt at the time the "primal needs" were not met. An example of primal need would be frustration created by lack of love and warmth.

primary drive—An aroused condition that motivates the individual to satisfy a physiological need. Deprivation of warmth, food, water, or oxygen may be the cause of such physiological needs.

primary hunger—Hunger that occurs in response to the actual needs of the animal as opposed to hunger that may be caused by habit, such as customary time of eating.

primary memory—The nineteenth-century philosopher William James's term for information still in our consciousness.

primary reinforcement—A situation in which an object or condition does not require prior association with

589

other reinforcers in order to have reinforcement properties. Primary reinforcement often satisfies biological needs.

proactive interference—The process by which earlier learning can interfere with the ability to recall newly learned material.

progesterone—Female sex hormone produced by the ovaries. It is important in developing female sex characteristics and also in the menstrual cycle.

projection—The psychoanalytic defense mechanism of repressing undesirable impulses or characteristics and attributing them to someone else.

projective tests—Tests that involve stimuli that are relatively unclear and ambiguous and that give subjects a wide range of possible responses. They have been used to study unconscious processes and are often used by psychodynamically oriented psychologists. Examples of projective tests are the Rorschach and Thematic Apperception Test.

proprioceptor—Specialized sensory organs located within the muscles, joints, and inner ear that are stimulated by the movement of the body itself.

proxemics—A method for study of the ways in which people use personal space. Developed by anthropologist E. G. Hall.

proximity, law of—Gestalt perceptual law that states that elements near each other are perceived as part of the same configuration.

pseudocommunity—A psychotic reconstruction of reality, peopled by real and imagined individuals who are part of a delusional system.

psychoanalysis—A system of psychological thought and a method of treatment of psychological disorders developed by Sigmund Freud. The technique used is free association by the patient. Special emphasis is given to feelings of which the patient may not be aware at the beginning of treatment.

psychoanalytic perspective—A view of behavior that focuses on inner causes, especially motivations, feelings, conflicts, and other unconscious factors in behavior. Freud's ideas formed the basis for this view.

psychokinesis (PK)—The ability to control matter through the mind. Studied by those interested in extrasensory perception.

psycholinguistics—The study of the way that sounds and symbols are translated into meaning and the psychological processes that are involved in this translation.

psychomimetic drug—Another term for hallucinogenic drugs. The term derives from the parallels that exist between drug effects and psychotic experiences.

psychopathic personality—A type of sociopathic personality disturbance in which individuals are chronically antisocial, are always in trouble, profit little from experience, and are unable to identify when to be loyal to other persons or groups. They often lack judgment and responsibility and demonstrate emotional immaturity.

psychopharmacology—The study of the effects of drugs on behavior.

psychophysics—The scientific study of the relationship between physical properties or stimuli and the perceptual experience to which they give rise. These stimuli are measured in physical terms.

psychophysiological disorder—Also called psychosomatic disorder. Tissue or structural change apparently caused by emotional factors. Stomach ulcers and high blood pressure are examples.

psychosexual stages—A series of specific stages believed by Freud to make up a universal pattern of sexual development.

psychosis—A disorder that involves major intellectual and/or emotional distortions often accompanied by delusions and hallucinations. Often requires hospitalization and includes the most serious forms of maladaptive behavior.

psychosurgery—Surgical procedures designed to alter brain functioning in an attempt to reduce undesirable behavior. Controversy surrounds the use of these techniques.

psychotherapy—The use of psychological methods in the treatment of disorders.

punishment—A negative consequence that follows an undesirable response and that decreases the future occurrence of that response.

Q-sort—A technique used to categorize statements. These are printed on a large number of cards and a person is asked to sort the statements into separate piles, ranging from those that are most descriptive to those that are least descriptive. A specific number of items usually must be sorted into each category to conform to a forced normal distribution. Frequently used to measure the self-concept.

random sampling—Procedure in which the probability of each person in the population being included in the sample is independent of whether or not any other member is selected. Chance plays a greater role in random sampling than representative sampling.

range—A simple measure of variability that gives the difference between the highest and lowest score.

rapid eye movement (REM)—REMs occur about 20 times per second during a fifth sleep stage that begins about an hour after falling asleep and that occurs approximately every 90 minutes thereafter. REM periods seem to coincide with periods of dreaming.

rating scale—A type of measuring instrument similar to a multiple-choice item except that the options on the rating scale represent different degrees of a particular characteristic rather than completely different characteristics.

ratio reinforcement—See *response dependent reinforcement*.

rational-emotive therapy—A type of psychotherapy developed by Albert Ellis that focuses on changing irrational beliefs that cause maladaptive feelings and behaviors.

rationalization—A psychoanalytic term for the defense mechanism in which socially approved logical reasons for behavior are presented rather than the real reasons or motives for the behavior.

reaction formation—Defense mechanism that involves repression of an impulse and the expression of its opposite, often in exaggerated form.

reality principle—In psychoanalytic theory, a guide by which the ego functions at the conscious level. It takes into account reality demands and restrictions in obtaining gratification.

recall—The technique by which persons recover and reproduce material that they have previously learned.

recency effect—Describes a situation in which the last information received is most influential on an individual's behavior.

recessive characteristic—A hereditary characteristic that is not apparent unless both genes in the gene pair are recessive. If the individual has only one recessive gene in the pair, its effect is masked by its dominant partner gene. A recessive gene may be passed on to the individual's offspring.

recognition—A technique used in verbal learning in which the subject is asked to pick out from a list of old and new items those he or she has previously learned.

reference group—A term describing that social group with whose standards and beliefs an individual identifies.

refractory period—The brief period after the passing of a nerve impulse during which the membrane of the cell is not excitable and cannot discharge another impulse.

rehearsal buffer—According to one theory of memory, a special section of short-term memory that can store information indefinitely by rehearsing it.

reinforcement—In classical conditioning, each pairing of the conditioned stmulus with the unconditioned stimulus. In operant conditioning, the following of the operant by the reinforcing stimulus. In general, any stimulation that serves to strengthen a response.

reinforcement contingency—In operant conditioning, the relationship between a behavior and its consequences.

relearning—A technique used in verbal learning experiments. The difference between the number of trials needed to learn the material originally and the number needed to relearn the material, the "savings score," measures degree of previous learning.

releasing stimulus (sign stimulus)—A term used by ethologists to refer to specific stimuli that trigger innate behavior patterns in animals.

reliability—The consistency of a test as a measuring instrument or its lack of measurement error. Reliability is measured by the coefficient of correlation between scores on two halves of a test, on alternate forms of a test, or on retests with the same test.

repeated-measures design—An experimental design in which the same behaviors are measured on two or more occasions. Used to study behavior over time or as a result of certain experience(s).

representative sampling—A sampling technique in which the number of individuals sampled from various groups is proportional to the size of these groups in the popula-

tion. This type of sampling is used by most public opinion polling firms.

repression—In psychoanalytic theory, a defense mechanism that guards against anxiety and guilt by excluding unacceptable ideas or impulses from consciousness. Motivated forgetting.

repressors—Individuals who deal with threatening events by avoiding them and trying to minimize the possibility of experiencing negative emotions. Repressors are likely to exhibit strong perceptual defense reactions.

resocialization—Ways of providing additional social development for individuals whose knowledge of one or more social roles is incorrect, not just incomplete. Resocialization may be applied to groups as different as criminals and middle-class neurotics through such techniques as adult education or training programs.

response dependent reinforcement—A kind of partial reinforcement schedule used in operant conditioning in which reinforcement is contingent on the number of responses that the subject makes.

resting potential—The voltage generated by unequal distribution of ions inside and outside the cell membrane when the neuron is in its resting state.

reticular formation—A large bundle of neurons in the mid-brain that controls the activation level of the cortex. It seems to be involved with control of certain aspects of motor behavior and to have a central role in consciousness, attention, and sleep.

retina—Portion of the eye that contains the visual receptors.

retinal disparity—The slightly different view of any object from each of an individual's two eyes. It occurs because the eyes are slightly separated from each other.

retroactive interference—The phenomenon in which new learning can interfere with ability to recall previously learned material.

reversal shift—A type of problem often used in experiments. Subjects are presented with pairs of stimuli and asked to choose one of each pair. They are reinforced for choosing by some characteristic, such as color or size. Then they must learn to reverse their response to exactly the opposite of what they have previously done. For example, if reinforcement was given for choosing the black object from each pair of black and white objects, after the shift the choice of the white object would be reinforced.

risky shift—The phenomenon that occurs in group decision making when a decision acceptable to all members of the group is found to be considerably riskier than the average of individual decisions that the group members would make.

rods—Structures within the retina of the eye that are sensitive to light and movement but not to color.

Rorschach test—A series of ten inkblots that are shown to subjects one at a time. Subjects are asked what the blot looks like and what it might be. Many scoring systems have been developed for the Rorschach test.

rote learning—The learning of material verbatim without regard for meaning.

sample—The limited number of subjects collected from a large group or population and used for testing and statistical treatment. The assumption is made that the sample may be representative of the whole group.

savings score—A measure in verbal learning experiments that use the relearning method. The savings score equals original trials minus relearning trials, the result divided by original trials and then multiplied by 100.

scapegoat theory of prejudice—States that frustrated individuals sometimes displace their aggression onto groups or individuals that are relatively powerless. The form the aggression takes depends on what is deemed appropriate by the person's reference group.

schizophrenia—A type of psychosis that includes several subtypes. Characterized by a loss of contact with reality, blunting of emotions, and disturbance of thinking. Behavior is often so bizarre that individuals must be hospitalized. The four major subtypes of schizophrenia are catatonic, paranoid, hebephrenic, and simple.

secondary drive—A motive that develops as a result of learning, presumably by virtue of being associated with satisfaction of biologically based (primary) drives.

secondary memory—Contains information stored outside our consciousness, according to the theory of memory of nineteenth-century philosopher William James. Finding information in secondary memory may involve a difficult and perhaps unsuccessful search.

secondary reinforcement—The situation in which reinforcing properties are acquired by one object or situation by being associated with other reinforcers.

selective breeding—A procedure used by animal breeders that involves mating animals with selected characteristics with other animals having the same or different selected characteristics in order to produce offspring with certain specific traits.

self-concept—The organized perceptions of the "I" or "me" and also perceptions of the relationship of the "I" or "me" to others and to various aspects of life.

self-desensitization—A program whereby persons can gain greater self-control of emotional responses. It involves training oneself in deep muscular relaxation and then using this coping response to control emotional responses to imagined and real-life problem situations.

self-fulfilling prophecy—Adoption by the individual of the unfavorable assumptions of others in order to rationalize a lower status or unfavorable position.

semantic memory—The organized knowledge we have about words and other verbal symbols, including their meaning and the things to which they refer; about relationships among them; and about rules for manipulating them.

semantics—The scientific study of the meanings of words.

semicircular canal—Three curved tubes located in each inner ear that serve as sense organs for equilibrium. They respond to left-right, backward-frontward, or up-down movements.

sensation—The physical process of detecting environmental stimuli and transmitting them through the nervous system.

sensitizers—Individuals who seem to be on the lookout for threatening events and are sensitive to their occurrence. They deal with an anxiety-arousing situation by approaching it and seeking to master it. These individuals fail to demonstrate perceptual defense.

sensorimotor period—The term used by Piaget for the first of four major stages in the continuous process of growth and change in cognitive development during childhood. The period begins at birth and lasts until about 18 months of age. Children's functioning in this period is at the action level involving sensing and motor movement. They have not fully developed internal representation of things or mental images.

sensory store—According to one theory, this is one of three major components of memory. It holds large amounts of information for a particular sense organ for a few seconds. The information is lost unless it is quickly transferred to another component, the short-term memory.

serial recall—The technique used in verbal learning experiments in which the subject is asked to reproduce material previously learned in the order in which it has been learned.

serial ordering, principle of—One of the skills Piaget calls operations that develop during the concrete operations period. The ability to arrange or order a group of objects according to some given characteristic (e.g., height).

serotonin—A chemical synaptic inhibitor important in the regulation of brain centers concerned with autonomic functions, such as temperature, blood pressure, and wakefulness.

sex-linked characteristics—Hereditary characteristics carried only by the female sex chromosome. Examples are red-green color blindness and hemophilia.

sexual dysfunction—Detrimental effect on a couple's sexual relationship caused by sexual difficulties experienced by the man or the woman or both.

shadowing—A technique for studying shifts of attention. Subjects are asked to listen to two messages simultaneously and to repeat or shadow one of them word for word.

shaping—A method used to train animals and humans to perform novel and complex behaviors. The process involves finding a behavior that the subject can already perform and reinforcing him or her to make gradual changes in the direction of the desired behavior. Also called the *method of successive approximations*.

short-term memory—One of three major components of memory, according to one theoretical system. It has limited capacity and can hold only about the amount of information contained in one telephone number. It can hold information for only about 15 seconds.

sign stimulus—See releasing stimulus.

signal detection theory—The idea that there is no fixed probability that a subject will detect a signal of a particular intensity and that the concept of "fixed absolute threshold" is largely meaningless. The subject's decision criterion or standard is far more influential than the actual physical intensity of the stimulus.

similarity, law of—Gestalt perceptual law that states that when parts of the stimulus configuration are perceived as similar they will also be perceived as belonging together.

simple schizophrenia—A type of psychosis characterized by gradual withdrawal from contact with other people. Usually without hallucinations or delusions.

simulation model—A program or set of instructions delivered to an electronic computer to mirror or simulate the processes presumably used by human subjects.

Skinner box—A piece of scientific apparatus designed by B. F. Skinner for use in operant conditioning studies. The typical box contains a lever that the animal may press and a method of delivering some kind of reinforcement, usually a food pellet.

sleeper effect—A decrease in attitude change produced by a high credibility source and an increase in attitude change produced by a low credibility source as time passes.

social attitude—A relatively enduring combination of beliefs, feelings, and behavioral tendencies toward individuals, objects, or events of a social nature.

social design—A concept that architectural design must be concerned not only with efficiency and aesthetic criteria but also with such factors as privacy and social interchange.

social desirability—The concept that individuals sometimes respond not to the content of test items but to the social acceptability of the answer choices.

social intelligence—A special kind of intelligence defined by some theorists. A sensitivity to other people and to social situations that falls under the heading of intelligence.

social movement—An attempt at change started by an interaction of people concerned with deprivation or unequal treatment of some group. Includes both an ideology and an organization and directs efforts both to publicize the problem and the desired changes. Methods used include slogans, rallies and more active measures, such as strikes, boycotts, and riots.

social psychology—The branch of psychology that studies the behavior of the individual in relation to his or her social environment. Psychological conditions that lead to the development of social groups are studied, as are such topics as attitude formation and change, affiliation, interpersonal attraction, conformity, and group processes.

socialization—The developmental process by which the individual (especially the child) comes to recognize and identify with basic values and attitudes of the dominant institutions and representatives of the society in which he or she lives and to practice them as a part of ordinary behavior.

soma—The cell body of a neuron that contains its nucleus.

somatic nervous system—A division of the peripheral nervous system that provides input from the sensory system and output to the skeletal muscles that are responsible for voluntary movement.

span of apprehension—The amount of visual material that can be recalled after one glance.

species-specific—Referring to the idea that each species has its own pattern of maturation or growth controlled by its own internal mechanisms.

specific hunger—The result of a deficiency of a specific mineral or vitamin that results in an innate tendency to consume large quantities of the needed material at the first opportunity.

specificity theory of pain—Holds that the location, intensity, and quality of pain is determined by the activity of the specific fibers in the central nervous system that are stimulated.

split-brain patients—Patients whose corpus callosum has been severed surgically to prevent the spread of a type of epileptic seizure from one side of the brain to the other hemisphere. Examination of these patients has indicated that the two halves of the brain have somewhat different functions.

split-half reliability—Correlation coefficient calculated by dividing the items of a test into two sets and comparing subject scores on the two halves.

spontaneous recovery—The reappearance of a classically conditioned response after a period of time when it has previously been extinguished.

spontaneous remission—Improvement in symptoms that seems unrelated to therapeutic efforts.

standardized test—A test for which the instructions, administration procedures, materials, and scoring procedures are so explicit that it can be administered at virtually any time and any place with comparable results. Norms for interpreting scores are usually available also.

stereotype—An idea based not on experience, but on selective observation of behavior that fits in with earlier expectations. These selective observations are then used as proof that certain behaviors exist.

simulation technique—Methodology used by environmental psychology in which subjects are presented with a scale model or some other accurate representation of the environmental setting that the investigators wish to evaluate. By measuring the reactions of subjects to models researchers try to determine how people would react to the real environment.

stage four rhythm—A brain wave pattern characterized by slow brain waves of large amplitude that occurs during deep sleep.

stage one rhythm—A brain wave pattern characterized by

a fast irregular rhythm. It is shown by individuals while in light sleep.

standard deviation—A measure of variation computed by finding the difference or deviation between each score and the mean, squaring and summing the deviations, dividing them by the total number of scores minus 1, and then finding the square root of this value.

statistical significance—A statistical concept that indicates the likelihood that the results obtained from a sample occurred by chance alone and do not reflect a finding that is characteristic of the population from which the sample was drawn. Psychologists consider a finding reliable if the chances are only 1 in 20 that it occurred by chance (.05 level of significance).

stereoscope—An apparatus for combining two different views of the same object into a three-dimensional picture.

stereotyping—The process by which characteristics of a group are attributed to an individual who is assumed to be part of that group. Stereotypes do not recognize individual differences but assume that the individual possesses *all* the traits or characteristics previously perceived in members of the group.

stimulus control procedures—Behavior modification procedures that involve arranging the environment so that specific stimuli will come to elicit desired behaviors.

stimulus-response specificity—One of two basic principles involved in physiological disorders. Certain psychologically based physiologic reactions may occur only in response to a very specific stimulus situation that constitutes a problem area for the individual. (Contrast with *individual response stereotyping*.)

stress—A concept that refers to a person's perception of a situation as demanding, challenging, and requiring some sort of response.

stuttering—A speech disorder characterized by a blocking or convulsive repetition of initial sounds of words.

sublimation—The process by which an individual channels unacceptable impulses into disguised socially acceptable behavior. For example, aggressive impulses may be expressed through such activities as competitive sports, hunting, or political activities.

subliminal perception—Perception of stimuli that are so weak or brief that they cannot be consciously perceived. The question as to whether subliminal stimuli can affect behavior is still unsettled.

superego—In psychoanalytic theory, that part of the psyche that is developed by internalized parental standards and parental identification. There are two parts to the superego: the *ego ideal*, which represents identification with parents and desired standards of conduct, and the *conscience*, which includes moralistic attitudes and values.

surface structure—The linguistic term that describes the words and organization of a spoken or written sentence. Two sentences may have quite different surface structure but the sentences may mean the same thing.

surgical ablation—A technique for studying the function of particular structures in the brain by systematic surgical removal of parts of the brain.

survey of recent experience (SRE)—Scale originated by Thomas Holmes for measuring the degree of change in people's lives. These scores may be related to the individual's chances of becoming ill.

survey study—Technique used to obtain information about opinions and attitudes by directly questioning individuals about these.

synapse—The junction between nerve cells across which the nerve impulse must pass.

syntax—The linguistic term that refers to the way morphemes are put together in coherent phrases or sentences.

tachistoscope—A projectorlike instrument that presents visual stimuli to subjects for very brief intervals of time.

telepathy—A type of extrasensory perception that refers to the ability to read another person's thoughts.

temporal lobe—One of the four lobes in each cerebral hemisphere. It lies beneath the lateral fissure and contains the reception area for hearing.

territoriality—A behavior common to many animal societies in which each individual or group marks off a living space or territory that is defined against intruders.

testosterone—Male sex hormone produced by the testes. Important in puberty for the growth of the male sex organs and development of secondary sex characteristics.

test-retest reliability—A correlation coefficient obtained by administering a test to the same subject on two occasions and correlating the separate scores.

T-group (also called Training, Sensitivity, or Encounter Group)—A type of group psychotherapy that emphasizes feedback among participants with emphasis on social relationships in the here and now. A procedure directed largely at "normal" persons, because the primary purpose is to improve the functioning of an already adequate individual.

thalamus—A large group of nuclei located above the midbrain that are an important sensory relay system.

Thematic Apperception Test (TAT)—A projective test developed by Henry Murray that consists of 30 pictures, including one blank card. The subjects are told to tell a story for each somewhat ambiguous picture. A number of scoring systems have been developed for the TAT.

time-dependent reinforcement—See *interval reinforcement*.

tip of the tongue phenomenon—An inability to remember that occurs in ordinary, everyday behavior. It is characterized by an inability to remember a particular thing but at the same time an ability to produce clues to the correct answer. It implies that the fact is not forgotten but that the retrieval mechanism is temporarily faulty.

token economy—An attempt to improve social behavior or work habits in members of a group, such as patients on a hospital ward. Reinforcement for certain behaviors is given by awarding patients a specified number of

594

tokens for each behavior. The tokens are then redeemable for privileges or merchandise.

trait—A reasonably stable characteristic of a person that can be observed and measured.

transactional analysis—A type of group therapy in which the leader focuses on transactions or basic units of social relationships. The process examines important transactions in which one person does something to another and the other person does something in return. Transactional analysis was originated by Eric Berne.

transcendental meditation—A quasi-religious technique founded by Maharishi Mahesh Yogi that involves dwelling on a thought, sensation, word, or object in an attempt to achieve inner peace.

transference—In psychoanalysis, the emotional attitude, either positive or negative, that the patient develops toward the analyst. Transference reactions may be excessive because of the patient's irrational needs and perceptions.

transformational grammar—A linguistic theory formulated by Noam Chomsky based on the distinction between surface and deep structure of language.

transitivity, principle of—One of the skills (called operations by Piaget) acquired during the concrete operations period from the ages of 7 to 12. The principle that if two things are each related to a third they are also related to each other. For example, if *A* is greater than *B* and *B* is greater than *C*, then *A* is also greater than *C*.

transsexual—One who feels an intense desire to change his or her body to that of the opposite sex.

transvestite—One who obtains sexual satisfaction by dressing in the clothing of the opposite sex (cross-dressing).

trial and error—A method of problem solving in which the individual tries alternative possibilities and discards those that do not work.

Turner's syndrome—A condition in which a female has only 45 chromosomes with one X chromosome missing from pair 23. She has female external genitalia but her ovaries, uterus, and breasts do not develop normally and she is almost always incapable of reproduction.

twin studies—The method most often used in psychological research on heredity. Identical and fraternal twins are compared to see whether one group has closer behavior resemblances than the other. If the monozygotic, or identical, twins show closer behavior resemblances than do dizygotic twins, difference in heredity may be inferred as a causal factor.

two-factor theory of avoidance learning—Incorporates both classical and operant conditioning factors. The warning stimulus evokes a classically conditioned fear response. The fear response motivates the operant avoidance behavior. The resulting anxiety reduction is a powerful reinforcer.

type A personality—A term used by Friedman and Rosenman for people prone to operate under high pressure and to be hard-driving and demanding of themselves and others. Such people are believed to run a high risk of having heart attacks.

unconditioned stimulus (UCS)—A stimulus that unconditionally evokes an unconditioned response. A neutral stimulus that is paired with a UCS may become capable of evoking a conditioned response.

unconscious—In psychoanalytic theory, a dynamic body of wishes, feelings, and impulses of which the individual is unaware.

validity—The degree to which a test measures what it is supposed to measure or accomplishes the purpose for which it is intended. Validity is measured by the coefficient of correlation between a test and some criterion.

variability, measures of—Measures of the dispersion of values in a distribution of scores. The range and standard deviation are two measures of variability.

variable reinforcement schedule—A procedure used in operant conditioning under partial reinforcement schedules when the required number of responses or the time interval for reinforcement varies around an average.

verbal protocol—The transcript of verbal thought processes obtained by asking people to "think out loud" while they are solving a problem.

vestibular sacs—Structures located in the inner ear at the base of the semicircular canal that respond to the position of the resting body and tell us whether we are upright or tilted at various angles.

visual cliff—An apparatus for determining the existence of depth perception in infants.

voyeurism—The obtaining of sexual gratification from looking at or watching sexually stimulating objects or acts.

waxy flexibility—A characteristic of some catatonic schizophrenics. If their arms or legs are placed in one position they will leave them there indefinitely until someone moves them again.

Weber's law—States that there is a constant ratio between the intensity of the stimulus and the amount that a second stimulus must differ from it before the perceiver can detect the difference. It is also expressed as $\Delta I/I = k$, in which I is initial intensity of the stimulus, ΔI is the amount that the second stimulus must be different in order to be distinguished, and k is constant for the particular sense through which we perceive the stimulus.

white-collar crime—Illegal activity carried out by one or more individuals in connection with a business or occupation. Included are individual activities by professionals, embezzlement by employees who have access to corporate funds, organized illegal activities by the management of a corporation. Those who commit such crimes usually do not consider themselves criminals, and are less often sentenced to prison or prosecuted than other offenders.

Whorfian hypothesis (also called *linguistic relativity* or *linguistic determinism*)—The idea that people's lan-

595

guage determines the ways in which they perceive and think about their world. Named for Benjamin Whorf, a noted linguist.

XYY syndrome—An abnormal condition in which an extra Y sex chromosome attaches to the male's XY chromosome pair. Sometimes suggested to be related to criminal or aggressive behavior, but this is not proved.

Yerkes-Dodson law—States that there is an optimal level of arousal for the performance of any given task. This optimal level can be expected to vary from person to person. At levels of arousal above and below the opti-mal, performance is less effective. For difficult tasks the optimal level of arousal for performance is lower than for easy tasks.

Young-Helmholtz theory—The theory of color vision that assumes that there are three types of color receptors in the retina, one sensitive to blue, one to green, and one to red.

zygote—The group of cells produced after several days of cell division of a fertilized egg. It travels down the fallopian tube to the uterus and implants itself in the uterine wall about two weeks after conception.

Bibliography

Adler, A. *Understanding human nature.* New York: Premier Books, 1959.

Adorno, T. W., Frenkel-Brunswick, E., Levinson, D. J., & Sanford, R. N. *The authoritarian personality.* New York: Harper & Row, Publishers, 1950.

Ainsworth, M. D. S. The development of infant-mother interaction among the Ganda. In B. M. Foss (Ed.), *Determinants of infant behavior.* Vol. II, New York: John Wiley & Sons, Inc., 1963.

Ainsworth, M. D. S., Bell, S. M., & Stayton, D. J. Individual differences in the development of some attachment behaviors. *Merril-Palmer Quarterly,* 1972, *18,* 123–143.

Alcohol and alcoholism. Washington, D.C.: U.S. Government Printing Office, 1972.

Alcohol and Health. Washington, D.C.: U.S. Government Printing Office, 1974.

Aldrich, C. K. *An introduction to dynamic psychiatry.* New York: McGraw-Hill Book Company, 1966.

Allen, V., & Levine, J. Social support and conformity: The role of independent assessment of reality. *Journal of Experimental Social Psychology,* 1971, *7,* 48–58.

Anastasi, A. *Psychological testing.* (4th ed.) New York: Macmillan Publishing Co., Inc., 1976.

Anderson, N. Averaging versus adding as a stimulus combination rule in impression formation. *Journal of Experimental Psychology,* 1965, *70,* 394–400.

Ardrey, R. *The territorial imperative.* New York: Atheneum Publishers, 1966.

Arnold, M. B. On the mechanisms of suggestion and hypnosis. *Journal of Abnormal and Social Psychology,* 1946, *41,* 107–128.

Aronfreed, J., & Reber, A. Internalized behavioral suppression and the timing of social punishment. *Journal of Personality and Social Psychology,* 1965, *1,* 3–16.

Aronson, E., & Linder, D. E. Gain and loss of esteem as determinants of interpersonal attractiveness. *Journal of Experimental Social Psychology,* 1965, *1,* 156–171.

Aronson, E., & Mills, J. The effect of severity of initiation on liking for a group. *Journal of Abnormal and Social Psychology,* 1959, *59,* 177–181.

Asch, S. E. Effects of group pressure upon modification and distortion of judgment. In E. E. Maccoby, T. M. Newcomb, & E. L. Hartley (Eds.), *Readings in social psychology.* (3rd ed.) New York: Holt, Rinehart and Winston, 1958.

Asch, S. Forming impressions of personality. *Journal of Abnormal and Social Psychology,* 1946, *41,* 258–290.

Aserinsky, E., & Kleitman, N. Regularly occurring periods of eye motility and concomitant phenomena during sleep. *Science,* 1953, *118,* 273–274.

Asher, J. Geller demystified? *APA Monitor,* Feb., 1976, p. 4.

Atkinson, R. C. & Shiffrin, R. M. Human memory: A proposed system and its control processes. In K. W. Spence and J. T. Spence (Eds.), *The psychology of learning and motivation: Advances in research and theory.* Vol. 2. New York: Academic Press, 1968.

Axelrod, S., Hall, R. V., Weis, L., & Rohrer, F. Use of self-imposed contingencies to reduce the frequency of smoking behavior. In M. J. Mahoney & C. E. Thoresen (Eds.), *Self-control: Power to the person.* Monterey, Calif.: Brooks/Cole Publishing Company, 1974.

Ayllon, T. & Azrin, N. H. The measurement and reinforcement of behavior of psychotics. *Journal of the Experimental Analysis of Behavior,* 1965, *8,* 357–383.

Ax, A. F. The physiological differentiation between fear and anger in humans. *Psychosomatic Medicine,* 1953, *15,* 433–442.

Badger, E. A mother's training program—the road to a purposeful existence. *Children*, 1971, *18* (5) 168–173(a).

Badger, E. A mother's training program—a sequel article. *Children Today*, 1972, *1* (3) 7–12.

Bales, R. F., & Slater, P. Role differentiation in small decision-making groups. In T. Parson & R. F. Bales (Eds.), *Family, socialization, and interaction process.* New York: The Free Press, 1955. Pp. 259–306.

Baltes, P. B., & Goulet, J. R. Exploration of developmental variables by manipulation and simulation of age differences in behavior. *Human Development*, 1971, *3*, 149–170.

Bandura, A. Influence of models' reinforcement contingencies on the acquisition of imitated responses. *Journal of Personality and Social Psychology*, 1965, *1*, 589–595.

Bandura, A. *Principles of behavior modification.* New York: Holt, Rinehart and Winston, 1969.

Bandura, A. *Aggression: A social learning analysis.* Englewood Cliffs, N.J.: Prentice-Hall, Inc., 1973.

Bandura, A. Behavior theory and the models of man. *American Psychologist*, 1974, *29*, 859–869.

Bandura, A. & Menlove, F. L. Factors determining vicarious extinction of avoidance behavior through symbolic modeling. *Journal of Personality and Social Psychology*, 1968, *8*, 99–108.

Bandura, A, & Walters, R. H. *Adolescent aggression.* New York: The Ronald Press Company, 1959.

Bandura, A., Grusec, J. E., and Menlove, F. L. Vicarious extinction of avoidance behavior. *Journal of Personality and Social Psychology*, 1967, *5*, 16–23.

Bannister, D., & Fransella, F. *Inquiring man: The theory of personal constructs.* Baltimore: Penguin Books, Inc., 1971.

Barber, T. X. Suggested ("hypnotic") behavior: The trance paradigm vs. an alternative paradigm. In E. Fromm & R. E. Shor (Eds.), *Hypnosis: Research developments and perspectives.* Chicago: Aldine Publishing Company, 1972. Pp. 115–182.

Barber, T. X., & Calverley, D. S. Experimental studies in "hypnotic" behavior: Suggested deafness evaluated by delayed auditory feedback. *British Journal of Psychology*, 1964, *55*, 439–446.

Barber, T. X., & Hahn, K. W., Jr. *Suggested dreaming with and without hypnotic induction.* Medfield, Mass.: Medfield Foundation, 1966. (mimeo.)

Barber, T. X., Spanos, N. P., & Chaves, J. F. *Hypnosis, imagination, and human potentialities.* New York: Pergamon Press, Inc., 1974.

Barclay, A. M. Sexual fantasies in men and women. *Medical aspects of human sexuality*, 1973, *7*, 205–216.

Barker, Roger. *Ecological psychology.* Stanford, Calif.: Stanford University Press, 1968.

Barker, R. G., & Gump, P. *Big school, small school.* Stanford: Stanford University Press, 1964.

Barnett, L. D. Women's attitudes toward family life and U.S. population growth. *Pacific Sociological Review*, 1969, *12*, 95–100.

Baron, R. A., Byrne, D., & Griffitt, W. *Social psychology: understanding human interaction.* Boston: Allyn and Bacon, 1974.

Barraclough, B. M. Differences between national suicide rates. *British Journal of Psychiatry*, 1973, *122*, 95–96.

Bateson, G., & Mead, M. *Balinese character.* New York: The New York Academy of Sciences, 1942.

Beach, F. A. It's all in your mind. *Psychology Today*, 1969, *3*, 33–35, 60.

Beary, J. F., & Benson, H. A simple psychophysiologic technique which elicits the hypometabolic changes of the relaxation response. *Psychosomatic Medicine*, 1974, *36*, 115–119.

Beck, A. T. Role of fantasies in psychotherapy and psychopathology. *Journal of Nervous and Mental Disease*, 1970, *150*, 3–17.

Becker, W. C. Early indications of positive outcomes. Washington D.C. National Follow-Through Sponsors Presentation, Educational Staff Seminar, 14 February 1974, quoted in Hunt, J., McV. Reflections on a decade of early education. *Journal of Abnormal and Child Psychology*, 1975, *3* (4), 275–330.

Bee, H. *The developing child.* New York: Harper & Row, Publishers, 1975.

Beecher, H. K. Generalization from pain of various types and diverse origins. *Science*, 1959, *130*, 267–268.

Bem, D. J., & Allen, A. On predicting some of the people some of the time: The search for cross-situational consistencies in behavior. *Psychological Review*, 1974, *81*, 506–520.

Berger, S. M. Conditioning through vicarious instigation. *Psychological Review*, 1962, *69*, 450–466.

Bergin, A. E., & Garfield, S. L. *Handbook of Psychotherapy and Behavior Change.* New York: John Wiley & Sons, Inc., 1971.

Bereiter, C. & Engelmann, S. *Teaching disadvantaged children in the preschool.* Englewood Cliffs, N.J. Prentice-Hall, 1966.

Berkowitz, L. Impulse, aggression and the gun. *Psychology Today*, September, 1968, 18–22.

Berkowitz, L. The frustration-aggression hypothesis revisited. In L. Berkowitz (Ed.), *Roots of aggression: A reexamination of the frustration-aggression hypothesis.* New York: Atherton, 1969.

Berkowitz, L., & LePage, A. Weapons as aggression-eliciting stimuli. *Journal of Personality and Social Psychology*, 1967, *7*, 202–207.

Berne, E. *Games people play.* New York: Grove Press, Inc., 1964.

Bettelheim, B. *The informed heart.* New York: The Free Press, 1960.

Binet, A., & Féré, C. *Animal magnetism.* Englewood Cliffs, N.J.: Prentice-Hall, Inc., 1901.

Blake, R. R., Rheod, C. C., Wedge, B., & Mouton, J. S. Housing, architecture and social interaction. *Sociometry* 1956, *19*, 133–139.

Blakemore, C., & Cooper, G. F. Development of the brain

depends on visual environment. *Nature*, 1970, *228*, 477–478.

Boisen, A. *The exploration of the inner world.* New York: Harper & Row, Publishers, 1952.

Bolles, R. C. Reinforcement, expectancy, and learning. *Psychological Review*, 1972, *79*, 394–409.

Bolles, R. C., *Theory of Motivation.* (2nd ed.) New York: Harper & Row, Publishers, 1975.

Boneau, C. A., & Cuca, J. M. An overview of psychology's human resources: Characteristics and salaries from the 1972 APA Survey. *American Psychologist*, 1974, *29*, 832–840.

Botwinick, J. *Cognitive processes in maturity and old age.* New York: Springer, 1967.

Boudreau, L. A., & Jeffrey, C. J. Stuttering treated by desensitization. *Journal of Behavior Therapy and Experimental Psychiatry*, 1973, *4*, 209–212.

Boulougouris, J. C., Marks, I. M., & Marset, P. Superiority of flooding (implosion) to desensitization for reducing pathological fear. *Behavior Research and Therapy*, 1971, *9*, 7–16.

Bourne, P. G. *Men, stress and Vietnam.* Boston: Little, Brown and Company, 1970.

Bower, G. H., & Clark, M. C. Narrative stories as mediators for serial learning. *Psychonomic Science*, 1969, *14*, 181–182.

Bower, M. B., Jr. *Retreat from sanity: The structure of emerging psychosis.* Baltimore: Penguin Books, Inc., 1974.

Bowlby, J. *Maternal care and mental health.* Monograph series, No. 2. Geneva: World Health Organization, 1951.

Brackbill, Y. Research and clinical work with children. In R. Bauer (Ed.), *Some views on Soviet psychology.* Washington, D.C.: American Psychological Association, 1962.

Bramwell, S. T. Masuda, M., Wagner, N. N., and Holmes, T. H. Psychosocial factors in athletic injuries. *Journal of Human Stress*, 1975, *1*, 6–20.

Broadcasting yearbook, 1971. Washington, D.C.: Broadcasting Publications, Inc., 1971.

Broden, M., Hall, R. V., & Mitts, B. The effect of self-recording on the classroom behavior of two eighth-grade students. *Journal of Applied Behavior Analysis*, 1971, *4*, 191–199.

Bronfenbrenner, U. Is early intervention effective? *Teacher's College Record*, Dec. 1974, *76*, pp. 279–303.

Bronfenbrenner, U. Reality and research in the ecology of human development, *Proceedings of the American Philosophical Society*, 1975, *119*, 439–469.

Brookes, M., & Kaplan, A. The office environment-space planning and affective behavior. *Human Factors*, 1972, *14*, 373–391.

Broverman, I. K., Broverman, D. N., Clarkson, F. E., Rosenkrantz, P. S., & Vogel, S. R. Sex role stereotypes and clinical judgments of mental health. *Journal of Consulting and Clinical Psychology*, 1970, *34*, 1–7.

Brown, R. *Social psychology.* New York: The Free Press, 1965.

Brown, R. *A first language: The early stages.* Cambridge, Mass.: Harvard University Press, 1973.

Bucher, B., & Lovaas, O. I. Use of aversive stimulation in behavior modification. In M. R. Jones (Ed.), *Miami symposium on the prediction of behavior, 1967: Aversive stimulation.* Coral Gables, Florida.: University of Miami Press, 1968. Pp. 77–145.

Burris, R. W. The effect of counseling on achievement motivation. Unpublished doctoral dissertation, Indiana University, 1958.

Burtt, H. E. An experimental study of early childhood memory. *Journal of Genetic Psychology*, 1941, *58*, 435–439.

Bushell, G., Jr. *The behavior analysis classroom.* Lawrence, Kansas: University of Kansas, Department of Human Development, 1970.

Buss, A. H., & Plomin, R. *A temperamental theory of personality development.* New York: Wiley, 1975.

Byrne, D., & Blaylock, B. Similarity and assumed similarity of attitudes between husband and wife. *Journal of Abnormal and Social Psychology*, 1963, *67*, 636–640.

Byrne, D., & DeNinno, J. A. Response to erotic movies as a function of contextual effects. Unpublished manuscript, Purdue University, 1973.

Byrne, D., & Lamberth, J. The effect of erotic stimuli on sex arousal, evaluative responses, and subsequent behavior. In *Technical report of the Commission on Obscenity and Pornography.* Vol. VIII. Washington, D.C.: U.S. Government Printing Office, 1971, pp. 41–67.

Byrne, D., & Nelson, D. Attraction as a linear function of proportion of positive reinforcements. *Journal of Personality and Social Psychology*, 1965, *1*, 659–663.

Byrne, D., Fisher, W., & DeNinno, J. A. *Sexual explicitness and thematic content as determinants of the behavioral effects of erotic films.* Unpublished manuscript, Purdue University, 1975.

Caldwell, B. M. The usefulness of the critical period hypothesis in the study of affiliative behavior. *Merrill-Palmer Quarterly*, 1962, *8*, 219–242.

Calhoun, J. B. Population density and social pathology. *Scientific American*, 1962, *206*, 139–148.

Calverley, D. S., & Barber, T. X. "Hypnosis" and antisocial behavior: An experimental evaluation. Harding, Mass.: Medfield Foundation, 1965. (Mimeo.)

Cameron, P., Robertson, D., & Zaks, J. Sound pollution, noise pollution and health: Community parameters. *Journal of Applied Psychology*, 1972, *56*, 67–74.

Cannon, W. B. The James-Lange theory of emotions: A critical examination and an alternative theory. *American Journal of Psychology*, 1927, *39*, 106–124.

Carlson, R. F., Kincord, J. P., Lance, S., & Hodgeon, T. Spontaneous use of mnemonics and grade point average. *Journal of Psychology*, 1976, *92*, 117–122.

Caro, R. *The power broker: Robert Moses and the fall of New York.* New York: Vintage Books, 1975.

Carpenter, B., Wiener, M., & Carpenter, J. T. Predictability of perceptual defense behavior. *Journal of Abnormal and Social Psychology*, 1956, *52*, 380–383.

599

Cerbos, G. Seasonal variation in some mental health statistics: Suicides, homicides, psychiatric admissions, and institutional placement of the retarded. *Journal of Clinical Psychology*, 1970, *26*, 61–63.

Cerletti, U. Electroshock therapy. In A. M. Sackler, R. R. Sackler, & F. Marti-Ibanez (Eds.), *The great physio-dynamic therapies in psychiatry: An historical reappraisal.* New York: Harper & Row, Publishers, 1956. Pp. 91–120.

Chapman, L. J., & Chapman, J. P. *Disordered thought in schizophrenia.* Englewood Cliffs, N.J.: Prentice-Hall, Inc., 1973.

Chomsky, N. The general properties of language. In C. H. Millikan & F. L. Darley (Eds.), *Brain mechanisms underlying speech and language.* New York: Grune & Stratton, Inc., 1967. Pp. 73–88.

Chomsky, N. *Language and mind.* New York: Harcourt Brace Jovanovich, 1968.

Christian, J. J. Adrenocortical, splenic and reproduction responses of mice to inanition and groupings. *Endocrinology*, 1959, *65*, 189–197.

Christian, J., Flyger, V., & Davis, D. Factors in the mass mortality of a herd of Sitka deer (cervus nippon). *Chesapeake Science*, 1960, *1*, 79–95.

Clark, K., & Clark, M. Racial identification and preference in Negro children. In T. Newcomb & E. Hartley (Eds.), *Readings in social psychology.* New York: Holt, Rinehart and Winston, Inc., 1947. Pp. 169–178.

Clore, G. L., & Jeffery, K. Emotional role playing, attitude change, and attraction toward a disabled person. *Journal of Personality and Social Psychology*, 1972, *23*, 105–111.

Cohen, A. Effects of Noise on psychological state, in W. D. Ward & J. E. Fricke (Eds.), Proceedings of the American Speech and Hearing Association conference on Noise as a public health hazard. Vol. I. Washington D.C.: Speech and Hearing Association, 1969.

Cohen, L. H., Hilgard, E. R., & Wendt, G. R. Sensitivity to light in a case of hysterical blindness studied by reinforcement-inhibition and conditioning methods. *Yale Journal of Biology and Medicine*, 1933, *6*, 61–67.

Colby, K. M., & Enea, H. Heuristic methods for computer understanding of natural language in the context-restricted on-live dialogue. *Mathematical Biosciences*, 1967, *1*, 1–25.

Coleman, J. C. *Abnormal psychology and modern life.* (4th ed.) Glenview, Ill.: Scott, Foresman and Company, 1972.

Coleman, J. C. *Abnormal psychology and modern life.* (5th ed.) Glenview, Ill.: Scott, Foresman and Company, 1976.

Collins, A. M., & Quillian, M. R. Retrieval time from semantic memory. *Journal of Verbal Learning and Verbal Behavior*, 1969, *8*, 240–247.

Craik, F. I. M., & Lockhart, R. S. Levels of processing: A framework for memory research. *Journal of Verbal Learning and Verbal Behavior*, 1972, *11*, 671–684.

Crombag, H. F. M., de Wijkerslooth, J. L., van Tuyll van Serooskerken, E. H. On solving legal problems. *Journal of Legal Education.* 1975, *27*, 168–202.

Crowne, D. P., & Marlowe, D. *The approval motive: Studies in evaluative dependence.* New York: John Wiley & Sons, Inc., 1964.

Culbertson, F. Modification of an emotionally held attitude through role playing. *Journal of Abnormal and Social Psychology*, 1957, *54*, 230–234.

Dale, P. S. *Language development: Structure and function.* (2nd ed.) Hinsdale, Ill.: The Dryden Press, Inc., 1976.

Daniels, R. S. Psychotherapy of depression. *Postgraduate Medicine*, 1962, *32*, 436–441.

Dank, B. M. Coming out in the gay world. *Psychiatry*, 1971, *34*, 180–197.

Darley, J. M., & Latané, B. Bystander intervention in emergencies: Diffusion of responsibility. *Journal of Personality and Social Psychology*, 1968, *8*, 377–383.

Darwin, C. *The expression of emotions in man and animals.* New York: Philosophical Library, Inc., 1872.

Darwin, C. T., Turvey, M. T., & Crowder, R. G. An auditory analogue of the Sperling partial report procedure: Evidence for brief auditory storage. *Cognitive Psychology*, 1972, *3*, 255–267.

Dashiell, John F. *Fundamentals of objective psychology.* Boston: Houghton Mifflin Company, 1928.

Davids, A. Therapeutic approaches to children in residential treatment. *American Psychologist*, 1975, *30*, 809–814.

Davis, C. M. Self-selection of diets by newly weaned infants. *American Journal of Diseases of Children*, 1928, *36*, 651–679.

DeCharms, R., & Moeller, G. H. Values expressed in American children's readers: 1800 to 1950. *Journal of Abnormal and Social Psychology*, 1962, *64*, 135–142.

Deci, E. L. *Intrinsic motivation.* New York: Plenum Publishing Corp., 1975.

Dekker, E., & Groen, J. Reproducible psychogenic attacks of asthma. *Journal of Psychosomatic Research*, 1956, *1*, 58–67.

Delgado, J. M. R. Social rank and radio-stimulated aggressiveness in monkeys. *Journal of Nervous and Mental Disease*, 1967, *144*, 383–390.

De Mause, L. The evolution of childhood. In L. De Mause (Ed.), *The history of childhood.* New York: Harper & Row, Publishers, 1974. P. 51.

Dement, W. C. *Some must watch while some must sleep.* San Francisco: W. H. Freeman and Co., Publishers, 1974.

Dennis, W. Causes of retardation among institutional children: Iran. *Journal of Genetic Psychology*, 1960, *96*, 47–59.

Dewald, P. A. *The psychoanalytic process: A case illustration.* New York: Basic Books, Inc., Publishers, 1972.

Dimond, E. G. Acupuncture anesthesia: Western medicine and Chinese traditional medicine. *Journal of the American Medical Association*, 1971, *218*, 1558–1563.

Dion, K., Berscheid, E., & Walster, E. What is beautiful is good. *Journal of Personality and Social Psychology,* 1972, *24,* 285–290.

Dixon, N. F. *Subliminal perception: The nature of a controversy.* New York: McGraw-Hill Book Company, 1971.

Dobelle, W. H., Mladejovsky, M. G., & Girvin, J. P. Artificial vision for the blind: Electrical stimulation of visual cortex offers hope for a functional prosthesis. *Science,* 1974, *183,* 440–444.

Dohrenwend, B. S., & Dohrenwend, B. B. (Eds.) *Stressful life events: Their nature and effects.* New York: John Wiley & Sons, Inc., 1974.

Dollard, J., Doob, L. W., Miller, N. E., Mowrer, O. H., & Sears, R. R. *Frustration and aggression.* New Haven: Yale University Press, 1939.

Donner, L., & Guerney, B. Z. Automated group desensitization for test anxiety. *Behavior Research and Therapy,* 1969, *7,* 1–13.

Dornbusch, S. M., Hastorf, A. H., Richardson, S. A., Muzzy, R. A., & Vreeland, R. S. The perceiver and the perceived: Their relative influence on the categories of interpersonal cognition. *Journal of Personality and Social Psychology,* 1965, *1,* 434–440.

Douglas, W. O. *Go east, young man.* New York: Random House, Inc., 1974.

Drenth, P. J. D. Psychological tests for developing countries: Rational and objectives. In *Nederlands Tijdschrift Voor de Psychologie,* 1975, *30,* 5–22.

Dubois, P. H. *A history of psychological testing.* Boston: Allyn & Bacon, Inc., 1970.

Duncker, K. On problem solving. *Psychological Monographs,* 1945, *58,* No. 5 (Whole No. 270).

Dwarnicka, B., Jasienska, A., Smolarz, W., & Wawryk, R. Attempt of determining the fetal reaction to acoustic stimulation. *Acta Oto-larynogologica,* 1964, *57,* 571–574.

D'Zurilla, T. Recall efficiency and mediating cognitive events in "experimental repression." *Journal of Personality and Social Psychology,* 1965, *1,* 253–257.

Easton, K. An unusual case of fugue and orality. *Psychoanalytic Quarterly,* 1959, *28,* 505–513.

Edwards, A. E., & Acker, L. E. A demonstration of the long-term retention of a conditioned galvanic skin response. *Psychosomatic Medicine,* 1962, *24,* 459–463.

Edwards, A. L. The relationship between the judged desirability of a trait and the probability that the trait will be endorsed. *Journal of Applied Psychology,* 1953, *37,* 90–93.

Eibl-Eibesfeldt, I. The fighting behavior of animals. *Scientific American,* 1961, *205,* 112–122.

Eibl-Eibesfeldt, I. *Ethology: The biology of behavior.* New York: Holt, Rinehart and Winston, Inc., 1970.

Eiseley, L. *The immense journey.* New York: Random House, Inc., 1946.

Ekman, P. & Friesen, W. V. *Unmasking the face.* Englewood Cliffs, N.J.: Prentice-Hall, Inc., 1975.

Elliot, C. D. Noise tolerance and extroversion in children. *British Journal of Psychology,* 1971, *62,* 375–380.

Ellis, A. *Reason and emotion in psychotherapy.* Secaucus, N.J.: Lyle Stuart, Inc., 1962.

Ellis, A. Rational-emotive therapy. In L. Hersher (Ed.), *Four psychotherapies.* Englewood Cliffs, N.J.: Prentice-Hall, Inc., 1970. Pp. 47–72.

Ellis, E. *Humanistic psychotherapy.* New York: McGraw-Hill Book Company, 1973.

Elstein, A. S., Kagan, N., Shulman, L. S., Jason, H., & Loupe, M. J. Methods and theory in the study of medical inquiry. *Journal of Medical Education,* 1972, *47,* 85–92.

Epstein, A. W. Fetishism. In R. Slovenko (Ed.), *Sexual behavior and the law.* Springfield, Ill.: Charles C Thomas, Publisher, 1965. Pp. 515–520.

Epstein, J. The last days of New York. *New York Review of Books,* Feb. 19, 1976.

Eriksen, C. W. Discrimination and learning without awareness: A methodological survey and evaluation. *Psychological Review,* 1960, *67,* 279–300.

Erikson, E. *Childhood and society.* New York: W. W. Norton & Company, Inc., 1963.

Erikson, E. *Identity: Youth and crisis.* New York: W. W. Norton & Company, Inc., 1968.

Evans, J. R., Selstad, G., & Welcher, W. H. Teenagers: Fertility control behavior and attitudes before and after abortion, childbearing, or negative pregnancy test. *Family Planning Perspectives,* 1976, *8,* 192–200.

Evans, M. B., & Paul, G. L. Effects of hypnotically suggested analgesia on physiological and subjective responses to cold stress. *Journal of Consulting and Clinical Psychology,* 1970, *35,* 362–371.

Evans, R. I., Rozelle, R. M., Lasater, T. M., Dembroski, T. M., & Allen, B. P. Fear arousal, persuasion, and actual vs. implied behavioral change: New perspectives utilizing a real-life dental hygiene program. *Journal of Personality and Social Psychology,* 1970, *16,* 220–227.

Eysenck, H. J. *The IQ argument: Race, intelligence, and education.* La Salle, Ill.: Open Court Publishing Company, 1971.

Eysenck, H. J. Obscenity—officially speaking. *Penthouse,* 1972, *3* (11), 95–102.

Eysenck, H. J. *The inequality of man.* Glasgow, Scotland: Fontona Collins, 1975, p. 146.

Fanning, D. M. Families in flats. *British Medical Journal,* 1967, *4,* 382–386.

Fantz, R. L. Pattern vision in newborn infants. *Science,* 1963, *140,* 296–297.

Farrell, B. Scientists, theologians, mystics swept up in a psychic revolution. *Life,* March 25, 1966.

Feldman-Summers, S., & Kiesler, S. B. Those who are number two try harder: The effect of sex on attributions of causality. *Journal of Personality and Social Psychology,* 1974, *30,* 846–855.

Felipe, N. J., & Sommer, R. Invasion of personal space. *Social Problems,* 1966–67, *14,* 206–214.

601

Ferster, C. B., & Skinner, B. F. *Schedules of reinforcement.* Englewood Cliffs, N.J.: Prentice-Hall, Inc., 1957.

Festinger, L., & Carlsmith, J. M. Cognitive consequences of forced compliance. *Journal of Abnormal and Social Psychology,* 1959, 58, 203–210.

Festinger, L., Riecken, H. W., & Schachter, S. *When prophecy fails.* Minneapolis: University of Minnesota Press, 1956.

Festinger, L. Schachter, S., & Back, K. *Social pressures in informal groups.* New York: Harper & Row, Publishers, 1950.

Fiedler, F. *A theory of leadership effectiveness.* New York: McGraw-Hill Book Company, 1967.

Fields, S. Ounces of prevention. *Innovations,* 1976, 3, 2–25.

Finkelman, J. M., & Glass, D. C. Reappraisal of the relationship between noise and human performance by means of a subsidiary task measure. *Journal of Applied Psychology,* 1970, 54, 211–213.

Fixsen, D. L., Phillips, E. L., & Wolf, M. M. Achievement Place: Experiments in self government with pre-delinquents. *Journal of Applied Behavior Analysis,* 1973, 6, 31–47.

Flavell, J. H. Cognitive changes in adulthood. In L. R. Goulet & P. B. Boltes (Eds.), *Life-span developmental psychology.* New York: Academic Press, 1970.

Fleming, J. F. Field report: The state of the apes. *Psychology Today,* 1974, 7, 31–38.

Fowles, J. *The French lieutenant's woman.* Boston: Little, Brown and Company, 1969.

Frank, J. D. Therapeutic components of psychotherapy. *Journal of Nervous and Mental Disease,* 1974, 159, 325–342.

Frankenburg, W. K. & Dodds, J. B. The Denver developmental screening test, *Journal of Pediatrics,* 1967, 71, p. 185.

Frankl, V. E. *Man's search for meaning: An introduction to logotherapy.* Boston: Beacon Press, Inc., 1962.

Fraser, S., Gouge, C., & Billig, M. Risky shifts, cautious shifts, and group polarization. *European Journal of Social Psychology,* 1971, 1, 7–29.

Freedman, Jonathan. *Crowding and behavior.* New York: The Viking Press, Inc., 1975.

Freedman, J. L., Klevansky, S., & Ehrlich, P. The effect of crowding on human task performance. *Journal of Applied Social Psychology,* 1971, 1, 7–25.

Freedman, J. L., Levy, A. S., Buchanan, R. W., & Price, J. Crowding and human aggressiveness. *Journal of Experimental Social Psychology,* 1972, 8, 528–548.

Freedman, J. L., & Loftus, E. F. Retrieval words from long-term memory. *Journal of Verbal Learning and Verbal Behavior,* 1971, 10, 107–115.

Freud, S. *A general introduction to psychoanalysis,* trans. Joan Riviere. London: Hogarth Press, 1935. Pp. 353–362.

Freud, S. *Selected papers.* Vol. 3. London: Hogarth Press, 1950 (originally published 1909).

Freud, S. Analysis of a phobia in a five-year-old boy (1909). In *Collected works of Sigmund Freud.* Vol. 10. London: Hogarth Press, 1955.

Freud, S. *The standard edition of the complete psychological works of Sigmund Freud.* Vol. XXII. *New introductory lectures on psychoanalysis.* London: Hogarth Press, 1964.

Friedman, C. N., Greenspan, R., & Mittleman, F. The decision-making process and the outcome of therapeutic abortion. *American Journal of Psychiatry,* 1974, 131, 1332–1337.

Friedman, M., & Rosenman, R. H. *Type A behavior and your heart.* New York: Alfred A. Knopf, Inc., 1974.

Fuhrer, M. J., & Baer, P. E. Differential classical conditioning: Verbalization of stimulus contingencies. *Science,* 1965, 150, 1479–1481.

Funkenstein, D. H., King, S. H., & Drolette, M. E. *Mastery of stress.* Cambridge, Mass.: Harvard University Press, 1957.

Galanter, E. Contemporary psychophysics. In Brown, R., et al. (Eds.) *New directions in psychology.* New York: Holt, Rinehart and Winston, 1962.

Galle, O. R., Gove, W. R., & McPherson, J. M. Population density and pathology: What are the relations for man? *Science,* 1972, 176, 23–30.

Galton, F. *Hereditary genius: An inquiry into its laws and consequences.* London: Macmillan & Company Ltd., 1869.

Ganzer, V. J. & Sarason, I. G. Variables associated with recidivism among juvenile delinquents. *Journal of Consulting and Clinical Psychology,* 1973, 40, 1–5.

Gardner, R. A., & Gardner, B. T., 1969. Teaching sign language to a chimpanzee. *Science.* 165, 664–672.

Garmezy, N. Children at risk: The search for the antecedents of schizophrenia. I. Conceptual models and research methods. *Schizophrenia Bulletin.* Rockville, Md.: Center for Studies of Schizophrenia, National Institute of Mental Health, Spring 1974.

Gaudia, G. Race, social class, and age of achievement of conservation of Piaget's tasks. *Developmental Psychology,* 1972, 6, 158–167.

Gazzaniga, M.S. The split brain in man. *Scientific American,* 1967, 217, 24–29.

Geen, R. G., & Berkowitz, L. Name-mediated aggressive cue properties. *Journal of Personality,* 1966, 34, 456–465.

Geen, R. G., & Pigg, R. Acquisition of an aggressive response and its generalization to verbal behavior. *Journal of Personality and Social Psychology,* 1970, 15, 165–170.

Gesell, Arnold. The ontogenesis of infant behavior. In L. Carmichael (Ed.), *Manual of child psychology.* New York: John Wiley & Sons, Inc., 1946. Pp. 295–331.

Gibson, E. J., & Walk, R. D. The "visual cliff." *Scientific American,* 1960, 202, 64–71.

Ginsburg, H. *The myth of the deprived child.* Englewood Cliffs, N.J.: Prentice-Hall, Inc., 1972.

Glass, D., & Singer, J., *Urban stress: Experiments on noise and social stressors.* New York: Academic Press, Inc., 1973.

602

Glueck, S., & Glueck, E. *Unraveling juvenile delinquency.* New York: The Commonwealth Fund, 1950.

Gochman, I. R. Causes of perceived crowding unrelated to density. Unpublished Ph.D. dissertation, University of Washington, 1976.

Goldfried, M. R., & Davison, G. C. *Clinical behavior therapy.* New York: Holt, Rinehart and Winston, Inc., 1976.

Goldsmith, J. R., & Jansson, E. Health effects of community noise. *American Journal of Public Health,* 1973, 63, 782–793.

Goldstein, A. P. *Structured learning therapy: Toward a psychotherapy for the poor.* New York: Academic Press, 1973.

Goldstein, M., Kant, H., Judd, L., Rice, C., & Green, R. Experience with pornography: Rapists, pedophiles, homosexuals, transsexuals, and controls. *Archives of Sexual Behavior,* 1971, 1, 1–15.

Goranson, R. E., & King, D. Rioting and daily temperature: Analysis of the U.S. riots in 1967. Unpublished manuscript, York University, 1970.

Gottesman, I. I. Heritability of personality: A demonstration. *Psychological Monographs,* 1963, 77, No. 9 (Whole No. 572).

Gove, W. R., & Tudor, J. F. Adult sex roles and mental illness. *American Journal of Sociology,* 1973, 78, 812–835.

Graham, C., & Leibowitz, H. W. The effect of suggestion on visual acuity. *International Journal of Clinical and Experimental Hypnosis,* 1972, 20, 169–186.

Green, E. Biofeedback for mind/body self-regulation: Feeling & creativity. *Biofeedback and self control.* Chicago: Aldine Publishing Company, 1972. Pp. 152–166.

Green, R. *Sexual identity conflicts in children and adults.* New York: Basic Books, Inc., Publishers, 1974.

Green, R., & Money, J. (Eds.) *Transsexualism and sex reassignment.* Baltimore: The Johns Hopkins University Press, 1969.

Gregory, R. L. *Eye and brain.* New York: McGraw-Hill Book Company, 1966.

Griffitt, W. Response to erotica and the projection of response to erotica in the opposite sex. *Journal of Experimental Research in Personality,* 1973, 6, 330–338.

Griffitt, W., & Veitch, R. Hot and crowded: Influences of population density and temperature on interpersonal affective behavior. *Journal of Personality and Social Psychology,* 1971, 17, 92–98.

Grings, W. W., & Lockhart, R. A. Effect of "anxiety-lessening" instructions and differential set development on the extinction of GSR. *Journal of Experimental Psychology,* 1963, 66, 292–299.

Grossack, M. M., & Gardner, H. *Man and men: social psychology as a social science.* Scranton, Pa.: International Textbook, 1970.

Groves, W. E., Rossi, P. H., & Grafstein, D. Study of life styles and campus communities. A preliminary report for students who participated. Department of Social Relations, Johns Hopkins University, 1970.

Guilford, J. P. *The nature of human intelligence.* New York: McGraw-Hill Book Company, 1967.

Gustavson, C. R., Garcia, J., Hankins, W. G., & Rusiniak, K. W. Coyote predation control by aversive conditioning. *Science,* 1974, 184, 581–583.

Haas, H., Fink, H., & Hartfelder, G. Das placeboproblem. *Psychopharmacology Service Center Bulletin,* 1959, 2 (8), 1–65 (translation) U.S. Public Health Service.

Haavio-Manilla, E. Sex-role attitudes in Finland 1966–1970. *Journal of Social Issues,* 1972, 28, pp. 93–110.

Haber, R. N., & Haber, R. B. Eidetic imagery: I, Frequency. *Perceptual and Motor Skills,* 1964, 19, 131–138.

Hall, E. T. *The silent language.* Garden City, N.Y.: Doubleday & Company, Inc., 1959.

Hall, E. T. *The hidden dimension.* Garden City, N.Y.: Doubleday & Company, Inc., 1966.

Halsell, G. *Soul sister.* New York: Fawcett World Library, 1969.

Hamblin, R. L., Buckholdt, D., Ferritor, D., Kozloff, M., & Blackwell, L. *The humanization processes: A social, behavioral analysis of children's problems.* New York: John Wiley & Sons, Inc., 1971.

Hansel, C. E. M. *ESP: A scientific evaluation.* New York: Charles Scribner's Sons, 1966.

Hariton, E. B., & Singer, J. L. Women's fantasies during sexual intercourse: Normative and theoretical implications. *Journal of Consulting and Clinical Psychology,* 1974, 42, 313–322.

Harlow, H. F. and Zimmerman, R. R. Affectional responses in the infant monkey. *Science,* 1959, 130, 422.

Harlow, J. M. Recovery from the passage of an iron bar through the head. *Publication of the Massachusetts Medical Society,* 1868, 2, 327.

Harris, T. A. *I'm ok-you're ok.* New York: Harper & Row, Publishers, 1967.

Hartley, S. F. Our growing problem: Population. *Social Problems.* 21(2), Fall, 1973.

Hartshorne, H., & May, M. A. *Studies in deceit.* New York: Macmillan Publishing Co., Inc., 1928.

Hastorf, A., & Cantril, H. They saw a game: A case study. *Journal of Abnormal and Social Psychology,* 1954, 49, 129–134.

Heath, R. G. Pleasure and brain activity in man. *Journal of Nervous and Mental Disorders,* 1972, 154, 3–18.

Heber, R., Garber, H., Harrington, S., and Hoffman, C. Rehabilitation of families at risk for mental retardation. Unpublished progress report, Research and Training Center, University of Wisconsin, Madison, Wisconsin, December, 1972.

Hendin, D. Is acupuncture today's medical miracle? In *Acupuncture: What can it do for you?* New York: Newspaper Enterprise Association, 1972. Pp. 4–7.

Hersen, M., Gullick, E. L., Matherne, P. M., & Harbert, T. L. Instructions and reinforcement in the modification of a conversion reaction. *Psychological Reports,* 1972, 31, 719–722.

Hilgard, E. R. *Hypnotic susceptibility.* New York: Harcourt Brace Jovanovich, 1965.

603

Hilgard, J. R. *Personality and hypnosis.* Chicago: University of Chicago Press, 1970.

Hindelang, M. J., Dunn C. S., Sutton, L. P., & Aumick, A. *Sourcebook of criminal justice statistics, 1975.* Washington, D.C.: U.S. Government Printing Office, 1976.

Hiroto, D. S. Locus of control and learned helplessness. *Journal of Experimental Psychology,* 1974, *102,* 187–193.

Hoffman, A. Psychotomimetic agents. An A. Burger (Ed.), *Drugs affecting central nervous system.* Vol. 2. New York: Marcel Dekker, Inc., 1968. Pp. 169–236.

Hoffman, M. L. Power assertion by the parent and its impact on the child. *Child Development,* 1960, *31,* 129–143.

Hoffman, M. L. Moral development. In P. H. Mussen (Ed.), *Carmichael's manual of child psychology.* (3rd ed.) Vol. 2. New York: John Wiley & Sons, Inc., 1970, pp. 261–359.

Hogan, R. A., & Kirchner, J. H. Preliminary report of the extinction of learned fears via shortterm implosive therapy. *Journal of Abnormal Psychology,* 1967, *72,* 106–109.

Hohm, Charles F. A human-ecological approach to the reality and perception of air pollution. *Pacific Sociological Review,* 1976, *19,* 21–43.

Hollander, E. P., & Webb, W. B. Leadership, followership, and friendship. *Journal of Abnormal and Social Psychology,* 1955, *50,* 163–167.

Holmes, T. H., & Rahe, R. H. The social readjustment rating scale. *Journal of Psychosomatic Research,* 1967, *11,* 213–218.

Homme, L. E. Perspectives in psychology XXIV: Control of coverants, the operants of the mind. *Psychological Record,* 1965, *15,* 501–511.

Honzik, M. P., Macfarlane, J. & Allen, L. The stability of mental test performance between two and eighteen years. *Journal of Experimental Education,* 1948, *17,* 454–455.

Horan, J. J., & Johnson, R. G. Coverant conditioning through self-management application of the Premack principle: Its effect on weight reduction. *Journal of Behavior Therapy and Experimental Psychiatry,* 1971, *2,* 243–249.

Horn, P. (Ed). Newsline. *Psychology Today,* 1975, *9,* 26–27.

Horner, M. S. A psychological barrier to achievement in women—the motive to avoid success. Symposium presentation at the Midwestern Psychological Association, May, 1968, Chicago.

Horner, M. S. The motive to avoid success and changing aspirations of college women. In J. M. Bardwick (Ed.), *Readings on the psychology of women.* New York: Harper & Row, Publishers, 1972. Pp. 62–67.

Horner, M. S. Toward an understanding of achievement-related conflicts in women. *Journal of Social Issues,* 1972, *28,* 157–175.

Hovland, C. I., & Sears, R. R. Minor studies of aggression: Correlation of lynchings with economic indices. *Journal of Psychology,* 1940, *9,* 301–310.

Hovland, C. I., Janis, I. L., & Kelley, H. H. *Communication and persuasion.* New Haven: Yale University Press, 1953.

Hovland, C. I., & Weiss, W. The influence of source credibility on communication effectiveness. *Public Opinion Quarterly,* 1951, *15,* 635–650.

Howard, J. L., Reifler, C. G., & Liptzin, M. B. Effects of exposure to pornography. In *Technical report of the Commission on Obscenity and Pornography.* Vol. VIII. Washington, D.C.: U.S. Government Printing Office, 1971. Pp. 97–132.

Hraba, J., & Grant, G. Black is beautiful: A re-examination of racial preferences and identification. *Journal of Personality and Social Psychology,* 1970, *16,* 398–402.

Hudson, L. *The cult of the fact.* New York: Harper & Row, Publishers, 1972.

Hunt, M. *Sexual behavior in the 1970's.* Chicago: Playboy Press, 1974.

Ikemi, Y., & Nakagawa, S. A psychosomatic study of contagious dermatitis. *Kyushu Journal of Medical Science,* 1962, *13,* 335–350.

Institute for Social Research *Newsletter.* Boring jobs are hardest on health, a study of 23 occupations reveals. Ann Arbor, Mich.: Spring, 1975, 3–4.

Ittelson, W. H., Proshansky, H. M., Rivlin, L. G., & Winkel, G. H. *An Introduction to environmental psychology.* New York: Holt, Rinehart and Winston, Inc., 1974.

Izard, C. E. Personality similarity, positive affect, and interpersonal attraction. *Journal of Abnormal and Social Psychology,* 1960, *61,* 484–485.

Jacobs, J. *The death and life of great American cities.* London: Pelican Books, 1965 (originally published 1961).

Jacobs, P. A., Brunton, M., & Melville, M. N. Aggressive behavior, mental sub-normality and the XYY male. *Nature,* 1965, *208,* 1351–1352.

James, W. *The principles of psychology.* New York: Holt, Rinehart and Winston, Inc., 1890.

Janis, I. *Victims of groupthink: A psychological study of foreign-policy decisions and fiascos.* Boston: Houghton Mifflin Company, 1972.

Janis, I. L., & Feshbach, S. Effects of fear-arousing communications. *Journal of Abnormal and Social Psychology,* 1953, *48,* 78–92.

Janis, I. L., & Mann, L. Effectiveness of emotional role playing in modifying smoking habits and attitudes. *Journal of Experimental Research in Personality,* 1965, *1,* 84–90.

Jensen, A. R. How much can we boost IQ and scholastic achievement? *Harvard Educational Review,* 1969, *30,* 1–123.

Johnson, R. N. *Aggression in man and animals.* Philadelphia: W. B. Saunders Company, 1972.

Jones, E. E., & Nisbett, R. E. The actor and the observer: Divergent perceptions of the causes of behavior. In E. E. Jones et al. (Eds.), *Attribution: Perceiving the causes of* behavior. Morristown, N.J.: General Learning Press, 1972.

Jones, K. L., Shainberg, L. W., & Byer, C. O. *Sex and people.* New York: Harper & Row, Publishers, 1977.

Kaats, G. R., & Davis, K. E. The dynamics of sexual behavior of college students. *Journal of Marriage and Family,* 1970, 32, 390–399.

Kagan, J. Reflection-impulsivity and reading ability in primary grade children. *Child Development,* 1965, 36, 609–628.

Kahn, M., & Baker, B. Desensitization with minimal therapist contacts. *Journal of Abnormal Psychology,* 1968, 73, 198–200.

Kallmann, J., & Jarvik, F. Individual differences in constitution and genetic background. In James E. Birren (Ed.), *Handbook of aging and the individual.* Chicago: University of Chicago Press, 1969.

Kanellakos, D. T., & Lukas, J. S. *The psychobiology of transcendental meditation: A literature review.* Menlo Park, Calif.: W. A. Benjamin, Inc., 1974.

Kanfer, F. H., & Goldstein, A. P. (Eds.) *Helping people change.* Elmsford, N.Y.: Pergamon Press, Inc., 1975.

Kanter, A. M., & Zelnick, M. Contraception and frequency: Experience of young unmarried women in the United States. *Family Planning Perspectives,* 1973, 5, 21–35.

Kaplan, B. (Ed.) *The inner world of mental illness.* New York: Harper & Row, Publishers, 1964.

Kaplan, H. S. *The new sex therapy.* New York: Brunner/Mazel, 1974.

Kasamatsu, A., & Hirai, T. An EEG study on the Zen meditation. *Folia Psyckiatria Neurologica Japonica Journal,* 1966, 20, 315–336.

Katchadourian, H. A., & Lunde, D. T. *Fundamentals of human sexuality.* (2nd ed.) New York: Holt, Rinehart and Winston, Inc., 1975.

Keating, J. P., & Snowball, H. The effect of crowding and depersonalization on group atmosphere. Paper presented at the Western Psychological Association Convention, San Francisco, 1974.

Kelley, H., & Thibaut. J. Group problem solving. In G. E. Lindzey & E. Aronson (Eds.), *The handbook of social psychology.* (2nd ed.) Vol. 4. Reading, Mass.: Addison-Wesley Publishing Co., Inc., 1969. Pp. 1–101.

Kelman, H. Processes of opinion change. *Public Opinion Quarterly,* 1961, 25, 57–78.

Kelman, H. C., & Hovland, C. I. "Reinstatement" of the communicator in delayed measurement of opinion change. *Journal of Abnormal and Social Psychology,* 1953, 48, 327–335.

Kenyon, F. E. Studies in female homosexuality: Psychological test results. *Journal of Consulting and Clinical Psychology,* 1968, 32, 510–513.

Kenyon, F. E. Homosexuality in the female. *British Journal of Hospital Medicine,* 1970, 3, 183–206.

Kerckhoff, A. C., & Davis, K. E. Value consensus and need complementarity in mate selection. *American Sociological Review,* 1962, 27, 295–303.

Kerner, O. et al. *Report of the National Advisory Commission of Civil Disorders.* New York: Bantam Books, Inc., 1968.

Kimmel, D. C. *Adulthood and aging.* New York: John Wiley & Sons, Inc., 1974.

King, M., & Sobel, D. Sex on the college campus: Current attitudes and behavior. *Journal of College Student Personnel,* 1975, 16, 205–209.

Kinsey, A. C., Pomeroy, W. B., & Martin, C. E. *Sexual behavior in the human male.* Philadelphia: W. B. Saunders Company, 1948.

Kinsey, A. C., Pomeroy, W. B., Martin, C. E., & Gebhard, P. H. *Sexual behavior in the human female.* Philadelphia: W. B. Saunders Company, 1953.

Kintsch, W. *Learning, memory and conceptual processes.* New York: John Wiley & Sons, Inc., 1970.

Kinzel, A. F. Body-buffer zone in violent prisoners. *American Journal of Psychiatry,* 1970, 127, 59064.

Kleinmuntz, B. *Essentials of abnormal psychology.* New York: Harper & Row, Publishers, 1974.

Kleitman. N. *Sleep and wakefulness.* Chicago: University of Chicago Press, 1939.

Kohlberg, L. Development of moral character and moral ideology. In M. L. Hoffman & L. W. Hoffman (Eds.), *Review of child development research.* Vol. 1. New York: Russell Sage Foundation, 1964.

Kohlberg, L. A cognitive-developmental analysis of children's sex-role concepts and attitudes. In E. E. Maccoby (Ed.), *The development of sex differences.* Stanford, Calif.: Stanford University Press, 1966. Pp. 82–172.

Kohlberg, L., & Zigler, E. The impact of cognitive maturity on the development of sex-role attitudes in the years 4 to 8. *Genetic Psychology Monographs,* 1967, 75, 84–165.

Kohlenberg, R., & Phillips, T. Reinforcement and rate of litter depositing. *Journal of Applied Behavior Analysis,* 1973, 6, 391–396.

Köhler, Wolfgang. *The mentality of apes.* (2nd ed. rev.) London: Routledge & Kegan Paul, 1956. (First published in German in 1917.)

Korchin, S. J. *Modern clinical psychology.* New York: Basic Books, Inc., Publishers, 1976.

Kosambi, D. D. Living prehistory in India. *Scientific American,* 1967, 216, 105.

Kroeber, A. L. *Anthropology.* New York: Harcourt Brace Jovanovich, 1948.

Kuo, Z. Y. *The dynamics of behavior development.* New York: Random House, Inc., 1967.

Kutschinsky, B. The effect of pornography: A pilot experiment on perception, behavior, and attitudes. In *Technical report of the Commission on Obscenity and Pornography.* Vol. VIII. Washington, D.C.: U.S. Government Printing Office, 1971. Pp. 133–169.

Lacey, J. I., & Lacey, B. C. Verification and extension of the principle of autonomic response stereotypy. *American Journal of Psychology,* 1958, 71, 50–73.

Lagerspetz, K. Y., Tirri, H. R., & Lagerspetz, K. M. J. Neurochemical and endocrinological studies of mice selec-

605

tively bred for aggressiveness. *Scandinavian Journal of Psychology,* 1968, 9, 157–160.

Laing, R. D. *The divided self.* New York: Pantheon Books, Inc., 1969.

Lakin, M. Personality factors in mothers of excessively crying (colicky) infants. *Monographs of the Society for Research in Child Development,* 1957, 22, No. 64.

Lawrence, J. E. S. Science and sentiment: Overview of research on crowding and human behavior. *Psychological Bulletin,* 1974, 81, 712–822.

Lazarus, A. A. *Multimodal behavior therapy.* New York: Springer-Verlag New York, Inc., 1976.

Lazarus, R. S. *Psychological stress and the coping process.* New York: McGraw-Hill Book Company, 1966.

Lazarus, R. S. Emotions and adaptation: Conceptual and empirical relations. In W. J. Arnold (Ed.), *Nebraska Symposium on Motivation.* Lincoln: University of Nebraska Press, 1968.

Lazarus, R. S., & McCleary, R. A. Autonomic discrimination without awareness: A study of subception. *Psychological Review,* 1951, 58, 113–122.

Lefkowitz, M. N., Eron, L. D., Walder, L. O., & Huesmann, L. R. Television violence and child aggression: A follow-up study. In G. A. Comstock & E. A. Rubinstein (Eds.), *Television and social behavior.* Vol. III. *Television and adolescents' aggressiveness.* Washington, D.C.: U.S. Government Printing Office, 1972. Pp. 35–135.

Lekberg, C. The tyranny of qwerty. *Saturday Review,* September 30, 1972, pp. 37–40.

Lepper, M. R., Greene, D., & Nisbett, R. E. Undermining children's intrinsic interest with extrinsic reward: A test of the "overjustification" hypothesis. *Journal of Personality and Social Psychology,* 1973, 28, 129–137.

Lerner, M. J., & Simmons, C. H. Observer's reaction to the "innocent victim." *Journal of Personality and Social Psychology,* 1966, 4, 203–210.

LeShan, L. An emotional life-history pattern associated with neoplastic disease. *Annals of the New York Academy of Sciences,* 1966, 125, 780–793.

Lester, D. Social disorganization and completed suicide. *Social Psychiatry,* 1970, 5, 175–176.

Lester, G., & Lester, D. *Suicide: The gamble with death.* Englewood Cliffs, N.J.: Prentice-Hall, Inc., 1971.

Levenstein, P. The mother-child home program. In M. C. Day and R. K. Parker (Eds.). *The preschool in action* (2nd ed.). Boston: Allyn and Bacon, 1976.

Levenstein P., & Sunley, R. Stimulation of verbal interaction between disadvantaged mothers and children. *American Journal of Orthopsychiatry,* 1968, 38, 116–121.

Levinger, G., & Breedlove, J. Interpersonal attraction and agreement: A study of marriage partners. *Journal of Personality and Social Psychology,* 1966, 3, 367–372.

Levy, L. H. *Conceptions of personality.* New York: Random House, Inc., 1971.

Liebert, R. M., Poulos, R. W., & Strauss, G. D. *Developmental psychology.* Englewood Cliffs, N.J.: Prentice-Hall, Inc., 1974.

Linder, D. E., & Worchel, S. Opinion change as a result of effortfully drawing a counterattitudinal conclusion. *Journal of Experimental Social Psychology,* 1970, 6, 432–448.

Lion, J. R., Bach-y-Rita, G., & Ervin, F. R. Enigmas of violence. *Science,* 1969, 164, 1465.

Lipsitt, L. P. Learning in the first year of life. In L. P. Lipsitt and C. C. Spiker (Eds.), *Advances in child development and behavior.* Vol. I. New York: Academic Press, 1963.

Loehlin, John C. Lindzey, G., & Spuhler, J. R. *Race differences in intelligence.* San Francisco: W. H. Freeman and Co. Publishers, 1975.

Loftus, E. F., & Palmer, J. C. Reconstruction of automobile destruction: An example of the interaction between language and memory. *Journal of Verbal Learning and Verbal Behavior,* 1974, 13, 585–589.

London, P. *Behavior control.* New York: Harper & Row, Publishers, 1969.

Loo, C. M. The effects of spatial density on the social behavior of children. *Journal of Applied Social Psychology,* 1972, 2, 372–381.

Lorayne, H., & Lucas, J. *The memory book.* New York: Ballantine Books, Inc., 1974.

Lorenz, K. *On aggression.* New York: Harcourt Brace Jovanovich, 1976.

Lovitt, T. C., & Curtiss, K. Academic response rate as a function of teacher- and self-imposed contingencies. *Journal of Applied Behavior Analysis,* 1969, 2, 49–53.

Luchins, A. S. Primacy-recency in impression formation. In C. I. Hovland (Ed.), *The order of presentation in persuasion.* New Haven: Yale University Press, 1957. Pp. 33–61.

Luria, A. R. *The mind of a mnemonist.* New York: Basic Books, Inc., Publishers, 1968.

Lynch, K. *The image of the city.* Cambridge, Mass.: The M.I.T. Press, 1960.

Lynch, K., & Rivkin, M. Walk around the block. *Landscape,* 1959, 8, 24–32.

Maccoby, E. E., & Feldman, S. S. Mother-attachment and stranger-relations in the third year of life. *Monographs of the Society for Research in Child Development,* 1972, 37, No. 1 (Whole No. 146).

Maccoby, E. E., & Jacklin, C. N. *The psychology of sex differences.* Stanford, Calif.: Stanford University Press, 1974.

Maccoby, E. E., & Maccoby, N. The interview: A tool of social science. In G. Lindzey (Ed.), *Handbook of social psychology.* Cambridge, Mass.: Addison-Wesley Publishing Co., Inc., 1954. Pp. 449–487.

Maccoby, E. E., & Masters, J. C. Attachment and dependency. In P. H. Mussen (Ed.), *Carmichael's manual of child psychology.* (3rd ed.) Vol. 2. New York: John Wiley & Sons, Inc., 1970.

MacKinnon, D. W. The nature and nurture of creative talent. *American Psychologist,* 1962, 17, 484–495.

MacKinnon, D. W. Assessing creative persons. *Journal of Creative Behavior,* 1967, 1, 291–304.

MacLeod, J. Lipe ignored obvious hypothesis (comment). *American Psychologist*, 1972, 27, 233.

Mahoney, M. J. Self-reward and self-monitoring techniques for weight control. *Behavior Therapy*, 1974, 5, 48–57.

Mahoney, M. J., Moura, N. G. M., & Wade, T. C. The relative efficacy of self-reward, self-punishment, and self-monitoring techniques for weight loss. *Journal of Consulting and Clinical Psychology*, 1973, 40, 404–407.

Maier, N. R. F. Reasoning in humans. II. The solution of a problem and its appearance in consciousness. *Journal of Comparative Psychology*, 1931, 12, 181–194.

Mallick, S. K., & McCandless, B. R. A study of catharsis of aggression. *Journal of Personality and Social Psychology*, 1966, 4, 591–596.

Maltz, M. *Psycho-cybernetics*. Englewood Cliffs, N.J.: Prentice-Hall, Inc., 1960.

Man, P. L., & Chen, C. H. Acupuncture "anesthesia"—A new theory and clinical study. *Current Therapeutic Research*, 1972, 14, 390–394.

Mann, J., Sidman, J., & Starr, S. Effects of erotic films on sexual behavior of married couples. In *Technical report of the Commission on Obscenity and Pornography*. Vol. VIII. Washington, D.C.: U.S. Government Printing Office, 1971. Pp. 170–254.

Mansson, H. H. Justifying the final solution. *Omega*, 1972, 3, 79–87.

Marcus, J. Obedience. *New York Times Book Reviews*, March 17, 1974. Pp. 5–6.

Mark, V. H., & Ervin, F. R. *Violence and the brain*. New York: Harper & Row, Publishers, 1970.

Marks, I., & Lader, M. Anxiety states (anxiety neurosis): A review. *Journal of Nervous and Mental Disease*, 1973, 156, 3–18.

Marlatt, G. A., & Kaplan, B. E. Self-initiated attempts to change behavior: A study of New Year's resolutions. *Psychological Reports*, 1972, 30, 123–131.

Marshall, G. *Unexplained arousal*. Unpublished manuscript, Stanford University, 1974.

Marston, A. R. Self-reinforcement and external reinforcement of visual-motor learning. *Journal of Experimental Psychology*, 1967, 74, 93–98.

Martin, R. The experimental manipulation of stuttering behaviors. In H. H. Sloane, Jr., & B. D. MacAulay (Eds.), *Operant procedures in remedial speech and language training*. Boston: Houghton Mifflin Company, 1968. Pp. 325–347.

Maslach, C., Marshall, G., & Zimbardo, P. G. Hypnotic control of peripheral skin temperature: A case report. *Psychophysiology*, 1972, 2, 600–605.

Masserman, J. H. *Principles of dynamic psychiatry*. (2nd ed.) Philadelphia: W. B. Saunders Company, 1961.

Masters, W. H., & Johnson, V. E. *Human sexual response*. Boston: Little, Brown, & Co., 1966.

Masters, W. H. & Johnson, V. E. *Human sexual inadequacy*. Boston: Little, Brown and Company, 1970.

McCandless, B. R., Parsons, W. S., & Roberts, A. Perceived opportunity, delinquency, race, and body build among delinquent youth. *Journal of Consulting and Clinical Psychology*, 1972, 38, (2), 281–287.

McClelland, D. C. *The achieving society*. New York: Van Nostrand Reinhold Company, 1961.

McClelland, D. C., Atkinson, J. W., Clark, R. A., & Lowell, E. L. *The achievement motive*. Englewood Cliffs, N.J.: Prentice-Hall, Inc., 1953.

McClelland, D. C., & Steele, R. S. *Human motivation: A book of readings*. Morristown, N.J.: General Learning Press, 1973.

McClelland, D. S. *Search for power*. New York: Irvington Publishers, Inc., 1975.

McDougall, W. *An introduction to social psychology*. London: Methuen & Co. Ltd., 1908.

McGinnies, E. Emotionality and perceptual defense. *Psychological Review*, 1949, 56, 244–251.

McGinniss, J. *The selling of the presidency, 1968*. New York: Simon & Schuster, Inc., 1969.

McGuire, W. J., & Papageorgis, D. The relative efficacy of various types of prior belief-defense in producing immunity against persuasion. *Journal of Abnormal and Social Psychology*, 1961, 62, 327–337.

McIntyre, J. J., & Teevan, J. J., Jr. Television violence and deviant behavior. In G. A. Comstock & E. A. Rubinstein (Eds.), *Television and social behavior*. Vol. III. *Television and adolescents' aggressiveness*. Washington, D.C.: U.S. Government Printing Office, 1972. Pp. 383–435.

McKellar, T. *Imagination and thinking*. London: Cohen & Wast, 1957.

McNally, R. *Biology: An uncommon introduction*. San Francisco: Canfield Press, 1974.

Mead, M. *Sex and temperament in three primitive societies*. New York: William Morrow, 1935.

Mednick, B. R. Breakdown in high-risk subjects: Familial and early environmental factors. *Journal of Abnormal Psychology*, 1973, 82, 469–475.

Mednick, S. A. Breakdown in individuals at high risk for schizophrenia: Possible predispositional perinatal factors. *Mental Hygiene*, 1970, 54, 50–63.

Mednick, S. A. Birth defects and schizophrenia. *Psychology Today*, 1971, 4, 48–50, 80–81.

Mednick, S. A., Schulsinger, F., Higgins, J., & Bell, B. *Genetics, environment, and psychopathology*. New York: American Elsevier Publishing Co., Inc., 1974.

Megargee, E. I. Undercontrolled and overcontrolled personality types in extreme anti-social aggression. *Psychological Monographs*, 1966, 80 (Whole No. 611).

Megargee, E. I., Cook, P. E., & Mendelsohn, G. A. Development and validation of an MMPI Scale of assaultiveness in overcontrolled individuals. *Journal of Abnormal Psychology*, 1967, 72, 519–528.

Meichenbaum, D. Cognitive modification of test anxious college students. *Journal of Consulting and Clinical Psychology*, 1972, 39, 370–380.

Meichenbaum, D. H., & Goodman, J. Training impulsive children to talk to themselves: A means for developing self-control. *Journal of Abnormal Psychology*, 1971, 77, 115–126.

Melzack, R. *The puzzle of pain*. New York: Basic Books, Inc., Publishers, 1973.

Mercer, C. *Living in cities*. Harmondsworth, England: Penguin Books, 1975.

Milgram, S. *Obedience to authority: An experimental view*. New York: Harper & Row, Publishers, 1974.

Miller, N. E., & Bugelski, R. Minor studies in aggression: II. The influence of frustrations imposed by the in-group on attitudes expressed toward out-groups. *Journal of Psychology*, 1948, 25, 437–442.

Miller, N. E., & DiCara, L. V. Instrumental training of visceral functions. *Mental Health Program Reports, No. 6*. (DHEW) Publication No. (HSM) 73-9139. Chevy Chase, Md.: National Institute of Mental Health, 1973.

Milner, B., Corkin, S., & Teuber, H. L. Further analysis of the hyppocampal amnesia syndrome: 14-year follow-up study of H.M. *Neuropsychologia*, 1968, 6, 215–234.

Miner, G. D. The evidence for genetic components in the neuroses. *Archives of General Psychiatry*, 1973, 29, 111–118.

Mischel, W. *Personality and assessment*. New York: John Wiley & Sons, Inc., 1968.

Mischel, W. *Introduction to personality*. New York: Holt, Rinehart and Winston, Inc., 1971.

Mischel, W. Toward a cognitive social learning reconceptualization of personality. *Psychological Review*, 1973, 80, 252–283.

Mischel, W. Cognitive appraisals and transformations in self-control. In B. Weiner (Ed.), *Cognitive views of human motivation*. New York: Academic Press, 1974.

Mischel, W. *Introduction to personality*. (2nd ed.) New York: Holt, Rinehart and Winston, Inc., 1976.

Money, J., & Ehrhardt, A. A. Prenatal hormonal exposure: Possible effects on behavior in man. In R. P. Michael (Ed.), *Endocrinology and human behavior*. London: Oxford University Press, 1968.

Montgomery, R. Comment on fear and house-as-haven in the lower class. *Journal of the American Institute of Planners*, 1966, 32, 31–37.

Moore, N. Behavior therapy in bronchial asthmas: A controlled study. *Journal of Psychosomatic Research*, 1965, 9, 257–276.

Morganstern, K. P. Cigarette smoke as a noxious stimulus in self-managed aversion therapy for compulsive eaters. *Behavior Therapy*, 1974, 5, 255–260.

Mosak, H. H., & Dreikurs, R. Adlerian psychotherapy. In R. Corsini (Ed.), *Current psychotherapies*. Itaska, Ill.: F. E. Peacock Publishers, Inc., 1973.

Mowrer, O. H. An experimental analogue of "regression," with incidental observations on "reaction formation." *Journal of Abnormal and Social Psychology*, 1940, 35, 56–87.

Mowrer, O. H. *Learning theory and personality dynamics*. New York: The Ronald Press Company, 1950.

Mowrer, O. H. *Learning theory and the symbolic processes*. New York: John Wiley & Sons, Inc., 1960.

Murdock, B. B. The retention of individual items. *Journal of Experimental Psychology*, 1961, 62, 618–625.

Murray, E. J. A case study in a behavioral analysis of psychotherapy. *Journal of Abnormal and Social Psychology*, 1954, 49, 305–310.

Mussen, P. H., Conger, J. J., & Kagan, J. *Child development and personality*. (4th ed.) New York: Harper & Row, Publishers, 1974.

Newcomb, T. Persistance and regression of changed attitudes: Long-range studies. *Journal of Social Issues*, 1963, 19, 3–14.

Newman, O. *Defensible space*. New York: Macmillan Publishing Co., Inc., 1972.

Nisbett, R. E. Hunger, obesity and the ventromedial hypothalamus. *Psychological Review*, 1972, 79, 433–453.

Nisbett, R. E., Caputo, C., Legant, R., & Maracek, J. Behavior as seen by the actor and as seen by the observer. *Journal of Personality and Social Psychology*, 1973, 27, 154–164.

Norman, P. A. *Memory and attention*. New York: John Wiley & Sons, Inc., 1969.

O'Connell, D. N., Shor, R. E., & Orne, N. T. Hypnotic age regression: An empirical and methodological analysis. *Journal of Abnormal Psychology Monograph Supplement*, 1970, 76, No. 3, Part 2, 1–32.

O'Connor, R. D. Modification of social withdrawal through symbolic modeling. *Journal of Applied Behavior Analysis*, 1969, 2, 15–22.

Orme-Johnson, D. W. Autonomic stability and transcendental meditation. *Psychosomatic Medicine*, 1973, 35, 341–349.

Orne, M. T. The nature of hypnosis: Artifact and essence. *Journal of Abnormal and Social Psychology*, 1959, 58, 277–299.

Orne, M. T. Hypnosis. In G. Lindzey, C. Hall, & R. F. Thompson *Psychology*. New York: Worth, 1975.

Orne, M. T., & Evans, F. J. Social control in the psychological experiment: Anti-social behavior and hypnosis. *Journal of Personality and Social Psychology*, 1965, 1, 189–200.

O'Sullivan, M., Guilford, J. P., & de Mille, R. Measurement of social intelligence. *Psychological Laboratory, University of Southern California Reports*, 1965, No. 34.

Oswald, I. Induction of illusory and hallucinatory voices with considerations of behavior therapy. *Journal of Mental Science*, 1962, 108, 196–212.

Pagano, R. R., Rose, R. M., Stivers, R. M., & Warrenburg, S. Sleep during transcendental meditation. *Science*, 1976, 191, 308–310.

Page, E. B. Miracle in Milwaukee: raising the IQ. *Educational Researcher*, 1972, 1, 8–16.

Parrish, M., Lundy, R. M., & Leibowitz, H. W. Hypnotic age-regression and magnitudes of the Ponzo and Poggendorff illusions. *Science*, 1968, 159, 1375–1376.

Patterson, G. R., Littman, R. A., & Bricker, W. Assertive behavior in children: A step toward a theory of aggression. *Monographs of the Society for Research in Child*

Development, 1967, 32 (Whole No. 5).

Peale, N. V. *The power of positive thinking.* Englewood Cliffs, N.J.: Prentice-Hall, Inc., 1960.

Peeples, D., & Teller, D. Y. Color vision and brightness discrimination in two-month-old infants. *Science*, 1975, 189, 1102–1103.

Perl, E. R. Is pain a specific sensation? *Journal of Psychiatric Research*, 1971, 8, 273.

Perls, F. S. *Gestalt therapy verbatim.* Lafayette, Calif.: Real People Press, 1969.

Peters, H. N., & Jenkins, R. L. Improvement of chronic schizophrenic patients with guided problem solving, motivated by hunger, *Psychiatric Quarterly Supplement*, 1954, 28, 84–101.

Peterson, L. R., & Peterson, M. J. Short-term retention of individual verbal items. *Journal of Experimental Psychology*, 1959, 58, 193–198.

Pettigrew, T. F. Social psychology and desegregation research. *American Psychologist*, 1961, 16, 105–112.

Phillips, E. L., Phillips, E. A., Wolf, M. M., & Fixsen, D. L. Achievement Place: The modification of the behavior of predelinquent boys within a token economy. *Journal of Applied Behavior Analysis*, 1971, 4, 45–59.

Piaget, J. *The moral judgment of the child.* New York: Collier Books, 1962.

Piaget, J. Piaget's theory. In P. H. Mussen (Ed.), *Carmichael's manual of child psychology.* (3rd ed.) Vol. I. New York: John Wiley & Sons, Inc., 1970. Pp. 703–732.

Pickering, G. *Creative malady.* New York: Oxford University Press, 1974.

Poincaré, H. *The foundations of science.* G. B. Halstead (trans.) New York: Science Press, 1924.

Polin, A. T. The effects of flooding and physical suppression as extinction technique on an anxiety motivated avoidance locomotor response. *Journal of Psychology*, 1959, 47, 235–245.

Pollio, H. R. *The psychology of symbolic activity.* Reading, Mass.: Addison-Wesley Publishing Co., Inc., 1974.

Pomeroy, W. B. Homosexuality. In R. W. Weltage (Ed.), *The same sex.* Philadelphia: Pilgrim Press, 1969. Pp. 3–13.

Pomeroy, W. B. *Dr. Kinsey and the Institute for Sex Research.* New York: Harper & Row, Publishers, 1972.

Porter, R. P. *The recovery of American cities.* New York: Sun River Press, 1976. P. 91.

Power, J. Avoiding urban mistakes, cities fit for man. *International Herald Tribune*, May 23, 1976.

Premack, A. J. *Why chimps can read.* New York: Harper & Row, Publishers, 1976.

Premack, A. J., & Premack, D. Teaching language to an ape. *Scientific American*, October, 1972.

Premack, D. Reinforcement theory. In D. Levine (Ed.), *Nebraska Symposium on Motivation: 1965.* Lincoln, Neb.: University of Nebraska Press, 1965. Pp. 123–180.

Prince, V. C. *The transvestite and his wife.* Los Angeles: Argyle Books, 1967.

Rahe, R. H., & Holmes, T. H. Life crisis and major health change. *Psychosomatic Medicine*, 1966, 28, 774.

Rainwater, L. Fear and the house-as-haven in the lower class. *Journal of the American Institute of Planners*, 1966, 32, 23–31.

Rapoport, A. & Watson, N. Cultural variability in physical standards. In Robert Gurman (Ed.), *People and buildings.* New York: Basic Books, Inc., Publishers, 1972. Pp. 33–53.

Razran, G. Ethnic dislikes and stereotypes. *Journal of Abnormal and Social Psychology*, 1950, 45, 7–27.

Reiss, I. *The social context of premarital sexual permissiveness.* New York: Holt, Rinehart and Winston, Inc., 1967.

Richardson, L. S. *Statistics of deadly quarrels.* Pittsburgh: Boxwood Press, 1960.

Rimm, D. C., DeGroot, J. C., Boord, P., Heiman, J., & Dillow, P. V. Systematic desensitization of an anger response. *Behavior Research and Therapy*, 1971, 9, 273–280.

Rimm, D. C., & Masters, J. C. *Behavior therapy: Techniques and empirical findings.* New York: Academic Press, 1974.

Roe, A. *The making of a scientist.* New York: Dodd, Mead & Company, 1952.

Roe, A. A psychological study of eminent psychologists and anthropologists, and a comparison with biological and physical scientists. *Psychological Monographs*, 1953, 67, No. 2.

Rogers, C. R. *Client-centered therapy.* Boston: Houghton Mifflin Company, 1951.

Rogers, C. R. A theory of therapy, personality and interpersonal relationships, as developed in the client-centered framework. In S. Koch (Ed.), *Psychology: A study of a science.* Vol. 3. New York: McGraw-Hill Book Company, 1959. Pp. 184–256.

Rogow, A. A. *James Forrestal: A study of personality, politics, and policy.* New York: Macmillan Publishing Co., Inc., 1964.

Rogow, A. A. Private illness and public policy: The cases of James Forrestal and John Winant. *American Journal of Psychiatry*, 1969, 125, 1093–1097.

Rosenhan, D. L. On being sane in insane places. *Science.* 1973, 179, 250–258.

Rosenthal, D. (Ed.) *The Genain quadruplets: A case study and theoretical analysis of environment in schizophrenia.* New York: Basic Books, Inc., Publishers, 1963.

Routtenberg, A., & Lindy, J. Effects of the availability of rewarding septal and hypothalamic stimulation on bar pressing for food under conditions of deprivation. *Journal of Comparative and Physiological Psychology*, 1965, 60, 158–161.

Rundus, D., Loftus, G. R., & Atkinson, R. C. Immediate free recall and three-week delayed recognition. *Journal of Verbal Learning and Verbal Behavior*, 1970, 9, 684.

Russell, C. & Russell, W. M. Violence . . . What are its roots? *New Society*, 1961, 317, 595–600.

Rutter, M. Children of sick parents: An environmental and psychiatric study. *Maudsley Monograph* No. 16, 1966.

609

Sabin, L. Why I threw out my TV set. *Today's Health*, February, 1972.

Saegert, S., Swap, W., & Zajonc, R. B. Exposure, context, and interpersonal attraction. *Journal of Personality and Social Psychology*, 1973, *15*, 234–242.

Saghir, M. T., & Robins, E. *Male and female homosexuality: A comprehensive investigation.* Baltimore: The Williams & Wilkins Company, 1973.

Sarason, I. G. Verbal learning, modeling, and juvenile delinquency. *American Psychologist*, 1968, *23*, 254–266.

Sarason, I. G. *Personality: An objective approach.* (2nd ed.) New York: John Wiley & Sons, Inc., 1972.

Sarason, I. G. *Abnormal psychology: The problem of maladaptive behavior.* (2nd ed.) Englewood Cliffs, N.J.: Prentice-Hall, Inc., 1976.

Sarason, I. G., & Ganzer, V. J. Modeling and group discussion in the rehabilitation of delinquents. *Journal of Counseling Psychology*, 1973, *20*, 442–449.

Sawry, W. C., Conger, J. J., & Turell, R. B. An experimental investigation of the role of psychological factors in the production of gastric ulcers in rats. *Journal of Comparative and Physiological Psychology*, 1952, *45*, 143–149.

Schachter, S. *Emotion, obesity and crime.* New York: Academic Press, 1971.

Schachter, S., Goldman, R., & Gordon, A. The effects of fear, food deprivation, and obesity on eating. *Journal of Personality and Social Psychology*, 1968, *10*, 91–97.

Schachter, S., & Singer, J. E. Cognitive, social and physiological determinants of emotional state. *Psychological Review*, 1962, *69*, 379–399.

Schaffer, H. R., & Callender, W. M. Psychologic effects of hospitalization in infancy. *Pediatrics*, 1959, *24*, 528–539.

Schaffer, H. R., & Emerson, P. The development of social attachments in infancy. *Monographs of the Society for Research in Child Development*, 1964, *20* (Whole No. 94).

Schimel, J. L. Dialogic analysis of the obsessional. *Contemporary Psychoanalysis*, 1974, *11*, 87–101.

Schizophrenia: Is there an answer? Washington, D.C.: National Institute of Mental Health, 1972.

Schlosberg, H. The description of facial expressions in terms of two dimensions. *Journal of Experimental Psychology*, 1952, *44*, 229–237.

Schlosberg, H. Three dimensions of emotion. *Psychological Review*, 1954, *61*, 81–88.

Schmeidler, G. R., & McConnell, R. A. *ESP and personality patterns.* New Haven, Conn.: Yale University Press, 1958.

Schmidt, C., Sigusch, V., & Schafer, S. Responses to reading erotic stories: Male-female differences. *Archives of Sexual Behavior*, 1973, *2*, 181–199.

Schmitt, R. C. Implications of density in Hong Kong. *Journal of the American Institute of Planners*, 1963, *29*, 210–217.

Schmitt, R. C. Density, health and social disorganization. *Journal of the American Institute of Planners*, 1966, *32*, 38–40.

Schneider, J. Civil commitment of the mentally ill. *American Bar Association Journal*, 1972, *58*, 1059–1063.

Schoenfeld, W. N. Notes on a bit of psychological nonsense: "Race differences in intelligence." *Psychological Record*, 1974, *24*, 17–32.

Schwartz, G. E. The facts on transcendental meditation. Part II. TM relaxes some people and makes them feel better. *Psychology Today*, 1974, *7*, 39–44.

Sears, D. O., & McConahay, J. B. *The politics of violence: The new urban black and the Watts riot.* Boston: Houghton Mifflin Company, 1973.

Sears, R. R. Experimental studies of projection: I. Attribution of traits. *Journal of Social Psychology*, 1936, *7*, 151–163.

Seeman, W., Nidich, S., & Banta, T. H. Influence of transcendental meditation on a measure of self actualization. *Journal of Counseling Psychology*, 1972, *19*, 184–187.

Segal, M. W. Alphabet and attraction: An unobtrusive measure of the effect of propinquity in a field setting. *Journal of Personality and Social Psychology*, 1974, *30*, 654–657.

Seiden, R. H. Suicide capital? A study of the San Francisco suicide rate. *Bulletin of Suicidology*, U.S. Department of Health, Education and Welfare, Public Health Service. Washington, D.C.: U.S. Government Printing Office, December, 1967.

Seligman, M. E. P. Depression and learned helplessness. In R. J. Friedman & M. M. Katz (Eds.), *The psychology of depression: Contemporary theory and research.* Washington, D.C.: V. H. Winston & Sons, 1974. Pp. 83–108.

Seligman, M. E. P. *Helplessness: On depression, development, and death.* San Francisco: W. H. Freeman and Co., Publishers, 1975.

Selye, H. *The stress of life.* New York: McGraw-Hill Book Company, 1956.

Selzer, M. L., & Vinokur, A. Life events, subjective stress, and traffic accidents. *American Journal of Psychiatry*, 1974, *131*, 903–906.

Senden, M. von. *Space and sight: The perception of space and shape in the congenitally blind before and after operation.* P. Health (trans.) New York: The Free Press, 1960.

Shannon, C. E. Programming a computer for playing chess. *Philosophical Magazine*, 1950, *41*, 256–275.

Shepherd, M. Pollution, noise and mental health. *The Lancet*, Feb. 8, 1975, p. 322.

Sherif, M. On the relevance of social psychology. *American Psychologist*, 1970, *25*, 144–156.

Sherif, M., Harvey, O., White, B., Hood, W., & Sherif, C. *Intergroup conflict and cooperation: The Robbers Cave experiment.* Norman: Institute of Group Relations, University of Oklahoma, 1961.

Sherrington, C. S. The physical basis of mind. In P. Laslett (Ed.), *The physical basis of mind.* New York: Macmillan Publishing Co., Inc., 1950.

Sherrod, D. R. Crowding, perceived control, and behavioral aftereffects. *Journal of Applied Social Psychology*, 1974, *4*, 171–186.

Singer, J. L. *Daydreaming*. New York: Random House, Inc., 1966.

Skinner, B. F. *Walden two*. New York: Macmillan Publishing Co., Inc., 1948.

Skinner, B. F. *Verbal behavior*. Englewood Cliffs, N.J.: Prentice-Hall, Inc., 1957.

Skinner, B. F. In E. G. Boring, & G. Lindzey (Eds.), *A history of psychology in autobiography*. Englewood Cliffs, N.J.: 1967. Pp. 387–413.

Skinner, B. F. *Beyond freedom and dignity*. New York: Alfred A. Knopf, Inc., 1971.

Smith, R. E., Vanderbilt, K., & Callen, M. B. Social comparison and bystander intervention in emergencies. *Journal of Applied Social Psychology*, 1973, 3, 186–196.

Smith, R. M. World arms bill: Trillion since '64. *The New York Times*, March 22, 1970.

Smith, S., & Haythorn, W. W. Effects of compatibility, crowding groups size, and leadership seniority on stress, hostility and annoyance in isolated groups. *Journal of Personality & Social Psychology*, 1972, 22, 67–79.

Solomon, J. Aural assault. *The Sciences*, 1970, 10, 26–31.

Sommer, R. *Personal space*. Englewood Cliffs, N.J.: Prentice-Hall, Inc., 1969.

Sommer, Robert. Environmental psychology. In M. H. Siegel & H. P. Zeigler, *Psychological research: The inside story*. New York: Harper & Row, Publishers, 1976.

Sonders, W. B. *Juvenile offenders for a thousand years*. Chapel Hill: University of North Carolina Press, 1970.

Sontag, L. W. The significance of fetal environmental differences. *American Journal of Obstetrics and Gynecology*, 1941, 42, 996–1003.

Sorenson, R. *The edge of the forest land, childhood and change in a New Guinea Proto-Agricultural Society*. Smithsonian Institution, Washington, D.C., in press.

Spanos, N. P. Goal-directed phantasy and the performance of hypnotic test suggestions. *Psychiatry*, 1971, 34, 86–96.

Speisman, J. C., Lazarus, R. S., Mordkoff, A. M., & Davidson, L. A. The experimental reduction of stress based on ego-defense theory. *Journal of Abnormal and Social Psychology*, 1964, 68, 367–380.

Sperling, G. The information available in brief visual presentations. *Psychological Monographs*, 1960, 74, No. 11 (Whole No. 498).

Sperry, R. W. Perception in the absence of neocortical commissures. In *Perception and its disorders*. The Association for Research in Nervous and Mental Disease, 1970.

Spielberger, C. D., & DeNike, L. D. Descriptive behaviorism versus cognitive theory in verbal operant conditioning. *Psychological Review*, 1966, 73, 306–326.

Staats, A. W., & Staats, C. K. Attitudes established by classical conditioning. *Journal of Abnormal and Social Psychology*, 1958, 57, 37–40.

Stein, A. H., & Friedrich, L. K. Television content and young children's behavior. In J. P. Murray, E. A. Rubinstein, & G. A. Comstock (Eds.), *Television and social behavior*. Vol. II. *Television and social learning*. Washington, D.C.: U.S. Government Printing Office, 1972. Pp. 202–317.

Stevenson, H. W. *Children's learning*. Englewood Cliffs, N.J.: Prentice-Hall, Inc., 1972.

Stokols, Daniel. The experience of crowding in primary and secondary environments. *Environment and Behavior*, 1976, 8, 49–86.

Stoller, R. J. Male transsexualism: Uneasiness. *American Journal of Psychiatry*, 1973, 130, 536–539.

Stone, L. J., & Church, J. *Childhood and adolescence*. New York: Random House, Inc., 1968.

Strongman, K. T. *The psychology of emotion*. New York: John Wiley & Sons, Inc., 1975.

Strupp, H. H., Fox, R. E., & Lessler, K. *Patients view their psychotherapy*. Baltimore: The Johns Hopkins University Press, 1969.

Swan, J. Public response to air pollution. In J. F. Wohlwill & D. C. Carson (Eds.), *Environment and the social sciences: Perspectives and application*. Washington, D.C.: American Psychological Association, 1972. Pp. 66–74.

Sweet, W. H., Ervin, F., & Mark, V. H. The relationship of violent behavior to focal cerebral disease. In S. Garattine & E. Sigg (Eds.), *Aggressive behaviour*. New York: John Wiley & Sons, Inc., 1969.

Szasz, T. S. *The myth of mental illness*. (rev. ed.) New York: Harper & Row, Publishers, 1974. (Perennial Library Edition.)

Tanner, J. M. Physical growth. In P. H. Mussen (Ed.), *Carmichael's manual of child psychology*. Vol. 1. New York: John Wiley & Sons, Inc., 1970.

Tart, C. T. *Effects of posthypnotic suggestion on the process of dreaming*. Doctoral Dissertation, University of North Carolina, 1963.

Task Force Report. *Organized Crime*. President's Commission on Law Enforcement and Administration of Justice. Washington, D.C.: U.S. Government Printing Office, 1967.

Terman, L. M. *The measurement of intelligence*. Boston: Houghton Mifflin Company, 1916.

Terman, L. M., & Merrill, M. A. *Measuring intelligence*. Boston: Houghton Mifflin Company, 1937.

Terman, L. M., & Merrill, M. A. A Stanford-Binet Intelligence Scale: Manual for the 3rd revision. Form L-M. Boston: Houghton Mifflin Company, 1960.

Tharp, R. G., & Gallimore, R. What a coach can teach a teacher. *Psychology Today*, January, 1976, 75–78.

Thiery, A. Uber geometrisch-optische tauschungen. *Philosophisches Studien*, 1896, 12, 67–126.

Thiessen, D. D. Role of physical injury in the physiological effects of population density in mice. *Journal of Comparative and Physiological Psychology*, 1966, 62, 322–324.

Thigpen, C. H., & Cleckley, H. M. A case of multiple personality. *Journal of Abnormal and Social Psychology*, 1954, 49, 135–151.

Thigpen, C. H., & Cleckley, H. M. *The three faces of Eve*. New York: McGraw-Hill Book Company, 1957.

611

Thompson, R. F. *Introduction to physiological psychology*. New York: Harper & Row, Publishers, 1975.

Thomson, W. R. The inheritance and development of intelligence. Research publications of the Association for Research in Nervous and Mental Disorders, 1954, 33, 209–331.

Thorndike, E. L. Animal intelligence: An experimental study of the associative processes in animals. *Psychological Review Monograph Supplement*. 1898, 2, 1–9.

Thurstone, L. L. Primary mental abilities. *Psychometric Monographs*, 1938, No. 1.

Timeros, P. S. *Developmental physiology and aging*. New York: Macmillan Publishing Co., Inc., 1972.

Todd: F. J. Coverant control of self-evaluative responses in the treatment of depression: A new use for an old principle. *Behavior Therapy*, 1972, 3, 91–94.

Toffler, Alvin. *Future shock*. New York: Random House, 1970.

Tognacci, L. N., Weigel, R. H., Wideen, M. F., & Vernon, D. T. A. Environmental quality. How universal is public concern? *Environment and Behavior*, 1972, 4, 73–86.

Ubell, E. *How to save your life*. New York: Harcourt Brace Jovanovich, 1973.

Valenstein, E. S. *Brain Control: A critical examination of brain stimulation and psychotherapy*. New York: John Wiley & Sons, Inc., 1973.

Van Praag, H. M. (Ed.) *On the origin of schizophrenic psychoses*. Amsterdam, The Netherlands: DeErven Bohn, 1975.

Von Sydow, G., & Rinne, A. Unequal identical twins, *Acta Paediatrica*, 1958, 47, 163–171.

Wall, P. An eye on the needle. *New Scientist*, July 20, 1972, Pp. 129–131.

Wallace, R. K. Physiological effects of transcendental meditation. *Science*, 1970, 167, 1751–1754.

Wallace, R. K., & Benson, H. The physiology of meditation. *Scientific American*, 1972, 226, 84–90.

Warrington, E. E. Neuropsychological studies of memory. *British Medical Bulletin*, 1971, 27, 143–247.

Wason, P. C., & Johnson-Laird, P. M. (Eds.), *Thinking and reasoning*. Harmondsworth, England: Penguin Books, 1968.

Watson, D. L., & Tharp, R. G. *Self-directed behavior: Self-modification for personal adjustment*. Monterey, Calif.: Brooks/Cole Publishing Company, 1972.

Watson, J. B. Experimental studies on the growth of emotions. In C. Murchison (Ed.), *Psychologies of 1925*. Worcester, Mass.: Clark University Press, 1926.

Watson, J. B., & Rayner, R. Conditioned emotional reactions. *Journal of Experimental Psychology*, 1920, 3, 1–14.

Watson, O. M., & Graves, T. D. Quantitative research in proxemic behavior. *American Anthropologist*, 1966, 68, 971–985.

Wechsler, D. *The measurement and appraisal of adult intelligence*. (4th ed.) Baltimore: The Williams & Wilkins Company, 1958.

Wei, T. T., Lavatelli, C. B., & Jones, R. S. Piaget's concept of classification: A comparative study of socially disadvantaged and middle-class young children. *Child Development*, 1971, 42, 919–928.

Weil, R. J. Psychiatric aspects of disaster. In S. Arieti (Ed.), *The world biennial of psychiatry and psychotherapy*. (Vol. 2). New York: Basic Books, Inc., Publishers, 1973. Pp. 112–135.

Weinberg, M. S., & Williams, C. J. *Male homosexuals: Their problems and adaptations*. New York: Oxford University Press, 1974.

Weiner, B. *Theories of motivation: From mechanism to cognition*. Chicago: Markham Publishing Co., 1972.

Weiss, T., & Engle, B. Operant conditioning of heart rate in patients with premature ventricular contractions. *Psychosomatic Medicine*, 1971, 33, 301–321.

Weitzman, B. Behavior therapy and psychotherapy. *Psychological Review*, 1967, 74 (4), 300–317.

Weitzman, L. J., Eifler, D., Hokada, E., & Ross, C. Sex role socialization in picture books for children. *American Journal of Sociology*, 1972, 77, 1125–1149.

Wender, P. H., Rosenthal, D., Dety, S. S., Schulsinger, F., & Weiner, J. Crossfostering: A research strategy for clarifying the role of genetic and experimental factors in the etiology of schizophrenia. *Archives of General Psychiatry*, 1974, 30, 121–128.

Wenger, M., Bagachi, B., & Anand, B. Experiments in India on "voluntary" control of the heart and pulse. *Circulation*, 1961, 24, 1319–1325.

Whimbey, A. E., & Whimbey, L. S. *Intelligence can be taught*. New York: E. P. Dutton & Co., Inc., 1975.

White, R. K. *Nobody wanted war*. Garden City, N.Y.: Doubleday & Company, Inc., 1968.

Whitehead, A. N. *Adventures of ideas* (2nd ed.). New York Free Press (paperback), 1967, p. 13 (orig. published 1933).

Whitmont, E. C., & Kaufmann, Y. Analytical psychotherapy. In R. Corsini (Ed.), *Current psychotherapies*. Itasca, Ill.: F. E. Peacock Publishers, Inc., 1973.

Winkel, G. H., & Sasanoff, R. *An approach to an objective analysis of behavior in architectural space*. Architecture/Development Series No. 5., University of Washington, College of Architecture and Urban Planning, Seattle, 1966.

Wicker, A. Undermanning theory and research: implications for the study of psychological and behavioral effects of excess populations. *Representative Research in Social Psychology*, 1973, 4, 185–206.

Winter, D. G. *The power motive*. New York: The Free Press, 1973.

Wishner, J. Reanalysis of "impressions of personality." *Psychological Review*, 1960, 67, 96–112.

Witt, P. N. Drugs alter web-building of spiders: A review and evaluation. *Behavioral Science*, 1971, 16, 98–113.

Witty, P. Studies of the mass media, 1949–1965. *Science Education*, 1966, 50, 119–126.

Wohlwill, J. F., Nasar, J. L., DeJoy, D. M., & Foruzani, H. H.

Behavioral effects of a noisy environment: Task involvement versus passive exposure. *Journal of Applied Psychology*, 1976, *61*, 67–74.

Wolf, M., Risley, T., & Mees, H. Application of operant conditioning procedures to the behavior problems of an autistic child. *Behavior Research and Therapy*, 1964, *1*, 305–312.

Wolf, S., & Wolff, H. G. *Human gastric function.* (2nd ed.) New York: Oxford University Press, 1947.

Wolfgang, M. E., Figlio, R. M., & Sellin, T. *Delinquency in a birth cohort.* Chicago: The University of Chicago Press, 1972, pp. 68–69.

Wolpe, J., & Rachman, S. Psychoanalytic "evidence," a critique based on Freud's case of Little Hans. *Journal of Nervous and Mental Disease*, 1960, *131*, 135–147.

Woodruff, R. A., Jr., Goodwin, D. W., & Guze, S. B. *Psychiatric diagnosis.* New York: Oxford University Press, 1974.

Yablonsky, L. *The violent gang.* New York: Macmillan Publishing Co., Inc., 1962.

Yalom, I. D. *The theory and practice of group psychotherapy.* (2nd ed.) New York: Basic Books, Inc., Publishers, 1975.

Yalom, I. D., & Elkin, G. *Every day gets a little closer: A twicetold therapy.* New York: Basic Books, Inc., Publishers, 1974.

Yancey, W. L. Architecture, interaction, and social control. *Environment and Behavior*, 1971, *3*, 3–21.

Yarrow, L. J. Separation from parents during early childhood. In M. L. Hoffman & L. W. Hoffman. *Review of child development research.* Vol. 1. New York: Russell Sage Foundation, 1964. Pp. 89–136.

Yarrow, L. J. Attachment and dependency: A developmental perspective. In J. L. Gewirtz (Ed.), *Attachment and dependency.* Washington, D.C.: V. H. Winston & Sons, 1972. Pp. 81–96.

Yerkes, R. M., & Dodson, J. D. The relation of strength of stimulus to rapidity of habit-formation. *Journal of Comparative Neurology and Psychology*, 1908, *18*, 459–482.

Young, R. K. *Human learning and memory.* Module A-6, Personalized Psychology. New York: Harper & Row, Publishers, 1975.

Young, R. K., & Thompson, W. J. Retention of single- and double-function lists. *Journal of Verbal Learning and Verbal Behavior*, 1967, *6*, 910–915.

Zajonc, R. B. Attitudinal effects of mere exposure. *Journal of Personality and Social Psychology Monograph Supplement*, 1968, *9*, 1–27.

Zajonc, R. B. Family configuration and intelligence, *Science*, 1976, *192*, 227–236.

Zborowski, M. Cultural components in responses to pain. *Journal of Social Issues*, 1952, *8*, 16.

Zelditch, M. Role differentiation in the nuclear family: A comparative study. In T. Parsons & R. F. Bales (Eds.), *Family, socialization, and interaction process.* New York: The Free Press, 1955.

Zelnik, M., & Kantner, J. S. Sexuality, contraception and pregnancy among young unwed females in the United States. In C. F. Westoff & R. Parke, Jr., (Eds.), *Demographic and social aspects of population growth.* Vol. I. Research reports of the Commission on Population Growth and the American Future. Washington, D.C.: U.S. Government Printing Office, 1973.

Zimbardo, P. G., Haney, C., Banks, W. C., & Jaffe, D. The mind is a formidable jailer: A Pirandellian prison. *The New York Times Magazine*, April 8, 1973, pp. 38–60.

Indexes

Name Index

Subject Index

Tell Us What You Think . . .

We are committed to making *Psychology: The Frontiers of Behavior* a valuable tool for the teaching and learning of psychology. Because we want to be sure that *Psychology: The Frontiers of Behavior* continues to meet the needs and concerns of instructors and students, we would like your opinion of this edition. We invite you to tell us what you like about the text—as well as where you think improvements can be made. Your opinions will be taken into consideration in the preparation of future editions. Thank you for your help.

Please indicate whether you are ☐ an instructor ☐ a student

Your name _____

School _____ City and State _____

Course Title _____

How does this text compare with texts you are using in other courses?

☐ Excellent ☐ Good ☐ Fair ☐ Poor ☐ Very Poor

Please circle the chapters that were required in the course.

Section One:	Chapters	1 2	Section Four:	Chapters	9 10 11 12
Section Two:	Chapters	3 4 5	Section Five:	Chapters	13 14
Section Three:	Chapters	6 7 8	Section Six:	Chapters	15 16 17 18

What chapters did you read that were not assigned by your instructor? (Give chapter numbers.) _____

Please tell us your overall impression of the text.

	Excellent	Good	Adequate	Poor	Very Poor
1. Did you find the text to be logically organized?					
2. Was it written in a clear and understandable style?					
3. Did the graphics enhance readability and understanding of topics?					
4. Did captions contribute to a further understanding of the material?					
5. Were difficult concepts well explained?					
6. Were the issues valuable to a further understanding of psychology?					
7. Did the boxes contribute to the text?					

Which chapters did you particularly like and why? (Give chapter numbers.) _____

Which chapters did you dislike and why? _____

After taking this course, are you now interested in taking more courses in this field? ☐ Yes ☐ No

Do you feel that this text had any influence on your decision? ☐ Yes ☐ No

How can this text be improved? _____

What topics did the instructor discuss that were not covered in the text? _____

Did you use the Study Guide? ☐ Yes ☐ No Comments _____

Thank you very much

We need your advice

Because this book will be revised regularly, we would like to know what you think of it. Please fill in the brief questionnaire on the reverse of this card and mail it to us.
